Benjamin Franklin Bache and the Philadelphia *Aurora*

Benjamin Franklin Bache and the Philadelphia *Aurora*

James Tagg

upp

University of Pennsylvania Press

Philadelphia

Library of Congress Cataloging-in-Publication Data
Tagg, James.
    Benjamin Franklin Bache and the Philadelphia Aurora / James Tagg.
        p.   cm.
    Includes bibliographical references and index.
    ISBN 0-8122-8255-8
    1. Bache, Benjamin Franklin, 1769–1798.   2. Bache's Philadelphia
Aurora.   3. Journalists—United States—Biography.   4. Press and
politics—United States—History—18th century.   5. Washington,
George, 1732–1799—Relations with journalists.   6. United States—
Politics and government—1789–1797.   I. Title.
E302.6.B14T34   1991
070.92—dc20
[B]   91-6829
                                                               CIP

For
June, Nat, and Ike

Contents

Preface

HIS CONTEMPORARIES labeled him a peddler of "filth," "a base and unnatural miscreant," and an "impudent dog," who "outraged every principle of decency, of morality, of religion and of nature." "He is an ill-looking devil," William Cobbett proclaimed, "of sallow complexion, hollow-cheeked, dead-eyed, and has a toute en semble, just like that of a fellow who has been about a week or ten days in a gibbett." Abigail Adams simply described him as having the "malice & falshood [sic] of Satan."[1] Although Benjamin Franklin Bache's successor as editor of the Philadelphia *Aurora* would later remember him for his "timely and able developments and expositions of public measures, foreign and domestic," and as "the most formidable check upon ambition and false policy, which this nation has possessed for five years past," Washington declared that Bache attacked his administration with "malignant industry, and perservering [sic] falsehoods . . . in order to weaken, if not destroy, the confidence of the Public." Most of his enemies would have agreed that he was "Printer to the French Directory, Distributor General of the Principles of Insurrection, Anarchy and confusions," and "the greatest fool, and most stubborn sans culotte in the United States."[2]

Steeped in the paranoid style, most of these same enemies had little difficulty analyzing the motives behind his behavior. Some, like John Quincy Adams, a schoolmate of Bache's in France who was attacked in the *Aurora* in 1797, were not altogether wrong in finding Bache "too thoroughbred a democrat to suffer any regard for ancient friendship, or any sense of generosity for an absent enemy to suppress his patriotic scurrility." Adams's friend William Vans Murray displayed some insight as well in attributing Bache's character to having "had a philosopher for a grandfather [Benjamin Franklin], for that idea was the food of much of his extravagance of mind, and placed him in a state of pretence where he was obliged to act a part for which he had not talents."[3] But most were less charitable. Timothy Pickering claimed Bache was a mere opportunist who opposed the federal administrations of the 1790s to shock readers and gain subscribers. Those devoted to the thesis that he was nothing more than a follower of Franklin, or a "right chip of the Old Block," as Cobbett liked to put it, were more common. With sycophancy as their criterion for judging character development, these opponents easily moved on to claim that the *Aurora*'s editor was a "born hireling" who had "been as faithful to the cut-throats of Paris, as ever a dog was to his master," and "a miserable tool of the most abandoned faction that ever disgraced a free country."[4]

Modern commentators have not been much kinder. Bernard Faÿ suggested in his 1933 study of Bache, tellingly entitled *The Two Franklins: Fathers of American Democracy,* that Franklin and Bache were inseparably linked. "Benny Bache had only one idea," Faÿ contended in his light and melodramatic style, "to follow in the footsteps of his grandfather and keep on following them."[5] The myth has remained. As one recent student of the press in America has put it, Bache "found himself putting that energy into filiopiety that other men put into a career."[6] Although several authors have attempted to rescue the 1790s press and figures like Bache from such one-dimensional distortions, the standard authorities usually provide no more than one or two lines about Bache or the *Aurora,* most suggesting Bache's debt to Franklin or merely his journalistic virulence.[7]

Bache's contemporaries and modern scholars have not been entirely wrong about some aspects of Bache's character and style. Bache seldom came across as an especially pleasant journalist. Though he embraced much of Jefferson's philosophy, he did not possess Jefferson's profundity or appreciation of nuance; he engendered the same response in his own time as did his ideological mentor, Thomas Paine. His attacks on policies and personalities were often outrageous in style, and sometimes in argument as well. He did have deep ties to Franklin. He was a thorough democrat. And he remained an unrepentant francophile up to his death in 1798 at the young age of twenty-nine.

But in large measure the significance and context of Bache's life and an analysis of his newspaper, the Philadelphia *General Advertiser* (his paper's usual name from 1790 to November 1794) and *Aurora* (1794–1798), have not been investigated with much sophistication. Unlike the case for many historical figures, his social and intellectual development as a child and adolescent can be studied through extant sources, including a childhood diary and letters, as well as through sources dealing with Franklin. In the first four chapters of this work, I attempt to trace critical psychological developments in his youth. The ideology he embraced and the broader paradigm in which that ideology was expressed and evolved are discussed in the fifth and subsequent chapters. The remainder of the book investigates Bache's search for a means of articulating representative democracy; his passionate desire to defeat all vestiges of monarchy, aristocracy, and the antique ethos of traditionalism; and his vision of maintaining the sister-hood of the American and French republics through a narrative history of Bache's newspaper. My hope is that through examining social contexts of Bache's childhood and adulthood, defining ideological paradigms, and placing all these within a developing narrative will reveal a more realistic picture of Bache, politics, and the press.

Like all books, this one has its own history, some of which may be of interest to its readers. This study began over twenty years ago when Richard D. Miles suggested that Bache was worthy of re-examination. Although I have had many moments of frustration dealing with a subject who lived for hardly more years than the time I have been studying him, I have always been grateful for Professor Miles's suggestion, and for the kind—dare I say Franklin-like—manner in which he helped me see my initial study of Bache through to completion as a doctoral dissertation in 1973. From the mid-1970s through the mid-1980s, I put aside the Bache work, concentrating on a long research project on the image of the French Revolution in America (research that is dealt with briefly in the seventh chapter of this work). Uncomfortable with the interpretive focus of the original dissertation, and discouraged somewhat by the celebrity of social history alone in the 1970s, I did not revive my interest in Bache until 1984. By that time it was clear that political and narrative history was going to be revived (in what I believe is an improved form), and I felt that I could offer some useful comments on issues like identity, ideology, and political developments in the 1790s. Unlike the original dissertation, this work takes a different analytic approach and places a different stress on most elements of Bache's life.

This book has a somewhat unusual research history as well. Readers will note throughout the following chapters references to Bache Family Papers, B. F. Bache Papers, and Franklin Papers containing manuscript material relating to B. F. Bache. These materials—relatively few in number—are part of the archive materials held by the American Philosophical Society in Philadelphia. Other Bache material is scattered and fragmentary. Readers will also note references to the Castle Collection—a collection available on microfilm from the American Philosophical Society that contains the core of B. F. Bache and Bache Family material.

It was, in fact, the Castle Collection that would provide the eleventh-hour climax to the completion of this book. In 1970, after searching for letters described by Faÿ, I finally came across typescripts of some of these letters in the possession of Mrs. J. Manderson Castle of Wilmington, Delaware. The late Mrs. Castle kindly sent me some fifty-odd individual typescripts, and I employed them in my dissertation manuscript, thinking I had seen the main body of material. Then, in September, 1990, as this book entered the galley proof stage, I learned that the remainder of the Castle Collection—containing over two hundred original and typescript items that were of value, and new, to me—had been donated to the American Philosophical Society. This book, therefore, contains many last-minute additions of quotations and other material—especially regarding Benjamin's adolescence in Philadelphia and his courtship with Margaret Hartman Markoe—that came from this invaluable source.

I am indebted to the American Philosophical Society for its effort to make this valuable collection available to scholars. I am also indebted to the Society's Archivist, Ms. Beth Carroll-Horrocks, and its Assistant Archivist, Mr. Martin Levitt, for informing me about the Castle Collection, and allowing me early access to this material. Mr. Simon P. Newman did an expert job of organizing and indexing this material in what must be record time. No one who is familiar with the American Philosophical Society will be surprised when I note what a pleasure it is to be allowed to work with the Society's archival materials and their staff.

Several other persons also deserve special mention for their confidence, generosity, or help in bringing this work to completion. Claude-Anne Lopez has attempted to give me direction in locating sources, and I am indebted to her and her colleague Eugenia Herbert for their study of *The Private Franklin,* cited herein. My colleagues at the University of Lethbridge in general, and in the Department of History in particular, have also given me considerable encouragement and material aid. A small research grant from the University of Lethbridge helped me complete this manuscript, while the Department generously granted me course relief in 1988–89 to aid in writing this book. In 1989, the University of Lethbridge Research Fund generously granted me money to aid in the production of this book.

On the intellectual side of things, wide-ranging conversations with Malcolm Greenshields in my home department have helped me sort out contextual problems. Many discussions of Paine, Burke, and Cobbett with Ian Dyck of Simon Fraser University have done much to inform my discussion of these figures in this work. A former student of mine, David

Cavilla, did some important reading for me in secondary sources, especially alerting me to useful ideas regarding Bache's moral development as a child. At a small university remote from many materials, it is critical to employ (I should better say stretch) the services of our inter-library loan department. Over the years, Ms. Rosemary Howard has cheerfully responded to my tiresome—and sometimes unreasonable—demands for materials. She not only tolerates me (and others like me), but treats the urgency of the work as if it were her own (which in part it is).

Finally, I wish to thank the University of Pennsylvania Press for publishing this work. Dr. Alison A. Anderson, Managing Editor, and her staff have aided me greatly through their attention to the details of publication and with their professional advice. I am particularly indebted to Mr. Jerome Singerman who, although technically in charge of acquisitions for the Press, has skillfully played the role of kindly adviser and consultant as well as trouble-shooter through the long process of bringing this book forward.

University of Lethbridge   *James Tagg*
October, 1990

Permission is gratefully acknowledged to quote correspondence and other material from the following sources.

American Philosophical Society: Bache Family Papers; Benjamin Franklin Bache Diary; B. F. Bache Papers; Castle Collection; James S. and Frances M. Bradford Collection of Franklin Papers; Franklin Papers; William Temple Franklin Papers; Hewson Family Papers; Thomas Jefferson Papers; Miscellaneous MSS Collection

Historical Society of Pennsylvania: Society Collection; Simon Gratz Collection; Mathew Carey Papers; Etting Papers; Franklin Papers; Markoe Family Papers; Society Collection Transcriptions; Minutes of the Democratic Society of Pennsylvania

Massachusetts Historical Society: Timothy Pickering Papers

New York Public Library: Emmet Collection, Rare Books and Manuscripts Division, Astor, Lenox and Tilden Foundations

Pierpont Morgan Library: Franklin Papers

Princeton University Library: George S. Eddy Collection, Franklin Bache Papers

University of Virginia Library: James Monroe Papers (#2119), Manuscripts Division, Special Collections Department

William R. Perkins Library, Duke University: Jefferson Papers

Notes

1. For these quotations see respectively *Gazette of U. S.*, Nov. 8 ("corres."), 1794; May 29, 1798; *Porcupine's Gazette*, Dec. 13, 1797; Apr. 20, 1798; Nov. 16, 1797; and Abigail Adams to Her Sister, Apr. 21, 1798, Stewart Mitchell, ed., *New Letters of Abigail Adams, 1788–1801* (Boston, 1947), 159.

2. See respectively William Duane, *Aurora*, Sept. 21, 1799; G. Washington to Benj. Walker, Jan. 12, 1797, John C. Fitzpatrick, ed., *Writings of George Washington* (Washington, D. C., 1931–44), XXXV, 363–65; and "Extract" from the *Federal Gazette* repub. in *Porc. Gaz.*, Mar. 12, 1798.

3. See respectively J. Q. Adams to Charles Adams, Aug. 1, 1797, Worthington Chauncey Ford, ed., *The Writings of John Quincy Adams* (New York, 1913–1917), II, 196; and William Vans Murray to J. Q. Adams, Worthington Chauncey Ford, ed., "Letters of William Vans Murray to John Quincy Adams," *Annual Report of the American Historical Association for the Year 1912* (Washington, D. C., 1913), 489–90.

4. See respectively Timothy Pickering, "Manuscript Notes on Various Historical Subjects Composed in 1828," 34–35, in the Timothy Pickering Papers, Massachusetts Historical Society, Boston; William Cobbett, *A Bone to Gnaw for the Democrats* (Philadelphia, 1795), 9; *Porc. Gaz.*, Nov. 16, 1797; *Gaz. of U. S.*, Sept. 22, 1797.

5. Bernard Faÿ, *The Two Franklins: Fathers of American Democracy* (Boston, 1933), 159.

6. Thomas Leonard, *The Power of the Press: The Birth of American Political Reporting* (New York, 1986), 68–69.

7. For the slight and stereotypical coverage of Bache and the *Aurora* in standard works on the era see John C. Miller, *The Federalist Era, 1789–1801* (New York, 1960), 198, 233; and Richard Buel, Jr., *Securing the Revolution: Ideology in American Politics, 1789–1815* (Ithaca, N. Y., 1972), 225–26. For thorough and even-handed analyses of the press and politics, see especially Jeffrey Alan Smith, "Printers and Press Freedom: The Ideology of Early American Journalism" (unpub. Ph.D. diss., University of Wisconsin-Madison, 1984); William David Sloan, "The Party Press: The Newspaper Role in National Politics, 1789–1816" (unpub. Ph.D. diss., University of Texas, 1981); John Bixler Hench, "The Newspaper in a Republic: Boston's *Centinel* and *Chronicle*, 1784–1801" (unpub. Ph.D. diss., Clark University, 1979); William Frank Steirer, Jr., "Philadelphia Newspapers: Years of Revolution and Transition, 1764–1794" (unpub. Ph.D. diss., University of Pennsylvania, 1972); and Richard Moss, "The Press during the Federalist Era," *Journal of Popular Culture*, 15 (Fall, 1981), 3–12.

1. Franklins and Baches

"Remember, for your Encouragement in good oeconomy, that whatever a Child saves of its Parents' Money, will be its own another Day."
(Benj. Franklin to Sarah Bache, April 6, 1773)

WHEN BENJAMIN FRANKLIN BACHE was born on August 12, 1769, he entered two significant worlds, which together, defined and shaped his brief life. The larger of these was a public world, driven by rationalist hopes and reformist fervor. It was a revolutionary world, and, insofar as revolution produced republican ideals and anxieties, libertarian faiths in world reformation, and an expression of romantic rage, Benjamin Bache would become both an example and an author of the new age. But from 1769 to 1790 a more primary significant world—the private world of the family—dominated Benjamin Bache's life. Even under unexceptional circumstances, in an unremarkable environment, Bache's childhood would have been inescapably marked by familial influences. But Benjamin Bache was not only born into the age of the emergent intimate and affectionate family, into the family in the process of modernization; he also entered the world as Benjamin Franklin's grandson.

For Benjamin Bache, Franklin was not just an eminent grandfather. He was Benny's guardian, teacher, mentor, and business partner. But even as *pater familias* of the Franklin-Bache household Franklin could not claim exclusive dominion in young Benny's childhood development. Although under his parents' charge only intermittently during his childhood years and politically estranged from them in later years, Benjamin Bache was also influenced by his father and mother, Richard and Sarah Bache.

As Benjamin Franklin's only daughter and as a product of the mid-eighteenth-century "affectionate family," Sarah ("Sally") Franklin (1743–1808) experienced the tensions of love and discipline, autonomy and dependence, that she and her father eventually applied to Benjamin Bache as well. Perhaps influenced by Lockean notions of child-rearing, in which the necessity of paternal affection was counterbalanced by demands for discipline, Benjamin Franklin as a father and a grandfather pursued a mixed path of flattering affection, chastisement, and lectures on duties and responsibilities. He expressed, as one scholar puts it, the moderate Protestant temperament of both "duty and desire," the "affectionate family" that is ever wary of over-indulging its progeny, the family that seeks for its members both autonomy and freedom on the one hand and obedience to familial morals on the other.[1]

Absent during most of his daughter's adolescent years, Franklin exaggerated Sally's qualities and abilities and occasionally lavished on her gifts such as fine clothes and accessories, once even a harpsichord to allow her to pursue her musical talent. Eager for his daughter to become "an ingenious, sensible, notable and worthy woman," Franklin often admonished Sally to "mind her Learning and Improvement." Sally responded with affection, a pleasant gregariousness, and unwavering loyalty to what she imagined her father wished of her.[2]

Beyond this, the ties of father and daughter were confused and complex, just as the ties between Sarah and her eldest son Benjamin would later become. Franklin was never entirely clear about what he expected in a daughter. He encouraged her independence of mind, her pursuit of French, and even her political curiosity. But he also steered his daughter toward domestic skills, and away from any significant social role beyond wife and mother. Industry and frugality remained in his catechism for all women, along with some concern that Sally develop the cosmopolitan skills necessary to become a lady in society and a helpmate in his old age. More cruel was the fact that Franklin—absent from Philadelphia from 1757 to 1762, from 1765 to 1775, and again from 1776 to 1785—seems to have felt that his daughter sometimes paled next to his surrogate daughter in London, Polly Stevenson (later Hewson). Polly was, as one biographer puts it, "closer and brighter and more comforting than Sally." It is possible, in fact, to believe that Franklin was occasionally embarrassed by his plain American wife, Deborah, and his daughter—an embarrassment complicated by his long absences, his celebrity, and his opportunity to focus his attention only occasionally on domestic life in Philadelphia.[3]

No matter how Franklin might view his daughter's future, the fact remained that Sally was the daughter of a famous man in a changing age. The small but significant and unique contributions of her life were grounded in both of these factors. Although she came to portray herself as no more than a modest mother, she would in fact take some of the first steps toward independent action for American women. Her insistence on learning French, despite her mother's apparent lack of interest, may have represented her early insistence on some personal autonomy. By the 1760s, Sally's independence had spilled over into the public domain of politics. When a petition for her father's removal as agent for Pennsylvania was laid on the communion table at Christ Church in 1764, Sally openly threatened to leave the church. Only her astonished father's stern admonitions to desist and remain an obedient attending member of the congregation stopped her. Later interests in political issues like the Stamp Act and the Society of Cincinnati exemplify her keen, if not insightful, interest in the political world around her.[4]

But two larger events would define her as an example of the emerging, independent woman of the late eighteenth century. One of these was her decision to marry Richard Bache out of affection, despite the lack of Franklin's approval or of Bache's ability to prove that he could support a family. The other was her active involvement in the Revolution.

Sarah Franklin's symbolic importance as a new, more independent, self-reliant woman stood out in her marriage. Franklin, ever the paradoxical father, had half-heartedly attempted to arrange his daughter's marriage. Always dreaming of bringing symmetry and convenience to his personal life, Franklin had jokingly proposed marriage between his seven-year-old daughter and William Strahan's son William, Jr. in 1750. But Franklin seldom merely joked. An easy personality with a deft ability to deflect the serious into the humorous, a man determined to get his way but temperamentally wary of direct and threatening tactics to accomplish it, Franklin cultivated the idea of "our Daughter [Sally]," marrying "my Son [Billy Strahan, Jr.]" in his letters to Strahan senior. By 1757, with Sally only fourteen, Franklin was unabashedly promoting his daughter's virtues. But when Strahan, Sr., made a concrete marriage proposal in 1760, Franklin hesitated. The hard reality was that Deborah would have to agree to cross the ocean (which she dreaded), and that they would both have to leave Pennsylvania (which Franklin dreaded). Unspoken was the fact that he had established a dual life for himself—one in England, one in Philadelphia—and that this marriage would disrupt both. The decision was shifted to Deborah, and she declined the proposal.[5]

Although Franklin tried to keep some control as match-maker, he lost not only the initiative but virtually any influence in Sally's decision to marry. Sally met her husband-to-be in unpropitious circumstances, at the bedside of her dying friend Peggy Ross, to whom Richard Bache was betrothed. Bache's meager finances and his uncertain commercial future as a dry-goods merchant did not improve the picture when Sally and Richard announced their seriousness about one another in 1767. Deborah liked Bache's personality and tried to remain optimistic, but felt besieged and powerless.[6]

Franklin understood the threat clearly but moved cautiously. At first he used distance as an excuse for delay. But then he was shaken by a report from his own son William, who concluded that "If Sally marries him they must both be entirely on you for their Subsistence."[7] Franklin, never temperamentally suited to utter "No!" forthrightly, calculated on the strategy of convincing Bache that there would be little to inherit from the Franklins. Thus, he could generously admit to Deborah that "if he [Bache] proves a good Husband to her, and a good Son to me, he shall find me as good a Father as I can be." But how "good" could he be? The Franklins could give the young couple some clothes and furniture, and for the rest "they must depend as you and I did, on their own Industry and Care; as what remains in our Hands will be barely sufficient for our Support, and not enough for them when it comes to be divided at our Decease."[8] Franklin waited for the courtship to wither on the vine. If William was right about Bache's opportunism, and if Bache's recent disaster regarding a bankruptcy with the ship *Charleston* was as severe as William contended, Franklin could easily believe the issue was dead.

By the end of the summer of 1767, however, it was not over. Both Sarah and Deborah had become more independent of patriarchal authority and were championing the courtship. To Deborah, Franklin wishfully forecast that Bache would "forbear entering hastily into a State that must require a great addition to his expence, when he will be less able to supply it." With desperation tactics, he resurrected the idea of bringing Sarah to England, even though there had been no recent ploys for a Strahan-Franklin match.[9] Finally, addressing Richard Bache directly, he lamented the young man's losses, advised Bache that "industry and good management may in *a few years* [emphasis added] replace what you have lost," alerted the young man to the expenses of a family, declared that the Franklin estate was too small to support everyone, and attempted to warn Bache off directly:

> I am obliged to you for the regard and preference you express for my Child and wish you all prosperity; but unless you can convince her friends of the probability of your being able to maintain her properly, I hope you will not persist in a proceeding that may be attended with *ruinous consequences to you both* [emphasis added].[10]

Franklin made no attempt to influence his daughter. Why? Although Franklin may not have analyzed his own behavior, it is probable that he was following two contradictory paths: a traditional one of *pater familias,* yet paradoxically and correctly identifying his daughter as the chief, and very able, protagonist of the whole issue, an independent agent from whom he could win little ground.

As one work puts it, Sarah "had the women on her side." But when Sarah married Richard Bache on October 9, 1767, it was a symbol of something more than the victory of a strong circle of women. It was a declaration for the primacy of affection over marital convenience despite paternal opposition.[11] It exemplified the independence and individuality of Sarah Franklin—and of her mother, Deborah, who shared in the decision. The marriage also stood as a prototype for a new realm of autonomy for family members that would become more evident in the decades following the Revolution. In 1767, the autonomy of Sarah Bache was unusual, and along with her revolutionary activism in 1780, her experience suggests the tentative first beginnings of a new conception of American womanhood.

And where did Richard Bache fit into the private politics of the Franklin family? In several ways Bache always had been, and would remain, one of life's willing captives. Less the opportunist than a genial, easy-going "hanger-on," Richard Bache was born in 1737, six years before Sarah. The son of William Bache, a collector of the excise in the town of Settle in Yorkshire, he had apparently been apprenticed in English counting houses, as had his brother Theophylact. A better follower than leader, Richard came to America in 1760, after Theophylact had achieved some success as a New York merchant.[12]

Theophylact had arrived in New York in 1751, a boy of seventeen. By good fortune he was taken into the merchant house of Paul Richards, mayor of the city from 1735 to 1737. Upon Richards's death, Theophylact improved the business in the 1750s and 1760s, expanding his dry goods trade, purchasing ships, speculating in real estate, and writing marine insurance (which Richard sold for his brother in Philadelphia). Marrying well, he slipped into the conservative New York elite with ease. A generous and hospitable man, he became an avid supporter of charitable and civic causes and was one of the founders of the New York City Chamber of Commerce.[13]

Above all, Theophylact seemed to dislike controversy. He apparently supported Non-importation in 1765, and when Non-importation was re-instituted in 1768 he served on a Committee of Inspection. In 1774, he was appointed to the prestigious Committee of Fifty-One, a conservative committee of leading New Yorkers who hoped to redress grievances with England and counter the more militant demands of radicals and moderates. When revolution approached, Theophylact drew back. He was temperamentally unsuited for strife, and he retained strong English ties. He recognized some justice in the American cause, but after his ship, the *Sally,* ran afoul of the Association in 1775, and after one of his personal letters, complaining that no one could freely speak or write any longer, fell into the hands of the Committee of Safety in September 1775, he sought self-imposed exile in Flatbush on Long Island.[14]

Aside from being temporarily "kidnapped" during the Revolution, he came through the war relatively unscathed. During British occupation of New York, he accepted appointment to a committee of eighteen that administered poor relief in the city. Alexander Graydon, interned as a captive on Long Island, reported that, "His [Bache] being an Englishman and a determined royalist did not prevent him from accosting us very civily, and manifesting a disposition to maintain friendly intercourse with us, notwithstanding the difference in our political sentiments." His behavior, Graydon added, "was altogether free from intolerance and party rancour: it was more, it was hospitable and kind." And, Graydon concluded, Bache's moderation came from his knowing "that the opposition to the mother country was not confined to a low and desperate faction, as it was the fashion among the loyalists to represent it."[15]

After the Revolution, he eased back into the mercantile mainstream of New York, reviving his dry-goods trade, increasing his land speculations, and resuming charity work. The only ripple on the water was his desire to be re-admitted to the Chamber of Commerce in 1784; it did not re-admit loyalists until 1787. As Vice-President of the Chamber from 1788 to 1792, Theophylact helped welcome the establishment of the new federal government in New York in 1789. Although his later politics are unknown, he was probably active in the Chamber in 1795 when that body presented a petition to President Washington in support of the Jay Treaty. (Ironically, Theophylact's nephew Benjamin was at the same time leading the fight against the Jay Treaty.) When Benjamin took a tour of the northern states to excite opposition to the treaty, he went out of his way to visit his uncle in New York.[16]

It seems that Richard Bache shared his brother's equable, inoffensive, and cooperative personality. He did not share his success. Always longing for inclusion in the social elite, he at least pretended success. He joined the

Mount Regale Fishing Company and fêted its prominent members during a 1762 outing. He undoubtedly met Peggy Ross at a city assembly dance or some equivalent entertainment by and for Philadelphia's elite. But, although he may have striven to establish his business as determinedly as his social life, he never gained a permanent foothold. By the mid-1760s, he was struggling. He may have lacked the necessary business connections in England; he may have lacked cleverness. In 1765, he was in England acting as an agent for his brother and trying to improve his connections. In 1766, he tried to open a dry-goods store. Then, on the eve of marrying Sarah Franklin, with his prospects unimproved, he met disaster in a ship speculation. Having purchased the *Charleston,* he outfitted the ship for a Jamaica to London voyage, expecting his London partner, Edward Green, to assume the expenses and share the profits. Green reneged. Bache was left with a debt of £3,620 to be paid in five years at seven percent interest.[17]

Richard Bache made furtive attempts to recoup his business and his independence after marrying Sarah in 1767, but apparently never came close. He may have formed a partnership in 1770 with John Shee, the son of a prominent merchant, and by 1773 he was involved in a small wine importing trade.[18] Having faced the *fait accompli* of the marriage and having failed to accept his son-in-law for a depressing year, Franklin eventually tried to guide Richard toward the ever-receding horizon of economic independence. "If you prove a good Husband and Son, you will find in me an Affectionate Father," Franklin stated in his first cautious gesture of conciliation, suggesting several possible layers of meaning to any careful reader. Thus, Richard and Sarah lived in Franklin's house rent-free (where they could conveniently care for Deborah). The birth of Benjamin Franklin Bache in 1769 and Sally's belated pledge to remain Franklin's "dutiful and affectionate daughter" softened Franklin more.[19]

The final step toward conciliation came in 1771, when Richard sailed for England to convince Franklin of his worth and seek his aid. Everyone except Franklin anticipated the meeting with anxiety. When father-in-law and son-in-law actually met, not only did Richard and his English relatives manage to charm the great man, but Franklin accepted Richard into the family without apparent hesitation as well. Privately, behaving as if no problem had ever existed, Franklin described Bache as a "very agreeable" person, adding, "I very much like his behavior."[20] The commendation was for character, not accomplishment. Although concerned about his son-in-law's financial state, Franklin henceforth saw the economic dilemma as secondary. He must have realized that he had regained patriarchal control through patience. With an eye cocked to his and Deborah's future, he now placed the security and happiness of his Philadelphia family first, Sarah's and Richard's independence and prosperity second.

Yet Franklin was not ready to abandon entirely Bache's prospect for independence. He first refused to seek a government appointment for Bache, although Richard had brought £1,000 to England to assist that purpose. "I am of opinion that almost any profession a man has been educated in is preferable to an office held at pleasure, as rendering him more independent, more a freeman, and less subject to the caprices of superiors," he told Sarah, showing no signs of criticizing her husband. Hoping to eliminate William's previous skepticism about Bache, and to drive home to his own son, as well as his son-in-law, the pertinent issue of industry, frugality, and independence, Franklin reported that he had advised Bache "to lay out the Money he brought with him (£1,000 sterling) in Goods, return and sit down to Business in Philadelphia, selling for ready Money only, in which way I think he might, by quick Return, get forward in the World." Franklin dispassionately outlined the same course to Deborah and Sarah, some of the moralizing edge gone from his previous admonitions to industry; he reassured his daughter that other merchants had started as low and encouraged her not to be too proud to help, while telling his wife to grant Bache use of the North Room as a store.[21]

The textile business that Bache subsequently opened, as well as the wine and grocery business begun in 1773 went nowhere, and a new partnership begun with John Shee in 1779 apparently never prospered. Deborah's frailty and illness, coupled with the dislocations of troubled times, reoriented Sarah and Richard Bache, no matter what their previous initiatives. Franklin also had to see Richard's and Sarah's role in a new light. As if all parties had anticipated the direction things would take, Bache had begun in 1772 to manage some of Franklin's business matters, collecting rents, paying for repairs to property, and checking on defaulted debts and mortgages owed to Franklin. With Deborah failing, Franklin had granted Bache power of attorney by 1773. When Deborah died in 1774, Bache managed the problems concerning her funeral and estate.[22]

When Franklin returned to Philadelphia in 1775, he had suffered political disappointment and personal loss. So, for a brief time at least, he enjoyed finding how well his properties had been cared for by Bache, basked in the warmth of family reunion, and found delight and renewed purpose in his namesake and grandson, Benjamin Franklin Bache. Ambitious in his own conventional sense, Richard apparently continued to press Franklin for aid and support. Franklin, always quick to understand another person's strengths as well as weaknesses, began to see the value to the Baches and himself in exploiting Richard's chief aptitude, his ability to perform routine administrative tasks loyally.

In 1774, Franklin had once again tried to deflect Bache's interest in public office, declaring in regard to the colonial post office, "I am displac'd and consequently have it no longer in my Power to assist you in your Views relating to the Post Office, and as things are I would not wish to see you concern'd in it." And, he bluntly added, intending to eliminate any lingering hopes on Bache's part, that it would be wrong for either of them to hold office in the British post again. But after his return in 1775 Franklin was put at the head of a committee of the Second Continental Congress to establish a post office. Adapting a model already formulated by William Goddard, Franklin brought forth a plan that, when adopted, left Franklin as Postmaster General, Goddard as Surveyor, and Bache, at a salary of $340 a year, as Controller. When Franklin left for France in 1776, Bache, much to Goddard's disappointment, became the acting Postmaster.[23]

At the Post Office, Bache's successes remained meager. Members of Congress, especially Jefferson and Charles Lee, criticized the operation of the new system. Postal rates lagged behind spending and inflation. By 1779, the cost of postal riders was eight times what it had been in 1775. Postal riders went unpaid and, most of the time, so did Bache.[24] Bache's petitions to the Continental Congress were usually requests for advances of money to keep the Post Office operating. As in other business affairs in his life, circumstances overwhelmed a modest competence. Although he had not mismanaged Post Office affairs, he was identified with a failing system. More importantly, he was rightly seen as Franklin's surrogate by Franklin's enemies and, when some New England members of Congress united to further their patronage, they managed to engineer Bache's dismissal and replacement by Ebenezer Hazard. Bache vacillated between philosophical detachment and bitter hurt feelings. On the eve of dismissal, the confusion of emotions showed through:

> This matter was put to vote before I knew a title about it; thinking myself ill-used, I had determined to have resigned, but upon consulting some of my friends was dissuaded from it; there the matter rests, and thus I am to be requited for my past services. All that gives me concern in this business is, that if I am displaced, it will convey to the world an idea that I have not done my duty; but, thank God, nothing of the sort can be alleged against me. I shall, therefore, endeavour to reconcile myself to the worst that can happen.[25]

Resilient and persistent, Bache sought the postmastership again in 1789, when he along with a multitude of others applied for the position under Washington. He had improved the productivity of the post, he argued, while adding "Facility, Quickness & Extent to correspondence." Only difficult times and inveterate prejudice against Franklin, he explained, had led to his unexpected dismissal in 1781, and "Malpractice, Misconduct, Neglect or Incapacity" had not been proved.[26] His statement was as much a bitter lament and defense as it was an application. For thirty years, Bache had anticipated that some system of natural justice would bring him success, status, and independence. When Washington failed to appoint him, Bache was once again bitterly hurt; he apparently held a grudge against Washington through the 1790s and undoubtedly supported at least the early stages of Benjamin Franklin Bache's assault on Washington.[27]

The Post Office was not Richard's only occupation during the Revolution. Hoping to establish those social and political connections that he perceived as critical to success in his deference-dominated world, Bache did not worry about charges of nepotism. He accepted appointment in January, 1775, as a delegate from Philadelphia to a Provincial Convention established to endorse the Continental Congress and its actions. A few months later, he assumed the task of supervising the printing of bills of credit for the Congress. More importantly, he was appointed to the Pennsylvania Board of War in April, 1777. A creature of the Pennsylvania Supreme Executive Council, the Board was less imposing than its name, handling minor administrative and quarter-mastering tasks. In 1778, for example, Richard supervised the supply of flour and cattle to the army from one of the quarter-master districts.[28]

The Pennsylvania Board of War did not remain only a petty administrative body; it became an engine for political activity as well. The object was the Pennsylvania Constitution of 1776 itself. Supported by Franklin in 1776, because he was skeptical of "mixed" constitutions, and mildly defended by an ill, distracted Franklin in 1788, the Constitution of 1776 continued the old democratic structure of a unicameral legislature and a plural executive while ushering a class of new men into the state's political life. Displaced conservatives and moderates, eventually calling themselves the Republican Society, opposed the 1776 "Constitutionalists" and began a ten-and-a-half-year campaign to amend the Constitution. The first Republican effort came from the Board of War. In a mid-1776 petition signed by Bache as chairman, the Board lamented the dissension in Pennsylvania over the Constitution and suggested that certain "defects and disorders" had resulted. The times demanded united action against a common enemy, they said, and this required a convention to alter, amend, or confirm the Constitution. The "Constitutionalists" agreed; then Philadelphia was invaded by Howe, and by the time further action could take place the state was quite evenly divided into opposing political camps.

In late 1778, under James Wilson's leadership, the Republicans renewed a campaign for revision, calling for efficiency in government and in the war effort. In March, 1779, Bache's name again appeared as chairman of the Republican Society and at the head of a petition for revision, apparently in order to refute the more radical "Constitutionalist" charge that Republicans were actually Tories. When this petition failed in the face of overwhelming petition support for the Constitution, the Republicans rebuked the Assembly for vacillating in first supporting a convention and then opposing one in the face of petitioners. This last protest, again signed by Bache as chairman of the Republican Society, criticized the Assembly for not putting the issue to a popular vote. But when the Constitution was revised in 1790, Bache was no longer active.[29] If Richard Bache was sincere and firm in championing the Republican Society's views on the proper constitution of government, he must have clashed with his eldest son Benjamin. In 1797, and even before in various newspaper editorials, Benjamin had promoted the benefits of a unicameral legislature and defended a plural executive with a blunt insistence that his grandfather would never have exercised.[30]

The Board of War and the campaign over the 1776 Constitution locate Richard Bache in the landscape of late-eighteenth-century thought and life. He was frequently assigned routine administrative tasks that required no imagination but did require day-to-day scrutiny. When political issues arose, he was emblematically useful, as a representative either of Franklin, or of the independence movement. He never appeared as a man with his own mind; he was always someone's surrogate. Born into a world of ascribed status, of deference and patronage, Bache seemed untroubled in doing the bidding of others to enhance or ensure his own social position.

No matter what the task, Richard Bache was primarily Franklin's agent. He assumed, by default and without fanfare, the management of almost every facet of Franklin's holdings. In the 1780s, he exercised his own discretion by investing some of Franklin's money in Robert Morris's Bank of North America while sitting, from 1784 to 1792, as a director of the Bank. Altogether, Franklin's estates prospered under Bache's management (and wartime inflation). Between 1775 and Franklin's death in 1790, rents collected on Franklin's properties exceeded taxes by over £2,000.[31] Richard and Sarah were also social managers for Franklin. In 1774, Franklin had recommended that Bache give his "advice and countenance" to "an ingenious, worthy young man" named Thomas Paine, so that Paine might find employment as a clerk, tutor, or surveyor. Thus began a long association between Paine and the Baches. With the introduction of France into the Revolution, Franklin encouraged the Baches to look after the new French Minister, Conrad Alexander Gérard, and make him feel at home.[32]

Meanwhile, Richard's position in the complex musical chairs of family politics was changing. When Benjamin Franklin rambled off on a useless mission to Canada in 1775, and then when William Franklin embraced the Crown and disgraced the family in 1776, Richard was cast briefly in the additional role of family diplomat and then permanently in that of only son. He stood anchored in the eye of the storm, the temporary custodian of William's petulant, foppish illegitimate son, William Temple. After Franklin departed for France in 1776 with Benjamin Franklin Bache and William Temple Franklin in tow, Richard faced the difficult task of being Franklin's eyes, ears, and political informant. He and Sarah also faced the dislocations of war, fleeing first to Goshen in Chester County, then in the fall of 1777 to Manheim near Lancaster. In mid-1778 Richard returned to Philadelphia only to find many of Franklin's treasured belongings gone and the house damaged and looted.[33]

Upon her return to Philadelphia, Sarah—perhaps seeking relief and reassurance in a tumultuous world—seemed to react with a kind of hedonistic release. In 1779, for example, she informed her father that "there never was so much dressing and pleasure going on; old friends meeting again, the Whigs in high spirits, and strangers of distinction among us." She flaunted her new-found friendship with French minister Gérard and bragged that she had "lately been several times invited abroad with the General and Mrs. Washington." When she also asked her father for some lace and feathers, he exploded, replying that her request "disgusted me as much as if you had put salt into my strawberries." "You seem not to know, my dear daughter," he added, "that of all the dear things in this world idleness is the dearest, except mischief."[34]

Chastised, Sarah shifted her energies. Always willing to indulge her desire for popularity, she was equally able to heed the call to duty. In 1780, responding to her father's criticism, she helped Mrs. Esther Reed found an association of Philadelphia women with the purpose of collecting contributions in aid of Washington's army. When Mrs. Reed died, Sarah led this group, including four other women, in a zealous collection campaign. Social pretense and, according to some, social decency failed to deter them from door-to-door solicitations from servant and householder alike. One observer claimed that the "ladies were so importunate that people were obliged to give them some thing to get rid of them, . . . nor did they let the meanest ale house escape."[35] By late 1780, the group had collected over $300,000 (Continental currency) from 1,645 donors. When Washington suggested that the Army needed shirts, the women bought the linen cloth and cut most of the shirts at the Franklins' (or Sally's) home. The day after Christmas, Sarah informed Washington that 2,005 shirts had been made and delivered. The campaign had been so successful that Sarah had urged the organization of similar associations in Bethlehem, Germantown, and Lancaster. Washington was effusive in his praise of the Philadelphia association, proclaiming that their work "intitles [sic] them to an equal place with any who have preceded them in the walk of female patriotism." Subsequent observers have noted that this was the most independent and "best organized political action" by women in the Revolution.[36]

Sarah's activities in 1780 say much about Franklinian morals as practiced in the private Franklin family. Personal comfort and ease were set aside (not abandoned) in favor of public duty. Initiative and industry took precedence over a quest for social status. Artisanal craftsmanship (shirtmaking) combined with obliviousness to class (door-to-door solicitation) in pointed disregard for conventional public morality. Fame and acclaim followed a seemingly selfless act. A kind of full circle often seen in Franklin's own life—self-satisfied ease wedded to moral purposefulness, followed by determined industry, followed by celebrity—was accomplished this once by Sarah. She briefly knew the patriotic fame her father experienced so easily, an achievement that stood in marked contrast to the stolid, mundane endeavors of her husband Richard.

Sarah's achievement in 1780 not only became part of a family legacy of sacrifice and republican virtue, it also became an instrument of moral education for young Benjamin Franklin Bache, who had been sent to Geneva by his grandfather to mature in a republican and protestant country. In 1781, Franklin informed young Benjamin about his mother's recent patriotic activities, reminding the boy that he had to be diligent in his studies to be worthy of such an eminently good woman.[37] The underlying messages were not lost on young Bache. A few years later, he too would trace the circle of vanity and morality, celebrity and industry that had been fostered in him early through his grandfather's and mother's examples.

No matter how domestic the episode of 1780 appeared, Sally had participated in one of the few political activities accomplished by women in eighteenth-century America. The window of political opportunity for American women had opened only briefly. Raised in the morally charged atmosphere of Franklin's family, Sally had moved beyond Franklin's ambivalent ideas on womanhood. He had seemed wistfully attached to a traditional domestic ideal of the woman in the home and woman as ornament, while undermining that subtle desire with his catechisms on industry and usefulness. Perhaps Sally hoped to play the role of ornament and traditional domestic womanhood, but her love of finery, parties, and luxuries could not compensate for her plainness and, more importantly, her need to live up to a social and political moral standard and to pursue that standard vigorously.

After 1780, however, with avenues to political service shut for women, even for those whose political consciousness had been raised during the Revolution, Sally accepted the role of domesticity again. She did so for two compelling reasons. On the moral side, she seems to have embraced the validity of the "moral mother's" importance to the new republic. By 1785 she was the mother of seven children, and that circumstance alone could have provided her with the rationale to seek civic virtue through educating her children.[38] On the private domestic side, her father cleverly wielded the carrot and the stick of domestic life's advantages. Aware of his own need to be cared for in old age, and equally aware of his daughter's love of ease and comfort even though Richard faced a failed business, Franklin had already reminded his daughter and son-in-law in 1773, "Remember, for your Encouragement in good oeconomy, that whatever a Child saves of its Parents' Money, will be its own another Day."[39]

Sarah Bache, then, experienced virtually the full range of opportunities open to women in the revolutionary age, only to slip quietly in her later years into the more conventional garb of middle-class domesticity. Later commentators noted some of that spirit in describing Sarah. Samuel Vaughan described her as strong-minded, educated, and affectionate. The Marquis de Chastellux proclaimed that, "Simple in her manner, like her respectable father, she also possesses his benevolence." In 1798, the Polish traveler Julian Niemcewicz remarked that "her natural wit and her conversation does not belie the origin from which she descends." Although the severe New Englander Manasseh Cutler once described her as "a very gross and rather homely lady," almost all observers seemed to see her possessed of the same self-confidence that Deborah Franklin had seen in her daughter in the 1760s and 1770s.[40]

The post-revolutionary period brought an end to any prominence Richard and Sarah had achieved as public figures. By the time Franklin arrived home from France in 1785 with Benny Bache in tow, Richard and Sarah were living in domestic tranquility with their other six children. A tone of ease and leisure returned to the Franklin-Bache household. Franklin doted on his grandchildren and planned additions to the house. Richard apparently continued to manage Franklin's properties, as much his now as Franklin's. Richard and Sarah continued their pursuit of social distinctions and pleasures as well, although the spirited social life of the Revolution was gone.[41] Richard seems to have remained submissive to Franklin's lead. Perhaps genuinely interested in political science (although we have no record to suggest it), he joined Franklin's new creation, the Society for Political Inquiries, upon its establishment in 1787. A year later, he rode at the head of a "federal procession" in Philadelphia, again as Franklin's surrogate, in celebration of the adoption of the Constitution by ten states and the dawning of a new era.[42]

When Franklin died in 1790, Richard and Sarah Bache found themselves financially independent for the first time. It was an independence built on Franklin's will. Written in 1788, it left Richard and Sarah in possession of Franklin Court, the printing office, most of Franklin's other real estate in the city, and almost all the household goods and treasures. Richard received Ohio lands, some lots in Philadelphia, a cancellation of some old debts to Franklin and the right to collect others, Franklin's gold watch and chain, and his musical instruments, all on the condition that the family's black slave, "Bob," be set free (Franklin died as President of the Pennsylvania Abolition Society never having manumitted his own slave). In the 1790s "Daddy Bob," who apparently found his latecoming freedom unbearable, was taken back into the Bache household as a servant.[43] Sarah received her own money from Franklin's accounts in Paris and London banks. She also received Franklin's miniature of Louis XVI set with 408 diamonds on the condition that she not remove the diamonds or have jewelry made out of them and "thereby introduce or countenance the expensive, vain, and useless fashion of wearing jewels in this country." Understanding his daughter's weaknesses, Franklin tried to extend the long hand of Franklinian morals from the grave. It did not work. In the early 1790s, the Baches violated the spirit, if not the letter, of the will, removing the outer ring of diamonds to finance an extended tour of Europe, a tour that Sarah had long anticipated as a young woman but had never received because it never suited her father's agenda.[44]

Little is known of the later life of Richard and Sarah Bache, partly because they wished to lead uneventful lives. During their European tour, Richard wrote from England to a friend in Philadelphia that he enjoyed the amusements and sports of "this Land of pleasure & dissipation."[45] Sometime after returning from Europe, Richard managed to add gentrification to his desire for ease. The Baches purchased a farm in Delaware and named it "Settle" after Richard's birthplace in England—an appropriate name referring to the Baches' Anglo-American orientation and semi-retirement. The Polish traveler Niemcewicz described the family as living in bucolic ease on a farm of 270 acres where five men and a gardener handled the work. "Mr. Bache," he reported, "has completely the air of a Country Esquaire [sic], frank countenance and with a rather jovial humour." Other Bache family members, including the by then radical newspaper publisher Benjamin, all assembled during Niemcewicz's visit, were similarly described. "This whole family appeared to know good fortune," he concluded, "that is to say enjoying easy circumstances, independence, and tranquillity." It seemed to him that "With these people domestic harmony is as much a virtue as a custom."[46]

No one can understand fully the role that family dynamics play in the evolutionary history of a family. In most ways, Benjamin Franklin Bache's life reflected fragmentation and deep divisions between generations, which might be described in twentieth-century psychological terms as showing autonomy coupled with alienation. But subtle ties did exist; family circumstances and events, at least before 1790, must have had significant effects upon him. Sarah's independent spirit and her commitment to a marriage of affection must have shaped her actions as a mother and influenced her first-born son during his infancy and boyhood (1769–1776). And by 1780 even Franklin was using Sarah's patriotic achievements to encourage young Benjamin toward initiative, industry, moral commitment, and worthiness. The events of the Revolution as reflected in his mother's life, seen from afar by an impressionable young boy, might have also given him the confident sense that a place in history and family celebrity were goals to be sought.

Richard's influence as father is less obvious. Aside from both men's ability to work hard at routine tasks, father and son held little in common. Richard was the product of eighteenth-century cultural "sensibility," not political enlightenment. He accepted without question the conservative Anglo-American world of social convention and class, of deference to a social order that changed only in a slow evolutionary fashion. He was no visionary; the only autonomy he sought was that of the middle-class merchant attempting economic, not political, independence. So, in the realm of ideas and ideology, he stood at a great distance from his radical son. As real flesh and blood, he was equally distant. To young Benjamin, he was a subordinate of his much more dominant grandfather. As a failed merchant, he had no legacy of industry and achievement to leave. The faithful servant of others, his accomplishments were neither unique nor remarkable; they set no standard for imitation. What young Benjamin saw was a father attempting to live a life of ease. Benjamin made clear his own vision of his father in a 1789 letter, while Richard was away in New York City:

> I can see you running all morning to pay your visits *de ceremonie*. You are so fond of making your bows, paying your court and all that kind of stuff; dress and then dine with your old friends, a pack of jovial, clever fellows . . . and in the evening the Ladies, if you happen to rise from table [in] time enough. . . .[47]

Franklin's pattern of behavior in regard to his dependent family—from his daughter Sarah to his grandson Temple—reveals important clues for his later role in raising young Benjamin to adulthood. But the pattern was usually one of paradox. He understood, and even shared, Richard's and Sarah's desire for ease and comfort and acceptance of conventional society, while admonishing himself and others to duty and industry. At the same time, he had an equally intense desire for autonomy and a vision of political progress, though he was seldom passionate about that vision. Franklin's parental behavior could seem ambivalent. Love and affection were checked by uncertainty, neglect, and distance. Admonitions for industry and morality produced independence and autonomy, not paternal control. Franklin's attempts at intervention in the lives of William, Sarah, Richard, Temple, and Benjamin were on a grand scale that suggested great expectations. But he was unable to shape their ultimate characters or their beliefs. In part, his temperament and other factors stymied him. Although he was eager to get his way, he was seldom so guileless as to disclose fully what ends he desired, and he never demanded that his family accept his views on family issues as closed and final. Thus, both directly through design on Franklin's part, and indirectly through his behavior, those intimately tied to him tried to interpret Franklin's wishes, and more often, to fashion their own desires within a framework they imagined would be acceptable to him. Their freedom, within the broad moral paradigms he had constructed and made clear, was to act as free agents in relation to particular events. Franklin, not fully realizing this consequence and not fully committed to consistent, attentive parental direction, was often left as the somewhat bewildered patriarch. If he had lived past 1790, he might have been even more astounded at the conduct of his namesake grandson.

Notes

1. See Philip Greven, *The Protestant Temperament: Patterns of Child-Rearing, Religious Experience, and the Self in Early America* (New York, 1977), 13, 149–261. Greven places Franklin on the more "modern" end of the spectrum of temperament toward the efficacy of self-love and freedom. While this may have been Franklin's tendency, the fact is that he frequently exhibited the ambivalence of the moderate when it came to moral instruction in regard to both his daughter and later his grandson. See *ibid.*, 194, 205–206, 216, 253.

2. For Franklin's admonishments see Benj. Franklin to Abiah Franklin, April 12, 1750, Leonard W. Labaree, *et al.*, eds., *The Papers of Benjamin Franklin* (New Haven, Conn., 1959–), III, 475, hereafter cited as Labaree, *et al.*, eds., *Franklin Papers;* and Benj. Franklin to Deb. Franklin, June 2, 1757, *ibid.*, VII, 232. For other positive encouragements see Benj. Franklin to Deb. Franklin, Nov. 22, 1757, and Feb. 19, 1758, *ibid.*, 276, 383. On musical encouragement see Benj. Franklin to Jane Mecom, June 19, 1763, and Benj. Franklin to Sir Alex. Dick, Dec. 11, 1763, *ibid.*, X, 292, 385. For Franklin's analysis of his daughter's strengths, and on his gifts to her, see Benj. Franklin to Abiah Franklin, Oct. 16, 1747; Benj. Franklin to Wm. Strahan, June 2, 1750, *ibid.*, III, 179–80, 479; Benj. Franklin to Deb. Franklin, June 10 and Sept. 6, 1758, *ibid.*, VIII, 91, 306–307; and Benj. Franklin to Wm. Strahan, Jan. 31, 1757, *ibid.*, III, 475, VII, 415. See also Claude-Anne Lopez and Eugenia W. Herbert, *The Private Franklin: The Man and His Family* (New York, 1975), 74, 133, which contains the best and most subtle description of family relations among the Franklins.

3. On Polly see Esmond Wright, *Franklin of Philadelphia* (Cambridge, Mass., 1986), 110. On Franklin's general attitude see Lopez and Herbert, *Private Franklin*, 70–77, and Wright, *Franklin*, passim.

4. Lopez and Herbert, *Private Franklin*, 119–20, 122; Wright, *Franklin*, 326; Elizabeth F. Ellet, *The Women of the American Revolution* (New York, 1851), I, 333; and Benj. Franklin to Sally Franklin, Nov. 8, 1764, Labaree, *et al.*, eds., *Franklin Papers*, XI, 448–49.

5. Lopez and Herbert, *Private Franklin*, 76–77. For interesting insights into Franklin's personality patterns see Richard L. Bushman, "On the Use of Psychology: Conflict and Conciliation in Benjamin Franklin," *History and Theory*, V (1968), 225–40. On Franklin's promotion of his daughter see Benj. Franklin to Wm. Strahan, Jan. 31, 1757, Labaree, *et al.*, eds., *Franklin Papers*, VII, 115. For the collapse of the "arranged" marriage see Benj. Franklin to Deb. Franklin, Mar. 5, 1760, *ibid.*, IX, 32; and Lopez and Herbert, *Private Franklin*, 82–83.

6. The entire issue of Sarah's courtship and marriage is discussed thoroughly in Lopez and Herbert, *Private Franklin*, 133–46.

7. Wm. Franklin to Benj. Franklin, [May ?, 1767], Labaree, *et al.*, eds., *Franklin Papers*, XIV, 174–75.

8. Benj. Franklin to Deb. Franklin, June 22, 1767, *ibid.*, 193.

9. Benj. Franklin to Deb. Franklin, Aug. 5, 1767, *ibid.*, 225.

10. Benj. Franklin to R. Bache, Aug. 5, 1767, in Copies of Letters, Miscellaneous Collection, Historical Society of Pennsylvania, Philadelphia. It must be remembered that the events of the American Revolution had not yet separated Franklin from his loyalist son William. Franklin was undoubtedly estimating the amount of his estate that would go to William both before and after his death, and concluding that Richard and Sarah could expect little. Franklin's almost total disinheritance of his son after the Revolution changed this picture.

11. The quotation is from Lopez and Herbert, *Private Franklin*, 138. On the concept of affection see Mary Beth Norton, *Liberty's Daughters: The Revolutionary Experience of American Women, 1750–1800* (Boston, 1980), 59–60.

12. Austin S. Stevens, ed., *Colonial Records of the New York Chamber of Commerce, 1768–1784, with Historical and Biographical Sketches* (New York, 1867), II, 41; and Walter Barrett, *The Old Merchants of New York City* (New York, 1885), II, 90.

13. Biographical material on Theophylact may be found in *Appleton's Cyclopedia of American Biography*, James G. Wilson and John Fiske, eds. (New York, 1887), I, 126; Stevens, *Colonial Records*, I, 21, 53, 57–59, 63–64, 75, 177, 299–300, II, 41–45; Barrett, *Old Merchants*, III, 234, 239, IV, 164, 218, 226, 281; James G. Wilson, ed., *The Memorial History of the City of New York from Its First Settlement to the Year 1892* (New York, 1893), II, 466, IV, 525; Lorenzo Sabine, *Biographical Sketches of Loyalists of the American Revolution* (Boston, 1864), I, 199–200; and Virginia D. Harrington, *The New York Merchant on the Eve of the Revolution* (New York, 1935), 12–13, 52, 261–62.

14. On the "Sally" incident see Theo. Bache, *The General Committee for the City and County of New York . . . , June 23, 1775* [Broadside] (New York, 1775); and Stevens, *Colonial Records*, I, 202. On his clash with the Committee of Safety see [Theo. Bache] to Major Moncrieff, Sept. 3, 1775; and [Theo. Bache] to the Provincial Congress of New York, July 7, 1776, *ibid.*, II, 47–48.

15. Alexander Graydon, *Memoirs of a Life Chiefly Passed in Pennsylvania within the Last Sixty Years . . .* (Harrisburg, Pa., 1811), 230. On Theophylact Bache during the Revolution see *New York City During the American Revolution, A Collection of Papers from Manuscript* (New York, 1861), 154; and Oscar T. Barck, *New York City during the War of Independence* (New York, 1931), 55.

16. Stevens, *Colonial Records*, II, 51–53, I, 296, 306; Wilson, *Memorial History*, IV, 536; Joseph B. Bishop, *A Chronicle of One Hundred and Fifty Years: The Chamber of Commerce of the State of New York, 1768–1918* (New York, 1918), 34–47; and New York Chamber of Commerce, *Charter and By-Laws*, 15–17. For allusions to Benjamin's visit see M. H. Bache to B. F. Bache, July 4, 1795; and B. F. Bache to M. H. Bache, July 18, 19, 21, 1795, Bache Papers, Castle Collection, American Philosophical Society, Philadelphia.

17. "The Mount Regale Fishing Company of Philadelphia," *Pennsylvania Mag-*

azine of History and Biography, XXVII (1903), 88–90; and Lopez and Herbert, *Private Franklin,* 134–37.

18. "Note," *PMHB,* XLIX (1925), 184n and 185n; and John C. Campbell, *History of the Friendly Sons of St. Patrick and of the Hibernian Society for the Relief of Emigrants from Ireland, 1771–1892* (Philadelphia, 1892), 140.

19. See respectively Benj. Franklin to R. Bache, Aug. 13, 1768, Labaree, *et al.,* eds., *Franklin Papers,* XV, 186; and S. Bache to Benj. Franklin, May [1770], *ibid.,* XVII, 153.

20. Benj. Franklin to Jane Mecom, Jan. 13, 1772, *ibid.,* XIX, 349.

21. See respectively Benj. Franklin to S. Bache, Jan. 29, 1772, *ibid.,* 46; Benj. Franklin to Wm. Franklin, Jan. 30, 1772, *ibid.,* 50–51; Benj. Franklin to S. Bache, Jan. 29, 1772; and Benj. Franklin to Deb. Franklin, Jan. 28, 1772, *ibid.,* 46–47, 45.

22. Lopez and Herbert, *Private Franklin,* 170–73; Benj. Franklin to R. Bache, Oct. 7, 1772; Mrs. Jenny Bedford to Benj. Franklin, Feb. 2, 1773; Benj. Franklin to Wm. Franklin, Sept. 7, 1774, Labaree, *et al.,* eds., *Franklin Papers,* XIX, 314–16, XX, 35, XXI, 286; and Penrose R. Hooper, comp., "Cash Dr to Benjamin Franklin, *PMHB,* LXXX (1956), 47.

23. Benj. Franklin to R. Bache, Feb. 17, 1774, Labaree, *et al.,* eds., *Franklin Papers,* XXI, 101. On the Post Office in general see Wesley Everett Rich, *The History of the United States Post Office to the Year 1829* (Cambridge, Mass., 1924), 46–51.

24. *Ibid.,* 52–56.

25. R. Bache to Benj. Franklin, Nov. 24, 1781, [William Temple Franklin], *Letters to Benjamin Franklin from His Family and Friends, 1751–1790* (New York, 1859), 119.

26. R. Bache to G. Washington, April 21, 1789, Presidential Papers on Microfilm, George Washington Papers, Library of Congress, Series III, Vol. II, 1.

27. The Polish traveler Niemcewicz, who visited the extended Bache family in 1798, claimed that after Richard's failure to gain appointment in 1789, "the whole family since then [was] very embittered against G1. Washington and in general against the power of the executive." Julian Ursyn Niemcewicz, *Under Their Vine and Fig Tree, Travels through America in 1791–1799, 1805 with some Further Account of Life in New Jersey,* trans. and ed. Metchie J. E. Budka (Elizabeth, N. J., 1965), 61.

28. *Pennsylvania Archives,* Series 2, Vol. III (1896), 549–50; and Worthington C. Ford, ed., *Journals of the Continental Congress, 1774–1789* (Washington, D. C., 1904–1933), II, 194. On the Board of War see Minutes of the Board of War, *Pennsylvania Archives,* Ser. 2, Vol. I (1879), 3–72; See also Minutes of the Supreme Executive Council, *Colonial Records. Pennsylvania Archives,* Ser. 1, Vol. VI, 234–35.

29. On the Board of War, Constitution issue see Allan Nevins, *The American States During and After the Revolution, 1775–1789* (New York, 1924), 105–56, 185–86; Wright, *Franklin,* 239, 250–52; "The Petition and Remonstrance of the Board of War. . . . To the Honorable Representatives of the Freemen of the Commonwealth of Pennsylvania in Assembly . . . , June 12, 1777," Minutes of the Board of War. *Pennsylvania Archives,* Ser. 2, Vol. I (1879), 54; C. Page Smith, "The Attack on Fort Wilson," *PMHB,* LXXVIII (1954), 177–78; J. Thomas Scharf and Thompson Westcott, *History of Philadelphia, 1689–1884* (Philadelphia, 1884), I, 396; Phila-

delphia, Constitutional Society, *To the Citizens of Pennsylvania . . .* [Broadside] (Philadelphia, 1780).

30. Benjamin Franklin Bache, *Remarks Occasioned by the Late Conduct of Mr. Washington as President of the United States* (Philadelphia, 1797), 34–41.

31. Lawrence Lewis, Jr., *A History of the Bank of North America* (Philadelphia, 1882), 133; Hooper, "Cash D^r to Benjamin Franklin," *PMHB*, LXXX (1956), 48.

32. On the Paine introduction see Benj. Franklin to R. Bache, Sept. 30, 1774, Labaree, *et al.*, eds., *Franklin Papers*, XXI, 325–26. On Gérard see Benj. Franklin to R. and Sarah Bache, Mar. 31, 1778, *ibid.*, XXVI, 202–203.

33. Lopez and Herbert, *Private Franklin*, 193–94, 208–209, 218–20, suggest the difficulty of Richard's position.

34. See respectively Sarah Bache to Benj. Franklin, Jan. 17, 1779, [Franklin], comp., *Letters*, 91–92; Benj. Franklin to Sarah Bache, June 3, 1779, Albert Henry Smyth, ed., *The Writings of Benjamin Franklin* (New York, 1905–1907), VII, 346–50, hereafter cited as Smyth, ed., *Writings of Franklin*. See also Frederick D. Stone, "Philadelphia Society One Hundred Years Ago," *PMHB*, III (1879), 373–76.

35. Anna Rawle to Mrs. Benj. Shoemaker, June 30, 1780, in Wm. Brooke Rawle, "Laurel Hill and Some Colonial Dames Who Once Lived There," *PMHB*, XXXV (1911), 398.

36. G. Washington to Mrs. Anna Francis, Mrs. Harrietta Hillegas, Mrs. Mary Clarkson, Mrs. Sarah Bache, and Mrs. Susan Blair, Feb. 13, 1781, John C. Fitzpatrick, ed., *The Writings of George Washington from the Original Manuscripts, 1745–1799* (Washington, D. C., 1931–44), XXI, 221–221n, hereafter cited as Fitzpatrick, ed., *Writings of Washington*. The modern comment is from Linda K. Kerber, *Women of the Republic: Intellect and Ideology in Revolutionary America* (Chapel Hill, N. C., 1980), 99. On the association's accomplishments see also "Itinerary of George Washington, June 15, 1775 to Dec. 23, 1783," *PMHB*, XV (1891–92), 144n; *Notable American Women, 1607–1950: A Biographical Dictionary,* ed. Edward T. James (3 vols.; Cambridge, Mass., 1971), I, 75–76; Kerber, *Women*, 99–103; Linda K. Kerber, "The Republican Mother—Women and the Enlightenment—An American Perspective," *American Quarterly*, XXVIII (Summer, 1976), 201; and Norton, *Liberty's Daughters*, 179–87.

37. Benj. Franklin to B. F. Bache, April 16, 1781, Franklin Papers, American Philosophical Society, Philadelphia.

38. On moral motherhood as a syphon for growing female awareness of the public world, see Kerber, *Women of the Republic*; Kerber, "Republican Mother," *Am. Quar.*, XXVIII (1976), 187–204; Paula Baker, "The Domestication of Politics: Women and American Political Society, 1780–1920," *American Historical Review*, 89 (June 1984), 620–47; and Ruth H. Bloch, "American Feminine Ideals in Transition: The Rise of the Moral Mother, 1785–1815," *Feminist Studies*, 4 (June 1978), 100–26. Norton, *Liberty's Daughters*, 228–29, believes that gains in liberated views persisted after the Revolution in many individual cases and in subtle ways, and denies that all women were held captive in the narrow domestic confines of moral motherhood.

39. Benj. Franklin to Sarah Bache, April 6, 1773, Labaree, *et al.*, eds., *Franklin Papers*, XX, 142.

40. Sarah P. Stetson, "The Philadelphia Sojourn of Samuel Vaughan," *PMHB*, LXXIII (1949), 461; Marquis de Chastellux, *Travels in North America in the Years 1780, 1781, and 1782,* trans. and intro. by Howard C. Rice, Jr. (Chapel Hill, N. C., 1963), II, 135; Niemcewicz, *Under Their Vine and Fig Tree,* 61; "New York and Philadelphia in 1787. Extracts from the Journals of Manasseh Cutler," *PMHB*, XII (1888–89), 110; and, on Deborah's view of her daughter, Lopez and Herbert, *Private Franklin,* 139.

41. Richard apparently participated in lavish dinners and fox hunts. For allusions to these see "Notes and Queries," *PMHB*, XXIV (1900), 383; and Benj. Franklin to Le Ray de Chaumont, Oct. 20, 1785, in Carl Van Doren, ed., *Benjamin Franklin's Autobiographical Writings* (New York, 1945), 662. Sarah enjoyed the company of dignitaries and in 1787 is mentioned giving a tea attended by General Washington. See Joseph Jackson, "Washington in Philadelphia," *PMHB*, LVI (1932), 143.

42. Society for Political Enquiries, *Rules and Regulations . . . , 9th February, 1787* (Philadelphia, Aitken, 1787); Minutes of the Society for Political Inquiries, 1787–1789, Historical Society of Pennsylvania; Lopez and Herbert, *Private Franklin,* 284.

43. See *ibid.,* 306; and Niemcewicz, *Under Their Vine and Fig Tree,* 61.

44. "Franklin's Will," Smyth, ed., *Writings of Franklin,* X, 494–96, 496n, 500–501; Lopez and Herbert, *Private Franklin,* 306–307.

45. R. Bache to Peter Baynton, July 23, 1792, in the Autograph Collections of Simon Gratz, Hist. Soc. Pa.

46. Niemcewicz Journal, April 19, 1798, Niemcewicz, *Travels,* 61.

47. B. F. Bache to Richard Bache, May 7, 1789, Bache Papers, Castle Coll., Am. Philos. Soc.

2. Identity and Youth, 1769–1785

"... as he is destined to live in a Protestant Country, and a Republic, I thought it best to finish his Education where the proper Principles prevail."
(Benj. Franklin to John Quincy Adams, April 21, 1779)

ON OCTOBER 27, 1776, a less than reliable ship, the *Reprisal*, quietly left Philadelphia for France with a cargo of indigo, one of America's new commissioners to France—Benjamin Franklin—and two boys, William Temple Franklin and the undoubtedly bewildered seven-year-old, Benjamin Franklin Bache. It was an unusual manifest and it would prove to be a dangerous voyage. For the three principal passengers, it was also a voyage marking momentous personal and emotional changes.

Temple was leaving his loyalist father, William, in a futile search to discover himself. Witty, clever, cynical, often sly, frequently irresponsible to others and himself, he was a young man who sought status and position under Franklin through attachments and connivance. Knowing full well the future disadvantages Temple would suffer by not acquiring the well-directed education that could give him true independence, Franklin ignored the consequences and insisted on keeping Temple by his side as a comfort and aid. Unbeknownst to anyone at the time, Temple's service to the American commissioners would turn out to be "competent, diligent, honest and patriotic," the one noble achievement of his life.[1] But Franklin knew that he played a dangerous game in both tolerating and exploiting Temple's weaknesses. When it came to Benny Bache he could not afford such conduct; he had to make certain that Benny's education did not fail, that Benny did not follow Temple down the road of insouciant bad habits.

For Franklin, the voyage to France would prove to be the start of his most successful public service, an eight-year sojourn in which he brought to bear all of the reason, self-confidence, temperamental equanimity, and subtle knowledge of the human condition that he had garnered over his previous seventy years. Accomplishment demanded resolve and understanding. Furthermore, Franklin had come to see the value in subduing ego through flexibility and restraint. He was an old man who had found the fame and fortune he had always sought, but who had also come to enjoy the fruits of those rewards, particularly if he did not appear to seek them. Thus, it was not surprising that his whole approach to French diplomacy was, as one historian points out, immersed in "a style of calculated passivity."[2]

Always better at accommodation than confrontation, Franklin hid his mixed emotions, although his grandsons probably picked up many of his half-spoken or unspoken signals of bitterness and approval. With the influential French aristocracy expecting either rustic charm or scientific sophistication, and with the French Foreign Minister, Vergennes, and the French Court navigating a dangerous foreign-policy course, Franklin was willing to become a caricature of himself and, when necessary, of America. Busied by a mountain of mundane business, Franklin sometimes experienced physical weariness and illness, distractions, and self-doubts. But like the good actor he was, he usually rose to the occasion at court or as host at Passy (the then small French suburb of Paris where Franklin lived) playing the several engaging roles of natural man enlightened and republican American embodied, and undoubtedly retaining the genuine and consistent charm that he had so long cultivated.[3]

For Benny Bache, such a grandfather must have communicated an array of mixed messages. It was certainly unclear to the young boy why his grandfather was taking him to France. Nor did Franklin and the Baches probably know entirely. Keeping Benny safe from the vagaries of the Revolution was surely a practical reason. Offering the boy a chance at a European education—something that seems to have been important to Franklin despite his earlier drives for "English" language and useful arts in education in America—was clearly appealing to parents who realized in 1776 that their lives were to be beleaguered by hardships and responsibilities that would leave them little opportunity to raise their youngster properly. And Franklin seems to have been determined, after his brief return to the warmth of hearth and home prior to 1776, to hang onto at least some remnant of family joy. By taking along Temple and Benny, by looking after them and directing them toward useful adulthood, he could rationalize the friendly kidnapping of two youngsters who might offer him comfort in France in a way that the Stevensons had offered it in England. He might have also felt that the boys would provide re-invigorated reminders of his own youth at a time when he felt old and tired. Perhaps he did not even think about the decision very much, reacting more automatically to a familiar twinned pattern of desire and duty.[4]

Yet, for all of the vagueness about why Benny Bache left Philadelphia in 1776, and what his immediate reaction to the removal entailed, we find in Benny's childhood and adolescence a fertile field for investigating the development of personal identity, as well as for discovering the origins of intense political and moral radicalism. Benny's progress through childhood to adolescence is better documented than that of most eighteenth-century youth, and the evolution of identity, the impact of emotions, the call to responsibility, and the fashioning of a peculiar moral development can be extrapolated from the evidence. From his birth in 1769 to his adulthood in 1790, his life was an example of the rapid changes in the nature of youth in the late eighteenth century.

In 1776 Benny at the age of seven obviously had a better idea of what he was leaving than of what he was approaching. From infancy, he had been exposed to several new tendencies in child-raising—the centrality of the child in the family, unabashed adult affection and love of the infant, anxious parental concern for the child's social environment, the very idea of child psychology itself—all supercharged by the celebrity of the Franklin household. In accord with the new pleasure in seeing children as "sweet, tender, promising, pretty little birds," Deborah Franklin lovingly described her grandson as her "little kingbird," an energetic, playful little gentleman. Jane Mecom, Franklin's warmly affectionate sister, told Deborah, "Mrs. Foxcroft & myself have often Pleas'd ourselves with talking of Little King Bird she Agrees with us that He is an Extroydinary [sic] Fine Child, God Bless Him, may He live to be a Blessing to Grand Papah & all the rest."[5]

In England, Franklin vicariously shared family affections for Benny. In 1771, he helped celebrate his grandson's second birthday, agreeing to hold a birthday party for Benny at the home of the Bishop of St. Asaph, complete with the Bishop's traditional "floating island" dessert and toasts. With amusement as well as an anxious eye to the future, Franklin reported that the Bishop's wife's toast was to the hope that Benny might become "as good a Man as his Grandfather"; Franklin replied that he hoped Benny would be better, while the Bishop cleverly added that everyone should "be contented if he should not prove quite as good." Franklin tried to substitute Polly Hewson's oldest child for Benny in his affections and in letters to Deborah, but generally these made him "long to be at home to play with Ben."[6]

Although Sarah apparently did not spare the rod on her eldest son on at least one occasion, the general tenor of the Franklin household suggests that Benny had every reason to feel loved, to feel that he was a special and unique member of the family. When Franklin returned in 1775, he reveled in his grandson, a boy with "big, dark eyes," and already a charmer who was "pretty, affectionate and gentle." No greater proof of his affection and concern could exist than his return to the symbolic fantasy of an arranged marriage, this time between Polly Hewson's daughter Elizabeth and Benny.[7] The boy was also a source of escape from more serious matters. In 1776, before leaving for France, Franklin told Temple he would have sent along a letter from Benjamin but,

> It was thought to be too full of Pothooks and Hangers, and so unintelligible by the dividing Words in the Middle and joining Ends of some to Beginnings of others, that if it had fallen into the Hands of some Committee it might have given them too much trouble to decypher it, on a Suspicion of its containing Treason, especially as directed by a Tory House. He is now diligent in learning to write better.[8]

Franklin would not live long enough to appreciate the ultimate irony of his little joke with Temple. But even without that irony, he continued to reveal his equivocation on the indulged child, countering the levity of the moment with the somber need for better handwriting.

Love and affection were the primary but not the sole elements of Benny's early childhood environment. As early as 1771, Sarah had reported that her eldest son was a grave infant, one who might be raised easily because "he will do a great deal out of affection."[9] His grandmother's illness and death in 1774, the arrival of a new brother, the death of an infant sister, the unsettled comings and goings of relatives, and the natural evolution of self-identity offered a sense of separation as counterpoint to affection, a sense that would be steadily enhanced through his youth. Attachment and separation, with their corollaries commitment and autonomy, would increasingly establish the essence of his childhood and adolescence. But before 1776 at least, Benny's childhood would likely be considered healthy by twentieth- as well as eighteenth-century standards.[10]

The journey to France in the *Reprisal* exaggerated the need for attachment and the force of separation while adding a third childhood element—excitement—to the significant aspects of his youth. Between Philadelphia and Paris, grandfather and grandson experienced cramped ship quarters, near interception by the British, the capture of two prizes by the *Reprisal,* a storm off the French coast, a rough row ashore, the danger of land travel through woods containing bandits, a difficult and slow 250-mile journey from Nantes to Paris, and the confusion of acclaim that greeted Franklin upon his unexpected arrival in Paris. Both were overwhelmed.[11]

Franklin was immediately busied by his celebrity and by the unfamiliar task that lay ahead of him. In addition to a preoccupied grandfather, Benny was confronted by a new landscape. Paris, with its contrasts of wealth and poverty, elegance and squalor, and wide, straight roads alongside narrow, dirty, twisting streets must have been large and confusing to him. Nor did confusion abate when it came to a domicile. The Franklin entourage lived briefly in the Hôtel d'Entragues, and then with Silas Deane at the Hôtel d'Hambourg in the rue Jacob, not moving to Passy until March 1777—a long two months of anxiety, insecurity, and readjustment for a seven-year-old. No wonder that Benny reacted by being "a special good boy," meaning a quiet, untroublesome boy.[12]

He was virtually lost in the shuffle of dignitaries, diplomats, petitioners, and celebrities. References to Benny in Franklin's correspondence henceforward seldom extended beyond obligatory comments on the child's health or the fact that he was not a burden or bother to his grandfather. The only big social episode for Benny in these years was his being "blessed" by Voltaire in 1778 before some twenty witnesses, including the Marquis de Condorcet. While observers were uncertain whether Voltaire pronounced the benediction "God and liberty" or some variant thereof upon Benny, it is doubtful that any immediate philosophical osmosis from one to the other took place. With a few significant exceptions like this one, Franklin did not pay consistent close attention to the youngster until 1783, a distant six years away.[13]

Benny was not the victim of material neglect, however. By March 1777, Franklin had arranged a nearly idyllic permanent residence for his household in the pastoral suburb of Passy, on the elegant estate of Jacques-Donatien le Ray de Chaumont. Chaumont, an ambitious, wealthy, pro-American shipper and munitions dealer, offered Franklin virtually every comfort that the now self-indulgent republican could have wanted. Living first in a modest garden pavilion slightly removed from the main house, and after 1779 in a wing of Chaumont's Hôtel Valentinois, which "stood on the crest of a bluff with terraces and formal gardens, a lake and avenues of clipped lindens, leading down to the Seine," Franklin slipped into a pattern of life well suited to his many interests and duties.[14] Though he reproached his daughter for an unrepublican desire for luxuries, Franklin spent lavishly on meals and wine even while dining abroad as often as six days a week, had no fewer than nine servants, and kept a carriage, horses, and a coachman. French aristocrats found Franklin's life at Passy simple and economical; John Adams was nearer the mark in calling it luxurious.

In a material sense, this setting did not bode poorly for a young, lonely boy separated from the more homely comforts of Philadelphia. Although Franklin may have remained preoccupied with other matters, Benny could share some of the privacy, security, and comfort of their Passy home. But in the first two years that Benny lived with or near Franklin at Passy, the boy's contact with his grandfather seems to have been primarily restricted to Sundays, the day Franklin had set aside to dine with Benny and Temple. And even these Sundays and other holidays were not entirely private, as ever-changing collections of dignitaries and children shared the fellowship.[15] Only after Benny returned from school in Geneva in 1783 did he participate more regularly and fully in the maelstrom of entertainment at Passy, or meet and dine with guests and notables. By then, however, he was a more composed young man, increasingly at Franklin's side, absorbed in the quieter aspects of Franklin's welfare, interests, and hobbies.

But even before Franklin settled in at Passy or received his grand reception, he had calculated that Benny would need more than a comfortable home and his grandfather's occasional charm; he would need attention and education. The solution was a boarding school where, he informed Silas Deane, Benny might "early learn the French language."[16] Almost upon arrival in Paris, Benny was enrolled in Le Coeur's *pension* in Paris. For nearly two years, he lodged at Le Coeur's. Except for Sundays and holidays at Passy, a mere half-hour carriage ride from Paris, he was absorbed in school work and playing with his schoolmates. The school regimen, though not harsh, was exacting for a boy his age. The school day began at 6:00 a.m. and ended at 7:00 p.m., with frequent intervals for play and amusement. Typical of the relatively new concept of the *pension,* the curriculum consisted of French, Latin, dancing, music, and drawing—that is, classical and ornamental education. Also typical was the school's clientele, the children of aristocratic and middle-class families who, through the boarding school, were segregating their children from their elders and the poor alike. Le Coeur's was atypical in that it apparently took some of its students from the small contingent of young Americans in Paris. Thus, Benny's closest friend in school would be Charles Cochran, who entered at about the same time he did; Jesse Deane, placed in Le Coeur's by Franklin in the spring of 1778, would also become a good friend. Along with John Quincy Adams, two years older than Benny, these youngsters made up the majority of the Americans at the academy.[17]

Altogether, Le Coeur's probably represented the best in French education and the steady evolution away from the cruel authoritarianism that had plagued French schools in the previous century. Its curriculum and regimen reflected a liberal desire to shape the morals of boys through careful and relatively personal tutelage. At the same time it reflected the aristocratic and middle-class desire to segregate and protect children that encouraged the emergence of the *pension* boarding schools instead of day schools. By the mid-eighteenth century, *pensions* embodied a "new spirit"; "a child's schooling was expected to provide more than preparation for adult life," it was to provide "the moulding of a type of individual (the gentleman in the English public schools)." In addition, *pensions* anticipated a more national education, less religious, more civic, and more accessible to the broad citizenry.[18]

For Benny, the impact of this liberal, aristocratic education was subtle in some ways and direct in others. He must have been influenced by the personal attention he received, by the school's apparent goal to produce young gentlemen, and by the curriculum's mixture of useful arts and ornaments. He could not have been unaware of the costs, especially as his form of dress shifted from young republican to young gentleman. Later in life he retained an interest in drawing and the aristocrat's love of dancing acquired in France and Geneva. More striking, however, was the most direct effect, the supplanting of English by French as his first language. Franklin told his daughter in 1779 (without the pride of a man who had sent his grandson to Le Coeur's to learn French) that Benny "speaks French better than English."[19] Benny's letters reveal that he wrote French exclusively from 1779 until at least the fall of 1782.

Franklin was shocked. He could not ignore the obvious conclusion that a few hours a week at Passy were not going to offset the youngster's total immersion in French, although he never admitted his own culpability in the personal neglect he had shown Benny. For a man who spoke French poorly, more to charm than to communicate, the specter suddenly loomed of a grandson whose attachments would necessarily be French, which to Franklin meant Catholic and monarchical, rather than Protestant and republican.

Franklin, therefore, made the second big decision in the boy's young life, the decision to send Benny to a place sanitized from monarchical and Catholic forms—Geneva. Franklin told John Quincy Adams, Benny's former schoolmate, that, "as he is destined to live in a Protestant Country, and a Republic, I thought it best to finish his Education where the proper Principles prevail."[20] The care that Franklin took to explain himself to everyone on this matter served several purposes. On an unspoken level, it rationalized his own neglect, casting blame for what had occurred on the opposing natures of France and America. It also revealed a momentary coolness and stagnation in Franco-American relations. By sending Benny off to Geneva, he could make a small point and satisfy his pique as a diplomat.[21] In a letter to Richard Bache, Franklin tried to soothe the family with a litany of soft words and rationalizations. Benny was a "good, honest lad," he said, who had the potential to be "a valuable man." But Le Coeur's (which may have offered only elementary education through what the French called the fourth course) could not provide him much more in education. Franklin had finally "fixed on sending him to Geneva." Fortunately, Franklin added, a native Genevan named Philibert Cramer had agreed to escort Benny to that city and to act as a kind of guardian for the boy. "He went very cheerfully," Franklin concluded, "and I understand is very happy." "I miss his company on Sundays at dinner," Franklin testified, "But if I live, and I can find a little leisure, I shall make the journey next spring to see him, & to see at the same time the old thirteen United States of Switzerland."[22]

Franklin's cheerful comments were attempts to disguise not only his neglect, but the risky business of sending a nine-year-old boy off to a strange country with unknown guardians. Torn between affections for her father and her son, Sarah told Franklin,

> We are all well satisfied with Your sending Benjamin to Geneva, knowing well that you would do every thing by him for the best; but I cannot help feeling very sensible when I consider the distance he is removed from you: I wish with all my heart that his brother Will [the Baches' second son] was with you, but much more so that you were with us.

Sarah's concerns suggest that Benny had been sent along in the first place as a comfort to Franklin, and that she believed young children were less important as autonomous individuals than as objects for adult affection. Jane Mecom, ever loving and empathetic, was both more sensible and more blunt, asking, "how will he support the loss of you both [Franklin and Temple]? Was he willing to go?"[23]

For Benny, separation was to be defined again by careful attention to his physical and educational needs accompanied by emotional and psychological neglect. The consequences would be mixed. He was well housed and clothed, and given such books as his guardian and tutor thought reasonable. Philibert Cramer, with whom young Benny traveled to Geneva, reputedly cared for the boy in a "friendly & fatherly" way. When Cramer died shortly after Benny's arrival in Geneva, Cramer's widow, Catherine, virtually adopted Benjamin as a son. Gabriel Cramer, Philibert and Catherine's son, soon became Benny's closest friend in Geneva. But the records suggest a coldness and a hollowness in Benny's removal, and he remained without any American companion or acquaintance until two years later when Franklin sent Samuel Johnnot to further his education with Benny in Geneva.[24]

For a grave boy with a need for affection, placement in a *pension* under the tutelage of Gabriel Louis Galissard de Marignac did not ease the transition. Marignac was a respected citizen of the city; he was a recognized poet and a long-time officer and regent of the college. Benny's correspondence and diary suggest that Marignac was attentive and careful but perhaps a bit aloof as well. During the school week, Benny boarded with Marignac and his wife in their comfortable, three story house near the college. On weekends and holidays, Benny usually stayed at the Cramer home, occasionally sleeping there Wednesday and Thursday nights as well since no classes were held on Thursdays.[25]

Having moved up from elementary courses at Le Coeur's *pension* to college (secondary) courses at Marignac's, Benny found his studies more rigorous. About 500 students attended the college, which was set on a hill in an old building. Here the routine was tedious and studies demanding. The students sat on wood benches, and regular school hours ran from 7:30 in the morning to 7:00 at night. The education they received was classical. Translation of various classical works, recitations on Cicero and the Old and New Testaments of the Bible, and studies in Greek grammar apparently occupied much of the students' time. By 1782, Benny reported that he was interpreting Telemachus, Terence, Sallust, the orations against Cataline by Cicero, Lucian, and the New Testament in Greek.[26] Meanwhile, still clumsy with English, he informed his father that, "I will try when I come to America to know perfectly the French, Latin and Greek enough to explain any Book with enough English to be understood."[27]

Finding time to complete translations and study texts forced Benny to work long hours out of school as well, a point that he tried to drive home again and again to his grandfather. In 1781, he told Franklin that the students had received a three-week holiday between terms, but that they had also received demanding assignments to complete. A year later, he recorded in his diary:

> Today begins our Vintage Holiday, which lasts a month; but one must not think that we are given nothing to do, quite the contrary. If one wished to do one's tasks well, there is more work to do than when it is not holiday.

In 1783, Johnnot and Benny emphasized their need to study when they bought candles to "work some hours longer" beyond their usual retirement at nine o'clock in the evening.[28] As Benny's later editorship of the *Aurora* would reveal, this early habit of long, hard work remained with him.

Although diligent and dutiful and an able translator, Benny was no scholar. Upon arriving in Geneva he promised Franklin, "I will do all [I] can . . . to be the first of the class." He did not become first in the class, but he succeeded well enough in a slow persistent way. A year after beginning his studies, he claimed that he was bending every effort in his English and Latin "interpreting," hoping throughout his first two years in Geneva to complete the curriculum rapidly and return to his "homeland." His antic- ipation of a swift completion of his studies did not last, but he kept up a brave front. By 1781, he optimistically told his grandfather that he had reached the third level and was certain that he would reach the first level and be finished at the college in two more years.[29]

Estranged from family and American friends, he sought some means of proving himself worthy. As he saw it, the best means to do so was by winning one of the yearly prizes offered at the college. In 1780, he won the prize for "having translated a piece of Latin into French better than the other students," and begged Franklin to allow him to hold the traditional tea-party celebration. The following year he was less fortunate. Although his expectations were high and he had put his best efforts into winning, he "didn't even approach the prize because the theme fell on a subject that I didn't expect at all." He was equally disappointed to receive no prize for good grades when none were awarded that year.[30] After 1781, he appar- ently came to the hard conclusion (especially for a twelve-year-old boy) that scholarly achievement at the highest levels would not prove his *forte,* and that it perhaps held no redemptive consequence with Franklin and the family in any case. He mentioned prizes only one more time, reporting unenthusiastically in 1783 that he had received the "last" prize for grades.[31]

Insofar as sober Geneva, a quiet town of a mere 25,000 persons in 1760, provided any environment for youthful distractions, it did so through political tension. Unlike Franklin's idealized vision of the "old thirteen United States of Switzerland," Geneva was a closed and hierarchical society where, if the "proper Principles" prevailed, they did so in theory more than practice. It was true that Geneva lacked a monarchy and nobility, and that eighteenth-century Calvinist states "like Geneva and the Dutch Republic were avid for learning."[32] It was true that in the 1760s Rousseau's *Social Contract* had produced a new spirit of free will, of the sovereignty of the "people," and had fostered the idea that governments are fictions relying on the general will of the citizenry. It was also true that Voltaire's liberal support of the unenfranchised "natives" of the city had established and forwarded a liberal ethos in the 1770s.

Rousseau's influence in particular had led to a seemingly successful, though partial, revolution in 1768 against a severely restricting Act of Mediation of 1738. The 1738 accord had made France a "guarantor" of Geneva's peace and order and had regimented Genevan society and politics along strict lines, with a handful of real "citizens" who held all of the power in a system of smaller and greater governing councils; an expanding, prosperous "bourgeois" class with voting rights; and the "native" class who constituted three-fourths of the population but held no political rights and were denied entry to liberal professions. By 1768 ambitious burghers on the one hand, and the artisans known as "natives" on the other, had expanded their social and political consciousness and demands. The burghers, named the "Représentants" and inspired by Rousseau's political philosophy, exacted concessions in the Edict of 1768, thereby elevating their political importance.

Having generally supported the burghers, the natives received little in 1768, although between 1768 and 1781 some "natives" were admitted to burgher status if their families had lived in Geneva for enough generations and they paid a fee. Relying on their stolid virtues as ordinary people and on Voltaire's humane sympathy more than on Rousseau's bourgeois general will, the "natives," aided by the General Council and burgher petitions, insisted on more democratic involvement and less aristocratic control. They besieged City Hall, locked up patrician leaders, and forced the government to resign. They also brought on the intervention of the "guarantor" French, who ringed Geneva with 10,000 troops, crushed the rebellion, arrested and exiled its leaders, stripped some "natives" of their hard-won rights, and established an Edict of Pacification ("Black Code") that restored aristocratic rule and the Mediation of 1738. Thus, when Benny left Geneva in 1783, there was no close correlation between the increasingly homogeneous Genevan commercial and middle classes, made up of burghers and aspiring "native" artisans, and the stratified aristocratic constitution of the city. As one commentator observed in 1789, Geneva would have to admit its people to the constitution or the constitution itself would be "smothered by the very ardor with which the excluded class tries to embrace it."[33]

When revolution seemed imminent in 1781, Marignac removed his family and Benny from the city and rented a small house in a neighboring village. For a time the college remained open and Benny commuted to Geneva every day. But when French troops moved in to suppress the rebellion, the college closed down. For several months in 1782 he took his instruction at the home of his professors and, when the college remained closed, he stayed at Marignac's retreat. Almost thirteen years old when the revolution broke out in 1782, Benny's overt response was to the excitement of violent events. The journalist-to-be recorded robberies, assassinations, quarrels between soldiers, conflicts among townspeople, and especially military comings and goings, all at a safe distance. By late July, 1782, conditions had improved in the city and within a month Benny was again living in Geneva and able to tell Franklin that the town was in "good order."[34]

Exciting events aside, it is unclear how strongly the Geneva environment as a whole influenced Benny's moral and intellectual development. Franklin must have been partially correct in assuming the ameliorative effects of a proud Protestant society, free of monarchical dominance and the worst forms of aristocratic privilege. The intimate nature of the Genevan city-state, the face-to-face, day-to-day relationships that Genevans necessarily shared, whether "citizen," "burgher," or "native," must have been obvious to even such a young boy. The fact that the "natives" were not a despised lower class but a vigorous, advancing foundation for that society, must have filtered through to him, helping to form his later trust and faith in the ultimate progress of ordinary men in society everywhere. Geneva's slow political evolution toward representation for its stalwart inhabitants, the diffuse expressions of Rousseau's new politics, the need for struggle to create constitutional change, all could have filtered through his consciousness, shaping his intuition if not directly establishing some of his later beliefs, forming selective memories to be drawn on later. The fact that Philibert Cramer had been a member of the burgher Council of Two Hundred and had been Voltaire's publisher, and that the Cramers admired Rousseau, must have produced more direct philosophical effects. And, finally, the visible might of France, its capacity to dictate Geneva's constitutional framework as "guarantor," contained powerful messages for a young boy who only eleven years later would declare, "Upon the establishment or overthrow of liberty in France probably will depend the permanency of the Republic in the new world."[35]

The routine of school and studies and the social and political scene in Geneva were not the only conditions shaping young Benny Bache. More private and subtle factors molded his character and personality as well. But these are difficult to define. It can be easy, on the one hand, to reduce his psychological development to simple categories or, on the other hand, to stress too much the exceptional circumstances of his boyhood. As for the dangers of generalization, Lopez and Herbert, in remarking on Benny's loneliness and estrangement in being packed off to Geneva, make an unclear and invidious comparison of Benny to "another boy," the same age as Benny, who "also left home to cross the water and study in a distant school: Napoleon Bonaparte." Later, in diagnosing Benny's shyness and poor academic achievement, they apply the modern labels of "introvert" and "underachiever" to him. But these oblique connections and modern labels are too fraught with multiple meanings to be helpful. This is not to deny that Benny did reflect some universal and general patterns of growth and behavior. His struggle against feelings of inferiority, his attachment to teachers and the parents of others, his desire for literacy and competence, and his capacity to perform routine tasks, are all recognized attributes of pre-pubescent childhood.[36]

But in other ways, Benny's personal development is not so easily categorized. He was, after all, a young boy twice torn from familiar surroundings—first in leaving Philadelphia at the age of seven, and again in being sent to Geneva at the age of nine. Placed in the care of strangers in a remote land, Benny would necessarily journey from childhood to the threshold of adolescence in a manner experienced by few children. To some degree his childhood was unique, and an important element in that uniqueness involved his relationship with Franklin. Although Franklin was concerned about Benny's development, he was busied by other matters, seldom writing to the youngster, never visiting Geneva as he periodically promised, and usually interceding only to react negatively or to lecture Benny on essential virtues.[37] Franklin was attentive to Benny's physical needs but neglectful of, or reckless with, his emotional ones. Most of his letters were filled with gratuitous moral advice that was too general for a youngster to apply, or instruction of the most mundane sort that resembled carping more than parental concern.

Simple affection and reassurance from Franklin, with no strings attached, did not occur. In an early letter, Franklin made it clear that "there is nothing I desire more than to see you furnish'd with good Learning, that I may return you to your Father and Mother so accomplish'd with such Knowledge & Virtue as to give them Pleasure, and enable you to become an honorable Man in your own Country." Benny was to obey Cramer and Marignac since "by so doing you will recommend yourself to me, and all

good People as well as we will love & esteem you for your dutiful Be-
haviour." Then came the blunt summation: "I shall always love you very
much if you continue to be a good Boy."[38] It was part casual dismissal of an
issue he could not, and did not wish to, dwell on; part an outdated piece of
conventional wisdom inappropriately applied to Benny's youth and somber temperament; part admonition only useful for parents physically close
by, where immediate disapproval or approval of moral actions can have
effect. No matter what Franklin's motive, the idea that affection and attachment must be earned undoubtedly produced in Benny anxiety, then striving, and perhaps eventual detachment.

Rather than play the role of confident parent, Franklin displayed his own
anxieties. Having already met miserable defeat with his only son, William,
he was also losing the moral battle with Temple as well. Yet, contrary to
Rousseau's concept of treating children individually and differently at
various stages of development, Franklin attempted fixed remedies. Worried
that Benny would not establish English as his primary language, or that he
would not establish habits of industry and morality, Franklin hauled out his
old moral recipes laden with guilt and foreboding for the unindustrious,
suggesting graphically what happens to one unprepared for the vagaries of
adulthood. In 1780, he pontificated,

> You see everywhere two Sorts of People. One who are well dress'd, live
> comfortably in good Homes, whose Conversation is sensible and instructive,
> and who are respected for their Virtue. The other Sort are poor and dirty, and
> ragged and ignorant, and vicious, and live in miserable Cabins or Garrets, on
> coarse Provisions, which they must work hard to obtain, or which if they are
> idle, they must go without and starve. The first had a good Education given
> them by their Friends and they took Pains when at School to improve their
> Time and increase their Knowledge; the others either had no Friend to pay
> for their Schooling and so were never taught, or else when they were at
> School they neglected their Studies, were idle and wicked and disobedient to
> their Masters, and would not be instructed, and now they suffer.[39]

Benny would come to appreciate this practical value of education, but also
its value for an enlightened citizenry. And he would also learn how to divide
society into the free and virtuous versus the poor and the ignorant, but
more for public, civic benefit than for his own personal status.

In regard to Benny, Franklin liked to employ comparisons with others to
affect results. As noted previously, Franklin remarked on how virtuous
Benny's mother was in the revolutionary cause and suggested that Benny

would have to be diligent in his studies to be worthy of such an obviously good woman.[40] In 1782 he told Benny,

> I am pleased that you keep an Account of your Expences. You will hereafter find it a great advantage, if you acquire the Habit of doing so, and continue the Practice thro' Life.
>
> I wish you would learn to write a fair round Hand. It is surprising what a Progress your Brother has made in such Writing—considering his Age. I have sent to London for some Copy Books of that Hand for you, which you will try to imitate. Fair legible Writing is of great Importance and I shall be much pleas'd to see you improve in it.[41]

Could comparisons to his brother, whom he hardly knew, have mattered much?

The only other subject that involved Franklin in the boy's life were Benny's two extravagant requests. In February, 1782, Benny asked if he could purchase an expensive twenty-eight volume work entitled *Le Voyager Français*. Five months later, after receiving no reply from his grandfather, he again requested these books, arguing that they would "give me much pleasure and will teach me much." In late August, Benny finally informed his grandfather that Marignac had bought the set because they had taken Franklin's "silence as agreement."[42] Given Franklin's usual reactions to such requests from his family, he was probably preoccupied, although he may have simply hoped that his silence would encourage his grandson to abandon the extravagance. In 1783, however, Benny requested a gold watch, an expensive luxury he may have seen as a memento of a Geneva already overflowing with watch-makers. Franklin chided him saying, "You should remember that I am at a great Expence for your Education, to pay for your Board & Cloathing and Instruction in Learning that may be useful to you when you are grown up, and you should not tease me for expensive things that can be of little or no Service to you." Benny truculently replied that every other boy in Geneva had a watch but promised to ask no more. There is no evidence that he ever asked Franklin or anyone else for a gift again.[43]

Benny's only other outside contacts were with his parents in Philadelphia. The correspondence was slight. Benny's letters were meager and stilted attempts to oblige his responsibilities. In a letter probably written to his parents sometime around his departure for Geneva, Benny admitted that he was "dying to see both of you," and asked that his brother William be sent to join him in Europe. But, he added, while he was trying to do all he could to "content you," he apologized that he could not "write to you in English because I am not in a position to do it." Sarah fumbled in search of the appropriate words and subjects to address to her distant son. Initially, she asked him to write on whatever he saw or heard that gave him "pleasure." But even here she could not avoid admonishment, encouraging him to "behave well," to recognize the "great care your Grand Papa takes of your Education and Morals," and to become a "wise and good man." On the subject of the English language, she declared pathetically that, "I hope you will endeavour to regain your English or how will you be able to converse with me when you see me, . . . as I am too old and too much engaged with your little brothers and sisters to learn French?" But without day-to-day, face-to-face contact, the conversation fell flat. In a letter written toward the end of his residence in Geneva, Benny told his father how he had determined not to write to him until his father had written first. But this was "too hard," he decided, and just resulted in self-punishment. Then he proceeded to offer the briefest possible news about his school life, reciting without emotion his demanding daily work schedule for his mother's benefit, and closing by noting that he had written them a joint letter because he had not time to write each of them separately.[44]

Franklin's involvement with Benny was sporadic and distant, and the ocean was both real and figurative in the psychological separation between Benny and the Philadelphia Baches. His emotional development through this period fell into several overlapping stages. In the first, stretching over his first two years in Geneva, Benny was confused and sullen, sometimes depressed, every bit the lonely youngster who craved affection and was uncertain of how to attain it. Probably still unsettled by his removal from his Philadelphia home, his second loss, this time of France and Franklin, immediately caused him to seek new ties. He apparently found them in his guardian Philibert Cramer. But Cramer died in August of 1779, and Benny must have felt three times removed from familial affection. Though assigned to the charge of Philibert's widow, Catherine, as a comfort for her in her loss, Benny himself was the person who desperately needed attention.

Catherine Cramer provided that eleventh-hour attention. Alarmed at first at Benny's extreme shyness and "indolence"—apparently the product of loss and depression coupled with his inherent somberness and need for affection—Catherine was won over by the boy's sensitivity, good heart, and common sense. Slowly, probably through Catherine's intercession and Marignac's tutelage, and also through the friendships of Gabriel Cramer, Catherine's son, and Samuel Johnnot, Benny's American classmate after

1782, Benny gradually moved from an initial period of defeat to the later stages of growing autonomy.[45]

The crisis of Benny's first two years in Geneva was his most emotionally traumatic experience until Franklin's death in 1790. Early on he tried to win worthiness in scholarship, as noted above. And his dutiful letters to Franklin and Philadelphia revealed a desire to please. Undoubtedly coached in the composition of his 1780 New Year's address to his grandfather, he assured Franklin,

> that I am aware of all the kindness that you have for me. I promise you, my dear papa that I will always hold the memory of it in my heart and you can be assured of the respect and of the most tender friendship that I have for you. I am doing everything possible to win yours and that of all our dear relatives is dear to me. I feel how I am responsible to you and how I must do things on my part to make me worthy of all the attentions that you have given me.[46]

In these early years, he frequently reassured Franklin that he was doing everything possible to satisfy his grandfather. As he once said, "I know too well my dear grandpa that I have too many obligations to you to not do all I can to make you happy."[47] He understood Franklin's formula of worth and affection well.

His correspondence gradually became less servile, more petitioning. He repeatedly mentioned Franklin's failure to write, and often asked for news about his parents, Philadelphia, and the war. Although very young when he left Le Coeur's, he did not forget his friends; he often requested news about Charles Cochran and asked if he might hear from him. Franklin seldom responded to these queries and Cochran did not write. As the shock of separation wore off, Benny began to worry more acutely about the practical side of his separation from the language and culture of America. As he put it in one letter, "it is troublesome for me that there isn't an American or at least a young man who knows English [here]." This lack and a simple desire for friendship led him to beg Franklin to send another American, preferably Cochran, to live and go to school in Geneva, as well as encourage his hopes for a quick completion of his studies.[48]

But petitioning alone did not replace submission. Depression was a factor as well in 1780 and 1781. He was "indolent." His enthusiasm for achievement declined. *Ennui* developed. Though not yet an adolescent, he apparently began to steel himself not to show dependence and need. In 1781, Marignac described Benny as someone "who makes himself loved by those he knows." But, he added politely, he was both a bit lazy and high strung, unwilling to be reproved. Hoping that Franklin could find time to write to the boy, and hoping to boost Benny's spirits, Marignac assured Franklin that he was encouraging Benny to write to his grandfather and to understand how busy his grandfather was.[49]

Catherine Cramer was more direct. "He is cold," she claimed in 1781. "He has few needs, no whims. Even though I had offered to ask you to give him a somewhat larger allowance (all his friends receive more than he does) he showed no great interest in the suggestion." He was taciturn and uninclined toward youthful competition like fighting and playing cards. Catherine Cramer concluded "that unless he has one of those temperaments that mature quite late, he will never display the kind of fire that leads young men into such trouble, much to their parents' chagrin, but then he won't develop those great talents either that are sometimes associated with excess but gratify the parents' pride."[50] She could not know that his somber demeanor would not dampen his intensity, and that his morose personality was an unpleasant but temporary by-product of his growing autonomy.

A fine line was crossed between a small, lonely boy full of poignant insecurities and a young person coming to terms with his alienation, independence, and internal resourcefulness. This latter stage was slowly and inexplicably established. It probably began in 1781, but it can be more confidently dated from roughly August 1782, when Benny undertook the self-conscious act of writing a diary. Though he was still purposeful and serious, a buoyancy also began to appear in his personality, marked by a delight and curiosity about the world. His resignation over scholastic standing and the drab routine of school gave way to broader amusements and distractions—drawing, the purchase of *Le Voyager,* and the gold watch mentioned above, playing with and interpreting for Samuel Johnnot, who had arrived in 1782, and the tumult of the Genevan revolution. (His interest in drawing actually reached back to an earlier stage when, to curry Franklin's elusive favor, he had presented his little sketches to his grateful grandfather.) He and his friends occasionally went fishing, and they were always attracted to parades and other public entertainments. In December 1782, he discontinued his diary for a month in order "to do nothing but skate."[51] Like most boys his age, he had found formal occasions annoying, boring and uncomfortable, and they had added to his grief during his first two years in Geneva. Because he was Franklin's grandson, he received invitations that his peers did not receive. He was a guest on more than one occasion at the home of the aristocrat Robert Pigott and met such notables as the Duke of Gloucester. But by 1783, when he was almost fourteen, he was more receptive to formal affairs. "I have been today to a Ball," he announced happily, "where from beginning to end I was not bored."[52]

Unbeknownst to Franklin, Benny's newfound ability to enjoy the world was not the kind that would lead to the hedonism of his cousin Temple or to the habitually undisciplined behavior of many of Benny's American acquaintances in France and Geneva. Nor is there even evidence that he found in amusements the gratification that his mother and father did. Instead, the joys of youth were more a proclamation of psychological liberation for Benny after a dark period of separation and uncertain identity. It was a liberation heavily paid for in lost affections and loneliness, but it was a liberation that encouraged moral self-reliance and true autonomy. Confidence had replaced dependency. Henceforth, he appears to have freely arrived at his attachments to and affections for Franklin and others, a maturity that could perhaps have been achieved, ironically, only through the process of detachment and separation that the Geneva years had provided.[53] Thus, when Benny remarked that it gave him "a great deal of pleasure" to learn of the news of peace between England and America in 1783 "because that gives me hope of seeing you soon," he was speaking, at 14, with what the eighteenth century would call a "manly" tone.[54]

Franklin probably failed to comprehend these subtle changes and, in any case, was distracted by the alarming news that Benny's physical well being was in jeopardy. Benny had reported in June, 1783, and again in July, that he had the "fever," implying that he was not recovering with much speed. Robert Pigott, the aristocratic English friend of Franklin's living in Geneva, reported in June 1783 that Benny was threatened by "his unhealthy dwelling, improper diet, and ignorance on the part of his tutors. His apartment is in no respects better than that of a Prisoner, it is so confined with Walls, included in a little Alley and crowded with other Contemporaries who sleep in the same Chamber that it would be almost a Miracle that he should escape some Pestilential Disorder."[55] This hardship may have toughened Benny for the impoverishment of newspaper publishing in the 1790s, or helped to shape his sympathy for the squalid sufferings of laboring classes. The immediate effects were to frighten Franklin. By July, 1783, Benny was back at Passy.

Franklin may not have known what to make of his returning fourteen-year-old grandson. As we have seen, out-of-sight, out-of-mind had been the prevalent mode of relationship for Franklin since their arrival in late 1776, except when Franklin had been startled into taking immediate action to forestall some crisis, such as those threatened by Benny's too proficient knowledge of French in 1779 and his living conditions in 1783. As a whole, Franklin did not see himself as a surrogate father. Thus, in 1782 he could wax eloquent on Polly Hewson's devotion and constant attention to raising her children according to the "natural environment" principles of Rousseau, principles to which Franklin apparently gave his avid academic attention, while at virtually the same moment he was absentmindedly asking Richard and Sarah what Benny's exact age was since he had "forgotten."[56]

Several considerations loomed large on Benny's return to Passy in 1783. Franklin was seventy-seven years old and suffered from gout and gallstones. He did not relish the idea of having to raise a youngster, especially since his tour of duty in France was not near its end, as he had anticipated upon Benny's recall in the summer of 1783. He apparently still worried about Benny's ability to speak English. And he did not like what he had seen in the recent development of Temple, or the boyish irresponsibilities of Samuel Johnnot. So, it was for his own convenience, the need to improve Benny's English, and a sign of his sense of promise in Benny, that he asked his trusted surrogate daughter, Polly Hewson, "You were once so kind as to offer to take him under your Care; would that still be convenient to you?" Polly was willing, but reminded Franklin that her children were much younger than Benjamin. And she wondered, apparently unaware of the kind of life Benny had been leading, "how will my young Friend like to lay aside his powder and curls, and return to the simplicity of a rustic schoolboy?" "I fear he will think us all so unpolished he will scarcely be able to endure us," she concluded modestly, perhaps confusing Benny with Temple, "but if English cordiality will make amends for French refinement we may have some chance for making him happy."[57]

"French refinement" was just what Franklin wanted Benny to avoid. But Polly had been politely reluctant, and Benny had been so upset at the prospect of beginning an utterly new life with new people for the fourth time, that Temple successfully pleaded Benny's cause in staying at Passy.[58] Franklin was not particularly unhappy with the decision to keep Benny at Passy. Even in his petition to Polly he had remarked with some sense of happy surprise that Benny had improved in Geneva, and that although "his English suffer'd for want of use," Franklin was certain this too would improve. Benny was described as "docile" with "gentle Manners." And, Franklin concluded with respect, "He gains every day upon my Affections." As one observer at Passy noted in 1783, Benny reciprocated with the warm but detached observation that "his G. Papa [was] very different from other

Old Person's, for they were fretful and complaining, and dissatisfied and my G. Papa is laughing & cheerful like a young person."[59]

In late 1784, Polly Hewson came to live at Passy with her three young children, and quickly divested herself of any "refined" notions about Benny's character, especially in contrast to Temple. The latter, she noted disapprovingly, "has such a love of dress and is so absorbed in self-importance and so engaged in the pursuit of pleasure that he is not an amiable nor a respectable character, he is just fit to be employed in a court and to be the galant of the French ladies, nothing else." Temple may have inherited Franklin's looks, she added, but Benny inherited his mind. Benny was "very high in my favor," she stated bluntly, "Indeed he is one of the most amiable youths I ever knew." He was "sensible and manly in his manner without the smallest tincture of the coxcomb." His simplicity of dress and "lovely simplicity of character" appealed to her, and although he was a tall, mature looking boy of sixteen when she met him, he had avoided the "foppery," "gaiety," and particularly the "licentiousness" so evident in other Parisian boys his age.[60]

Indeed, the confidence and maturity that had first begun to emerge in Benny's personality in 1782 appears to have steadily increased during these last two years in Passy. Living in luxurious surroundings at Passy, frequently surrounded by famous men and women, the advantaged spectator at everything from balloon ascensions to Mesmerist experiments, Benny kept his sense of childish wonder and an equally strong sense of detachment, both of which ultimately improved his journalist's eye for the episodic. While Passy could have led him toward the cultural pretense of the drawing room, he instead luxuriated in the outdoors, especially the river common to all, the Seine. He flew kites over the river, swam in it in the summer, and skated on it in the winter. Although old enough by 1783 to hold in awe mighty dignitaries and visitors—whether occasional ones like Lafayette or frequent ones like Jefferson and John Adams—Benny remained unimpressed. He even tried to avoid Prince Henry, brother of Prussia's Frederic the Great, and when finally cornered by the Prince, found him "very short" and "ugly."[61] He made no mention of the new men of France, like Condorcet, Robespierre, Mirabeau, and Marat, who sought Franklin's attention. Still very much a loner, he revealed little emotion about his household—Franklin, Temple, or the Hewsons—in his diary. He was not anti-social, however. He enjoyed accompanying Franklin in the latter's "official" investigation of Mesmerism and delighted in recording Deslon's dramatic magnetizing of the trees in Franklin's garden, remaining smugly skeptical himself of all but rational explanations. Substituting for an ailing Franklin, he dutifully took Polly Hewson and her flock on a tour of Paris, noting with detail but without judgment the splendor of Long-champs and Notre Dame and the scale of misery at the Foundlings' Hospital.

Above all, Benny was fascinated with the new "science" of balloon ascensions. He had not seen the very first launch by Montgolfier, but he did see the second by Jacques Charles on August 27, 1783. He watched subsequent launches as well, and eventually met Montgolfier in late 1783, and his English counterpart, Dr. John Jeffries, shortly after the latter's crossing of the Channel in 1785. Caught up in what would be a French craze for balloons in 1783–1784, Benny investigated the science further, attending lectures on natural philosophy by Charles (which he found "very interesting"), tracking flights, and recording measurements of airships. Having developed an historical consciousness of sorts for the significance of early aeronautics, he carefully recorded the details Jeffries related of his flight over the Channel.[62]

These leisure activities did not consume most of his time at Passy, however. Immediately upon his arrival at Passy, he told his parents, "I have left off my Latin and Gr—— to learn writing fencing dansing [sic] and Drawing."[63] Through the late summer and fall of 1783 he continued to pursue these studies and some mathematics as well with his cousin and a Mr. Munro. Privately tutored, he saw and met few other boys his age, his only acquaintances being Munro and Robert Montgomery, who lived and studied in Paris. From Benny there were few complaints. "I only want a few more companions of my age to be as happy as I can be in my present Situation," he concluded, undoubtedly recalling much more difficult times in Geneva.[64]

By early 1784, Franklin had determined, perhaps because of Benny's maturity, that it was time to introduce him to a useful trade. The way had already been prepared by Franklin's continuing interest in printing after his arrival at Passy in 1777. Having initially commissioned the leading type-founder of the time, Fournier, to cast type for him, Franklin added more type in 1778 and 1779, so that by 1783 he had accumulated a fine set ranging from Double Great Primer to Double Small-Pica. Employing the Passy press as a hobby, Franklin even experimented with casting his own type. By 1780, the press had expanded to official business and Franklin had installed two new presses, a foreman, and three assistants. Passports, commissions, bank orders, and information tracts about America as well as his famous bagatelles kept the Passy press busy.[65]

By early 1784 Benny was receiving intensive instruction on how to print under Franklin's master printer, Maurice Meyer, a move that momentarily rekindled Franklin's own interest in printing after he had grown tired of politics, Congress, and his long stay in France. Describing his decision to Benny's parents many months later, Franklin remarked that Benny was "a very sensible and a very good Lad, and I love him much." Having become convinced that Service is no Inheritance, Franklin had decided not to bring Benny up for public service as he had attempted to do with Temple. Instead, virtually repeating what he had told Richard Bache a few years before, Franklin was "determined to give him a trade that he may have something to depend on, and not be oblig'd to ask Favours or Offices of anybody." Benny was "very diligent in working and quick in learning," Franklin noted proudly, and he believed the boy would "make his way good in the World" as a printer.[66]

Neither money nor facilities were spared in developing Benny's career. The "Masters" Franklin hired were experts in both printing and type-casting. In addition to his own master printer, Franklin brought in Philippe Denis Pierres, a well-known printer from Versailles and a member of a number of scientific academies. Pierres taught Benny printing and intro-duced the young man to the difficult art of type-casting. Through the winter of 1784 and 1785 his life was very "regular," as he put it, and he was industrious and enthusiastic. He arose at seven in the morning and worked most of the day. He claimed he was so occupied that he made no visits outside Franklin's home at Passy during the entire winter. Polly Hewson further observed that "he [Benny] works with uncommon diligence, rising every morning before day, just comes into breakfast & dinner, returns immediately to his business which he never quits before seven o'clock in the evening."[67]

Given Benny's initial diligence and the infant industry status of type-founding in America, Franklin decided to give him better and more exten-sive training in type-casting, this time with the already famous Didot family. About 1775, François Ambroise Didot began producing a new type which used "accentuated 'thicks and thins'" in the lines of the letters. To standardize his type sizes, Didot also introduced a point system whereby seventy-two points equaled an inch. By 1785, when Benny was appointed to the Didot household, the Didots had revolutionized typefounding. At that time, François designed the types while his sons, Pierre and Firmin, cut the punches, managed the casting, and supervised printing. Under Pierre and Firmin, who were involved in teaching Benny, the family reached its peak in the craft in the late eighteenth century.[68]

Benny was more than appreciative of his good fortune, no matter how exhausting the instruction might be. He exclaimed in his diary,

> My grandfather has induced Mr. Didot, the best printer of this Century, or that has ever been seen, to take me into his house for a time to teach me his art. I take my meals at his house, and lodge at Mr. Le Roy's, a friend of my grandfather's. I have been there to-day with my cousin and made the acquaintance of the family, and besides of the forge, and foundery and the printing and engraving offices, all in the house. The family seemed to me very amiable, the repasts are frugal.[69]

For the next month, Benny's attention was riveted on his apprenticeship with the Didots to the exclusion of all else. The few diary entries he did make during this time referred to his progress in typefounding. With his attention riveted on this fascinating new trade, he attempted ancillary skills, keeping a careful list of his revenues (money given to him by Franklin) and expenses. Exploiting his gift for reporting details accurately, he also drew up his own manual of printing techniques, and recorded through drawings and prose how typefounding machinery operated.[70]

But the Didot apprenticeship was short-lived. By mid-May, a little more than a month after he had begun, Benny returned to Passy to supervise packing for his and Franklin's return to America. His training in typefounding would remain rudimentary. But Franklin held out hope for Benny's future in typefounding in America, purchasing the necessary equipment from Didot before departure. When the Franklin party sailed for Philadelphia an enormous amount of equipment and material had been gathered, including type-casting and cutting equipment, thirty-four different sets of type—much of it cast at Passy—and miscellaneous materials for printing.[71]

From mid-May until their departure on July 12, Benny conducted the packing for the trip "home" to Philadelphia. The task suited his symbolic status in the family—peripatetic student, unbegrudging servant to his grandfather, and, by 1785, honest, responsible apprentice. Altogether, 128 boxes had to be made, packed, sealed, and labeled for shipping. By June 29, the task was complete and the shipment ready to be sent to Le Havre. All other responsibilities were carried out by July 12, and the journey home, this time to much official fanfare, was underway.[72]

As Benny's diary attests, it was a departure of confusion, sadness, and mixed emotions for him. Knowing that he was "destined" to live his adult life in America, everyone, including Benny, refused to admit that Passy had been his true boyhood home. At first, the trip promised to be trying as well, with slow progress from Rouen to Le Havre, and a diversion to Southampton that allowed Franklin his last, uncomfortable visit with his son William. But then the party, comprised of Franklin, Benny, and Jean-Antoine Houdon, the sculptor, was soon under sail for Philadelphia on the *London Packet*. Benny slipped back into curiosity about all he saw. He noted sea life and ships that they met, sketched the beauty of a dolphin and the way it changed color after being caught and taken from the water, and was amused at the enthusiasm of sailors on a New York whaler when they were offered some bottles of wine.[73] He was thrilled more than terrified when they encountered a severe storm in late August near what he called the "Gulf of Florida," allowing himself full journalistic enthusiasm in recording the event.

> The sea was in a frightful state of agitation. The waves rose to such a height that the main mast plunged three times into the water, and the water was so blown about by the winds that we could not see 50 feet ahead of us. . . . the sailors and the Captain acknowledged, they had never seen anything to equal it.

The next day he added, "I believe that all my life I shall keep in remembrance that moment, rendered so interesting by its danger."[74]

The same momentary excitement awaited his arrival in Philadelphia three weeks later. After nine years' absence, he would admit, "The joy that I received at the acclaim of the people, in seeing father, mother brothers and sisters can be felt, not described."[75] It was the flush of reunion and hope, and it would not last. Still an adolescent, he was culturally a fish out of water, with no clear role in the family and no predictable future.

Those uncomfortable with Bache's later radicalism, or those who have always felt that radicalism as a whole is unnatural, can craft a too easy, too convenient "analysis" of Bache's European years. Here was a young boy who craved affection. Isolated in a strange culture with a celebrated grandfather, he became bonded to Franklin to a perversely sycophantic degree. Never an American, they would argue, he attempted to foist on the young republic his "foreign" views, insensitive to anything but French enlightenment thought and his own personal cult of Franklin.

At the other extreme we might place those persons who claim nothing for processes of socialization, those who by acquiescence agree to the pervasive influence of innate cognition, and those who circumscribe all human conduct within the implicit or explicit argument that human action is the consequence of received knowledge applied to particular events. For them, Bache's childhood could hold little significance beyond what he read or was taught in the realm of philosophy and politics, a subject to be dealt with later. Bache's subsequent radicalism, then, might be the simple consequence of his intelligence and learning, of conscious choices rationally and freely made.

Both views contain some truths. But the evidence suggests that both psychological and rational analyses are false taken alone. In 1776, at age 7, Benny Bache was too young to be anything but confused, perhaps frightened, and certainly lonely. The effects of the changes in his life were undoubtedly traumatic. From the Le Coeur years until at least 1781 or 1782, insecurity, shyness, and timidity resulted. At the outset, Franklin loomed large in the boy's life, but more as a source of control over him than as a figure to whom the boy was hopelessly attached. Distance rather than intimacy prevailed, as Franklin at first saw his grandson only on Sundays and holidays, and then, with Benny's removal to Geneva, not at all. He seldom wrote to Benny except to admonish him to strive to be better, a not inconsequential influence since instructors like Marignac and guardians like Catherine Cramer understood well what kind of behavior Franklin expected from the youngster. Franklin never visited Benny in Geneva, and his interest in the boy was almost singularly directed at establishing in him habits of industry. Benny reciprocated with dutifulness before 1783, and even to a large degree afterward. He strove to win Franklin's and anyone's affections with his work. By 1783, Franklin's big success—one he did not fully realize—had come from Benny acquiring strong habits of industry.

Between 1781 and 1783, prior to his reunion with Franklin, Benny began to establish something much more valuable than pleasing his grandfather—a sense of self-confidence, individualism, and personal autonomy. He was not beholden to a neglectful Franklin. His Philadelphia family was too remote for too long to lay claim to directing his life. When he rejoined Franklin, he won over his grandfather by example rather than by special deeds or juvenile servility.[76] He would come to appreciate Franklin even while trying to gain his independence from him in the 1780s. He would adopt some of Franklin's philosophical views, perhaps even to the point of interpreting American society as a national enlargement of his grandfather, but he came to this position from a state of psychological maturity. More significantly, he had acquired the ability to choose and act independently of others, to judge circumstances and events on his own, and to ignore those ordinary social perspectives that formed conventional wisdom. And this ability, in turn, undoubtedly produced a premature autonomy—the force behind radical philosophical and political, commitment.[77]

Notes

1. Jonathan R. Dull, *Franklin the Diplomat: The French Mission,* Transactions of the American Philosophical Society, Vol. 72, Part 1 (Philadelphia, 1982), 41. Benjamin Franklin Bache will be called "Benny" throughout this chapter because the entire Franklin Bache family used that name in their mention of him. It is likely that they continued to use "Benny" throughout his life.

2. *Ibid.,* 11.

3. For suggestive views on the behaviorist psychology revealed in and promoted by Franklin see Jesse Bier, "Benjamin Franklin: Guilt and Transformation," *PMHB,* CVI (1982), 89–97; Richard L. Bushman, "On the Use of Psychology: Conflict and Conciliation in Benjamin Franklin," *History and Theory,* V (1968), 225–40; and especially Norman S. Fiering, "Benjamin Franklin and the Way to Virtue," *American Quarterly,* XXX (1978), 199–223. None of this is to deny that the familiar and friendly Franklin is to be understood as part of the essential Franklin as well. For a work that sympathetically captures this aspect of Franklin see Esmond Wright, *Franklin of Philadelphia* (Cambridge, Mass., 1986).

4. Many actions taken in regard to Benny after 1776 suggest reactive rather than active planning. Dull, *Franklin the Diplomat,* 42, and 42n, suggests that Franklin liked bright young men around him to remind him of his youth.

5. See respectively Deb. Franklin to Benj. Franklin, June 30, 1772 (?), [William Temple Franklin], comp., *Letters to Benjamin Franklin from His Family and Friends, 1751–1790* (New York, 1859), 51; and Jane Mecom to Deb. Franklin, Sept. 2, 1771, Carl Van Doren, ed., *The Letters of Benjamin Franklin and Jane Mecom* (Princeton, N. J., 1950), 129. On the general promise of children quoted see Philip Greven, *The Protestant Temperament: Patterns of Child-Rearing, Religious Experience, and the Self in Early America* (New York, 1977), 156.

6. See respectively Benj. Franklin to Deb. Franklin, Aug. 14, 1771, Leonard W. Labaree, *et al.,* eds., *The Papers of Benjamin Franklin* (New Haven, Conn., 1959–), XVIII, 204–205, hereafter cited as Labaree, *et al.,* eds., *Franklin Papers;* and Benj. Franklin to Deb. Franklin, Feb. 2, 1773, *ibid.,* XX, 34.

7. The quotations are from Faÿ, *The Two Franklins,* 8–9. On arranged marriage see Benj. Franklin to Mrs. Mary Hewson, July 8, 1775, Labaree, *et al.,* eds., *Franklin Papers,* XXII, 100. Franklin would return to this match two years later, when Elizabeth was two and a half. Benj. Franklin to Polly Hewson, Jan. 12, 1777, *ibid.,* XXIII, 156. And, as with Sarah earlier, a serious level to the Hewson connection would eventually emerge, replacing Franklin's romantic and impractical ideal union of real and surrogate families, when he later attempted to send off an adolescent Benny to live with Polly.

8. Benj. Franklin to Wm. Temple Franklin, Sept. 19, 1776, *ibid.,* XXII, 612–13.

9. Sarah Bache to Richard Bache, Dec. 2, 1771, cited in Claude-Anne Lopez and Eugenia W. Herbert, *The Private Franklin: The Man and His Family* (New York, 1975), 216.

10. There is no definitive standard for developmental norms, but it is useful to employ even vague theoretical concepts of childhood development for purposes of individual contrast. Thus, Benjamin appears to have satisfied the standards of basic trust and autonomy that Erik Erikson described in his familiar stages of identity. See his *Childhood and Society* (New York, 1950), 247–58; and *Identity: Youth and Crisis* (New York, 1968), 96–122.

11. See especially Lopez and Herbert, *Private Franklin,* 215–16.

12. Benj. Franklin to Mrs. Mary Hewson, Jan. 12, 1777, Labaree, *et al.,* eds., *Franklin Papers,* XXIII, 156.

13. The dispute over Voltaire's precise pronouncement, which was quoted in the *Journal de Paris,* is closely detailed in A. Owen Aldridge, *Voltaire and the Century of Light* (Princeton, N. J., 1975), 400. On Benny's inconspicuous status as a youngster see Benj. Franklin to R. Bache, April 14, 1777, Labaree, *et al.,* eds., *Franklin Papers,* XXIII, 582; and Jane Mecom to Benj. Franklin, May 5, 1778, *ibid.,* XXVI, 402. On Franklin's many duties and preoccupations in these years see Dull, *Franklin the Diplomat,* 45–46.

14. Wright, *Franklin,* 263. Wright's description of Franklin's Paris and Passy is the best available. See especially *ibid.,* 256–70.

15. On Franklin's attention to his grandsons on Sundays see Benj. Franklin to Mrs. Margaret Stevenson, Jan. 25, 1779, Albert Henry Smyth, ed., *The Writings of Benjamin Franklin* (New York, 1905–1907), VII, 223, hereafter cited as Smyth, ed., *Writings of Franklin.* The variety of persons in attendance on holidays and Sundays is suggested in Carl Van Doren, *Benjamin Franklin* (New York, 1938), 637–38; and John Adams, Diary, May 3, 1778, in Lyman H. Butterfield, ed., *The Adams Papers,* Ser. I. *Diary and Autobiography of John Adams* (New York, 1964), II, 308. Benny's role in the Passy household after 1783 is documented in Benjamin Franklin Bache's Diary, Aug. 1, 1782 to Sept. 14, 1785, American Philosophical Society, Philadelphia. See especially Feb. 2, May 7, 19, 22, July 11–12, 15, Aug. 24–29, Sept. 19, 30, 1784, and Jan. 15, 1785.

16. Benj. Franklin to Silas Deane, Dec. 7, 1776, Labaree, *et al.,* eds., *Franklin Papers,* XXIII, 30.

17. On Benny's enrollment see Wm. Temple Franklin to Silas Deane, April 24, 1778, *The Deane Papers* (New-York Historical Society, *Collections* [New York, 1886–1890]), II, 461. See also Sums Paid by Benj. Franklin for B. F. Bache, Dec. 27, 1776–Sept. 6, 1780, Franklin Papers, Bache Family Papers, Am. Philos. Soc. A description of Le Coeur's and Benny's American schoolmates can be found respectively in J. Q. Adams to Abigail Adams, April 20, 1778, Letters Received and Other Loose Papers, April–Dec., 1778, Adams Papers microfilm, Reel 349; John Adams, *Diary,* II, 301; and J. Q. Adams to Charles B. Cochran, July 18, 1814, letter published in the *American Historical Review,* XV (April 1910), 572.

18. The quotation is from Philippe Ariès, *Centuries of Childhood: A Social History of Family Life,* trans. Robert Baldick (New York, 1962), 284. For a discussion of the

evolution of French schools through this period see *ibid.*, 241–336. On the more national orientation of French education see R. R. Palmer, *The Improvement of Humanity: Education and the French Revolution* (Princeton, N. J., 1985), 8–69.

19. Benj. Franklin to Sarah Bache, June 3, 1779, Smyth, ed., *Writings of Franklin*, VII, 348.

20. Benj. Franklin to J. Q. Adams, April 21, 1779, *ibid.*, 289. Franklin repeated these motives for sending Benny away in almost identical language to Jane Mecom and to Sarah Bache. Benj. Franklin to Jane Mecom, April 22, 1779, Van Doren, ed., *Letters*, 191; Benj. Franklin to Sarah Bache, June 3, 1779, Smyth, ed., *Writings of Franklin*, VII, 348.

21. On this latter point see Dull, *Franklin the Diplomat*, 16.

22. Benj. Franklin to R. Bache, June 2, 1779, Smyth, ed., *Writings of Franklin*, VII, 345–46.

23. See respectively Sarah Bache to Benj. Franklin, Sept. 14, 1779, [Franklin], ed., *Letters*, 105; and Jane Mecom to Benj. Franklin, Sept. 12, 1779, *ibid.*, 104.

24. On Benny's physical needs and Philibert Cramer's role see, respectively, Benj. Franklin to B. F. Bache, Aug. 19, 1779; and Benj. Franklin to Mr. Cramer, Aug. 19, 1779, Smyth, ed., *Writings of Franklin*, VII, 368, 369. For a general but useful summary of Bache's life in Geneva see Lucien Cramer, *Les Cramer, une famille génévoise. Leurs relations avec Voltaire, Rousseau et Benjamin Franklin Bache (Génève, 1952)*. For the relationship of Benny, Gabriel and Johnnot see *ibid.*, 61–61; B. F. Bache Diary, Aug. 1, 1782 to April 19, 1783, B. F. Bache Papers, Am. Philos. Soc.; and B. F. Bache to [Benj.] Franklin, Sept. 29, 1781, Bache Papers, Castle Collection, Am. Philos. Soc.

25. *Ibid.*, Aug. 3, 1782; B. F. Bache to [Benj.] Franklin, Oct. 15, 1782, Bache Papers, Castle Coll., Am. Philos. Soc.; and Cramer, 60.

26. Cramer, 61; and B. F. Bache to Benj. Franklin, Aug. 30, 1782, B. F. Bache Papers, Am. Philos. Soc.

27. B. F. Bache to R. Bache, Sept. 15, 1782, *ibid.*

28. B. F. Bache to Dr. Franklin, June 30, 1781, *ibid.*, and B. F. Bache Diary, Oct. 5, 1782, and Mar. 8, 1783, B. F. Bache Papers, Am. Philos. Soc.

29. See respectively B. F. Bache to Benj. Franklin, May 30, 1779; May 30, 1780; and June 30, 1781, *ibid.*

30. B. F. Bache to Dr. Franklin, June 19, 1780, Sept. 12, [1781], Mar. 26, and June 30, 1781, *ibid.*

31. B. F. Bache Diary, Jan. 19, 1783, B. F. Bache Papers, Am. Philos. Soc. See also [Benjamin] Franklin Bache to [Benj.] Franklin, Oct. 15, 1782, Bache Papers, Castle Coll., Am. Philos. Soc.

32. Peter Gay, *The Enlightenment: An Interpretation: The Science of Freedom* (New York, 1969), 58.

33. Francis d'Ivernois, cited in R. R. Palmer, *The Age of the Democratic Revolution: A Political History of Europe and America, 1760–1800*. Vol. II, *The Challenge* (Princeton, N. J., 1959), 361. On Geneva in general see *ibid.*, 110–39, 358–61; William Oeschsli, *History of Switzerland, 1499–1914*, trans. Eden and Cedar Paul (Cambridge, 1922), 277–86; George Rudé, *Europe in the Eighteenth Century:*

Aristocracy and the Bourgeois Challenge (London, 1974), 233–35; and Gay, *The Science of Freedom*, 47, 58, 463–65.

34. See especially B. F. Bache Diary, Aug. 1, 1782 to April 19, 1783, B. F. Bache Papers, Am. Philos. Soc., and B. F. Bache to Dr. Franklin, Mar. 26, 1781, July 27, 1782, and Aug. 30, 1782, *ibid*. Franklin failed to report the Geneva uprising to Benjamin's parents until over a year later, perhaps to avoid alarming them. Benj. Franklin to [R. and Sarah Bache], June 26, 1782, Franklin Papers, Am. Philos. Soc.

35. *Gen'l. Adv.,* July 26, 1793. On the relationship of memory to intuitive knowledge, and on "screen memories" as "iconic metaphors" of understanding, see Avery D. Weisman, *The Existential Core of Psychoanalysis: Reality Sense and Responsibility* (Boston, 1965), 122–24, and passim.

36. Lopez and Herbert, *Private Franklin,* 220, 222. One need not subscribe to any particular set of general observations about child psychology as an exact litany of truth to appreciate their broad usefulness. See Erikson, *Childhood and Society,* 258–61, and *Identity,* 122–28.

37. I have found only five letters from Franklin to Benny for this four-and-a-half-year period. If more were written, they could not have been delivered more often than every four to six months.

38. Benj. Franklin to B. F. Bache, Aug. 14, 1779, Smyth, ed., *Writings of Franklin,* VII, 368–69.

39. Benj. Franklin to B. F. Bache, Sept. 25, 1780, cited in Lopez and Herbert, *Private Franklin,* 228.

40. Benj. Franklin to B. F. Bache, April 16, 1781, Franklin Papers, Bache Family Papers, Am. Philos. Soc.

41. Benj. Franklin to B. F. Bache, Jan. 25, 1782, Smyth, ed., *Writings of Franklin,* VIII, 372–73.

42. B. F. Bache to Benj. Franklin, Feb. 21, July 27, and Aug. 30, 1782, B. F. Bache Papers, Am. Philos. Soc. See also B. F. Bache to [Benj.] Franklin, Oct. 1, 1782, Bache Papers, Castle Collection, Am. Philos. Soc.

43. On Benny's request for the watch see B. F. Bache to [Benj.] Franklin, n.d., *ibid*. Franklin's chastising response is in Benj. Franklin to B. F. Bache, May 2, 1783, Franklin Papers, Bache Family Papers, Am. Philos. Soc. Benny's curt acceptance of Franklin's decision is in B. F. Bache to [Benj. Franklin], May 30, 1783, Bache Papers, Castle Coll., Am. Philos. Soc.

44. See respectively, B. F. Bache to R. Bache, n.d.; and S. Bache to Benjamin F. Bache, Feb. 2, 1782, *ibid;* Sarah Bache to B. F. Bache, Oct. 1, 1782, cited in Lopez and Herbert, *Private Franklin,* 227; and, B. F. Bache to R. & S. Bache, Dec. 3 [1782?], Bache Papers, Castle Coll., Am. Philos. Soc. See also Sarah Bache to B. F. Bache, Oct. 19, 1781, cited in Lopez and Herbert, *Private Franklin,* 226.

45. Cramer, *Les Cramer,* 61; and Lopez and Herbert, *Private Franklin,* 221–22.

46. B. F. Bache to Dr. Franklin, Dec. 21, 1779, B. F. Bache Papers, Am. Philos. Soc.

47. B. F. Bache to Dr. Franklin, June 19, 1780, *ibid*. See also B. F. Bache to Dr. Franklin, Mar. 25, May 6, Sept. 20, 1780, *ibid;* and, B. F. Bache to Benj. Franklin, n.d., Bache Papers, Castle Coll., Am. Philos. Soc.

48. B. F. Bache to Dr. Franklin, Nov. 26, 1780, *ibid.* Although Johnnot Cooper eventually joined Benny in Geneva, he did not leave France until 1782. Johnnot was less serious than Benny, more prone to seek fun, less diligent in school work, and less habituated to industry. For full details on Johnnot's removal to, and ensconcement in, Marignac's *pension,* see Lopez and Herbert, *Private Franklin,* 228–29. Benny mentioned more than once that he wanted Franklin to send Cochran to Geneva. But he also revealed interest in the prospect that J. Q. Adams and Charles Adams might also be sent. See B. F. Bache to Dr. Franklin, May 30, July 18, Oct. 17, 1780, B. F. Bache Papers, Am. Philos. Soc. Mention of Franklin's failure to write, the shortage of news received in Geneva, and Benny's concern for Cochran can be seen in B. F. Bache to Dr. Franklin, Mar. 25, May 6, Sept. 20, Oct. 17, 1780; Mar. 26, Sept. 12, 1781; and Aug. 30, 1782, *ibid.;* and in, B. F. Bache to [Benj.] Franklin, Aug. 16, 1781; Oct. 1, 1782; n.d.; Mar. 10, 1783, Bache Papers, Castle Coll., Am. Philos. Soc.

49. G. L. de Marignac to [Benj.] Franklin, Aug. 16, 1781, Bache Papers, Castle Coll., Am. Philos. Soc.

50. Mrs. Cramer to Benj. Franklin, May 15, 1781, cited in Lopez and Herbert, *Private Franklin,* 227.

51. See B. F. Bache to Dr. Franklin, May 30, 1780; June 19, 1780; Sept. 12, [1781]; and, Sept. 20, 1780, B. F. Bache Papers; and, B. F. Bache Diary, Dec. 5, 1782, Am. Philos. Soc. See also B. F. B[ache], Illustrations of Coats of Arms, [1782–1783]; and, B. F. Bache to [Benj. Franklin], Mar. 10, 1783, Bache Papers, Castle Coll., Am. Philos. Soc.

52. *Ibid.,* Mar. 20, 1783. For descriptions of Benny's social activities as a boy in Geneva see *ibid.,* Aug. 1, 1782 to April 19, 1783; and Cramer, *Les Cramer,* 60–64.

53. We can never know if this progress is ascribable primarily, or in combination, to the influences of the Cramers, Marignac's *pension,* the Geneva environment, cognitive development, or some inherited, innate qualities. Developmental psychology is not especially useful in uncovering processes of identity formation and of emotional and moral development, as it either simply categorizes behavior into arbitrary and theoretical stages (see especially the many works of Erik Erikson on identity and Lawrence Kohlberg on moral development), or asserts reductionist faiths in cognitive development (Jean Piaget, Erikson, and Kohlberg) or socialization (e.g., the works of Justin Aronfreed) as the motive forces of psychological change.

54. B. F. Bache to Benj. Franklin, Jan. 30, 1783, Franklin Papers, Historical Society of Pennsylvania, Philadelphia. For other letters suggesting his desire to be reunited with Franklin, and to see England, see B. F. Bache to Benj. Franklin, n.d.; and, July 2, 1783, Bache Papers, Castle Coll., Am. Philos. Soc.

55. See B. F. Bache to [Benj.] Franklin, June 20, 1783; July 2, 1783; *ibid;* and, Robert Pigott to Benj. Franklin, June 27, 1783, cited in Lopez and Herbert, *Private Franklin,* 231–32.

56. Benj. Franklin to Polly Hewson, June 13, 1782, Smyth, ed., *Writings of Franklin,* VIII, 456. On Polly and child-rearing see also Lopez and Herbert, *Private Franklin,* 262–63. On Benny's age see Benj. Franklin to R. and Sarah Bache, June 26, 1782, Franklin Papers, Bache Family Papers, Am. Philos. Soc.

57. Benj. Franklin to Mrs. Mary Hewson, Sept. 7, 1783, Smyth, ed., *Writings of Franklin*, IX, 89. And Mary Hewson to M. Franklin, Sept. 28, 1783, in the James S. and Frances M. Bradford Collection of Franklin Papers, Am. Philos. Soc.

58. Lopez and Herbert, *Private Franklin*, 265–66. Bernard Faÿ, *The Two Franklins: Fathers of American Democracy* (Boston, 1933), 41–43, makes a too poignant scene out of Benny's desire to stay at Passy, implying a strong emotional and dependent bond to Franklin. The equally plausible view is that no adolescents, then or now, would want to be thrown among strangers in a strange culture, if they have long been removed from family and home and have anticipated for some time their return to the comforts and familiarities of family surroundings.

59. Benj. Franklin to Mrs. Mary Hewson, Sept. 7, 1783, Smyth, ed., *Writings of Franklin*, IX, 89. On reciprocated affection see D. M[Montgomery] to Mrs. [Sarah] Bache, July 26, 1783, in the Bache Family Papers, Am. Philos. Soc.

60. Mrs. M[ary Stevenson] H[ewson] to [Barbara Hewson], Jan. 25, 1785, Misc. MSS Collection, Am. Philos. Soc.

61. B. F. Bache Diary, Sept. 30, 1784, B. F. Bache Papers, Am. Philos. Soc.

62. For Benny's many activities see his diary, Jan. 2, 1784 to June 30, 1785. On the natural philosophy lectures see B. F. Bache to S. Bache, June 17, 1784, Bache Papers, Castle Coll., Am. Philos. Soc. For more detail on these activities see Lopez and Herbert, *Private Franklin*, 255–57, 266–71.

63. B. F. Bache to Mrs. Bache, July 27, 1783, Bache Family Papers, Am. Philos. Soc. For other mention of his studies see B. F. Bache to R. and Sarah Bache, Sept. 13, Oct. 30, Dec. 27, 1783, *ibid*.

64. B. F. Bache to Sarah Bache, Sept. 13, 1783, *ibid*.

65. Luther S. Livingston, *Franklin and His Press at Passy* (New York, 1914), 1–124; John Clyde Oswald, *Benjamin Franklin, Printer* (New York, 1917), 151–66; Van Doren, *Franklin,* 661, 709; and Benjamin Franklin, *The Bagatelles from Passy,* with notes by Claude Anne Lopez (New York, 1967), 63–71.

66. Benj. Franklin to R. Bache, Nov. 11, 1784, Smyth, ed., *Writings of Franklin*, IX, 279.

67. B. F. Bache Diary, Oct. 8–9, 11, 1784; and Jan. 21, Mar. 19, 1785, B. F. Bache Papers, Am. Philos. Soc.; and Mrs. M[ary Stevenson] H[ewson] to [Barbara Hewson], Jan. 25, 1785, Misc. MSS Collection, Am. Philos. Soc.

68. Douglas C. McMurtrie, *The Didot Family, Typefounders* (Chicago, 1935), 1–7; and Albert J. George, *The Didot Family and the Progress of Printing* (Syracuse, N. Y., 1961), 6–13.

69. B. F. Bache Diary, April 5, 1785, B. F. Bache Papers, Am. Philos. Soc.

70. On his expense ledger, printing techniques, and typefounding machinery see B. F. Bache, "Dépences de l'année 1784 à Passy"; "Variétés a Passy, 1785"; and "Explication des Machines nécessaires pour la Fonte des Caractères d'Imprimérie par Benjamin Franklin Bache durant son Apprentissage sous M. Emeri commencé de 1st Novembre, 1784," Bache Papers, Castle Coll., Am. Philos. Soc.

71. "Account of Contents of 34 boxes of printing letters, . . . cast at Passy," Franklin Papers, Bache Family Papers, Am. Philos. Soc.; and Livingston, *Franklin and His Press,* 128.

72. B. F. Bache Diary, May 14, 1785–Sept. 14, 1785; and B. F. Bache to Rob't Alexander, July 9, 1785, B. F. Bache Papers, Am. Philos. Soc. See also Charles F. Jenkins, "Franklin Returns from France—1785," *Proceedings of the American Philosophical Society*, XCII (1948), 421; Lopez and Herbert, *Private Franklin*, 276–83; and Van Doren, *Franklin*, 722–28.

73. B. F. Bache Diary, July 12–Sept. 10, 1785, B. F. Bache Papers, Am. Philos. Soc.

74. *Ibid.*, Aug. 23, 24, 1785.

75. *Ibid.*, Sept. 13, 1785.

76. Even Faÿ, who saw Benny as a clone of Franklin, had to admit that upon his return from Geneva, Benny was more "reserved, prouder, purer and shyer, he was also more courageous and more straightforward." Faÿ, *The Two Franklins*, 36.

77. Much literature on moral development is confident in its claim that a real transformation takes place in many persons in vague stages from "conventional morality" to "post-conventional morality," the latter heavily dependent upon autonomy, rationality, and the ability to approach problems abstractly and philosophically. The prime promoter of this position is Lawrence Kohlberg. See his *Essays on Moral Development. Vol. I. The Philosophy of Moral Development: Moral Stages and the Idea of Justice* (New York, 1981); "Development of Moral Character and Moral Ideology," in *Review of Child Development Research*, ed. Martin L. Hoffman and L. W. Hoffman (1964), 383–487; and "Moral Stages and Moralization: The Cognitive-Development Approach," in Thomas Lickona, ed., *Moral Development and Behavior* (New York, 1976), 31–53. Among those who assume an opposing view of socialization, Martin L. Hoffman argues that the use of shame and guilt (which Franklin employed in his letters to Benny in Geneva) can be effective to start the process of moral development, but that inductive examples (as in Franklin's letter comparing youngsters who get a good education to those who do not) establish the important step of empathy. See Martin L. Hoffman, "Development of Moral Thought, Feeling, and Behavior," *American Psychologist*, XXXIV (1979), 958–66; and "Parent Discipline and the Child's Moral Development," *Journal of Personality and Social Psychology*, V (1967), 45–57.

3. Coming of Age in America, 1785–1790

> "My principal object shall be to be esteemed virtuous, reputed learned, & to be useful thro' their means to my Country & Mankind. Ambition is, I think, my strongest passion. To be great, truly great, by my virtues, I want sufficient money to shew those virtues in their most brilliant appearance, & a Wife who may by partaking increase the Bliss I expect by their exercise."
>
> (B. F. Bache, "Melanges")

BENJAMIN RETURNED "HOME" with his childhood, and the European milieu that shaped that childhood, behind him. Adulthood was about to supplant adolescence. Although he undoubtedly shared a special social category and a permanent social alienation with many men who were later his political contemporaries and some his allies—men like Alexander James Dallas, John Beckley, Thomas Leiper, James Thomson Callendar, and Albert Gallatin—he never doubted that he was an American. He would make no attempts to return to Europe or to recreate Genevan or French culture in Philadelphia. As his childhood correspondence and diary attest, he recognized his European years as a sojourn, and clearly anticipated that his passage "home" in 1785 meant real and permanent residence in America.

Benjamin brought more than material baggage home, however. The liberal philosophical ethos in which he had been raised remained latent, but, as later events would prove, a broad body of ideas and ideology had been indelibly impressed on his beliefs and morals before 1785. Vocationally, he was already educated as a printer and typefounder; there was little prospect that he would turn away from the one thing that seemed to promise eventual autonomy and accomplishment. In any case, Franklin had it in his power from 1785 to 1790 to dictate Benjamin's future. Benjamin now depended on Franklin's economic legacy and his support in printing and typefounding to a degree he could not have anticipated while both remained in France. With Temple appearing more and more the wastrel, unable to gain government patronage or find satisfaction on his farm in New Jersey, Franklin tightened his grip on Benjamin. Worn and less combative, no longer a potent force in politics, increasingly exploited publicly for his prestige (by the Constitutionalists and Republicans alike in Pennsylvania and then by the authors of the United States Constitution), Franklin spent as much of his remaining energy on the improvement of his properties and the final shaping of Benjamin as he did on political affairs. In the pain of his last years, Franklin also sought the close companionship, comfort, and aid that he had previously charmed from others, and that he could now exact from a dependent grandson unfamiliar with and uncertain about the culture around him. From 1785 to 1790 what had been a predictable condition of childhood dependence and grandfatherly guardianship was exaggerated into a tighter symbiosis.

A whole new body of influences also bombarded the now adolescent Benjamin. The mixture of European culture, history, and education he had absorbed as a child was supplanted by the active, dynamic, and unsettled environment of Philadelphia. Visible before him was Quaker, Scotch-Irish, and German ethnic diversity; a vigorous, fluid, risk-taking mercantile community that had made Philadelphia "the second city in the British empire," at least in terms of prosperity; a politically rambunctious citizenry still unresolved on the proper frame of government for the state and nation; a society of "new" men competing with an educated aristocracy for sovereign authority and the opportunity to set the tone for the future; and a growing city imbued with a spirit of social reform in the areas of slavery, crime and punishment, benevolence, and education.[1] New family and new acquaintances, cultural nuances, social divisions and social habits, postrevolutionary political subtleties, all remained to be absorbed and understood.

By Benjamin's own testimony, his and Franklin's initial response to their home-coming was both gratifying and distracting. Franklin had not expected to be "received by a crowd of huzzas" or to be "accompanied with acclamations quite to my door." For a month, the Franklin-Bache household remained in euphoric turmoil with a steady stream of well-wishers greeting Philadelphia's most famous citizen.[2] But then the excitement subsided, and young Benjamin discovered that passage to Philadelphia was only a preamble to rites of passage in America.

The first step was a familiar one—further education. Without delay Franklin enrolled Benjamin in the University of Pennsylvania "to compleat his Studies."[3] No longer pressed by necessity to place his grandson in the custody of a school, Franklin's motives for arranging for more formal education for Benjamin, when the latter's career and wishes might have been satisfied by simply furthering his education in printing and type-founding, were unclear. And the University had certainly not acquired any record of special achievement, or improved so considerably since Franklin's earlier involvement in its founding and governance as to warrant Franklin's eagerness to see his grandson enrolled.

Yet Franklin may have had concrete and philosophical reasons to see his less than scholarly grandson complete a baccalaureate degree. First, the University of Pennsylvania in the 1780s seemed committed anew to English language education as opposed to what Franklin saw as the frivolities of Greek and Latin. Who needed English language education more than a grandson whose first language was French and whose formal education had been European and classical? Second, with the departures of William Smith, former provost of the temporarily defunct and superseded College of Philadelphia, and Jacob Duche, the classical languages teacher, the University not only had begun to play down the classics but had rid itself of two persons cool to the Revolution as well. The new University, itself a product of Pennsylvania's revolution, was staffed by men like John Ewing, the natural scientist, and David Rittenhouse, the astronomer, who were committed to Franklin's much loved sciences. And this new orientation of the University to English language studies and science, coupled with that institution's long anti-sectarian emphasis, made advanced studies at the University of Pennsylvania appear to be a fitting finish to Benjamin's education. As Franklin had written in 1751, young persons should leave formal education "fitted for learning any Business, Calling or Profession," and education should "qualify them to pass thro' and execute the several Offices of civil Life, with Advantage and Reputation to themselves and Country." Always the behaviorist who found habit, environment, and experience at the core of human growth, and a man who "saw his entire career as a series of problems in education," Franklin apparently hoped that the University's new liberal breadth and utilitarian orientation correlated with his "sense of an open-ended universe" of experiential possibilities.[4]

Benjamin was less enthralled. He implied in an early letter to Robert Alexander that it had not been his idea to attend the University, and that he was compelled to take a degree. A year later, in 1786, he told Alexander that he was disappointed in the education he received at the University, noting how inferior it was to what he would have received in Europe; his chief relief was that he hoped to complete the degree later that year and be free of the school.[5] Though always a hard worker, Benjamin was not able to complete the three-year curriculum so rapidly. In early 1787, Benjamin informed Le Veillard that he was "following a course in Mathematics" and expected to have a Bachelor of Arts degree by August. Franklin had earlier told Francis Childs, a prospective customer for type fonts, that Benjamin would have his degree in July, and in early 1788, Franklin remarked that Benjamin had completed his studies.[6] Throughout this vague trail of evidence, one senses that Franklin never fully appreciated why Benjamin worked so closely at his studies. Nor does one sense that Benjamin fully appreciated Franklin's concept of the value of a liberal education.

Benjamin's unenthusiastic view of the University did not translate into rebelliousness. As his course notebooks reveal, he could be an attentive student. While his notes on ancient history appear mostly as a series of run-on sentence fragments depicting important people and military events, his notes on Euclidean geometry were neatly laid out. More importantly, his two notebooks on moral philosophy, which he studied with the Reverend Magaw, reflect some academic interest in the subjects of ethics, nature, virtue, rights, and duties covered in the course. Yet the doodles in these same notebooks—including attempts to imitate Franklin's signature, and to sketch Franklin's profile—also suggest his pre-occupation with Franklin.[7] This, coupled with his apparent love of printing and his natural shyness and unfamiliarity with a new culture, seemed to drive him closer to Franklin's side. Grandfather and grandson seemed to reciprocate affection and dependence. In Philadelphia, with other family members to amuse the great man, Benjamin still remained his steadfast support. Samuel Vaughan, a guest of Franklin's, "spoke highly" of Benjamin and mentioned that he gave Franklin much pleasure. Franklin, to indicate his continued affection, kept up the charade of a Hewson-Bache match, declaring to Mrs. Hewson that Benjamin "continues to behave well as when you knew him, so that I think he will make you a good son."[8]

The strongest bond between Franklin and Benjamin Bache was the literal partnership they shared in typefounding, book publishing and selling, and printing. For Benjamin it meant the prospect of establishing invaluable commercial contacts, furthering his apprenticeship, and relying on Franklin's largesse in creating and equipping a typefoundry and printing shop. Franklin's generosity and his determination in furthering his grandson's prospects knew few bounds.

Even much of the re-development of Franklin Court and Franklin's properties on High Street after 1785 was tied to the Franklin-Bache partnership. From mid-century, Franklin had been acquiring and assembling properties along High Street. In 1763 he had built Franklin Court in the interior of the block bordered by High Street, Third and Fourth Streets, and Chestnut Street; access to his secluded home off busy High Street was through an alley lot that would later become the site of Benjamin Bache's home and office. Upon returning to Philadelphia in 1785, Franklin discovered several things about his properties, besides the fact that they had risen dramatically in value. If he were to enjoy his old age at Franklin Court, he wanted to keep some of the comfort he had experienced at Passy. He also wanted Richard and Sarah's large family to live with him. This meant expansion and improvements at Franklin Court. In 1786, therefore, he added a wing to the house, with a large dining room on the first floor, a long library on the second, and two bedrooms on the third.

Franklin also owned four lots on High Street, three of which had decrepit houses on them, the fourth being the alley-carriageway (graveled in 1783) to Franklin Court. High Street, Franklin noticed upon his return, was becoming increasingly central to the busy world of the Philadelphia tradesman, with "market sheds" already extending by his properties, with ambitious tradesmen of every sort coming to occupy High Street's narrow houses and shops, and with institutions like the Bank of North America practically on his door-step. An incorrigible dabbler in both printing and building, Franklin determined to improve these properties, tearing down the three old houses and erecting three new ones, leaving an arched carriageway through the middle of the properties. All of the new structures stood on deep lots and were built with care, incorporating brick wall structures designed to retard the spread of fires. By mid-1787, these three houses were completed in addition to the changes to Franklin Court, and Franklin must have been aware of the rising costs that would lead him, a year later, to dun old debtors for payment.

But Franklin continued building in 1787. Faced with an enormous amount of typefounding equipment and fonts brought from France, he proceeded to build a two-story foundry, bindery, and print shop for Benjamin behind his properties at what would become 316–318 Market Street. By August 1787 Benjamin Bache would tell his grandfather, "My father's letter informs me, . . . to my great satisfaction, of the raising of the Printing Office & foundery."[9] With one large room on the top floor and the archway dividing two more work rooms on the second floor, Benjamin Bache should have been satisfied with Franklin's initiative. In mid-1788 Franklin also completed the structure at 112 High Street (later 322 Market Street) which Benjamin would make famous as the office of his newspaper and which would ultimately serve as his home from 1792 to his death in 1798.[10]

With this extensive investment in facilities, in equipment, in type fonts, and in Benjamin's training, the prospects for the Franklin-Bache partnership seemed good. But in fact the venture had begun to falter even before the printing shop and foundry were completed, and before Benjamin could take his degree and devote full attention to the business. Most of the illusory promise as well as the monumental problems involved in typefounding lay in the general nature of both printing and typefounding in late eighteenth-century America. Most printers needed three or four fonts of type, and a single font of Caslon type, the most popular style for Americans, cost about £50 sterling in this period. The Revolution, having restricted the normal importation of type from England, Holland, and France, stimulated local typefounding ventures. But few Americans entered the infant industry, and the states remained virgin territory for any persons who could satisfy the demands of printers on a large, national scale. While some men, like Abel Buell, David Mitchelson, and Christopher Sower, had cast type as early as the 1760s for local markets, none had taken the step toward filling the gap in a national way until Bache and Franklin attempted it in 1786. And while a few others like John Baine of New York made serious attempts after 1786, none achieved real success until 1796, when Archibald Binney and James Ronaldson formed a partnership that offered customers type and service equivalent to those of foreign suppliers.[11]

Reasons why typefounders failed were varied. They had to own matrices for type styles that were locally or currently popular. Printers expected low prices and high quality, and had a ready excuse for defaulting on their debt if the types contained any irregularities or imperfections. When typefounders tried to cast replacement type they often found it difficult to match the old type. Others were troubled by irregular and short supplies of metal for casting. Some were just slow or inefficient or did poor work in the casting itself. A skilled caster might do as many as 4,000 letters a day, but standardizing the product to satisfy the customer remained difficult if not impossible.[12]

The Franklin-Bache partnership had no immunity from these ordinary vagaries of the trade. Their uniqueness lay mainly in the large scale of their endeavor, and the oddity of a seventeen-year-old boy's entering business allied with an eighty-year-old man. Before August 1787, when Benjamin left the University, Franklin handled all matters except casting the type. Apparently, the partnership had only one customer before that time. That one customer, Francis Childs of New York, was troublesome. Franklin interviewed Childs some time in early 1786 and subsequently agreed to sell the printer more than one thousand dollars worth of type that had been cast at Passy, probably by Benjamin, some of Franklin's employees there, and perhaps a little of it even by Franklin himself.[13]

The sale signaled the start of a frustrating business transaction that would fail. Soon after the purchase Childs expressed dissatisfaction with the incompleteness and poor condition of some fonts. The trip from Passy had apparently taken its toll. Franklin promised to have imperfections corrected. In March, 1786, revealing the status and organization of their partnership, Franklin told Childs, "Benjamin will make new Puncheons, and cast for you some Petite W's as soon as we can get the Foundry in Order."[14] Childs ordered other replacements in 1786, but it proved difficult for Benjamin to find time for such extensive work while still attending the University. Franklin brought in help, informing Childs in the fall of 1786 that he was having some work done in Germantown (probably by Justin Fox) but that the work proceeded at a disappointing pace. "All the other [corrections of] Imperfections were cast by my Grandson during his vacation from College in July," Franklin added, "but he had not time to do these."[15] Childs continued to complain, first about one imperfection and then another. By the spring of 1787, Franklin was exasperated. He wrote Childs a long letter politely but condescendingly discussing the use and care of type and printing materials but promising to make whatever types Childs wanted. "My Grandson will cast them," Franklin concluded, "as soon as he had taken his Degree and got clear of the College; for then he purposes to apply himself closely to the Business of Letter Founding and this is expected in July next."[16]

Just as Childs had difficulty obtaining the type he wanted, Franklin and Benjamin had difficulty getting Childs to pay his bill. In July, 1787, Benjamin traveled to New York City (staying with his Uncle Theophylact's family whose solicitousness put him ill at ease) but had difficulty locating Childs, who, as Benjamin put it, "keeps out of the way" and had "acquired the character of a very shuffling fellow." The visit must have had some effect, because within the month Childs told Franklin, "I have wrote to B. F. Bache, informing him of my expectations of money in the hands of Mr. Mitchard, in a few days, when I shall order his payment of his account."[17] But by early 1788 Childs had requested a one year extension of credit with the implicit justification that there were still many imperfections in his type. Although he promised to make some payment, Childs stalled through 1788 and the first part of 1789. Franklin, having spent heavily on his own house, as well as on the building of other houses and on the printing equipment and typefoundry, was "now in real and great want of money." He even sent Richard Bache to New York to collect. When this failed, Franklin finally agreed to cancel Childs's debt in exchange for some of the type. The matter was closed by early 1790.[18]

The Childs affair did more than take the bloom off the rose of a new business. It spotlighted the critical problems that successful typefounding would have to overcome. Yet, with Franklin's support, Benjamin seems to have remained cautiously optimistic, declaring confidently to his grandfather that in regard to typefounding, "in all probability we shall succeed at least as well as M. Barrie & Son . . . provided we make a few alterations in the several founts, so as to suit them a little better to the English taste." In accordance with his observation, Franklin ordered £150 of Caslon type to comport with "English taste."[19]

Undated correspondence also indicates that Benjamin attempted to sell some type to Matthew Carey, probably in the late 1780s. Carey, whose printing shop was only two blocks from Bache's, had begun publication of the *Columbian Magazine* in 1786 and soon thereafter began the *American Museum*. Perhaps this second venture created a need for a greater variety and quantity of type. In trying to sell type to Carey, Benjamin again experienced difficulty in meeting his customer's demands. Apparently purchasing some small pica for Carey from elsewhere, Benjamin first apologized for interruptions caused by transportation problems. In a later letter, Benjamin was "astonished" at Carey's complaint of imperfections in the type he had sold, promising nevertheless to recast them when he could get his small pica mold and some matrices back from Mr. Fox. Carey-Bache business dealings apparently never went beyond this point.[20]

Acquiring all of the type, printing equipment, and the letter foundry upon Franklin's death—materials that amounted to more than £1,000 in value—Benjamin necessarily had visions of making the typefoundry profitable. In 1790, he published the first typefounding specimen sheet ever printed in America, advertising both the type he had for sale and the type he could cast. Ranging from the smallest fonts to billboard-size lettering, the specimen revealed Benjamin's talent for design and appearance, a talent he simultaneously employed in designing his own Great Seal for the United States.[21] But customers did not beat down the door. Bache probably remained unable to supply and cast the type his customers specified, and the characters of his French designs and matrices may have also been no help. During the 1790s he sometimes cast type for his own newspaper but the foundry lay dormant. In 1802, William Duane, Benjamin's successor at the *Aurora* would attempt to revive the foundry but ultimately, and ironically, finally gave all of the equipment to Binney and Ronaldson in 1806. These later pioneers in American typefounding considered the equipment a treasure, finally depositing it with the Smithsonian Institution.[22]

Franklin fell silent about the promise of typefounding by 1788, a fact that suggests a re-orientation of focus and perhaps a broader view of Benjamin's prospects in other fields related to printing. To a friend in France, Franklin simply stated, "He [Benjamin] has finish'd his Studies at our University, and is preparing to enter into Business as a Printer, the original Occupation of his Grandfather."[23] Undoubtedly with Franklin's aid and advice, Benjamin made his tentative entrance into the book publishing field in 1788 with works that, at first glance, appear far removed from his political radicalism of the 1790s. All of these books were "readers" for young children by Anna Letitia Aikin Barbauld. The daughter of Dr. Aikin, a leading English Dissenter and friend of Joseph Priestley and other Dissenters, Barbauld was part of that intricate web of progressive thinkers with whom first Franklin and then Benjamin Bache were connected. A minor figure in late-eighteenth-century literature, a follower of "post-Lockean associationist psychology," and a well-traveled liberal, she may have met Franklin and even Benjamin, although Franklin most probably came to know her work through his revived interest in education during the last decade of his life.[24] For Benjamin, the Barbauld books were a modest beginning. In the advertisement to the first volume Bache simply proclaimed that these books succeeded where others failed because the traditional "speller" was abandoned in favor of teaching vocabulary through stories about familiar objects, noting as an aside his special use of high quality paper and large print.[25]

Franklin consigned some of these books to Boston, part to his sister, Jane Mecom, and part to his grand-nephew, Jonathan Williams, Jr. But Williams was apparently guilty of "some Miff," as Franklin put it, by making little effort to sell the books. Franklin eventually had Jane Mecom return all of the books to Philadelphia, and offered to pay her forty dollars for her trouble. With another foray into modern entrepreneurship by the Franklin-Bache partnership failing before it had really begun, Franklin again expressed his frustration.

As to the Books themselves, how much soever your People may despise them, they are really valuable for the purpose of teaching Children to read. The largeness and plainness of the Character, and the little Sentences of common occurrence which they can understand when they read, make them delight in reading them, so as to forward their Progress exceedingly. Our little Richard, not yet 5 years old, has by their Means outstript his Brother Lewis in Reading, who is near nine.[26]

Even with this miscalculation in the market for children's books, Benjamin plunged ahead into other book publishing ventures, showing the same determination to try again as he had after failing with Childs in typefounding. Perhaps on his own initiative, perhaps at Franklin's insistence, Benjamin agreed to publish two books edited by his classics professor at the University, James Davidson. The first of these, a selection of Aesop's tales and Erasmus's writings, was designed to teach the Greek and Latin classics. According to its advertisement, it had already been chosen as a text by the faculties of the College of Philadelphia and by Washington College in Maryland. In equally positive terms he promoted the second volume, containing Old Testament selections, which he boldly "suggested for the use of Schools on this Continent." In contrast to the simplicity of format and crispness of type found in the Barbauld books, these works were a showcase for Benjamin's ability to handle complex printing tasks involving several styles and sizes of fonts, an elaborate format, a delicately engraved frontispage, and, in the first volume, the careful arrangement of Latin and English in parallel columns.[27]

His reach again exceeded his grasp. The Reverend Charles Nisbet, principal of Dickinson College, a classics scholar and later a political opponent of Benjamin, told the young printer that he had found fifty mistakes in the book without reading it, and concluded by condemning Franklin for helping to destroy the classics in America. Benjamin's haughty reply was that he no longer intended to publish Latin or Greek books, perhaps rebelling against Franklin's heavy-handed management of the printing business.[28]

Aside from his newspaper, Benjamin printed only two other items before 1791. One of these printing jobs involved two denominations of species tickets printed for the Bank of North America, an institution Franklin had defended after his return in 1785 and which Richard Bache had also supported. The other was a twenty-three-page pamphlet advertising a yearly subscription scheme to the Reverend William Smith's best and most important sermons.[29] Since none of these sermons reached the public under Bache's imprint, the project was probably abandoned. Until his successes with political works in the 1790s, such as Paine's *Rights of Man,* Benjamin made little headway in the book market. Even the aid of men like Jefferson, who had met Benjamin in 1785 and three years later had offered to send him popular English books through a French bookseller in France, did little good. But Benjamin remained surrounded by books. Franklin would leave him some works as well as his share in the Library Company, and an inventory in William Temple Franklin's papers lists a large number of titles in both French and English, covering a wide variety of subjects, as belonging to Benjamin.[30] After 1790, some excerpts would appear in Bache's newspaper suggesting further his contact with a wide and disparate body of literature.

Both the typefounding business, culminating in the production of his elaborate type specimen, and book publishing, resulting in the production of obscure texts of little demand, were attempts at establishing a profit. In addition, the type specimen, the Barbauld books, and the classical works were all opportunities for Bache to display and advertise his printing skills. The adolescent desire to be, or appear to be, accomplished in something— anything—runs as a clear theme through this failed entrepreneurship. At the same time, perhaps to show that he could be more determined than his grandfather and certainly to show that he could act independently of Franklin, he pursued typefounding when the pitfalls of that industry and the tastes of its customers made the attempt futile. And publishing obscure classical texts at the very time when Franklin was repeating his charge that classical language studies were no more than "ornaments" suggests some necessary distance between Franklin's ideals and the practical matters of establishing Benjamin's independence.[31]

By the late 1780s, Benjamin's availability and his skill in handwriting also kept him employed by his grandfather as a secretary. Ever since he had been a small boy, Benjamin had received constant harping advice about handwriting from his grandfather; Franklin undoubtedly interceded to show the youngster just what constituted a good hand. The instruction succeeded. By the 1780s Benjamin Bache had even adopted a signature entirely imitative of his grandfather's.[32]

As for dictation, Benjamin had written down, as early as 1784, a plan devised by Franklin for daylight savings time. The plan was subsequently sent to the *Journal de Paris,* but when Franklin later decided to broadcast the plan through Jonathan Williams, he sent what he thought were more readable printed copies, suggesting that Benjamin's transcription may not

have been free of errors.[33] In Philadelphia, Benjamin became more conspicuous as Franklin's occasional aide and secretary. After Franklin suffered a
bad fall in his garden in early 1788, and began to suffer more severely from
gallstones, he began to confine himself first in his home and then in his
bedroom, occasionally calling upon Benjamin for writing assistance rather
than scratching words out with his own pen. Most of this assistance apparently involved minor secretarial help. Upon his grandfather's death Benjamin reported that Franklin was, in fact, "little in the Habit of dictating"
during the last stages of his illness, although Bache had written a letter to
Thomas Jefferson for his grandfather just before Franklin's death.[34]

By the late 1780s Franklin was, in fact, less in the habit of dictating and
more in the habit of having Benjamin make both "press" and "fair hand"
copies of longer works that Franklin felt would constitute his historical
legacy. Probably first among these was Benjamin's "fair hand" transcription
of a one-hundred-ninety-six-page manuscript on Franklin's negotiations
with the British ministry in 1774–1775. Later, Benjamin's copy of this
manuscript would cause confusion for its temporary guardian, Thomas
Jefferson, and a suspicion of intrigue on the part of its ultimate owner,
William Temple Franklin. Jefferson would fear that he had given up an
important historical state paper, given him in trust, when he released it to
the less than reliable Temple in 1790. Temple was ultimately suspected of
suppressing both the original and Benjamin's copy of this document to save
the British embarrassment. Although Benjamin was innocent of any blame
in this affair, aside from not informing Jefferson in 1790 that another copy
of the manuscript existed, he was blamable in making a horrendous botch
of the "fair hand" copy itself. Julian Boyd, who studied the document
thoroughly, has remarked that Bache "committed almost all of the errors of
omission, repetition, and misconstruction of which an incompetent copyist
is capable—including such nonsense readings as *tine pish* for time past."
Benjamin also used "*would* for *could, have* for *hence, nearly* for *merely.*" One
page was done so badly that the entire page had to be re-copied. Franklin,
ever the vigilant tutor, meticulously corrected Benjamin's mistakes in red
ink, even inserting missing paragraph markers. Boyd further believes that
another copy of the manuscript was made at some time. Boyd reasons that
"If such a copy had been needed for no other purpose, it could have served
as salutary discipline for a youth who sorely needed it in the art of accurate
transcriptions."[35]

Benjamin's chief role, however, was in assisting Franklin with the *Autobiography*. The *Autobiography* had a long and complex history. It was written

in several stages between 1771 and 1790. The famous first section had been lost by Joseph Galloway during the Revolution, and was only found and returned in 1785. In either 1784 or 1785, Franklin had regained his interest in the work, beginning the second section. Franklin did not immediately resume work on the manuscript upon returning to Philadelphia. He re-read it in 1786, but did not take the work up in earnest until 1788, probably completing the third section in early 1789 and working on the very short fourth section in the winter of 1789–1790.

Sometime in 1789 Benjamin was instructed to make two "fair" copies of the first three sections. Franklin then sent one to Benjamin Vaughan in England and the other to Le Veillard in France. Neither person was to reveal or lend these copies for any purpose, but Le Veillard certainly showed his to La Rochefoucauld in 1789 and was given permission to show it to Condorcet in 1790, so the latter could prepare his eulogy to Franklin. By 1790, three copies of the autobiography existed: the two copies containing three sections each, and Franklin's original containing four sections. Franklin wanted to keep the *Autobiography* out of press because Temple was to inherit Franklin's papers and the autobiography. Neither wise nor swift in taking advantage of his inheritance, and unwilling to edit his tangled holographic original manuscript, Temple traded it for Le Veillard's copy, unwittingly short-changing himself of section four as well as receiving a "fair" copy of Part One which was already flawed and which Temple would proceed to flaw further with his own changes. In fact, by 1791 part of the *Autobiography* had leaked out, and by the time Temple finally published his edition in 1817, the entire work had been printed and reprinted several times. All editions had been taken from either the Vaughan or the Le Veillard copies, or from pre-1784 fragments of Part One.[36]

What was Benjamin's precise role in this confusion? While the answer cannot be definitive, Lemay and Zall argue that Benjamin simply made a "press" copy of parts two and three, thus retaining the pristine originality of the holographic copy for those sections. But because the holographic copy of the first part was on hard paper, it probably had to be recopied in a "fair hand," a circumstance allowing Benjamin to proceed carelessly in transcribing the first fifty-seven pages of text. In all probability, Franklin then sent Benjamin's "fair hand" copy of part one with the press copy of two and three to Benjamin Vaughan. Le Veillard then probably received a press copy of the Vaughan copy. When the original came to light in 1867 it became clear that Benjamin Bache's copies were not exact duplicates of the original but contained careless errors, omissions, and even gibberish. Benjamin also copied two of "Uncle Benjamin Franklin's Poems," which were sent to Le Veillard with the *Autobiography*. In one of these he mutilated Franklin's punctuation and substituted the word "tears" for Franklin's earthier "scars." Furthermore, all but one page of the original holographic autobiography is in Franklin's hand, so, again, Benjamin had not acted as a meticulous secretary loyally taking dictation.[37]

Taking Benjamin's role regarding the manuscript on negotiations together with the *Autobiography* no longer suggests a clinging grandson, the bedside "amanuensis" of a dependent grandfather. The image of a loyal Benjamin taking dictation disappears, and his sloppy copying unsurprisingly suggests a young man distracted by other things while simply compelled to do his grandfather's bidding.[38]

But what were the distractions of this young man who had (with his grandfather's help) bungled his way through typefounding, bookselling, printing, and copying? All of those things that preoccupy most intelligent persons moving swiftly from adolescence to adulthood. First, there was the matter of mental and moral maturity. In August, 1786, he began a notebook appropriately labeled "Melanges." It was to be, he proclaimed, a book in which he could transcribe curious incidents, anecdotes, maxims, and any new thing that interested him. All were intended to provide him with a background for a later diary memoir; all were—in perfect Franklinian order—to improve his English, his writing style, and his clarity of mind.[39]

The "Melanges" notebook was an intellectual and literary side-show of sorts—often trivial and usually sophomoric in style and content. But it was more. It was a discourse on nature, religion, perfection, virtue, happiness, pleasure, and young women. Extolling the primacy of "Nature" and natural human instinct, Benjamin outlined his deistic belief in a multiplicity of peopled universes, all begun by a master watchmaker (or watchmakers), that "once put into movement . . . are governed by themselves." He denied that God exercised any supernatural power in this universe—except that of "taking us from it when he pleases"—and suggested a bizarre kind of reincarnation as well, in which individual souls were refitted or improved upon bodily death in order to make them more suited—one might say more perfect—for their new life. Jesus was inconsequential. He may have existed, Benjamin admitted, "but I'll never believe he was the son of a Supreme Being." Christianity and other religions had the salutary effect of compelling morality out of fear, he conceded, but they fell far short of making humankind "love virtue."

Virtue, standing opposite "Nature," was the other pillar of Benjamin's moral philosophy. "Virtue," he concluded in one essay, "is the fairest pastport [sic]" to "happiness," and because of this he further argued that "it is easier for me to be really virtuous than to merely appear so; therefore let me be truly virtuous in order to obtain that Happiness that can be derived from it thro' Men." Already a product of Franklin's behaviorist influence, with its insistence on habit and industry, he determined to be "temperate in all things," to "keep things in order," and to follow the rule that, "what ever you undertake do it well." Unsurprisingly, he endorsed the maxim that upon "the impressions we receive when we are young depend the character we will have in maturity." When Benjamin discovered his grandfather's thirteen-point program for "perfection"—the one soon to become famous with the publication of Franklin's *Autobiography*—he declared himself "astonished & much pleased to find many of his Ideas coinciding nearly with mine." In 1789 he established his own checklist and notebook for self-improvement—one that tellingly remained blank—plagiarized entirely from Franklin.[40]

But willing enslavement to Enlightenment epistemology or to Franklinian morals was not what Benjamin intended in his "Melanges." He sought intellectual and social independence. In the privacy of this notebook, he began to argue with his eminent grandfather. In an essay on religion he began by noting that "G[rand] P[apa] seems to think that God has an influence over us while in this world. Here we differ." Even in saluting Franklin's program to reach perfection, he found that Franklin differed "in some respects totally from my way of thinking." Benjamin went on to complain that,

> He [Franklin] says a Man ought to have one, & but one design in view in human affairs, that if he studies to make a fortune he should sticking closely to his Business abandon every sort of amusement; & if he aims at honours every thing else should be laid aside. I think with him that a Man should have one principal design in view but also apprehend he should not sacrifice to it all his time, but allow himself amusement & variety for the last is grateful to human nature & the former necessary.

In fact, he had made his exasperation with his grandfather clear in an earlier essay as well:

> G[rand] F[ather] tells me, I should stick to my Business. I should not seek pleasure, should remain at home, not enjoy good company, that it is not the

way to grow rich, to divide my time between Business & Pleasure, that I cannot be a Printer & a Gentleman too, that I may if I please be a Gentleman but he don't [sic] see when I shall get money to support the character of one, that I had better be a Printer till I have got enough money to be substantial Gentleman, that I had better believe him, that he has Experience.

But, Benjamin retorted, "I answer that I find always work with more pleasure and satisfaction, when I have been, or expect to be, entertained." And, he declared himself willing to work "all the working hours, provided I may then have 2 or 3 hours to visit my Friends [once] or twice in the course of a Week." As for becoming a gentleman—an idea Bache embraced as a goal until sometime in the early 1790s—he claimed he would work "two or three years longer for a fortune, & enjoy myself in the Mean time, that Youth is the only time to enjoy certain pleasures & that the enjoyment of pleasure is Happiness & that Happiness is the only thing we do, or should, aim at." When Franklin protested that the frivolous entertainments Benjamin sought were "not pleasures," Benjamin simply noted to himself that, "The Difference of our Sentiments is owing to the Difference of our Ages." He might have added that it was owing to the difference of the historical "ages" in which they lived.

Among other things, the "Melanges" was, therefore, a statement of faith and philosophy, a dialogue with himself about what mattered in his own life, an argument with his grandfather, and a proclamation of self-identity. In one of the last essays of the notebook, he summarized his goals and ambitions:

> My principal object shall be to be esteemed virtuous, reputed learned, & to be useful thro' their means to my Country & Mankind. Ambition is I think my strongest passion. To be great, truly great, by my virtues, I want sufficient money to shew those virtues in their most brilliant appearance, & a Wife who may by partaking increase the Bliss I expect by their exercise. I shall aim at being a public character to shew how I could choose the good of my Country in opposition to my private interest, which is a rare thing now a days.

Taken out of context the "Melanges" notebook could be seen as a diary of unalloyed egoism or hedonism. But set against the approval adults had already expressed in his character and his attempts to act responsibly, the "Melanges" convey a more laudatory message. He had not ruined himself, as Temple had. And, he could not be expected, at the age of seventeen, to join Franklin's monastery of industry and frugality without some leaven to his life. But in many ways, his contemporaries and modern critics failed to appraise him as the adolescent or young adult that he was, preferring to contrast him with men decades older than he.

Complicating matters, and adding further to the list of things distracting Benjamin, was the obvious fact that he was reaching sexual maturity. As the "Melanges" and his later letters attest, his world had expanded out of Franklin Court by 1786 or 1787. He apparently developed new friendships with a number of Philadelphia's young men, and he had begun to notice the young women as well. At dances and the Dancing Assembly he worked at converting his former boyish charm to a more manly version.[41] His French accent and French sophistication, to say nothing of his connection with a celebrated household, must have made him appear both debonair and dangerous to many of the young "ladies."

Benny had experienced a kind of forced precocity, both as a small child whisked away to Passy and Geneva and as a sixteen-year-old business partner with Franklin. Precocity was to mark his romantic life as well. By the summer of 1788, not yet nineteen, he began to fall in love with Margaret Hartman Markoe, one year his junior.

Margaret was the granddaughter of Isaac Hartman and the daughter of Francis Markoe, both of whom were sugar planters on the Danish Island of St. Croix. After her father's death, she lived with her mother in Philadelphia, perhaps residing for a time with Margaret's uncle, Abraham Markoe, Sr., an aristocratic member of Philadelphia's economic elite who had himself come to the city from St. Croix in 1771. In 1783, Abraham, Sr., built a mansion between Market and Chestnut streets, perhaps helping to bring Benjamin and Margaret together. As a Markoe, Margaret stood to inherit a quarter share—along with her brothers Francis and Peter and her sister Elizabeth—in the St. Croix Hartman family estate called "Clifton Hill." But Abraham Markoe, Sr., had appointed his own son, Abraham, Jr., to manage "Clifton Hill" and other Markoe properties in the 1780s. By the 1790s, when Margaret and her new husband Benjamin desperately needed the money and could lay claim to their share, it had long been obvious that Abraham had so badly mismanaged the property that there was little inheritance to claim. In the end, Margaret and Benjamin would receive less than $1,500 from the Hartman-Markoe inheritance. Margaret's real legacy was a strong family bond with, and affection for, her brothers—Peter and Francis—who spent the 1790s trying to untangle family finances.[42]

In 1780, well before Benjamin met Margaret, Margaret's mother, Elizabeth Hartman Markoe, had married Dr. Adam Kuhn, a renowned Philadelphia physician. Kuhn had studied botany under Linnaeus but abandoned botany in favor of medicine in Philadelphia. Eventually recruited for the Faculty of Medicine at the University, he was a prominent member of the Pennsylvania Hospital and a founder of the College of Physicians. He was clearly part of Philadelphia's intellectual elite, and before 1800 he may have been part of its economic elite. In the 1790s, the generally obscure and apolitical Kuhn emerged as a supporter of the Federalist orthodox view on yellow fever, advocating its "foreign origin" source rather than the local environs interpretation. After Benjamin's death in 1798, William Cobbett claimed that the *Aurora* had been kept afloat in part through money provided by Adam Kuhn. And, Kuhn did appear as one of the executors of Benjamin's estate in 1798. But in regard to the courtship of Benjamin and Margaret, Kuhn remained largely a silent figure in the background.[43]

By the late 1780s, therefore, Margaret Hartman Markoe was part of a Markoe family whose wealth was falling into disarray, and she was the stepdaughter of a man whose world was remote from that of the Markoes. Already in a kind of kin and culture limbo, she undoubtedly felt further estranged and uncertain about what constituted "home" when her mother died in 1790. Fond of her brothers, she might have returned to her St. Croix roots—except for the intrusion of her eager suitor, Benjamin Bache.

The courtship spanned three and a half years. According to Benjamin's "history of my heart"—part of a letter written to Margaret in the summer of 1791—he had first gotten to know her in the spring of 1788, had known he could love her by that summer, and had, by June 14, 1789, become her "professed lover."[44] For Benjamin, it was a passionate love from that date forward. If Sarah Bache had shown initiative and independence in selecting Richard Bache, her son pushed the evolution of modern courtship a step further, foreshadowing the new era of romantic love of the nineteenth century.

His early letters to Margaret as well as unsent drafts of letters contained every emotion—passion, anticipation, fear, and jealousy. A still very young Margaret Markoe drew back. Realizing he had frightened her, Benjamin was torn between passion and the need to offer reassurances. On the one hand, he promised not to press her for the declaration he wanted to hear, and promised to "keep the Secret" of his affection to protect both of them. "I never could think of sacrificing your Happiness to my most ardent Wishes," he promised. On the other hand, he wallowed in "wretched uncertainty." He wondered, "Is your Heart engaged? Has ——— gained your Affection? Am I to be unhappy?" He criticized, and then magnanimously withdrew and corrected his criticism of, a young rival he was certain she admired. He lay awake at night, his imagination and fears running riot. "Hope & Fear, in fact, rise and sink in my breast like buckets in a well," he admitted.[45]

Rational or calculating arguments occasionally intruded. Perhaps he should "have endeavoured first to obtain the Doctor's [Kuhn's] good Graces?" he ruminated at the outset of the courtship. And, when Margaret argued that before a woman is twenty-two or twenty-three it was impossible for her "to have acquired all the Knowledge she ought to have to become a good Wife," Benjamin countered with the observation that at eighteen or nineteen a young woman's "Habits" were not so well formed and were more "flexible," allowing young couples to grow in their compatibility. Yet, he continued, young women of that age also know themselves well enough to know who not to marry.[46]

Benjamin was too young, too eager, and too imploring. In late 1789, Elizabeth Markoe Kuhn, ill and undoubtedly worried about the vulnerability of her daughter, decided to return to St. Croix. Eager to avoid the pressure being applied by Benjamin, and feeling a genuine need to care for her mother, Margaret escaped with her. From late 1789 until June, 1790 Benjamin was forced to wait. In fact, he was forced to do more. Believing he had formed his "attachment" in "haste," Margaret apparently compelled him to cease and desist on the issue of an engagement. He was heartbroken. A girl friend of Margaret wrote in November that Benjamin had been to the Dancing Assembly: "Caro Bene [Benny] was there & danced it is true; but his heart did not, I am sure, keep pace with his feet. Indeed I believe it was not in the Room."[47]

Unable to press his devotion to her, he decided to flood her with letters. Above all, he wanted her to know his character and intentions. He was not wealthy nor did he expect to be, he admitted, adding that "I never was intended to be made a Man of Fortune, but rather to endeavour at becoming one."[48] Usually he skirted the issue of courtship. He reported on the Dancing Assembly, conveyed gossip, told her of his growing interest in music over dance, recited Hume on balancing work and pleasure, and reassured her that absence makes the heart grow fonder. She refused to reply, and as late as April, 1790, he recorded that he had received no letter from her.[49]

Franklin's death on April 17, 1790, with Temple and Benjamin at his bedside in his last moments, furthered Benjamin's anxiety and grief. His loss was "irreparable," Benjamin told Margaret. Testifying to the closeness he and Franklin felt to the very end, even when Franklin was no longer able to speak, Benjamin reported that, "Whenever I approached his Bed he held out his Hand & having given him mine he would take & hold it for some time; this shows that he was not insensible." Pain and confusion prevailed. Benjamin confessed:

> I have spent a Spring of great uneasiness. Fatigue, Anxiety, & Fear, Trouble & Grief. 'Tis time Summer should come to restore my Spirits & Strength, to bring some happy Moments that may efface those Hours of Pain that are even now gliding along, but won't fly swift enough.[50]

Franklin's will, he said bravely, hoping to convince her that the will was generous and left him sufficient resources to support a wife, "squares perfectly with the Expectations I had." According to his own estimate he had received property worth fifteen hundred pounds sterling, "chiefly in tools that his Industry are to put in Motion assisted by his Fathers Aid." And, he noted, this legacy was free and clear since there were, "No Marriage Conditions relating to him."[51] Benjamin's estimation of the will was fair. In receiving all of the printing and typefounding equipment as well as the share in the Library Company and the books, he acquired a large and potentially valuable legacy. But, as Franklin clearly intended, it was a legacy that only became valuable as Benjamin put it to use, as he applied industry to these materials.

Benjamin's legacy was categorically different from that left to Benjamin's parents. They received real property of established value and the Louis XVI miniature with its 408 diamonds, which they did not hesitate to turn into ready cash. It was also categorically different from Temple's legacy, which included Franklin's autobiographical writings, materials that should have required little originality on Temple's part in order to produce a large publishing revenue, as well as the title to the farm in New Jersey (when he married). By comparison, and even by any absolute standard, Benjamin had a right to feel proud of his inheritance. Like the biblical parable of the talents, Benjamin was, after all, the only beneficiary of the will in whom Franklin placed real confidence, apparently being the only one who Franklin believed had the ability and the industry to turn an otherwise limited inheritance into a continuing legacy.[52]

But Benjamin felt no such confidence in the spring and summer of 1790. What he sought was relief from his grief. What he got was increased anxiety. By late June, he had composed a letter to Margaret in which he defended his own industry but bitterly criticized his grandfather for not letting him establish an independent printing business earlier. He reassured her that Richard and Sarah were fond of her. And, he asked on what basis she would allow him to see her on her return, acknowledging that he had only Sundays and an hour or so a day free time. He did not send this letter. Instead, he pathetically inquired, "Will you leave the Island without much Regret? Who will you leave to lament your Departure?"[53]

The trail of anxious letters ended with her return in the summer of 1790. His industry and diligence in courtship paid off. Perhaps he looked more reliable and worthy after Franklin's death. He had certainly matured. When Margaret moved to Somerset, New Jersey, between April, 1791, and her marriage to Benjamin on November 17, 1791, he declared that he did not "know why I do not feel as I did when you were at S[t.] C[roix]. Not that I love you less; but that more." The earlier anxieties were gone, as he told her how much he "admired, esteemed, loved and adored" her since he had first seen her. She, out of genuine modesty and embarrassment, demanded that he quit writing about her virtues. Although he visited her twice in Somerset, once by riding all day and night to see her, the Somerset months led to what he called being "Somerset sick."[54]

By September he had also screwed up his courage to ask his father and mother for financial assistance to allow him to marry. Having broached the issue to his mother in conversation, he repeated to his father his devotion to Margaret, putting it all in writing so that he would not be misunderstood and would be on-the-record. "For my part," he said, "I can never be happy without her." For her part, she was brought up to "enjoy an independent fortune," he admitted, but she "would be content to exchange comfort for elegance." In asking what support Richard could give them, he admitted that his "youth" had been "a considerable obstacle to my advancement" in business, that his expenses at the newspaper were high, and that Margaret could expect little inheritance because the St. Croix estate was mismanaged and in debt. Three weeks later, after a favorable response from his father, Benjamin asked for one of the "Front Houses at least," and some money to "brighten my prospects or my business." Above all, he thanked his father for removing "a great deal of anxiety off my mind."[55]

Most of the details of Benjamin's and Margaret's married life have disappeared. After Margaret's sister Elizabeth had suggested that Margaret showed "want of taste" in marrying Benjamin Bache, Margaret replied with confidence that the Markoe family's "big House does not make me regret having changed my name." She never looked back. In 1792, Benjamin remarked on his marriage and newfound maturity in a shy and jocular yet self-satisfied manner. After poking fun at his frantic but meager efforts in newspaper publishing, he added,

> "But the good news, . . . which you must know, I am no longer Little Benjamin, I am the large, bearded Benjamin, and what is worse—married. Yes at 22. Whether badly married or well married—well then, what they call well I'll call well, that is to say to my taste—yes and to the taste of my friends too. If you know her, you would like her very much, you'll like her, without knowing her."

In the couple's few extant letters of the later 1790s—letters written during Benjamin's brief sojourn to New England and New York to fight the Jay Treaty—a strong sense of love and true partnership prevailed.[56]

A small woman of intelligence, will, and determination, Margaret ignored the hardships of journalistic poverty and political contention that shaped her life in the 1790s. She strove with stoic determination to support the two causes she shared with her husband, the improvement and education of her family and the political education of a people. During Benjamin's brief absence in 1795, Margaret published the *Aurora*. Whenever her name did emerge from the obscurity of family life, it appeared in alliance with her husband's. In 1796 Elizabeth Hewson (who was to have been Benjamin's wife, in Franklin's earlier fantasies) reported condescendingly,

> I have staid with Mrs. B. Bache since I have been in town. She has frequently asked me. Poor woman, her old acquaintance have almost all deserted her. She is luckily of opinion that her husband is quite in the right. She does not therefore suffer the pain of entertaining a mean opinion of him which I am sorry to say most people do.[57]

Imbued with a Federalist sense of politics and propriety, Hewson remained astonished at Margaret's commitment, especially in 1798 when Benjamin contracted yellow fever and Margaret—pregnant and exhausted—dutifully nursed him. When Benjamin died, Margaret proudly proclaimed that he "knew no anxieties but what were excited by his apprehensions for his country—and his young family."[58] Margaret survived the subsequent newspaper war with her husband's enemies, and eventually married William Duane, Bache's successor on the *Aurora*. Duane's admiration for her would be as great as Bache's had been, and after twenty-five years of marriage Duane described her as an intelligent, courageous woman with the qualities of a "Roman Matron."[59]

In the midst of the turmoil of the 1790s, Benjamin and Margaret would have four children. The young couple first lived at Franklin's mansion, Margaret caring for Sarah's offspring while Richard and Sarah toured Europe, Benjamin undertaking the sale of some of the mansion's furnishings and the ultimate rental of the mansion. With the mansion rented in 1792, Benjamin and Margaret established housekeeping at 112 High Street, taking some of their furnishings from the mansion. Benjamin and Margaret managed to raise their fledgling family in the comfort of this modest tradesman's house which served as subscription office, printing shop, and home. On October 25, 1792, their first child, Franklin Bache, was born. Named after his great-grandfather at the insistence of Richard Bache, Franklin Bache would gain fame as a chemist, physician, and teacher, eventually holding a professorship at Jefferson Medical College and once being elected President of the American Philosophical Society. Richard Bache III, born two years later in 1794, died before he was forty, a Captain of Ordnance in the U. S. Army and the author of a volume on his travels in South America. Benjamin, born in 1796, would lead a life of relative obscurity, but Hartman Bache, born shortly after his father's death in 1798, would distinguish himself as an 1817 graduate of West Point and as the highest ranking officer in the United States Army Corps of Topographical Engineers. As the achievements of their children attest, Margaret must have followed the precepts of Benjamin's will, in which he recommended "that she will bestow on our dear Children a Suitable and enlightened Education, such as shall be worthy of us, and advantageous to themselves, and render them virtuous, generous, and attached to the immutable principles of Civil Liberty."[60]

Benjamin Bache's first five years in Philadelphia after his return from France were ones of personal, vocational, and philosophical preparation. The personal and vocational lessons were divided between the ordinary and the hidden, the obvious and the psychological. First, one cannot ignore several facts of his mundane life. He dutifully followed his grandfather's direction as student, secretary, typefounder, and printer and publisher. He remained diligent if not accomplished in all of these tasks, sometimes absorbing failure with equanimity and even less frustration than his grandfather. He appeared almost physically anchored in Franklin's house, study, bedroom, and workshop, at least until the late 1780s when Margaret

Markoe appeared on the scene. Some observers, therefore, have been satisfied in dismissing him as "Lightning Rod, Jr." (William Cobbett, 1798); as merely the second of the "Two Franklins" (Bernard Faÿ, 1933); as "aimless" and "led" if not quite "herded" by Franklin (John D. R. Platt, 1971); and as a "pliant" youngster who inexplicably became a "bold" man (Lopez and Herbert, 1975).

There is no denying that Benjamin Bache was more attached to Franklin between 1785 and 1790 than he had been from 1776 to 1785 in Passy and Geneva. Yet in both periods Benjamin dodged the worst implications of dependency. In Europe, he did not remain a pathetic boy without a sense of self-identity and worth. In America, he did not become a sycophant of the great man, a toady or promoter of a cult of Franklin. His behavior was what one might expect of any curious and dutiful adolescent who lived with a grandfather of Franklin's absorbing breadth. Franklin was, after all, an omnibus man, embracing every item of interest around him as his own, collecting books and ideas with tireless curiosity, drawing those around him to his heuristic example. Some cynical, frustrated adults could see Franklin as a man hard to pin down.[61] An idealistic grandson, full of hope, must have seen him as a mirror of America, less chameleon than empathic prophet of the country's future.

If there was nothing pathological in Benjamin's attachment to Franklin, there was nothing slavish in it either. He attended the University of Pennsylvania because Franklin, and probably the Baches, insisted that he do so. But instead of rebelling, he did an equally reasonable thing: he worked hard to get free of the University in as short a time as possible. In printing and typefounding, he displayed what might have been tentative attempts at independence as well. And in courting and proposing marriage to Margaret Markoe he followed no family leads. Nor was attachment a one-way street. Franklin sought and found comfort in his grandson, relied on Benjamin as his secretary, and vicariously relived his youth in trying to establish Benjamin's career.

Benjamin's personal and emotional attachments were those one might expect of a young person approaching adulthood. Benjamin clearly suffered through Franklin's death: the close of an intimate relationship in the loss of a surrogate parent, a friend, and a colleague combined. And the fact that Benjamin's intimacy was not exclusive to Franklin before the latter's death, that it included a healthy desire for sexual partnership and commitment to Margaret Markoe, suggests ongoing psychological evolution into adulthood.[62]

Benjamin's vocational ties were no more or less than might be expected as well. He had acquired a genuine interest in printing and its associated trades in Europe. He naturally followed Franklin's generous lead in furthering that career in America. Why would he not cast type, or print what Franklin advised? Chief among the "role confusions" that have been seen by some developmental psychologists as threatening the establishment of a real identity during adolescence has been "the inability to settle on an occupational identity."[63] But in the broader sense, Benjamin resolved this crisis in adolescence, never revealing any signs that he wished to pursue another vocation.

All this is not to claim that Benjamin Bache in 1790 stood heroically untouched by the travails of human imperfection and youth. He was, and continued to be, narrowly serious and sober (despite his love of pleasure), inflexible in his search for virtue and truth, with a tincture of smug pretense in his character. Throughout his twenties, he would keep, as Erikson defines young adulthood, an "ideological mind," forever testing others "within a defined world image and a predestined course of history"; he demanded, as Erikson characterizes this "ideological mind," that the "best people" rule while insisting that the authority to rule should develop "the best in people."[64] But in 1790 his prime focus was anxiously cast on how to combine his newfound independence with his commitment to printing to produce a useable liberty for the future.

Notes

1. On eighteenth-century Philadelphia see J. Thomas Scharf and Thompson Westcott, *History of Philadelphia, 1609–1884* (Philadelphia, 1884), I; Carl and Jessica Bridenbaugh, *Rebels and Gentlemen: Philadelphia in the Age of Franklin* (New York, 1942); and Thomas Doerflinger, *A Vigorous Spirit of Enterprise: Merchants and Economic Development in Revolutionary Philadelphia* (Chapel Hill, N. C., 1986).

2. Benj. Franklin's Journal, Sept. 14, 1785, Albert Henry Smyth, ed., *The Writings of Benjamin Franklin* (New York, 1905–1907), X, 471, hereafter cited as Smyth, ed., *Writings of Franklin*. For Benjamin's testimony to home-coming confusion see B. F. Bache to [Robert Alexander], Oct. 30, 1785, B. F. Bache Papers, and B. F. Bache's Diary, Sept. 13, 1785, American Philosophical Society, Philadelphia. Franklin's return is detailed in Carl Van Doren, *Benjamin Franklin* (New York, 1938), 731–33; and Charles F. Jenkins, "Franklin Returns from France—1785," *Proceedings of the American Philosophical Society,* XCII (1948), 432.

3. Benj. Franklin to Mrs. Mary Hewson, Oct. 30, 1785, Smyth, ed., *Writings of Franklin,* IX, 474.

4. Benj. Franklin, "Idea of the English School Sketch'd Out for the Consider-

ation of the Trustees of the Philadelphia Academy," cited in Wilson Smith, ed., *Theories of Education in Early America, 1655–1819* (Indianapolis, Ind., 1973), 183. The quotations on Franklin's broad, liberal view of education are from Bernard Bailyn, *Education in the Forming of American Society: Needs and Opportunities for Study* (Chapel Hill, N. C., 1960), 34–35. On the University of Pennsylvania itself see Edward Potts Cheyney, *History of the University of Pennsylvania, 1740–1940* (Philadelphia, 1940), 171–175. On college professors and university governance in this period see respectively William D. Carrell, "American College Professors: 1750–1800," *History of Education Quarterly,* VIII (1968), 289–305; and Jurgen Herbst, *From Crisis to Crisis: American College Government, 1636–1819* (Cambridge, Mass., 1982). The Presbyterian motif of the University of Pennsylvania, and the corresponding importance of Scottish common-sense philosophy in the University (which may have influenced Bache's moral and political philosophy) are discussed in Howard Miller, *The Revolutionary College: American Presbyterian Higher Education, 1707–1837* (New York, 1976); and Douglas Sloan, *The Scottish Enlightenment and the American College Ideal* (New York, 1971). The best work blending pedagogy and social environment for this period is David W. Robson, *Educating Republicans: The College in the Era of the American Revolution, 1750–1800* (Westport, Conn., 1985). More general social and cultural works on education are Frederick Rudolph, *The American College and University* (New York, 1965); and Lawrence A. Cremin, *American Education: The National Experience, 1783–1876* (New York, 1980).

5. B. F. Bache to [Robert Alexander], Oct. 30, 1785; and B. [F. Bache] to R. Alexander, Oct. 16, 1786, B. F. Bache Papers, Am. Philos. Soc.

6. B. F. Bache to M. Le Veillard, April 18, 1787, B. F. Bache Papers, Am. Philos. Soc. And Benj. Franklin to Francis Childs, May 8, 1787; Benj. Franklin to M. Brillon, April 19, 1788; and Benj. Franklin to Ferdinand Grand, Mar. 5, 1786, Smyth, ed., *Writings of Franklin,* IX, 581, 644, 492.

7. See respectively [B. F. Bache], Notes on History (n.d.); B. F. Bache, 5th Book of Euclid (n.d.); and, B. F. Bache, Moral Philosophy, Vols. I and II (1786), Bache Papers, Castle Collection, American Philosophical Society, Philadelphia.

8. On Vaughan see Jane Mecom to Sarah Bache, May 29, 1786, Carl Van Doren, ed., *The Letters of Benjamin Franklin and Jane Mecom* (Princeton, N.J., 1950), 271. Franklin's comments are in Benj. Franklin to Mrs. Mary Hewson, May 6, 1786, Smyth, ed., *Writings of Franklin,* IX, 512.

9. B. F. Bache to Benj. Franklin, Aug. 1, 1787, Bache Papers, Castle Coll., Am. Philos. Soc.

10. On Franklin's building ventures see Benj. Franklin to Jane Mecom, Sept. 21, 1786, and May 30, 1787, Carl Van Doren, *Benjamin Franklin's Autobiographical Writings* (New York, 1945), 674–75, 680; Van Doren, *Franklin,* 737, 740; Edward M. Riley, "Franklin's Home," *Transactions of the American Philosophical Society,* XLIII (1953), 158. For the best account see John D. R. Platt, *The Home and Office of Benjamin Franklin Bache (America's First Modern Newsman)* (Washington, D. C., 1970). The typefounding and printing shop is described in Robert Carr to J. A. McAllister, May 25, 1864, in Scharf and Westcott, *Philadelphia,* I, 460n.

11. The best description of typefounding in early America is in Rollo G. Silver, *Typefounding in America, 1781–1825* (Charlottesville, Va., 1965), 3–23, 38, 54, 109. See also Lawrence C. Wroth, *The Colonial Printer*, 2d ed. (Portland, Me., 1938), 83, 87–114.

12. Silver, *Typefounding*, 54, 91–92.

13. Material on the Childs affair is taken largely from Luther S. Livingston, *Franklin and His Press at Passy* (New York, 1914), 125–76.

14. Benj. Franklin to Francis Childs, Mar. 26, 1786, cited in *ibid.*, 140.

15. Benj. Franklin to Francis Childs, Oct. 15, 1786, cited in *ibid.*, 159–60.

16. Benj. Franklin to Francis Childs, May 8, 1787, Smyth, ed., *Writings of Franklin*, IX, 581.

17. Benjamin also reported that he had met Mr. and Mrs. John Jay while in New York. See respectively B. F. Bache to R. Bache, July 31, 1787; B. F. Bache to Benj. Franklin, Aug. 1, 1787, Bache Papers, Castle Coll., Am. Philos. Soc.; and Francis Childs to Benj. Franklin, Aug. 21, 1787, cited in Livingston, *Franklin and His Press*, 168.

18. Benj. Franklin to Francis Childs, April 27, 1789, *ibid.*, 173.

19. B. F. Bache to Benj. Franklin, Aug. 1, 1787, Bache Papers, Castle Coll., Am. Philos. Soc. On the Caslon type order see Platt, *The Home and Office of Benjamin Franklin Bache*, 58.

20. B. F. Bache to M. Carey, Feb. 21, ?, B. F. Bache Papers, Am. Philos. Soc.; and B. F. Bache to M. Carey, undated, Matthew Carey Papers, Historical Society of Pennsylvania, Philadelphia.

21. For Benjamin's specimen see Douglas C. McMurtrie, *Benjamin Franklin, Typefounder. A Note to Accompany a Facsimile Reproduction of the Type Specimen of Benjamin Franklin Bache* (New York, 1925). See also Platt, *The Home and Office of Benjamin Franklin Bache*, 58–59.

22. McMurtrie, *Benjamin Franklin, Typefounder* 10; Silver, *Typefounding*, 35–57; Livingston, *Franklin and His Press*, 175; and Platt, *The Home and Office of Benjamin Franklin Bache*, 59n.

23. Benj. Franklin to M. Brillon, April 19, 1788, Smyth, ed., *Writings of Franklin*, IX, 644.

24. See the biographic sketch of Barbauld in Janet Todd, ed., *A Dictionary of British and American Women Writers, 1660–1800* (Totowa, N.J., 1985), 37–38; and on behaviorist pedagogy and Barbauld, Jacqueline S. Reinier, "Rearing the Republican Child: Attitudes and Practices in Post-Revolutionary Philadelphia," *WMQ*, 3d Ser., XXXIX (Jan., 1982), 153.

25. Charles Evans, *American Bibliography . . .* (New York, 1903–59), VII, 193–94, 238, lists six works advertised for sale by Bache in 1788, five being children's readers, the last a short story in the form of a puzzle; Anna Letitia Aikin, *Hymns in Prose, for Children;* A. L. A. Barbauld, *Mrs. Barbauld's Lessons for Children, From Two to Four Years, Part I. With Alterations Suited to the American Climate, by a Lady;* A. L. A. Barbauld, *Mrs. Barbauld's Lessons for Children of Four Years Old. Part II. . . . ;* A. L. A. Barbauld, *Mrs. Barbauld's Lessons for Children Four to Five Years Old. Part III. . . . ;* and *Moral and Entertaining Labyrinth.* Evans lists no extant

copies for the first and last two books on the list. Bache's advertisement was enclosed in the preface to Barbauld, *Mrs. Barbauld's Lessons . . . Part I. . . .*

26. Benj. Franklin to Jane Mecom, Feb. 22, 1789, Van Doren, *Franklin's Autobiographical Writings,* 768.

27. Mathuria Cordier, *Quaedam Ex Colloquiis Corderii, Fabulis Aesope, & Colloquiis Erasmus Selectae. With English Translations, As Literal As Possible. . . .* (Philadelphia, 1789); and [Biblia. Old Testament], *Selectae e Vetere Testamente et e Profanis Scriptoribus Historiae. . . .* (Philadelphia, 1789).

28. This no longer extant letter is reported in Faÿ, *The Two Franklins,* 105–106. While its authenticity cannot be verified, it fits a familiar pattern for the curmudgeon, Nisbet, who later in life gratuitously took swipes at Franklin and at Bache.

29. See The Bank of North America [Th. Willing] to Benjamin Franklin Bache, Aug. 6, 1789, Franklin Papers, Am. Philos. Soc.; and William Smith, *Proposals for Printing by Subscription a Body of Sermons Upon the Most Important Branches of Practical Christianity* (Philadelphia, 1789).

30. On Jefferson's offer see Benj. Franklin to Th. Jefferson, Oct. 24, 1788, Van Doren, *Franklin's Autobiographical Writings,* 761 and 761n. On Bache's book inheritance see "Franklin's Last Will and Testament," Smyth, ed., *Writings of Franklin,* X, 498–99; and [W. T. Franklin], "A List of Books for B. F. Bache," [1790], in the William Temple Franklin Papers, Am. Philos. Soc.

31. Franklin wrote his "Observations Relative to the Intentions of the Original Founders of the Academy in Philadelphia" in June 1789 as the college was being reorganized. See Smyth, ed., *Writings of Franklin,* X, 9–32; and Van Doren, *Franklin,* 769.

32. Compare their reproduced signatures in Faÿ, *The Two Franklins,* 118.

33. See Benj. Franklin to Jonathan Williams, Jan. 27, 1786, Smyth, ed., *Writings of Franklin,* IX, 481.

34. See [B. F. Bache] to [Margaret H. Markoe], May 2, 10, 1790, B. F. Bache Papers, Am. Philos. Soc.

35. Julian P. Boyd, *et al.,* eds., *The Papers of Thomas Jefferson* (Princeton, N.J., 1950–), XVIII, 86n–97n.

36. Material in this and the preceding paragraph is from the history of Franklin's autobiography in the introduction to *The Autobiography of Benjamin Franklin,* ed. and intro. Leonard Labaree, *et al.* (New Haven and London, 1964), 22–40. See also the "Introduction" to Franklin's autobiography in Smyth, ed., *Writings of Franklin,* I, 32–33. Verification of Benjamin Bache's role in copying the memoir can be found in Benj. Franklin to M. Le Veillard, Sept. 5, 1789, *ibid.,* X, 35.

37. See J. A. Leo Lemay, Jr., and P. M. Zall, *The Autobiography of Benjamin Franklin: A Genetic Text* (Knoxville, Tenn., 1981), xl–xliv, 177.

38. On Benjamin as "amanuensis" see Platt, *The Home and Office of Benjamin Franklin Bache,* 46. Claude-Anne Lopez and Eugenia W. Herbert, *The Private Franklin: The Man and His Family* (New York, 1975), 288–89, describe a Benjamin who "spent long hours as his grandfather's secretary," implying that Benjamin was always ready by Franklin's side when, in fact, he probably spent lonely hours

scribbling out Franklin's autobiography and only occasionally taking dictation for letters.

39. Unless otherwise noted, material in this and the next six paragraphs are from B. F. Bache, "Melanges," (Aug., 1786–[?]), Bache Papers, Castle Coll., Am. Philos. Soc.

40. [B. F. Bache], Notebook of "Resolutions and Plan for Self-Improvement," (Sept. 29, 1789).

41. Benjamin became one of the "managers" of the Dancing Assembly some time around 1793. For mention of the dancing assembly see B. F. Bache to R. Bache, Feb. 3, 1793. The non-elitist character of the Dancing Assembly is studied in Robert James Gough, "Towards a Theory of Class and Social Conflict: A Social History of Wealthy Philadelphians, 1775 and 1800 " (unpub. Ph.D. diss., Univ. of Pennsylvania, 1977), 427.

42. Sketchy genealogies and histories of the Markoe family can be found in *Appleton's Cyclopedia of American Biography,* III, 577, and IV, 211; Joseph Jackson, "Abraham Markoe," *DAB,* VI, 286–87. A. C. B., "Peter Markoe," V, 287–88; Gough, "Toward a Theory of Class and Social Conflict," 279, 347–49, 513; and Mary Chrysostom Diebels, *Peter Markoe (1752?–1792): A Philadelphia Writer* (Washington, D. C., 1944), 1–20. The Markoe Family Papers, Hist. Soc. Penn., deal primarily with the plantation business on St. Croix of Abraham Sr. and Jr.

Benjamin and Margaret knew even before their marriage that her inheritance was in jeopardy. A long exchange of letters among Benjamin, Margaret's brothers, and various agents details the poignancy of Benjamin's moral and practical interest in trying to retrieve that legacy. See Peter Markoe to B. F. Bache, June 12, 1790; Aug. 17, Sept. 10, 1792; and, July 26, 1796; B. F. Bache to Peter Markoe, July 6, 8, 1790; and, Mar. 20, 1793; B. F. Bache to Administrators of the Estate of Isaac Hartman, July 21, 1792; Peter Markoe to M. H. Markoe, Aug. 29, 1790; William Markoe to B. F. Bache, Sept. 15, 1792; Apr. 10, May 9, 1793; June 12, and 14, 1795; B. F. Bache to William Markoe, Mar. 26, May 4, 1793; and, Oct. 4, 1794; Francis Markoe to B. F. Bache, Sept. 29, 1796; and, Mar. 27, 1797; Francis Markoe to M. H. Bache, Jan. 8, 1797; Francis Markoe to A. J. Dallas, Sept. 22, 1800; and, W. H. Krause to B. F. Bache, Sept. 30, Oct. 22, Nov. 13, Dec. 7, 1796; Jan. 8, May 7, July 24, 1797; and, July 14, 1798. Bache Papers, Castle Coll., Am. Philos. Soc.

43. Willis L. Jepson, "Adam Kuhn," *DAB,* V, 510–11; Gough, "Towards a Theory of Class," 412, 534, 645. On yellow fever see Martin S. Pernick, "Politics, Parties, and Pestilence: Epidemic Yellow Fever in Philadelphia and the Rise of the First Party System," *WMQ,* 3d. Ser. XXIX (1972), 559–86. On Kuhn and Benjamin Bache see *Porcupine's Gazette,* July 8, 1799; and B. F. Bache's will, Sept. 7, 1798, B. F. Bache Papers, Am. Philos. Soc.

44. [B. F. Bache] to [M. H. Markoe], July 1, [1791], Bache Papers, Castle Coll., Am. Philos. Soc.

45. See respectively B. F. Bache to M. H. Markoe, [June 13 & 14, 1789] [draft]; and, three letters with no date, *ibid.*

46. B. F. Bache to M. H. Markoe, June 17[?], 1789, [draft], *ibid.*

47. See respectively B. F. Bache to M. H. Markoe, n.d., [draft]; and, Mary Coxe to M. H. Markoe, Nov. 22, [1789?], *ibid.*

48. B. F. Bache to M. H. Markoe, Dec. 6, 1789, *ibid.*

49. Although some letters were written over two or three days, Benjamin wrote to Margaret on the following days, B. F. Bache to M. H. Markoe, Jan. 28, 29, Feb. 4, 20, Mar. 16, 20, 21, 22, 24, 27, 28, 29, Apr. 1, 7, 1790, *ibid.*

50. [B. F. Bache] to [Margaret H. Markoe], May 2, 10, 1790, *ibid.*

51. *Ibid.*

52. "Franklin's Last Will and Testament," Smyth, ed., *Writings of Franklin*, X, 498–99. Lopez and Herbert, *The Private Franklin*, 305, find Benjamin's legacy "much less than he might have expected," but their view is also of a young man who was pliant to the point of sycophancy, a young man tied to Franklin out of abject dependency rather than for the fuller and more varied reasons noted in this and the preceding chapter.

53. See respectively B. F. Bache to M. H. Markoe, June 23, 1790 and [May 2, 1790?], Bache Papers, Castle Coll., Am. Philo. Soc.

54. See especially B. F. Bache to M. H. Markoe, Apr. 20, June 5, 15, 21, 27, Aug. 17, 18, 23, 27, Sept. 8, 15, 19, 23, Oct. 3, 4, 1791, *ibid.*

55. B. F. Bache to R. Bache, Sept. 1, 20, and Oct. 10, 1791, *ibid.*

56. M. H. Bache to Eliz. Markoe, n.d., *ibid.*; B. F. Bache to Le Veillard, Apr. 6, 1792, Franklin Papers, Pierpont Morgan Library, N. Y. See the couple's exchange of letters during the Jay Treaty battle, July 2–21, 1795, Bache Papers, Castle Coll., Am. Philos. Soc.

57. Eliz. Hewson to Thos. T. Hewson, Oct. 24, 1796, Hewson Family Papers, Am. Philos. Soc.

58. For Margaret's devotion, fortitude, and strong sense of responsibility see Eliz. Hewson to Thos. T. Hewson, Aug. 31, Oct. ?, 10, 1798, and May 10, 1799, *ibid.* Margaret's death notice for Benjamin appeared only hours after Bache's death. A copy of the notice is in the Castle Collection.

59. See Kim Tousley Phillips, "William Duane, Revolutionary Editor" (unpub. Ph.D. diss., Univ. of California, Berkeley, 1968), 83–84.

60. "Genealogy of the Bache Family," Leonard Labaree, *et al.*, eds., *The Papers of Benjamin Franklin* (New Haven, Conn., 1959–), I, lxiii, hereafter cited as Labaree, *et al.*, eds., *Franklin Papers;* and Platt, *The Home and Office of Benjamin Franklin Bache*, 73–75; and Benjamin Franklin Bache's Will, Sept. 7, 1798, B. F. Bache Papers, Am. Philos. Soc.

61. The famous Federalist commentator, Alexander Graydon, observing Franklin's conduct in Pennsylvania politics in the 1780s, remarked that Franklin's "demeanor to both parties was so truly oily and accommodating that it always remained doubtful to which he really belonged; and while president of the executive council . . . he sedulously avoided voting on questions which partook of the spirit of party." Alexander Graydon, *Memoirs of a Life Chiefly Passed in Pennsylvania* (Harrisburg, Pa., 1810), 266–67.

62. On intimacy see Eric H. Erikson, *Childhood and Society* (New York, 1950), 263–66; and *Identity: Youth and Crisis* (New York, 1968), 135–36.

63. Erikson, *Childhood and Society*, 262.

64. *Ibid.*, 263.

4. The Paradoxes of Practical Liberty, 1790–1798

> "The Freedom of the Press is the Bulwark of Liberty. An impartial Newspaper is the useful offspring of that Freedom. Its object is to inform."
> (*General Advertiser*, Oct. 2, 1790)

BENJAMIN BACHE OPENED HIS FIRST ISSUE of the *General Advertiser* by emphasizing the reciprocal relationships between "Freedom of the Press" and "Liberty." In part, this view of the press represented a broad shared rhetoric of his own time coupled with a centuries-old and ever-expanding sentiment of public and private liberty. In part, these words reflected a personal political creed and ideological faith. But in another sense they expressed the significance of practical liberty, of liberty applied to the material aspects of life. Although Bache would not have agreed with Edmund Burke that "Abstract liberty, like other mere abstractions, is not to be found," he would have had some appreciation for Burke's follow-up: "Liberty inheres in some sensible object."[1]

"Liberty" was a charged word of mixed definition in 1790. It could mean merely a passive and elemental release from another's authority. Several events of 1790 had almost simultaneously accomplished this release for Bache—Franklin's death, the provisions in Franklin's will, and, finally, Benjamin's reaching the age of majority. As a printer Benjamin could even have understood "liberty" in its ancient definition as the guild-like rights and privileges of a free artisan. But those liberties were akin to the seventeenth-century idea of ascribed civil liberties, liberties allowed within the ordered confines of a traditional society, where liberty primarily consisted in the right to occupy an established station in life. The liberties of passive freedom and of ascribed status implied a world of the past, a traditional world of fixed rights and relationships, and of fixed institutions through which those rights were exercised.[2]

While Benjamin Bache possessed to some degree this older, more traditional liberty, it was one that better belonged to Edmund Burke. Always concerned with the corporate nature of society, Burke, in addressing the "loose" definition of liberty, denied that liberty was "solitary, unconnected, individual, [or] selfish." "As if every Man was to regulate the whole of his Conduct by his own will," he observed. "The Liberty I mean is *social* freedom."[3] Meanwhile, American revolutionaries one generation Benjamin's senior embraced their own brand of "social freedom" or liberty, a brand that found expression in civic humanism and classical republicanism. Rather than an individualistic release from obligation, this liberty presumed a clear and unchanging virtue, a perennial essence of virtue that appealed to both the conservative mind and the Calvinist soul. Fixed concepts of liberty and virtue stood joined against their Manichean opposites, power and corruption.[4]

Liberty was generally of a broader, more liberal, more modern concept for Bache. For him, liberty from ascriptive status was a powerful and sometimes cruel reality. Admittedly, Benjamin's parents remained important to him through their material support (as Franklin had directed them to be in his will). But that aid and comfort never compromised the independence and detachment that he had already acquired by 1790. He was not intellectually or psychologically enslaved to the extended family, and although we must assume that he was financially beholden to them, he never acted as though money placed him under other obligations. His comings and goings during the 1790s were those of a man committed to his small family but personally free to perform the new journalistic role of independent observer, reporter, and commentator. With his mixed cultural background and his private political relationships with a few intimate associates during the 1790s, Bache exemplified the private man, the man who has detached himself from the collective associations of an organic traditional society and whose autonomy and freedom eventually verge more toward alienation than toward a defined niche in the social order.[5]

Bache was a participant in this liberty in a less abstract, more concrete and positive way as well. Raised under the tutelage of a grandfather who saw liberty and virtue as the consequences of industry and frugality, Bache had become habituated to hard work. He had succumbed to the one enslavement that Franklin insisted upon, a behavioral bonding to industry that, when consistently put into practice, paradoxically returned the rewards of liberty and virtue.[6] Thus, Bache was poised in 1790 to benefit from the consequences of Franklin's influence and identify his own personal education with a new liberal ideal of liberty. First articulated by John Trenchard and Thomas Gordon as a radical Whig idea of the early eighteenth century, the liberal ideal did not demand that liberty find definition merely as a residual corollary of the limits of social authority or private rights to property. By the 1790s, as Joyce Appleby succinctly puts it, a new comprehension of liberty had become widespread: "Instrumental, utilitarian, individualistic, egalitarian, abstract, and rational, the liberal concept of liberty was everything that the classical republican concept was not."[7] This liberty was the very definition of "modernity" itself, containing the potential to achieve success, to shape one's future, as well as to discover both private and public virtue through enlightened self-interest.

But in practice, the way was not entirely free for such applications of modernity in the 1790s. Both Philadelphia and publishing promised the potential to fail miserably accompanied by the new opportunity to succeed, while the vision of individualism, abstraction, and rationality carried the potential seeds of social alienation as much as benign detachment.

From a distant view, Philadelphia in the 1790s may have appeared the city of progress, the epitome of the pre-industrial city. Its dynamism and commercial vibrancy and its hardy artisan classes suggested a city ready to achieve bourgeois maturity. But while the cityscapes, drawings, and paintings of late-eighteenth-century Philadelphia suggested a blend of prosperity and ordered comfort, the economic and cultural transitions underway actually held discomforting portents. Some artisans may have appeared as emerging entrepreneurs, but any new ethic of egalitarian improvement was severely compromised by lingering class divisions and social and economic stratification. Philadelphia had no economically cohesive elite in the 1790s. Social conditions determined elite membership, with occupational and religious interest groups slowly eroding these traditional social determinisms.

Yet a "hierarchical, organically integrated society of ranks, where every man knew his place and deferred to his betters, had not disappeared."[8] Both traditional and modern forces seemed to maintain a highly differentiated pattern of wealth. By 1800, the upper 23.2 percent of the city's taxpayers owned 76.8 percent of the city's taxable property for those with a ratable estate above $50, while perhaps half of the city's working class "lived on or just above subsistence levels."[9] The loosening ties of a modern economy did not have entirely positive side effects. Wage earners replaced unfree or semi-free labor, and this fact coupled with a rise in immigration placed heavy pressures on Philadelphia's lower classes. One study concludes that "Unskilled workers and journeymen artisans in the 'lesser' crafts in Philadelphia often encountered very serious difficulties in meeting their families' basic needs. Many, if not most, lived in poverty or on its edge."[10] Meanwhile, those upper classes still adherent to traditionalism abandoned their earlier charitable view of the poor, insisted on a new deference from lesser sorts, pressured the poor to live up to more rigorous standards of industry, and attempted to stem "the flow toward a more egalitarian society."[11] Philadelphia's ambitious artisans and entrepreneurs like Bache thus contemplated the prospect of the poverty and failure of an insecure lower class encroaching on the artisan class from below while the wealth and security of an upper class appeared clearly beyond the middling man's reach.

Bache learned of these social and economic realities early. In 1786, twenty-six of the journeymen printers of Philadelphia organized to protest a reduction in wages. Franklin and young Benjamin could not have been unaware of this earliest example of occupational response to Philadelphia's emergent free wage economy. Two years later, a very ill Franklin and an ambitious Bache formed the Franklin Society, the first attempt to create an on-going organization for printers with regular meetings and the regular payment of dues, and with schemes for loans, workmen's compensation, and insurance.[12]

Although political and ideological issues dominated Bache's newspaper through the 1790s, the necessity of honest labor and industry producing a society of general equality remained important to him. In the early years of the *General Advertiser,* he sometimes sounded conventionally conservative in his pronouncements. "The idle are not only useless," he claimed early on in perfect Franklinian style, "but mischievous members of society." He occasionally exhorted readers to embrace frugality and thrift, short of miserliness, as the avenue to personal morality, thereby parroting the sentiments of not only Franklin but the other classical purveyors of republican virtue as well.[13]

Generally a more radical liberalism emerged in his editorials. He usually commented on the evils of luxury and seldom on the moral deficiencies of the poor. Luxury was "the moth of public happiness"; it "extinguishes the courage and military spirit of a nation" through dissipation and enervation, making all actions mercenary.[14] Above all, his utopian vision of the ideal socio-economic order grew to be one of equality. "Let the division of property be made so nearly equal as possible, or advantages given that will form an equivalent," he said while contemplating the deprivations of poverty in England, "and mankind will become virtuous instantaneously."[15]

Thomas Paine or the radical William Godwin, who might have inspired that editorial, could not have been more blunt or extreme. Increasingly critical of the maldistribution of wealth and the insecurities of wage earners and touched by the disease and poverty that plagued the working poor, Bache asked the following rhetorical question only one week before his own death: "Is it not heart rending, that the labouring poor should almost exclusively be the victims of the disease [yellow fever] introduced by that commerce, which, in prosperous times, is a source of misery to them, by the inequality of wealth which it introduces?"[16]

Privately and personally, Bache spoke of a qualified liberalism for those already possessing means other than their own labor. In a long letter to Louis Gabriel Cramer in 1794 he outlined what Cramer's personal prospects might be if he emigrated to the United States. The prospectus was part Crèvecoeur, part caution. America was, Bache testified, a country of "perfect peace, complete religious and political freedom, just laws, good morals, a healthy climate, abundant land," and "respectable people," but it was also "the best country in the world to exploit any industry and one of the worst, . . . for 'eating' money." "Industry and ability" were "therefore the best capital to be brought" to America. Predicting a great increase in land values, Bache did not recommend simple money management or speculation. Rather, he urged Cramer to buy a small farm, hire a farmer to share-crop the land, and there, "with your farmer, your farm, little worry, you will produce the necessities, and the surplus products the objects of comfort." With the clear vision of his father's farm at Settle in mind, Bache urged upon Cramer a kind of aristocratic-democratic, half-way house of practical liberty, while for himself he promised to "succeed in laying the foundations of a solid and considerable fortune by attaching myself to business affairs with perseverance for several years."[17]

But clear and consistent rhetorical support of practical, pecuniary liberty for others obviously engaged his attention less than his need to establish a niche for himself. His primary focus was on the establishment of a successful newspaper in the midst of a highly volatile, competitive, and uncertain journalistic environment. And here the liberty and success Bache sought were qualified by the history of the press in America, by material constraints imposed on all printers, and by the loaded implications which the word "impartial" carried for all would-be newspaper publishers.

The historical legacy for journalists of the 1790s was not a clear one. The colonial period represented little more than a dim past of cautious printers seeking a meager living by seizing whatever publishing opportunities they could. Newspaper publishers emerged and maintained themselves almost exclusively through picking up scraps of printing patronage thrown their way by the constituted authorities. Until the mid-eighteenth century, publishers were primarily poor printers, plagued by inadequate aid, little patronage, and decrepit equipment. They were generally timid and visionless. Neither the legal constraints of licensing in the seventeenth century nor those of prior restraint in the first half of the eighteenth were really necessary to control most of these mere mechanics of the colonial period. Their primary liberty was the "liberty" to pack up and leave for healthier economic or political environs elsewhere. Only by the mid-eighteenth century did printers begin to sense vaguely a practical liberty of toleration that had begun to compromise the legal "legacy of suppression" of the colonial period.[18]

The era of the American Revolution brought significant changes to American journalism. Until mid-century, publishers had tried "to be all things to all men," but popular sentiment and self-interest, in the Stamp Act crisis in particular, produced newspapers that were self-confident and aggressive "engines of opinion." Patriot printers frequently made "early and relatively unambiguous political moves, accompanied by ardent expressions of high constitutional principle."[19] Within the paradigm of the classical republicanists, they felt charged with the responsibility of rousing the people and uniting them on behalf of liberty and virtue against power and corruption.[20] Yet the constitutional cause that preceded the Revolution left newspapermen impartial and "free" in a limited sense. They had become the willing conduits for an ethic of republicanism more than they were the source for defining that republicanism. Both literally and metaphorically speaking, they remained skilled craftsmen rather than creative artists.

Even Benjamin Franklin's journalism, which bridged the entire development span from the early part of the century to the post-revolutionary stage, reflected the circumscribed achievements, the restraints on journalism, that marked the editor and the entrepreneur up to the 1790s. Franklin was a remarkable innovator in combining useful knowledge, philosophy and ideas, morality, wit, and even political satire in his newspaper ventures. But Franklin proceeded cautiously and kept himself in check. Temperament as well as the pitfalls of publishing prevented him from replying to most attacks. As the Revolution approached, he shifted from passive reporter to advocate slowly and carefully. Virtually the author of balanced journalism, he believed firmly in the duty of the press to inform and enlighten, and in its moral responsibility to bolster republicanism. Yet he seemed almost wistfully attached to the impartial ideal of the press as well. And by 1789 he was even prepared to react to what he saw as too much power and too little legal restraint on the press, and was advocating some modest limits to press freedom.[21]

The force of the Revolution was too great, however, to leave American newspapermen as mere humble mechanics and servants of a pre-defined republicanism. Many successful new-generation printers of the 1770s and 1780s discovered that they were no longer viewed by others or themselves as "printers" and "mechanics" but as "journalists" and "editors." Having achieved intellectual respectability, they also began to discover, as Franklin had much earlier, tactics and strategies that might result in entrepreneurial success. In addition to shaping public political opinion and a public interest in the progress of American governments, editors of the 1780s sought to enlarge their readership through the variety found in advertisements, commercial news, shipping intelligence, articles on science and the "useful arts," international news, and even items to entertain. While some states continued legal restraints that retarded press development, Pennsylvania's constitutional battles in the 1780s generally aided the fast developing political tone of that state's press.[22]

The prospect of intellectual and economic prosperity, combined with the liberty to be "free" of even impartiality, led to the rapid growth of newspapers from the 1760s through the 1790s. The exact number of newspapers in operation in the nation depends on the source one cites. One source has newspapers expanding from a meager twenty-one in 1763 to forty-two in 1775.[23] Mott claims as many as seventy papers published during the Revolution but with only twenty making it through the war. He further suggests that sixty new papers began operation in the mid-1780s, with ninety-one papers publishing in 1790, and an enormous two hundred thirty-four in print in 1800.[24]

But this dramatic increase in newspapers must not be misread. Behind the statistics lay two qualifiers that at first glance appeared to cancel each other out. First, while there were many newspapers, most were weeklies, bi-weeklies, or tri-weeklies; only eight were dailies in 1790, although that number swelled to twenty-four by 1800. Furthermore, one source contends that only about a dozen newspapers in existence in 1783 were still in existence in 1801.[25] The upshot is that newspapers died as swiftly as a hatch of insects, leaving in their brief cycle of emergence, maturity, and death few individual issues of each newspaper. The ratio of newspaper copies to readers, therefore, was low, with probably less than one copy of one newspaper per adult reader in 1790.[26] But this limited number of copies was offset by another qualifier; Americans were, by all testimony, avid newspaper readers. Each copy might be read by several people, and readers probably consumed and digested a high percentage of the news and opinion actually printed. These circumstances suggest that newspapermen faced an uncomfortable paradox. Though the status of the printed word was high, and the editor's selections and opinions were influential, editorial success did not necessarily translate into entrepreneurial success, as Bache would find—a condition that must have confused and frustrated more than one would-be journalist.[27]

Costs of material and labor must have dampened the spirits of the ambitious publisher as well. Modern visitors to Bache's printing shop in Philadelphia—a National Historic Park Site since the early 1970s—are hard pressed to locate in time the historic period of the shop. Most of them probably identify it as a colonial rather than an early republican enterprise. The fault is not theirs. The printing trade changed little in terms of equipment and process from colonial times to the early nineteenth century. The central object, the printing press itself, saw "no essential change in construction . . . from the common English printing press."[28] Bache was lucky; he inherited good and ample press equipment, and while some printers had to get by with one press, he operated at least two presses through the decade. Nor did Bache suffer as much as others in obtaining relatively good type. He undoubtedly possessed more fonts than other newspaper publishers and probably cast and cut some type when needed. When long Congressional debates or extensive news or opinion demanded more coverage, he had the flexibility to set more columns of small type than did others. But when it came to paper, Bache was just as captive as his fellow printers. Isaiah Thomas claimed that sixty paper mills operated by 1810. But production was irregular, and it was not unusual to see printers make a common plea to the public for old discarded linen rags. As one author notes, "paper and ink were dear," and the "continuing costs [of newspaper publishing] were high."[29]

Skilled labor was another factor in persistently high costs. By the 1790s most journeymen printers were receiving the rather high wage for that period of six to eight dollars a week. Even with the extensive use of cheaper apprentices, the work force on a reputable newspaper often had to be numerous to offset the deficiencies of technology. Competent pressmen could only turn out about 200 impressions an hour, and total press time needed to turn out 1,800 copies of a paper would take fifteen to thirty hours. Less than one year into publication of the *General Advertiser,* Bache told his father that the cost of labor and materials stood at forty dollars a week. Bache could not have been exaggerating when he declared in 1793 that seven workmen and assistants made up the staff for the *General Advertiser,* although he privately informed his father that the core of his assistance came from apprentices. Though a modern advocate and practitioner of liberal liberty, Bache was not exempt from employing indentured apprentices who, being subservient to the printer, were given the dirtiest, meanest tasks and were prone to run away. In 1795, he offered an eight dollar reward for a runaway apprentice who had stolen some cloths, "not that he is worth half the money to his master, but because he is a notorious villain, that should be brought to condign punishment."[30]

The revenue side of the ledger was as problematic as the cost side. Bache and others began the movement toward daily papers at a time when the average of 200 to 600 subscribers during the revolutionary era was about to rise to 600 to 700 subscribers for the 1790s.[31] The increase in both the subscription rate and the number of issues should have fostered the development of a new economy of scale and a new entrepreneurial enthusiasm. It did so only in part. Not only did the material limitations cited above compromise this development, but so did distribution problems. The full potential of a cheap newspaper directed at the broadest possible audience was never realized, although Bache made tentative moves in this direction. Problems of distribution to rural areas, Post Office regulations, and the easy access to newspapers at coffee shops and taverns further hindered this development. Circulations remained low by modern standards, subscription rates high, and advertising revenue small. Mott claims that, at their peak, the *Columbian Centinel* had 4,000 subscribers, *Porcupine's Gazette* had 2,000, and Bache's *Aurora* had 1,700. But even if these figures are accurate, it is certain that these publishers had one-third of that number, or even fewer subscribers at other times in the decade.[32]

Translating subscriptions into profit was another major problem. Subscription rates for daily papers were five to ten dollars a year; weeklies and semi-weeklies charged three dollars on average. Getting subscribers to meet their payments was difficult; so was holding subscribers over a long period of time. Well before the decade of the 1790s closed, individual politicians subscribed to numerous newspapers themselves and urged the political faithful to do the same, as well as to pay their bills. But subscribers in remote areas frequently ordered a paper, put the publisher to great trouble to deliver it, and then refused to pay the subscription. Bache finally had to stipulate that subscribers outside the city should pay a year in advance or appoint an agent in the city who could pay their bills as they came due. This policy apparently discouraged many potential subscribers, and in 1796 Bache instituted a policy whereby the paper would "be sent for a short period, and soon again discontinued, if, having received thro' its medium notice of the terms of subscription, they are not complied with."[33] One authority claims a printer had to recover seventy-five percent of his debts to keep printing, with perhaps fifteen percent of a subscription rate going to profit. Advertisements were more profitable in that they were prepaid. But the competition in newspapers made it relatively cheap to advertise. The average charge was about three shillings (about sixty-five to seventy-five cents) for the first "square"—a space of about twelve lines in one column—and two shillings (forty-five to fifty cents) for each additional square.[34]

And then there were those apparently secondary issues that were really central to the new hope of journalism in the new republic—issues of format, layout, editorial content, and the post office. Most 1790s papers were of generally larger dimension than their colonial counterparts, with pages measuring about seventeen to twenty-one inches in length. This added size combined with small type led to surprisingly extensive newspaper coverage on international news, debates of Congress and the state legislature, letters to the editor, miscellaneous useful knowledge, and editorial comment. In virtually all of these categories, Bache improved the press by his thorough and extensive coverage. He, more than anyone, established a regular column for editorial comment, although in this, as in other things, he only offered a transition to the next century's clear designation of editorial opinion. Along with such leaders as the *Gazette of the United States* and the *Minerva,* Bache often allotted half, and sometimes more, space to the editorials of letter writers and "correspondents," as well as to unsigned editorials by himself or one of his closer associates. These associates varied from the eminent, like James Madison and Albert Gallatin, to the scurrilous, like James Thomson Callender and William Duane, to the political insiders, John Beckley, Michael Leib, Dr. James Hutchinson, and Dr. James Reynolds.

Postal issues also reflected the ambiguities of a supposedly new era of practical liberty. Keenly aware of the significance of the Post because of his grandfather's and father's intimate connections to the post office, Bache advocated reforms that combined this legacy with his self-interest. Franklin had admitted newspapers to the colonial mails on an equal basis. In the 1780s, private postal riders served those printers who could afford it, while

Congress publicly placated journalists by allowing the free exchange of one copy of a printer's paper with any and all printers in the country. Newspaper delivery was further facilitated in 1788 when the cross-posts or east-west routes were opened to papers as well as the main north-south routes. Yet in 1790 and 1791 the new Congress simply extended the inadequate acts of the earlier period, although their debates encouraged the public and newspapermen alike to discuss the merits of a flat postal fee per paper or of a graduated fee by distance delivered, or the wisdom of any fee at all. In the debate over the 1792 Postal Act, Elbridge Gerry and James Madison favored a low flat fee, or ideally, no fee at all, arguing that a postal fee was a tax on the dissemination of the knowledge necessary to maintain a free people.[35]

Bache and Fenno had already plunged into the debate in 1791, before ideological or partisan overtones were clearly perceived. Both demanded postal improvements. In reply to the suggestion that newspapers were already liberally treated, Bache argued that papers were not treated equitably, that many exchange papers did not reach their legitimate destination because the Post Office would not guarantee the delivery if the cost was exorbitant. Bache also went beyond these swipes at the current administration to second the *Gazette*'s demand for the nationwide distribution of all papers and the subsidization of their delivery through a small charge to the subscriber.[36]

At the time of the debate on a new postal act, Bache ran a long editorial on the relationship between the broad dissemination of newspapers and a free people.

> In a government by representation, like this, the people are the foundation of power. The value and permanence of this government will therefore depend upon the people being enlightened. Newspapers are the best, the only channel of information to the numerous classes of citizens; newspapers ought therefore to be rather encouraged than otherwise.

Charging postage, he now concluded in line with Madison's arguments, would be "contrary to the spirit" of federal and state constitutions that recommended the dissemination of "useful knowledge" and would "check" the spread of that knowledge. "A bounty upon newspapers," he proudly proclaimed, "would be more consistent with the principles of our government." Then, employing a political mathematics that would become one of his trademarks later in the decade, he argued that a one-half-cent-an-issue rate of postage on 500 papers a day for 312 days in the year, would garner the government a meager 780 dollars revenue a year. In any case, with even a low flat fee a taxing precedent would be set that might later entail the power to exclude and destroy.[37] For the next two months, as the Congressional debate proceeded on what would become the 1792 Postal Act, he argued that postal charges on newspapers were dangerous and would bring trifling revenues. Newspapers would not circulate equally, postage might later be increased, and sparsely populated areas would get poor service and have poor post roads since they would provide few revenues.[38]

To Bache's disappointment, the new Act provided a flat fee of one cent for delivery within 100 miles and one and a half cents for delivery beyond that distance. Before passage of the Act, Bache predicted that the discriminatory charge for distant subscribers would create sectional divisions between North and South. When he assessed the situation ten months later, he was convinced the Act had "materially cramped the circulation" of newspapers. He took comfort in Washington's similar conclusion and incorrectly predicted Congressional repeal of postage on newspapers.[39] After 1792, Bache continued to criticize the post, claiming that delays, poor roads, and irregular deliveries left many papers little better than "waste paper" by the time they reached their destination.[40] He was much more disturbed when Congress began to debate that same year, and finally passed in early 1797, a bill requiring publishers to dry their papers before delivery in order to reduce their weight. Such a policy, he pointed out, would not lighten newspapers much, would force printers to establish expensive drying rooms where fires would have to be maintained winter and summer, and would cause delays since morning papers like his own would have to stop collecting news earlier in the evening in order to accomplish printing and drying. Even worse, papers like the *Aurora,* decidedly in opposition to the government of the day, would be subject to arbitrary censorship by postal employees who could refuse his papers if they were not dry enough.[41]

The postal issue stands as an analog for the ambiguities in Bache's entrepreneurial career. He was interested in those elements of business practice that would further his commercial venture. However, his myopic interpretation of first principles, morality, and political righteousness frequently qualified his own success and self-interest in ways that more profit-minded newspaper men could never tolerate. A brief chronology of his entrepreneurial career is instructive.

Bache's journalistic start was inauspicious. A friend predicted that the removal of the national capital to Philadelphia in 1790 would not only bring "Satisfaction" to a young man "fond of good Fellowship, tho' by no Means a giddy Youth; It may likewise throw great business into your Hands & your Natural Industry will prompt you to embrace it."[42] Bache made a try. He petitioned Thomas Jefferson, who had undoubtedly met Bache in France in the mid-1780s and who had recently assumed his post as Secretary of State, for government printing jobs. He observed that Childs & Swaine had decided not to move to Philadelphia and timidly offered, "Perhaps you may have not yet fixed upon a person to print the laws here; in this case permit me to offer myself."[43] Jefferson did not take him up on the offer. Thus, partially by default, Bache turned to the profession of his grandfather. In fact, he had discussed the prospect of founding a newspaper with Franklin before the latter's death.[44] Publishing meant his equipment would not lie idle and useless. It would keep him occupied and, even with few subscribers, it might prime the pump for more customers.

Several people were apprehensive about his proposal. Perhaps already aware of Bache's liberal political and philosophical orientation, perhaps eager to maintain John Fenno's chances at government patronage against any competition, Robert Morris dressed his blunt discouragement in the clothing of an older morality.

> Some of your friends here are rather sorry for your intention of Printing a News paper. There are already too many of them published in Philadelphia, and in these days of Scurrility it is difficult for a press of such Reputation as you would choose yours to be to maintain the Character of Freedom and Impartiality, connected with Purity. They seem to entertain the opinion that you might be more Honorably and more lucratively employed by the Printing of Books, but of this you are the best Judge, and I have only mentioned the substance of a conversation that arose upon my producing the prospectus of your intended News Paper.

The family probably agreed with Jane Mecom. "I hope my nephew will succeed in his undertaking of a daily paper," she remarked, "but it seems to me a vast one. May he inherit all his grand-father's virtues, and then He will be likely to succeed to his honours."[45]

At the outset, Bache was like the restauranteur who specializes in nothing and therefore offers everything; humbly offering a menu of domestic politics, foreign politics, agriculture, commerce, manufactures, useful arts, fine arts, the sciences, works of wit, humor, and fancy, anecdotes and poetry. Unable to perceive his niche in the market, he accepted the advice of his grandfather and friends "that more attention should be paid to the

Sciences, Literature in general, and more particularly the Useful Arts."
Perhaps he hoped to make his way through the use of little more than a
fresh style. While in university he had written an "Essay on Writing" in
which he promoted writing that established a voice, that used "stress" in
word selection, and that employed capitals and italics liberally as a means to
overcome the "monotony" of written language. In this ambition for an
aural language, he was fully in step with his political mentor, Thomas
Paine.[46] His one creative flourish was to promise a weekly edition to be
printed Tuesdays in which abstracts of the news and material of "rural
concern" would be offered. He then set his prices. The daily would cost five
dollars a year; the country edition would sell for two dollars; and a single
issue of the daily would cost three cents. Advertisements were to be printed
for the lower than market fee of one shilling ten pence for the first square
and eleven pence for each square thereafter. Boldly optimistic, he promised
to print 400 copies at the start.[47]

Nothing happened. Having set a fragmented and bland menu for himself, he soon found little to do beyond the scissors-and-paste plagiarism of
the period. There was too little routine news, and it was too routine. He
noted with mock sadness the decline of political violence in France as the
National Assembly completed its framing of the constitution. Reverting to
his diary style, he half-jokingly complained that "there was something of a
bustle—heads cut off, a little fighting, all very good. They soon got quiet
again, and the printer's hopes were sadly disappointed." There was little
fresh foreign news from elsewhere, while in America there were "no party
disputes to raise the printer's drooping spirits . . . not even so much as a
piece of private abuse to grace a paper. Zounds, people now have no spirit
in them." Ever the modernist in his quest for the eventful and the crisis, he
concluded with false passion: "Now not even an accident, not a duel, not a
suicide, not a fire, not a murder, not so much as a single theft worthy of
notice. O! tempora, O! mores."[48]

By early 1791, Bache had decided to reorganize. There would be no
more attempts to follow in Franklin's precise footsteps. It is significant that
he began by dropping the word "Agriculture" from the masthead. The
paper became the *General Advertiser and Political, Commercial and Literary
Journal;* nine months later, as Bache began to sense the niche he was to fill,
it became merely *General Advertiser.* He candidly acknowledged the need to
increase coverage of Congressional debates and European news, and to
sacrifice variety. To serve this end, he enlarged the paper from twelve to
sixteen columns per page and employed smaller type. Such enlargement, he

boasted, would make his paper "a complete MUSEUM of every important transaction in the History of the times."[49] The weekly paper was dropped. Advertisements in the daily did not interest the distant customer. When the weekly was long it was considered "tedious"; when it was short it was "too concise." The "fatigue and anxiety" of publishing a daily was enough. The price went up by one dollar a year, and advertising charges also rose.

Changes in format were accompanied by less abrupt, but still obvious, qualitative improvements. At the federal level, this meant ever more accurate and fuller accounts of the debates in the House of Representatives. In late 1790, he had first promised an accurate sketch of those debates. For the next eight years the young man who had been such a sloppy copyist for Franklin strove to maintain the high level of reportage he had early set for himself. He reveled in congressional debates and always tried to secure the best listening area he could for himself on the floor. He opposed Senate secrecy from the start, and when the House threatened to remove reporters from the floor he promised to transcribe debates from the gallery, where distance and noise would inevitably deprive readers of full or accurate accounts.[50] His reports of debates, compared to those of others, were more accurate, more detailed, and yet, often more economically written than theirs. His strength in this pursuit, according to Bache, was his steady adherence to "candour and impartiality," his concern for "brevity" and "accuracy," and his careful recording of votes on all major issues.[51] In the turbulence of the partisan strife of the 1790s he remained proud that Republican and Federalist papers alike chose to copy his debates. Although he sought credit as the source for others' debates and later boasted about the many who did admit to copying from him, he was self-confident enough in 1794 to claim that "the satisfaction of finding a correct statement of congressional proceedings circulated, will amply repay him for his trouble in giving it." And although other Philadelphia newspapers had the same access to the House as he did, they—along with virtually all other long-lived papers of the 1790s—borrowed his debates.[52]

Meanwhile, the virtue of having French as a first language began to emerge. Though he continued through the decade to take foreign news (the most significant news to readers) from liberal British papers like the London *Star* and the London *Morning Chronicle,* he frequently turned to the French language papers, like the Paris *Moniteur,* for news as well. Jefferson was so impressed by Bache's catholic taste for the foreign press that he made an effort to supply the *Leyden Gazette* to Bache beginning in April, 1791. Here, too, Federalist and Republican newspapermen alike eagerly copied Bache's accurate translations on the momentous issues of the day in France.[53]

Even by early 1791, although Bache's reputation for covering debates and for translating and publishing foreign news was still ahead of him, it appeared that he was finding his niche. He was developing habits of news-gathering, writing and reportage, and translation that would exceed the standards that almost all other American newspapermen set or reached. At the level of "impartial" reporting as opposed to political opinion-making, he was at least as important as any other single journalist of the period. He was probably more often cited for his translations and transmissions of foreign news than for his debates, although his coverage of Congressional debates may have come in a close second, and he was frequently cited also for the candor and colorfulness of his editorials among fellow Republican editors who undoubtedly found it prestigious to invoke the *Aurora*'s name. This does not mean that he conducted a 1790s "press service," but it does mean that he initiated a broad range of qualitative and quantitative changes in journalism.[54]

From 1791 to 1794 the *General Advertiser* maintained the format adopted in early 1791. It appeared that Bache had won Jefferson's endorsement and support. But Jefferson's support—as Freneau, Callendar, William Duane, and William Harrison Smith could attest—was often transient and impermanent. In Bache's case, that support was usually indirect and always something far less than substantial financial aid. In April 1791 Jefferson congratulated Bache on what he perceived as steady "improvement" of the paper. Already certain of Bache's political principles, Jefferson desired "seeing a purely republican vehicle of news established between the seat of government & all its parts," and was convinced that the *General Advertiser* could become "a paper of general distribution, thro' the states." With the weekly edition discontinued months earlier, Jefferson wondered if another abbreviated version might be started and suggested a plan whereby advertisements "could be thrown into the last half sheet (say pages 3 & 4.) which might be torn off or omitted for distant customers."[55] Whether material circumstances, over-work, or Bache's already established pattern of letting golden opportunities slip away caused the failure of this plan is unknown. All we know is that Jefferson declared, in his long letter to Washington during the Jefferson-Hamilton feud in the Cabinet, that Bache had "tried, at my request, the plan of a weekly paper of recapitulation, from his daily paper, in hopes that that might go into the other States; but in this too we failed."[56]

Always impatient when it came to the press, Jefferson shifted his main support to Phillip Freneau and the newly created *National Gazette* in October, 1791. In no uncertain terms, Jefferson told his daughter that he was enclosing "Freneau's paper instead of Bache's, on account of the bulk of the latter which, being a daily paper was too much for the post. And Freneau's two papers contain more good matter than Bache's six."[57]

Bache's best chance for patronage outside the financial support his family was obliged to give him was lost. And with that loss Bache actually achieved a kind of "impartial" press that he might not have been contemplating in 1790, a newspaper that owed no obligations to financial contributors, at least until 1798.

Unfortunately, this autonomy and utilitarian "liberty" caused his journalistic progress to grind along slowly, no matter what improvements he accomplished in recording debates or translating foreign news. In 1791, he reported to Margaret that Claypoole, a powerful rival, was about to start an evening paper. And, while claiming he had been "gaining ground," admitted that "it will require my personal and again unremitting exertions not to loose [sic] ground." Although he said he received "liberal encouragement" from his patrons and promised to exert every effort to satisfy them, there is no evidence that subscriptions increased greatly.[58] Privately, he admitted hardship. He told his father in early 1793,

> By the help of apprentices I may now say, with the present run of business, I may keep the mill going. I work hard, that's clear yet perhaps am not as economical as I ought to be, and want regularity in my business. Not having been brought up as a man of business has proved a considerable disadvantage to me. Sad experience has taught me the absolute necessity of more precision in my arrangements, and in time, I shall, I think, bend to method.[59]

He did what he could to make ends meet. In 1792 and 1793, while his parents toured Europe, he managed his father's estate and the complex business interests it entailed, much as Richard Bache had fallen back on managing Franklin's properties out of necessity two decades earlier. By August, 1793 he despairingly toyed with the idea of diversification again, confiding to his father, "I have a prospect of setting my foundry in motion if I can scrape up a little assistance; I find I must have two strings to my bow."[60] Bache, like many others, was beginning to feel the limitations of affective liberty and entrepreneurial opportunity in the new republic.

But the events of 1793 would begin an alteration in Bache's fame and, to some degree, his fortune. Well schooled in French affairs, he became more critical and aggressive on such issues as neutrality, the Genet affair, the

French Revolution itself, and American foreign policy as a whole. Having served his tutelage as a journalist, and having established his abilities at accurate reportage and translation, he was ready in 1793 to apply a broad Enlightenment ideology to current events with some confidence. Without a patron or an extensive clientele to satisfy, he could cast aside timidity. Federalist opponents later seized on Bache's "nothing-to-lose" financial condition to prove the insincerity of his aggressiveness. Nearly two decades after Bache's apparent transformation, John Marshall indicted Bache for the supposed radical change of 1793.

> [Bache] found it extremely difficult to maintain his family with all his industry. That he had determined to adopt a bold experiment & to come out openly against the administration. He thought the public temper would bear it.[61]

Coupled with claims that Bache was in the pay of the French, Marshall's summary represented a well-known and hackneyed creed of the Federalists in the 1790s.

In 1794 Bache himself admitted the connection between profits and politics, but not personal contrivance at popularity, by attributing "the rapid encrease of encouragement his paper has experienced, especially of late, more to the importance of the present political crisis, than to any particular merit to which his publication may have a claim."[62] A buoyancy returned to his vision of the future as he finally anticipated some journalistic success. He told his readers that with the list of subscribers "daily increasing," he saw "no reason for a deviation from his present plan," although he welcomed suggestions for improvements with feigned humility. He lamented, without apparent grief, "some friends lost and some enemies made," but, still claiming the objectivity of his position, he felt he could not "shrink" from the duties of an "impartial" editor. With youthful arrogance he proclaimed, "Public men are all amenable to the tribunal of the press in a free state," admitting at the same time that while subject to scrutiny, "the brighter their virtues are, the fairer their character will appear after a public investigation of their conduct." In late January, 1794, he reported with pride that he had gained one hundred new subscribers in the last two months, many of whom were congressmen or legislators.[63]

If real economic improvements occurred in 1794, they were apparently modest or temporary. In the fall, Bache accidentally killed an expensive saddle horse while trying to determine whether it would suit his father's needs. The "vexed and impatient" owner decided Bache was financially responsible. Already low on funds because no revenues came in at the end of the year for subscriptions, he requested a two-hundred-dollar loan from his father to cover the one hundred forty dollars charged for the horse, the investments needed in the printing shop until the new year, and the purchase of fifty reams of paper.[64]

Shortly thereafter Bache showed his growing attachment to a vision of political purity and radical beliefs over material advantage, as he changed the name of the newspaper to the *Aurora*. Although he claimed with practiced self-effacement that mere "whim and fancy" had led to the change, the new name accurately suggested his virtually religious vision of inevitable human progress and a new day for all men. The *Aurora*'s purpose was to "dispel the shades of ignorance, and gloom of error and thus tend to strengthen the fair fabric of freedom on its surest foundation, publicity and information." Denying material self-interest with the disdain appropriate to his youth and his ideology, he swore never to let the "frowns of men" or "allurements of private interest" alter his devotion to public duty. His new motto, *surgo ut prosim* (I rise to be useful), was to remind him of this duty.[65]

Whatever primacy he had once given to entrepreneurial success was receding. Although he alluded to increased subscriptions in early 1795, he was more intent on showing his opponents the paper's political capacity to survive and thrive than he was on convincing himself and others that he stood on the springboard of economic takeoff. And, when he enlarged the paper to twenty columns instead of sixteen, introduced smaller type, and bought new type from London in 1795, he made these changes primarily to accommodate more European news, not to enhance profits directly. At the same time, recognizing his lessening role as a commercial advertiser, he lowered his advertising rates and increased his subscription rate to eight dollars to offset the loss.[66]

Bache made one further innovative change in the area of format before his death in 1798. He introduced a tri-weekly newspaper. Jefferson, who had never lost interest in the "distant" subscriber, and who by this time was urging Republicans to support the *Aurora* through subscriptions, was pleased. Jefferson remarked that "it is doing a good office . . . to observe that Bache has begun to publish his Aurora for his *country customers* on 3 sheets a week instead of six." In the regular paper,

> the 1st. & 4th pages are only of advertisements. The 2d and 3d contain all the essays & news. He prints therefore his 2d & 3d pages of Monday & Tuesday papers on opposite sides of the same sheets, omitting the 1st & 5th so that we

have the news pages of 2 papers on one. This costs but 5 instead of 8 dollars & saves half the postage.

"Indeed five dollars instead of eight," Noah Webster sarcastically noted, "is reducing the price somewhat nearer the intrinsic value of the paper." Bache told James Monroe a few months after it had begun that "this . . . paper takes well in the country." The tri-weekly outlived Bache by many years.[67]

What role then did political patronage as opposed to autonomous entre-preneurship play in this last half of Bache's short business career? By 1795, Federalists had either convinced themselves or wished to convince others that a paper as deluded as Bache's could only survive on patronage or luck, not on its merits. Fenno's *Gazette* began these attacks early to discredit his chief rival. When Bache achieved his first journalistic *coup* by publishing the supposedly secret Jay Treaty in pamphlet form, the *Gazette* charged him with base economic motives. The *Gazette* asked if Senator Mason, who reputedly gave the Treaty to Bache, was going to share in the immense profits Bache must have garnered from selling a rumored 30,000 copies at twenty-five to fifty cents each. Bache did not rise to the bait and admit either an economic windfall or the sale of far fewer than 30,000 copies, although he did admit to his wife, while he was touring in New England, that sales were not as good as he had expected and would barely pay his expenses.[68]

At the same time, it could not have been a party secret that leading Republicans encouraged support of Bache's paper. Jefferson's support was quiet but it could not have been unknown. James Monroe, meanwhile, called the *Aurora* the "best political paper" in Philadelphia.[69] He and other Republicans must have made clear their private desire for subscribers to come forward. Monroe also loaned Bache an enormous six hundred dol-lars, mainly to defray costs toward the publication of Monroe's scathing attack on Washington, *A View of the Conduct of the President*. But no evidence appeared of direct financial grants for the ongoing publication of Bache's paper until the sedition crisis of 1798. And even Monroe's largesse was compromised by the fact that he pressed Bache very hard on the publication of his pamphlet, and even harder for prompt repayment of the loan.[70] Before 1798, Republican partisans were little more than word-of-mouth advertisers for a newspaper that had largely earned its prestige as the leading opposition journal. Within this category, even Federalists like Washington could claim sponsorship, since he subscribed to Bache's paper throughout his years as President.[71] Therefore, Bache had some claim to being "impartial" insofar as he was not materially indebted to these individuals.

Sensing or perhaps knowing this, Federalists looked for more clandestine support of the *Aurora,* and nothing seemed better suited, given Bache's clear francophilism, than to accuse him of being in the pay of the French. Such charges first came to the fore through the ever suspicious Timothy Pickering. Having heard a rumor about Bache's complicity with the French, Pickering requested a deposition from a Frenchman named Rochefontaine regarding the matter. Rochefontaine claimed that the French Foreign Minister, Fauchet, regularly purchased eight hundred copies of the *Aurora* with French government funds and had these papers sent to the several government departments in France. His information had come from a gentleman of high repute, Rochefontaine continued, and to avoid embarrassment to that gentleman and Fauchet, he asked Pickering to keep the information to himself. Pickering probably did not restrain himself, and the rumor spread. Bache periodically denied the charge, and the rumor, which circulated even among family and friends, was never substantiated.[72]

With the hysteria of 1797 and 1798, and the Federalists content to believe that Bache's alliance with the French was manifest to all, the Federalist charge turned to proving the paucity of Bache's political ideas by disclosing his financial poverty. Here too the Federalists probably had good reason to suspect the very real economic stress the *Aurora* was under by 1797. And with William Cobbett's entry into the fray as "Peter Porcupine," they had the perfect journalist for a personal assault of this type. Employing unrestricted tactics that disgusted even some Federalists, Porcupine claimed that Bache had failed to pay a five-dollar fine laid against him in Mayor's Court and, adding sacrilege to insult, declared gratuitously that it would be easier to raise Franklin from the grave than for Bache to raise one hundred dollars. Six months later Cobbett claimed that Bache could not pay his paper maker but added that no one should bemoan Bache's poverty since in this case it was "the wages of villainy." Another writer suggested that Bache's only escape was to find refuge in France since the French owed him a good deal for his support. Fenno was close to correct in hinting that "a gentleman of high station in our Government [Jefferson]" had been forced to procure subscriptions for Bache in Virginia in order to prevent the *Aurora*'s demise. When Bache faced prosecution for seditious libel, the *Gazette* accurately charged that the "Jacobin" party was paying the court and legal costs, implying that Bache could not afford to pay them.[73]

Contrary to popular mythology about Bache's skill in scurrility, he was not very adept at the give-and-take of journalistic attacks and gained fame along these lines primarily for his one-sided assaults on Washington and Adams. In terms of cutting invective and the short but severe blow to an opponent, he was relatively weak. He did charge Fenno with being supported by "land jobbers, lottery ticket mongers, and British agents," and with owing printer James Greenleaf five hundred dollars. And he made a nearly identical charge against Noah Webster.[74] But he left Cobbett relatively unscathed, perhaps on the advice of persons like Jefferson.

Bache's more usual response to Federalist charges was a hollow denial of poverty. Riding the crest of popular opposition to the Jay Treaty, he was able in 1795 to boast that "the *Aurora* for one subscriber lost, has gained TEN; about the proportion between the approvers and opposers of the British Treaty."[75] But fearing a collapse of Republican opposition in 1798 and resignation to Federalist anti-French policies, he put up a brave, but undoubtedly false, front in arguing that his circulation had never been more extensive and that it was as large as Fenno's. Then, getting closer to the sorry truth, he denied that the paper was about to fold if it did not gain more support. "It is true," he admitted in an effort to maintain at least the façade of entrepreneurial autonomy, "that it has never been a very lucrative establishment; but it may become so, and in the meantime it is able to support itself and the proprietor of it, without 'benefaction' from any individual whatever."[76]

Bache's hope to preserve utilitarian liberty and material autonomy was real. But his resources, meager for fighting the partisan and ideological cause he espoused, were never sufficient. Elizabeth Hewson claimed that Bache was said to be "very much embarrassed in his circumstances" and was "going fast to destruction," When Bache died, she showed sympathy for Bache's widow, not entirely for the latter's loss but because Mrs. Bache had inherited a paper with "trifling" profits, and one that might be difficult to sell.[77] The reality was that Bache had asked Tench Coxe, who had contributed a series of articles to the *Aurora* on democracy, national policy, and political economy, to help salvage the *Aurora*'s operation in September 1798. Furthermore, according to later testimony, Bache's paper lost between $14,700 and $20,000 in the years he published the paper.[78]

Did this mean that Bache was simply a casualty of an emergent capitalist economic order? The answer is no. But what Bache experienced in the new realm of liberty is filled with ambiguity and paradox. His editorials and correspondence suggest that he saw, at least dimly, the entrepreneurial opportunities of a daily paper broadly distributed. But attempts to seize that opportunity were stymied by everything from scarce materials and inadequate technology, to reading and spending habits that left little revenue in the printer's hands, to problems of distribution, to the struggle to discover modern and appealing contents and formats, to the too extensive competition from other small scale newspaper ventures, to the divisive and ruinous consequences of partisanship and its tendency to force printers into one camp or another.

Still, while Bache did not achieve economic success, he did achieve economic autonomy of a sort. Although his opponents thought otherwise, he was never subsidized to the degree that Freneau and Fenno were in the early 1790s or that Duane and Samuel Harrison Smith were at the turn of the century.[79] His support of Jeffersonian principles was voluntary, and the way he chose to support those principles was of his own choosing and direction, whether driven by ideology or by the advice he chose to take from his small circle of political friends. It was not driven by considerations of profit. As one critic of the press in the early republic puts it, there were two kinds of newspaper in the 1790s. "One was established and sustained through the support of politicians. The other was established independently and brought into the service of a party by its editor."[80] Bache's newspaper was clearly of the latter kind.

If monetary reward was an elusive aspect of useful liberty, social prestige was not. Bache did not attempt to trade economic hardship for social influence directly. But early on, the magnet of social autonomy and importance overwhelmed any primary quest for profits. The boy who wished to please others, the adolescent who, tied to a famous grandfather, unsuccessfully sought a niche for himself in a rapidly changing society, and the pretentious young man with a trans-Atlantic background, all found ultimate accomplishment in trying to shape and mold the opinions of others. And this accomplishment itself was a consequence of the general ethos of autonomy, utility, and rationality of the new liberal liberty.

The ambiguous manner in which liberty became a reality for Bache finally produced a far different definition of the word "impartial" than the definition Bache intended to give it in 1790. At the outset, he undoubtedly intended something akin to Franklin's view of a press with the capacity to represent several sides to an issue or belief, of one unattached to a specific party or faction and able to provide information objectively. But very early on, impartiality came to mean instead a lack of material dependence on others, no matter how much "encouragement" Jefferson, Madison, Monroe, Tench Coxe, or others gave him. This impartiality of economic and social condition did not result in some search for bland objectivity but freed Bache to make his attachments without coercion and without the need to satisfy family or friends. Later in the 1790s, when Bache proclaimed his continuing impartiality, he meant it in this modern context of free, rational choice.

Notes

1. Edmund Burke in a speech before the House of Commons, Mar. 22, 1775, cited in Michael Kammen, *Spheres of Liberty: Changing Perceptions of Liberty in American Culture* (Madison, Wis., 1986), 4.

2. On seventeenth-century ascribed liberty see esp. *ibid.*, 19–23. Kammen also discusses the mixed definitions of the term "liberty" as the consequence of both diachronic and synchronic circumstances. See *ibid.*, 17.

3. Burke to Depont, Nov., 1789, cited in *ibid.*, 84.

4. Liberty's more complex definition in the classical republican mind is discussed in many works. See especially J. G. A. Pocock, "Virtues, Rights and Manners: A Model for Historians of Political Thought," *Political Theory,* IX (Aug., 1981), 353–68; Bernard Bailyn, *The Ideological Origins of the American Revolution* (Cambridge, Mass., 1967), esp. 55–93, 280–301. The complex problem of semantics and definitions is handled with aplomb by Forrest McDonald, *Novus Ordo Seclorum: The Intellectual Origins of the Constitution* (Lawrence, Kan., 1985), 9–10, 36–53.

5. The loss of the "familial paradigm" as a whole, a loss in which "Independent republicans were no longer held together or in place by affective prescriptions," is described well in Melvin Yazawa, *From Colonies to Commonwealth: Familial Ideology and the Beginnings of the American Republic* (Baltimore and London, 1985), 3 and *passim.*

6. Franklin's views on habit, industry, behavior, and pedagogy have been discussed earlier. But on the point of industry, frugality, liberty, and virtue see as well Drew McCoy, *The Elusive Republic: Political Economy in Jeffersonian America* (Chapel Hill, N. C., 1980), 49–67; his article, "Benjamin Franklin's Vision of a Republican Political Economy for America," *William and Mary Quarterly,* 3d Ser., XXXV (Oct., 1978), 605–628; and Donald H. Meyer, *The Democratic Enlightenment* (New York, 1976), 61–89.

7. Joyce Appleby, *Capitalism and a New Social Order: The Republican Vision of the 1790s* (New York, 1984), 21. On Trenchard, Gordon, the radical Whigs, and the emergence of a more liberal definition of liberty see Kammen, *Spheres of Liberty,* 30–33. See also Gordon Wood, *The Creation of the American Republic* (Chapel Hill, N. C., 1969), 609–609n; and the debate between Appleby and Lance Banning in Lance Banning, "Jeffersonian Ideology Revisited: Liberal and Classical Ideas in the New American Republic," *WMQ,* 3d Ser., XLIII (1986), 3–19; and Joyce Appleby, "Republicanism in Old and New Contexts," *ibid.,* 20–34.

8. Robert James Gough, "Towards a Theory of Class and Social Conflict: A Social History of Wealthy Philadelphians, 1775 and 1800" (unpub. Ph.D. diss., Univ. of Pennsylvania, 1977), 636. Gough catalogs in detail the social versus the economic orientation of Philadelphia's elite.

9. Richard G. Miller, *Philadelphia, The Federalist City: A Study of Urban Politics, 1789–1801* (Port Washington, N. Y., 1976), 5–6.

10. Billy G. Smith, "The Material Lives of Laboring Philadelphians, 1750 to 1800," *WMQ*, 3d Ser., XXXVIII (April, 1981), 201. Smith estimates that one-fourth to one-third of the city's population was made up of laboring poor, percentages comparable to those of Europe. On the intrusion of wage labor see Sharon V. Salinger, "Artisans, Journeymen, and the Transformation of Labor in Late Eighteenth-Century Philadelphia," *ibid.*, XL (Jan., 1983), 62–84.

11. John K. Alexander, *Render Them Submissive: Responses to Poverty in Philadelphia, 1760–1800* (Amherst, Mass., 1980), 166.

12. On the 1786 typographers' strike see Salinger, "Artisans," *WMQ*, XL, 78; and Henry P. Rosemont, "Benjamin Franklin and the Philadelphia Typographical Strikers of 1786," *Labour History*, XXII (1981), 398–429. The famous printer Isaiah Thomas claims he aided Franklin and Bache in founding the Franklin Society in 1788. An extant copy of the Society's constitution verifies its birth, but the Society apparently faded out of existence some time in the 1790s. See Isaiah Thomas, *The History of Printing in America* . . . (Worcester, Mass., 1810. Cited here from *Transactions of the American Antiquarian Society*, V, 1874), I, 238. Franklin Society of Philadelphia, *Constitution . . . Instituted March 8, 1788* (Philadelphia). See also Rollo G. Silver, *The American Printer, 1787–1825* (Charlottesville, Va., 1967), 82–85.

13. On "idleness" see *General Advertiser*, Jan. 10, 1792. On frugality see, for example, *ibid.*, Feb. 12, Mar. 1 (ed. from the *Federal Gaz.*), 5 ("corres."), June 3, Nov. 21, 1791.

14. *Ibid.*, Jan. 26, 1792, and Sept. 23, 1791.

15. *Ibid.*, July 7, 1791; June 12, 1792.

16. B. F. Bache to R. Bache, Sept. 2, 3, 1798, in the Society Collection, Historical Society of Pennsylvania, Philadelphia. Bache subscribed to the foreign-commerce theory of yellow fever. One student of Philadelphia estimates that 27% of lower-class married adults died of yellow fever between the summer of 1793 and the fall of 1799, while only 6.8% of the upper-class married population died of the disease in the same period. See Susan Edith Klepp, "Philadelphia in Transition: A Demographic History of the City and Its Occupational Groups, 1720–1830" (unpub. Ph.D. diss., Univ. of Pennsylvania, 1980), 180.

17. B. F. Bache to Louis Gabriel Cramer, Dec. 20, 1794, in Lucien Cramer, *Les Cramer, une famille génévoise. Leur relations avec Voltaire, Rousseau et Benjamin Franklin Bache* (Génève, 1952), 65–69.

18. The standard works on the colonial newspaper are Sidney Kobre, *The Development of the Colonial Newspaper* (Pittsburgh, 1944. Cited here Gloucester, Mass., 1960); Lawrence C. Wroth, *The Colonial Printer* (New York, 1931); Douglas McMurtrie, *A History of Printing in the United States*. Vol II. *Middle and Atlantic*

States (New York, 1936); and Frank Luther Mott, *American Journalism: A History, 1690–1941* (New York, 1941). The best early contemporary account is Isaiah Thomas, *The History of Printing*. The most useful interpretive source on the colonial press is Stephen Botein, "Printers and the American Revolution," in Bernard Bailyn and John B. Hench, eds., *The Press and the American Revolution* (Worcester, Mass., 1980), 11–57. On the subject of liberty in a diffuse society see Richard Buel, Jr., "Freedom of the Press in Revolutionary America: The Evolution of Libertarianism, 1760–1820," in *ibid.*, 68–71. Leonard W. Levy, *Emergence of a Free Press* (New York, 1985) is a revised edition of his previously critical view of early American press freedom in which he cautiously admits some importance for a social ethic as well as the law in formulating a concept of freedom of the press.

19. See respectively Arthur M. Schlesinger, *Prelude to Independence: The Newspaper War on Britain, 1764–1776* (New York, 1958), 54, 82; and Botein, "Printers," in Bailyn and Hench, eds., *The Press and the American Revolution*, 42.

20. Buel, "Freedom of the Press," *ibid.*, 71–81.

21. See especially Botein, "Printers," *ibid.*, 11–32, 52–53; and Jeffrey Alan Smith, "Printers and Press Freedom: The Ideology of Early American Journalism" (unpub. Ph.D. diss, Univ. of Wisconsin, 1984), which is an interpretive biography of Franklin's publishing career. Smith argues that Franklin, like Jefferson, was primarily devoted to "the Enlightenment's ideal of widespread knowledge and the radical Whig belief that the people had to be informed in order to exercise their legitimate authority" (59). While giving primacy to Franklin's libertarian impulses, Smith also admits Franklin's caution, concluding that Franklin was essentially a "vendor" of "ideas and information" (253). Franklin protested the excessive liberty of the press in an essay he wrote for the *Federal Gazette* pamphlet entitled, "An Account of the Supremest Court of Judicature in Pennsylvania, viz. the Court of the Press." *Fed. Gaz.*, Sept. 12, 1789. Ironically, Robert Goodloe Harper used Franklin's words out of context to support his defense of the Sedition Act of 1798, the act designed to silence a list of Republican editors headed by Benjamin Franklin Bache. See Smith, "Printers and Press Freedom," 318n.

22. On this transformation see especially Botein, "Printers," in Bailyn and Hench, eds., *The Press and the American Revolution*, 41–48. See also Bernard Faÿ, *Notes on the American Press at the End of the Eighteenth Century* (New York, 1927); and Mott, *American Journalism*, 113–15.

23. Botein, "Printers," in Bailyn and Hench, eds., *The Press and the American Revolution*, 41.

24. Mott, *American Journalism*, 95, 113, 159. An earlier source puts the number of newspapers at 106 in 1790, with fifteen in Philadelphia alone by 1790. William A. Dill, *Growth of Newspapers in the United States* (Lawrence, Kan., 1928), 11, 28, 78–79. For a more modern breakdown of Mott's numbers see Donald H. Stewart, *The Opposition Press of the Federalist Period* (Albany, N. Y., 1969), 5.

25. Richard Moss, "The Press during the Federalist Era," *Journal of Popular Culture*, XV (1981), 15.

26. See *ibid.*, 4; and, for slightly less inflated figures, see Mott, *American Journalism*, 159; and William David Sloan, "The Party Press: The Newspaper Role in

National Politics, 1789–1816" (unpub. Ph.D. diss., Univ. of Texas, 1981), 54.

27. On the number of readers per copy see *ibid.*, 54–56. The many material and intellectual ambiguities of publishing in the early republic are traced well in John Bixler Hench, "The Newspaper in a Republic: Boston's *Centinel and Chronicle, 1784–1801*" (unpub. Ph.D. diss., Clark Univ., 1979).

28. Thomas, *History of Printing,* V, 36.

29. Hench, "The Newspaper in a Republic," 108–109. On paper see Thomas, *History of Printing,* V, 20–26; and Wroth, *Colonial Printer,* 122–51. On printing equipment in general see Kobre, *Colonial Newspaper,* 41; Silver, *American Printer,* 28–58; and Wroth, *Colonial Printer,* 62–86.

30. On journeymen and apprentices in general see Silver, *American Printer,* 1–26; and Wroth, *Colonial Printer,* 154–68. The capacity of print shops to produce is discussed well in Stewart, *Opposition Press,* 16, 653n. The cost of printing the *Advertiser* in 1791 is discussed in [B. F. Bache] to [R. Bache], Sept. 1, 1791, Bache Papers, Castle Coll., Am. Philos. Soc. Bache's employees are mentioned in B. F. Bache to R. Bache, Jan. 10, 1793, and *Gen'l. Adv.,* Nov. 25, 1793. Bache's runaway is noted in Advertisement, *Aurora,* Oct. 26–Nov. 17, 1795.

31. Clarence S. Brigham, *Journals and Journeymen: A Contribution to the History of Early American Newspapers* (Philadelphia, 1950), 19–20.

32. Mott, *American Journalism,* 159. William Duane, Bache's successor as editor of the *Aurora,* reported in 1834 that the paper had 1,700 subscribers in 1798. See Wm. Duane, "A Circular," in Worthington Chauncey Ford, ed., "The Letters of William Duane," *Proceedings of the Massachusetts Historical Society,* XX (1906), 392.

33. *Aurora,* Nov. 8, 1794; and July 28, 1796.

34. Stewart, *The Opposition Press,* 15; and Mott, *American Journalism,* 157–58. On party support see Sloan, "The Party Press," esp. 74–77, 99–100. On seventy-five percent recoverability see Hench, "The Newspaper in a Republic," 109–110.

35. On newspapers and the Post Office see Wesley Everett Rich, *The History of the United States Post Office to the Year 1829* (Cambridge, Mass., 1924); and especially Richard B. Kielbowicz, "The Press, Post Office, and Flow of News in the Early Republic," *Journal of the Early Republic,* 3 (Fall, 1983), 255–80, which both describes postal developments through the 1790s and links the debate over newspapers in the mails with a growing partisanship.

36. See "Occurrences on a Journey in 1791," *Gen'l. Adv.,* July 13, 1791; and Bache's rebuttal, July 14, 1791. Editorials from the *Gazette of U.S., ibid.,* Oct. 31, Nov. 3, 17, 21, 1791.

37. *Gen'l. Adv.,* Dec. 1, 1791.

38. *Ibid.,* Dec. 2, 5, 8, 1791; Feb. 23, 1792.

39. *Ibid.,* Jan. 9, Nov. 8, 1792. On Washington see his "Fourth Annual Address to Congress," Nov. 6, 1792, in James D. Richardson, ed., *A Compilation of the Messages and Papers of the Presidents* (New York, 1897), I, 120.

40. *Aurora,* Jan. 15, 1796.

41. *Ibid.*, May 19, 1796. The drying act passed Congress on Mar. 3, 1797. Kielbowicz, "The Press, Post Office . . .," *Jour. of Early Rep.,* 9 (Fall, 1983), 265.

42. Richard Smith to B. F. Bache, June 12, 1790, Autograph Collection, Hist. Soc. Penn.

43. B. F. Bache to Thos. Jefferson, Aug. 20, 1790, Julian Boyd, ed., *The Papers of Thomas Jefferson* (Princeton, N. J., 1950–), XVII, 397. Jefferson chose to have one newspaper in each of five cities—Boston, Philadelphia, New York, Richmond, and Charleston—publish the federal laws under a 1789 enabling act. With partisanship still in the dim future, Jefferson carelessly chose John Fenno's *Gazette of the United States,* as the Philadelphia representative.

44. *Gen'l. Adv.,* Oct. 2, 1790.

45. R. Morris to B. F. Bache cited in Bernard Faÿ, *The Two Franklins: Fathers of Democracy* (Boston, 1933), 147; and Jane Mecom to Sarah Bache, Sept. 6, 1790, Carl Van Doren, ed., *The Letters of Benjamin Franklin and Jane Mecom* (Princeton, N. J., 1950), 342.

46. *Gen'l. Adv.,* Oct. 2, 1790; and, [B. F. Bache], Essay on Writing, n.d., Bache Papers, Castle Coll., Am. Philos. Soc.

47. *Gen'l. Adv.,* Oct. 2, 1790.

48. *Ibid.,* Oct. 23, 1790.

49. *Ibid.,* Jan. 1, 1791.

50. *Ibid.,* Dec. 14, 1790; Feb. 13, 1792; *Aurora,* Feb. 14, 1798. For Bache's meticulousness in recording Congressional debates see his several notebooks of debates in Congress, Dec. 10, 1795–Jan. 6, 1796; Dec. 14, 1795–May, 1796; Mar. 7–17, 1796; Mar. 18–Apr. 10, 1796; Apr. 15, 1796; Apr. 27, 1796, Bache Papers, Castle Coll., Am. Philos. Soc.

51. *Gen'l. Adv.,* Nov. 3, 1792.

52. *Ibid.,* Feb. 4, 1794; *Aurora,* Feb. 1, 1796. It is impossible to know how many times Bache's reportage was copied by others since casual standards of plagiarism and journalistic "ethics" applied in the 1790s. For examples of other papers ascribing credit to Bache's paper see *Gaz. of the U. S.,* Mar. 29, 1794; *National Gazette,* Mar. 9, 1793; and, the Boston *Independent Chronicle,* April 10, 1794, and Mar. 10, 1796.

53. See Thos. Jefferson to B. F. Bache, April 22, 1791, Thomas Jefferson Papers, Am. Philos. Soc. See also Thos. Jefferson to G. Washington, Sept. 9, 1792, Paul Leicester Ford, ed., *The Writings of Thomas Jefferson* (New York, 1895), VI, 106, hereafter cited as Ford, ed., *Jefferson's Writings.* Bache also received British and London newspapers through Benjamin Vaughan. See Benj. Vaughan to [B. F. Bache], Sept. 1 and 3, 1790. Bache Papers, Castle Coll., Am. Philos. Soc.

For random samples of copying foreign news from Bache see *Gaz. of the U. S.,* Jan.–Feb., 1794, and Mar., 1795; Noah Webster's *American Minerva,* June, 1794, and July, 1795; *Ind. Chron.,* June–July, 1795, and Aug.–Sept., 1797; *Connecticut Courant,* April 8, 1793; Nov. 3, 1794; June 8, 1795; and Nov. 7, 1796, and many others, especially for the period 1793–1798.

54. No quantitative analysis has been attempted here even though I have surveyed the contents of twelve newspapers published during the 1790s. It is impossi-

ble to formulate any mathematical equation, any context of numerical comparison, that would not contain internal distortions and misleading conclusions. It is sufficient to observe that other editors did not hesitate to copy Bache's debates, translations, and foreign news whenever they had no other access to this material or when Bache's account was fuller and more accurate. After 1794 Republican newspapers were also unreserved in repeating his editorial comments, largely for the force and color employed in them. Thus, Bache's *General Advertiser* and *Aurora* was most often cited around critical events or issues, the leading ones being the French Revolution, the Jay Treaty debate, the XYZ Affair and the 1797–1798 crisis with France, and the Sedition Act.

55. Thos. Jefferson to B. F. Bache, April 22, 1791, Jefferson Papers, Am. Philos. Soc.

56. Thos. Jefferson to G. Washington, Sept. 9, 1792, Ford, ed., *Jefferson's Writings*, VI, 106.

57. Thos. Jefferson to Martha Jefferson, Nov. 13, 1791, cited in John D. R. Platt, *The Home and Office of Benjamin Franklin Bache (America's First Modern Newsman), 322 Market Street, Philadelphia, Pa.* (Washington, D. C., 1970), 78.

58. On Claypoole and circulation see respectively [B. F. Bache] to [M. H. Markoe], May 9 [1791], Bache Papers, Castle Coll., Am. Philos. Soc.; *Gen'l. Adv.*, Dec. 18, 1792.

59. B. F. Bache to R. Bache, Jan. 10, 1793, Bache Papers, Castle Coll., Am. Philos. Soc.

60. B. F. Bache to R. Bache, Aug. 22, 1793. For examples of managing his father's properties see B. F. Bache to R. Bache, Jan. 10, Feb. 3, 1793; R. Bache to B. F. Bache, July 23, 1792, Feb. 6, 1793.

61. John Marshall to Timothy Pickering, Feb. 28, 1811, in the Timothy Pickering Papers, Massachusetts Historical Society, Boston.

62. *Gen'l. Adv.*, Jan. 28, 1794.

63. See, respectively, *ibid.*, Jan. 1, 28, 1794.

64. B. F. Bache to R. Bache, Sept. 27 and [Oct. ?], 1794, Bache Papers, Castle Coll., Am. Philos. Soc.

65. *Aurora,* Nov. 8, 1794.

66. *Ibid.*, Jan. 1, April 1, 1795.

67. Thos. Jefferson to P[eregrine] Fitzhugh, June 4, 1797, Jefferson Papers, William R. Perkins Library, Duke University, Durham, N. C. Jefferson supported the *Aurora* both as subscriber and by urging others, like Fitzhugh, to subscribe. See, Thos. Jefferson to B. F. Bache, June 2, 1795, Franklin Papers, New York Public Library, New York; and Thos. Jefferson to B. F. Bache, December 26, 1795, Jefferson Papers, Am. Philos. Soc. Jefferson's material support apparently went no further. Webster's reaction is in *Am. Minerva.*, Mar. 9, 1797. Bache's appraisal of success in in B. F. Bache to James Monroe, Sept. 7, 1797, Presidential Papers on Microfilm, Series 1, Reel 2, James Monroe Papers, Library of Congress, Washington, D. C.

68. *Gaz. of U. S.,* July 14, 1795; and B. F. Bache to M. H. Bache, July 8, 1795, Bache Papers, Castle Coll., Am. Philos. Soc.

69. James Monroe to [?], April 23, 1794, Simon Gratz Collection, Hist. Soc. Penn.

70. James Monroe to B. F. Bache, Nov. 13, 1797, Monroe Papers, University of Virginia Library, Charlottesville, Va.; James Monroe to B. F. Bache, Jan. 28, 1798, Etting Papers, Hist. Soc. Penn.; and James Monroe to B. F. Bache, Mar. 26, 1798, Franklin Papers, Am. Philos. Soc.

71. See "Washington's Household Account Book, 1793–1797," *PMHB*, XXX, 459, 473, and XXXI, 70, 340.

72. M. Rochfontaine to T. Pickering, Dec. 6, 1795, Pickering Papers, Mass. Hist. Soc. An example of Bache's denials can be seen in the *Aurora*, May 12, 1798. Elizabeth Hewson, who knew the family better than did other Federalists, believed the rumor but could predicate her belief on nothing more than Bache's apparent poverty and need. See Eliz. Hewson to Thos. T. Hewson, June 5, 1797, Hewson Family Papers, Am. Philos. Soc.

73. For *Porcupine's Gazette* attacks see respectively, *Porc. Gaz.*, Nov. 20, 1797; Apr. 20, May 1 ("No Doctor Leib"), 1798. For the *Gazette* see *Gaz. of U. S.*, June 4 ("corres."), and Aug. 30 ("corres."), 1798. Thomas Leiper and Israel Israel paid Bache's bail, and Moses Levy and Alexander James Dallas defended him before Judge Richard Peters.

74. On Fenno see *Aurora*, April 4, 1798. On Webster see *ibid.*, April 19, 1798.

75. *Ibid.*, Sept. 15, 1795.

76. *Ibid.*, June 5, 1798.

77. Eliz. Hewson to Thos. T. Hewson, June 20, 1798, and May 10, 1799, Hewson Family Papers, Am. Philos. Soc.

78. See Jacob E. Cooke, *Tench Coxe and the Early Republic* (Chapel Hill, N. C., 1978), 345; and *Aurora*, Aug. 11, 1798; Apr. 23, 1800, and Aug. 11, 1802.

79. Fenno admitted in late 1793 that he had but two hundred subscribers and had to take a "loan" to keep afloat. See J. Fenno to Jos. Ward, Dec. 18, 1793, in John B. Hench, ed., "Letters of John Fenno and John Ward Fenno. Part 2: 1792–1800," *Proc. Am. Antiquarian Soc.*, XC (1980), 188.

80. Sloan, "The Party Press," 112. Sloan, throughout his thesis, clearly separates those papers heavily dependent upon patronage, or seeking it avidly, from those, like Bache's, that were more independent.

5. Radical Ideology, 1790–1798

> "In a Commonwealth, the PEOPLE are the Basis on which all power and authority rest. On the extent of their knowledge and information the solidity of that Foundation depends. If the PEOPLE are enlightened the Nation stands and flourishes; thro' ignorance it falls or degenerates."
> (*General Advertiser,* Oct. 2, 1790)

IN 1834, while contemplating the "backward" state of American education, Peter du Ponceau remarked "that the people will always be right in things that they understand, and as to what they do not, they will be the dupes of designing Men, who flatter their passions, start games for them to pursue and cry out Tally Ho!"[1] Du Ponceau's remarks differed little from Bache's declaration of faith cited above and made nearly forty-four years earlier in the first issue of the *General Advertiser.* But there were sharp differences of context, of time and place, of ideas and emotions, between the two statements. One of Bache's Republican colleagues in the 1790s and a fellow member of the controversial Democratic Society of Pennsylvania, du Ponceau glibly proffered his views in the Jacksonian era, when the coupling of the ideal of the people's genius and authority with the efficacy of public education were routinely accepted and already deeply encoded in a liberal American ideology.[2]

Bache's manifesto anticipated that democratic and populist ideology. But the radical ideology that issued from it, repeatedly and consistently affirmed by Bache and his newspaper correspondents, also stood apart from the later Jacksonian world in its origins and content. It arose from more immediate abstract, skeptical, and revolutionary Enlightenment roots, not a fifty-year history of representative democracy in practice. It was articulated amidst the vestigial remnants of classical republicanism, but was not captive of that ideology. It anticipated the full bloom of modern private man, of *homo oeconomicus,* the nascent capitalist end-product of Lockean liberalism, while at the same time advocating a more public role for man, envisioning a new, non-classical *homo civicus.*

The confusion over finding an ideological context for radicals like Bache and many others in the 1790s stems from many sources and demands some resolution. Seen as a consequence of the Revolution, the last decade of America's eighteenth century has been presented as the *dénouement* of classical republicanism. Cast in negative more than nostalgic terms, this view found reflection in Federalist Party pessimism over the future of republics, a pessimism confirmed by historical lessons as well as by repeated contemporary signs of lost virtue. John Adams's didactic defense of mixed governments, Madison's and Jefferson's attacks on the modern economic policies of Hamilton, and Jeffersonian adherence to the purist world of agriculture have seemed at first glance to confirm the persistence of a classical republican ethic, anti-modern and even reactionary.[3]

But classical republicanism could not claim paradigmatic monopoly in the 1790s. It did not set the tone and temper of the most radical political debate. In the dramatic and often violent political disputes of the decade, some combatants directly resurrected the nostalgic classical arguments; the classical word "virtue" was still employed. But by the end of the eighteenth century many former adherents to the substance of classical thought had become followers of Francis Hutcheson and advocates of Scottish moral philosophy, or had returned to a Calvinist conservatism that mimicked a republican vision of "virtue" but had become increasingly devoid of a classical, civic thrust. For many on Bache's end of the political spectrum, civic virtue had clearly lost its earlier essence, its association with an aristocratic, civic humanism begun in the Renaissance and embellished in the seventeenth and eighteenth centuries. For these radicals, "virtue" had become more the consequence of self-interest expressed than the pre-condition of right action. The encouragement of good individual habits, the elimination of impediments to knowledge, and the pursuit of social as well as economic self-interest—all dynamic processes exercised by free, individual, private men—provided the active basis of true virtue. Classical republicanism primarily provided a vague and obscure backdrop for the ideological battles of the era.[4]

Were the 1790s, therefore, primarily the harbinger of a new age of nascent capitalism, of private man replacing the classical republicanist's public man? The excitement and strife of the period did seem to swirl around the ineluctable forces of Federalist traditionalism and Jeffersonian modernism. And the French Revolution, Democratic Societies, and partisan battles were clearly important in exciting the desire for useable liberty and bringing passion to the individual's quest for autonomy and authority. But did a new liberal vision, more economic than political, entirely erase the collective and civic focus of the revolutionary era?[5] Bache and many others undoubtedly marched only part way down the road of modern economic individualism. Bache, his supporters, and his newspaper opponents continued to speak a language that was primarily political and civic; they continued to see themselves as public men, albeit with increased emphasis on individuals exercising free will.[6]

The 1790s may be better comprehended as a time of broader, more general, more abstract ideological transition than simply of one from classical republican to emergent capitalist. Diffuse yet strong Enlightenment elements remained at work. European ideas and influences remained important. Scottish common sense and moral philosophy—appealing to liberals with its emphasis on moral instinct and equalitarian common sense, appealing to conservatives and classical republicans through its emphasis on innate virtue and on seemingly divine origin—partially mediated ideological polarity while confusing any unity we might impose on the era. By the end of the decade, the resurgence of Calvinist theology absorbed some previously secular, classical energies. Variety was accompanied by synthesis. In the 1790s, religious, republican, and liberal traditions all persisted, but generally in a blended form. Liberalism had arisen, but it was a "restrained liberalism" that still advocated man's moral and civic virtues. A "revised republicanism" remained that was concerned with both the autonomy of the individual and the best means of articulating liberalism's popular sovereignty.[7]

Rather than focus on the ideological mists of modern analysis, it is more fruitful to comprehend the 1790s through the example of two central figures who best reflected the ideological conflict of the 1790s: Edmund Burke and Thomas Paine. Both men were the products of seventeenth- and eighteenth-century Whig thought, and both were influenced at least in part by classical republican and liberal ideas. By 1790 they had headed in diametrically opposed directions, Paine the liberal advocate of increased autonomy and popular sovereignty, Burke arguing for the restraints of authority and order. Over time, the Burke-Paine dichotomy would come to define many of the broad, apparently perennial outlines of American conservatism and liberalism.

Through the power of rhetoric if not philosophy, the ideological dialectic of the 1790s was really theirs. They excited the empathy and vicarious understanding of ordinary people throughout the English-speaking world in opposite ways, illuminating visions of the future while discussing the past or the present. In the 1790s their conflict seemed to demand immediate resolution. Both those like Bache, who envisioned the future as Paine did, and those extreme opponents of Bache, who often subscribed to Burkean principles more obliquely, believed with millenarian certainty that the ideological conflict would ultimately be resolved along the lines that either Paine or Burke had laid out.[8]

Burke and Paine developed their ideological beliefs around the dynamism of the French Revolution. Lesser figures like Bache and his opponents came to similar ideological conclusions either through their own reaction to the French Revolution, or through the influence of Burke and Paine. But the French Revolution was less important to any of them for its concrete realities than for the focus it provided in the universal ideological contest for the future. Burke self-admittedly knew little about France or its Revolution when he published his *Reflections on the French Revolution* in 1790, while Paine, a monolingual anglophone who spent most of the decade in France, was capable of naive beliefs about the Revolution, finally arriving, well before the end of the decade, at the conclusion that among established states the American republic, not France, represented mankind's best hope for the future. Bache's distance from France kept him naive about the Revolution longer, but even for Bache the issue was less "France" than the maintenance of more universal republican liberty.

The significance of Burke versus Paine, then, lay less in the events of France than in general ideological qualities. Chief among these was their creation of truly modern reductionist ideologies, more general and abstracted and universal in appeal than most that came before. For both men the issue centered less on formal analyses of human nature, systematic philosophical thought, or expert political science or political economy than it did on vague intuitions and all-engrossing visions of man in society.[9] Burke, of course, believed his own views denied ideology altogether, and he attacked those who "set up a scheme of society on new principles." In truth his traditional world of precepts and prejudice was as ideologically laden as Paine's facile vision of the future. Correspondingly, Paine was uninterested in formulating a careful science of human nature or in acknowledging intellectual indebtedness to the pantheon of seventeenth- and eighteenth-century theorists.[10] Paine paid little attention to the past, attracting adherents through his vision of society new-modeled on equality and security. Neither ideology depended on systematic philosophy at the same time, neither was explicitly culture-specific, neither was formulated in terms of something like the anthropologist's "face-to-face" community of shared experiences and encoded symbols. No matter how much Burke reveled in "his England," the precepts of his ideology and those of Paine's were put forth in terms of a generalized human experience, a presumed intuitive understanding of how all social intercourse operates at its most elemental level. Yet both were rigorously social in their universal perspectives; solutions for society took precedence over economics and religion. Even when Paine turned to the problem of economic competence in *Rights of Man*, Part Two, and later in *Agrarian Justice*, he did so to emphasize the need for individual social security in society.

Edmund Burke's ideological success flowed from his ability to synthesize feelings and prejudices already widely held. But it was less an analytic rigor and consistency of thought that bolstered this success than it was his robust use of metaphor. In fact, Burke was passive, obscure, or evasive on many pivotal philosophical points. A believer in the precepts of natural law as God's will, he could declare with confidence that all social contracts were "but a clause in the great primeval contract of eternal society, linking the lower with the higher natures, connecting the visible and invisible world, according to a fixed compact." But when it came to discovery of God's will, Burke waffled between reliance on natural feelings and reliance on reason (neither of which he totally dismissed), frequently settling on a weak theory of intuition. He more generally concluded that nature was simply "wisdom without reflection, and above it."[11]

Adhering to a radical Protestant-Calvinist outlook, Burke's writings served to define the "modern conservative" vision of society. He believed that social decisions were best based on their probable consequences, and consequences depended on already established circumstances. "The circumstances are what render every civil and political scheme beneficial or noxious to mankind." Circumstances demanded acknowledgment of the significance of the accumulated past. Tradition, experience, and ancestorism—what Burke called "the ancient, permanent sense of mankind"—were the only proper foundations for happy societies.[12]

While he admitted that revolution could be legitimate on rare occasions, as it was in England in 1688, gradual reform carried out with due respect for the past was more likely to succeed because such gradualism was a careful amalgam of reason and tried experience. The elements that generally marked this gradualism were natural aristocracy, mixed government, the protection of property, and a modicum of civil rights, including a right to life, liberty in a very reserved and docile sense, and the fruits of one's labor. The alternative to gradualism, which he discovered in the French Revolution, was "will," the intellectual arrogance of fanciful theories, and social "experiments" by "schemers." Such schemers "abandon wholly to chance," he declared, "I say to chance, because their schemes have nothing in experience to prove their tendency beneficial."[13] Revolution, then, could open the floodgates of destruction more readily than it could provide reform and reconstruction.

Taken this far—and many Americans may have taken him no further—Burke's social philosophy offered an ideological vision that synthesized conservative American religious and classical republican views. Burke was a Whig after all, and had appreciated the bases upon which the American Revolution had been fought. His philosophy allowed conservative Americans to see their own revolutionary cause as both necessary and completed, much as Burke had seen England's Glorious Revolution. Nor did Burke condemn any particular form of government, as long as that form was compatible with tradition, experience, and social necessity. "I reprobate no form of government merely upon abstract principles," he declared in the *Reflections,* "There may be situations in which the purely democratic form will become necessary. There may be some (very few, and very particularly circumstanced) where it would be clearly desirable. This I do not take to be the case of France or of any other great country."[14]

The extremes in Burke's philosophy—his promotion of "manners" rather than virtues, his support of "prejudice" rather than tradition—have usually made Burke seem inaccessible to American sentiments. Above all, his seemingly inflexible adherence to "an inheritable crown, an inheritable peerage, and an house of commons," to Church and State, would appear to make his political recipes unacceptable in America. But as Paine observed in the *Rights of Man,* "He [Burke] does not mean some one particular church, or some one particular state, but any church and state; and he uses the term as a general figure to hold forth the political doctrine of always uniting the church with the state in every country."[15] By extension, it can be argued that Burke, who defended monarchy and hereditary aristocracy for Britain and France, did not suggest the superimposition of those institutions in societies where they were not a part of the ancient agreement. He can be and was read as simply insisting on the binding force of tradition and experience, the permanent and independent existence of the state, and the necessity of religion as the mainstay for any and all societies. The Revolution and Constitution were the icons of American and Burkean traditionalism; they were articles of faith that many Americans in the 1790s, seeking to halt further change and maintain established social distinctions, sought to keep in place.

While Burke offered a template for modern conservatism, he coincidentally inspired Thomas Paine's counterattack in the *Rights of Man*. Paine was the epitome of Burke's "schemers." Bent on a new-modeled vision of man in society, he consciously ignored any philosophical debt that he may have owed to Locke, Rousseau, and others. Like Burke's, Paine's ideological success rested on simplicity, imagery, and metaphor, his appeal on vague yet shared intuitive impulses across cultures. Paine stripped "the veil of sanctity from tradition." And, as Bache fully realized, he linked "the linear rationality of the emerging typographically literate society" to the predominantly oral-aural culture from which he emerged.[16]

By the 1790s the essential core of Paine's ideology centered on the perfectibility of man in society. Unlike philosophers like Hobbes and Locke, Paine began with positive assumptions about both nature and society. Nature established a basic equality among men, he declared, and natural equality was the basis for all subsequent natural rights, while "every civil right grows out of a natural right." Natural rights, for Paine, include all "which appertain to man in right of his existence," including "intellectual rights . . . and also all those rights of acting as an individual for his own comfort and happiness, which are not injurious to the natural rights of others."[17]

Although recognizing that "it is impossible to control Nature in her distribution of mental powers," and that talent and merit should be given opportunity, Paine contended that there exists in all men "a mass of sense lying in a dormant state" that requires release and excitement to action. "Reason, like time," Paine predicted, "will make its own way, and prejudice will fall in a combat with interest."[18] In agreement with Enlightenment ideas, Paine saw reason as the free exercise of self-interest. By the time he published *Agrarian Justice* in 1797, he believed that self-interest also implies the end to Burke's vaunted social deference, the immutability of property, and the sanctity of inherited inequality of wealth.

Yet Paine did not dwell on his vague state of nature, nor did he ruminate on the philosophical implications of his post-Lockean psychology of reason and self-interest. He was simply interested in man in society.

As Nature created him for social life, she fitted him for the station she intended. In all cases she made his natural wants greater than his individual powers. No one man is capable, without the aid of society, of supplying his own wants; and those wants, acting upon every individual, impel the whole of them into society, as naturally as gravitation acts to a centre.

Above all, nature had "implanted in him [man] a system of social affections, which though not necessary to his existence, are essential to his happiness."[19] Paine's equation was clear: Nature demanded society; society was positive; only through man in society could self-interest and a broader human interest be satisfied.

Society demanded that government be constituted so that benefits could be enhanced as much as preserved. But government was a problematic thing. According to Paine, it could only be based on "Superstition," "Power," or "The common interest of society, and the common rights of man." Therefore, he condemned Burke's government by precedent because "without any regard to the principle of the precedent," it was "one of the vilest systems that can be set up." Mixed government was "an imperfect everything, cementing and soldering the discordant parts together by corruption, to act as a whole." In it, there was "no responsibility: the parts cover each other till responsibility is lost; and the corruption which moves the machine, contrives at the same time its own escape."[20]

Paine's solution to the problem of government was to wipe the slate clean of historical encumbrances, the baggage of the past, and to consider modern processes rather than antique substances. Defining society as the "Nation," Paine concluded that sovereignty "appertains to the Nation only, and not to any individual." Unwilling to give natural permanence and authority to government as Burke had, and fearful of governments adapting and changing unchecked, Paine promoted a constitutional argument. "A constitution is a thing *antecedent* to a government, and a government is only the creature of a constitution." Government was, therefore, nothing more than an agent for the improvement of its citizens; it was a fiction established to implement the reality of society and nation. For Paine, it followed that "a Nation has at all times an inherent indefeasible right to abolish any form of Government it finds inconvenient, and establish such as accords with its interest, disposition, and happiness."[21]

Given government's purpose, republican government was superior because it was "established and conducted for the interest of the public, as well individually as collectively." Furthermore, it was "not necessarily connected with any particular form, but it most naturally associates with the representative form, as being best calculated to secure the end for which a nation is at the expense of supporting it." While democracy was most ideal in translating society's needs, wants, and interests, it was "incapable of extension, not from its principles, but from the inconveniences of its form." But the Americans had solved the problem, Paine contended, because they established a system whereby "representation" was "ingrafted upon democracy."[22]

Even here, Paine did not wish to be misunderstood. Representation was a constant process, not something merely decided upon at times of election. "It is not because a part of the government is elective, that makes it less a despotism, if the persons so elected possess afterwards, as a parliament, unlimited powers. Election, in this case, becomes separated from representation, and the candidates are candidates for despotism." There were no classical republican calls to virtue here or reliances on Bolingbroke's patriot king; elected representatives were simply bound to heed public need continuously.

Bache embraced this catechism closely and tried to find a vehicle for its implementation in the Democratic Society of Pennsylvania. But Bache seconded even more emphatically Paine's ultimate position, that no parliament, government, generation, or group "possessed the right or the power of binding and controlling posterity to the '*end of time*,' or of commanding for ever how the world shall be governed, or who shall govern it. . . . Every age and generation must be as free to act for itself, *in all cases,* as the ages and generations which preceded it."[23]

Having moved naturally from Nature to Society to Nation, Paine would develop his ascending stages to include a vision of international cooperation. The final stage of international harmony would apparently flow from representative democracy, social tolerance built on the common qualities of mankind, and religious toleration. Here, too, Bache's own transAtlantic experiences would reinforce his support of Paine's vision. Like Paine, Bache would see the ultimate success of international unity as the consequence of national successes for many nations.

The elements of Paine's ideology outlined above were constantly and consistently promoted in Bache's newspaper. Unlike those of Philip Freneau, who had begun publishing the *National Gazette* in 1790 as well, Bache's ideological concerns did not originate with Hamilton's economic policies. Only the French Revolution and the publication of Paine's *Rights of Man* ignited Bache's ideological fervor. Having published two articles critical of Burke in early 1791, Bache eagerly republished Part One of the *Rights of Man* in serial form beginning in May, 1791, only two months after its initial publication. A year later he began an irregular series of excerpts from the *Rights of Man,* Part Two.[24] From the outset, Bache's praise was florid.

> Tho' unadorned with all the tropes and figures which bedizen the page of his antagonist [Burke], he informs—he interests—he convinces. Intelligible to every capacity, he is read extensively, and with pleasure—and having truth and justice on his side, he finds a friend in every uncorrupted & well-disposed heart.

At the same time Bache condemned Burke, finding that Burke's declamation "in support of the most abominable heresies that ever disgraced politics or literature, is in the highest degree offensive to every liberal and benevolent mind." "The appetite for liberty, like that of hunger is derived from nature, it is universal and ineradicable," Bache added, and "the man . . . who would voluntarily surrender this exalted right to another for 'himself and his posterity for ever,' as Burke contends the English nation have done, richly deserves a bastile [sic] for life, and a total exclusion from the privileges of ever being accosted by the endearing salutation of *father.*"[25]

The "Publicola" debate that ensued during the summer of 1791 simply sharpened Bache's focus on the Burke-Paine dichotomy. He carried all of "Publicola's [John Quincy Adams]" letters, added rebuttals by "Brutus" from the *New York Daily Advertiser,* and submitted his own criticisms for good measure. Believing as did others that "Publicola" was John Adams, Bache had no reason to be shocked. He had already read Adams's *Defence of the Constitutions . . .,* and indexed all passages where Adams spoke in derogatory terms about the "people" or "democracy." But "Publicola's" arguments, echoing Burke's proclamation defending the binding authority of the past, awakened in Bache for the first time a note of fear, the fear of a real battle line being drawn between traditionalists and republicans. "Publicola's" defense of the English constitution, his contention that France had no constitution, and his condemnation of Paine as a simple majoritarian were met directly by Bache and "Brutus." Both were unapologetic in claiming full sovereign majority rights for the people of a nation. And Bache claimed an immediate right of revolution that did not require any sovereign people to wait until revolution was absolutely necessary, as both

Burke and "Publicola" had claimed they should do, before they re-formed their government.[26]

Bache's attachment to Paine was not solely dependent on shared philosophical impulses. After all, Franklin had introduced Paine to America in 1775 through a letter to Richard Bache. And although Sally Franklin and Paine apparently antagonized one another, Paine had become a part of the private Franklin's life. Franklin considered Paine his "adopted political" son and urged Paine to write *Common Sense*. Paine reciprocated the affection and even left Philadelphia in 1781 to visit Passy for three months (while Bache was in Geneva). After Franklin returned to Philadelphia in 1785, Paine visited his elderly mentor at Franklin Court. Bache undoubtedly overheard philosophical conversations between the two men and may have attended some meetings of Franklin's Society of Political Inquiries, before which Paine once delivered an essay that would become part of the *Rights of Man*.[27]

Paine left Philadelphia for France in 1787, carrying a letter of introduction from Franklin to Jefferson, and would not return to America again in Bache's lifetime. But the family ties remained. In the *Rights of Man*, Paine paid tribute to Franklin for his service in France as "not the diplomatic of a Court, but of MAN." Not surprisingly, Bache became Paine's quasi-official publisher, distributor, and book-seller in America in the 1790s. Bache printed the second (the last interesting) part of *The Age of Reason* (printed in separate editions in 1795 and 1796), *The Decline and Fall of the English System of Finance* (printed for Bache by John Page, 1796), and *Agrarian Justice* (1797). In 1796 he published Paine's letter to George Washington, wherein Paine condemned the latter for ingratitude in allowing Paine to languish in a French prison and refusing to recognize Paine's American citizenship. Although a London publisher reputedly offered Paine £300 for the manuscript, Paine sent it through an intermediary to Bache. Employing the material as carefully as he could, Bache issued the letter in "salvos" intended to influence the election, and then published it as a pamphlet, *A Letter to George Washington . . . on Affairs Public and Private* (1796).[28]

Always eager to gain a wide readership, Paine also imposed some difficult demands on young Bache. In 1795 Paine sent 5,000 copies of his *Dissertations on First Principles of Government*, instructing Bache to sell it for twenty cents a copy or less and in quantities of a dozen or more. Later that year Paine dispatched a staggering 12,000 copies of the second part of *The Age of Reason* to Bache, and ordered him to sell it for thirty-three cents a copy with a twenty-five percent discount on wholesale purchases. Paine even requested Bache to seek an act of Congress to get copyright protection from pirates who were reprinting the work incorrectly and charging too much for it.[29]

Yet Bache was not Paine's toady, nor did Paine have any real claims on Bache. Bache sought acclaim but did not try to live from Paine's fame (or infamy). They both were bonded to Franklin, but they were a generation as well as an ocean apart. Bache admired Paine but exploited Paine's ideas and writings as eagerly as he did any others for what he thought was an advantage in public opinion or electioneering. Where Bache and Paine met was in the similarity of their ideas. It excited Bache to learn in the early 1790s that his view of nature, society, and government was so nearly approximate to that of Paine and a host of others.

If Bache was excited by this shared radical vision in the 1790s, it should not have surprised him or anyone else that his views were so ideologically similar to Paine's. In many ways, Bache had been more thoroughly, consistently bathed in radical Enlightenment thought than had Paine. And before the *Rights of Man* became Bache's theme, French ideas, screened and transmitted through Franklin, had provided the foundation for Bache's later adherence to Paine's ideology.

The people, events, and interests in Franklin's life could not have made a very lasting impression on young Benjamin Bache until the latter returned to Passy in July 1783. Nearly fourteen years of age that summer, Bache returned to a grandfather who had been preoccupied with diplomacy but was about to take a renewed interest in society, science, and politics. By 1783, Franklin's eminence had led him to know virtually the entire pantheon of France's great eighteenth-century progressive thinkers. As an active member of the Masonic Lodge of the Nine Sisters from 1777 onward, he knew a wide range of anti-absolutist free-thinkers and constitutionalists, including Brissot, Danton, Camille Desmoulins, Condorcet, and the Abbé Sieyès. He discussed science with Marat and Robespierre, was often visited by the chemist Lavoisier, played chess with the physicist Jean-Baptiste Le Roy, and discussed economics with the Abbé Morellet. He undoubtedly discussed social and political matters extensively with Condorcet. And after Thomas Jefferson arrived in Paris in August 1784, he and Franklin renewed a warm and harmonious friendship. None of these relationships could have escaped young Bache's notice. Who can know what casual comments by or about one of these men influenced Bache's philosophical development?

Franklin's other activities in France could not have escaped Bache's notice either. In 1782, Franklin published and spoke highly of *A Project of Perpetual Peace* by Pierre André Gargaz, which outlined a plan for a league of united nations. The idea fit squarely with Paine's and Bache's later view of nationalism and the harmony of republican nations. In 1784, Franklin published his own *Information to Those Who Would Remove to America*, a work lauding America's middle-class society of men who were establishing their individual economic competence. That same year in a letter to Benny's mother, Franklin wrote a stinging attack on the newly formed Society of Cincinnatus. Loathing the artifice of hereditary honors, he more circumspectly yet actively encouraged his unicameralist and anti-nobility friend Mirabeau to write and publish *Considérations sur l'ordre de Cincinnatus*. The philosophical messages of these publications must have been clear to young Bache.

Above all, Benny had the opportunity to learn the lessons of scientific rationalism in his Passy years. Benny was present to observe Charles Deslon's attempts to prove the mysteries of animal magnetism and Mesmerism, and undoubtedly heard Franklin talk of the need for methodical proofs to claims of men like Mesmer. Furthermore, Benny and his grandfather shared an attraction to the technological wonder of the hot-air balloon craze and the promise of progress that such developments held.

Franklin's intellectual influence undoubtedly continued after their return to Philadelphia. During these years Franklin was elected to Pennsylvania's Supreme Executive Council and, although he avoided granting partisan blessings to either the Constitutionalists or the more conservative Republicans, he re-affirmed his confidence in a unicameral legislature and a plural executive, ideas that Bache repeatedly endorsed in the 1790s. In helping to found the Society for Political Inquiries in 1787 (a group that met in Franklin's home), Franklin promoted the idea of establishing governmental principles through group political science rather than leaving the process in the hands of individual, elitist theoreticians or partisan politicians. The idea antedated Bache's own eventual support and view of the Democratic Societies. And, finally, Franklin's involvement in the Constitutional Convention in 1787 occurred at an impressionable time for the adolescent Benjamin Bache. Franklin's arguments in 1787—his promotion of nationalism, his denial of the lessons of antiquity for modern republics, his support of proportional representation and universal manhood suffrage, his desire to circumscribe executive authority, and his wish to see citizenship easily acquired by immigrants—contained ideas important to Bache in the 1790s. Because Franklin appeared doddering during the

Convention and seldom intruded in the debate except to play the grand-fatherly role of friendly sage, his radical nationalism, his increasingly demo-cratic views, and his belief that no constitution was holy writ to last for all time did not make a very lasting impression on the history of American political theory. But it did on Benjamin Bache.[30]

Franklin's temperament, especially his desire to avoid conflict, confused his contemporaries and has led a disparate group of modern critics to have their way with him in interpreting his larger ideology. Thus, Franklin's preoccupation with virtue, his physiocratic tendencies, his belief in the primacy of agriculture, and his obsessive interest in an industrious citizenry have made him a prime candidate for the classical republicanists.[31] But to recognize this narrow view of Franklin is to admit no more than that Franklin absorbed an ideological world in transition.

A broader view of Franklin reveals a man of more radical and modernist elements. His natural optimism and early success in life led him toward a vision of the perfectibility of man and a belief in free will. Franklin's notion of this free will was not purely intellectual. He respected the significance of feelings as well. Mind and emotion shaped men's lives, while man in turn was shaped by the generally benign and beneficent environment around him. The greatest freedom was his opportunity to fashion one's own life within this environment, to make habitual such things as industry and frugality, and thus to be virtuous. Education and a free press played critical roles in this habituation. This self-imposed behavior modification was, therefore, little more than the first step toward recognizing true self-interest. Self-interest was essentially moral; through it one discovered social and religious toleration and found the need to establish open, equitable societies of individuals imbued with autonomy and agency in both a private and public capacity.

In arriving at these positions, Franklin homogenized the radical Whig tendencies of his early years with the European thought of the philosophes of his later years, retaining a notion of pragmatism and utility through it all. By the time he died in 1790 he embraced radical political ideas not out of bitterness and disappointment but through his persistent optimism and his long perspective on the century about to end. Yet over the whole of Franklin's life, his cosmopolitan acceptance of many diverse ideas remained offset by ambiguities on free will and necessity, on religion, and on appro-priate political forms and structures.[32]

Because Franklin conceived of his own philosophy as one to be lived as much as stated, young Benny Bache could not avoid its subtle reflection in

Franklin's daily life nor, being under Franklin's governance, escape the application himself. Only near Franklin's death did Benny try to resist his grandfather a bit and push Franklin's ideas to more radical extremes, promoting a more radical philosophical line: that Nature was to be the guide in all things, and that that Nature was rational and predictable. The deist vision of God as author of the universe was similar to Franklin's but it was extended to deny all further divine intervention and, by implication, the importance of religion. Morality and virtue were entirely the consequence of natural man's acting out of self-perceived self-interest, and natural desires for pleasure and happiness should be followed. The moderate, skeptical, utilitarian tone of Franklin was absent; a more demanding, uncompromising radicalism replaced it. If Franklin more passively assumed an evolutionary improvement in society, encouraging a gradualist vision, Bache seemed to feel more urgently the "logic of the enlightenment: if most men are not yet ready for autonomy, they must be *made* ready for it."[33] The moral imperative of the Enlightenment that man must "act" made the strongest impact on Bache.

Unlike Franklin, Bache came to radical ideas before personal maturity could mellow his confidence. In the vast, diffuse fiction called the Enlightenment, "unabashedly paradoxical" in its capacity to be "didactic and frivilous [sic], primitive and progressive, reforming and determinist, coolly rational or, on principle, passionate," Bache belonged by temperament and ideas to the "Revolutionary Enlightenment" along with Rousseau, Condorcet, Paine, and Godwin, an Enlightenment marked by its emphasis on "will" and a secular millennium. According to Henry May, it was a "quasi-romantic, millennial, supremely optimistic dream of the universal republican future" that "roused only occasional echoes in America."[34]

It was no accident that, aside from Paine, the only philosophers spoken of favorably by Bache during the 1790s were themselves advocates of a revolutionary enlightenment. Having been raised at a critical stage of his youth in the Cramer household, a family with close ties to Jean-Jacques Rousseau, Bache probably encountered Rousseau's writings early on. Bache had access to Rousseau's ideas through his grandfather's library and through the Library Company of Philadelphia, which held much Rousseau material. William Duane, Bache's assistant editor and successor at the *Aurora,* owned twenty-eight volumes of Rousseau's works in 1798, and these may have originally belonged to Bache. Although Bache never articulated a view of the general will as anything other than a majoritarian will, he probably acquired some of his sense of republican rage through Rousseau.

In 1792, he printed "A Sketch of Jean Jacques Rousseau" in the *General Advertiser*.[35]

Bache's passions were more clearly aligned with the Marquis de Condorcet. He undoubtedly met Condorcet at Passy. Having been a mathematics student at the University of Pennsylvania, Bache may have shared with Condorcet—the mathematician turned social mathematician—both a simplistic vision of human perfectibility and a naive dialectical view of the past versus the future. Bache sold and distributed Condorcet's book on the ten epochs of man. He also published a speech and an article by Condorcet, and printed a short biography and eulogy of Condorcet upon the latter's execution. And in a letter to his father Bache hinted that he placed great faith in Condorcet's opinions and judgments.[36]

Other radical Enlightenment figures received even less mention as Bache became, like Paine, unwilling to designate a lineage of ideational inheritance. He published an address by George Logan proclaiming the perfectibility of man, and sold copies of Joel Barlow's *Advice to Privileged Orders* (1792) and Joseph Priestley's *Letters on Religion* (1793) at his Market Street printing office. Priestley, alone among prominent English radicals, enjoyed occasional mention in the newspaper.[37] Though many of Bache's ideas agreed with Thomas Jefferson's and though Bache was undoubtedly closeted with Jefferson on several important political matters, Bache never referred to Jefferson directly as a philosopher.

Nor, with the exception of Paine, did Bache fill the columns of the *General Advertiser* and *Aurora* with a roll-call of philosophers' names. But in editorials of his own and in the material he chose to print, he did not fail to paint a clear portrait of his social and political ideas. Like others in the eighteenth century, Bache began from assumptions about nature. Embracing Newton's mechanistic universe, he envisioned a nature in which everything had a role; nothing was extraneous. Although nature provided no moral assistance in discovering her truths, "the dominion of man over matter is incontestable," so that nature "is continually suffering her mysteries to escape." Combining a Lockean view of the mind with radical deist thought, Bache concluded along with Paine, that God was "the impartial father of the whole human race; that the rights of all men therefore must be equal." Furthermore, all men were imbued with reason by God. "Men are not brutes," he declared in 1797, "the meanest of men, unless a lunatic, is endowed by divinity with reason, with a capacity of discerning good from evil."[38] As early as 1791, when he began publishing the *Rights of Man* in serial form, he declared that ignorance was not a natural condition of man but was only the "absence of knowledge," adding that "though man may be kept ignorant yet he cannot be made ignorant." He concluded in perfect Lockean symmetry that "When once any object has been seen, it is impossible to put the mind back to the same condition it was before it saw it."[39]

Yet underlying this progressive philosophy were remnants of classical republicanism. He maintained a belief in the dual nature of man, in the dichotomies of power versus liberty, of virtue versus corruption. Well before he entered the political fray against Washington or Adams, he argued that "strong power is requisite to curb the strong passions of man." In one editorial, he lamented man's desire for distinction and argued with the cynicism of John Adams that dread of a supposedly wrathful God was all that prevented men from accepting "infamy and disgrace, rather than remain in oblivion." And by 1795 his "political profession of faith" began with the statement that, "He believes all men fallible, and considers officers of government as men."[40]

Bache generally revealed his strong impulse toward a liberal view by suggesting that man has a natural tendency toward virtue. Virtue, he claimed, was self-interest, and true self-interest was not crass and selfish. Echoing the Scottish moral philosophers and Jefferson, he claimed that virtue results from a "pure impulse" which found satisfaction in "doing good."[41] Never consistent nor clear in his theory, Bache seemed to remain confused between "passions" and "interests." His natural impulse was to see man's capacity to pursue enlightened self-interest. But, like his grandfather, he could never entirely exclude man's "passions" nor man's capacity to abandon his rights. When summarizing his political creed in 1797, he asserted that since God had created all men equally, "he who tamely resigns those rights [of equality], wrongs his posterity, degrades himself, and ought to be ashamed to live."[42]

Bache's concern over man's "passions" and human corruptibility was never discussed at length in his newspaper because Bache essentially believed with Paine that environmental and educational change could ameliorate individual tendencies toward corruption. Few issues of the *General Advertiser* and *Aurora* failed to mention how artificial distinctions, privilege, inequality, hereditary monarchy, titled nobility, and aristocracy kept man ignorant, prejudiced, superstitious, enslaved, and incapable of improvement. The enormous weight of these social elements had originally fed his skepticism about man's ability to avoid his "passions." As he put it, he found "it . . . really astonishing to observe how mankind have suffered themselves to be led quietly in ecclesiastical trammels, without once conceiving themselves at liberty to think agreeably to the powers of reason within them. Owing to these slavish systems, the vigor of the human mind has been lost." The solution was the free exercise of individual and social attentiveness. "Want of watchfulness in the people, the arts of ambition and artifices of sycophants have enslaved most," he concluded by 1796.[43]

Monarchy led the list of pernicious environmental influences corrupting man's natural equality and freedom. Some monarchies, like Prussia's, were supported entirely by brute force. All were imperialistic, fostering wars that cost lives. There was, indeed, a slippery slope from monarchy to individual degradation because

> where there is a king, there must be a nobility: where there is a nobility there must be a standing army. A standing army is always composed of those wretches who are unwilling to endeavour to procure a living any other way; they are the vilest rascals of the mob; their only principle is obedience to their officers and their only trade murder.[44]

Nobility was the crutch that supported monarchy and inequality. Although the nobles of Europe seemed to be "merely . . . a flock of noisy parrots, or gaudy peacocks," who could do no harm, they were actually "ravening vultures, that prey on the vitals of every country, where they are permitted to exist." And those who thought that nobility and the titles of distinction that went with nobility were necessary "for preserving decorum in and éclat to a nation" were only deceiving themselves.[45]

Because the United States had neither monarchy nor nobility, Bache spent much more time attacking titles of distinction and the Burkean ethic that stood behind them. Titles, "like craws and bishops in the female dress, or like large cravats and high collars in the dress of gentlemen, were introduced only to supply the absences of real beauties, or to cover some existing defects."[46] As early as 1791, he condemned laudatory addresses made to President Washington because they favored "too much of Monarchy to be used by Republicans, or to be received with pleasure by a President of a Commonwealth." A month later, after John Adams had posed the question of how the President should be addressed, Bache opened his newspaper to attacks on the use of titles. In answer to "Publicola's" charge of "political heresies" against Paine, Bache suggested that a majority of Americans were repulsed by titles and orders of nobility and that advocacy of such forms should be an American political heresy.[47] Answering a writer in John Fenno's *Gazette of the United States* who advocated titles, Bache simply replied,

Does not the name of the office convey an idea of the trust which is reposed in the office? and what more dignified title could be bestowed on our supreme executive Magistrate than George Washington? Would the epithet Honor, or even Excellency, annexed to his name express as much as his Name itself? Does Excellency call to mind the services he has rendered to his Country?[48]

If eradication of monarchy, nobility, aristocracy, and titles of distinction were the first steps toward liberty and equality, education was the second step. It, too, stood to sweep away the ignorance and superstition that had kept men in chains and despotic governments from falling. "Royal government is plainly calculated for ignorance," he argued, and "friends to genuine republican government and the rights of man" should "promote true and rational knowledge among the individuals of a nation." Without an educated citizenry, the fruits of victory from the American Revolution would be overcome by "local prejudices" and "inveterate habits." Above all, Bache firmly believed "that the more the world is enlightened and true philosophy gains ground, the more the governments of every people will necessarily verge towards, & at length embrace the republican system."[49]

There was also a social economy to education. "Men, well taught, will earn more than ignorant men; skill will be as gainful as hard work. Such men too will be more enterprizing." With education, men's minds would rapidly improve; "though at first, it cannot creep, it will learn to fly; the higher it mounts, the wider its prospects; till, at last, the world, and all its means of happiness, are brought within its reach." Put bluntly, "men are what education makes them." In perfect Franklinian form he concluded, "Who can say how many vices will be eradicated, how many social habits will be formed," through universal education?[50]

Bache promoted two methods for the dissemination of "true philosophy": free, universal, public education and the wide distribution of newspapers. Early in his newspaper career, Bache made it clear that he believed the unity of the separate states and the smooth operation of the new government depended on public intelligence flowing from an "early education" and sustained by the "stream of public information" made available by the public gazettes. The support of formal education was a patriotic duty.

On knowledge and virtue . . . are raised the pillars of this rising republic— these must support the edifice—and it is the first of legislative duties to make provision to encrease, as our numbers encrease, and to perpetuate the means of knowledge among the people, and he is unworthy the name of patriot, let his pretensions be what they will, who discovers a lukewarmness on this subject.[51]

Bache was never lukewarm. He went out of his way to commend educational reforms in Germany and France, published French revolutionary pamphlets on new policies toward education, copied editorials on education from John Fenno's *Gazette of the United States* even though Fenno was Bache's hated rival, and while on his death bed was unequivocal in demanding that his wife provide their children with an "enlightened education."[52]

Not surprisingly, he scorned economic arguments against public education, haughtily noting that some people preferred to spend larger sums on seeing bears that had been taught to dance or parrots taught to speak than they did on schools for their children. Public schools were a necessity for the poor and they were cheap compared to the ills produced by the persistence of ignorance. But he believed schools organized along county lines would only result in inequitable education favoring the rich. Instead, he advocated a state system that would guarantee an equal right to education for all, supported by a progressive tax system that would fall heavily on the rich. The poor and the middle classes would gain opportunity and equality; the wealthier classes would enjoy the comfort of supporting a system that would respect and protect property.[53]

Bache willingly recognized the legitimate gradualness of formal education but felt that grown men should be informed without delay. This could best be achieved through newspapers. He admitted that bad newspapers should be discouraged, but he believed that newspapers were more generally undervalued and unfairly compared to books.[54] No matter how valuable books were, the fact remained that, "A newspaper is cheap, of small bulk, and goes everywhere . . . it tells us facts at the minute we are curious to know them—it tells also the opinion of the world upon them."[55] For Bache, books clearly represented an aristocracy of learning, newspapers a democracy. Still an advocate of the Constitution in the early 1790s and always a supporter of nationalism, Bache claimed that the press was the "principal instrument" that allowed Americans to win independence as well as "preparing the public mind for a more energetic government" and the United States Constitution.[56]

Yet Bache's final focus was never on the mere eradication of ignorance or the establishment of education. "Of all the countries on earth," he declared, "America is in the best condition to regenerate man by education: We have the most to do with, and the least yet to do."[57] "Regeneration" was the goal: not a Calvinist regeneration but a modern, democratic one. To some degree, this regeneration was private, individual, and economic. Shortly after establishing the *General Advertiser,* Bache glowed with his grand-father's optimism, declaring that "nature has done everything on her part to render the United States more fully competent to support an independent empire, than any other country whatever." Less the physiocrat than Frank-lin, he nevertheless claimed in 1790 that agriculture was "the basis of all real power in a state." After encountering the first part of Paine's *Rights of Man,* he broadened his views on economic issues as he would on others. "We have too frequently heard invidious and altogether ideal distinctions be-tween the agricultural, manufacturing, and commercial interests of a com-munity," he said, "which on a proper and candid view of the subject will be found to spring from each other to be intimately and efficiently connected, and not easily separated in their principles or effects, and to flourish best while going hand in hand." He also embraced Paine's view, as did Jefferson, that property was not antecedent to society, as Locke would have it, but was in fact an incidental product of it. For example, when Bache described the nature of crimes against property, he called these "an artificial crime" which, in a certain manner, was "created by society."[58]

Bache's personal economic success in benefiting from the new liberal liberty of his age was qualified. But he was a nascent capitalist at least. He argued broadly for both domestic self-sufficiency and commercial potential, urging American farmers to diversify into maple sugar as a substitute for foreign cane sugar, and encouraging Americans to pursue a silk culture in agriculture and manufacturing, both for self-sufficiency and for an export trade. In 1791, he unapologetically supported manufacturing, believing that the old roadblocks to manufacturing success—scarcity of labor, unset-tled lands, and weak state governments—had been overcome by good, just, and equitable government.[59] He did not praise Alexander Hamilton's *Report on Manufactures* directly, but many of the ideas in it comported with Bache's own views. In fact, Bache was not opposed to funding, or to Hamilton's Bank of the United States. Long after other observers had joined the fray, Bache slowly began to accept Philip Freneau's charges that Hamilton's policies led to speculation, corruption, and the creation of unhealthy economic conflict.[60]

But Bache's personal interest never lay in commerce or manufacturing. As conflict with Britain grew in the 1790s, he increasingly linked commerce with problems in foreign affairs. On the practical level, he spent much more time than before advocating the mundane economic advantages of receiving more immigrants from Europe, creating an intelligent western land policy and encouraging internal improvements.[61] At a theoretical level, he clung to one ideal: "No truth is better proved," he argued, "than that trade should be free." Or, as he put it in 1791, "When will nations follow the laws of nature and depend, for the prosperity of trade, on the abundance of the sources of individual industry, from which it is to be supported."[62]

Political economy did not fascinate him or hold his attention. His primary vision, a diluted and more glib version of Paine's, was social, civic, political, revolutionary, and international. Part of his frustration as a radical arose from his political belief that, "The science of government is not as abstruse as some men would wish to make it. The principles of fair, equal government are easily understood, and within the comprehension of the meanest capacity." He simply contended that the "appetite for liberty" was "universal and ineradicable," and that "the light of heaven-born liberty" would point out to those enslaved "the plain road to political happiness."[63]

That "plain road" was republicanism. Like Paine, Bache denied that republicanism existed in Venice, Genoa, Geneva, or Holland; they "were in fact tyrannical aristocracies." Throughout the 1790s, Bache seconded Paine's simple definition of republican government as "no other than government established and conducted for the interest of the public." "It is not connected with any particular form," Paine declared, "but it most naturally associates with the representative form, as being best calculated to secure the end for which a nation is at the expense of supporting it."[64] On at least one occasion, Bache attempted to elaborate that "end," stating that republicanism

> while it preserves order, industry, and subordination, secures human right, checks exorbitant ambition, discourages immense accumulation of wealth, promotes a spirit of peace and concord, distributes the beneficence of the God of nature with an equal hand, and acting from an impulse of a benevolent Providence becomes that subordinate Deity [nature], which was certainly designed to regulate the concerns of the globe.[65]

Thus, government was primarily a negative force of restraint; its primary function was to preserve "to each member of the society his person, the liberty of doing whatever is not inconsistent with the rights of others, and all the fruits of his honest industry."[66]

Because all were born with equally shared natural rights, the social compact was designed to protect those equal rights. Members of the social compact were sovereign, and sovereignty, for Bache, meant a general will.

Although Bache never hinted at any Rousseauan *Volksgeist,* no point was more strongly stressed in his political philosophy than the primacy of the general will.[67] Never a strong advocate of minority rights, Bache boldly stood by his declaration in reply to "Publicola" "that whatever they [the majority] may do will be right; unless the fundamental principle is erroneous, and it can be proved that wisdom is in the minority."[68] He held no sympathy with the large minority in France who opposed the Revolution. Even as he lost political battles in the mid-1790s and found himself in the minority, he declared either that he was not truly in the minority or that if the majority were well informed they would agree with him. When the Sedition Act rose as a specter over his press career, he seldom fell back on state sovereignty or minority protection arguments, preferring to argue broad national rights and the need for the majority to see the pernicious effects of the Act.[69]

The translation of sovereignty into government was little different for Bache than it had been for Paine. A constitution was a necessity, and it had to originate from the whole sovereign people; it could not be formed by mere legislative representatives.[70] Once a constituted system of government was in place, sovereignty was delegated from the people to their representatives. Bache was eager to emphasize the need for restraint and restrictions on these representatives, but was never able to articulate a theory of sovereignty that did not include absolute delegation. In 1791 he declared, "Power ought ever to spring from the People—and being delegated for a given time—those who use it, must at the expiration of that time, revert to the general mass, and thereby, be subject to every act which in the execution of that power, they may have made." Later that year he declared even more emphatically that "not a particle" of sovereignty ought to remain anywhere else than in the elected representatives; "these delegates are to dispose of that power in such a manner as they conceive will best suit the convenience of their constituents, without check or control." And in 1797 he further added that "the representative system, founded on frequent elections and universal suffrage, is the perfection of political wisdom."[71] Bache remained consistent on this theme even during his activities in the Democratic Society of Pennsylvania. It is little wonder that Bache—having painted himself into the corner of absolute majoritarian sovereignty and the absolute legislative authority of representatives—became one of the first to recognize the significance of shaping public opinion, not just for elections but for day-to-day government, and one of the first to find political organization as the ultimate solution to his theoretical conundrum.[72]

When the subject turned to more specific forms of government, Bache was less interested. Early on he endorsed checks and balances and government with three branches. By mid-decade he had reverted to unicameralism, claiming that three branches of government would simply fight among themselves for dominance. He further noted that Franklin had felt bicameralism was "absurd and prejudicial," while the Yazoo land fraud in Georgia showed how ineffectual checks really were.[73]

Bache simply believed that forms of government were subordinate to the principles of popular sovereignty and representative supremacy. Once, while praising the various forms of government employed by the American states, England, and France, he asked, "Who has a right to decide dogmatically that there is but one right way in politics?"[74] Forms of government, what he called "principles," "vary and should vary with a change of circumstances," he argued elsewhere. A majority of the people "may certainly whenever they think fit undo what they have done," and establish new "principles." The Constitution of 1787 was good, he claimed in a long 1791 editorial published just as Paine's *Rights of Man* was being serialized,

> but should a majority of the people at any time think that they could enjoy greater political happiness by a change of government, the principles of the Constitution would not be looked upon as fixed principles. The security we have that a change will not speedily take place, is not that the principles are fixed but good; that there is reason in the majority; and also that it would be better to bear with some small political inconvenience than to risk the fate of a change.[75]

In the early part of the decade, Bache was frequently gratuitous, condescending, and patronizing in his praise for the American system of government. He promised grandly to overlook "political inconveniences." "No country in the world can boast a constitution so wisely constructed," he boasted in 1790, "or whose departments are conducted by men of more ability and integrity."[76] Republican government meant future prosperity, improvements in inventions and the mechanical arts. Confidence in the government was so high that everyone anticipated that America was "maturing to a perfection, hitherto unknown." He even chastised state governments for their jealousy of the federal government. Employing classical republican ideas, he prescribed vigilance by the people, since "without frequent pruning of vicious shoots, the most virtuous governments will degenerate, and bear bad fruit."[77]

Beginning in 1792, Bache became more openly critical of American government. Senate secrecy and the failure of that body to make their debates public worried him and his readers. With the Jay Treaty debate in 1795, Bache began to claim that the Senate acted as if the people were inferior and that sovereignty had been transferred to the Senate in "fee simple."[78] By late 1795, he remarked that he thought "the Constitution a good one; but cannot see that it is stampt with the seal of perfection." Two years later he was certain the French were right in praising the American people while condemning the government of the United States, since the administration no longer truly represented the people.[79]

The fullest expression of Bache's discontent came with his pamphlet, *Remarks Occasioned by the Late Conduct of Mr. Washington*, published in 1797. Primarily interested in how the executive and legislative branches of government failed to protect the public interest, Bache dismissed the judicial branch as of "secondary weight" and one which did not "preponderate against the people."[80] The executive, he claimed, was far too powerful. Although the framers of the Constitution and Washington himself had called for extensive constitutional checks in government, the Constitution provided very few in regard to the presidency. No one would allow a general a command of an army near the seat of government for four years, yet as Commander-in-Chief the President had that power. The power of the veto, the authority to grant pardons and reprieves, and the opportunity to run for re-election opened the doors to abuses and corruption. Even worse, the control over foreign affairs in a single person was dangerous,

> since the negative here given is direct and universal; and by imitation or carelessness it may often operate positively. It is therefore greater in its effect, than the power in internal affairs; and by occasioning wars, by preventing peace and also alliances and treaties for other purposes, or by disturbing advantageous relations which actually subsist, and thus affecting the leading lines of foreign connection and trade, it may endanger the tranquility, fortunes, and lives of each individual of the United States.[81]

Bache's preference was for a plural executive modeled on the French Directory. The Directory's attributes of "vigor, secrecy, and celerity," as well as its ability to unite the country compared favorably to European monarchy and was certainly preferable to Washington's divisive policies. If such a plan were instituted, Bache argued, the vice-presidency would no longer remain "inert" and cabinet members might be less active in usurping presidential functions. The present Constitution had been written "before the United States had sufficiently un-monarchized their ideas and habits,"

Bache claimed. And since the American and French revolutions had been conducted by committees, Americans might expect success from a plural executive. With this arrangement, "The executive government would no longer exhibit the fluctuating character of an individual, but approach nearer to the fixed abstract of the American nation."[82]

Meanwhile, the "American Senates," both national and state, had also been created on false premises and, Bache declared—invoking the specter of Burke—"dictated under the influence of habit." Americans had conceived of senates as replacements for the dual functioning colonial councils, which performed an advisory role to the governor as well as being second branches of the legislature. And, Bache suggested, many persons probably thought of a senate as Montesquieu had, as a body to preserve not only the Constitution but manners as well. Convinced that senates were not necessary at all, Bache charged senators with failing to uphold even the Constitution or manners, and with being "more advanced in political corruption" than any class of men in America.[83]

The number of branches of government was inconsequential, he concluded. A single-branched government separated from the people would surely militate against the public interest. A two- or three-branched government where the people were separated from the government might protect the public interest. But the salient point for Bache was whether all branches of the government were elected by the people and were thus in "union with the WHOLE PEOPLE." Popular government was the real necessity. And a popular government was "one which is representative, and of which the parts are in their composition plural and rotary; for thus only will a government have common objects with the people." Political systems should be based on reason and philanthropy, not history, he argued. But history did offer two negative lessons: avoid having governors whose interests were separated from the governed, and "never trust too much power in the hands of a single man."[84]

Bache's political science was thoroughly national. But his ideology was international and was supported by his extraordinary faith in human progress through world revolution. The American Revolution was necessary in this progress but not sufficient; it was too mild, too remote from Europe. The brave new world he envisioned had really begun with the French Revolution. That was a revolution he could only know in an abstract way, but it served him well in an ideological sense. Partially alienated from his own country to begin with, Bache was driven even farther from the American "revolutionary center," by the events of the 1790s. In regard to the

French Revolution, he could combine the very real physical memories of his boyhood with the visionary, millenarian qualities of his ideology. Ideological impulses and remembrances of real places and persons allowed him to reify the French Revolution and give it a romantic gloss. In 1792, therefore, Bache would ask rhetorically, "Can you seriously suppose that the present struggle of that nation [France] is not the beginning of that universal reformation which is about to take place in the world for the general benefit of the human race, & which will unfold itself into successful reality?"[85]

France had been the great absolutist state. Yet among all European powers, it was the one to experience a full and permanent reformation. And, unjust as it might seem, it had had to defend itself not only against internal foes but against the united despots of Europe. French military success, in Bache's eyes and those of most others caught in the spirit of the times, was of more than symbolic importance: on it hung the ultimate success of reason, liberty, equality, and enlightenment everywhere. As early as 1792, Bache had become convinced that the liberal, enlightened future of America depended on France's success against her enemies.[86] The vision was so powerful that Bache was literally enraptured.

> Contemplate the expansive energy of principles, and eye the universe! Then estimate the course of events, and consider what the prospect portends! The associating of the champions of Liberty, against the conspiring supporters of despotism, the assembling of their respective powers, in various quarters of the globe, the conflicts of their numerous forces—now strike the mind, as approaching CONVULTIONS of the WORLD, and a GENERAL EARTH QUAKE, Undoubtedly, must overthrow the Colossus of despotism.[87]

Bache and his contributors repeatedly emphasized that the rise of reason, knowledge, and science would provide the basis of impending world revolution. Once the mass of men had been led out of darkness, false appeals to nationalism and the manipulation of superstitious persons would have no effect; despotic governments would fall from the weight of their wars and expenses.[88]

To follow the inevitable course of progress, Bache frequently checked the world's political barometer, unfailingly finding a rising spirit of reformation. He identified Italy as ready for revolution as early as 1791, claiming that traditional abuses (apparently Roman Catholic paternalism and Italian government censorship of French revolutionary material) could not be tolerated much longer. When Napoleon hastened Italy's "liberation" late in the decade, Bache boasted that liberty and enlightenment would "rise on the ruins of the Vatican" within days. The Polish Constitution of 1791, condemned by Bache initially for its maintenance of monarchy, was eventually praised as a first step toward complete liberty.[89] By 1797 he felt that India, maladministered and exploited by a degenerate British ruling class, was ripe for independence. That same year, he claimed that if France gained a foothold at the mouth of the Mississippi River, Mexico would become free. He hinted that the ascension of a new king in Sweden who was cool toward the aristocracy might be significant. He even reported rumors of possible rebellion against Mandarin authority in China.[90]

Great Britain and her dominions were a more constant source of fascination in Bache's vision of the secular millennium. He had been interested in India partly because it could strike an economic blow at the "totering [sic] fabric" of Britain's "rotten government."[91] But he worried over Britain's capacity to defeat natural developments. He saw the Canada Act of 1791, for example, as a clever constitutional ploy to separate English-French and Protestant-Catholic Canada and allow England to play both sides off against each other. When aristocrats dominated Canada's legislative assembly in 1792, Bache could only take comfort in a prospect of revolution when those aristocrats failed to reform abuses. When David McLane (spelled McLean by Bache) tried to subvert British rule in Canada in 1797, and was tried and hanged under a severe sedition act, Bache celebrated McLane's martyrdom as the beginning of Canadian liberty and revolution.[92]

Ireland represented a more realistic candidate for revolution. When the Irish responded to the French Revolution by forming the United Irish Society and other revolutionary clubs, Bache took an immediate interest. By 1795, Bache believed that the defenders of Ireland's liberty "appear to want but a leader to demolish the ancient system of tyranny and superstition in that infatuated country." To generate further sympathy and momentum for the cause, he emphasized the miserable condition of the Irish peasantry. With the French and Dutch navies supposedly poised to invade Ireland and England in 1797, Bache speculated that "if even 300 men have at last arose against their oppressors, . . . this will be a signal for a general rising, and we are sure they must eventually conquer." When news of the Irish rebellion reached Philadelphia, Bache boasted that "for a people to be free, it is sufficient they will it," and when subsequent news of the failure of the rebellion arrived, Bache refused to accept defeat.[93]

From 1790 on, Bache refused to believe that even England could long remain immune to the infection of revolution. The war against France waged by England would only destroy England's national character at home. England's best people, he argued, were emigrating to the United States. The war would lead to discontent in the army and navy, increased emigration, and economic dislocation; hunger alone might bring on the revolution.[94] In 1797, when John Fenno charged that it was inhumane to pray for a revolution in England, Bache admitted he prayed for such a course of events and denied that such prayers were inhumane. "What are the temporary evils of a revolution, to the silent deadly effects of such a weight of government, as that under which the unfortunate people of Great Britain stagger?" he asked. He cited disease, starvation, and debtors prison as far worse fates than revolution. If the wealthy and privileged did not try to impede the people's inalienable rights, the revolution could even be bloodless. And, he concluded, although some property would be lost, it had been "ill-gotten" in the first place; it would do more good if used for the people's benefit instead of being hoarded by a few.[95]

The sweeping generalization of Bache's radical rhetoric, as it progressed from specious deism to democratic certitude to revolutionary romanticism, differed from the rhetoric of his chief journalistic competitors—John Fenno, Noah Webster, and William Cobbett—in content more than intensity. John Fenno, Bache's elder by eighteen years, appeared to agree with Bache in the early 1790s regarding the importance of education, a free press, and a popular energetic federal government. But even here, Fenno and his correspondents in the *Gazette of the United States* stressed peace, order, and "fixed principles" in opposition to Bache's vaunted adherence to popular sovereignty.[96] Public opinion, one *Gazette* writer claimed, made "Government the most capricious idea in nature," while another argued that "the majority is as much bound by the Constitution as individuals are by the laws—and even where no written Constitution exists—the minority possesses unalienable Rights which cannot be invaded without violating the principles of nature and reason."[97]

Although Fenno's universalist and rationalist argument may have shared an Enlightenment base with Bache's, the implications of his arguments for the supremacy of law and "Liberty" as "order," without which man's passions and excesses take over, gave a Burkean hue to the ideological whole. Bache certainly saw Fenno as an apostle of Burke, claiming that Fenno felt that, "so long as the government exists the power of the people is delegated and the moment that power is resumed by the people the government is extinct."[98] Fenno continually argued for the need to recognize permanent orders, groups, and distinctions in society, and the need to enlist mixed government in order to check the human avarice behind them.[99] For Bache, evolutionary progress of man in society was unavoidable; for Fenno the inevitable reality was the permanence of passions and necessary institutions. Thus, Fenno was appalled at Bache's call for world revolution, believing that enlightenment had to precede liberation. Throughout his private correspondence Fenno would maintain that American nationalism had to remain entirely separate from the corruptions of European influence, that France was an enemy to ordered or real liberty, and that the French Revolution was largely about the destruction of the Christian religion.[100] Unwilling to agree with Bache that enlightenment occurred immediately upon liberation and was a result of unleashing man's true self-interest, Fenno predicted that "the lapse of a century will be necessary to bring back society to a state of real freedom, security and tranquillity [sic]" after the French Revolution.[101]

Noah Webster was Bache's other chief rival among the moderate Federalist journalists. From December, 1793, when he began publication of the *American Minerva,* and later as editor of the New York *Commercial Advertiser,* Webster developed a sophisticated ideological opposition to Bache's radical faith. As a young man, however, Webster displayed a radical vision similar to Bache's. Educated in Enlightenment ideas, he could still be termed an American *philosophe* in the 1780s. More the modern economic man-on-the-make than Bache, he argued that property was the substitute for virtue. Socially, he defended an enlightened self-interest, one free of passion. The cornerstone of his political philosophy was not unlike Bache's: the preservation of "this union of private with public interest." Furthermore, he echoed Bache in believing the revolution had just begun in 1787, and subsequently defended the early stages of the French Revolution.[102]

Yet, already by 1793, he had come to believe that the language of the French Revolution had confused American objectives. Partisan divisions and strife troubled him in the 1790s. As the decade progressed, Webster lost his nerve and faith in all revolutionary promise, calling for a halt to change, a freezing of habits, a return to classical virtue, and the imposition of social and self-discipline. Strident in maintaining his editorial independence from the Federalists, Webster nevertheless became, by temperament as well as logic, an early architect of American conservatism.

As the specter of revolutionary rage increasingly troubled Webster during the mid-1790s, Bache failed to comprehend the subtleties of Webster's ideas. When Webster argued that man's rational pursuit of self-interest was legitimate but that human passion, even including patriotism, demanded restraint, Bache countered that as man was freed to pursue his self-interest he became virtuous and wise, that the emergence of purer passions sustained republican principles.[103] This difference in confidence in man's moral perfectibility led to further disagreements in the realm of politics. While Bache supported the Democratic Societies, Webster stridently denounced parties, factions, and clubs that distorted his vision of some pristine public interest.[104] Webster subsequently defended John Adams's theory of balanced government, chastised the French Constituent Assembly for failing to establish bicameralism and an elected senate, proclaimed the superiority of laws over men, and continually remarked on Bache's naive optimism about the French and world revolutions. At one point, when Bache continued to be surprised at political violence in France, Webster chided him for being too young to understand the true principles of the American Revolution, and too poorly read in history to understand the need for restraints and mixed governments.[105]

The Jay Treaty battle only intensified this split, with Webster condemning the excessive powers and few responsibilities of the "complaining branch" of government, the House of Representatives. Bache could only charge Webster with giving aid-and-comfort to the enemy, the "British faction," and with defending monarchy. Webster retorted that monarchies were not necessarily tyrannical nor republics necessarily free. Tyranny was simply "a violation of right." "The idea that a republican government alone can secure freedom, is political bigotry," he argued, turning Bache's own support of political-structural relativism against him.[106] As criticism of the administration intensified in 1798, Webster sounded like Burke in concluding that the "irreligious and anarchical principles of modern theoretical philosophers" like Rousseau and Godwin were bad and that democracy was a sham.[107]

William Cobbett completed the triumvirate of Bache's political protagonists. Cobbett shared few classical republican or Enlightenment values with Fenno and Webster. He was "a popularizer of Edmund Burke" with no "coherent vision" of his own, an observer who "focussed more upon individuals than upon ideas" while refusing "to assess American culture, society and politics on its own terms."[108] Cobbett's behavior was compulsive, and this trait, coupled with his habituation to writing and seeing his prose in print, frequently resulted in extreme language and imagery in *Porcupine's Gazette* (1797–1799) and his other publications.

Bache's revolutionary rage and Cobbett's contemptuous disdain of that rage left no ground for ideological discourse. Bache initially attempted to engage Cobbett in a simple exchange of abuse but was no match for his adversary and apparently became frightened and wary of an all-out assault on Cobbett. In any case, Cobbett freely and unapologetically admitted his advocacy of England and his contempt for American society. He openly supported the Burkean precepts of a class-ordered society, hereditary monarchy, parliamentary government, and established Christian religion.[109] Bache was left with little to expose but much to attack, if he had had the nerve. Cobbett, who never considered giving verbal quarter to any man or woman, diligently continued his attacks on Bache as a quisling of the French and defined Bache with bemusement as a moral coward whose "eyes never get above your knees."[110] Mutual loathing admitted no serious ideological debate; utter alienation from each other's ideas and beliefs was the prevailing state of affairs.

Ronald Formisano has presented the political ideological dichotomy of the early Republic, as a conflict between a desire for "liberty" among those who became Jeffersonian Republicans, and a quest for "order" or "law" among those who became Federalists. Yet in doing so, he has emphasized the shared revolutionary experience of the combatants, dwelling on how the Revolution of 1776 created a "revolutionary center" that bonded friend and foe together in experience. The partisan strife of the 1790s, therefore, reflected factional differences within a shared ethic and past, rather than modern party division.[111]

But the "revolutionary center" clearly did not apply to Benjamin Bache. Peter Hoffer, in narrowing the definition of a shared "collective identity" or "revolutionary center" and applying it strictly to the generation of Americans born before 1758, restores some of its application to Bache. Revolutionary Americans, Hoffer claims, in tying all of their personal ideological and emotional commitments to their own revolution against England, consumed this generation's capacities for "alienation and rebellion, the search for wholeness and uniqueness, and visions of universes of possibilities."[112] But as time passed, the generation grew conservative and ethnocentric, saluting American uniqueness, rejecting the universal potential or applicability of American revolutionary ideals elsewhere, and embracing a fast receding but seemingly protective past. Some, like Bache, were not imbued with this identity, did not feel the urge of the older generation in the 1790s to rely on experience more than on universal principles. This new group continued to look to the future and to emphasize the continued unfolding of political progress. Much of the rivalry between Bache and Fenno, Webster, Cobbett, and others can be explained by these clashing identities or something closely approximating them. Differences in age and generation, in education, and in cultural experience led to ideological division even among Jeffersonian Republicans.

Yet Bache's passions and beliefs bespoke a profound personal psychology and rage that was not driven solely by rational disagreements over political theory, by differences produced by age or identity status, or by cleavages between his trans-Atlantic experiences and a hardening American ethnocentrism. In 1790 he was a very young man trying to establish a personal autonomy that he had long worked toward in his childhood and adolescence. Before mid-decade, that narrow personal autonomy had given way to a broader dream regarding world revolution and liberation. He created a liberation creed, virtually reifying the abstract principles of the French Revolution. In the controversy and events surrounding the Jay Treaty, he discovered frightening challenges to this dream, and he seemed genuinely surprised at the extent and depth of opposition to his own political and social beliefs. He renewed and intensified his commitments, codifying his ideology and ferreting out all who stood against it, be they Hamilton, Washington, John Adams, or lesser lights. Late in the 1790s he would cast off all restraints: any internalized uncertainties ended, the past was denied, conspiracies were disclosed, and extraordinary claims for the secular millennium were proclaimed in the midst of crisis. Action alone stood as the necessary radical solution.[113]

Howard Mumford Jones has best summarized this revolutionary romanticism that infected Bache. Acknowledging that nothing in the French Enlightenment makes "consistent sense," Jones nevertheless agrees that the late eighteenth century was the last period in which the prospect of full "human omniscience" was considered attainable. The "main tenet" of this enlightenment vision was

> the identical quality of sensory experience and of rationality among all human beings. This identity made for atomism and for egalitarianism. Men were separated by the truth that every person's sensory experience was unique and private; men were united in their common power of rational thought. . . . Men of course differed in customs and opinions, but this was not because rationality was untrustworthy but because of climate, or a backward education, or bad government, or a perverse theology. Each man was an island of self-rule, independent of all other souls, a self-sufficing physiological and nervous mechanism . . . functioning in an environment admirably suited to him.[114]

For Americans who came of age with an American rather than the French revolutionary ethic, this enlightenment credo suggested only reforms of limited scope and utilitarian ends. Not so with Bache and his romantic revolutionaries, filled with their rage for completion. "Victory and remorse were here and now; the development of advanced thought, if it isolated the individual revolutionary leader, also permitted him to picture a perfected society and a rational future as an enlarged image of himself." The romantic rebel took on a Promethean role, becoming the "incarnation of a will to resist" and displaying "a capacity for infinite endurance."[115] Bache played this role fully, his brief life and career ending after a decade long crescendo of ideological commitment and emotional frenzy.

Notes

1. Peter du Ponceau to Sam'l Breck, Mar. 14, 1834, Historical Society of Pennsylvania, Philadelphia.

2. See, for example, Benjamin Franklin Butler, *Representative Democracy in the United States: An Address Delivered Before the Senate of the Union College on the 26th, July, 1841* (Albany, N. Y., 1841). "Man" and "mankind" as used in this work are to be read as encompassing both men and women. Bache in particular did not suggest that he meant to exclude women in his ideological vision.

3. The three most significant works in this regard are Richard Buel, Jr., *Securing the Republic: Ideology in American Politics, 1789–1815* (Ithaca, N. Y., 1972); Lance Banning, *The Jeffersonian Persuasion: Evolution of a Party Ideology* (Ithaca, N. Y., 1978); and Drew McCoy, *The Elusive Republic: Political Economy in Jeffersonian America* (Chapel Hill, N. C., 1980).

4. For classical republican versus populist concepts of "virtue" see J. G. A. Pocock, "Virtues, Rights and Manners: A Model for Historians of Political Thought," *Political Theory*, IX (August, 1981), 353–68; and Linda K. Kerber, "The Republican Ideology of the Revolutionary Generation," *American Quarterly*, XXXVII (1985), 494. Joyce Appleby bluntly concludes that "by the end of the century virtue more often referred to a private quality, a man's capacity to look out for himself and his dependents—almost the opposite of classical virtue." See her book, *Capitalism and a New Social Order: The Republican Vision of the 1790s* (New York, 1984), 15. Melvin Yazawa identifies a changing definition of virtue beginning with the Revolution in which "virtuous citizens were by definition autonomous in their personal bearing and independent in the exercise of their wills." Melvin Yazawa, *From Colonies to Commonwealth: Familial Ideology and the Beginnings of the American Republic* (Baltimore, 1985), 4. Joseph Ellis, "Habits of Mind," *Am. Quar.*, XXVIII (1976), 159, notes for the late eighteenth century that, "Perhaps words like 'virtue' or 'moral,' or even a term like 'natural law' became so popular because they allowed a writer to refer simultaneously to both spiritual and rational realms, to fuse opposites in a language that all Americans found meaningful and enlightening." Even classical republicanism's chief advocate insists that the ideology be seen as "no

more than a winding and knotted thread in a complex and tangled texture." See J. G. A. Pocock, "Between Gog and Magog: The Republican Thesis and the *Ideologia Americana*," *Journal of the History of Ideas*, XLVIII (1987), 332.

For Bache's modern view of virtue as dependent on liberating education and self-interest see, for example, *Gen'l. Adv.*, Aug. 6, Nov. 19, Nov. 21 ("corres."), 1791; Jan. 11 ("Extracts"), Dec. 24, 1792; *Aurora*, May 19, 1795. For those contemporaries of Bache who shared his views see Michael Durey, "Thomas Paine's Apostles: Radical Emigrés and the Triumph of Jeffersonian Republicanism," *William and Mary Quarterly*, XLIV (1987), 661–88.

5. For the liberal argument see the several articles of Joyce Appleby and especially her book, *Capitalism and a New Social Order*. Appleby acknowledges in this work a broad "principle of hope" that "animated" Republican Party ideology in the 1790s (86). But she more often talks of a new "benign and visionary" capitalism (50), of a "new commercial age" (87), and of self-interest in market, rather than communal terms (31). She speaks of "the democratization of opportunity" in "The Social Origins of American Revolutionary Ideology," *Journal of American History*, LXIV (Mar., 1978), 953, and has tended to speak of liberal liberty, private man, and individual self-interest in economic terms in her subsequent articles: "Commercial Farming and the 'Agrarian Myth' in the Early Republic," *JAH*, LXVI (1982), 833–49; "What Is Still American in the Political Philosophy of Thomas Jefferson," *WMQ*, XXXIX (April, 1982), 287–310; "Republicanism and Ideology," *Am. Quar.*, XXXVII (1985), 461–73; and "Republicanism in Old and New Contexts," *WMQ*, XLIII (Jan., 1986), 20–34.

6. In analyzing Thomas Jefferson, Richard K. Matthews, *The Radical Politics of Thomas Jefferson: A Revisionist View* (Lawrence, Kan., 1984), 14, notes that Jefferson was closer to *homo civicus* than to *homo oeconomicus*, adding that "Neither wealth nor capital ever constitutes the conceptual core of Jefferson." The same could be said for Bache, many of his allies, and many of his foes.

7. On this synthesis see James T. Kloppenberg, "The Virtues of Liberalism: Christianity, Republicanism, and Ethics in Early American Political Discourse," *JAH*, LXXIV (1987), 9–33. Besides Kloppenberg's, various attempts at synthetic resolution of the ideological morass can be seen in Robert Kelley, "Ideology and Political Culture from Jefferson to Nixon," *AHR*, LXXXII (1977), 531–62; Daniel Walker Howe, "European Sources of Political Ideas in Jeffersonian America," *Reviews in American History*, X (1982), 28–44; Matthews, *Radical Politics of Thomas Jefferson*; Forrest McDonald, *Novus Ordo Seclorum: The Intellectual Origins of the Constitution* (Lawrence, Kan., 1985); and Kerber, "Republican Ideology," *Am. Quar.*, XXXVII (1985), 474–95.

The best single introduction to competing ideas and ideologies is Howe, "European Sources," *Rev. in Amer. Hist.*, X (Dec., 1982), 28–44. European ideas and Enlightenment impulses are also surveyed in several articles on the Enlightenment in the *Am. Quar.*, XXVIII (1976); Donald H. Meyer, *The Democratic Enlightenment* (New York, 1976); Henry F. May, *The Enlightenment in America* (New York, 1976); Donald S. Lutz, "The Relative Influence of European Writers on Late Eighteenth-Century American Political Thought," *American Political Science Review*,

78 (Mar., 1984), 189–97; and Paul Merrill Spurlin, *The French Enlightenment in America* (Athens, Ga., 1984). The significance and role of Scottish philosophy is seen in Howe, "European Sources," *Rev. in Amer. Hist.*, X (1982), 28–44; Gary Wills, *Inventing America: Jefferson's Declaration of Independence* (New York, 1978); Louis Schneider, ed., *The Scottish Moralists on Human Nature and Society* (Chicago, 1967); and Douglas Sloan, *The Scottish Enlightenment and the American College Ideal* (New York, 1971). The Calvinist element is argued critically by John Patrick Diggins, *The Lost Soul of American Politics: Virtue, Self-Interest, and the Foundations of Liberalism* (New York, 1984). Those who see classical republicanism persisting through the 1790s include Linda K. Kerber, *Federalists in Dissent: Imagery and Ideology in Jeffersonian America* (Ithaca, N. Y., 1970); Lance Banning, "Republican Ideology and the Triumph of the Constitution, 1789 to 1793," *WMQ*, XXXI (1974), 167–88; Banning, *The Jeffersonian Persuasion;* Lance Banning, "Jeffersonian Ideology Revisited: Liberal and Classical Ideas in the New American Republic," *WMQ*, XLIII (1986), 3–19; and Daniel Walker Howe, *The Political Culture of the Whigs* (Chicago, 1979). Significant works arguing a new liberal ethos include Richard D. Brown, *Modernization: The Transformation of American Life, 1600–1815* (New York, 1976); Isaac Kramnick, "Republican Revisionism Revisited," *AHR*, LXXXVII (1982), 629–64; Appleby, *Capitalism;* Appleby, "Republicanism in Old and New Contexts," *WMQ*, XLIII (1986), 20–34; and Diggins, *Lost Soul of American Politics.*

8. As Eric Foner, *Tom Paine and Revolutionary America* (New York, 1976), 214, puts it: "The Burke-Paine debate was the classic confrontation between tradition and innovation, hierarchy and equality, order and revolution." Paine's ideological importance is discussed in Michael Durey, "Thomas Paine's Apostles: Radical Emigrés and the Triumph of Jeffersonian Republicanism," *WMQ*, XLIV (1987), 661–88. Howe, "European Sources," *Rev. in Amer. Hist.*, X (1982), 39, finds Burke "was more widely admired than most historians realize."

9. E. P. Thompson has observed that "neither writer was systematic enough to rank as a major political theorist. Both were publicists of genius, both are less remarkable for what they say than for the *tone* in which it is said." E. P. Thompson, *The Making of the English Working Class* (Harmondsworth, Eng., 1968), 98.

10. Edmund Burke, *Reflections on the Revolution in France,* intro. by Conor Cruise O'Brien (orig. pub., 1790; cited here, Harmondsworth, Eng., 1968), 275. On Burke's ideas as ideology see Reinhold Bendix, "The Age of Ideology: Persistent and Changing," in David E. Apter, ed., *Ideology and Discontent* (New York, 1964), 300–301. On Paine's intellectual inheritance see Caroline Robbins, "The Lifelong Education of Thomas Paine (1737–1809): Some Reflections upon His Acquaintance Among Books," *Proceedings of the American Philosophical Society,* vol. 127, No. 3 (1983), 135–42. David Freeman Hawke, *Paine* (New York, 1974), 144, claims that, "Books bored him; he never was and never would be much of a reader, except of newspapers."

11. See respectively Burke, *Reflections,* 195 and 119. Most of the analysis of Burke contained herein is taken from the *Reflections,* and from Michael Freeman, *Edmund Burke and the Critique of Political Radicalism* (Oxford, 1980). Free-

man argues that Burke maintained a consistent ideological opposition to radical thought.

12. Burke, *Reflections.*, 90 and 275.

13. *Ibid.*, 277.

14. *Ibid.*, 228.

15. See respectively *ibid.*, 119; and Thomas Paine, *Rights of Man,* intro. by Eric Foner (New York, 1984), Pt. 1, 87.

16. Jack P. Greene, "Paine, America, and the 'Modernization' of Political Consciousness," *Political Science Quarterly,* 93 (1978), 73–92.

17. Paine, *Rights of Man,* 68–69. Some modern literature makes much of Paine as the progenitor of modern economic liberalism, as the friend of the emergent private man, as a bourgeois liberal, when Paine can also be seen defending freedom, equality, and security on a broader social and political plane. See Foner, *Paine;* and Isaac Kramnick, "Tom Paine: Radical Democrat," *Democracy,* I (1981), 127–38. Other useful works on Paine's social and political ideas are A. Owen Aldridge, *Thomas Paine's American Ideology* (Newark, N. J., 1984); Paul F. Boller, "Thomas Paine and Natural Rights: A Reconsideration," *Social Science,* 52 (1977), 67–72; Jett B. Conner, "Thomas Paine and the First Principles of Democratic Republics," (unpub. Ph.D. diss., Univ. of Colorado, 1980); Hawke, *Paine;* and Staughton Lynd, *Intellectual Origins of American Radicalism* (London, 1969), 35, 51, 54, 75–77.

18. See respectively Paine, *Rights of Man,* 176 and 161.

19. *Ibid.*, 163.

20. See respectively *ibid.*, 69, 196, and 141.

21. See respectively *ibid.*, 143, 71, and 143.

22. *Ibid.*, 178 and 180.

23. See respectively *ibid.*, 193 and 41. For Bache see *Gen'l. Adv.*, June 4, July 1, 2, 1791.

24. On Burke see *ibid.*, Mar. 7, April 15, 1791. On Aug. 4, 1791, Bache carried a rebuttal of Burke by Joseph Priestley. Extracts of the *Rights of Man,* Part One, are in *ibid.*, May 7, 9, 10, 11, 12, 14, 16, 20, Dec. 6, 1791. Extracts of the *Rights of Man,* Part Two, are in *ibid.*, May 26, June 1, 8, 27, July 10, Aug. 3, Sept. 4, 1792; and *Aurora,* Oct. 26, 1795.

25. *Gen'l. Adv.,* June 4, 1791.

26. See [B. F. Bache], Notes on John Adams's *Defence of the Constitution of the U.S.,* Bache Papers, Castle Collection, American Philosophical Society, Philadelphia. The "Publicola" letters appeared in *ibid.*, June 30, July 1, 2, 4, 5, 12, 15, 20, 24, 28, and Aug. 2, 1791. "Brutus's" comments are in *ibid.*, July 1, 2, 21, 24, 1791. Bache's editorials are in *ibid.*, June 30, July 1, 2, 13, 1791.

27. Hawke, *Paine,* 25, 93, 107, 115, 117, 119, 162–63, 169–70. On *Common Sense,* see also Owen, *Paine's American Ideology,* 21, 38.

28. See respectively Paine, *Rights of Man,* 95; and Hawke, *Paine,* 320–21. On the second part of *The Age of Reason,* and Paine's *A Letter to George Washington,* see respectively Thomas Paine to B. F. Bache, Sept. 24, 1795; and, Aug. 7, 1796, Bache Papers, Castle Coll., Am. Philos. Soc.

29. Thomas Paine to B. F. Bache, July 13, Sept. 20, 21, 1795, Bache Papers, Castle Coll., Am. Philos. Soc.

30. For aspects of Franklin's life that could have influenced Bache's development see Carl Van Doren, *Benjamin Franklin* (New York, 1938), Claude-Anne Lopez and Eugenia W. Herbert, *The Private Franklin: The Man and His Family* (New York, 1975), and Esmond Wright, *Franklin of Philadelphia* (Cambridge, Mass., 1986).

31. For this view see especially Drew McCoy, "Benjamin Franklin's Vision of a Republican Political Economy for America," *WMQ*, XXXV (1978), 605–28; or McCoy, *The Elusive Republic*, 49–67.

32. Among the many works that address Franklin's social and political philosophies see Malcolm R. Eiselen, *Franklin's Political Theories* (Garden City, N. Y., 1928), 1–12, 51–96; Clinton Rossiter, "The Political Theory of Benjamin Franklin," *PMHB*, LXXV (July, 1952), 259–93; Paul W. Conner, *Poor Richard's Politicks: Benjamin Franklin and His New American Order* (New York, 1965); Gerald Stourzh, *Benjamin Franklin and American Foreign Policy* (Chicago, 1969); Donald H. Meyer, *The Democratic Enlightenment* (New York, 1976), *passim;* Horst Dippel, "Franklin and Condorcet: Revolution and Social Order; Some Remarks on their Social Theories," in *La Révolution Américaine et l'Europe* (Paris, 1979), 431–47; Merle Curti, *Human Nature in American Thought: A History* (Madison, Wis., 1980), 99–102; and Jeffrey Alan Smith, "Printers and Press Freedom: The Ideology of Early American Journalism" (unpub. Ph.D. diss., Univ. of Wisconsin-Madison, 1984), *passim.*

33. The quotation is from Peter Gay, *The Enlightenment: An Interpretation*. Vol. II. *The Science of Freedom* (New York, 1969), 499. On Bache's 1790 philosophy see B. F. Bache, "Melanges" (Aug., 1786–?), Bache Papers, Castle Coll., Am. Philos. Soc.

34. May, *Enlightenment in America*, 108 and 251. On the "Revolutionary Enlightenment" in general see *ibid.*, 153–251.

35. See respectively Paul Merrill Spurlin, *Rousseau in America, 1760–1809* (University, Ala., 1969), 35–38, 57–59; and *Gen'l. Adv.*, Nov. 17, 1792.

36. See Marie Jean Antoine Nicolas Caritat, Marquis de Condorcet, *Outline of an Historical View of the Progress of the Human Mind* (Philadelphia, 1796); *Gen'l. Adv.*, July 13–14, 1791; Dec. 7, 1792; April 21, 1795; and B. F. Bache to R. Bache, Jan. 10, 1793, Castle Transcripts. On Condorcet's dialectic and naiveté see Gay, *The Enlightenment*, II, 112–33.

37. George Logan, *An Address on the Natural and Social Order of the World . . .* (Philadelphia, 1798). Bache advertised Priestley's and Barlow's works in the preface of France, Convention Nationale, 1792–1795, Comité d'instruction publique, . . . *Report on the . . . National Library* (Philadelphia, 1794). On Priestley see *Gen'l. Adv.*, Aug. 4, 1791; April 14, 1792; and May 25, 1793.

38. See respectively, *Gen'l. Adv.*, Dec. 5, 7, 1791, and Dec. 15, 1792; and *Aurora*, Oct. 27, 1797. Bache may have been influenced by the Scottish common sense philosophy of Francis Hutcheson, expounded to Benny when he was a student of the Reverend Magaw at the University of Pennsylvania. See B. F. Bache, Notes on Moral Philosophy, Bache Papers, Castle Coll., Am. Philos. Soc.

39. *Gen'l. Adv.*, May 9, 1791.

40. See respectively *ibid.*, June 4, 1791; May 3, 1792; and *Aurora*, Nov. 27, 1795.

41. See Bache's reply to Noah Webster's contention that patriotism was "imaginary," in *Gen'l. Adv.*, May 19, 1795. An earlier editorial argues essentially the same thing. See "Extracts," *Gen'l. Adv.*, Jan. 11, 1792.

42. *Aurora*, Sept. 8, 1797. On the evolutionary change from a traditionalist concept of "passions" to a modernist view of "interests" see especially A. O. Hirschman, *The Passions and the Interests: Political Arguments for Capitalism before Its Triumph* (Princeton, N. J., 1977).

43. *Gen'l. Adv.*, Dec. 2, 1791; and *Aurora*, May 21, 1796.

44. The quotation is from *Gen'l. Adv.*, Aug. 12, 1793. See also *ibid.*, Oct. 20, 1791; Nov. 13, 1792.

45. *Ibid.*, Sept. 5, 1791; and Jan. 20, 1792.

46. *Ibid.*, June 7, 1791.

47. See respectively *ibid.*, April 23, May 17 ("A Recluse Man"), 1791; May 1, 1792; and June 30, 1791.

48. *Ibid.*, June 7, 1791.

49. *Ibid.*, Oct. 19, 1791; and Dec. 24, 1792. For other editorials on much the same theme see *ibid.*, June 7, Nov. 10 (ed. repr. from *Gaz. of U. S.*), 21 ("corres."), 1791; Mar. 8, Dec. 24, 1792; Feb. 1, 1793; and Jan. 29, 1795.

50. See respectively *ibid.*, Dec. 8, 1791; and Nov. 3, 1791.

51. *Ibid.*, Dec. 24, 1792. The editorial on "early education" is in *ibid.*, July 7, 1791.

52. Bache's praise of German and French educational reform is in *ibid.*, Aug. 15, 1792; and May 28, 1796. See also his publications, France. Convention Nationale, 1792–1795. Comité d'instruction Publique, . . . *Collections of the Heroic and Civil Actions of the French Republicans* (Philadelphia, 1794); and France. Convention Nationale, 1792–1795. Comité d'instruction Publique, . . . *Report on the Organization of Public Schools* (Philadelphia, 1794). Bache republished the following editorials on education and schools from the *Gazette of the United States: Gen'l. Adv.*, June 23, Nov. 10, Dec. 15 ("corres."), 1791; Nov. 27 (quotation from John Adams's *Defense of the American Constitutions*), 1792; Aug. 1 ("E."), and 11, 1796. See also Benjamin Franklin Bache's Will, Sept. 7, 1798, B. F. Bache Papers, Amer. Philos. Soc., Philadelphia.

53. *Gen'l. Adv.*, Dec. 5, 8, 1791; Mar. 8, 1792.

54. *Ibid.*, Feb. 21, July 15, Aug. 6, Nov. 14, and Dec. 1, 1791.

55. *Ibid.*, Dec. 5, 1791.

56. *Ibid.*, Jan. 2, 1792.

57. *Ibid.*, Dec. 8, 1791.

58. For the quotations cited see respectively *ibid.*, Oct. 12, Nov. 19, 1790; and July 8, 1791. On the commitment of many Jeffersonian-Republicans to this post-Lockean, Paine ideal see David M. Post, "Jeffersonian Revisions of Locke: Education, Property-Rights, and Liberty," *Jour. of the Hist. of Ideas*, 47 (1986), 147–57.

59. *Ibid.*, April 21, 23, 27, Aug. 5, 18, Oct. 6, Nov. 30, 1791.

60. For Bache's mild support of Hamiltonian policies see, for example, *ibid.*, Dec. 23, 1790; April 11, July 4, 1791; Jan. 6, May 25, 1792. For representative examples of Freneau's attacks on these economic policies between 1791 and 1793 see the *National Gazette*, June 28, July 4, Aug. 1, 11 ("corres."), 1792; and Mar. 16 ("An American Farmer"), Sept. 11 ("Reflections on Several Subjects"), 1793. For a

more general survey of opposition to Hamilton's policies see Donald H. Stewart, *The Opposition Press of the Federalist Period* (Albany, N. Y., 1969), 33–70.

61. *Gen'l. Adv.*, Nov. 9, 1790; April 13, June 18, 24, Sept. 15, Oct. 6, 1791; Mar. 26, April 1, 1793. For his support of Pennsylvania projects specifically see *ibid.*, Aug. 8, Oct. 5, 6, 1791; Mar. 18, Sept. 13, 1792.

62. *Ibid.*, Jan. 9, 1792; and Dec. 5, 1791.

63. See respectively *Aurora*, Oct. 27, 1797; and *Gen'l. Adv.*, June 4, 1791.

64. See respectively *Aurora*, Dec. 18, 1797; and Paine, *Rights of Man*, 178.

65. *Aurora*, Dec. 18, 1797.

66. *Gen'l. Adv.*, June 12, 1793. See also "Speculator" and Bache's reply in *Aurora*, Feb. 19, 1796.

67. On natural equality see *Gen'l. Adv.*, Jan. 4 ("Government"), 1792; and June 12, 1793. On the sovereign will of the people see *ibid.*, May 24, June 13, July 2, 11, Oct. 5, 1791; Aug. 16 ("A Republican"), 1793; Sept. 8 ([Bache's] "Political Creed"), 1797; Nov. 28 and Dec. 11, 1797.

68. *Ibid.*, July 2, 1791.

69. On national rights see Bache's reply to Noah Webster's views on the French Revolution, *Aurora*, Nov. 28, 1797.

70. *Gen'l. Adv.*, May 24, 1791.

71. See respectively, *ibid.*, July 11, Oct. 5, 1791; and *Aurora*, Sept. 8, 1797.

72. For examples of Bache's emphasis on the importance of public opinion see *Gen'l. Adv.*, Dec. 20, 1791; July 30, 1798.

73. On three branches of government see *ibid.*, Jan. 16 and Feb. 7, 1792. On unicameralism see *ibid.*, Jan. 29, April 14, 1795.

74. *Ibid.*, April 12, 1792. See also Bache's assertion that liberty is rightfully sought in different ways in different places. *Ibid.*, Sept. 22, 1791.

75. *Ibid.*, May 24, 1791.

76. *Ibid.*, Nov. 17, 1790.

77. For the quotations see respectively *ibid.*, Nov. 20, 1790; and May 29, 1792. Criticism of state governments is in *ibid.*, Jan. 24, June 13 ("corres."), Oct. 27, Nov. 3, and Dec. 26, 1791.

78. *Aurora*, June 22, 1795. On Senate secrecy and shortcomings in general see *Gen'l. Adv.*, Nov. 16 ("corres."), 17 ("corres."), 20 ("corres."), 28, Dec. 19 (art. from *American Museum*), 1792; Feb. 7 ("X."), 28 ("Philo-Philadelphiensis"), 1793.

79. *Aurora*, Nov. 27, 1795; and July 19, 1797.

80. B. F. Bache, *Remarks Occasioned by the Late Conduct of Mr. Washington* (Philadelphia, 1797), 40n.

81. *Ibid.*, 37–38, and more generally on the presidency, 35–39.

82. *Ibid.*, 35–36, 38–39.

83. *Ibid.*, 39.

84. *Ibid.*, 39–40.

85. *Gen'l. Adv.*, July 17, 1792. For similar declarations see *ibid.*, Oct. 5, 30, 1790; Aug. 18, Oct. 26, 1792; Jan. 15, 29, Mar. 26 ("Cato"), 1793; Mar. 15 ("corres."), 1798.

86. On the latter point see *ibid.*, June 22, 1792; and Jan. 29, 1793. For other points discussed in this paragraph see *ibid.*, Oct. 5, 1790; Aug. 18, Oct. 26, 1792; and Jan. 15, 1793.

87. *Ibid.*, Aug. 16, 1793.

88. See for examples *ibid.*, May 9, June 11, July 1 (M. le Merciér, "Tableau de Paris"), 1791; Jan. 6, 19, 1792; Jan. 18 (Extract), 1793; and April 7 ("The Progress of Justice and Reason"), 1798.

89. *Ibid.*, Jan. 29, 1791; Feb. 25, 1797. On the Polish Constitution see *ibid.*, July 22, Aug. 11, 1791.

90. *Ibid.*, Oct. 3, 1792; Feb. 25, April 8, and May 4, 1797.

91. *Ibid.*, Feb. 25, 1797.

92. *Ibid.*, July 9, 1791; Aug. 1, 1792; and Aug. 15, 1797. On McLane see Robert R. Palmer, *The Age of Democratic Revolution: A Political History of Europe and America, 1760–1800.* Vol. II, *The Struggle* (Princeton, N. J., 1964), 515–18.

93. *Aurora*, Oct. 19, 1795; July 21, 1797; and Aug. 11, 1798. See also on the Irish issue *ibid.*, Aug. 20, 1792; Jan. 25, May 24 (letter), 30 (art. from Belfast paper), 1793; Feb. 2, 1796; Aug. 14, 15, and 16, 1798. On the Irish rebellion see Palmer, *Age of Democratic Revolution*, II, 491–505.

94. *Gen'l. Adv.*, Oct. 26, 1791; Sept. 27, 1792; July 1, 10, Oct. 27, 29, 30, 1794; May 6, Dec. 21, 1795; and Aug. 3, 1797.

95. *Ibid.*, Aug. 5, 1797.

96. See for example *Gaz. of U. S.*, Nov. 17, 1790; Feb. 8, May 21 ("corres."), 25, 1791; Aug. 11 and Nov. 7, 1792.

97. *Ibid.*, July 30 ("corres."), and Jan. 1 ("corres."), 1794. Privately, Fenno admitted in 1794 that most of the challenge to his concept of the rule of law came from America's "exiles from Europe," who "suppose they should get rid of all restraints in this free & happy country—the majority of this class are persons that cannot be quiet under any government whatever & we shall find, that they will oppose the just & wholesome laws of this Country as long as they can do it with impunity." J. Fenno to Jos. Ward, Sept. 14, 1794, in John B. Hench, ed., "Letters of John Fenno and John Ward Fenno. Part 2: 1792–1800," *Proc. of Am. Antiquarian Soc.*, XC (1980), 196.

98. For Fenno and order see *Gaz. of U. S.*, Jan. 23 ("corres."), 1793. For Bache see *Gen'l. Adv.*, July 28, 1794.

99. See *Gaz. of U. S.*, Dec. 8, 1790, May 7, June 4, 1791; Jan. 14, 1792.

100. See especially J. Fenno to Jos. Ward, Apr. 6, May 26, Aug. 24, 1793; Feb. 23, Sept. 14, 1794; and July 9, 1796, in Hench, ed., "Letters of John Fenno," *Proc. of Am. Antiquarian Soc.*, XC (1980), 167, 169, 172, 192, 198–200, and 216.

101. For this disagreement see *Gaz. of U. S.*, Aug. 3, 1797; and *Aurora*, Oct. 27, 1797.

102. *Am. Minerva*, May 15, 1795; and also May 5, 6, 13, 14, 1795. On the evolution of Webster's character and philosophy in general see especially Richard Rollins, *The Long Journey of Noah Webster* (Philadelphia, 1980); Gary Coll, "Noah Webster, Journalist: 1783–1803," in Donovan H. Bond and W. Reynolds McLeod, eds., *Newsletters to Newspapers: Eighteenth-Century Journalism* (Morgantown, W.Va., 1977), 303–18; and Joseph J. Ellis, *After the Revolution: Profiles of Early American Culture* (New York, 1979), 161–212.

103. *Am. Minerva*, May 13, 15, 1795, and Bache's direct reply to Webster in *Aurora*, May 19, 1795.

104. *Am. Minerva,* Dec. 26, 1793; Feb. 8 ("corres."), 1794; May 6, July 28, 1795; Feb. 9, 1796.

105. On the philosophical disagreements with Bache see *ibid.,* May 7, Oct. 20, 21, 1794; and Dec. 4, 1795. On the exchange over violence see *ibid.,* Mar. 27, 1795; and *Aurora,* April 14, 1795.

106. *Am. Minerva,* Mar. 17 and June 13, 1796. For Bache's weak reply see *Aurora,* June 16, 1796.

107. *Comm. Adv.,* Feb. 7, Mar. 5, 1798.

108. Ian Dyck, "From 'Rabble' to 'Chopsticks': The Radicalism of William Cobbett," *Albion,* 21 (1989), 58.

109. On Cobbett's Burkean beliefs see George Spater, *William Cobbett: The Poor Man's Friend* (Cambridge, Eng., 1982), I, 94; and especially Karen K. List, "The Role of William Cobbett in Philadelphia's Party Press, 1794–1799," (unpub. Ph.D. diss., Univ. of Wisconsin-Madison, 1980), 109–41 and *passim.*

110. *Porcupine's Gaz.,* Nov. 16, 1797. Few of Cobbett's references to Bache fail to describe the *Aurora's* editor as anything less than an agent of the French. On Cobbett's willingness to attack any man or woman who disagreed with him see List, "Role of William Cobbett," 41–74; and especially Karen K. List, "Two Party Papers' Political Coverage of Women in the New Republic," *Critical Studies in Mass Communications,* II (1985), 152–65.

111. See Ronald P. Formisano, "Deferential-Participant Politics: The Early Republic's Political Culture, 1789–1840," *Amer. Pol. Sci. Rev.,* LXVIII (June, 1974), 473–87; and Ronald P. Formisano, *The Transformation of Political Culture* (New York, 1983), esp. 3–85.

112. Peter Hoffer, *Revolution and Regeneration: Life Cycle and the Historical Vision of the Generation of 1776* (Athens, Ga., 1983), 25.

113. The systematic psychological rejection of traditional authority and the radical evolutionary imperative from fantasy-wishes to revolutionary action is argued best, and traced historically in relationship to revolutionary France, in Fred Weinstein and Gerald M. Platt, *The Wish to Be Free: Society, Psyche, and Value Change* (Berkeley, 1969), esp. 1–44.

114. Howard Mumford Jones, *Revolution and Romanticism* (Cambridge, Mass., 1974), 31, 34, and 63.

115. *Ibid.,* 243, 248, 251.

6. In Search of the Cause, 1791–1792

"When it [the line between republican and anti-republican senti-
ment] comes to be struck definitely I hope I shall be found on the
right side of it."
(B. F. Bache to R. Bache, Feb. 3, 1793)

PHILOSOPHY AND PSYCHOLOGY bound Benjamin Bache to act and to
advocate action. If environment determined men's lives, if it was all that
stood between enlightenment and slavery, right action had to be undertaken to create and sustain freedom, to keep public opinion correctly
informed, and to prevent the re-infection of the body politic with old
despotic elements. But in 1790 the twenty-one-year-old editor seemed
unclear about what constituted right action. Through the early years of the
1790s, Bache seemed to cast about for authentic, unambiguous causes.

In the brief hiatus between the establishment of the second new nation
in 1789 and the excitement aroused by revolutionary visions in 1792–
1793, Bache shared with many other Americans a semi-conscious kind of
political self-restraint and pursued a myth of the "promised land" through
national self-congratulation and self-exaltation. Some of Bache's early rhetoric was, therefore, full of patronizing, rhapsodic, and transparently flattering attempts to join the mythic celebration:

A new, a happy series of years commences. Justice descends from the skies,
where too many had compelled her to take refuge. The hands of the manufacturers are beneficially employed. Our ports abound in our own vessels. Agriculture is encouraged. A WASHINGTON presides over us with as much dignity & wisdom as man is capable of exerting. The sound policy of ADAMS
shall again be manifested; & the distinguished talents of JEFFERSON ad-
vantageously displayed.
  With these prospects, which rest on as much security as humanity can effect,
what evils have we to fear? or rather what blessings may we not hope for?[1]

The immediate task of reform, therefore, seemed to involve little more
than the discovery of those small elements of useful knowledge that would

marginally improve an already basically reformed society. At the very outset Bache had observed that his grandfather and other friends "were desirous that more attention should be paid to the Sciences, Literature in general, and more particularly to the Useful Arts."[2] But what Bache published was more trivial than useful: an article on soil erosion, a method to establish the quality of gunpowder, a promotion of steam cooking, an easy formula for calculating tariff charges, a new way to heat greenhouses, and so on. He even briefly tied the memory of his grandfather, who "toil'd for the good of the whole human race," into this feeble promotion. But in reality, Bache put little effort into the cause and Franklin's name appeared in the *General Advertiser* only occasionally after 1792.[3]

If Bache tried to give a gloss of usefulness to trivia, he also tried to apply a veneer of enlightenment importance to a miscellany of events and issues. He defended drama in general, and the Chestnut Street Theatre in particular, finding moral utility in the arts. In 1793, he also tried (and failed) to puff Jean Pierre Blanchard's balloon ascent over Philadelphia as a landmark in scientific advancement.[4]

Ranging widely in his search for journalistic causes and personal identity, he attempted to excite interest in broader social issues—especially in penal reform and anti-slavery. But, unwilling to go beyond restitution of the criminal through such devices as hard labor, he hardly turned any heads in a state already known for its liberal penal code and ideas.[5] Slavery was more complex. In 1794 he would declare boldly that "Every man, however slenderly provided with common sense," could see how slavery and the slave trade were "iniquitous and attrocious [sic], as it is repugnant to the laws of nature and the principles of morality and religion, and militates against the very intentions of society, and the happiness of the human race."[6] But his insistence on a Franklin-like work ethic among slaves as a condition for release and his support of gradual emancipation only, coupled with unclear and under-developed ideas about racial equality, did not make him a radical champion of this cause either. The revolt of Saint Domingue's Blacks against liberal rule by a republicanized France confused his moral loyalties, forcing him ultimately to decide in favor of benevolent French rule and against the idea of a Black-dominated Caribbean nation. Later in the decade, his support of Jeffersonian Republicans hardly allowed him the luxury of attacking an institution defended and practiced by his political allies.[7]

Partisan politics also failed to afford Bache any easy or early editorial direction. From 1790 to the spring of 1792, Bache pursued non-partisanship consciously at both the state and the national levels. In regard to state politics, he went no farther in 1790 and 1791 than to condemn political lethargy while failing even to discuss the partisan split between western Pennsylvania demands for a district election law and eastern proposals for at-large representation. In the fall of 1791, he naively supported the selection of a United States Senator through concurrent elections in the separate houses of the legislature rather than through a joint vote of both houses, even though concurrent election was favored by conservatives and aristocrats who wished to preserve a Senate veto over the more democratic house.[8] Even the dramatic election of 1792—which witnessed the founding of two opposing parties to fight over all thirteen congressional seats as a consequence of a state-wide, at-large election process—resulted in mixed partisan signals from Bache. Though he defended the Correspondence group—labelled "anti-federalists" by their opponents and headed by the politically astute Alexander James Dallas and Dr. James Hutchinson—as pro-artisan and mechanic and not "anti-federalist" at all, the *General Advertiser* continued to pose as an impartial press, publishing editorials on all sides of the issue, including strong editorials supporting the Conferees (or "federalist") group. In the end, Bache merely urged the people to vote.[9]

Bache was equally timid (and sometimes almost sycophantic) when it came to national politics and personalities. The young man who would later gain infamy for his attacks on George Washington, grandly stated on the President's sixtieth birthday in 1792 that, "As long as Americans feel the blessings of Liberty, & of pure republican government this day will be remembered as one of the most auspicious in their calendar."[10] John Adams fared less well, but even here Bache was cautious, applying his opposition to Adams's philosophical positions rather than the man. Thus, while condemning Adams's "title campaign," he also condemned a severe satire against Adams from a Connecticut newspaper, warning, "Such gross abuse of a Man whose Services and patriotism were engraven on the hearts of his countrymen, almost before his traducers had existence—needs no comment."[11] And, although Jefferson admitted to clipping editorials from the *General Advertiser* because they attacked "Publicola," Bache always kept those attacks on the plane of principle, not personality, assaulting the ideas of aristocracy, devotion to orders of nobility, and advocacy of titles rather than attempting—as Jefferson had done in writing of "political heresies" in the foreword to Paine's *Rights of Man*—to suggest that there were persons in America deliberately trying to undermine republicanism.[12]

Hamiltonian economic policies regarding the public credit, funding and assumption, and the Bank of the United States also failed to stir Bache's partisan emotions. In fact, Bache shared with Tench Coxe (another soon-to-be Jeffersonian) a strong nationalist view of fiscal policy that admitted little criticism of Hamilton in the early part of the decade.[13] Thus, in late 1790, Bache praised the "rapid appreciation" in funded notes and certificates, "which has done more for the public credit in a few months than they anticipated for many years," while six months later he urged Pennsylvania's "monied men" to invest in the new Bank of the United States because any "plan that will in its operations reduce the interest on money—encrease the circulating medium—facilitate business in every line and profession—enhance the debt, and diminish the public burdens, must, and will meet the approbation of every friend to his country."[14] This did not mean, of course, that the consequences or ancillary effects of such policies went uncriticized. While applauding the rapid extinguishing of the debt through funding, the *Advertiser* attacked the baneful effects which speculation in public securities had on public morality and personal industry. And the rage of speculation that followed establishment of the Bank of the United States, a speculation that frightened and worried even Hamilton, was met in the *Advertiser* with predictable moral contempt. Unlike Philip Freneau, whose *National Gazette* had begun to make probing attacks on Hamilton's fiscal policies through his popular "Brutus" series in early 1792, Bache was unable to find in Hamiltonian policies the great cause for which he yearned.[15]

It is true that by 1792 the *Advertiser* was ultimately drawn into more of an oppositional stance on fiscal policies, and began to criticize more broadly the ill-effects of Hamilton's policies. But even here Bache was drawn in by reaction. The background to this modest transition could be found in early 1791. At that time, Bache had made clear where he stood on partisan conflict by publishing an editorial entitled "Party Spirit." "Truth is everywhere," that editorial proclaimed, "do you wish to find it? Separate it from the spirit of party which so often obscures it." After cataloguing the ill effects of party, the editorial concluded that, "If one wishes to be just to every body, and not guilty of gross errors, he must not adopt party spirit."[16] But as the battle between John Fenno and Philip Freneau began to heat up over Hamiltonian policy in early 1792, Bache reluctantly began to agree with Freneau that partisan disagreements were "unavoidable" in political societies. When Fenno followed with the broad hint that Bache might be part of an illegitimate opposition, Bache began to challenge Fenno's uncritical support of administration policies.[17] On May 3, Bache printed two more editorials protesting Fenno's accusations. "Some newspaper writers," he pointed out, "who indiscriminately praise the measures of government, for solid reasons, no doubt, treat writers in opposition to the sentiments they profess, & all those who venture in any degree to find fault, or [are] in any particular [involved] with a reform, as enemies of all government." After denying his own disloyalty, Bache stated,

> Certain paragraphists appear to ground their political belief upon the principle, that whatever is, is right—that a government established by the people, must ever act for the best good of the people. They appear to think, that such a government is as invariable in its operations as the planets are steady in their course. Such doctrine is near kin to the old doctrine of passive obedience and non-resistance, now almost universally exploded, even in Europe.[18]

In the wake of this exchange, the *Advertiser* began to come out more strongly against a public debt which seemed to divide the nation into two parties, one which "thought favorably of a great public debt" and "considered speculation as the very soul of public credit," and the other which saw a large debt as an "evil" and speculation the "child of unruly avarice, and the prolific parea [sic] of idleness, dissipation and fraud." A month later, another editorial mocking the mutability of public opinion virtually traced the migration of Bache's own sentiments about a public debt.

> 1789 - Public debt may be made a public blessing
> 1790 - Public debt is a public blessing
> 1791 - Public debt is not a public evil
> 1792 - (January) - Public debt may become a public evil
> 1792 - (November) - Public debt is a public evil
> 1793 - Public debt is among the greatest of public evils
> 1794 - It is wonderful that so great a folly of opinion should have ever existed in a free & enlightened country, as that a public debt & perpetual taxes were the means of public liberty & public prosperity, & that, both debts & taxes ought to be increased for their own sakes, instead of establishing the latter by paying off the former, for the sake of public credit & public honour.[19]

Bache refused to abandon impartiality altogether, however, reprinting a long series of essays in 1792 from the *American Museum* which essentially defended Hamilton and the administration on manufactures, commerce, the Bank, funding and assumption, the public debt, and America's political and economic potential for prosperity.[20]

Initiated into some oppositionist activity as a consequence of the Freneau-Fenno clash over Hamiltonian fiscal policies, Bache finally revealed some journalistic passion, rivaling Freneau for the first time in the breadth and power of his journalism, (in the quiet presidential election of 1792). Following Freneau's lead, many *Advertiser* contributors joined the campaign to replace John Adams with George Clinton, concentrating on condemnations of Adams's avowed love of titles and mixed government, and his hatred of equality.[21] With this contest between Adams and Clinton in progress, Bache unveiled his new, more candid, views of the political contest. Echoing Freneau's analysis of a few months earlier, Bache declared that "the question in America is no longer between federalism and anti-federalism, but between republicanism and anti-republicanism." The Constitution was no longer an issue; it was "firmly established" and uniformly supported, and had gained more than requisite "efficiency and strength," he added. Yet "some who have passed under the name federalists, have views far beyond those of the friends to the constitution in its present form." Clearly alluding to Adams's re-election, but taking a broader view as well, Bache accused Federalists of desiring a potentially dangerous "system of anti-republican orders and artificial balances." In staking out his new stand on political morality, he offered a thoroughly Whig conclusion:

> The progress of its [Federalists] leaders, in inculcating their doctrines and maturing their councils, is become too serious to be disregarded. A language in praise of monarchical and aristocratical institutions, and in derogation of our republican systems, which would not have been whispered a few years past, is becoming so familiar in certain scenes as scarcely to call forth observation. In this posture and prospect of things all true friends to liberty ought to be on their constant guard against insidious attempts to divide them by an abuse of names, and to be united firmly in checking the careers of monarchy, by bearing testimony against its advocates.[22]

Unmoved by the intricate details of Hamilton's policies, Bache warmed to the cause when it appeared that monarchy, aristocracy, or privilege loomed as threats. Who, after all, could deny sympathy with attacks on these traditional forms, except those not yet baptized in an Enlightenment faith or a radical Whig past? To a large degree, Bache safely attacked only the vestigial symbols of monarchy and aristocracy. "Mirabeau"'s political satire, "Forerunners of Monarchy and Aristocracy," carried the Bache-Freneau attack forward. Launching Bache's assault on Washington, "Mirabeau" catalogued ten vices practiced by the federal administration that could destroy republicanism: titles, levees, birthday celebrations for public servants, arrogance in the government, pomp, exaggerated status for department heads, high government salaries, "profligacy" in public servants, public servants monopolizing the management of society, and "an irre-deemable debt." "Condorcet" seconded "Mirabeau"'s accusations, la-mented the fact that France had surpassed America in the cause of liberty, and added two more indicators of approaching monarchy and aristocracy: office holders using their titles as badges in social life, and the Senate deliberating behind closed doors.[23]

By early 1793, Bache's dedication to eliminating the last vestiges of monarchy and aristocracy was complete. President Washington, saluted a year earlier in the *Advertiser*, became the object of satire in a mock advertise-ment for a "poet laureate." To qualify for the post, a candidate had to demonstrate "dexterity in composing birthday odes," had to have a com-plete knowledge of the decline and fall of all the republics that ever existed (an obvious allusion to Adams's pessimism about republics), and must be good at writing about such "Monarchical prettinesses" as "LEVEES, DRAWING ROOMS, STATELY NODS INSTEAD OF SHAKING HANDS, TITLES OF OFFICES, SECLUSION FROM THE PEOPLE, &c., &c."[24]

With Bache's publication of his first newspaper "scoop" the same day—"Mirabeau"'s revelation that Jefferson was planning to resign from the Cabinet—the campaign against Washington was begun. Contributors ex-posed the cold, monarchical formality of presidential levees and Wash-ington's love of luxury and birthday celebrations, insisting that if the President really sought public opinion he should frequent coffee-houses and similar public places.[25] One wag told of a farmer who, coming home from Philadelphia, reported he had seen Prince Edward in a cream colored coach drawn by six bay horses. Hearing of this, the narrator traveled to Philadelphia to see this novel sight, but instead

> I met the coach, and to my utter surprize and disappointment, who should it be but the President of the United States: Ah! thought I to myself the times are changed, and have changed with them the plain and republican General Washington into a being which my neighbour Tribble took to be a Prince.[26]

Determined to bring some aristocratic bearing to the office, an always too sensitive, too self-pitying and alarmist Washington worried about the bad and "diabolical" criticisms of the government and its servants.

> The publications in Freneau's and Beeche's [sic] papers are outrages on common decency; and they progress in that style, in proportion as their pieces are treated with contempt, and are passed by in silence, by those at

whom they are aimed. The tendency of them, however, is too obvious to be mistaken by men of cool and dispassionate minds, and, in my opinion, ought to alarm them; because it is difficult to prescribe bounds to the effect.[27]

Alarmed at having someone in addition to Freneau to contend with, Fenno did not have to be coached in answering Washington's confidential call. Claiming that the President's calumniators refused to allow virtue and dignity to rise above some low, general equality, he accused Washington's attackers of being self-seeking intriguers and politicians. And then, in order to embarrass and humiliate Bache personally, he attacked the whole Franklin clan.

> If your venerable Grandsire views from his abode the mockery of Patriotism exhibited in your paper, it may console him for the follies which He committed, the servility and sycophancy he practised at the court of France; and for the disappointment He met with in not being able to place an idle sing song [Richard Bache] at the head of the Post-Office.[28]

Bache may have seethed over the counter-attack by Fenno. But in the give-and-take of this episode, he may also have comprehended the underlying irony in Fenno's ill-fated attempt to silence the *Advertiser* through an attack on family—on Franklins and Baches—an attack that probably had less impact on young Bache in early 1793 than an attack on representative democracy would have had. Bache's mild response was that he ran an impartial paper and that, since "sumptuary laws" sometimes governed "forms and manners" in a republic, discussion of the President's social behavior was legitimate.[29]

Long after Bache's death, his enemies, looking back at the young editor's apparent transition to partisanism, took a cynical view of the self-interest that drove Bache. In 1800, John Ward Fenno's *Gazette of the United States* claimed that when Bache began publishing, his mediocre, uncontroversial style left him with a paper that grew at a "tardy pace." After inaccurately claiming that Bache's father had been relieved at the Post Office in 1791, and remarking that Bache's cousin Temple was embittered over loss of government patronage, the *Gazette* argued that Bache simply decided to abuse the President. "From being the avowed personal enemy of George Washington," the writer reasoned, "the transition of hatred and opposition was both easy and natural, to the government over which he [Washington] presided."[30] Bound by the traditionalist's attachment to the inviolability of kin, young Fenno was wrong about the spirit that drove Benjamin Bache's oppositionist politics. Equally wrong was Timothy Pickering, who in opting for the more cynical pecuniary-advantage motive, argued that Bache chose to move from impartial journalist to radical partisan and to come out in opposition to the government, in order to boost sagging subscriptions. Reductionist that he was, Pickering curtly concluded: "He did so; and succeeded to his wishes."[31]

But in reality, impartiality versus the defense of republican purity, pragmatism and expediency versus moral righteousness, the quest for personal autonomy versus the desire to discover and join the republican cause, were the real dialectics that motivated Bache's publishing decisions in the early 1790s. Privately, he admitted to moving farther into opposition than editorial comment in the *General Advertiser* revealed. In early 1793, in a letter to his father, he analyzed the political situation in America. Federal politics had changed much, he reported, not admitting how much his own views on persons and policies had changed over the past two years. In the federal legislature, "the danger of a moneyed interest growing out of past measures is seen." The majority in favor of Hamilton's programs was "neither so great or bold" as before, he noted. The minority opposing Hamilton was growing and might even succeed in unearthing evidence damaging to Hamilton in the congressional investigation of the Treasury. The new members of Congress promised to have better political principles and might "turn, or direct, at least, the current of publick measures." "The spirit of republicanism is reviving," he noted, "and the President, of whom no one, six months ago would have thought disrespectfully, is now freely spoken of, and in *print* found fault with, his levees, his six horses, etc., etc., are generally censured." And then, looking to the future, he defined the era as "a critical period in our politics." Remembering that his mother, before she had left for her European tour, had seen attempts to "strick [sic] a line" between republican and anti-republican sentiment in America, he closed anxiously, "When it [the line] comes to be struck definitely I hope I shall be found on the right side of it."[32]

Notes

1. *General Advertiser*, Nov. 27, 1790. On the "promised land" issue in general see Lawrence J. Friedman, *Inventors of the Promised Land* (New York, 1975), xiv–xvii, 4–43.

2. *Gen'l. Adv.*, Oct. 2, 1790. On this general theme see Meyer Reinhold, "The

Quest for 'Useful Knowledge' in Eighteenth-Century America," *Proceedings of the American Philosophical Society,* CXIX (1975), 108–32.

3. For examples of references to Franklin see *Gen'l. Adv.,* Oct. 2 ("Character of Dr. Franklin," from *St. James Chronicle*), 11, 1790; Oct. 14, 1791. The only thing Bache managed to publish on Franklin was William Smith, *Eulogium on Benjamin Franklin* . . . (Philadelphia, 1792). Thomas C. Leonard, *The Power of the Press: The Birth of American Political Reporting* (New York, 1986), 68–69, is a recent work that perpetuates the long-standing error that Bache "found himself putting that energy into filiopiety that other men put into a career."

4. On drama, the theater, and dance see the *Gen'l. Adv.,* for the months of Feb., 1791, and Dec., 1793. For Bache's opinions see especially *ibid.,* Jan. 29 (review of "Julius Caesar"), Feb. 24, 1791; and Dec. 28, 1793. The Chestnut Street Theatre was the most expensive and elaborate theater of the period. Along with Rickets Circus Amphitheatre, it insured the continuance of stage performances in Philadelphia. See also Brooks McNamara, *The American Playhouse in the Eighteenth Century* (Cambridge, Mass., 1969), 104–31.

On Blanchard's flight see especially "Aerostation," *Gen'l. Adv.,* Dec. 18, 1792. On Bache's early interest in balloon flight see B. F. Bache, Diary, Jan. 14–15, 1785, American Philosophical Society, Philadelphia. Bache's closeness to Blanchard is cited in B. F. Bache to R. Bache, Jan. 10, 1793, Bache Papers, Castle Collection, American Philosophical Society, Philadelphia. On Bache's several calls for financial aid see *Gen'l. Adv.,* Jan. 10, May 10, 28, June 8, 1793.

5. For editorials on penal reform see *ibid.,* Oct. 9, 12, 18, 1790; Mar. 1, 24, April 14, June 8, 9, July 8, 22, Aug. 5, Sept. 16, Nov. 8, 1791; and Aug. 23, 1793.

6. *Ibid.,* Aug. 8, 1794.

7. On slavery and race in general see *ibid.,* Dec. 28 (Alexandria, Va., heading), 1790; Aug. 5, 18, Nov. 24 (letter by James McHenry repr. from *Pennsylvania, Delaware, Maryland and Virginia Almanack*), 1791; Feb. 20, June 29, Oct. 16, 1792; Dec. 13, 1794; Feb. 1, 1797. See also Bache's remarks on a proposed English colony at Sierra Leone, *ibid.,* Aug. 19, 1791. On Saint Domingue see especially *ibid.,* July 8, 9, 1793. For other editorials on St. Domingue see *ibid.,* Sept. 21, 1791; Oct. 6, 8 (Extract), 31, 1792; July 12, 1793; and July 26, Dec. 13, 1794. For a good short survey of the material impact of the revolt in St. Domingue see Donald R. Hickey, "America's Response to the Slave Revolt in Haiti, 1791–1806," *Jour. of the Early Republic,* II (1982), 361–79. A broader consideration of the revolt and of racial issues is in Winthrop D. Jordan, *White Over Black: American Attitudes Toward the Negro, 1550–1812* (Chapel Hill, N. C., 1968), 375–86, 434.

8. See respectively *Gen'l. Adv.,* Oct. 8, Nov. 2, 1790; Mar. 8, 12, and Sept. 10, 1791. On the representation issue see Harry M. Tinkcom, *The Republicans and Federalists in Pennsylvania, 1790–1801* (Harrisburg, Pa., 1950), 45–46. He also supported the re-election to Congress of Frederick Augustus Muhlenberg as a nonpartisan man. See *Gen'l. Adv.,* Oct. 11, 1791.

9. For editorials on the congressional election of 1792 see *ibid.,* July 30, Aug. 1, 3 (ed. from *Am. Daily Adv.*), 4, 9 ("Sidney"), 10 ("Argus"), 14 ("Common Sense"), 16 ("Mirabeau" from *Nat'l. Gaz.*), Sept. 8 ("Argus"),12 ("Many"), 15 ("Hydra"),

26, 27, Oct. 9, 1792. "Cerberus"'s defense of the Conferees and his attack on Dallas and Hutchinson for being a conspiratorial elitist faction are in *ibid.*, Sept. 5, 7, 14, 1792.

The election of 1792 is discussed in Raymond Walters, Jr., "The Origins of the Jeffersonian Party in Pennsylvania," *PMHB,* LXVI (1942), 440–58; Tinkcom, *Republicans and Federalists in Pennsylvania,* 51–68; Richard G. Miller, *Philadelphia, The Federalist City: A Study of Urban Politics, 1789–1801* (Port Washington, N. Y., 1976), 43–51; Raymond Walters, Jr., *Alexander James Dallas* (Philadelphia, 1943), 35–40; Noble E. Cunningham, Jr., *The Jeffersonian Republicans: The Formation of Party Organization, 1789–1801* (Chapel Hill, N. C., 1957), 38–45; and John H. Frederick, "James Hutchinson," *Dictionary of American Biography,* V, 438–39.

10. See *Gen'l. Adv.,* Feb. 22, 1792. For earlier praise of Washington see *ibid.,* Mar. 4 ("corres."), June 18, July 7, Nov. 14 ("Sonnet" by Dr. Aitken), 1791; and Feb. 22, 1792. One correspondent questioned such flattery; see *ibid.,* Feb. 24, 1791.

11. *Ibid.,* June 7, 27 ("Antifederalist Abuse"), 1791. On Adams's title campaign see James H. Hutson, "John Adams' Title Campaign," *New England Quarterly,* XLI (1968), 30–39.

12. Bache even tried to soften the implications of Jefferson's allusions to "political heresies" by saying that very few persons embraced such heresies. See *Gen'l. Adv.,* June 30, 1791. On Jefferson's clipping editorials see Thos. Jefferson to Wm. Short, July 28, 1791, Paul Leicester Ford, ed., *The Writings of Thomas Jefferson* (New York, 1895), V, 361, hereafter cited as Ford, ed., *Jefferson's Writings.* On Jefferson and the "Publicola" affair in general see Dumas Malone, *Jefferson and the Rights of Man* (Boston, 1951), 354–59; and Cunningham, *Jeffersonian Republicans,* 10.

13. On Coxe see Jacob E. Cooke, *Tench Coxe and the Early Republic* (Chapel Hill, N. C., 1978), 132–256. Richard Buel, Jr., *Securing the Revolution: Ideology in American Politics, 1789–1815* (Ithaca, N. Y., 1972), 8–17, and Lance Banning, *The Jeffersonian Persuasion: Evolution of a Party Ideology* (Ithaca, N. Y., 1978), 126ff, argue the significance of Hamilton's debt policies in the formation of ideology, as do many who adhere to the classical republican interpretation. But that significance, by their own admission, came later in the decade, with sectional unhappiness, rather than ideological division, driving Jefferson and Madison in the early months. Donald H. Stewart, *The Opposition Press of the Federalist Period* (Albany, N. Y., 1969), 33, speaks only of "the first glimmerings of displeasure with the fledgling administration" being revealed over financial policies. Philip Freneau's *National Gazette* and Thomas Adams's Boston *Independent Chronicle* did not attack funding until 1792.

14. See respectively, *Gen'l. Adv.,* Dec. 23, 1790; June 24, July 4, 1791. For other early editorials that praised funding and assumption while only mildly criticizing their effects see Apr. 11 ("Extract"), July 20 ("corres."), Aug. 23, 1791; Jan. 8 ("Cincinnatus"), 16, 1792.

15. Early attacks on speculation in Bank "scrip" can be found *ibid.,* July 11 ("C."), 14 (ed. and "Square Toes"), Aug. 4, 10, 12 (letter and "C."), 13, 15, 1791. For Hamilton's concern about speculation and a "bubble," see Alex. Hamilton to

Rufus King, Aug. 17, 1791, Harold C. Syrett, *et al.*, eds., *The Papers of Alexander Hamilton* (New York, 1961–1979), IX, 75–76, hereafter cited as Syrett, *et al.*, eds., *Hamilton Papers*. Bache republished Hamilton's anonymous concerns in *Gen'l. Adv.*, Aug. 13, 1791. For Bache's later re-affirmation of the Bank, and his desire for its stability see *ibid.*, Aug. 17, Oct. 20, 1791; Jan. 18, Mar. 10, 1792. Freneau published extensive attacks on Hamiltonian policy between February and April, 1792, in the *National Gazette*.

16. "Party Spirit," *Gen'l. Adv.*, Mar. 31, 1791.

17. On the "unavoidable" quality of politics see *ibid.*, Jan. 24 (fr. *Nat'l. Gaz.*), 1792. Bache supported Freneau *ibid.*, Apr. 17, 1792. Fenno immediately replied with six editorials condemning opposition politics. See *Gaz. of U. S.*, Apr. 18, 1792. For Fenno's other early attacks on opposition writing see *ibid.*, Feb. 25 ("corres."), Apr. 21, May 2, 1792. On the over-celebrated Freneau-Fenno clash of 1792 (a clash that also involved the competing wills of Hamilton and Jefferson) see Philip Marsh, *Philip Freneau: Poet and Journalist* (Minneapolis, Minn., 1967), 165–66, 169–71; Cunningham, *Jeffersonian Republicans*, 24–27; Broadus Mitchell, *Alexander Hamilton: The National Adventure* (New York, 1961), 206–211; John C. Miller, *Alexander Hamilton: Portrait in Paradox* (New York, 1959), 344–46; Malone, *Jefferson and the Rights of Man*, 457–86; and Noble E. Cunningham, Jr., *In Pursuit of Reason: The Life of Thomas Jefferson* (Baton Rouge, La., 1987), 169–71.

18. *Gen'l. Adv.*, May 3, 1792. Fenno scoffed at Bache's suggestion that the press had been shackled, noting that for every paragraph supporting the government in the public newspapers, columns were written against it. *Gaz. of U. S.*, May 5, 1792.

19. *Gen'l. Adv.*, May 1, 30, 1792. Other editorials critical of the debt can be seen in *ibid.*, Apr. 20, May 25, 28, June 8, Oct. 12 ("Ebenezer Stevens"), 1792.

20. "Reflections on the State of the Union," from the *Amer. Museum*, *ibid.*, May 5, 7, June 4, 6, July 7, 9, 10, Aug. 15–17, Sept. 5, 1792.

21. On the Adams-Clinton issue in particular see *ibid.*, Dec. 1 ("Portius"), 4 ("Otsego"), 5 ("Portius" and "Otsego"), 1792. For other editorials, see *ibid.*, Dec. 6 ("A. B." and Fenno's reply), 12 ("A. B."), 21, and 22 (letter), 1792. On Fenno's replies see especially three editorials in the *Gaz. of U. S.*, Dec. 15, 1792.

22. *Gen'l. Adv.*, Dec. 1, 1792. For Freneau's earlier contention that the issue was between republicans and anti-republicans see *Nat'l. Gaz.*, Aug. 1, 1792. While Federalists argued publicly that the opposition was disloyal (see for example, *Gaz. of U. S.*, Jan. 9, 16 (poem), June 5, 1793), astute Federalists recognized the change from consensus to conflict that was taking place.

23. "Forerunners of Monarchy and Aristocracy," by "Mirabeau," *Gen'l. Adv.*, Dec. 7, 1792; and "Condorcet," *ibid.*, Dec. 15, 1792. For the first time a major editorial contributor published with Bache first, with Freneau reprinting the editorial in *Nat'l. Gaz.*, Dec. 12, 1792. Responding to rumors, "Mirabeau" denied that he was Freneau. See *Gen'l. Adv.*, Feb. 11, 1793.

24. *Ibid.*, Jan. 5, 1793.

25. The hint of Jefferson's retirement is in "Mirabeau," *ibid.*, Jan. 5, 1793. For further praise of Jefferson's republicanism at this time see *ibid.*, 12 (anonymous), 21 ("Mirabeau"), 22 (two letters), 25 ("Mirabeau" and a member of the Philadelphia

militia), 1793. For condemnations of Washington see *ibid.*, "Sidney," *Gen'l. Adv.*, Jan. 23 ("Sidney"), 26 ("Sidney"), 29 ("A Farmer"), Feb. 4 ("Sidney"), Feb. 5 ("Equality" and "Franklin"), 16 ("A Subscriber"), 18 ("Equality" and "A Democrat"), 21 (letter), Apr. 3 ("Hortensious"), 1793.

26. "A Farmer," *ibid.*, Jan. 29, 1793.

27. G. Washington to Gen'l. Henry Lee, July 21, 1793, John C. Fitzpatrick, ed., *The Writings of George Washington* (Washington, D. C., 1931–1944), XXXIII, 23–24, hereafter cited as Fitzpatrick, ed., *Writings of Washington*. On Washington's style and conduct see Freeman, *Washington*, VI, 226, 252, 295.

28. Letter, *Gaz. of U. S.*, Feb. 23, 1793. For Fenno's more general criticisms see *ibid.*, Feb. 13, Mar. 6, 1793.

29. *Gen'l. Adv.*, Jan. 30, 1793.

30. "Mutius Scœvola," *Gaz. of U. S.*, Sept. 1, 3, 1800.

31. Timothy Pickering, "Manuscript Notes on Various Historical Subjects Composed in 1828," 34–35, in the Timothy Pickering Papers, Massachusetts Historical Society, Boston. See for a similar analysis John Marshall to Timothy Pickering, Feb. 28, 1811, *ibid.*

32. B. F. Bache to R. Bache, Feb. 3, 1793, Bache Papers, Castle Coll., Am. Philos. Soc.

7. French Virtue, 1793

"Upon the establishment or overthrow of liberty in France probably will depend the permanency of the Republic in the new world."
(*General Advertiser*, July 26, 1793)

DOMESTIC EVENTS FAILED to "strike the line" clearly between republicanism and anti-republicanism for Bache before 1793, but the French Revolution had already begun to strike that line for him well before 1793. While
the early years of the French Revolution had been important for Bache, as
they were for most other Americans, in sorting out the ideological contest
and the moral cause of the Revolution, it would be the opening of war
between France and the First Coalition in early 1792 that would make the
Revolution a reality rather than a misty vision. The establishment in late
1792 of a French republic that embraced popular sovereignty made the
success of this really all the more imperative to men like Bache. For Bache,
the French Revolution established a republican and democratic yardstick
with which to measure all subsequent events in the 1790s.

Most Americans of the 1790s realized that they were witnessing in the
French Revolution events more monumental for the western world than
any other distant events they would encounter in their lifetimes. But that
realization did not translate into a profound depth of understanding or an
application of analytic rigor among most observers. Few considered the
Revolution in its full social, economic, or cultural contexts. Aside from
diplomats and those who had encountered French culture in France, fewer
still were competent to analyze it through such contexts. Prominent intellectuals like John Adams, James Madison, and Noah Webster sometimes
used the Revolution as a backdrop against which to test their pre-set radical
Whig or classical republican or Humean ideologies in a rationalist, universalist, academic mode. But academic and sociological frames of reference
were not of prime importance to Americans in the 1790s. When it came to
understanding the Revolution, most Americans fell silent or threw up their
hands in wonder.[1]

For many Americans, the French Revolution was deflected to serve local or parochial purposes. The French assault on the Roman Church and its clergy excited in some New England Calvinists a pre-millennialist vision of the union of liberty, republicanism, and Protestantism. But by 1794 the image of a corrupt, immoral, anti-clerical, secular, atheistic France and the threat of a loss of authority by New England's clergy over their own congregations had turned the image around, with anti-French hysteria and paranoia driving New Englanders back to a purely American variety of piety, morality, and striving that would ultimately find release in the Second Great Awakening.[2] A shallow fashion in favor of things French occasionally prevailed elsewhere. In the middle and southern states, an interest in the French language, in French literature, fashions, and dance had already begun in mid-century and expanded in the 1770s and 1780s. Although the dimensions and importance of this courtly and aristocratic orientation have been exaggerated, the cultural enthusiasms of these earlier decades undoubtedly stood in stark and hostile contrast to revolutionary sensibilities of the 1790s. Yet many Americans, some of whom had participated in this earlier francophilism, easily redirected their enthusiasm by donning the tri-colored cockade, singing French patriotic songs, or attending public dinners and fêtes celebrating French accomplishments. At the most superficial level, some of these enthusiasts swore that gratitude toward France was a prime motivator. But for most, the self-contradiction in transferring gratitude from Louis XVI's monarchy to the republican France that killed him, was too difficult a sentiment to maintain. Francophilism, appearing disproportionately large in its display and color, was a relatively insignificant element, important only where it was driven by stronger motives.[3]

Francophilism and gratitude were often polite rationalizations for a more profound force—national narcissism. Parochial and ethnocentric, many Americans who thought lightly but felt deeply about liberty and the virtues of a republic could see the French Revolution as a kind of reflecting pool. As long as the French seemed to verify and confirm the American Revolution in a liberal, reformist, and peaceful way, Americans happily discovered their own reflection. When the pool was disturbed by gusts of violence, many turned away. For example, George Washington, never analytic or contemplative in regard to the ideological dimensions of the Revolution, admitted gratitude and love for France on a personal level and became worried early about the rise of violence and instability in France. But like most Americans, Washington waited for the end of violence and the clearing of the pool. Violence and instability, in and of itself, has been exaggerated as a factor in making Americans feel their Revolution was different from that in France, or in discouraging them from believing in the ultimate success of the French Revolution. The serious issue that drove Americans from the reflecting pool was not violence but the realization that France would not fashion its government in the American image, and that French notions of popular sovereignty, equality, and national statism admitted few of the checks and balances or restraints of Anglo-American whiggism. A substantial minority of ordinary persons abandoned hope, or at least ceased to feel understanding or empathy for the French Revolution.

Meanwhile, between 1790 and 1793, Federalists or those soon-to-be Federalists began to discover earlier than did the general populace the evils inherent not only in the French but in all revolutions. By late 1792, overwhelmed and confused by continental events beyond his ability to understand, Washington had turned his total attention to national survival through American isolation from Europe. By contrast, John Adams, who admitted privately as early as 1790 that he could only "rejoice with trembling" over the progress of the French Revolution, came to condemn French simplicity and naiveté as embodied in its pursuit of the fiction of equality and in its adherence to political unicameralism. Unable to modify his classical republicanist fears about power and liberty and the need for mixed governments, Adams had almost lost hope by the time the republic was declared in late 1792.[4]

Other Federalists retreated at various paces. Alexander Hamilton, always cynically attached to the belief that all men pursue their basest passions and interests, had joined Burke in opposing the Revolution very early. Condemning from the outset Jefferson's attachment to France as "womanish," Hamilton concluded what Washington and others did not until late 1792 or early 1793—that French liberty was really anarchy and an invitation to tyranny. Gouverneur Morris, the United States minister to France, began his opposition earlier, blasting French excesses, attacking the deficiencies of the 1791 Constitution, and conspiring to maintain Louis XVI's monarchy against the rising tide of republicanism. Lesser Federalists, horrified more than ordinary Americans by the specter of violence and excesses, eventually outdid Hamilton in their hatred of the French. Rufus King, Theodore Sedgwick, and Harrison Gray Otis repeatedly charged the French with barbarity, violence, anarchy, and licentiousness. Noah Webster maintained his intellectual curiosity and hope for the Revolution until 1793 and then became so paranoid about French anarchy that he abandoned all hope for the goodness of man or the success of liberty without authority.[5]

Why did the Federalists turn away from the French Revolution so early and so vehemently? They and their later defenders claimed that the reason was less the Revolution itself than matters of American security—the need for non-entanglement and neutrality, the pragmatic elements of foreign relations, and the fragility and vulnerability of the new republic. But the same might have been said of the Jeffersonians. Jefferson, who clearly defined the French Revolution as the cause of mankind, the hope of liberty and republicanism in the old and new world alike, did not advocate an alliance with France and remained as wary as the Federalists of entangling alliances. James Madison, always anxious to hedge his intellectual bets and never as willing to cast aside the past as more radical republicans were, was more anxious about the final outcome of the Revolution than was Jefferson; he too desired friendship, not alliance, with France. Even James Monroe, a true radical in defending the cause of France as the cause of liberty in America and the world, never called for an offensive or defensive alliance with France.[6]

The really crucial conflict over the French Revolution in America was begun with the Burke-Paine debate of 1791–1792 and brought fully to life with the establishment of the French Republic in September 1792. What John Adams and other thoughtful opponents of the Revolution discovered was that the Revolution drew a distinct line between the restrained rationalism of radical Whig and Enlightenment thought, and a new impulse to implement Rousseauist will. Whereas Americans had initiated a representative republicanism with clear roots in the past, the French Revolution promised the direct democratic sovereignty of the people. The French Revolution aspired to do more than merely make men into citizens with a modicum of useful liberty; it aspired to unchain men's souls, to allow mankind to achieve immediate enlightenment, to unleash the powerful passions of nationalism, and to carry forward liberation through arms, not just moral persuasion. It was a millennialist view which stripped away evolutionary connections with the past.[7] Years later Friedrich Gentz would attempt to delineate these dichotomies between the American and French Revolutions. The American Revolution, he declared in Burkean tones, was defensive. It respected the past and the rule of law. It was a revolution of "right" and was fixed on a definite object, representative republicanism. The French Revolution was willful and "frivolous." It had no object. It had no restraint. It was abstract, anarchical, and offensive.[8]

All of Bache's energy was devoted to these most radical, virtually religious, precepts of the French Revolution, precepts he could cast in his imagination through his familiarity with many of the faces and places of the Revolution itself. He was a secular millenialist who found in the Revolution the chance for all of mankind to be immediately liberated and reformed within their national states. With that reformation, national and international peace would be built on democratic nationalism and the implementation of a new but clearly perceived collective self-interest. Among leading Jeffersonians, only Monroe occupied this radical position with Bache publicly. Jefferson sometimes agreed privately. Madison, intellectually indebted to David Hume, would only go so far in rejecting the past, never fully agreeing with the most radical elements of French revolutionary ideology.

If contemporaries of Bache had been asked to differentiate his editorial tone on the French Revolution from that of others they might have been hard pressed to discover rhetorical distinctions. But in terms of naive infatuation, romantic rage, and stubborn insistence, he had no equals. Outrageous in his simplistic faith from the beginning of the decade to the end, he declared as early as 1790 that the revolutionary cause was so irresistible that aristocrats would willingly give up their titles to win "popular favor." "Liberty is a plant of quick growth," he observed, "takes root in a short time, and spreads rapidly." Only a few weeks later, he was regretting that "liberty has met with so many difficulties and obstructions to oppose her wherever she has set up her standard."[9] The tactic of proclaiming a pretended consensus on the easy reformation of mankind, and then feigning disbelief when such reformation occurred more slowly than anticipated also remained a consistent element of his style. On other occasions his francophilism showed at a superficial level, as when he proclaimed the National Assembly superior to England's Parliament because many men spoke in the Assembly and few in Parliament.[10]

Yet until mid-1791, most Americans were only too willing to tolerate and even support Bache's kind of simplistic and boyish optimism. The establishment of factions and popular clubs in France, the flight of the émigrés, and conspiratorial attempts to bolster the monarchy through foreign aid, ended the happy consensus surrounding the moderate, bourgeois reformist revolution. It also meant the sudden need on Bache's part to explain how division could arise in France and thus challenge his faith in the irresistible and inevitable reformation of mankind. In 1791 he defined factional divisions quite simply. One party, the "Friends of the Constitution" (not to be confused with the Jacobins), were in the majority in the Assembly and among the people at large, he claimed. The other two parties were the "Aristocrats" and the "Mad Democrats," both of whom desired anarchy in order to reach their ends. Then, without warrant, he predicted the rapid extinction of parties in France and a return to perfect unity.[11]

From here on, Bache clung to the notion that there was collective agreement among all persons left or made fully free to see and pursue their interest. Like other eighteenth-century men who believed in individual agency, Bache was capable of ascribing any disruption of his millennial vision to conspiracies promulgated by France's internal and external enemies. The King's attempted flight from France and his capture at Varennes on June 25, 1791 were explained by the "weakness" of the King and the "wickedness" of the Queen. But above all, Bache wanted to emphasize "the absolute tranquility which reigned in Paris when the news of his flight was universally spread, and the perfect order preserved upon his entry into the capital."[12] Echoing Paine's condemnation of Burke for pitying the plumage rather than the dying bird, Bache attacked British newspapers for always bemoaning the king's misfortune in being held captive by the revolutionaries, noting that twenty-five million Frenchmen had suffered harder miseries for centuries. The French people were congratulated again for their moderate and generous policy toward Louis. Although Bache hedged his bets by declaring the right of France to execute Louis XVI, Bache further claimed that European states that anticipated the King's execution as an excuse to invade had been foiled by French magnanimity. Six months later, he was pleased to announce that Louis's affirmation of the new Constitution had again brought the king into conformity with "the spirit of the times."[13]

But Louis's adoption of the Constitution in September 1791, and the subsequent establishment of the new Legislative Assembly, were not the final resolutions that Bache might have anticipated. Prussia and Austria still loomed as future external foes, while internally the factional divisions promised continued dissension among Feuillants, Constitutionalists, the radical Jacobins, and their more moderate Girondist brothers in the Assembly. Bache's reaction to the external threat was bold and childishly naive. Austria would not be able to force on the French people a new constitution acceptable to Leopold and Louis because,

> If it came to this, the French need only say to the German troops—Had you rather die all slaves, than live all free men; and they will turn about and proceed towards Vienna, there to assist in framing a Constitution for themselves—taking as fundamental principles, the rights of men, rejecting the pretended rights of sovereigns when incompatible with the first, and teach Leopold, that Sovereignty is in the People, and Kings are only Kings as long as it is the interest of the People that they should be Kings.

He stretched credulity again a month later, claiming the French government under the new constitutional monarchy was so secure that most Europeans would recognize it. The only enemies France faced were three thousand servile and insolent émigrés who, camped on the border, were furtively searching for a chance to restore the monarchy.[14]

Bache's hollow predictions were wrong. Fearing a conspiracy among Leopold, Louis, the Queen, and the émigrés, the Girondists convinced the Assembly to isolate Austria and to rally popular support for revolution outside France's boundaries. On April 20, 1792, France declared war on Austria and invaded Belgium. Austria, joined by Prussia, then formed coalition armies under the Duke of Brunswick. Issuing a manifesto on July 25 threatening severe retribution on the French people if they harmed the King and Queen, Brunswick struck the line neatly between the maintenance of monarchism and the sovereignty of the people, rallying liberal sentiment throughout the western world against the coalition. But on the battlefield the coalition prevailed through the summer. By August 19, Brunswick had entered France. Facing imminent defeat and incited by Brunswick's manifesto, French revolutionaries under General Dumouriez proceeded to turn back Austria and Prussia at Valmy on September 20, driving on from there to invade Belgium and occupy the left bank of the Rhine. This dramatic victory re-ignited revolutionary enthusiasms worldwide. With Prussia and Austria preoccupied with Russia over the partition of Poland, France basked in its revolutionary success for a brief period in late 1792 and early 1793.[15]

The war caused Bache to sober up. In June, relying on news already almost two months old and apparently not fully informed about the European theater, Bache published a prospectus on the coming conflict. Like the Girondists, he felt the war might produce a "general Revolution" in Europe. He accurately predicted an Austrian-Prussian alliance and concluded that France would strike quickly in the Austrian Netherlands where "the spirit of liberty" would aid in French liberation. He admitted that France had "most to fear from the want of experienced officers; but all to hope from the justice of her cause, and the patriotism of her citizens."[16]

Through the summer and fall of 1792, Bache was primarily occupied trying to argue that France was not being defeated. In July, he tried to convince readers that France was on the offensive, while hoping that Americans would show their "patriotic gratitude" to France by sending "two thousand of our hardy and valiant woodsmen" to aid and instruct the French armies in the art of Indian warfare. A month later he was arguing that the coalition appeared "more formidable" than it really was, that world revolution remained imminent, and that French armies were beginning to combine "order and system" with their "ardent love of liberty."[17] In September, while analyzing likely consequences of Brunswick's manifesto, he admitted for the first time that "Jacobin rabble" might execute the King and drive some moderates away from the Revolution. But, he claimed, such an act would strengthen the republican party and unite the nation against the "inroads of the conspirators." Admitting that negotiation and stalling tactics would serve France best, and acknowledging that the disturbances in Paris, the violence of party, weak armies on the frontier, and a lack of ministers hampered French success, Bache nevertheless returned to his blind faith in liberty and the rights of man:

> Take another view of the picture; examine the justice of the French Cause— that of freedom; the base motives of the invaders—to forge chains for thousands; compare the situation of the French with the situation of this country at the commencement of the war here; the manifesto of the commander in chief of the conspiring forces with the proclamation of General Burgoyne, view the effects of our glorious struggle,—then need we one moment doubt the issue of a contest between Liberty and Despotism. That hand which enabled us to surmount every difficulty under every disadvantage, will support the French and bring confusion on the enemies of the RIGHTS OF MAN.[18]

Not learning of the cannonade of Valmy until December, 1792, Bache and his correspondents continued to hammer away at old themes: revolutionary patriotism, the justice of the French cause, and unity among the people. Exasperated at battlefield losses, Bache again compared Brunswick to Burgoyne in December, claiming the coalition could not occupy and hold every town, and calling on reasonable persons to realize that four million "free men . . . all fired with a divine enthusiasm," must certainly be able to defend their own country against 400,000 Austrians, Russians, and Prussians.[19]

On December 16, one day after reporting the French victory at Valmy, Bache proudly pointed out how his newspaper had kept faith in the power of the French people and the justice of the revolutionary cause. He predicted that if Brunswick were completely thrown out of France, the "liberty pole" might soon be planted in the Austrian Netherlands. "Then the winter will brew wonders," he added, "and in the spring the flame of liberty will burst forth in more than one spot hitherto devoted to the tyranny of kings."[20]

While Bache fought a holding action against the specter of French defeat in 1792, he tried to keep pace with and justify the turbulent internal changes in France. The Girondists' enthusiasm for war had begun to ruin their influence, and throughout the summer of 1792 both the Parisian proletariat and the rural peasantry became more enamored with the patriotic frenzy of more radical Jacobins like Marat, Danton, and Robespierre. On August 10, 1792, these more radical elements, filled with suspicion of the monarchy, caused the imprisonment of the King, and the elevation of the Paris commune to dominance over the Assembly. The popular revolution had begun. More radical Jacobins began to supplant fumbling Girondists, who were increasingly associated with war and even with royalism. In September, universal manhood suffrage was instituted, the Republic was proclaimed, the National Convention replaced the Legislative Assembly, and Danton headed a new executive council (which in effect constituted provisional leadership before the establishment of the Committee of Public Safety in April, 1793). By November, 1792 the new regime, still adherent to many Girondist principles, invited the world to throw off the monarchical yoke.[21]

As early as June, 1792, Bache defended the Jacobins (the Mountain remaining a minority, after all, in a party that also included the Girondists). Anticipating his later view of the Democratic Societies, he argued that although the Jacobins were a faction, a club designed to exert political influence outside the regular channels of authority, they were legitimate. They were really friends of the Constitution, a "majority of the leading men in the nation" belonged to it, and their actions were purely reformist. Bache calmly observed that in France "Ministers are changed, the views of the society are fulfilled, decisive measures are adopted; the opposition of the Jacobins will die away, until a fresh cause calls it into action." Continuing to receive his news two months late, in mid-summer he discovered five classes of people in France: the nobility and clergy, dupes of the nobility and clergy, and those who would lose property through the Revolution stood in opposition; in support of the Revolution stood two-thirds of the population, pure republicans who disavowed party politics, and certain zealous patriots who—though some were troublemakers—were "true friends to liberty and equality." Popular satisfaction with the Revolution prevailed, he contended, for few from the common classes emigrated from Paris to America in contrast to the flood of like emigrants from England and Ireland.[22]

American reactions to the August Revolution were not negative before the spring of 1793 even in the Federalist press. Fenno and Russell could still agree with Bache's claim in October that "the cause of the French is still that of humanity—is still the cause of freedom."[23] But Bache continued to make the same predictive errors he had in the past. In January 1793 he foresaw a new French constitution and administration establishing peace and tranquility. The King would be tried and found guilty but permitted to live; the Queen's "disappointed ambitions," however, would lead to her execution. Revolutionary excesses might remain for awhile, "but with them [the French] the reign of revolutions is over." Yet, as Bache waited for it to be "over," he and his editorialists routinely defended violence and turmoil as the natural consequence and vestige of centuries of despotic monarchy. Before the execution of Louis and Marie Antoinette became the issue of the day, Bache was primarily worried about two things. First, he was troubled by Lafayette's alienation from the Revolution and thus admitted condemnations of the French into the *General Advertiser* for forgetting Lafayette's contributions to republicanism. And, second, while congratulating Boston's citizens for celebrating French successes at home and abroad, he was troubled about how this stood in "striking contrast to the indifference and coldness with which the news has generally been received at the seat of the federal government."[24]

Although the execution of Louis in January, 1793 did divide American public opinion and ended sympathy for the Revolution from its weakest American supporters, it was not as significant an element in deciding sides as has often been suggested. At one end of the spectrum, lukewarm Federalist supporters of France had been fretting since the Fall of 1792 about the King's predicament. At the other end, Jefferson privately praised the end of monarchy, although he was troubled after the execution by continued violence since he feared this would cause a corresponding increase in the "zealous apostles of English despotism" in America.[25] Bache's views were close to Jefferson's, although it is important to note that he did not yet link the rising threat of "English despotism" to the execution as had Jefferson. Bache privately confided to his father,

> I have great hopes that the French for humanity sake, not for the sake of royalty, will forbear sacrificing Louis & Antoinette to their just vengeance; but from the drift of the English prints it appears and it seems to be your opinion that they must die martyres in a bad cause.

These were the sentiments that Thomas Paine, unbeknownst to Bache, was about to fight for in the National Convention in a courageous and dangerous attempt to save Louis's life. Richard Bache, writing to his son from

England, also expressed his appreciation for Paine's "humane American" attitude in voting against Louis's execution.[26]

When news of the execution reached America, the *General Advertiser* began a long series of articles on the King's trial and execution. The need to be politic plus genuine ambivalence probably encouraged Bache to publish editorials on both sides of the issue. "Cato" apologized for the execution, claiming that any private citizen committing the crimes for which Louis was guilty would have been executed, while asserting that sympathy for royalty was unbecoming behavior for republicans. On the other hand, "L." believed Louis could have been imprisoned, reminded Americans of the gratitude they owed that monarch, and accused any who applauded the execution of having a "heart of stone."[27]

Bache's concern about, and extensive coverage of, Louis's demise ended by April. On April 24, employing the largest type font he would ever set for his newspaper, Bache published the new republican constitution of France, the so-called Constitution of 1793. But the Constitution also quickly receded as the issue of the moment with France's declaration of war on Great Britain and Holland in February, 1793; the further rise of the Mountain; the defection of Charles François Dumouriez, France's leading general, to the Austrians; the establishment of the Committee of Public Safety in April, 1793; Robespierre's ascension to power; and the introduction of the Terror.[28]

Impending prospects of the war, France's moral and political justification in declaring war, England's weaknesses and corruption, and the expanded war's implications for America became the compelling topics for Bache in the first half of 1793. In January, Richard had informed his son that the British ministry was so "high-toned" that war was "inevitable." A month later, not knowing war had been declared, Benjamin's father speculated that the English were arming to protect the Dutch or to stop the diffusion of revolutionary principles; in either case, he claimed, a large majority of Englishmen opposed interfering with France. And in April he finally announced the opening of the war with the ominous observation that, "How far the event of war will prove either favourable or unfavourable to our interests, will depend upon the prudence of our government."[29]

From April on, Bache attempted to undermine support for England. England was so repressive, Bache claimed, that Englishmen could not safely admit they had ever read Paine's works. A correspondent argued that England had never fought a war for noble purposes but was an "intolerant, proud, illiberal, sullen, revengeful" country. In subsequent editorials, a litany of English cruelties from the seventeenth century through the American Revolution were exposed. Meanwhile, Bache tried to suggest that Britain was paying the price for her attitude against France and revolutionary principles: manufacturers were going bankrupt; English markets were failing; the government needed a loan; and unemployment was rampant.[30]

Renewed attempts were made to prop up the cause of France. Bache squarely defended France's justification in declaring war first and in playing the role of aggressor. "Must they [the French] wait till the British Court had ripened their measures to attack them with success?" he asked. An extract from another source put the case succinctly. "It is not against Frenchmen that Europe is combined; but against the great principles of Freedom." "Because the French have beheaded their king, and because massacres have taken place in Paris," Bache added, "are we to abandon that nation, or condemn the justice of their cause?"[31] Other writers placed their faith in France's popular army and its do-or-die policies. The more problematic issues of anarchy and violence in France were swept aside again as vestigial cruelties produced by monarchy and aristocracy in general before the Revolution, and by the King and Queen in particular during it. Dumouriez's defection was handled unconvincingly with a similar reliance on conjecture. Bache claimed Dumouriez's personal principles had changed, not the principles in the Convention or among the people. Another writer claimed the defection of France's hero of Valmy was a victory over despotism and over those who hoped to restore monarchy.[32]

By mid-1793, Bache had defended the French Revolution with unremitting devotion. His periodic predictions for the impending end of the Revolution demonstrated his ignorance of the dynamism of radical political change. His attempt to proclaim the unity of true republicans in France rang more and more hollow as time passed. Yet he never doubted the monumental significance of the French Revolution for the world as a whole. In July, 1793, he summarized his broad view of the situation, a view undoubtedly shared by all American radical republicans.

> Upon the establishment or overthrow of liberty in France probably will depend the permanency of the Republic in the new world. It is not very absurd to suppose that if complete success attends the arms of the combined powers, that they will endeavor directly or indirectly totally to extinguish the fire of freedom in every part of the globe; hence this country is much deeper concerned in the politics of the European world than might appear to a superficial observer.[33]

Bache was "deeper concerned" than most. But neither his perception of European affairs nor his understanding of a proper basis for relations among nations gave him any acuity of vision as to how the United States should conduct itself. Bache was in good company. Aside from Hamilton, who by inclination and understanding refused to consider any evolutionary potential of the modern law of nations, most Americans possessed vague and imprecise notions about how the United States should act to remain "friendly" or "impartial" or "neutral." They were unclear about the relationship between treaty obligations and impartiality, between commerce and military alliances, and between executive and congressional authority in foreign affairs. Only Hamilton, blending his own definition of American self-interest with a passionate dislike for the French Revolution, was cold and calculating enough to advocate complete neutrality, non-recognition of the new French Republic, and at least a temporary suspension of the Alliance of 1778 with France. Others were less clear. Washington desired non-entanglement, an apparently fluid concept that became more restrictively anti-French in his eyes as time passed. John Adams had called for an "honest neutrality," whatever that was, since early 1790.[34]

Jefferson, Madison, Monroe, and most of their political friends advocated impartiality as well. Jeffersonian sophisticates may have comprehended the advanced theory of separating commercial affairs, long blamed as a cause for war, from political and military alliance, but they did not conceptualize that theory clearly in 1793 nor did their supporters harbor any more than a vague understanding of the concept. In the Cabinet debates preceding the President's proclamation, Jefferson stood alone in questioning the constitutional authority of the executive initiative in this foreign policy area (although he quietly acquiesced), and never managed to exact any favoritism for France from his colleagues. A jumble of complexities, the idealist Jefferson foresaw a "benevolent neutrality" and resisted any abrogation of treaty obligations, while the realist Jefferson wanted to retain the capacity to apply or withhold neutral status as a bargaining element with the belligerents—hence his double impulse to exclude the word "neutral" from the Proclamation. No wonder other Jeffersonians, even Madison and Monroe—both of whom favored impartiality but opposed a neutrality that would antagonize France—were somewhat timid in their initial reactions. Only with the press debate between Madison ("Helvedius") and Hamilton ("Pacificus") could the essential rift between sentiment for and against France appear. Washington's pledge on April 22, 1793 of "conduct friendly and impartial toward the belligerent powers" thereby served many interpretations.[35]

General Advertiser editorials innocently embraced neutrality well before the Proclamation, although Bache and his writers assumed, as did many other ordinary citizens, that neutrality would not interfere with continued friendship and gratitude toward France. Thus, in February, Bache reported an anniversary celebration of the 1778 alliance. But later he confidently claimed that "Policy incontestably dictates a strict neutrality on our part," while speculating how far the French Treaty might militate against America's "best interests." The following day, trying to set the table for a pro-French neutrality, he predicted that France would declare her West Indies islands independent when war with Britain began, releasing the United States from its obligation to protect and defend France's sugar islands.[36] Yet, three days after Washington's proclamation was announced, Bache claimed he was "relieved" to learn that existing treaties did not stand in the way of peace.

> It is extremely happy for this country, that no treaty exists interfering with the system of neutrality which it is our interest to keep at the present juncture. Had we been obliged to take part with the French our pecuniary resources would have been impaired by a diminution of our imports, and the credit of the United States would have sustained a proportionate shock. A great happiness it is, that our plighted faith does not stand in the way of those arrangements on which our credit is supported, and that while Europe is rent by the fiend of war, we can nurse the bantling in the arms of peace.[37]

For almost three months the *Advertiser* supported the proclamation. Editorials flowed from the press emphasizing France's generosity in not insisting on protection for her West Indian islands; castigating war as an unthinkable alternative to impartiality; describing in gloomy detail the chaotic effect war would have on the American economy; suggesting that America was too weak militarily to aid the French effectively; and supporting the wisdom of the President's proclamation.[38] Implicit throughout was a neutrality (generally not referred to as such after the proclamation) that was friendly to France and that also supported the inviolability of treaties and the unspoken certainty that if the United States were dragged into war it would be on the side of France.

The arrival of the new French minister, Edmond Genet, did not cause Bache to revoke these innocent views but it did change his definition of neutrality. Above all, it supercharged his already keen enthusiasm for France. Genet's character, ideology, and purpose combined to support and further Bache's prejudices. Labeled an "upstart" with "more genius than ability" by Gouverneur Morris, Genet was an energetic, enthusiastic, pretentious dilettante—not unlike Bache. His middle-class background, his privileged associations (his father had met Franklin and Adams in France, and Genet's advancements had come through personal patronage), his love of music and dance and hot-air balloons, his abilities as a translator, and his temperament and "superficial education" which resulted in a lack of "steadiness of application," were personal characteristics strikingly similar to Bache's. As a product of Girondist *mentalité*, Genet was religiously wedded to the immediate sovereignty of the people and, like Bache, could not comprehend most constitutional and structural interferences with that sovereignty.

More an American Girondin than a Jacobin, Bache shared with Genet and the Girondists the vision of a world revolution of sovereign peoples. Although he may not have completely supported the French strategy of clandestinely exciting western filibusters into Louisiana, Florida, and Canada—a strategy embodied first in Genet's instructions—Bache did support at one time or another Genet's other instructions: to create a new treaty based on the need to extend the "Empire of Liberty"; to remind Americans that the fate of republicanism in the United States depended on its success in the old world; and to obtain compliance with Articles 17, 21, and 22 of the Treaty of Commerce and Amity while not invoking provisions of the 1778 treaty of alliance to defend each other's territory. Bache probably even cooperated with the French foreign ministry in publishing anonymous pieces to counteract pro-English propaganda. When Genet later tried to vindicate his conduct through publishing his correspondence, Bache published and sold that correspondence. And, much later, when Bache traveled to New York to attack the Jay Treaty, he went out of his way to visit his Girondist colleague.[39]

With Genet's arrival imminent in April and May, 1793, Jefferson and his colleagues anxiously hoped for an expression of affection and gratitude for France from the American people, while Hamilton worked to separate affection for Louis XVI's *ancien régime* from Genet's republic. In helping to effect this Jeffersonian reception, Bache attempted to rival Freneau on something other than the French Revolution per se. As early as April 11 a writer in the *Advertiser* predicted that Genet's arrival would be saluted by cannon, and urged all true republicans to display the tri-color and all women to wear patriotic ribbons and emblems in their hair as a way of showing American affection "in the noblest of all causes, the success of our French allies; who are giving up all that is near and dear to them for the general interests of human nature." "A Freeman" subsequently took up the more disagreeable task of claiming the government would prohibit a cannon salute. This was not surprising, he added, "for France is not only waging war against the despotism of monarchy, but the despotism of aristocracy, and it would appear rather uncommon to see men welcoming the ambassador of republicans who are warring their darling Aristocracy."[40]

Genet's unexpected landing at Charleston delayed his arrival in Philadelphia and added difficulty to the task that Bache had clearly left for himself—to bring popular sentiment for Genet and the Republic to its peak upon that arrival. To emphasize American enthusiasm for France, Bache declared on May 2 that the "whole city" had expectantly turned out to welcome the French privateer *L'Embuscade,* on which Genet was thought to be a passenger. Already developing the "politico"'s keen sense for a public opinion numbers game, Bache emphasized that "the wharves were lined with our citizens." But the ship did not arrive that day. When it did arrive a day late, Bache noted the thirteen-gun salute it received and how the ship was "ornamented with many republican emblems."[41] On the eve of Genet's arrival, Bache carried full details concerning the time and place of embarkation as well as expected salutes, celebrations, and addresses. When Genet entered the city from an unexpected direction on May 16, it did not dampen Bache's optimism, especially when Genet responded with such warmth and gratitude to the reception. Bache concluded,

> The crowds of citizens that flocked from every avenue of this city to meet the ambassador at Gray's ferry was a proof to him that the Pennsylvanians are not behind hand with their fellow citizens of other states. We have no doubt that the affability and popularity of Citizen Genet will gain him the esteem of the inhabitants of this county and city, and awaken in them sentiments of gratitude for our generous allies, the defenders of the rights of man.

Jefferson was pleased, and estimated that at least one thousand people received the French minister. Hamilton tried to suggest that the reception was only half as large as Jeffersonian enthusiasts claimed.[42]

Through May and June, as Genet cavalierly issued commissions for privateers, authorized his consuls to decide prize cases, interpreted the 1778 treaty broadly in favor of France, plotted a filibuster against New Orleans with the aid of George Rogers Clark and discontented westerners, and arrogantly assumed that the immediate sovereignty of the people supported his actions against executive restraints, Bache continued to feed Genet's infatuation and self-deception. Two days after Genet's arrival, Bache reported the address of the French Benevolent Society to Genet with

Genet's reply, promising at the same time to publish news of other Philadelphia celebrations "as proofs of gratitude, patriotism and liberality that
do honor to the American character." On May 20, he published the addresses of a committee headed by Rittenhouse and Charles Biddle, and of
the German Republican Society, with Genet's replies, all contrived to sway
American opinion. Three days after more than a hundred people celebrated
Genet's arrival publicly at Oeller's Tavern on May 18, Bache reported the
entire proceedings—all fifteen toasts, an ode written by Peter Du Ponceau,
the singing of the Marseillaise, and Genet's rendition of a patriotic song in
honor of the sailors of *L'Embuscade*. Subsequent addresses and celebrations
were reported faithfully to sustain the impression of unanimity behind the
French cause.[43] Although the evidence is circumstantial, Bache and Genet
almost certainly spoke with one another in these early months and undoubtedly contributed to each other's exaggerated expectations for Franco-
American comity and mutual interest.

Bache did far less well trying to defend Genet in the diplomatic crisis that
ensued. In mid-May he defended Genet's issuance of commissions to
privateers with the ridiculously inappropriate argument that Genet was
merely following instructions. On the other hand, when the administration
tried to prosecute the American Gideon Henfield for enlisting on a French
privateer, the *General Advertiser* failed to embrace the liberal and correct
legal argument that Henfield was not restrained by any American statute
from such an enlistment. Instead, Bache backed off, acquiescing to the
administration's view that such actions threatened American neutrality and
peace, and thereby losing the groundswell of support for Henfield, who re-
enlisted with the French and was even given a public dinner. Bache's desire
to woo the administration and his consistent emphasis on republicans
fighting the same cause but in individual nationalist garb, were at the root
of some of these tactics. But confusion and uncertainty were also factors.
For example, Bache frequently published only straightforward summaries
on privateering incidents, prize cases, or recruitment problems, simply
promising on one occasion to report "any question which may in the least
degree appear to implicate . . . neutrality."[44]

As events would prove, Bache was not being warned off from Genet by
Jefferson, who as early as late June and early July was telling Monroe and
Madison that Genet's conduct was "indefensible" and his ministry beyond
rescue. In June Jefferson had already denied to Genet a broad definition of
rights for privateers and disposal of prizes in American ports, and in early
July Genet had already threatened, in the presence of A. J. Dallas and

Jefferson, to appeal to the people over the President. Bache was apparently not on intimate enough terms with Jefferson at this time to know the magnitude of the diplomatic rift. Instead, Bache was swimming upstream, re-directing the *General Advertiser* toward even more uniform support for Genet. In early July, one writer bitterly contested the administration's seizure of the *William,* a prize captured and sold by the French in early June: the ship was kept under government seizure for a month as the administration tried to determine if it was a legitimate prize. This writer condemned the administration for secrecy and for trying to return the vessel to the British without public knowledge. Such actions, he concluded, revealed the "coolness" of the administration toward France, and the "fear or favoritism" it showed toward Britain and Spain.[45]

The case of the *Little Sarah,* a prize reported captured in the *Advertiser* on April 30 and subsequently outfitted as the privateer *Petite Démocrate,* caused the unraveling of the complex strands that held together American neutrality and Franco-American relations. It also marked the great dividing line in the emergence of Bache's political opposition to the administration. Although Genet had been told by Jefferson in May that the United States would not allow the outfitting of privateers in American ports or the condemnation of prizes in those ports by French consuls, Genet had never acceded to Jefferson's "interpretation" of the 1778 treaty, nor to what he saw as a new and peculiar definition of neutrality that appeared to abrogate treaty provisions, nor to the concept that the executive, rather than Congress, could have such authority over treaties. Genet was on dubious ground in boldly asserting the rights of French consuls in prize cases and in interpreting the limits of executive authority (or even assuming the right to do so). But he was also confused by an American policy not fully articulated, and one that took liberties in its interpretation of Article XXII regarding privateers. That article prohibited privateers of enemies of either France or the United States from outfitting in either French or American ports but did not necessarily prohibit French or American outfitting. And the administration was not clear about the extent of American waters or jurisdiction or what, therefore, constituted a legitimate prize, finally allowing France prizes condemned before June 5.[46]

Yet while the public remained ignorant of this diplomatic turmoil, the administration remained ignorant of the gradual outfitting of the *Little Sarah* into a new privateer, the *Petite Démocrate.* Only on July 6 did Governor Mifflin become alarmed and inform Jefferson of the impending departure of a French privateer leaving an American port. Jefferson assigned Dallas the task of asking Genet to detain the vessel. It was at this meeting that Genet refused to agree and threatened to carry his case to the people over the President. A day later, Genet exploded in rage at Jefferson as the two men disagreed again over constitutional authority and the inviolability of treaties. By July 8, informed by Jefferson on some aspects of the Genet affair, Hamilton, Knox, and a delegation of Philadelphia merchants urged military detention of the *Petite Démocrate,* a move that Jefferson considered extreme. On July 10, Jefferson assembled a packet of documents for the President on the affair including the suggestion that Genet would appeal to the people, which Washington, just returned from Mount Vernon, received on July 11.[47]

On July 10, Bache belatedly reported the intentions of the merchants to stop the ship from sailing (the *Petite Démocrate* had already slipped down the bay to Chester on July 9). The following day, "Brother Tory," posing as a conspiring anglophile, began the assault on the administration. Sarcastically commenting on how things were getting better and better in the United States, he claimed he had found it "necessary to smother emotions of gratitude, silence justice, mislead the national interest, destroy treaties the most sacred," and lull the people to sleep. In the end, he had prepared "the public mind to receive that great work of darkness, that specimen of the crooked policy of courts, the President's proclamation." With it, he concluded, a French prize had been kept from leaving port even though the French had a perfect treaty right to take it out of port. Another writer, perhaps aware that the administration had asked the Supreme Court for a ruling on the extent of French treaty rights, argued that the United States had no right to decide unilaterally in the case. He concluded with the *Advertiser*'s new interpretation of the proclamation and the treaty:

> If the right is acknowledged to outfit ships to be given by the treaty of alliance, of consequence the permission of exercising that right is no breach of neutrality. As for contravening the President's proclamation, the merchants might have known that any proclamation is merely a declaration which owes its little force to the laws, and if it is contrary to treaties, the supreme law of the land, is a perfect nullity.[48]

Bache had quickly severed support for the administration and embraced Genet's interpretation of the treaty, neutrality, and constitutional authority in foreign policy application. On July 12, "A Jacobin" summarized the matter, declaring that Washington intended to nullify the French Treaty in opposition to the will of Congress and the people. He charged the President's proclamation with "changing the sacred treaty between the French and Americans into a treaty between the Federal Government and the king of England." He then offered an extended analysis of the French treaty, arguing that Article XXII gave France the right to arm ships in American ports, and that Article XVII guaranteed the condemnation and sale of prizes in America. In defiance of the Treaty, however, the executive had detained French privateers, had seized prizes at the last minute before sale and without explanation, and had allowed British ships but not French ones to arm in American ports. Fenno's *Gazette* immediately denied these charges, claiming that the treaty had been intentionally written in ambiguous language to allow for later interpretations, while adding that the treaty had never been, as "A Jacobin" wanted it, an "explicitly offensive treaty."[49]

Already successfully rivaling Freneau's *National Gazette*, Bache closed the *Little Sarah* affair by reprinting an exchange between "Juba" and "Metellus" (a pseudonym employed by Hamilton) from Freneau's paper. "Juba" erroneously claimed that the *Little Sarah* had once been a British ship that the United States government had allowed to arm in an American port. But as a French ship she had been prevented from sailing in contravention of the Treaty. Hoping to disclose the perfidy of administration policy, Bache reprinted "Metellus"'s inflexible position. Hamilton denied that the *Little Sarah* had ever been a warship with the British, and was adamant in denying the French any right to arm ships in American ports. He further attacked "Juba" for calling the militia dupes of the administration in trying to keep French prizes in American ports. Finally, "Metellus" undoubtedly guaranteed Bache's enmity by concluding that the time would soon arise when Americans would have to support a government of their own choice, "or submit to a new order of things forced upon them by JUBA, VERITAS [one of Freneau's pseudonyms], a JACOBIN, little BEN BADGE [Bache], the translator of foreign languages [Freneau], and other numerous descendants of the first declaimer and remonstrator upon record."[50]

Although the *Little Sarah* case marked the *General Advertiser*'s final separation from the administration, it fast receded from public view. Meanwhile, Bache's writers had already begun forming a partisan phalanx which charged the administration with divorcing France and marrying Great Britain. In late May, writers attacked the "insolence" and brutality of British sailors assaulting French sailors on Philadelphia's streets. From mid-June through early July, correspondents further predicted an arrogant, unlawful attack on American shipping by the British. The British, they implied, wished to embarrass American trade and did not respect modern principles of neutrality. "Brutus," anticipating more extreme arguments of 1794, even advocated war against Britain if the British tried to seize neutral goods going to France, and "A Farmer" argued that British possession of the western posts was in and of itself an act of war.[51]

During the *Little Sarah* crisis, *Advertiser* writers spent much time trying to prop the French cause. Most played on American sentiments, morality, or fears, although some did stress treaties, laws, and logic. A popular argument, usually implied but sometimes stated outright, was that Americans owed gratitude to France for aiding American independence. This argument was embellished by an emphasis on France's continued friendship and her generosity in not demanding execution of the treaty. Yet, as one writer declared on July 11, "Many persons in this country, republicans merely by chance or avowed enemies of democracy have stepped forth the champion of political perfidy, and have generously endeavored to convince their countrymen that they are not bound to favor the French cause in any manner whatever."[52] When a writer in a rival paper claimed the French treaty was buried in the grave with Louis XVI, Bache lost his temper and exclaimed, "Well said political honesty and gratitude!" Using Solon's definition of good government as that in which an injury done to one citizen is seen as an insult to the whole community, Bache raised the specter of French retaliation: "What must that government be, which suffers insult to be added to injury, & permits both to remain not only unpunished but unnoticed?" "A Republican" called the proclamation a "fire-brand" which would ignite divisions in the country, and claimed it would become a "party word." With England applauding neutrality and the French seeing neutrality as an insult and breach of the treaty, the government, the *Advertiser* predicted, would waver; war with France would eventually ensue, America would turn to England for military support, and England would again enslave America.[53]

In late July Hamilton counter-attacked against Genet, Bache, and Freneau. Believing the *Advertiser*'s "A Jacobin" letters were authored by Genet (as they may have been), Hamilton began a series called "No Jacobin" which attempted to finish the job of discrediting Genet. Allowed to use government documents, Hamilton proceeded to manipulate public opinion in a manner that he denied was legitimate for Genet or others. Disclosing both Genet's silly insolence and his threat to appeal to the people, Hamilton succeeded. Public meetings and resolutions condemning Genet flowed from Boston and elsewhere in New England, from New York (through the influence of Rufus King and John Jay) and Virginia, where John Marshall rallied the opposition. Madison and Monroe offered counter-resolutions couched in the vague language of gratitude for France, but only John Taylor of Caroline was able to get resolutions of a radical nature passed—negative ones that declared that the Proclamation of Neutrality was driving America "closer to union with Britain." The Jeffersonians failed in their defense even in the South. Genet, distracted during some of the summer and fall with the need to prove himself to the new Jacobin foreign affairs minister, with his filibuster operations, and with the arrival of the French fleet in New York, kept a lower profile. While occasionally fêted by now more subdued supporters, he remained ignorant of the American government's decision on August 1 to have his recall discreetly engineered.[54]

Facing a crisis nearly equal to those he would later encounter in the XYZ affair, yet still a novice in partisan conflict, Bache did not fare well trying to defend Genet and France in the last five months of 1793. But the "No Jacobin" letters did offer him the opportunity to redefine his political position for his readership. Although "No Jacobin" had sent him communications, Bache declared that they were unsuitable for printing. He had printed "Metellus" essays before, he admitted, but "No Jacobin" went too far in attacking the "inviolable" character of a foreign minister and his charges were "totally unfounded."

> Our ideas of 'a free and impartial press,' however are so widely different from those of our correspondent, that we should hold ourselves unjustifiable in publishing injurious personal charges, against a private citizen or even a governmental officer, when we knew such charges to be false. Neither do we conceive it to be consistent with our duty to bring before the tribunal of the American public, the character or conduct of a foreign minister, over whom they have neither jurisdiction nor controul.

Bache insisted that he still conducted a free press—one where both sides of great public questions might be aired: "To a free and impartial investigation . . . this paper is always open."[55] But from this time on, unwilling to recognize the legitimacy of his "aristocratic" opposition, Bache showed no qualms about narrowing his definition of impartiality within the paradigm of democratic, pro-French republicanism.

Bache's correspondents largely fell silent regarding Genet in the late summer and fall. A few offered editorials trying to retrieve lost support by defending neutrality in very general terms, but there were no spirited essays. Bache quietly reported some naval and privateer activities. But he also remained loyal to Genet. He reprinted the New York letter in which Jay and King, using information given them by Hamilton, claimed that Genet intended to appeal to the people over the President's head. He then reprinted two others in rebuttal. One claimed that Jay and King had been unspecific in their charges. The other anticipated Dallas's claim in December that Genet simply meant he would appeal to Congress, not to the people directly. A week later, Bache republished Genet's letter to Washington in which Genet denied the appeal statement, charging certain persons with trying to undermine French-American relations. Bache finally offered the feeble argument that those who proclaimed Genet guilty of bad conduct for trying to by-pass the President were themselves guilty of unscrupulous, illegitimate conduct.[56] But, as a letter to his father testified, he was fully aware of the tenor of the times and subscribed to the same dualistic analysis of politics as did other emergent Jeffersonians:

> Our Federal Executive carry things with a high hand. We are all engaged in interpreting our treaty with France. The interpretation put on it by the Secy. of Tr. for the executive is as much narrowed as was possible as far as the French interest is concerned, that is, the British interest has by far outweighted the French with the government, the commercial, the monied interest carries all before it.[57]

The yellow fever outbreak of 1793 provided a tragic climax and interruption to the partisan rift so clearly established in the Genet affair. So potent was the political dimension of life in Philadelphia that even the city's worst health disaster, one that killed as many as 14,000 of its citizens by late October, became an arena for ideological and partisan dispute. Federalists fled the city; Jeffersonian Republicans "dominated relief work" among a lower class that became increasingly impoverished from disruptions in the economy. Federalists argued that the disease was imported by French refugees; Republicans claimed local origins. Federalist "cures" for the disease included quinine bark and wine; Republicans generally clung to Benjamin Rush's ultimate "cure"—purging of the blood. Though predictably disturbed by the flight of the wealthy to the countryside, Bache speculated on many local sources and cures for yellow fever (once advocating lightning rods as a preventative!), attacked Rush's bleeding, and was probably influenced by his stepfather-in-law, Dr. Adam Kuhn, in maintaining an open, if not very carefully analytic, mind. Attempting to prove his courage and his seriousness, Bache stuck it out in the city longer than most who had the chance to escape. He closed down his shop on September 26 and re-opened it again on November 23. In late December, undoubtedly alluding to more than yellow fever, he summed up the crisis as "a most critical time."[58]

With resumption of publication, Bache turned again to the issue of France and a final futile attempt to salvage Genet. Genet himself tried to emphasize France's good intentions in his own bizarre fashion by promising to find and punish "counter-revolutionists" in America, and by promising to investigate and punish any French privateers illegally seizing ships. Bache, meanwhile, offered thin comfort to his readers and stretched the boundaries of truth, by claiming that Genet had not authorized the formation of an armed military force on American territory.[59] On December 6, Bache reprinted from a New York newspaper the repeated charges of Jay and King against Genet. Implicating Dallas and Jefferson for the first time as witnesses to Genet's appeal to the people, Jay and King knew of Jefferson's July 10 summary of his meetings with Genet. They also knew this summary, which could only be released by Jefferson, would damn Genet completely and badly damage Jefferson and the Republican cause. Jefferson refused to be drawn out, although Genet's threat in mid-December to prosecute Jay and King for libel, if it had been carried out, might have forced revelation of the document. Dallas responded in the American press immediately, trying to lessen the damage by claiming that he believed Genet was only intending to appeal to Congress and that, if this did not succeed, Genet planned to publish his appeal and withdraw from the entire issue. Trimming all the way, Dallas denied that he had ever heard Genet say he would appeal from the President to the people.[60] Sympathetic to Genet's belief that foreign policy was an issue for Congress in America just as it was for the National Convention in France, and increasingly sympathetic for direct appeals to public opinion, Bache supported Genet down the line. The same day he published Dallas's letter, Bache declared that commerce and relations with Europe were at a crisis because of the administration's cool policies toward France and its handling of Genet's recall. Bache sarcastically congratulated the President for his "very seasonable" suggestion to place the country in a state of defense.[61]

The big guns deployed in the final defense of Genet were not Bache's. Four long letters by "Cato" from New York claimed that the "enemies of France and freedom have been dragged from their hiding places." Comparing England and France, "Cato" catalogued again the reasons why Americans should support France while listing American grievances against Great Britain. In conclusion, he argued that England went to war with France for either "revenge for the aid she gave to the United States, or aversion to a Republican form of government"; in either case, the United States had an interest in supporting France since England, through her actions, had already proven that she would turn on the United States next.[62] Other editorialists attempted to analyze the progress of the conspiracy. "An Old Soldier" concluded that:

> The minister's principles of republicanism were not in concord with the principles of certain agents of our own; his sentiments were too unadulterated, his conduct too undesigning, his enthusiasm too great, and his probable influence too extensive for the benefit of men, who contemplated a system, at war with the innate principles of freedom.

But he admitted he did not know the cause of this anti-Genet conspiracy, unless Genet was simply "too democratic" for them.[63]

"A Farmer from the Back Settlements" ended the year with a long analysis of the Genet affair, presenting an excellent summary of the political views that had come to separate Bache and his correspondents from the administration. He began by describing the slight impact the French Revolution had made on the minds of American agents and ministers in Europe, especially the minister to France, Gouverneur Morris. And he alluded to the anti-revolutionary, anti-French position of the Vice-President and the Secretary of the Treasury. Genet was well received in Charleston when things were going well for the French Republic, he argued; when they began to go poorly, Genet was "coldly" treated. The proclamation of neutrality that followed was a means of placating the British, as was the interpretation of that document to prevent Americans from enlisting in the French service and in seizing French prizes. But most importantly, the "intimate connections" of blood, commerce, and culture between England and American prevented the development of more intimate ties between France and America. Americans "retained the idea so flattering to our self love, that England was the most powerful, the most enlightened nation, and her government the most perfect that existed in our time." The consequences were destructive. Vestiges of aristocracy and monarchy remained in the Constitution and government; two firm advocates of aristocracy, Adams and Hamilton, attained high public office. Although supporters of Great Britain were appointed to the government, no Frenchman or francophile was appointed. Pro-British prejudices among American diplomats thus combined with an already biased administration to lead the government as a whole to assume that France could not win the war. And, he concluded a day later, the despotic powers would never allow the United

States to remain neutral. The war in Europe was a war against the people and the elective power. Americans should, therefore, supply France with all needed provisions and urge other nations to join the cause as well.[64]

The Genet affair lingered on in scattered editorials after 1793. But by late 1793 Genet was beyond salvage, even for loyalists like Bache. In fact, Genet would represent an early warning of how difficult it would be to defend radical ideals through friendship with France. The twists and turns and terror of the Revolution made it difficult for those less radical than Bache to attach to the great republic their heartfelt hopes for the democratic sovereignty of the people. From 1794 onward France may have received the enthusiastic support of part of the American population, but it was an oppositionist part, far smaller than the more universal support France had received in late 1792 or early 1793. In early 1794 Bache reported a considerable increase in customers as a result of his outspoken republicanism and obvious support of France.[65] But these were readers eager to choose sides. They probably did not represent a net increase in American supporters of France. For the rest of the decade, therefore, Bache was primarily occupied as an apologist for France and only secondarily as a celebrator of French accomplishments.

The events of 1793 had confirmed the political ideology and partisan cause that Bache and his newspaper would support in the future. The French Revolution had produced the panoramic prospect and vision of the sovereignty of the people. Genet's ebullient, outrageous commitment to that vision had given Bache a personal embodiment of that cause to defend. In 1800 a writer in Fenno's *Gazette* caught some of the significance of Genet to Bache.

> Very early after the arrival of Citizen Genet, the facility with which young Bache spoke and translated the French language, independent of his affinity to Monsieur Franklin, recommended him to the notice and the patronage of that factious French Minister. He always had the earliest intelligence of any new commotions in the interior of the French Republic, or of the external victories of their armies. He was the earliest to catch the watch word of the triumphant faction at Paris, and to pass it over through his newspaper to the enamoured partisans of the Republic, here. Civic festivals were continually advertised, and all the Sans Culottes were invited to attend the celebration.[66]

Bache's devotion to the French cause was beyond dispute, but even this writer drew back from an open charge of dependence and sycophancy on Bache's part. Although later charged with being in the pay of France or the

Republicans, Bache, like most other press figures of the 1790s, came to support his cause willingly. Neither Genet nor Jefferson nor anyone else needed to, or could, direct him. And the rhetoric used by those whose ideological consciousness was shaped through the radical Whig and classical republican mind-sets of an earlier era, did not form the dominant mood in the *Advertiser*'s discourse in 1793. Republican zeal and romantic nationalism often pushed radicals beyond their earlier cynicism of conspiracy and sycophancy, ushering in new fears and infatuations. Bache and others were passing from eighteenth-century rationalism into an emotional, strident reductionism, identifying in the elevated self—the new egocentric *moi*—the needs and will of all. Not only was the impulse democratic rather than merely republican, it was emotional rather than merely rational.[67]

Notes

1. Press coverage in America of the French Revolution is detailed in Davis R. Dewey, "The News of the French Revolution in America," *New England Magazine*, I (1887), 84–89; Huntley Dupré, "The Kentucky Gazette Reports the French Revolution," *Mississippi Valley Historical Review*, XXVI (1949), 163–80; Beatrice F. Hyslop, "The American Press and the French Revolution of 1789," *Proceedings of the American Philosophical Society*, CIV (1960), 54–85, and her "American Press Reports of the French Revolution, 1789–1794," *New-York Historical Society Quarterly*, XLII (1958), 329–48. Statements about American failure to analyze the French Revolution carefully, and the subsequent bewilderment displayed by Americans over that revolution, are drawn generally from my own survey of archival manuscript collections in the United States for the 1790s.

2. The Second Great Awakening was, in fact, a Calvinist reaction against deism and the "infidelity" of French revolutionary ideas. New England's view of the French Revolution in general is considered in Ann Butler Lever, "Vox Populi, Vox Dei: New England and the French Revolution, 1787–1801" (unpub. Ph.D. diss., Univ. of North Carolina, 1972). The New England clergy and the Revolution are analyzed well in Gary B. Nash, "The American Clergy and the French Revolution," *William and Mary Quarterly*, XXII (1965), 392–412; Ruth H. Bloch, *Visionary Republic: Millennial Themes in American Thought, 1756–1800* (New York, 1985), esp. 151–209; Nathan O. Hatch, *The Sacred Cause of Liberty: Republican Thought and the Millennium in Revolutionary New England* (New Haven, Conn., 1977), 141–160; and James W. Davidson, "Searching for the Millennium: Problems for the 1790s and the 1970s," *New England Quarterly*, XLV (1972), 241–61.

3. French cultural influences in America are discussed most thoroughly in Howard Mumford Jones, *America and French Culture, 1750–1848* (Chapel Hill, N. C., 1927), and his articles, "The Importance of French Literature in New York City, 1750–1800," *Studies in Philology*, XXVII (1931), 235–51; "The Importance of French Books in Philadelphia, 1750–1800," *Modern Philology*, XXVII (1934), 157–77; Bernard Faÿ, *The Revolutionary Spirit in France and America* (New York,

1927); and Edward G. Everett, "Some Aspects of Pro-French Sentiment in Pennsylvania, 1790–1800," *Western Pennsylvania Historical Magazine,* XLIII (1960), 23–41.

For the impact of the French Revolution in America in general the central work remains Charles D. Hazen, *Contemporary American Opinion of the French Revolution* (Baltimore, 1897). Hazen's title promises a wider scope than his book delivers as he primarily focuses on the reactions to the Revolution by a few prominent Americans. See also Morrell Heald and Lawrence S. Kaplan, *Culture and Diplomacy: The American Experience* (Westport, Conn., 1977), 19–45, as well as scattered references throughout Lawrence Kaplan's many other works; and Ralph L. Ketcham, "France and American Politics, 1763–1793," *Political Science Quarterly,* LXXVIII (1963), 198–223. Richard James Moss, "The American Response to the French Revolution, 1789–1801" (unpub. Ph.D. diss., Michigan State Univ., 1974), makes the psychological argument that the French Revolution caused Americans guilt over their own revolutionary past and the desire to seek order and stability in the 1790s.

4. On Washington see Louis Martin Sears, *George Washington and the French Revolution* (Detroit, 1960); Douglas Southall Freeman, *George Washington. A Biography* (New York, 1954), VI, 237, 325, 327–28. On John Adams's "trembling" see J. Adams to Richard Price, Apr. 19, 1790, Charles Francis Adams, ed., *Works of John Adams,* IX, 563–65, hereafter cited as Adams, ed., *Works of John Adams.* See also J. Adams to Thomas Brand-Hollis, June 11, 1790, and J. Adams to Benjamin Rush, Aug. 28, 1811, *ibid.,* 570, 635; and J. Adams to Thos. Jefferson, July 15, 1813, in Lester Cappon, ed., *The Adams-Jefferson Letters: The Complete Correspondence between Thomas Jefferson and Abigail and John Adams* (Chapel Hill, N. C., 1959), II, 357; and Hazen, *Opinion of the French Revolution,* 152–56.

5. On Hamilton see John C. Miller, *Alexander Hamilton: Portrait in Paradox* (New York, 1959), 363–65; and Forrest McDonald, *Alexander Hamilton: A Biography* (New York, 1979), 265, 270–73. On Morris see Hazen, *Opinion of the French Revolution,* 54–119; and G. Morris to R. King, Oct. 23, 1792, in Charles R. King, *The Life and Correspondence of Rufus King* (New York, 1971), I, 434. For Morris's intimacy with Louis XVI see Morris's Diary, July 24, 1792, in Anne Cary Morris, ed., *The Diary and Letters of Gouverneur Morris* (New York, 1970), I, 555–56. On King, Sedgwick, Otis, and Webster respectively see Robert Ernst, *Rufus King, American Federalist* (Chapel Hill, N. C., 1968), 182; Richard E. Welch, Jr., *Theodore Sedgwick, Federalist. A Political Portrait* (Westport, Conn., 1965), 117, 121–22; Samuel Eliot Morison, *Harrison Gray Otis, 1765–1848. The Urbane Federalist* (Boston, 1969), 89–91; Richard M. Rollins, *The Long Journey of Noah Webster* (Philadelphia, 1980), 71–86; and Moss, "American Response," 96–98. Webster's changing attitudes can be seen in a series of articles entitled "Revolution in France," *American Minerva,* Oct. 1–Nov. 24, 1794. These were later republished in Noah Webster, *A Collection of Papers on Political, Literary, and Moral Subjects* (New York, 1843. Cited here, N. Y., 1968), 1–41.

6. McDonald, *Hamilton,* 265, 270–73, describes Hamilton's concerns over the French Revolution almost solely in terms of non-entanglement, charging Jefferson with being the real ideologue and Hamilton the cool rationalist. On Jefferson's support of the French Revolution see Samuel Bernstein, "Jefferson and the French

Revolution," *Science and Society*, VII (1943), 115–40; Paul C. McGrath, "Secretary Jefferson and Revolutionary France, 1790–1793," (unpub. Ph.D. diss., Boston Univ., 1950); Hazen, *Opinion of the French Revolution*, 1–53; and Dumas Malone, *Jefferson and the Rights of Man* (Boston, 1951) and *Jefferson and the Ordeal of Liberty* (Boston, 1962), *passim*. Jefferson's pragmatism in regard to Franco-American relations is generally acknowledged in the works cited above and is strongly emphasized in Lawrence Kaplan's many works, in particular, "Thomas Jefferson: The Idealist as Realist" and "Reflections on Jefferson as a Francophile," in *Entangling Alliances with None: American Foreign Policy in the Age of Jefferson* (Kent, Ohio, 1987), 3–23 and 24–34 respectively. On Madison's apprehension but support see Irving Brant, *James Madison: Father of the Constitution, 1787–1800* (Indianapolis, Ind., 1950), 371–77; and especially Ketcham, "France and American Politics," *Political Science Quarterly*, LXXVIII (1963), 198–223. Monroe first articulated his radical vision of the French Revolution's importance as "Aratus" in Freneau's *Nat'l. Gaz.* On Monroe and the French Revolution see Harry Ammon, *James Monroe: The Quest for National Identity* (New York, 1971), 87; and Hazen, *Opinion of the French Revolution*, 120–36.

7. Useful in understanding this definition are Harry Ammon, *The Genet Mission* (New York, 1973), 10–31; Bloch, *Visionary Republic;* Clarence Crane Brinton, *Americans and the French* (Cambridge, Mass., 1968); Alfred Cobban, "The Enlightenment and the French Revolution," in Earl R. Wasserman, ed., *Aspects of the Eighteenth Century* (Baltimore, 1965), 305–15; Gerald Stourzh, "The Declaration of Rights, Popular Sovereignty and the Supremacy of the Constitution: Divergencies Between the American and the French Revolutions," in *La Révolution Américaine et l'Europe* (Paris, 1979), 347–67; and especially Regina Morantz, "Democracy and Republic in American Ideology, 1787–1840" (unpub. Ph.D. diss., Columbia Univ., 1971); and Howard Mumford Jones, *Revolution and Romanticism* (Cambridge, Mass., 1974).

8. Friedrich von Gentz, "The French and American Revolutions Compared," in *Three Revolutions*, ed. Stefan T. Possony (Chicago, 1959).

9. *General Advertiser*, Oct. 5, 30, 1790. Interestingly, Bache had been critical of the early mob activities of the French Revolution. See B. F. Bache to [R. Bache], Sept. 21, 1789, Bache Papers, Castle Collection, American Philosophical Society, Philadelphia.

10. *Gen'l. Adv.*, Nov. 6, 1790.

11. *Ibid.*, Aug. 22, 1791. On France in 1791 see Georges Lefebvre, *The French Revolution*. Vol. I. *From Its Origins to 1793*, trans. Elizabeth Moss Evanson (London, 1962), 173–205.

12. *Gen'l. Adv.*, Aug. 26, 1791. Bache printed extensive details on the King's flight *ibid.*, Aug. 24–30, 1791. On the King's flight see Lefebvre, *French Revolution*, I, 206–10.

13. *Gen'l. Adv.*, Sept. 5, 14, Dec. 22, 1791.

14. See respectively *ibid.*, Oct. 21, Nov. 29, 1791. On the Legislative Assembly see Lefebvre, *French Revolution*, I, 210–19.

15. *Ibid.*, I, 206–63.

16. *Gen'l. Adv.*, June 18, 1792.

17. *Ibid.*, July 17, Aug. 16, 1792.

18. *Ibid.*, Sept. 18, 1792.

19. See, for example, *ibid.*, Sept. 29 ("Cursory Observations on the March of the Combined Powers to Paris"), Oct. 1, 5 ("French Politics . . ."), 15, 26 ("Libertus" from N. Y. *Daily Gaz.*), Nov. 1, 3, Dec. 3, 5, 1792. For the latter quotation see *ibid.*, Dec. 12, 1792.

20. *Ibid.*, Dec. 16, 1792. See also *ibid.*, Dec. 26, 1792. For other exaltations over French success see *ibid.*, Jan. 5, Feb. 8, 9 ("A Republican"), 1793.

21. Lefebvre, *French Revolution*, I, 227–47, 264–73.

22. See respectively *Gen'l. Adv.*, June 21, July 5, Aug. 9, Sept. 20, 1792.

23. *Ibid.*, Oct. 26, 1792. See a similar comment on the end of monarchy on Oct. 8, 1792. Fenno, Russell, and other Federalist journalists generally remained cautiously hopeful for the Revolution until March 1793.

24. *Ibid.*, Jan. 15, 1793. See also *ibid.*, Nov. 15 ("Phil Elutheria"), Dec. 12 ("Situation of France"), 1792; Jan. 1 ("corres."), 15, Mar. 15 ("Approved by the Ghosts of Warren, Mercer and Montgomery") ("corres."), 16 (ed. from *Ind. Chron.*), 1793. On Lafayette see *ibid.*, June 21, Oct. 8, 25, 29 ("La Fayette. A Traitor?"), Nov. 1, 1792; Mar. 9, 1793. On the latter point see *ibid.*, Feb. 4, 1793.

25. On Federalist pessimism see G. Washington to G. Morris, Oct. 20, 1792, John C. Fitzpatrick, ed., *The Writings of George Washington* (Washington, D. C., 1931–1944), XXXII, 188, hereafter cited as Fitzpatrick, ed., *Writings of Washington;* R. King to J. Adams, Sept. 30, 1792, Charles R. King, ed., *Life and Correspondence of Rufus King* (New York, 1895–1899), I, 431; J. Adams to R. King, Oct. 11, 1792; and G. Morris to R. King, Oct. 23, 1792, *ibid.*, 432, 434. On Jefferson see Thos. Jefferson to Wm. Short, Jan. 3, 1793, and Jefferson to Jean Pierre Brissot de Warville, May 8, 1793, Paul Leicester Ford, ed., *The Writings of Thomas Jefferson* (New York, 1895), VI, 153–55, 249, hereafter cited as Ford, ed., *Jefferson's Writings.*

26. See B. F. Bache to R. Bache, Jan. 10, 1793; and, R. Bache to B. F. Bache, Feb. 6, 1793, Bache Papers, Castle Coll., Am. Philos. Soc. Richard reported in late 1797 that both the King and Queen had "acted most treacherously." But when the King was executed, Sarah was truly distressed, remarking on how the King had died like a "Christian," and lamenting such "unnecessary cruelty." See R. Bache to B. [F. Bache], Nov. 5, 1792; and, S. Bache to "My Dear Children," Feb. 5, 1793.

27. *Gen'l. Adv.*, Feb. 11, 25, Mar. 1, 20, 27, 28, 30, Apr. 1, 1793. See also *ibid.*, Mar. 26 ("Cato"), Apr. 5 ("L."), 1793.

28. *Ibid.*, Apr. 24, 1793. Lefebvre, *French Revolution*, I, 264–84, II, 39–136.

29. R. Bache to B. F. Bache, Jan. 9, 1793, Bache Papers, Castle Coll., Am. Philos. Soc.; *Gen'l. Adv.*, Feb. 8, Apr. 9, 1793.

30. See respectively *ibid.*, Apr. 20, 1793, May 25 and 27 ("Anti-Britannia"), 30 ("Cornwallis" and "Anti-Britannia"); and May 7, June 24, 1793.

31. *Ibid.*, May 9 (Bache and "Extract"), 1793.

32. *Ibid.*, May 31 ("Philo-Gallia," and "Extract" from a Southern paper), June 1 ("Impartialis"), 8 ("Observer, No. IV," and "corres." in *Ver. Gaz.*), 25 (ed. and "To Corres."), 1793. 25, 1793. On Dumouriez see May 22, June 25, 1793.

33. *Ibid.*, July 26, 1793.

34. On Hamilton, Washington, and Adams respectively see Broadus Mitchell, *Alexander Hamilton. The National Adventure, 1788–1804* (New York, 1962), 222–26; Miller, *Hamilton,* 368–69; McDonald, *Hamilton,* 272, 274–82; Freeman, *Washington,* VI, 325–26; Forrest McDonald, *The Presidency of George Washington* (Lawrence, Kan., 1974), 125–27; and J. Adams to Pres. Washington, Aug. 29, 1790, Adams, ed., *Works of Adams,* VIII, 497–98.

35. On Jefferson's support of neutral conduct and his desire to aid France see respectively Thos. Jefferson to the President, Apr. 7, 1793, and Thos. Jefferson to U. S. Minister to France, Apr. 20, 1793, Ford, ed., *Jefferson's Writings,* VI, 212, 217. On Madison and Monroe respectively see J. Madison to Thos. Jefferson, June 10, 1793, Gaillard Hunt, ed., *The Writings of James Madison* (New York, 1906), VI, 127–28n, hereafter cited as Hunt, ed., *Writings of Madison;* Brant, *Madison, Father of the Constitution,* 374–79; Ammon, *Monroe,* 99; and W. P. Cresson, *James Monroe* (Chapel Hill, N. C., 1946), 121. For a convenient summary of the "Helvedius" and "Pacificus" exchange see Richard Buel, Jr., *Securing the Revolution: Ideology in American Politics, 1789–1815* (Ithaca, N. Y., 1972), 43–45. On the issue of neutrality in general as well as the history of the President's proclamation see Charles Marion Thomas, *American Neutrality in 1793* (New York, 1931); Alexander De Conde, *Entangling Alliance: Politics & Diplomacy under George Washington* (Durham, N. C., 1958), 87–91; Malone, *Jefferson,* III, 68–79; Albert Hall Bowman, *The Struggle for Neutrality: Franco-American Diplomacy During the Federalist Era* (Knoxville, Tenn., 1974), 3–55; Ammon, *Genet Mission,* 44–64; and Daniel George Lang, *Foreign Policy in the Early Republic: The Law of Nations and the Balance of Power* (Baton Rouge, La., 1985).

36. *Gen'l. Adv.,* Feb. 7, Mar. 27, 28, 1793. For other early sentiment in favor of neutrality see *ibid.,* June 18, 1792; Mar. 22 ("Lucius Junius"), 1793.

37. *Ibid.,* Apr. 25, 1793. Public opinion was generally, and almost irresistibly, favorable for neutrality among all ranks of people. See especially Richard R. Beeman, *The Old Dominion and the New Nation, 1788–1801* (Lexington, Ky., 1972), 132; Norman K. Risjord, *Chesapeake Politics, 1781–1800* (New York, 1978), 428–29, 434; and Charles G. Steffen, *The Mechanics of Baltimore: Workers and Politics in the Age of Revolution, 1763–1812* (Urbana, Ill., 1984), 144–45.

38. *Gen'l. Adv.,* Apr. 29 ("corres."), May 18 (art.), 24 ("Numa"), June 10 ("A Friend to Order"), 13 ("An American"), 15 ("An Old Soldier"), 1793.

39. On Genet's character, Girondist ideology, and the French mission see Ammon, *Genet,* vii–x, 1–31. On Bache and Genet see *The Correspondence Between Citizen Genet, . . . and the Offices of the Federal Government . . .* (Philadelphia, 1793); and B. F. Bache to M. H. Bache, July 19, 1795, Bache Papers, Castle Coll., Am. Philos. Soc.

40. Jefferson's and Madison's desires are clear in Thos. Jefferson to J. Madison, Apr. 28, 1793, Ford, ed., *Jefferson's Writings,* VI, 232; J. Madison to Thos. Jefferson, May 8, 1793, Hunt, ed., *Writings of Madison,* VI, 27. Hamilton's attempt to smother enthusiasm through an anonymous essay can be seen in "On the Reception of Edmond Genet," Harold C. Syrett, *et al.,* eds., *The Papers of Alexander Hamilton* (New York, 1961–79), XIV, 449–50, hereafter cited as Syrett, *et al.,* eds., *Hamilton Papers.*

On the editorials see *Gen'l. Adv.*, Apr. 11 ("A Pennsylvanian"), 25 ("A Freeman"), 1793. "An Old Soldier," *ibid.*, Apr. 26, 1793, seconded "A Freeman's" views, but "Another Freeman," *Pennsylvania Gazette*, May 1, 1793, claimed that although Genet should be well received, the government of the United States should be obeyed.

41. *Gen'l. Adv.*, May 2, 3, 1793.

42. For *Gen'l. Adv.* editorials see May 14, 16, 1793. On Jefferson's and Hamilton's views of the reception see Thos. Jefferson to J. Madison, May 19, 1793, Ford, ed., *Jefferson's Writings*, VI, 260–61; and Alex. Hamilton to [?], May 18, 1793, Syrett, *et al.*, eds., *Hamilton Papers*, XIV, 473–75. On the reception as a whole see Ammon, *Genet*, 52–55.

43. *Gen'l. Adv.*, May 18, 20, 21, 1793. For subsequent addresses and celebrations see for example *ibid.*, May 29, 31, June 4, 14, 1793.

44. On commissions for privateers see *ibid.*, May 15, 1793. On the Henfield case see June 3, 4 ("corres."), 19 ("An Old Soldier"), 1793; and Ammon, *Genet*, 70–71. On Bache's comment on matters affecting neutrality see *Gen'l. Adv.*, June 19, 1793.

45. On the *William* affair see "Extract of a letter . . . June 26, 1793, *ibid.*, July 2, 1793; and Thomas, *Neutrality*, 103–107. On the issue of privateers, prizes, and Jefferson's disenchantment see Ammon, *Genet*, 44–79; Thomas, *Neutrality*, 86–98, 103–117, 125–217; and Charles S. Hyneman, *The First American Neutrality: A Study of the American Understanding of Neutral Obligations During the Years 1792 to 1815* (Urbana, Ill., 1934), 55–132; and Malone, *Jefferson and the Ordeal of Liberty*, 114–19, 122–31, 135–40.

46. See especially Ammon, *Genet*, 66–70, 75–76; and Bowman, *Struggle for Neutrality*, 68–71.

47. Ammon, *Genet*, 86–91; Bowman, *Struggle for Neutrality*, 73–75; Thomas, *Neutrality*, 137–45; and De Conde, *Entangling Alliance*, 217–26.

48. *Gen'l. Adv.*, July 10, 11 ("Brother Tory" and "A Friend to the French Revolution"), 1793.

49. "A Jacobin," *ibid.*, July 12, 1793; and "Corres.," *Gazette of U. S.*, July 13, 1793.

50. "Juba" and "Metellus," *Gen'l. Adv.*, July 22, 1793.

51. *Ibid.*, May 23 and 28 ("A Citizen"), June 4, June 11 ("Brutus"), 14 ("A Farmer"), 18 ("Equality"), 24, 25 ("A Republican" from the *N. Y. Jour.*), July 2 ("corres." from the *Nat'l. Gaz.*), 1793.

52. *Ibid.*, July 2 ("corres."), 11 ("A Friend to the French Revolution"), 1793. Similar arguments appear in *ibid.*, July 11 (extract from *Va. Gaz.*), and 15 ("corres."), 1793.

53. *Ibid.*, July 17, 1793. For a similar charge of dishonesty and injustice see *ibid.*, July 18, 1793. For "A Republican," see *ibid.*, July 15, 1793.

54. On Hamilton's "No Jacobin" letters see Miller, *Hamilton*, 377; McDonald, *Hamilton*, 280–81; and Ammon, *Genet*, 102–103. For general discussion on Genet's demise and the resolutions undermining support for him in America see Ammon, *Genet*, 94–146; De Conde, *Entangling Alliance*, 283–96; Thomas, *Neu-*

trality, 137–44; John A. Carroll and Mary W. Ashworth, *George Washington: First in Peace* (New York, 1957), 100–109; Mitchell, *Hamilton*, 237–43; Malone, *Jefferson*, III, 114–19, 122–31, 135–40. On Marshall and the Richmond resolutions see Leonard Baker, *John Marshall: A Life in Law* (New York, 1974), 188, 196. On Taylor's resolution see Risjord, *Chesapeake Politics*, 428–29.

55. *Gen'l. Adv.*, July 25, 1793.

56. On neutrality see *ibid.*, July 29, Aug. 7 (letter), 15 ("corres."), 20 ("corres."), 22 ("Priscus"), 1793. On naval and privateer actions see *ibid.*, Aug. 6, 9, 13, 17 (letter), 19 ("An American"), 22, 1793. On the Jay-King letter see *ibid.*, Aug. 15 (Jay and King to the N. Y. *Jour.*), 16 ("Impartial" and "A Citizen" from the N. Y. *Jour.*), 24 (E. Genet to Pres. Washington from the N. Y. *Jour.*), 26, 1793.

57. B. F. Bache to R. Bache, Aug. 22, 1793, Bache Papers, Castle Coll., Am. Philos. Soc.

58. On the social and medical side of the yellow fever issue see John Harvey Powell, *Bring Out Your Dead, The Great Plague of Yellow Fever in Philadelphia in 1793* (Philadelphia, 1949); Larry Gragg, "'A Most Critical Time': Philadelphia in 1793," *History Today*, XXIX (1979), 80–87; and Mark Workman, "Medical Practice in Philadelphia at the Time of the Yellow Fever Epidemic, 1793," *Pennsylvania Folklore*, 27 (1978), 33–39. Martin S. Pernick, "Politics and Pestilence: Epidemic Yellow Fever in Philadelphia and the Rise of the First Party System," *WMQ*, 3d. Ser., XXIX (1972), 559–86, argues the political dimension of the fever. Susan Edith Klepp, "Philadelphia in Transition: A Demographic History of the City and Its Occupational Groups, 1720–1820" (unpub. Ph.D. diss., Univ. of Pennsylvania, 1980), 180, claims that because of yellow fever 27% of married adults in the city's lower classes died between the summer of 1793 and the final epidemic's end in the fall of 1799, while only 6.8% of the upper classes died in the same period. The *General Advertiser* was given over to extensive discussion of yellow fever from Sept. 2–26, 1793. For Bache's December comment see *ibid.*, Dec. 23, 1793.

59. *Ibid.*, Nov. 30 (Genet), Dec. 4, 26, 1793.

60. *Ibid.*, Dec. 6 (Jay and King to the Public, from the N. Y. *Daily Adv.*), A. J. Dallas to the Public, Dec. 7, 1793, in *ibid.*, Dec. 10, 1793. See also Ammon, *Genet*, 147–52.

61. *Gen'l. Adv.*, Dec. 10, 1793.

62. "Cato" from the N. Y. *Diary* in *ibid.*, Dec. 14, 16, 19, 21, 1793.

63. *Ibid.*, Dec. 21 (ed.), 23, and 27 ("An Old Soldier"), 1793.

64. "A Farmer from the Back Settlements," *ibid.*, Dec. 30, 31, 1793. A writer for Fenno implied that Bache's correspondent could not be a native of the United States. See *Gaz. of U. S.*, Dec. 31, 1793.

65. *Gen'l. Adv.*, Jan. 1, 28, 1794.

66. "Mutius Scævola," *Gaz. of the U. S.*, Sept. 3, 1800.

67. On the independence of the press in the 1790s see especially William David Sloan, "The Party Press: The Newspaper Role in National Politics, 1789–1816" (unpub. Ph.D. diss., Univ. of Texas, 1981), 112–58. Leonard A. Granato, "Freneau, Jefferson and Genet: Independent Journalism in the Partisan Press," Donovan H. Bond and W. Reynolds McLeod, eds., *Newsletters to Newspapers: Eighteenth-*

Century Journalism (Morgantown, W. Va., 1977), 291–301, claims that Freneau acted completely independently of Jefferson during the Genet affair. On the role of conspiracy and rational agency see Gordon S. Wood, "Conspiracy and the Paranoid Style: Causality and Deceit in the Eighteenth Century," *WMQ*, 3d. ser., XXXIX (1982), 401–41. The emotional and behavioral transition from the rationalist world of the eighteenth century to the romantic nineteenth is richly discussed by Jones, *Revolution and Romanticism*.

8. A Democratic Society, 1794–1795

> "If a law is obnoxious to any part of the country, let the citizens there petition for its repeal, expose its defects, or injustice through the medium of the press; let them change their representation, put into their legislature men whom they know will be active to procure its repeal."
>
> (*General Advertiser*, July 26, 1794)

BACHE'S NAIVE ADVOCACY of closer relations with revolutionary France could not have struck a responsive chord even among those most infatuated with the French cause. But in 1794 and early 1795 Bache happened on issues that rescued him from the alienation inherent in an international vision too extreme to be taken seriously and too remote to promise resolution. The crisis with Great Britain in early 1794, and the threat of commercial retaliation against that nation by Congress, had opened the way.[1] As Federalists proclaimed the commercial necessity of peaceful relations with that country, Bache and his correspondents were awakened to the domestic root of this evil—a public debt that tied the fortunes of a few aristocratic creditors to the British commercial system and thereby strangled American independence as well as the ideal of democratic equality. Although Bache had affirmed his liberal advocacy of funding, banks, trade, and manufacturing earlier in the decade, he and most of his contributors saw American liberty compromised through the British commercial connection and the needs of a small creditor aristocracy. As one writer put it, "If to have a public debt is to produce the blessing of the influence and instrumentality of British policy, to little purpose has America contended; to little purpose have her patriots dyed the soil with their blood."[2]

As another put it, national autonomy and identity were at stake.

When we were without a national debt, as was the case in the late revolution, we acted with vigour against an enemy; we resisted oppression and with effect; but now we have a debt, we are unmanned, pusillanimous and servile, unfit to maintain those rights which we acquired, and pliant to injuries and insults, that would once have given indignation and resistance to every American heart.

An old Oppositionist saw other long-term consequences of a public debt.

> What means public credit? A readiness to get in debt, and what means a public debt? The means of causing a distinct interest from that of the whole community, and enabling government to adopt systems, and pursue measures, which they could not, nor dare not attempt without this pretext. Public credit means further, a yoke for posterity.[3]

Convinced that the public debt had subverted American liberty, Bache's writers began to look for new Hamiltonian subversions. A Republican-sponsored tax on public securities transactions, opposed by Hamilton as a violation of contract, was supported by the *General Advertiser* because it hit rich speculators, and because it avoided the need for more general excise taxes which undermined the honest industry of the mechanic class and of dignified labor as a whole. In like manner, paper money was identified as the handmaiden of credit and speculation. With early reports of the Yazoo land fraud in Georgia, land speculation was added to the list of potentially corrupting economic issues. And many correspondents began to condemn high public salaries for burdening honest industry and encouraging bribery, corruption, and patronage.[4]

But although economic issues became more prominent in Bache's newspaper in 1794, they were ancillary to, and a mere catalyst for the core of Bache's political focus. In 1794 that focus remained primarily civic. It involved Bache's half-conscious quest for a means to excite and release mankind's natural sense of justice, to articulate that natural perfection into effective public opinion, and to impose that public opinion in turn on the decisions of elected representatives. The issue that allowed that focus in 1794 was nominally economic—the excise on spirituous liquors. But the excise was only part of a much broader conflict involving emergent Democratic Societies, new suspicions about Hamiltonian and Federalist motives, and the Whiskey Rebellion.

Although admitting the extremist rhetoric of the 1790s, Republican fears of government tyranny, and Federalist fears of an unruly people, it might be argued that the essential character of the Democratic Societies excited less scrutiny among those living in that decade than it would later among modern historians. Historians have often worried over peripheral issues—the European versus the indigenous American origins of the societies, the class structure of the membership of the societies, and the position of the societies on the evolutionary tree of emergent political parties. We now know that the societies believed they were imitating the revolutionary societies of the American Revolution, and that they were prepared to call themselves the Sons of Liberty until Genet recommended the name Democratic Societies; but we also know that the societies identified with the Jacobin clubs of France and other radical democratic societies in England and Europe. Although we can identify Democratic Society members as the new men of the 1780s and 1790s—political outsiders and upstarts, ambitious merchants, and especially mechanics and artisans—we should also remember that these new men were not mere opportunists or people interested in promoting class advantage, but men determined to transform the process of political decision-making. And, while we may be curious about the societies as embryonic political parties, or as a "way-station" between "revolutionary and egalitarian party politics" as Sean Wilentz puts it, we should not analyze these societies solely by looking backward with our knowledge of party development. In recommending candidates for election and in promoting policies, the societies were not just modern parties in the making. They were, above all, struggling to discover in a radical and creative way, how to articulate representative democracy and popular sovereignty in the face of established political forces that stood to maintain deference, permanent social and economic class divisions, and a traditional, Burkean hierarchy of society.[5]

Although the German Republican Society of Philadelphia and the Democratic Society of Pennsylvania were both born in the spring of 1793, Bache seldom referred to the societies in that year, only reprinting Freneau's notice of the German Society and briefly reporting the formation of the Philadelphia Society he would eventually join.[6] But upon joining the Society on January 2, 1794, he was immediately elected to its correspondence committee. As a member of this committee and others, he was involved in every significant club activity in 1794. He was selected to obtain publication of the club's January 9 statement of philosophy and purpose. On the club's behalf, he unsuccessfully tried to recruit David Rittenhouse to return as the Society's president. In March, he helped draft a letter to the French National Convention. A month later, with the aid of Leib and Du Ponceau, he composed and arranged for publication a statement on "The Present State of Our National Affairs," which condemned neutrality, British depredations, and British influence in America, while calling on Americans to insist on complete indemnification, release of the western posts, and economic independence from Great Britain.

Meanwhile, Bache and his fellow members of the correspondence committee worked to encourage newly founded societies in Washington County, Pennsylvania, and in South Carolina, New York, Vermont, and New Jersey. In April Bache and this committee composed a circular letter accusing the British faction (which Bache seldom called the "Federalists") of selling out American liberty, and another letter asking for national support in their effort to oppose the appointment of John Jay as envoy to England. During the summer of 1794, before the Whiskey crisis, Bache also served on three other committees: one to prepare an address to the public urging the selection of public servants responsive to the people; another to establish a suitable means to celebrate the 4th of July; and a third to look into the Presque Isle incident in western Pennsylvania.[7]

The only men in the Society of equal importance to Bache were Alexander James Dallas, Dr. Michael Leib, Dr. George Logan, and Peter Stephen Du Ponceau. All but Leib, who was born of German parents and maintained contact with the German community, could claim some trans-Atlantic ties; all were firm friends of France. Unfortunately, all were also part of a day-to-day, face-to-face world of political conversation and calculation whose candid discussions have been lost to us forever. Dallas, a Scot born in the West Indies, was most eminent among his contemporaries as Secretary of the Commonwealth. Although he had been a cautious public defender of Genet, he undoubtedly was more extreme as the political confidant and adviser to Pennsylvania's Jeffersonian political activists. After the death of Dr. James Hutchinson in the yellow fever epidemic of 1793, Dr. Michael Leib, a physician who had trained under Benjamin Rush and been involved with both the Philadelphia Dispensary and the Almshouse, had joined Dallas as the chief mover-and-shaker in Republican partisan politics in Philadelphia. A street politician well before modern politics emerged, Leib actively organized the mechanics and artisans of the Northern Liberties. Scattered references also suggest Leib was a frequent loiterer around Bache's printing shop, undoubtedly writing or inspiring many of the editorials that appeared in the *General Advertiser* and *Aurora* in the 1790s. Dr. George Logan, an old republican and agrarian advocate who had studied at the University of Edinburgh, surely closeted himself with Bache far less frequently, especially as the more commercial and mechanic-oriented Leib began to fall out with Logan after 1794. Peter Du Ponceau, another immigrant and francophile, was more reserved than the rest, but his knowledge of language and international law must have made him a valuable asset to Republican writers. Leib, Dallas, Logan, and Du Ponceau were leaders in a network of political advisors to whom Bache could turn for political ideas and material. Only John Beckeley and William Duane would exert equal political influence on Bache as the decade progressed. In the summer of 1794, Fenno satirized the "anarchic" activities of Bache and his colleagues in a poem entitled "THE TRIO":

The leaders of the Demon frantic club,

Who Congress with their condine labels drub,

Are Doctors L[oga]n, L[ei]b and F[ranklin] B[ach]e,

These learned cacklers nightly take their stand,

With leathern bell, and goose-quill in their hand,

Lord, how of rapes on Liberty, they preach.[8]

But although his activities on behalf of the Democratic Society were extensive and important, Bache probably served the societies more through his editorial defense of their right to exist and their role in civic improvement. It was a task made necessary by Federalist attacks on the legitimacy of the societies, begun even before the Whiskey Rebellion. The central Federalist argument was that the clubs were private, secret organizations which usurped power from legitimate authority and from the people. Even John Adams, who admitted the political legitimacy of the clubs more than most, told his wife in 1794 that, "A man drawn between two horses is a neat image of a nation drawn between its government and self-created societies acting as corporations and combining together."[9] While Adams, unable to shake the traditionalist dialectic of rulers and ruled or his classical republican beliefs in a hierarchy of inevitable orders, did not understand the societies' quest for a means to articulate public opinion, the societies did give themselves the appearance of exclusivity. The Philadelphia Society initially required that no one could become a member unless the other members "concur in the Nomination and Vouch for his democratical principles." And in March the Society decided to expel anyone who had "principles inimical to this Institution."[10] In practice, the societies were more open in their admissions and their activities than these resolutions suggest. Nevertheless, many Federalists chose not only to condemn the societies as illegitimate but to see in them a pro-French conspiracy as well. Some, like Washington, were never able to understand why the societies might be considered legitimate organs of opinion. As early as April, as the societies attacked England, Washington believed that "the first fruit of the Democratic Society begins more and more, to unfold itself." Other Federalists, more advanced in partisan understanding, simply saw the societies as coterminous with the French faction.[11]

Early editorials attempted to brush aside criticisms with mild sarcasm and ridicule. One correspondent suggested that if the clubs had been made up of "officers of government, speculators, stockholders, stock-jobbers, bank-directors, or British agents, their opinions would have weight." Another added that the societies "must be a set of political infidels, who are so lacking in faith as to believe our government capable of doing wrong." And a third sarcastically concluded, "The present state of human perfection must make it entirely superfluous to have societies to guard against encroachments upon the people's rights."[12] But when Fenno's writers persistently charged, as one did in mid-April, that the societies were "aristocrats—a privileged order, not by law, or by the free consent of others, but by your own usurpation and intrigue," Bache and his writers responded by asserting the right of individuals to meet, discuss, and offer opinions on political matters; by demanding the government's respect for the voice of the people; by pointing out that public servants were elected and therefore open to criticism and scrutiny; and by appealing to the concept of free speech and assembly.[13]

For the first half of 1794, riding the crest of the public opinion wave in favor of retaliation against Great Britain, *Advertiser* correspondents and others were largely able to fend off Federalist attacks. But the crisis surrounding the excise, the impending Whiskey Rebellion, and the executive administration's eager use of military force against the rebels forced the Democratic Societies into a defensive posture, and never allowed them to recover fully or become permanent vehicles of public opinion.

Early in the decade, during his cautious years, Bache had defended a whiskey excise in no uncertain terms. In 1791, when the excise bill finally passed Congress, Bache apparently identified himself first as a publisher of an "advertiser" which catered to merchants who preferred the excise as an alternative to burdensome external taxes. But Bache's spoken reasons for supporting the excise and condemning its protestors had little to do with self-interest. Although the *Advertiser* alluded to the debilitating effects of drink in general, Bache's primary thrust was to emphasize that the excise had been legislated by democratically elected representatives of the people.[14]

When the public meetings and protests of the whiskey excise began in mid-1791, Bache did not hesitate to lecture the protestors. He scolded the Germantown Society for promoting Domestic Manufactures and its president, George Logan, for their denunciation of the excise as a violation of natural rights and an obstacle to the growth of industry. Although his own correspondents took him to task on his arguments, Bache pointed to Congress's constitutional right to impose such a law, claimed the German-town Society was trying to label the law "dangerous and arbitrary" while accusing Congress of "ignorance and precipitancy," and hinted that the Society was trying to set itself above the Constitution.

> Do these gentlemen live under, and enjoy the benefits of the federal constitu-tion, and yet, do they claim rights which are expressly given up by the adoption of that Constitution? And while they enjoy the blessings of govern-ment, are they justifiable in refusing their support to the constitutional measures of their lawful representatives?[15]

Bache re-affirmed this position in reaction to the famous Brownsville protest meeting of July 27, 1791, in which state representative William Findley participated. "In a private citizen such conduct would be extremely blameable," Bache began, "but it becomes unpardonable" when exercised by a representative of the people. As for the meeting as a whole,

> To oppose the passing of a law, in its progress through the legislature, or even to make exertions to procure its repeal, when once passed, is the duty of every representative of the people, who is convinced that such a law would be injurious to the interests of his constituents; but the constitutional mea-sures of lawful representatives, every citizen should lend a hand to sup-port.[16]

For the next two months, as opposition to the excise divided between peaceful petitioning and violent protest, Bache and his correspondents broadened their criticism. They emphasized the constitutionality of the act but also argued that the excise was not inequitable or immoral, labeled the protestors as selfish men inspired by anti-federalist sentiments, and noted the immense expense incurred by the federal government in protecting the frontier.[17]

By early 1792 Bache was sounding virtually like a Federalist. Those who opposed a constitutional measure in a country as free as the United States were the "worst enemies to liberty," he claimed. It was hard for him to understand how men could be so "wicked and foolish" as to oppose laws that their own elected representatives had framed. Two weeks later he added,

Liberty like any other good thing, is to be used with discretion. Cry huzzas, & down with government—is there any liberty in this? The few who govern the many often raise this cry, & possess themselves of the power of the multitude who join in it. But again, is this liberty, or the power of a few? In sober times, when the laws have no passions, the multitude really governs. The people, therefore, by supporting the laws, support liberty & equal right, which they already possess—by opposing the laws with force, they put all at risk. Are the opposers of the excise sons of liberty?[18]

Although he re-published from Freneau's *National Gazette* a series of "Sidney" letters which criticized the tax because it was indirect, inequitable, and burdensome to westerners who hardly considered whiskey a luxury, Bache did not abandon his first commitment to representative and majoritarian government. When President Washington privately condemned the second Pittsburgh protest meeting—which resolved not to comply with the excise until repeal was effected—as "subversive of good order . . . and of a nature dangerous to the very being of a government," Bache was not far behind, declaring:

Is not every measure tending to obstruct the operation of a constitutional law passed by legal representatives blameable and illegal? If so, what can excuse the last [resolves] but one of the above resolves [the petition for repeal]? Does it appear the result of a dispassionate and full deliberation?[19]

Not fully appreciative of the federal government's inability to contend with western grievances over navigation of the Mississippi River, or the threat of Indian attacks, or the west's disgust with internal taxes that stretched back to American revolutionary ideology, Bache apparently remained unable to comprehend the social, economic, and political realities and needs of the west.

When violence erupted in the west in 1794 and re-awakened debate over the excise, Bache maintained his consistency in condemning it. The impetus for that violence had been a legal process issued on May 31 for the arrest of sixty western distillers, and their summons to Philadelphia for federal trial. In fact, the writs were a "bluff" contrived to "induce compliance with the law" because on June 6 a new law was signed allowing trial of tax evaders in local state courts. Although no westerners were carried off for federal trial in the east, the consequences were the same. After John Neville, the federal tax collector, accompanied U. S. Marshall David Lenox in the latter's quest to serve summonses, Neville's Bower Hill home was attacked on

July 16 by an army of 500 fearful and paranoid anti-excise insurgents. An "unthinking, uncalculated, emotional rebellion" had begun. For a month the leaders of calmer, constitutional protest like Hugh Henry Bracken-ridge, William Findley, and Albert Gallatin were overwhelmed by the warlike enthusiasm of men like David Bradford and the Mingo Creek residents who, on July 23, advocated war on the east and the excise, and by the 7,000 largely poor and propertyless residents of the Pittsburgh area who met on Braddock's Field on August 1 in quest of some economic re-form and relief. Not until the moderates regained some foothold at the Par-kinson's Ferry meeting of August 14, did the rebellion—more renowned for its meetings than its fighting—begin to subside toward peace.[20]

Responding to the Bower Hill incident, Bache lamented the use of violence to counteract the "will of the majority." "If a law is obnoxious to any part of the country," he contended, "let the citizens there petition for its repeal, expose its defects, or injustice through the medium of the press; let them change their representation, put into their legislature men whom they know will be active to procure its repeal." Bache continued to ignore the fact that the excise protestors had in large measure attempted this very remedy, but his posturing also revealed that he had learned some lessons about political persuasion from the Genet affair, as he lectured the public further, demanding that the law be maintained as the wishes of the majority if legitimate protest failed. Violence was reversion to "anarchy and barba-rism," he added, especially when America's republican government pro-vided a system for correcting abuses.[21]

Yet perhaps the long debate over the excise between 1791 and 1794—a debate set by Thomas Slaughter within the "Country" and "Court" ideo-logical paradigm of "liberty" versus "order"—made some impact on Bache. Perhaps the passage of a Revenue Act in June, 1794—an act that through its taxes on snuff, sugar, and carriages badly affected lesser merchants like Thomas Leiper, who would later become one of Bache's political allies—persuaded Bache of the ill economic and political effects of an excise. And perhaps the influence of George Logan, who consistently indicted indirect taxes from an extreme opposition to interferences with personal liberty, had some effect upon him.[22] In any case, in the same editorial in which Bache condemned violence, he began to attack the heavy-handed application of the excise by the federal administration. "An excise was odious in many parts of the Union," he asserted, "and the executive should have endeav-oured to have consiliated [sic] the minds of the people to its execution, and not attempted to enforce it by rigorous means; we hope, this plan will in future be pursued, as severe measures can but irritate." A few days later, Bache added that the executive had seduced westerners into believing the law was not obnoxious by not executing it early but then executing it severely in 1794.[23] In early August, realizing that the excise issue was not dead, Bache and his contributors began to tie the excise to the evils of the Hamiltonian funding system and the introduction of British forms of taxation. In that context, it had increased the executive power in the Treasury and the usurpation of legislative authority, tied a wealthy plutocracy to the administration, shifted the tax burden to the poor, and caused the British to take advantage of the turmoil to encourage the western rebellion.[24]

The issue of pacification of the whiskey rebels was a greater problem for the *General Advertiser* than analysis of the excise protest. Although Washington, fearing anarchy, committed himself to err on the side of order from the outset, and although Hamilton sought armed reprisals against the protestors early on, Governor Mifflin argued against any precipitous military response. Amidst uncertainty, Secretary of State Edmund Randolph obtained what appeared to be a stay of execution for the rebellion by getting the President to agree to send a peace commission to the west in early August. But Washington was ambivalent, and Hamilton worked to undermine negotiations, claiming the rioters were trying to overthrow the government. Although Gallatin, Brackenridge, and Findley bent every effort to convince the protestors to accept the peace commission's terms, and although a majority of protestors signed an oath of loyalty, Washington and Hamilton proceeded with their military response, raising a 12,950 man army divided neatly into gentleman volunteers and poorly clad militiamen. With Hamilton as the "unofficial civilian head" of the expedition, the army marched west in October, rounded up a few pathetic captives in November (the main body of 2,000 "disloyal" protestors led by the bellicose David Bradford had headed into the wilderness), and had completed its work by the end of November. The escape of the 2,000, the Battle of Fallen Timbers (1794), the Treaty of Grenville with the Indians (1795), the Pinckney Treaty (1795) which opened the Mississippi River, and the Jay Treaty were the events behind the real "pacification" of the west, while the rebellion contributed simply "to widening the breach between self-styled friends of liberty and friends of order, and to the birth of the Republican and Federalist parties in the years following 1794."[25]

By mid-August, driven into a difficult political circumstance by western violence, almost all *General Advertiser* correspondents agreed that some means other than force should be employed in the west. One caustically recommended that "stockholders, bank-directors, speculators and revenue officers," or, in other words, those who benefited from the revenue acts, could put down the insurrection themselves if they desired force. In that case, he added, "the poor but industrious citizen will not be obliged to spill the blood of his fellow-citizens before conciliatory means are tried, to gratify certain resentments, and expose himself to the loss of life or of limb to supporting a funding order." Another pleaded to "not abandon the endeavor to reclaim and reform them [the rebels], by reason and good offices."[26]

Privy only to fragmentary reports, Bache vacillated in his reportage and commentary on problems in the west. On August 21, he sadly reported that the rebellion had spread beyond the excise to the issue of opening the Mississippi and even to independence of the west from the Atlantic states. He reversed this dismal picture on September 5 with an exaggerated report on an amnesty agreement being reached between the federal commissioners and representatives of the Parkinson's Ferry conclave. In the days that followed, perhaps employing his usual tactic of exaggerating both the gravity and the degree of resolution of a problem in order to embarrass the government if it failed, he congratulated the government on its successful and pacific termination of rebellion.[27] But when Bache learned that not all of the insurgents had capitulated, that some townships and counties in the west remained in turmoil, he was genuinely hostile toward the advocates of violent protest rather than disappointed in the government.

> Should the sense of the counties after this solemn trial, be in favour of violent opposition to the laws, no citizen who values the blessings that flow from government will refuse his most avid aid in suppressing so dangerous and despotic an attempt of a minority to rule, and we shall at a blow crush the hydra of anarchy and by a decisive line of conduct in this first instance destroy the germ of any future conspiracy against the constitution and laws.[28]

Although he wished that peaceful means had succeeded, Bache applauded Mifflin's promise to take stern action and claimed that the federal government was right in deciding to put the rebellion down in the autumn, before winter allowed time for it to spread.[29]

Ambivalence continued as the debate shifted to discussion of the militia. Many called for a spirited response from militia men, and applauded those who turned out for service. It was even recommended that the militia be used further to drive the British from the Northwest posts.[30] But questions were also asked about the military solution: would the "well-born" and rich fight, would the militia men be able to vote in the election and thereby voice their opposition to the excise, should all men be called up for service, would the low pay for the militia be raised, should eighteen-year-old boys ineligible to vote be pressed into service, and were the militia paraded out to suggest political support for the excise that never existed in their ranks?[31] Bache was worried that, by his estimate, it would cost 900,000 dollars to put the rebellion down in two months.[32] He and his correspondents were further concerned that Mifflin had authorized the mayor of Philadelphia to call out a five-hundred-man militia, leaving the city unprotected while the other militia companies were away. Bache claimed Mifflin had no authority to issue such an order, and other writers supported Bache's contention that Mifflin's move was politically motivated to intimidate those opposing the excise.[33]

By October, Bache's confusion and ambivalence regarding the crisis in general, his coy early support for suppressing the whiskey rebels, and his cat-and-mouse game with public opinion gave way to a more one-sided anti-administration stand. On October 3 he claimed that western fear of the militia had been the main reason for the federal government's success over the insurgents. But most criticisms avoided the pitfalls of the issue as to whether a show of military might was useful or proper. Instead, the *General Advertiser* turned on Washington, criticizing the commander-in-chief for accompanying the army to its staging area at Carlisle. The President had to be with Congress when it was sitting, Bache and others argued, and if he was not, he could not sign or veto legislation within ten days of its passage. Washington, growing less amused every day with Bache's style of attack, informed Randolph that he would return to Philadelphia before Congress met, "but not because of the impertinence of Mr. Bache."[34]

With Washington's return, Bache turned his attack against Hamilton for "usurping the station of the god of war and directing the avenging thunder of the nation." This was just the beginning of a prolonged editorial attack on Hamilton, the most severe Bache had launched against Hamilton to that time, which now identified the Secretary of the Treasury as a conspirator and potential despot. Hamilton was charged with harboring private and devious motives in joining the army. He had conspired to put opposers of his child, the excise, in a bad light and had stymied any opposition to the government or administration policies. Through a "deep laid scheme," Hamilton was trying to put himself at the head of all government. In Bache's mind, there was no justification for Hamilton's usurpation of War

Department responsibilities or for his abandonment of his fiscal duties in the Treasury Department, although "this absence may have the good effect of convincing those not already convinced that his labours in the financial career can be dispensed with, and that money bills can be originated without his instrumentality."[35]

Federalists were incensed. Washington, always sensitive to criticism, informed Hamilton on November 5 that Bache had "opened his batteries upon your motives for remaining with the Army." Fenno's *Gazette,* meanwhile, charged Bache with attacking Hamilton "behind his back," with erroneously calling the excise Hamilton's child when it was really the child of Congress, with abusively attacking a constitutional law, and with deceiving credulous Americans for political reasons. A correspondent complained on November 10,

> It is plain that nothing can satisfy these men with the Secretary but the evacuation of his office. That some little financier may have a chance to occupy it himself and fill the department with his miserable dependants [sic].

Webster's *Minerva* defended the Secretary as well, claiming that Hamilton was in the west merely to learn how best to handle the public revenue and serve the public interest.[36]

After the rebellion reached its less than glorious conclusion, Bache and his contributors discovered another political issue to add to their well justified suspicions about Hamilton's character and motives. This involved the Pennsylvania legislature's successful campaign in late 1794 and early 1795 to exclude from the state Senate and House legitimately elected legislators from the four western counties in rebellion. *Advertiser* writers angrily argued that party politics had motivated the exclusion, and that the elections had been conducted properly and peacefully. Bache believed the exclusion was unconstitutional and worried that the majority in the legislature could henceforward abolish the minority whenever it liked. He was obviously pleased when new elections in the west resulted in the re-election of all but one of the previously unseated representatives (that one declining to run for office again).[37]

But all contentions were finally subsumed under the big issue—the relationship of the Democratic Societies to the Whiskey Rebellion. At every opportunity during the insurrection crisis, Bache's Democratic Society tried to protect itself from the charge that the clubs supported rebellion and opposed the Constitution, the government, and the laws. On

July 3, with Bache in the chair *pro tem.*, the Philadelphia group took up an extensive discussion of the excise and taxes in general. Later that month, the Society issued a policy statement on the excise. The excise was "oppressive & hostile to the liberties of this country," and it created a "nursery of vice and sycophancy," they concluded. Yet, the Society was determined to continue only "legal opposition" to the excise. The Society resolved that they "highly disapprove of every opposition to them [the laws], not warranted by that frame of Government, which has received the sanction of the People of the United States." In early September, with Bache again in the chair, the club took up a letter from Philadelphian Israel Israel to the Democratic Society of Washington County which lamented the violence occurring in the west, attacked the excise, and called for a constitutional remedy to the problem.[38]

The crucial meeting of the Democratic Society, the meeting at which the excise and the Whiskey Rebellion issues came to a head, was held on September 11. Three resolutions were proposed. The first two, calling for approval of Mifflin's pacification plan and agreeing to support the use of force if reason proved "inadequate," passed easily. But the third resolution tore the Society apart. It stated that the rebels' refusal to accept a peaceful solution "augurs an enmity to the genuine principles of freedom, and that such an outrage upon order and democracy, will merit the proscription of every friend to equal liberty, as it will exhibit a rank aristocratic feature, at war with every principle of just and national government." In an initial vote, President Blair McClenachan and twenty-eight others voted against the resolution but were defeated by one vote. Angered at the manner in which this resolution criticized their western colleagues and at their apparent loss, McClenachan and his supporters walked out. With the possibility of the Society's disintegrating, Bache took the chair and the debate continued. In the end, it was agreed that the third resolution was too strong; only the first two resolutions were approved and published.[39]

Bache's role was revealing. While the Whiskey Rebellion was not, as Washington contended, directly caused by the Democratic Societies, many westerners involved in the rebellion were members of the western societies. McClenachan and his supporters, in passionately attacking a strongly worded resolution that condemned their western brethren's use of violence, clearly empathized with the western insurrection in a way that Bache did not. In the Society and in the *General Advertiser* Bache firmly condemned the excise but never defended unconstitutional means to eliminate it.

As the heat surrounding the Societies intensified in the late summer and fall, Bache's correspondents pointed out how the Democratic Society opposed the excise riot, how they opposed both anarchy and aristocracy, and how they boldly spoke out against the rioters instead of remaining silent.[40] Bache angrily charged that the insurrection was being made a "tool" to attack the societies, and claimed Hamilton was leading that attack. Hamilton was determined to erect an "artificial aristocracy," Bache argued, but would fail in trying to persuade the people "that they have not a right to assemble peaceably, discuss and give their opinion of public men and measures." Several days later, before Washington or anyone else in the administration had publicly attacked the societies, Bache added,

> Fain would our aristocrats discredit every establishment capable of keeping the people awake to their interests and throw light on the conduct of their servants; fain would they envelope the proceedings of government in impenetrable and mysterious secrecy, the people knew their rights and will assert them.[41]

Bache's democratic arguments were in vain. Although Hamilton privately admitted that there was no direct link between the societies and the rebellion, most Federalists, truly terrified by the rebellion, sought some means of establishing that link. They found a vigorous ally in the President. Unable to perceive any legitimacy in political debate external to the established offices of government, Washington had attacked the societies privately in early August and publicly in his message to Congress on November 19. In an address written by the sycophantic Edmund Randolph, the President charged "certain self-created societies" for assuming a "tone of condemnation" of the excise, and hinted at the societies' culpability in the insurrection. Federalists in the Senate rejoiced and moved to commend the President. Federalists outside Congress believed a serious threat to government and liberty had been averted. Most probably agreed with Noah Webster that the Democratic Societies had usurped the prerogative of the people's legitimately elected representatives to act and had thereby exercised tyranny over the majority. "They are a faction organized," declared Webster, "a civil army, officered, trained and disciplined, like the legions of Julius Caesar, and ready at the call of their leaders, to rally and prostrate the government of their country." In the House, Madison, who wrongly predicted that Washington had committed "the greatest error of his political life" in his attack on the societies, defeated moves to condemn the societies.[42]

The societies did not die, but they did fade away. By early 1795, the Democratic Society of Pennsylvania had already become inactive.[43] Until the spring of 1795, Bache desperately tried to vindicate and revive the Society. Enlisting even more spirit and determination than in his defense of Genet a year earlier, Bache claimed that "no sentiment or opinion has been expressed by the Society, that has not been uttered by a respectable minority in the Federal House of Representatives." The rebellion was once even predicted on the floor of Congress as a probable result of the excise, he added, a prophecy the Democratic Society had never been so bold as to make.[44] Meanwhile, Bache headed a Society committee established to draft a letter to the public. In that letter, the Society denied that club members were anarchists, opponents of the Constitution, or usurpers of the government's powers. But there was the necessity, they went on, to watch the government and to protect the right of free thought, speech, and expression. Although a plot had been put in motion to use the insurrection to destroy the societies, the letter concluded, the Society and its members had been conspicuous in opposing the insurgents. Bache was then appointed to arrange publication of the address, which appeared in his paper four days later.[45]

After the new year began, it became clear that Fenno and the Federalist propagandists would hammer away at the Democratic Society whenever it raised its head. Fenno and Webster eagerly told Americans how the French, suffering from the pressure and violence resulting from the activities of popular societies, had abolished them. Although the *Aurora* quibbled over the technical nature of the French decree, claimed a *Gazette* writer, the fact was that the French had banned all correspondence between self-created clubs. Bache maintained that the French decree could be blamed on the violence between contending factions. But although the *Aurora* first attempted to claim that the clubs had not been abolished, Bache finally had to admit that they had been outlawed. He weakly justified the abolition of the societies under revolutionary conditions but defended them in a "settled" country like the United States, where they were necessary to protect the right of free speech and petition.[46]

Equally devastating was the attack on the societies from Edmund Randolph, writing over the pseudonym of "Germanicus." A political chameleon devoted to Washington, Randolph was generally torn between not antagonizing others yet maintaining some semblance of independent moral choice. Perhaps he felt he had found the opportunity to satisfy all of these impulses in being the first to recommend to the President an attack on the Democratic Societies and by then defending that action in the press himself. The societies had denounced constitutional laws, "Germanicus" claimed, and had not been sanctioned by the people. They were like a meteor, he argued, "irregular in their course and dangerous in their approach." Perhaps because "Germanicus" at first assumed a moderate, almost impartial tone—even once claiming that the Society of Cincinnati would also have to defend itself from the "self-created" charge—and perhaps because Bache anticipated a different conclusion to "Germanicus"'s argument, Bache began to print the series in his newspaper. After the second letter, however, Bache claimed that he had been deceived; he thought that a reader had requested the publication of those two letters, whereas it had been "Germanicus" himself. Henceforward, Bache warned in a face-saving gesture, "Germanicus" would have to send his letters to the *Aurora* the same day they were sent to other papers.[47] Although Randolph's venture did not please Federalists, who saw his defense as too weak and vacillating, he was accused in the *Aurora* of deception through obloquy, feigned impartiality, falsely reporting the debate on the President's speech, and of offering vague, yet threatening, censures of society activities. Most concluded that "Germanicus" was trying to intimidate the people by implying that individuals and groups could not express their opinions on the laws.[48]

Pressured by Fenno and "Germanicus," Bache found himself defending the societies on many fronts, with the typical failures and frustrations he had experienced in the Genet affair. He accused Fenno of lying and trying to intimidate the people, and denied again that Genet had founded the Philadelphia society. He and his correspondents compared the Societies to the pro-administration Elizabethtown (N. J.) Society and the Tammany Society of New York. When Fenno wryly noted that "self-created Societies, to defend, uphold, and support, what the people have created, must be diabolical" while those "formed to undermine and destroy" were legitimate, a thin-skinned Bache began to call Fenno the "Witch of Endor," and turned on Webster for no longer printing resolves of the New York Democratic Society in the *Minerva*.[49]

Benjamin Bache probably found the Democratic Societies the best potential vehicles for translating the collective interest of society and fulfilling and maintaining the democratic revolution in America. He had learned in 1793 that mere revolutionary zeal and enthusiasm for the sisterhood of emergent republics were insufficient in establishing a democratic foundation. The failure of the Democratic Societies, therefore, eliminated an

important public source for shaping that opinion and threw political education back into the arena of the press. But even before this failure, while
preoccupied with the Democratic Societies and various public issues, Bache
did not fail to expand the partisan role of his newspaper. As early as 1794,
James Monroe, whose ideological views and sympathies for France were
very similar to those of Bache, declared that Bache's paper was "the lightest
and . . . best political paper" in Philadelphia.[50]

Having begun to draw increased attention from Federalist publicists like
Fenno, Webster, and William Cobbett in 1794, Bache found himself actively engaged in promoting Republicans, attacking prominent Federalists,
and trying to discredit his journalistic opponents. In one way, the task
involved only rhetorical volleys. He and his writers blasted Congressman
Samuel Dexter, for example, for allegedly declaring that "republicanism
was anything and nothing," and for claiming that the President was para-
mount to the people, while other New England congressmen drew fire for
their long-winded speeches, anti-republican sentiments, and arrogant sec-
tionalism.[51]

But Bache did not achieve his partisan fame or infamy attacking easy
New England Federalist targets. He did that by attacking George Washington. No less a political barometer than John Adams observed as early as
January 1794: "Bache's paper, which is nearly as bad as Freneau's, begins to
join in concert with it to maul the President for his drawing rooms, levees,
declining to accept of invitations to dinners and tea parties, his birthday
odes, visits, compliments, & etc."[52] Beginning with the President's birthday in February, Bache began to preview the kind of attack that would
become standard in the next few years. Everything depended on deper-
sonalizing the presidency, dissociating the celebrity of a person from the
authority of an office that threatened representative republicanism. A correspondent who opposed the monarchical farce of celebrating the President's
birthday put it clearly:

> If the birth day of the President is to be commemorated, that day ought to be
> chosen, that auspicious day, when nine States ratified the Constitution, and
> gave birth to the President, and every other branch of our government. The
> celebration of any other would be the celebration of an individual and not
> that of the first officer of our government.

In 1795, Washington's birthday again elicited ridicule of "monarchical
fashions," with comparisons made between celebrating Washington's and
the King of England's birthday.[53]

Yet there was a sham quality to these early birthday attacks, for Bache, for unexplained reasons, attempted a bizarre and silly pose of personal impartiality. Alongside attacks, Bache published accounts of public celebrations of the President's birthday, and in 1794 commented that these celebrations "evince that encreasing years have added to the general sentiment of respect and veneration in the minds of our citizens, for the father of his country and the friend of man."[54] In 1795, Bache astounded everyone by acting as manager of the birthday ball given by the City Dancing Assembly in honor of Washington. Whether youthful uncertainty or some strange vanity allowed him to participate is not clear. In a rare light mood, Fisher Ames ridiculed the scene.

> At the birthday ball, Ben. F. Bache acted as manager. Yet his paper teems with daily abuse of courtly sycophancy. The poor creature should not be brought into the danger of suffering by contact with courts.[55]

For once, Ames had a right to be cynical. On a more trivial level, Bache's correspondents attacked the playing of the President's march at the theater, and the President's habit of using the back door of the theater to reach his box, as examples of anti-republican behavior.[56] At a more serious level, writers worried that Washington's "infallibility" was being manipulated and employed in defense of Federalist measures. "Opinion has so far consecrated the President," remarked one, "as to make it hazardous to say that he can do wrong. Several acts of his have been incompatible with the spirit of free government and yet these acts have been regarded as right."[57] When a *Minerva* writer suggested giving the executive more discretionary powers during the British crisis of 1794, Bache quickly charged the *Minerva* with proposing "a visual king in our President." And when "An Unfeigned Democrat" accused Bache of protecting the Democratic Societies while allowing abuse of the President to fill his pages, Bache played the sophist, admitting the *Advertiser* contained "censure" of the President but claiming it would be arrogant on his part to decide for the people what was true or false in these arguments.[58]

The vast increase in shrill partisan rhetoric in the press in 1794 indicated the new value of elections. In late summer, 1794, the *Advertiser* tried to lay out what was at stake in the coming Congressional election. The best exposition was by "Franklin," who claimed that the present representatives should be turned out of office because they had faced British depredations with "a meekness that seemed to give birth to a question of the purity of the motives which led to such submission." The allusion was to incumbent

Congressman Thomas Fitzsimons and his commercial interests. On the home front, "Franklin" continued, "intestine divisions" leading to "the sword of civil war" had emerged from an "odious excise system." There was a "defect" in the government, he charged, one that flowed from "congressional stockholders marshalled in an impenetrable phalanx of opposition whenever their property is to contribute towards the general good." He concluded with a rhetorical question answered in the old Country-Oppositionist mode:

> Whence are all the clamours and disquietudes among the citizens? They arise from a funding system, founded upon injustice, engendered in corruption, the off-spring of the blood of our patriots, who have been spurned from the claims upon this country to make way for iniquity and speculation. . . . Let the men of your choice be the friends of justice, the enemies of inequality, the patrons of the rights of man, and the lovers of freedom, and America will become a land of promise where tranquility and contentment shall inhabit.

A month later, worrying that the people remained "unmindful" of the importance of the approaching election, Bache asked the public to scrutinize their representatives and "determine whether they have or have not acted as good and faithful servants; whether their votes on important questions have been blessed by their own interest." For both "Franklin" and Bache, elections had become a better means of altering the measures of government than trying to effect a sea-change of political sentiment throughout the nation.[59]

In early October, the campaign became specific as Bache moved to arouse support for John Swanwick, a liberal merchant, against the Federalist incumbent, Thomas Fitzsimmons. An opponent of both the whiskey excise and the Revenue Act of 1794, a supporter of the Democratic Societies, and a figure close to the German and mechanic elements in and around Philadelphia, Swanwick was a "pompous, vain little man" who nevertheless represented the new liberal ethic of free trade and the development of American industry.[60] Fenno, unaware of the approaching death of deference politics, ridiculed the Swanwick candidacy, publishing a long satirical account of a strategy meeting at Bache's printing shop. Paraphrasing the Democratic Society to the effect that "any man may run for any office he pleases" in a republic, the author concluded that Swanwick, being just any man, had a perfect right to run.[61]

Bache, meanwhile, seemed more concerned with strategy than answering Fenno. Facing a new district election law which seemed to necessitate having his man brought to broad public attention at the head of a ticket, Bache called upon the public to attend a nominating meeting where tickets would be drawn up. Still wistfully attached to some vague hope that a collective democratic osmosis would result in the public interest and morality being served without the promotion of candidates, Bache "regretted" the need for political tickets. On the more practical level, he worriedly apologized for the early hour of the meeting, since mechanics would find it difficult to attend. Bache's worries were confirmed. The mechanics arrived too late, and the meeting, designed as a Federalist nominating meeting in the first place and chaired by Charles Biddle, nominated Fitzsimmons.[62] Unnecessarily anxious over the outcome, Bache raised the issue of election tampering before the results were known. On November 1, the *Advertiser* reported that a person entrusted with returning the ballots of a militia company serving in the west had burned those ballots upon returning to Philadelphia rather than submit them. The accuracy of the report was never verified. Bache's correspondents claimed that thirty-six unanimous votes for Swanwick were thereby destroyed and lost. On November 6, however, Bache only seemed certain that the original ballots had not been returned. Swanwick's election, with 1,142 to 894 votes, ended the whole controversy.[63]

For the first time, the *General Advertiser* displayed intense interest in elections in other states as well—especially in Massachusetts, where Fisher Ames and Samuel Dexter seemed vulnerable—and wherever Federalists faced defeat. Although Bache cried fraud over Ames's victory over Jarvis, he was pleased that Dexter's defeat "seems to indicate that 'Republicanism means something' even in the Eastern states."[64] And by early 1795 Bache looked forward to the new political environment, laughing at what he obviously saw as an end to Federalist control at the national level.

It is a melancholy prospect and sad reflection that the Jacobins of America are thought so well of by the people as to be delegated to Congress. New York and Philadelphia have turned out their old and tried servants, the faithful supporters of federalism and every ministerial measure, and have placed in their room two horrid Democrats! And to add to the bitterness of our distress the Secretary of the Treasury has resigned!! What will become of the United States! . . . What will now become of the darling brats, that we have been nursing with so much care and tenderness, the excise and funding systems, now their parent has abandoned them to other hands! Horrid thought! . . . Ungrateful, degenerate Americans, is it thus you reward your servants for serving themselves and their friends first!

Two months later, Bache happily announced that Republicans would be in a "decided Majority" at the opening of the Fourth Congress.[65]

Through the 1794 partisan thicket of personal attacks and elections, Bache fashioned a new partisan rhetoric, defined party and faction, tried to define the Federalists, and developed tactics for countering his press opponents. Shallow allegory and unpolished satire were commonly used in these short editorials rather than extended analysis. In 1794, Bache suggested that since the terms "federal" and "anti-federal" were "worn-out," the Federalists were having a contest to find a replacement for these terms. The winning epithets, Bache argued,

> shall be rewarded with ten bank shares, and a contract to build a frigate. If the epithet designed to stigmatize the Republicans, could possibly be compounded of an allusion to French influence, it would be both sweet and politic. . . . Any veil which will hide 'a multitude of sins,' will suit the cidevant federals, alias, aristocrats. Enquire of Mr. Alexander Lovetitle, in Aristocracy Street, at the corner just as you are turning in to Monarchy alley.
>
> N. B. Secrecy may be depended on and payment to satisfaction, for the need is great.[66]

In a similar vein, Bache published "A Specimen of a New Dictionary" with words "Adapted to the existing circumstances." Among the definitions were:

> Opposition—Jacobins
> A treaty—a solemn engagement between two sovereign princes, never to be broken, except when convenient to either party.
> Liberty of the press—The liberty of praising the administration, and libelling their opponents.[67]

Satire and allegory suggested an appropriate quality to the partisan debate, appropriate in that neither Bache nor many others admitted their opponents' legitimacy. But although these clumsy satires lacked the aural clarity of Paine's rhetoric, satire was a bridge to the modern partisan world, with its non-deferential posturing and its strong suggestion of the absurdity of the opposition's point of view.

Bache's early partisan attacks were usually more blunt than subtle. In 1794, for example, the *Advertiser* tried to dismiss the Federalists as a faction. One writer distinguished between "party" and "faction," claiming the former applied to honest differences of opinion, as in the ratification fight over the Constitution, while the latter rested on "selfish passions and exclusive interests" and was most likely to be found in the executive department of governments, especially in the treasury branch, where corruption, graft, or interest encouraged sycophancy. In May the Federalists were summarized as a "paper junto" that increased taxes, manipulated currency, and excluded the vast majority of the people from political power. According to Bache, this editorial unveiled "the designs of a paper combination, and exposes to view the alarming situation to which an unsuspecting and honest people have been brought." A month later Bache only hoped that the 1794 election would destroy the "faction," adding that, "if their works are suffered to live after them, they will stand as the ruins of a monument reminding us of their perfidious designs and a proof of the danger of supineness in the people."[68]

As Bache's attacks on the administration decreased in the aftermath of the whiskey crisis, Noah Webster hoped Bache had begun to realize that the administration was not corrupt and evil.[69] It was a futile hope. "Benedict Arnold" charged the Federalists with trying to convert the Constitution into a "nose of wax," and stifling legitimate opposition. Another writer, labeling the Federalists "Johnny's Club" after John Fenno, said of Federalist principles:

> Their leading maxim appear to be 1. No limitation of power, if it can be kept in proper hands, viz. their own. 2. The most disciplined and implicit subjection to their leaders. 3. The varaciousness [sic] of canibals [sic] to devour all opposers. 4. Much reward to their faithful followers. They talk much of money being the oil of the political machine, they go so far as to maintain that it should if possible be all oil,—a mere ocean of oil,—and their principal officer like a tallow chandler, constantly employed in dipping in the whole club, till every part is kept always dripping with the fat of the land.[70]

Alexander Hamilton's resignation from the Treasury was occasion for special comment. When Fenno applauded the Secretary's God-like achievements, Bache found the panegyric "too much for the swallow of even the meanest toad-eater of administration." Instead of Hamilton's contributing to America's future, Bache added, "America will long regret, that his works live after him." Had the natural advantages of the country, the Constitution, the President, and Congress done nothing to aid the country? he queried.[71] In March, another writer summarized Hamilton's motives and accomplishments at length. Hamilton had not resigned his post out of patriotism, the author claimed, but because his salary of thirty-five hundred dollars was insufficient. During his public career, he went on, Hamilton had proposed a life term for the presidency and an unlimited term of office for senators, subject only to good behavior. He had sponsored funding and the excise and had said that "a public debt is a public blessing." He had written the proclamation of neutrality and had authored the "Pacificus" letters, which encouraged the United States to break her faith with France. Bache's correspondent found little comfort in the prospect that Hamilton might be used for consultation by the administration in the future.[72]

While Hamilton uniformly avoided public or private response to Bache's charges, John Fenno was obliged to be Hamilton's partisan surrogate in public debate with Bache. Their newspaper exchanges were usually as unenlightening as they were frequent. After Fenno labeled the Republicans "rabble" in early 1794, an *Advertiser* writer accused Fenno of "prostitution" and "abject servility to governmental men." Another, enraged by Fenno's castigation of the Republicans as an "incendiary faction," defined Fenno's faction in blunt terms as made up of

> Men bred in the schools of Britain and educated in the vile acts of sycophantic adulation; Speculators not worth one stiver previous to the funding system though now worth their tens of thousands, and lastly, men who, though born in America rambled all over Europe under pretence of education, until the die was cast and American independence acknowledged by Britain; when over they came piping hot patriots, full of fight; claimed their estates and got into Congress as a reward for not opposing their good friends the British; voted for the funding system to pay themselves for all those great services, and now, like a beggar on horseback, would willingly ride the people to the Devil.[73]

Having begun at a low level of accusation, Fenno and Bache seldom elevated the debate. In the spring of 1794 each accused the other of publishing a newspaper as abusive as the *Brussel's Gazette,* Bache accusing Fenno of sharing with that newspaper a contempt for the common man or what Burke had called the "swinish multitude." Petulant, Bache promised that he would no longer freely advertise the *Gazette of the United States* by reprinting any of Fenno's editorials or by replying to Fenno's abuse.[74]

Fenno's tactics varied. Early on, Bache was accused of having his editorials written and approved by the Democratic Society, of slandering office holders and a majority of Congress, and of lying, emitting "filth," and spreading "discord." Also, Fenno never doubted and emphatically argued that Bache was in the pay of a foreign nation.[75] When Bache added the name *Aurora,* and its symbol, to his masthead in late 1794, a *Gazette* writer said he first believed the rays of the *Aurora*'s half-risen sun were "emblematic of the vapour which continually arose in that paper." Instead of this emblem, he declared,

> I should have advised him to employ some eminent artist to purtray [sic] in type metal a full meeting of a certain club, and the features of a few might be delineated;—the Editor himself, might be introduced in the attitude of making a motion, or in the more vehement action of declamation, one hand might have grasped the Snakes of Envy carefully enfolded in the *General Advertiser*, and the other the torch of discord.[76]

Bache ascribed Fenno's bitterness to the military successes of France over the "set of reptiles" supported by the *Gazette*. Fenno was further described as an apologist for funding and speculation, an opponent of free speech and republicanism, a preacher of passive obedience to the government, a sycophant in the pay of the Federalists and the British, a supporter of titles and nobility, and a sponsor of limited monarchy. A typical editorial, commenting on Fenno's frequent use of poetical satire, stated that, "When our Senate becomes a House of Lords, and our President a King, we shall know where to look for a Laureat well practised in the art of court versification."[77]

A greater danger loomed in the figure of William Cobbett. An idiosyncratic man, Cobbett was both a compulsive writer of extraordinary volume, talent, and wit, and a combative person who apparently was unable to define his life except in conflict. Cobbett's better days were ahead of him, as a friend of the nineteenth-century English husbandman, defending a nostalgic agrarianism that contrasted with the Jeffersonian vision of a liberated yeomanry. But in 1792, arriving in America as an exile from England with a new wife, Cobbett struggled on in discomforting obscurity, teaching English to French immigrants and growing more and more opposed to the French Revolution. A Burkean through and through, Cobbett made no pretence about American republicanism. He boldly flaunted his pro-British, anti-French, and anti-republican opinions. In 1794, he launched a severe attack on the liberal ideas of his fellow-countryman, Joseph Priestley, in *Observations on Priestley's Emigration,* from which he won unexpected celebrity and success. He followed this in 1795 with a two-part work appropriately entitled *A Bone to Gnaw for the Democrats,* a work that condemned the French, ridiculed the Democratic Societies for encouraging subversion of the government, and argued for closer ties between England and the United States. Cobbett even made space to belittle Bache.

> Many have been the conjectures on the reason of this Print assuming the name of Aurora. The Editor after having, like a second Phaeton, driven the blazing car of democratic fury, till it was within an inch of burning us all up to cinders, has assumed the gentle gait and modest veil of the Goddess of the morning: 'A right chip of the Old Block;' as poor Richard says. Some think, that having seen the Sun of all his hopes and expectations set, in the west, he thought it was high time to rise upon us from the east. But, this is not the reason; the thing is an imitation of a French paper, conducted by 'Le veritable pere du chien.'[78]

Fearless and visceral, like a dog trained for combat, Cobbett began his reckless, unapologetic, sometimes even frightening exploration of political satire and assault.[79]

Adopting the too mild pseudonym "Peter Porcupine" soon after *A Bone to Gnaw* appeared, Cobbett was more than a formidable foe for Bache. He was an enemy without any American vulnerabilities, a seemingly free agent of invective. Bache instinctively and wisely feared him, only cautiously condemning Porcupine's referral to Washington as "our beloved President" when everyone knew that Cobbett was British. Eventually, the *Aurora* attacked *A Bone to Gnaw* as a "scurrilous" attempt to divide France and the United States, and "reconcile" Americans to Great Britain. Cobbett was also reproached for referring to Louis XVI as one of the "best of men" while speaking of the common people of America in demeaning terms.[80] But neither in this instance nor later did Bache show much enthusiasm for taking on Cobbett with energy and determination.

The domestic events of 1794, following the kindled excitement for France in 1793, forced Bache and his supporters to evaluate the limits of popular sovereignty. The Democratic Societies had seemed to represent a solution to the problem of informing and shaping popular opinion. But by late 1794 it was clear that they would not last as permanent engines of opinion. The Whiskey Rebellion had not only contributed to the Societies' downfall; it had also demonstrated to radicals like Bache that the line between peaceful protest and extralegal action was a fine one, a line difficult to draw and stay behind.

Nevertheless, the tenor of Bache's newspaper suggested that not all was lost as the Democratic Societies faded as vehicles of democratic action. Bache found within the Societies a new comradeship, a coterie of political activists with whom he would share all of his future partisan battles. More than that, he found a constituency for democracy. That constituency was made up of mechanics and artisans, not the degraded lower classes that Bache had seen in France, but a decent class who mirrored Franklin's vision of dignified labor and industry. Not yet politically alienated and still anticipating the possible fruits, both civic and economic, of a new democratic age, these men represented a community that would remain the object of Bache's radical republicanism in the years to come.

By late 1794 and early 1795, events had momentarily limited available areas of political action for Bache and his friends. Elections gave some sense of promise, but the gap between elections still had to be filled. It was increasingly filled by Bache through several editorial tactics: making invidious comparisons between England and France, condemning the growth of executive administrative powers, linking Hamiltonian fiscal policy with a conspiracy to subject America anew to British leadership, characterizing individual Federalists as enemies of the people and Federalist behavior as aristocratic, and attacking Federalist press opponents as founders and perpetrators of a minority faction, not a majority party. As a day-to-day journalist, Bache found that his task was to piece together fragmentary arguments and evidence, to make a whole cloth out of separate issues. He did not and could not know until the summer of 1795 that the Jay Treaty would provide that whole cloth so dramatically.

Notes

1. For more on this aspect of Anglo-American relations see Chapter 9.
2. "Corres.," *General Advertiser*, Feb. 5, 1794. For Bache's views see Chapter 6. Only a few of Bache's correspondents espoused a simple agrarian economy. Jacob E. Cooke, *Tench Coxe and the Early Republic* (Chapel Hill, N. C., 1978) is an excellent work that first demonstrated the unflagging commitment of one Jeffersonian to liberal economic policy; John R. Nelson, *Liberty and Property: Political Economy and Policymaking in the New Nation, 1789–1812* (Baltimore, 1988) extends the liberal argument and shows leading Jeffersonians, especially Albert Gallatin, to be firm friends of commerce and manufacturing. By contrast, promoters of a classical republican paradigm deny many of these liberal tendencies and see in Jeffersonian opposition to Hamilton's particular policies the continuing thread of antique, backward looking republicanism. For this latter view, see especially Lance Banning, "Jeffersonian Ideology and the French Revolution: A Question of Liberticide at Home," *Studies in Burke and His Time*, XVII (1976), 5–26; and Lance Banning, *The Jeffersonian Persuasion: Evolution of a Party Ideology* (Ithaca, N. Y., 1978), esp. 179, 187n. For Bache the French Revolution always remained primary, and the attack on Hamilton's policies looked forward toward a radical democratic future, not backward at seventeenth- or eighteenth-century oppositionist thought.

Forrest McDonald, an unapologetic neo-Hamiltonian, claims that Hamilton sought a hierarchical society based on economic class as well as a society whose political habits and social orientations would be formed for all time through the "monetization" of American society. Although saluting this economic realism, McDonald believes Hamilton kept the British economic connection only as a temporary, rather than as a permanent, solution to America's "monetization." See Forrest McDonald, *Alexander Hamilton: A Biography* (New York, 1979), 121–22, 135, 144, 161.

3. See respectively "Corres.," *Gen'l. Adv.,* Apr. 7 ("corres."), 17 ("corres."), 1794. For other variations on these themes see *ibid.,* Feb. 5 ("corres."), Mar. 24 ("corres."), Apr. 3 ("An American Sans-Culottes"), 7 ("corres."), 17 ("corres."), May 27 ("corres."), July 17 (ed. from a Boston paper), 1794; Feb. 9, 1795.

4. On the securities tax and Hamilton see John C. Miller, *Alexander Hamilton: Portrait in Paradox* (New York, 1959), 403–404. *Advertiser* responses are in *Gen'l. Adv.,* May 7 ("corres."), 8 ("corres."), 9 ("corres."), 17 ("Warren"), 24 (letter), June 12 ("corres."), 13 ("corres."), 16 ("corres."), 1794. On paper money see *ibid.,* Feb. 13 ("Honest Industry"), 14 ("Paper Credit"), 1794. On the Yazoo fraud see *ibid.,* Jan. 27 ("Caveto"), 28 ("Truth"), Feb. 16 (letter), 16 ("A Father" from the *Amer. Daily Adv.*), 21 (ed. from *Gaz. of U. S.*), Mar. 30 ("corres."), 1795. And on salaries of public servants see *ibid.,* Jan. 31 ("corres."), May 21 ("corres."), June 11 (letter), 12, 16 ("corres."), 17, 19 (two "corres."), July 31, 1794; Jan. 20 (letter), 24 ("A Citizen" and a letter), Feb. 13 ("A Lancaster Farmer"), Mar. 27 ("corres."), Apr. 2 ("corres."), 1795.

5. The history and historiography presented here are discussed at length in Eugene Perry Link, *Democratic-Republican Societies, 1790–1800* (New York, 1942); William Miller, "The Democratic Societies and the Whiskey Insurrection," *Pennsylvania Magazine of History and Biography,* LXII (1935), 224–49; and Philip S. Foner, ed. and intro., *The Democratic-Republican Societies, 1790–1800: A Documentary Sourcebook of Constitutions, Declarations, Addresses, Resolutions and Toasts* (Westport, Conn., 1976), ix–xi, 3–51. On the Societies as a "way-station" see Sean Wilentz, *Chants Democratic: New York City and the Rise of the American Working Class, 1788–1850* (New York, 1984), 71.

6. *Gen'l. Adv.,* Apr. 15 (repr. from *Nat'l. Gaz.*), July 13, 1793.

7. On Bache's many involvements see Minutes of the Democratic Society of Pennsylvania, Historical Society of Pennsylvania, Philadelphia, 27, 28, 38, 40, 68–76, 100–101, 116–17, 122, 125–26, cited hereafter as *HSP.* For Rittenhouse's refusal see David Rittenhouse to Mr. Bache, Jan. 10, 1794, Genealogical Notes of the Franklin Family, *HSP,* 23.

8. *Gazette of U. S.,* June 25, 1794. The political activities of Dallas, Leib, Logan, and Du Ponceau and the environment in which they practiced politics are traced generally in Harry M. Tinkcom, *The Republicans and Federalists in Pennsylvania, 1790–1801* (Harrisburg, Pa., 1950); and Richard G. Miller, *Philadelphia, The Federalist City: A Study of Urban Politics, 1789–1801* (New York, 1976). See also Kim T. Phillips, "William Duane, Philadelphia's Democratic Republicans, and the Origins of Modern Politics," *PMHB,* CI (1977), 365–87; Raymond Walters, Jr., *Alexander*

James Dallas: Lawyer, Politician, Financier, 1759–1817 (Philadelphia, 1943. Cited here, New York, 1969), 3–79; "Dr. Michael Leib," *Dictionary of American Biography*, X, 149–50; Frederick B. Tolles, *George Logan of Philadelphia* (New York, 1953), especially 105–204; and "Pierre Étienne Du Ponceau," *DAB*, III, 525–26, who is wrongly characterized as having "never evinced any interest in politics, local or national, and passed a somewhat sequestered life."

9. J. Adams to His Wife, Jan. 4, 1795, Charles Francis Adams, ed., *Letters of John Adams Addressed to His Wife* (Boston, 1841), II, 171. On Adams's moderate views see Gilbert Chinard, *Honest John Adams* (Boston, 1933), 250. For examples of the public Federalist argument see "Corres." *Gaz. of U. S.*, Dec. 14, 1793; Feb. 22 ("corres."), Apr. 4 (letter), 1794; and *American Minerva*, May 27, June 5, 1794.

10. Minutes of the Democratic Society of Pennsylvania, *HSP*, 22, 103–104.

11. G. Washington to the Sec. of State, Apr. 11, 1794, John C. Fitzpatrick, ed., *The Writings of George Washington* (Washington, D. C., 1931–1944), XXXIII, 321, hereafter cited as Fitzpatrick, ed., *Writings of Washington*. For other Federalist conspiracy views see G. Washington to Burges Ball, Sept. 25, 1794, *ibid.*, 506–507; and O. Wolcott, Jr. to O. Wolcott, Sr., Apr. 14, 1794, George Gibbs, ed., *Memoirs of the Administrations of Washington and Adams* (New York, 1846; cited here, N. Y., 1971), I, 133–34, cited hereafter as Gibbs, ed., *Wolcott Papers*.

12. *Gen'l. Adv.*, Jan. 17 ("corres."), 18 ("corres."), 20 ("corres."), 1794.

13. "L. E.," *Gaz. of U. S.*, Apr. 19, 1794; and *Gen'l. Adv.*, Apr. 16 (three "corres."), 17 ("corres."), May 5 ("corres."), 12, 16, (two "corres."), 22 ("corres."), June 26, Aug. 4 ("A Democrat"), 1794.

14. For Bache's early defense of the excise see *ibid.*, Jan. 27, 28, 1791. For later editorials in the same vain see *ibid.*, Feb. 15 ("corres."), Aug. 19, Nov. 16, 28, 1791. The best analytic work on the excise and Whiskey Rebellion is Thomas P. Slaughter, *The Whiskey Rebellion: Frontier Epilogue to the American Revolution* (New York, 1986). On the early period of the excise protest see *ibid.*, 3–170; and Leland D. Baldwin, *Whiskey Rebels: The Story of a Frontier Uprising* (Pittsburgh, 1939), 56–75. For other relevant sources for this discussion see James Roger Sharp, "The Whiskey Rebellion and the Question of Representation," in Steven R. Boyd, ed., *The Whiskey Rebellion: Past and Present Perspectives* (Westport, Conn., 1985); and William D. Barber, "Among the Most 'Techy Articles of Civil Police': Federal Taxation and the Adoption of the Whiskey Excise," *William and Mary Quarterly*, XXV (1968), 58–84.

15. For the Germantown protest and Bache's remarks see *Gen'l. Adv.*, July 11, 1791. For rebuttals against Bache's stand see *ibid.*, July 16 ("corres."), 19 ("A Farmer"), 1791.

16. *Ibid.*, Aug. 3, 1791.

17. *Ibid.*, Aug. 19 ("A Lover of Peace"), 31 (letter), Sept. 5, 20, 1791. On the progress of protest see Slaughter, *Whiskey Rebellion*, 109–24; and Baldwin, *Whiskey Rebels*, 76–85.

18. *Gen'l. Adv.*, Jan. 2, 16, 1792. For other editorials defending the excise see *Gen'l. Adv.*, Sept. 15, 28 ("corres."), Nov. 1, 10 ("A Friend of Good Laws," from the *Fayettesville Gaz.*), Nov. 13 (from the *Conn. Courant*), 1792. See the *Gaz.*

of U. S., and the *Columbian Centinel* for Sept.–Oct., 1792, for comparisons to Bache.

19. See Washington's Proclamation in James D. Richardson, *A Compilation of the Messages and Papers of the Presidents* (New York, 1897), I, 116–17. On Bache's comment see *Gen'l. Adv.*, Sept. 1, 1792. The original "Sidney" letters appeared in the *Nat'l. Gaz.*, Apr. 5–May 24, 1792. Bache carried most of them simultaneously. See *Gen'l. Adv.*, Apr. 16, 24, 26, 28, 30, May 2, 1792. On the Pittsburgh meeting see Baldwin, *Whiskey Rebels*, 86; and Slaughter, *Whiskey Rebellion*, 115–16.

20. On this stage of the rebellion see Baldwin, *Whiskey Rebels*, 76–182; and Slaughter, *Whiskey Rebellion*, 175–189. The "bluff" of the summonses and the "unthinking" rebellion are quotations from *ibid.*, 182 and 181 respectively.

21. *Gen'l. Adv.*, July 26, 1794.

22. On the "Country-Court" issue and Logan's vehement hatred of any excise see Slaughter, *Whiskey Rebellion*, 125–42, 131. On the Revenue Act of 1794 see Roland M. Baumann, "Philadelphia's Manufacturers and the Excise Tax of 1794: The Forging of the Jeffersonian Coalition," in Boyd, *Whiskey Rebellion*, 135–64.

23. *Gen'l. Adv.*, July 26, 29, 1794. The July 26 editorial also contained criticism of the federal administration's efforts to slow town and land development at Presque Isle—efforts which also angered westerners.

24. *Ibid.*, Aug. 1, 2 (Extract and "Excise"), 26 ("corres."), Sept. 5, 9 ("A Plain Dealer"), 1794.

25. Slaughter, *Whiskey Rebellion*, 221. For the pacification policy and process see *ibid.*, 190–221; and Baldwin, *Whiskey Rebels*, 183–258. For examples of the views of Washington, Hamilton, and the staunch Federalists see G. Washington to Henry Lee, Aug. 26, 1794, Fitzpatrick, ed., *Writings of Washington*, XXXIII, 475–76; Alex. Hamilton to R. King, Oct. 30, 1794, Charles R. King, ed., *The Life and Correspondence of Rufus King* (New York, 1894–1900. Cited here, N. Y., 1971), I, 575; and O. Wolcott, Jr. to O. Wolcott, Sr., Aug. 16, 1794, Gibbs, ed., *Wolcott Papers*, I, 157.

26. The two editorials quoted are respectively *Gen'l. Adv.*, Aug. 20 ("corres."), 25 (letter), 1794. Opposition to force can be seen in *ibid.*, Aug. 16 ("corres."), 18 ("Conservator"), 20 ("corres."), 25 (letter), 1794. One favored the use of the "sword," *ibid.*, Aug. 12 (letter), 1794.

27. *Ibid.*, Aug. 21, Sept. 5, 6, 8, 1794.

28. *Ibid.*, Sept. 9, 1794.

29. *Ibid.*, Sept. 10, 11, 1794. The *Gazette* cynically suspected Bache of taunting the government to act precipitously so that he could later attack the perpetrators of excessive force. See "Corres." *Gaz. of U. S.*, Sept. 15, 1794.

30. *Gen'l. Adv.*, Sept. 4 ("An Old Soldier"), 15 (Bache and "corres."), 16 (Bache and "corres."), 1794.

31. *Ibid.*, Sept. 4 ("An Old Soldier"), 15 (two "corres."), 16 ("A Militia Man"), Oct. 7, ("A Citizen"), Nov. 24 (letter), 1794.

32. *Ibid.*, Sept. 26. In November, using hindsight, a correspondent complained of the excessively large militia sent out to put down a small band of rebels. *Ibid.*, Nov. 10, 1794.

33. *Ibid.*, Sept. 27 (Bache and "corres."), 29 ("corres."), Oct. 7 ("corres."), 1794. One correspondent defended Mifflin's order. "No Friend of the Insurgents," *ibid.*, Oct. 20, 1794.

34. *Ibid.*, Oct. 3, 11 ("corres."), 15, 1794. G. Washington to the Sec. of State, Oct. 16, 1794, Fitzpatrick, ed., *Writings of Washington*, XXXIV, 2–3.

35. The central editorial is *Gen'l. Adv.*, Nov. 3, 1794. Variations on this theme are included in *ibid.*, Nov. 5, 6, 10, 14, 1794.

36. G. Washington to the Sec. of the Treasury, Nov. 5, 1794, Fitzpatrick, ed., *Writings of Washington*, XXXIV, 20; *Gaz. of U. S.*, Nov. 6 ("A Citizen and True Friend to the United States"), 10 (two "corres."), and 18 ("Peter Penitent"), 1794; and *Am. Minerva*, Nov. 7, 1794.

37. *Aurora*, Jan. 3 ("corres."), 13, 15 (letter and "Marcus"), 16 (three eds.), 18, 20 ("corres." and Bache), 21 (Bache and "corres."), 22 ("corres."), 24, 29 (two eds.), 30, Feb. 4 ("corres."), 13, 18 (letter and Bache), 1795. On the legislative episode see Baldwin, *Whiskey Rebels*, 262; and Tinkcom, *Republicans and Federalists in Pennsylvania*, 109–10.

38. Minutes of the Democratic Society of Pennsylvania, *HSP*, 127, 130–31, 134–37.

39. *Ibid.*, 141–45. The resolves were carried in the *Gen'l. Adv.*, Sept. 13, 1794. On this issue see Foner, *Democratic-Republican Societies*, 30.

40. *Gen'l. Adv.*, Aug. 9 ("A Convert"), 12 ("A Democrat" and "Humanitas"), Sept. 12 ("corres."), 1794. Two writers believed the Democratic Society was partially responsible for the rebellion. *Ibid.*, Aug. 21 ("Conservator"), Sept. 22 (letter), 1794.

41. *Ibid.*, Aug. 28, Sept. 8, 1794. For other editorials on a similar theme see *ibid.*, Sept 9, 25, 27, Oct. 20, 1794.

42. The President's message is in Richardson, *Messages and Papers of the Presidents* I, 154–60. On Webster see *Am. Minerva*, Jan. 14, 1795. On Madison's comments see J. Madison to J. Monroe, Dec. 4, 1794, and J. Madison to Thos. Jefferson, Dec. 21, 1794, Gaillard Hunt, ed., *The Writings of James Madison* (New York, 1906), VI, 22–24, 228, hereafter cited as Hunt, ed., *Writings of Madison*. For details on the attack on the clubs and the decline of the clubs see John Alexander Carroll and Mary Wells Ashworth, *George Washington. First in Peace* (New York, 1957), 219–24; Miller, *Hamilton*, 412–14; Link, *Democratic-Republican Societies*, 194–206; and Foner, *Democratic-Republican Societies*, 29–35.

43. Link, *Democratic-Republican Societies*, 200–206.

44. *Aurora*, Nov. 29, 1794. See also "L.," *ibid.*, Dec. 24 and 27, 1794. "Timothy Tinker" continued the charge that members of the Society were politically motivated and tried to press the wishes of a minority on the majority. *Ibid.*, Dec. 29, 1794.

45. Minutes of the Democratic Society of Pennsylvania, *HSP*, 170–71, 174–84; and *Aurora*, Dec. 22, 1794.

46. On the attack on the French societies by Fenno and Webster see *Gaz. of U. S.*, Jan. 12 ("corres."), 15 ("corres."), 1795; and *Am. Minerva*, Jan. 14, 1795. On the *Aurora*'s defense see Jan. 9, 14 ("An Enemy to Party Spirit"), Mar. 2 ("corres."), 1795.

47. "Germanicus" consisted of thirteen short essays. These essays appeared in the *Aurora* only on Jan. 21, 24, 29, 1795. Bache's public announcement to "Germanicus" regarding publication was carried on Jan. 24, 1795. On Randolph and these letters see John J. Reardon, *Edmund Randolph: A Biography* (New York, 1975), 280.

48. *Aurora,* Jan. 26 (letter), 31 ("A Friend to Truth"), Feb. 4 (letter), 7 ("Zenas"), 14 ("Claudius"), 1795.

49. *Ibid.,* Jan. 17, 22, 23, 29, 31, Feb. 2, 1795. For Fenno's comments see *Gaz. of U. S.,* Jan. 27, 1795. *Aurora* comparisons of pro- and anti-administration societies are in *Aurora,* Jan. 27 (Bache and "corres."), 30 (two eds.), Feb. 24, Mar. 19 (ed. from *Norfolk Herald*), 1795. On the "Witch of Endor" charge and condemnation of Webster see *ibid.,* Jan. 29, 31, Feb. 2, 1795.

50. James Monroe to (?), Apr. 23, 1794, in the Simon Gratz Collection, *HSP.*

51. On Dexter see *Gen'l. Adv.,* Jan. 1 ("Gracchus"), Mar. 4, 14, 1794. Federalist publicists denied Bache's accuracy. See Letter, *Col. Cent.,* Mar. 26, 1794; and "Corres.," *Gaz. of U. S.,* Apr. 17, 1794. Bache's insistence on his accuracy is in *Gen'l. Adv.,* Apr. 4, 25, 1794. On New England congressmen in general see *ibid.,* May 6 ("corres."), 6, 19 (two "corres."), Oct. 28, 1794; Mar. 10 ("A.B."), 1795. See also *Gaz. of U. S.,* May 8 ("corres."), 1794.

52. J. Adams to His Wife, Jan. 2, 1794, Adams, *Letters of John Adams,* II, 134.

53. "Corres.," *Gen'l. Adv.,* Feb. 5, 1794. See also *ibid.,* Feb. 14 ("corres."), 21 ("A Militia Man"), 1794. For 1795 see *Aurora,* Feb. 18 ("A Courtier"), 21 ("An Officer"), 27, 1795.

54. *Ibid.,* Feb. 22, 25, Mar. 14, 1794.

55. F. Ames to Chris. Gore, Feb. 27, 1795, Seth Ames, ed., *Works of Fisher Ames* (Boston, 1854. Cited here, N. Y., 1969), I, 167–68. See also F. Ames to Theo. Dwight, Feb. 24, 1795, *ibid.,* 168–69.

56. *Gen'l. Adv.,* Feb. 28 ("corres."), May 9 ("corres."), 1794.

57. "Gracchus," *ibid.,* Feb. 10, 1794. See also *ibid.,* Mar. 5 ("corres."), 7 ("corres."), 1794.

58. *Ibid.,* Mar. 31, 1794. On the *Minerva* incident see also, "Corres.," *ibid.,* June 2, 1794. The *Minerva* writer denied that he was a monarchist. Letter, *Am. Minerva,* Apr. 2, 1794. On "An Unfeigned Democrat," see *ibid.,* June 25, 1794.

59. "Franklin," *Gen'l. Adv.,* Aug. 22, 1794. For Bache see *ibid.,* Sept. 27, 1794. Another correspondent charged the public with apathy. "Corres.," *ibid.,* Oct. 7, 1794. Joseph Charles, *The Origins of the American Party System* (New York, 1956), has found a sudden emergence of party politics in Congress in 1794 with the introduction of Madison's resolutions. Mary Ryan, "Party Formation in the United States Congress, 1789–1796: A Quantitative Analysis," *WMQ,* XXVIII (1971), 539, has found an increase in partisanship in the Senate beginning only in December 1794 and in the House after the Whiskey Rebellion.

60. Roland M. Baumann, "John Swanwick: Spokesman for 'Merchant-Republicans' in Philadelphia, 1790–1798," *PMHB,* XCVII (1973), 131–82, convincingly promotes Alfred Young's thesis on the liberal, mercantile character of many 1790s Jeffersonian Republicans.

61. *Gaz. of U. S.*, Oct. 6, 1794.

62. *Gen'l. Adv.*, Oct. 11, 1794. One correspondent noted, however, that even with the absence of most mechanics, Swanwick nearly won the nomination. "Corres." *ibid.*, Oct. 14, 1794. On the Swanwick-Fitzsimmons election as a whole see Tinkcom, *Republicans and Federalists in Pennsylvania*, 138–42. Miller, *Philadelphia, The Federalist City*, 62–68, sees the Swanwick election as the break-through in creating an opposition party in Philadelphia. William Miller, "First Fruits of Republican Organization: Political Aspects of the Congressional Election of 1794," *PMHB*, LXIII (1939), 118–43, surveys the first significant, partisan Congressional election more broadly.

63. *Gen'l. Adv.*, Nov. 1 ("corres." and Bache), 6, 1794.

64. On the Ames-Jarvis race see *ibid.*, Nov. 11, 22 ("A Scrap for the *Aurora*"), 25 (ed. from Boston), 28 (two eds. from Boston), 1794. For editorials on the Varnum-Dexter election race see *ibid.*, Jan. 3, Apr. 8, 14, 30 (ed. from Boston), 1795. For Bache's comment on republicanism see *ibid.*, Apr. 14, 1795. The close contest for Massachusetts is discussed in Paul Goodman, *The Democratic-Republicans of Massachusetts: Politics in a Young Republic* (Cambridge, Mass., 1964), 61–62. Fisher Ames said that prospects of Republican success gave him the "hypo." See F. Ames to Theo. Dwight, Dec. 27, 1794, Ames, ed., *Works*, I, 158.

65. *Aurora*, Feb. 10, Apr. 14, 1795.

66. *Ibid.*, Feb. 13, 1794. Webster, in a satirical retort, hinted that Bache's editorial was in bad taste. *Amer. Minerva*, Feb. 15, 1794.

67. "A Specimen of a New Dictionary," *Gen'l. Adv.*, Sept. 27, 1794. Unlike Fenno, Bache seldom used the more antique form of poetic satire. For an exception see "Samuel Sweetbriar's Chaplet," *Aurora*, Mar. 13, 1795.

68. *Ibid.*, Mar. 6 (letter), May 8 ("A Definition of Parties" and Bache), and June 13, 1794.

69. *Amer. Minerva*, Dec. 20, 1794.

70. "Benedict Arnold," *Aurora*, Jan. 6, 1795. Another, seconding "Arnold," labeled the Federalists the new anti-federalists since they aimed at destroying the Constitution. "Corres." *ibid.*, Jan. 13, 1795. See also "Johnny's Club," *ibid.*, Jan. 14, 1795.

71. *Ibid.*, Feb. 11, 1795. Bache had previously attacked Hamilton for arrogance, aggressiveness, secrecy, and usurpation of governmental powers. See *ibid.*, Jan. 23, 1795.

72. "Duff," *ibid.*, Mar. 3, 1795.

73. *Ibid.*, Feb. 7 ("corres."), 24 (two "corres."), 1794.

74. *Gaz. of U. S.*, Apr. 25, May 2 ("B."), 1794; and *Gen'l. Adv.*, Apr. 29, May 6, June 2, 1794.

75. *Gaz. of U. S.*, June 3 (letter), Nov. 8 ("corres."), 1794; Feb. 12 ("corres."), 13 ("A Republican"), 17 ("corres."), 1795. On being in foreign pay see especially *ibid.*, May 9 ("B."), Nov. 6 ("corres."), 1794.

76. "Shakespeare," *ibid.*, Nov. 25, 1794.

77. *Gen'l. Adv.*, May 8, June 3, 7 (letter), 18 ("corres."), July 30, Oct. 10, Nov. 8 (two "corres."), 9 ("corres."), 10 ("E."), 12 (letter), 15 ("corres."), 16 ("Fellow

Citizens"), 17 ("Warren"), 19, 28, 1794; Feb. 12, 26 (letter), 28, 1795. On the "Laureat" editorial see "Corres.," *ibid.,* Jan. 17, 1795.

78. William Cobbett, *A Bone to Gnaw for the Democrats* (Philadelphia, 1795), 8–9.

79. This composite biographic portrait of Cobbett is drawn from G. D. H. Cole, *The Life of William Cobbett* (London, 1924), 51–59; William Reitzel, "William Cobbett and Philadelphia Journalism, 1794–1800," *PMHB,* LIX (1935), 223–35; Norman Victor Blantz, "Editors and Issues: The Party Press in Philadelphia, 1789–1801," (unpub. Ph.D. diss., Pennsylvania State Univ., 1974), 44–53; Karen K. List, "William Cobbett in Philadelphia, 1794–1799," *Jour. Hist.,* V (1978), 80–83; Karen K. List, "The Role of William Cobbett in Philadelphia's Party Press, 1794–1799," (unpub. Ph.D. diss., Univ. of Wisconsin-Madison, 1980); George Spater, *William Cobbett: The Poor Man's Friend* (Cambridge, 1982), I, 39–75; and Daniel Green, *Great Cobbett: The Noblest Agitator* (London, 1983), 107–67.

80. On Cobbett and Washington see *Aurora,* Jan. 20 ("corres."), 28 ("Marrow"), 1795. "A Constant Reader, " *Gaz. of U. S.,* Jan. 21, 1795, ridiculed Bache's timidity. On *A Bone to Gnaw* see *Aurora,* Jan. 24, 29 ("corres."), 1795.

9. The British Treaty, 1794–1796

> "This day leads in the 21st year since this country was declared independent of Britain. The wisdom and patriotism which dictated the declaration were well backed by the courage and fortitude that maintained it, and which after a glorious contest, finally effected a peace that had for its basis the independence of the United States.
>
> How far the lapse of a few years since that glorious period has brought us back towards the point whence we started in our career as a nation, let existing facts decide. Since the late treaty has become the law of the land it may be a doubt whether our independence be more than nominal."
>
> (*General Advertiser*, July 4, 1796)

IN EARLY 1795, Bache complained to his brother that no news was being either "made" or "hatched," sarcastically adding, "We have not yet seen the treaty—I suspect it has got frozen in the passage."[1] It thawed out soon enough. The heat of controversy raised by the Jay Treaty, pejoratively called the British Treaty by Bache, established the fundamental elements of American foreign relations for the remainder of the decade, led to an early but uneasy Anglo-American rapprochement, and undermined French-American relations. Equally important was that treaty's symbolic significance and its implications for cultural and political *mentalité* in an age of emergent American nationalism. In the long term of American history, it meant more than the first rapprochement: it meant reaffirmation of some elements of an older Anglo-American ethnocentrism, and the recognition that the United States was likely to find little in common with the cultures of the European continent. For all Americans of the 1790s, the Jay Treaty produced the great political schism. It brought to the forefront all of the partisan divisions of the decade. And, for Bache and his compatriots, it meant the redefining of American independence, the abandonment of a sister republic in France, and the establishment of an American quasi-republic built on order, aristocracy, and privilege as opposed to one founded on autonomy and democracy.[2]

The identification of Great Britain as the villain threatening French virtue had been fully made in Bache's paper in early 1794. Jefferson's Report on Commerce to Congress had set out American enslavement to British trade and commerce in December, 1793. The public disclosure of British Minister George Hammond's correspondence, with its contemptuous demands on American neutrality, coupled with Lord Dorchester's reckless speech in early 1794 to the western Indians, predicting imminent war with the United States, had further excited American anger. But it was the British Orders-in-Council—one of June 8, 1793, declaring foodstuffs as contraband as a means to entrap neutral vessels, and another of November 6, 1793, prohibiting neutral ships from taking produce or goods to or from the French West Indies—that compelled James Madison to offer retaliatory resolutions to Congress, eventually encouraged a more radical proposal to sequester British debts in America, and unleashed a broadly shared sentiment of outrage.[3]

Convinced that the British intended to wreck American commerce and enslave America anew, the *General Advertiser* took several approaches to the 1794 crisis. The most general of these was to suggest that the issue was once again that of independence. More specifically, the *Advertiser* tried to demonstrate broad support for Madison's resolutions, sequestration, and an embargo.[4] Contemptuous of critics who warned against British wrath or the prospect of war, Bache declared that

> The few among us, who, though sensible of the injuries heaped on us by the British, are not prepared to retaliate, because they have not actually declared war, put us in mind of Harlequin in the play, who being kicked gave as the reason for not resenting it, that when he turned round to see who had insulted him, he found that the offender did not look angry.[5]

British duplicity in regard to seizing American property was complete since,

> they [the British] have been in the practice, from time to time of permitting some small portion of our property, to be released, while another part of it, standing upon the same ground of right, has been peremptorily condemned. This agrees with the practice of the skillful fisherman, who sacrifices a piece of bait, to allure the scaly tribe. When therefore, we hear of an American vessel escaping from the grip of the West Indies plunderers, we must set it down to the account of a systematic rapacity, and not to any real and thorough change in their conduct toward us.[6]

Even after repeal of the noxious November Order-in-Council, Bache continued to push for American retaliation just short of war.

> It is time Americans had done with humbly petitioning the British Court to do them justice. If we mean to negociate with that arrogant nation, whose policy is plunder and whose law is power, we must first have a tie upon her interest by a sequestration of her debts here and then we shall be able to demand with effect a redress of our wrongs. By a continuance in a pusillanimous conduct we shall but encourage her insolence, decision alone can save us at this critical juncture from the horrors of war.[7]

The *Advertiser's* stridency in suggesting that Great Britain had done everything except officially declare war against the United States did not rally Americans to demand a declaration of war on Great Britain. It did, however, hurry Federalists in their campaign to persuade Washington to negotiate. As early as March 10, a delegation of Federalists had met to suggest a special mission to Great Britain. By mid-April, John Jay had accepted appointment. On May 12, Jay sailed for England.[8]

The rationality of negotiation rather than the rash retaliation that Bache had advocated had a broad general appeal, and Washington's avoidance of full republican rage by appointing Jay rather than Hamilton as the envoy extraordinary undoubtedly muffled some protest. Federalists rightly calculated that the nation would see the mission as the avoidance of war, and that the mission would place Republicans on the defensive. James Monroe led Senate resistance to the Jay appointment, but Madison watched from the sidelines, and Jefferson quietly sat at home at Monticello.[9]

Bache's newspaper attacked the appointment on the basis of John Jay's character, particularly his anglophilism and unfriendliness to France, as well as on the basis of his earlier defense of British retention of the western posts, and the partisan nature of an appointment that one correspondent claimed was designed to keep disgruntled eastern merchants in the Federalist fold. But the more general approach was to denounce the appointment on more technical and constitutional grounds.[10] Contributors argued that a Justice of the Supreme Court was being asked to negotiate a treaty on which he might later have to rule as a member of that court; and by early 1795 it was also being argued that the Chief Justice could not perform his duties on the court while absent in England, yet would continue to draw his salary of forty-five hundred dollars a year.[11] The most extravagant of these arguments was Bache's contention that Jay's absence denied Congress and the American people the right to impeach the President, since the Chief Justice was required to preside over all impeachment proceedings.[12]

Yet the attack lacked vigor and was never sustained. Perhaps the cause was the appointment of Monroe as minister to France in May, 1794. Bache was obviously pleased with this appointment of a man "so worthy the confidence of republicans." But Fenno immediately attacked the *Advertiser* for inconsistency; "if it was a deviation from the principles of the Constitution to take a judicial officer for an executive appointment, was it less so to take a legislative officer?" Fenno asked.[13] While Bache fumbled for a weak reply, his correspondents were quicker. Some noted that the two cases of nomination were dissimilar: Jay had retained his office as Chief Justice, they said, while Monroe had immediately resigned from the Senate. Others taunted Fenno's party for finally believing that the President was fallible after all in appointing a francophile minister to France.[14]

These two mutually off-setting appointments temporarily stalemated the controversy over negotiation. But the paucity of substantial news from England also left Bache and his correspondents with few issues to attack. About all that was known was Lord Grenville's apparently casual approach to the rift and his decision to flatter Jay's aristocratic and pro-British tendencies. American optimism based on the news that Jay had been warmly received in England was "built on fallacious ground indeed," Bache warned, since "bows and courtier's smiles cost nothing." He parodied the situation a month later:

> A favourable termination to Mr. Jay's negociation is augured, because with in the short space of one month after his arrival he has had the honour to make his bow to Lord Grenville, partake of dinner at his house, and appear in the presence of both their Majesties. At this rate of doing business what hopes can we entertain of ever seeing an end to the negociation. If to make two bows and eat one dinner a whole month is necessary, a year at least must elapse before our claims are fully stated and a century before they are finally adjusted, especially if the French continue to give as much business to the British cabinet as of late.[15]

Yet throughout the early months of the Jay mission, the *Advertiser* either honestly assumed that Jay was solely seeking restitution for British abuses, or else it left readers with that impression for purposes of political attack at a later date. No matter what connivance was involved, these men could not have known just how permissive Jay's instructions were, that Jay was authorized by the Cabinet and encouraged by Hamilton to gain closer commercial ties with Great Britain. Nor could they know that while Jay attempted to negotiate settlements on many fronts he was failing in many areas of restitution. But the breadth and flexibility of Jay's negotiation made it equally difficult for anyone to know how matters were proceeding. By late summer and early fall, just as the *Advertiser* began to complain of no news, the administration was receiving its first extensive correspondence from Jay, including the highly optimistic draft treaty (a draft never taken seriously by Grenville after Hamilton's assurances that the United States would not join the League of Armed Neutrality), a summary of negotiations, and Jay's correspondence with Grenville. The public face of things, therefore, suggested that negotiations were going well, and Bache had to resort to his straw-man tactic of humbly admitting that the "present administration of Great Britain is not supposed to be hostile to the United States," while hoping that overly optimistic news would only make the anger over failed negotiation all the more complete.[16]

In the meantime, after Bache's October 21 publication of some of the Jay-Grenville correspondence, contributors simply tried to attack Jay for wasting time, for lacking force and spirit in his dealings with Grenville, for relying too heavily on British "justice" and "magnanimity" rather than demanding reparations, and for praising the King and placing unwarranted confidence in the British government.[17] The most substantial criticisms of the published dispatches were directed against Jay's failure to mention recovery of the western posts, compensation for slaves taken during the Revolution, repeal of the Orders-in-Council, establishment of the modern law of nations regarding neutral rights, or the creation of trading advantages equal to those granted by France in the Treaty of Commerce and Amity of 1778.[18]

On January 31, 1795, Bache announced in bold block letters the signing of an Anglo-American treaty. For the next five months, Bache gradually intensified the assault on the Federalists and the undisclosed treaty. *Aurora* writers who believed rumors of a treaty favorable to the United States fell back on the argument that Madison's Resolutions and French military victories had accomplished the feat. Bache was able to conclude from general rumor only that the treaty relinquished the British hold on the western posts and opened trade with the British West Indies.[19]

Grudging belief in the "happy issue" of the negotiation did not last long. On February 6, Bache declared that Americans had lost more than they had gained. The next day he called the treaty "dishonorable" and accused Jay of not gaining reparations, of leaving indemnity cases to British courts, of not establishing a definition of neutral rights for at least a two-year period, and of not demanding immediate possession of the western posts. Discontent and suspicion soon infected the opinions of other contributors as well. Cautions against praise of an unknown document, charges of timidity, and worries about the impact of the negotiation on the French treaties and relations with France in general were raised. The most thorough editorial survey did not even come from one of Bache's own writers. "Franklin," whose editorials were copied from the Philadelphia *Independent Gazeteer,* also pushed the France-versus-England line, arguing that the treaty was merely a sop thrown out by Great Britain to hold off American retaliation, that it was negotiated in secret by a self-interested commercial faction, and that the election of 1794 proved that Madison's resolutions were preferable to treaties which tied Americans to European affairs.[20]

A year later, Washington interpreted the *Aurora*'s continual harping on the French themes as Bache's attempt to justify French seizures of American ships sailing to England by "preparing the public mind for the event as the 'natural' consequence of the ratification of the British treaty." Although the accusation was true, it is doubtful that the public mind needed as much preparation as Washington thought. Yet the *Aurora*'s suggestion of imminent French retaliation, coupled with actual increases in French seizures did lead Washington, in 1796, to ask Hamilton if a special envoy should also be sent to France.[21]

In the meantime, all *Aurora* comments on the treaty, though fired blindly, came close enough to the mark to worry the administration. Secretary of State Randolph pretended to take the matter lightly, telling John Adams,

> If you are not a subscriber to Bache's scandalous chronicle, it may be a subject of momentary amusement to be now informed, that it is filled with discussion on the treaty; not one word of which, I believe, is known thro' a regular channel to any person here, but the President and myself.[22]

In fact, the treaty had been a secret even to the administration until early March, at which time Washington and Randolph had decided the Senate should consider the merits of the treaty in a special session to be called for June 8. Although the administration maintained its silence on the treaty, no one was well pleased. Some historians, lavishly employing hindsight, would praise the precedents it set for peaceful negotiation. But in the broad context of the 1790s, in the irreversible course it gave to American foreign relations and cultural development, it was a decisive and bad treaty. Washington was immediately displeased with the treaty and was genuinely interested in the Senate's reaction to it. By March 30, Randolph had come to oppose it. Even Alexander Hamilton felt the articles on foodstuffs and contraband were bad and found the twelfth article, on trade with the British West Indies, totally unacceptable. Emerging High Federalists like Oliver Wolcott, Jr. and Timothy Pickering, the new secretaries of the treasury and war respectively, recommended ratification but had to rely on the weak argument that re-negotiation was probably impossible.[23]

Senate Republicans, disadvantaged by Senate secrecy, made strong efforts to recommend the treaty's defeat. After removing the obnoxious twelfth article, Federalists proceeded to get the treaty approved by the same vote of twenty to ten on June 24. In the meantime, Bache's *Aurora* spent most of June leading the public chorus against senatorial secrecy and approval. Secrecy not only prevented expression of the common will, correspondents argued, but demonstrated that the treaty was unfavorable as well. "What a pity it is that the Treaty cannot be kept secret after as well as before it is ratified," sneered one commentator.[24]

On June 24, the same day the Senate approved the treaty for ratification, Bache reported that the Senate had concluded its work but that it had also refused to approve some sections of the treaty. Apparently believing that refusal of some portion of the treaty would necessitate renegotiation, Bache speculated on the administration's supposed dilemma, wondering how the British would accept the "insult," speculating on the "judicial branch" being "stript" for a new negotiation, and concluding, "If the advice of the Senate had been asked before the negotiation was begun, affairs would not have come to this pass." A day later, he claimed that the British had not yet ratified the document, and reported that a new British Order-in-Council (April 25, 1795) had re-established the hated Order of November 6, 1793; foodstuffs headed for France on neutral ships were once again subject to seizure. Thus, he concluded, "the Treaty may have been thrown out as a last bait to lull us into security." "Surely, if they had agreed to the Treaty, or intend to ratify it," he added, "they would not thus sport with our most important commercial interests."[25]

When Bache learned of Senate approval on June 26, he bitterly noted that, "This imp of darkness, illegitimately begotten commanded but the bare constitutional number required for ratification." The following day he followed with a list of those ten senators who had voted against the treaty, calculating the population of those states decidedly opposed to the treaty, and declaring:

Upon this it is obvious that the remote representatives of a majority only of the people, have by adopting secrecy in their proceedings, passed an act more binding than the constitution, and more influential than any law. Such is the effect of the glorious system of checks and balances.[26]

On June 26, Bache had also gloomily predicted that the people would not even know how bad the treaty was until final ratification by the President had taken place and the treaty had become the supreme law of the land. In fact, disclosure was imminent. Even before Bache obtained a copy, Rufus King had shown the document to the British Minister, George Hammond, while Senator Pierce Butler had smuggled his copies, made from the secret Senate debate, to Madison. By late June, other copies may have been seen by people as far away as New York and Boston.[27] Most members of the administration favored disclosure, and even Hamilton believed further delay would simply cause "misrepresentation and misapprehension." According to Randolph, the plan was to publish the treaty in Andrew Brown's *Philadelphia Gazette* on Wednesday, July 1, and, he admitted, he would have done so even earlier had he not given his only copy to French Minister Pierre Adet in order to halt Adet's fears that the treaty damaged French interests.[28]

But the administration blundered. On June 29, without warning, the *Aurora* presented a detailed summary of the British Treaty which, as the introduction stated, had been transcribed from memory after an "attentive perusal" of the document. On July 1, after receiving a complete copy of the treaty from Virginia Senator Stevens T. Mason, Bache advertised it for sale in pamphlet form. Bache had accomplished the first major political disclosure by a newspaper in the new republic. In so doing, he had foreclosed any opportunity for that administration to prove its openness or candor on the issue. The image of a government separate from the people, uninterested in a well-informed people, lingered through the entire battle over the treaty.[29]

Bache had not accomplished this scoop alone. Although the treaty was known to several people, few had the motive or opportunity to reveal it to Bache. He was not on intimate terms with any of the ten senators opposed to the treaty. Mason freely admitted that he had provided Bache with an authentic copy of the treaty on June 29, but only after Bache had published a nearly accurate summary that same day. According to Mason, revelation of the treaty was necessary if the public were to gain "full and accurate knowledge" of the treaty. But who had first shown Bache the copy from which he made his June 29 summary? French Minister Pierre Adet privately claimed that he had. A quiet, private man, Adet sought a circumspect way to have the treaty revealed before the administration could take credit for its revelation. According to Adet's correspondence, he had purchased a copy of the treaty from a willing senator, and then clandestinely arranged to have the treaty shown to Bache without Bache's knowing that he, Adet, had been responsible. Adet never admitted that he held two copies of the treaty, the one he bought and the one Randolph gave him. He could hardly tell Randolph that he had another copy, but he may have contrived the scoop by knowing that Randolph could not proceed with publication until the administration's copy, which Adet held, had been returned to the Secretary.[30]

For a young man who had missed opportunities in the past through sloth and incompetence, Bache was remarkably swift in recognizing both his own advantage and the importance of the political moment. By July 1 he had already printed hundreds of copies of the treaty, and had left for New York and Boston with bundles of these copies. With Michael Leib managing the *Aurora* office in Bache's absence, Margaret Bache told her husband in a letter written on July 2 that people had lined up to purchase either the newspaper or the treaty from seven o'clock in the morning until noon. "It was more like a fair than anything else," she exalted. Reveling in their success, Bache wrote to his wife on July 3 that he anticipated selling the 800 copies he still had in Boston, and buying a horse with the proceeds. Other cities undoubtedly received copies of Bache's publication as well, although we cannot know how much he profited by their sale. On July 6, he simply reported that his personal sales of the treaty had covered his travel expenses. Fenno, perhaps attempting to attribute avaricious motives to Bache, risked convincing his readers of the widespread unpopularity of the treaty by reporting that the *Aurora* had distributed 30,000 copies of it, selling each for twenty-five to fifty cents. At that rate, Bache would have acquired a small fortune from the venture. But profits, if not sales, were more moderate than either side was willing to admit.[31]

Although he could not know it at the time, his trip to New York and Boston was to be his first and last chance to inspect the varieties of American life. Like the tourist he was, he enjoyed the "neatness" and "taste" of New York's small villages and admired the "elegance" of Boston. Yet, at the same time, he did not forget that his prime interest in his tour was political, not commercial or social. On July 6, while in Boston, he was visited by Dr. Charles Jarvis, whom he described as a man of as much "Jacobinic furor" as Doctor Leib, and Benjamin Austin, another Republican leader against the treaty in that city. "The treaty here is as much disliked as at Philadelphia and

New York," he reported on July 10, "and if the People make good use of the present moment of enthusiasm, I think it yet in their power to prevent its finally becoming the Supreme law of the land, and this only by a vigorous expression of their Sentiments." A public meeting was planned for Boston, he added, and if others were held in New York and Philadelphia, "the President, in my opinion will think it prudent to suspend, at least, the ratification."[32]

There was an edge of anxiety in his writing as he anticipated the Boston meeting. The treaty would be defeated, "if the people have fair play," he wrote on July 10, "but it is feared the well intentioned may be out man-uevered [sic]." Reporting on the outcome on July 15, he was somewhat re-lieved. He had met daily with Jarvis and Austin, he said, and had revealed what he could to these organizers about the Senate's secret proceedings. Re-marking again that this was a "momentous crisis in our affairs," he rejoiced at the Boston meeting's denunciation of the treaty, where "the voice of the toad-eaters of government was drowned in the universal disapprobation of the treaty." Not only had fifteen hundred townsmen condemned the treaty, he added, but when Jarvis tried to placate a minority by promising further inspection of details of the treaty at a later public meeting, the throng adamantly refused any delay in voting the treaty down.[33]

The Boston protest meeting was Bache's proudest and most optimistic hour. To Bache, that meeting proved the wisdom in popular sovereignty and the ability of all citizens to define and recognize their personal and collective self-interest. Confiding to his wife his most intimate sense of the meeting, he said,

> it was not the influence of this or that or any nature which commanded the decision of the People, but that they voted from a perfect understanding of the business—at least, that it was the free expression of the sentiments which must naturally arise in the breasts of Americans on the perusal of that infamous treaty. . . . I watched the countenance of the citizens assembled on the occasion, when not one instance of that stupid gaze was to be seen, so often to be observed among a people less enlightened, all appeared intelligent and to feel the force of every argument that was used. You may well imagine that I was highly delighted by the issue, and not less so, I can assure you, by the orderly and spirited manner in which the business was conducted.

The Federalist alarmist, Stephen Higginson, saw it differently, charging Bache with spreading "a collection of Lies" in order to enflame Boston's citizens, and claiming the Boston town meeting resolutions exhibited more "folly and absurdity than . . . dangerous influence."[34] Leaving Boston, Bache hurried to New York, where he visited his Uncle Theophylact and his friend Edmund Genet, and attended the New York protest meeting against the treaty. Apparently only an observer at the New York meeting, a meeting in which Hamilton attempted to defend the treaty but had to retreat in the face of an enraged mob, he described the results as "glorious."[35]

By late July, Bache was again in Philadelphia, ready to resume battle as editor of the *Aurora*. The Boston and New York meetings had created a nationwide atmosphere of anger, as protestors shouted down any who supported the treaty. In Philadelphia, three public meetings were held. Jay was burned in effigy at the first meeting, on July 4. At the second, held on July 23, a crowd of 500 established a committee to write a protest to the President. And, after a meeting on July 25, a riotous segment of the crowd, aroused by a speech by Blair McClenachan, marched with a copy of the treaty through the city streets, burned that copy in front of British Minister Hammond's house, and concluded the excursion by breaking some of the windows in Federalist Senator William Bingham's house. As smaller protests were held in the South, and as Federalists comforted themselves with the belief that public opinion would eventually shift, *Aurora* contributors for the months of July and August merely assumed that the Treaty's deficiencies were self-evident, using the 4th of July as a moment to reflect on independence lost. Details of protest meetings throughout the nation were published, with Boston held up as an example that other towns could follow so that they "might express their disapporbation in the strongest manner of an instrument, which reflects dishonor on America, and barters away her best interests and her dearest rights."[36]

Nothing demonstrated Bache's democratic ideology better than his preoccupation with the anti-treaty meeting held in the Philadelphia State House Yard on July 25. In a ridiculously drawn out debate with Fenno (who apparently conceded that only one person attending supported the treaty), everything centered on nothing more than how many people attended that meeting. Immediately after that gathering, one of Fenno's writers claimed that attendance had not been "general" or "numerous." In fact, he added, not even one-tenth of the city's citizens had turned out. "There were at this meeting about as many persons immediately round the scaffold as arrived in the last two ships from Ireland, interspersed with about 50 French Emigrants," another *Gazette* writer charged, while still another reported that there were only 1,500 persons present, of whom 500 or 600 were "spectators," and 200 or 300 "Frenchmen."[37]

The *Aurora* countered with its own adaptation of modern polling, arguing that there were no fewer than 5,000 in attendance, of whom only 1,000 were "not entitled to vote." In a maze of arguments dealing with how many men could stand within a circle of 360-feet circumference (the two agreeing on the size of the area in question), the debate was reduced to mathematics. *Gazette* writers, erroneously calculating 14,400 square feet in such a circle, maintained that each person required nine square feet to stand comfortably; because ample space existed at the State House Yard for persons to spread out, these writers believed that no more than 1,600 persons could have attended the meeting. The *Aurora,* calculating the size of the circle more accurately at 10,800 square feet, insisted that 5,400 persons could have attended, if one reasonably assumed that only two square feet were necessary for each.[38]

Those who defended the Treaty, like Theophylact Bache's New York City Chamber of Commerce and the citizens of Flemington, New Jersey, were denounced or ridiculed. When Federalists argued that the constituted authorities, not the people, should decide the matter of the treaty, the *Aurora* claimed that this denied Americans a constitutional right to petition the government and revealed how little confidence Federalists held in the intelligence of ordinary people to think for themselves.[39]

When tempers cooled in August and Federalists became more confident that sensible men would come to support the Treaty, the *Aurora* noted Great Britain's need for American trade, again defended the right of public protest, and labeled petitions supporting the Treaty as the work of "self-created societies." On August 14, Bache even reported the rumor that Virginia might secede from the union if the treaty was signed by the President. A few days later he asked, "if this detestable instrument is enforced, may we not anticipate the speedy dissolution of the Union?"[40] The biggest challenge in August was to combat a petition to the President supporting the treaty and signed by more than 400 Philadelphia merchants which received a thankful reply from Washington. Why should the opinions of a "select" few merchants carry more weight than those of the thousands of artisans and mechanics who opposed the treaty, *Aurora* correspondents asked. It was also contended that many individual merchants opposed the treaty but had been pressured into signing the petition by their peers. Meanwhile, Bache claimed that many of the Philadelphia signers were really mechanics who, dependent on merchant employers, had been coerced into putting their names to the petition. Merchants and other signers of pro-treaty petitions were uniformly labeled British agents, old Tories, and new emigrants from England.[41]

All Bache's efforts were directed at getting Washington to withhold his signature. In early August, Bache had correctly guessed that either the twelfth article of the treaty or renewed British seizures of foodstuffs had postponed Washington's approval. In an incredible defense of the President, the *Aurora* defended that postponement by arguing that the President had equal power with the Senate in ratification, even though Federalists like Fenno were trying to deprive Washington of his constitutional rights.[42]

Aurora analysis and advice had no influence on Washington's decision to sign the Treaty. Not happy with it initially, he nevertheless remained silent through Senate approval, and may have been willing to sign it. But the new British Order-in-Council, as Bache suggested, was seen by the President as an act of bad faith by the British. Then, in mid-August, came the interception of French Minister Fauchet's dispatches to his government—dispatches which, when crudely translated by Secretary of War Pickering, revealed Secretary Randolph's sharp criticisms of the administration in the Whiskey Rebellion and suggested that Randolph had asked Fauchet for a bribe in order to combat British influence in America. Pickering and Wolcott, eager to undermine the one Cabinet member who was decidedly opposed to the treaty, hurriedly called Washington back to Philadelphia and convinced the President of Randolph's subversion. Randolph's desire to serve Washington yet retain essentially Jeffersonian beliefs, his political trimming, and his chameleon-like personality had finally caught up with him. Washington, already unnerved by an uncomfortable uncertainty as to whether he should sign the treaty or not, and always willing to let matters of honor and character take precedence over rational scrutiny of issues, was outraged by what he saw as the duplicity of Randolph, his most consistent ally (and sycophant) in the Cabinet. Although historians would later wring their hands over Randolph's guilt or innocence in regard to the bizarre details of the affair, the significant fact was that Randolph had abused the President's trust by posing as a loyal minister when in spirit he was not. Feeling self-pity and betrayal, Washington allowed the Randolph issue to confuse his decision and signed the treaty.[43]

Washington's ratification of the British Treaty cemented partisan divisions and established clearly the Federalist nature of the executive administration. Bache was incredulous, unable to believe that the President had really ignored the general will of the people and signed the treaty.[44] Once he was convinced, the *Aurora* launched against the administration in general and Washington in particular a venomous war of anger that never ended. A correspondent launched the attack on August 22, declaring:

> The President has rewarded the people of the United States for their confidence and affection by violating their constitution, by making a treaty with a nation that is their abhorrence, and by treating their applications to him against the treaty with the most pointed contempt. Louis XVI, in the meridian of his power & his splendor never treated his subjects with as much insult, on a respectful application to him, as the President did the citizens of Boston and Philadelphia when they applied to him against the treaty.

Washington acted more like "the omnipotent director of a seraglio," he continued, than "the first magistrate of a free people." Since the President had treated the people with "disrespect," he could "no longer be viewed as a saint," nor could he "expect a blind devotion to his will." Washington's "new character," this writer proclaimed, "ought to awaken us to our situation, and teach us to shake off the fetters that his name has hitherto imposed upon the minds of freemen." A "new Era" had begun, Bache announced a few days later, one in which "blind confidence" in the President was "preached up" in opposition to "the constitution, to reason and republicanism."[45]

From August 1795 through the end of the British Treaty controversy in the spring of 1796, mention of the treaty never failed to inspire a flood of charges and attacks against Washington. Led by "Hancock," "Valerius," "Belisarius," "Atticus," and "Pittachus," writers repeatedly leveled their charges against Washington personally.[46] The President was accused of ignoring the advice of the people as expressed in town meetings and protest petitions, and listening to a handful of Tory merchants, a group that could not claim an exclusive interest in the treaty since it was only partly commercial.[47] When Webster dared to say that the President had been right and the people "duped by there [sic] artful leaders," Bache retaliated, claiming that Webster proclaimed, "as false, what 20,000 citizens of America have sanctioned as true," and adding, "The editor grants, that the people are opposed to the treaty, and that the President has disregarded their opinions. This is called a government of the people, framed by the people. The question now occurs who is to be understood by this we the people? The Editor of the Minerva explains it, it is now on a tour to Mount Vernon with the constitution." Portraying Washington as a man of modest political abilities who, deluded by the sycophantic praise and the trappings of royalty, had succumbed to the pro-treaty side and assumed an arrogant, aloof posture, *Aurora* writers discovered a Federalist campaign to set the President above the Constitution, and to create a cult of Washington's supposed infallibility.[48]

Old arguments about the Senate's not being consulted over Jay's instructions, and about the usurpation by the President of congressional authority in agreeing to a commercial treaty, were raised again. "Atticus" argued that the claims commission violated federal court authority, further noting that Congress was stripped of its power to make "needful rules and regulations" for the territories by granting British subjects the right to hold lands in those territories. He concluded with a condemnation of the Treaty for compromising the reserve powers of the states and the people as guaranteed under the Tenth Amendment. "Diplomaticus," discovering the dilemma of the treaty-making power and the supremacy clause of Article VI of the Constitution, lamented that if the President and two-thirds of the Senate "has an absolute power to make treaties, they may sweep away all the Laws and Constitutions of the several States, without any check," except the guarantee that the states would have republican forms of government.[49]

The publication of Randolph's *Vindication* encouraged Bache to pursue what he had suspected, Washington's vacillation and indecision in the ratification process. Bache did not waste this opportunity to describe Washington as both undemocratic and uncertain in signing the treaty.

> Mark the difference between the President of the United States in his closet and before the tribunal of the public. He doubted after the ratification of the treaty by the Senate, whether he should give it his sanction and tremblingly alive to his situation, 'expresses a wish, that the public opinion could be heard upon the subject.' (See RANDOLPH'S vindication, page 28). Here we see a weak man wavering in his determination and craving an expression of the public sentiment and judgement to assist his own, and wishing to lean on it for support. He however takes his determination from passion [the Randolph affair], and then to brave it out, not only slights but insults the public voice. 'I cannot substitute to my own conviction the opinions of others.' (See President's circular answer to sundry town meetings.) The plain language of all which is first 'I am at a loss to act, & know not which alternative to chuse, then let the public voice determine.' Afterwards, 'I have made up my mind: hold your tongue, think you I am to listen to you.'[50]

Randolph's *Vindication* was also used to emphasize the villainy of Wolcott and Pickering in the affair, to demonstrate the President's weak reliance on Hamilton for advice, and to accuse the President of conspiring with British Minister Hammond to have the obnoxious Order-in-Council lifted until the ratification was secure.[51]

Bache and his *Aurora* writers, through revelation of the Jay Treaty and impassioned anger against senate and presidential ratification, were among the leaders of the battle against the progress of the treaty toward implementation. They did less well in attacking the particulars of the treaty over the year that began in June, 1795. By August a disappointed James Madison, who complained of the efforts of men of lesser ability while at the same time failing to answer Jefferson's call to take up the pen against Jay Treaty defenders himself, declared that, "The only Philadạ paper that comes to me is the *Aurora* wch besides frequent miscarriages [irregular deliveries], is not I find the vehicle used by the regular champions on either side." Petty details needed to be avoided, Madison continued gratuitously, while important flaws in the treaty like the issue of neutral rights and definitions of contraband needed to be singled out. In the end, Madison would offer his own tardy opposition to the treaty in the House in 1796, but neither Madison nor Jefferson, who lamented that the Republicans had "had only middling performances to oppose" Hamilton, entered combat publicly.[52]

Jefferson and Madison were a bit unfair. Alexander James Dallas had written a 22,000-word essay against the treaty for the *American Daily Advertiser* in July and August as well as some other essays over the signature "Americanus" for the *Philadelphia Gazette* and the *Aurora,* but Dallas denied being the *Aurora*'s "Valerius" and ended his protest with Washington's ratification. Meanwhile, writers calling themselves the "Republican" and the "Constitutionalist" led the attack in Boston for the *Independent Chronicle,* while in New York "Decius" (Brockholst Livingston) and "Cato" (Robert R. Livingston) excited opposition, with the latter reputedly stimulating Hamilton's response in the "Camillus" letters. The *Aurora* carried the greatest number of writers, but neither the contributions of Bache's writers nor any other Republican series of letters could match the Federalist defense, led by Hamilton as "Camillus" and Webster as "Curtius." Both Hamilton and Webster argued their cases on the reductionist basis of pragmatic national self-interest.[53]

Aurora editorials and essays attacking the treaty between June, 1795 and the summer of 1796 took many forms, with criticisms of specific treaty provisions comprising the smallest part of the general assault. A few writers complained that British cession of the western posts by July 1, 1796, granted Americans nothing more than what they already owned, and that the British intended to repossess the western posts when the first "favourable opportunity" arose.[54] The burden and inequity of allowing British creditors to lay claims against American debtors was also attacked, as was the lack of compensation to Southern states for slaves taken during the

American Revolution.[55] Bache estimated the value of these slaves at six hundred thousand dollars, a sum which would have gone "a great way in paying off all debts due from this country to Britain." When the slave issue was raised in Congress in 1796, Bache agreed that the British could be praised if they had freed these slaves, as Federalists contended; but, he charged, the British had sold most of them into slavery again.[56]

Several other articles received scattered attention. Giving up sequestration of British property as a retaliatory weapon was condemned, as was the right of British subjects under Article IX to hold landed property in the United States. All of the commercial provisions of the Treaty—including Article XII on the British West Indies trade, American exclusion from the rich fur trade in the Hudson's Bay region, nonrecognition of neutral trade rights, and British privileges to enter American waters and navigate the Mississippi River—were seen as gross inequities. The Treaty was attacked also for still allowing the British to impress American seamen, to establish an unfair advantage in negotiating the boundary with Canada, and to define piracy to their advantage.[57]

The *Aurora* editorials infused with the greatest enthusiasm and vitality did not deal with the treaty's specific articles or with the likely particular consequences of its ratification; they dealt with general arguments and appealed to a spirit of nationalism. "Americanus," for example, castigated the treaty because

> I. It begets a base and unnatural political connection between a republican government and a monarch.
> II. It sacrifices to that connection, past injuries, a reparation for wrongs, and the most essential interests of commerce, that an independent nation can yield.
> III. It prostrates the constitution of the United States, at the feet of the President and Senate, . . .
> IV. It declares war against the independence and constitutional rights of Congress, ...

Besides creating constitutional conflict among the branches of government, the treaty

> records and perpetuates the dishonor of America, and the political depravity of her government; exhibiting the sad spectacle of the United States servilely cringing to the corrupt monarch of Great Britain, for a close and intimate alliance, at the sacrifice of the most essential political and commercial interests whilst pointing the finger of hostility to France.[58]

A discernible pattern emerged from these general views of the treaty between the summer of 1795 and the spring of 1796. First, Great Britain was portrayed as a dishonorable ally, willing to insult and injure Americans through continued seizures of ships on the high seas and to impress American seamen. Dishonor and hostility were evidenced in several ways: through the renewed interception of foodstuffs headed for the continent; by increased privateering activity directed from the British island of Bermuda; and by violation of American territorial waters when the British warship *Africa* attempted to capture the departing French Minister Fauchet even while Fauchet's ship lingered in American waters. President Washington rightly predicted that his efforts to chastise the *Africa* for its actions would not satisfy the *Aurora*. And Webster rebutted *Aurora* claims on seizures late in 1795 with the contention that more American ships were left unmolested by the British after the treaty than before it.[59]

Heaviest criticisms regarding British dishonor were directed at impressment. In addition to reporting incidents involving impressment of Americans, the *Aurora* ridiculed Federalists who dared to diminish the effects of impressment or who apologized for the lack of any clause in the treaty to prevent impressment. Bache noted

> that American citizens had not a right to expatriate themselves and then enter into the service of the French Republic; but we find . . . that American citizens may not only be recruited, but impressed and CARRIED IN IRONS on board a British Frigate. Does this look like a fair and impartial neutrality?[60]

Federalist apologists, like the *Columbian Centinel,* struggled to challenge Bache's "lies" by diminishing the incidence of impressment and defending its occasional use by Great Britain as a consequence of war. As one of the *Centinel*'s correspondents put it, American seamen seemed perfectly willing and eager to risk impressment, knowing "that not ten American-born seamen, out of a thousand, who gave regular and fair Protections, have ever been detained, much less impressed."[61]

A second strategy was to dispel the fear that rejection of the treaty would lead to war with Great Britain. The threat of war was a ruthless sham, *Aurora* critics suggested. There was no proof that rejection of the treaty would produce conflict, they claimed, suggesting that treaty supporters used this argument to deflect discussion of specific articles of the treaty. In any case, Great Britain was too weak to prosecute a war in America and could not risk losing its lucrative trade in America. The British already faced high taxes, internal dissension, and a corrupt monarchical government; they could not possibly be victorious over a willful republican country like the United States. Instead of timidly negotiating, they continued, Americans could have used commercial retaliation or joined the League of Armed Neutrality.[62] Bache, meanwhile, noted that "to believe" the Federalists "we are unable to maintain our rights against enfeebled Britain, and we must swallow a most disgraceful treaty with that nation, or be annihilated by her omnipotent arm."[63]

The *Aurora* also argued that the treaty would produce tragic consequences for American relations with France. As early as June, 1795, James Monroe had authorized George Logan, after consulting with John Beckley, to insert Monroe's observations on France in Bache's newspaper. Some of Bache's views on the dilemma must have stemmed from the information Bache surreptitiously received from Monroe and published in the *Aurora*. The *Aurora* held that the treaty violated neutrality, destroyed amity with France, and heightened the possibility of war with France. Even when the prospect of war was not addressed, contributors denounced treaty advocates for deserting America's sister republic; ignoring France's growing power and the advantages which could accrue to the United States by treating with France; and deceiving the French into believing the treaty was only directed toward adjusting grievances with Great Britain. This time the *Gazette* turned the war threat argument against Bache, declaring that France needed American provisions and did not have a strong enough navy to either "distress" American trade or attack the United States.[64]

Finally, the *Aurora*'s most sustained effort was applied to proving that the democratic will of the people stood against the treaty, ratification notwithstanding. An early opportunity to test the treaty's popularity came with the fall elections for the Pennsylvania legislature. *Aurora* writers attempted to bill the impending contest as a fight between pro-treaty Federalist aristocrats, and anti-treaty Democrats, with Bache claiming that the Federalists were approaching the election with "uneasiness." But with sixty percent of the City of Philadelphia vote going Federalist, Bache could only point out that half of the old Federalist legislators had been turned out. "Cleon" interpreted the Federalist majority in the city as the expected consequence of British influence, old Tories, banks, and speculators overwhelming the "free, uninfluenced, and unbiased electors," and he claimed that in Philadelphia County, where the vote had gone strongly anti-treaty, farmers and mechanics, who made up a majority of the electorate there, had acted freely and independently.[65]

More energy was spent analyzing the number of Americans who supported and opposed the Treaty than examining election results. Some of the *Aurora*'s contributors argued that opponents outnumbered supporters ten to one; all of them set very low numbers on those who actually petitioned for the Treaty. Fresh accounts of anti-treaty protests, were described, opponents of the Treaty were again identified as free and independent patriots, while supporters were again labeled old Tories, British merchants and agents, self-interested merchants and bank directors, and recipients of federal patronage.[66] Fenno's *Gazette* and Webster's *Minerva* strongly objected to the *Aurora*'s figures. In their view, the great mass of Americans quietly supported the treaty; very few had read the document, they implied, and even fewer had expressed an opinion on it. Nevertheless, when Webster cited James Sullivan as saying that nine-tenths of the population favored the treaty, the *Aurora* was quick to contradict Webster. Sullivan, in an open letter to the *Aurora*, stated that he had meant to say that many more might be opposed to the treaty but that only one-tenth of the people were truly hostile to Great Britain.[67]

When the House of Representatives took up the issue of the treaty after December 1795, the *Aurora* vigorously insisted that a new wave of anti-treaty sentiment had swept the nation. According to Bache, the South Carolina legislature opposed the treaty but failed to pass a resolution to that effect only because legislators felt the treaty was not a state issue. Virginia was applauded for offering constitutional amendments to place additional checks on the treaty-making powers of the federal government. And, although the *Aurora* lamented Massachusetts's refusal to support the Virginia amendments, the refusal was blamed on the fact that only one-fourth of that state's legislature was present for the vote. Massachusetts was redeemed, in Bache's eyes at least, when Samuel Adams's impressive gubernatorial victory was interpreted as a vote against the treaty.[68] In April, despite failing to arouse public enthusiasm for another anti-treaty meeting and demonstration, the *Aurora* again led Philadelphia's anti-treaty forces in an attempt to counter a new pro-treaty petition being circulated by the city's merchants and insurance underwriters. These new petitioners were charged with exercising economic pressure, political influence, and corruption in gaining signatures. Meanwhile, anti-treaty men circulated their own petition, asking Congress to deny passage of the appropriations bill which would put the treaty into effect. In the end, the *Aurora* claimed 2,600 signatures on the anti-treaty petition, with only 1,500 names on the pro-treaty list.[69]

The prospect that the House of Representatives might refuse to appropriate funds for the treaty's implementation, as some contributors to the *Aurora* predicted, was the central reason for the *Aurora*'s sustained campaign. In the four months between presidential ratification and the convening of Congress, these writers tried to create an atmosphere of anticipation. Congress was held up as the last bastion of defense against the destruction of republicanism and the usurpation of legislative power by the President and the Senate. Congressmen were urged to beware of Federalist intrigue; Southern congressmen in particular were warned against arriving late for such an important session.[70] Before debate even began on the treaty issue, "Scipio" encouraged Congress, while it was defeating the treaty, to impeach the President and the Cabinet for conspiring with the British. More moderate voices charged the Federalists with stalling, while Bache assured everyone at the end of February that if another congressional election were held in early 1795, the House would remain opposed to the treaty. Contributors reminded Congress that its power to legislate, appropriate monies, and regulate commerce as well as to follow the public will, would hang on their actions.[71]

When Edward Livingston laid before the House his motion that the President provide that body with all papers dealing with the Treaty, Federalists insisted on Congress's obligation to recognize the exclusive treaty-making power of the President and the Senate, pointing out that Congress could not withhold the President's or federal judge's salaries, and declaring that peace or war hinged on the outcome.[72] Sensing vulnerability in the Federalist apology, Bache's correspondents largely ignored Republican arguments and attempted to dismiss Federalist arguments as weak and unrepublican. In a mock "Advertisement Extraordinary," Bache proclaimed,

1000 Dollars Reward

———

Will be given to any man who invents a plausible story to help the British Treaty in its passage through the House of Representatives of the United States.

N. B. From past experience, the bugbear of a war is likely to prove most efficacious. But as this story is worn rather threadbare, it will require somewhat of a new dress.

Federalists, the *Aurora* charged again and again, were trying to make the House members into "automatons" and "puppets," and were accusing the

House of not being one of the government's "constituted authorities." Refusal to ratify would not lead to anarchy nor would it create a despotic House of Representatives, one writer argued.[73]

The passage of Livingston's motion requesting the President to lay the Jay Treaty papers before the House on March 24 did not deflect a growing cynicism and anger in the *Aurora*, especially when Washington declared he would take the matter into consideration. The *Aurora* compared this "consideration" with the considerations formerly given by the King of France to petitioners:

> 'Le Roi, s'avisera' was the answer of Louis; 'I will consider' that of our President. One thing however yet to be determined is, whether the two answers are of the same import; this is worthy of serious consideration; for if our executive by 'I will consider' means a refusal, it should be so understood, that the house might proceed without delay.[74]

Yet when Washington's consideration turned into a refusal at the end of March, the *Aurora* reacted with shock and outrage. For the *Aurora*, nothing short of a declaration of war between the two branches of government—a war that could destroy the House—had begun. The issue was again posed as the sovereign rights of the majority versus the prerogative of the President. "The President has taken the decisive step, which leads him to victory, or consigns him to defeat," pronounced one contributor. "He rises, if he rises at all, on the ruins of the Representatives of the People. The case admits not of accommodation."[75]

The President was accused of a long catalog of crimes and misdemeanors, such as adopting the language of the kings of France, of denouncing Democratic Societies and then attacking the democratic branch of the government, of treating Congress like a parliament that had to enroll his edicts, and of being as dictatorial as Cromwell.[76] The treaty papers were refused, declared one correspondent, because they would "unmask" the President and "produce horror in the mind of every true and virtuous American." When a rumor emerged in early April that Washington had changed his mind and intended to send the papers to Congress, Bache argued that this could "be believed only by those who are ignorant, that firmness and decision are prominent features in the President's character."[77]

As debate over approval of appropriations continued throughout April, the *Aurora* remained steadfast in its accusation that the Federalists were attempting to deprive the House, the only true representative of the people, of its rights and responsibilities and to transfer these to the President and

Senate.[78] When one congressman suggested that the House quit its exhaustive discussion of congressional rights in order to secure ratification and possession of the western posts by June 1, Bache chastised him:

> With equal propriety might a British press-gang say to an American seaman whom they attempted to entice out of a place of safety, 'Do but come aboard our vessels and then we will lend a willing ear to your arguments and protests against our power and rights.'—If once the sailor is put aboard, all his remonstrances will be in vain; and in like manner if the house were to abandon their rights in the present instance, all resistance in future would be vain.[79]

During the last week of April, as the Republicans began to lose their solidarity and the final contest over the Jay Treaty appropriations loomed near, Bache virtually threatened those members of the House, who, though opposing the treaty, planned to abstain on the final vote. Those guilty of such conduct "ought to be branded with the same ignominy as those who vote against their country," he argued, and a *Gazette* writer, equally impassioned, retorted that many members would vote for the treaty "however the Market street 'skunk of scurrility' may assert to the contrary."[80] In a last ditch stand, other *Aurora* writers denounced the Federalist war-whoop and rumors that the appropriation would pass. House members were again reminded that a rift with France would ensue and that American indebtedness to British creditors would rise by twenty million dollars.[81]

House passage of the appropriation bill on April 30 was a bitter defeat for Bache and his correspondents. Bache and his writers could do no more than explain their defeat and predict the consequences. The treaty had been ratified as a result of "design and fraud" by its supporters, declared a correspondent on May 3, while other editorials blamed Federalist petitioners raising the specter of war for the House's failure. Bache himself declared on May 5 that some Federalists conspired to have the treaty "crammed down the throats of the Republicans by the point of bayonet, if the House had not agreed to it." Two days later, Bache charged that Federalist ranting had been so extreme that an eastern paper had predicted "a revolutionary government, revolutionary tribunals, public accusers and guillotines," if the treaty failed. For Bache, such writings were proof

> that there is a faction in this country who will only adhere to the constitution as long as they can remain the ruling party, and who would tomorrow, if their influence was finally crushed under the present system of government, be vociferous for a King, and all the paraphernalia of royalism and aristocracy.

Slanders of Gallatin and other Republicans were held up as further proof of Federalist designs. Americans were again told of constitutional usurpations, and were warned that the House could expect a rapid decrease in its power.[82]

The battle over the Jay Treaty compelled Bache to employ a level of rhetoric, a tenacity of argumentation, and a method of combat he had not displayed before. Unlike his approach to earlier issues, he attempted to prepare the public mind against the treaty before its contents were known, and he recognized the value in disclosing and publicizing the text of the treaty to suggest the administration's secrecy. During the critical moments in June through August, 1795, he played a central role in fostering protests and petitions against the treaty. Although the *Aurora* failed to offer the sophisticated analytic arguments that intellectuals like Madison and Jefferson preferred, all other general and popular strategies were put into operation: attempting to prove consistent public opposition to the treaty; examining Federalist motives; de-fusing Federalist arguments and fear-mongering; and, above all, repeating general and diffuse arguments against closer ties with Great Britain.

Yet from the start of the controversy over John Jay's appointment, to the conclusion of the fight to defeat the treaty in the House, Bache and his *Aurora* had consistently promoted the same ideology, principles, and policies they had embraced during the battle over the Democratic Societies and the Whiskey Rebellion. The desire to foster a spirit of republican nationalism, to further that spirit through a new assertion of independence from Great Britain, and to identify liberal republican solidarity in closer ties with France were old and secure themes. Even more secure and central was the theme of popular sovereignty. Bache remained attached to an unflagging faith that a democratic majority of the people could arrive at collective, enlightened self-interest, at a kind of pure intuitive political morality, if they were properly informed and not deceived. For all of the obvious benefits of party politics and Republican organization, for all that Bache was thrown back on electing Republicans as the only democratic cure of the British disease, the Jay Treaty did not drive him into a modern faith in opposition party politics.

But something else did change. Bache was filled with a new level of rage and frustration. The last remnants of adolescent uncertainty were purged by the issue of the Jay Treaty. Absolutely convinced of the craven designs of the Federalists as well as the effects the treaty would have on relations between his two beloved countries, Bache would henceforward spend every ounce of hatred and radical rhetoric he could employ. To some degree his chief opponents, especially Fenno and Webster (who had accused him and the *Aurora* of being vengeful conspirators organized under the Democratic Societies banner to imitate the horrors and atrocities of the French Revolution) were responsible for this new level of rage.[83] But desperation, combined with a little more maturity and confidence in his political place in life, also allowed Bache to release his political emotions in an extravagant manner.

On July 4, 1796, Bache closed the *Aurora*'s assault on the British Treaty with an elegy to American independence lost. Remarking that there was to be an eclipse of the sun that day, he wondered if it might also be said that the sun of American liberty had been eclipsed by the British Treaty. He then added,

> This day leads in the 21st year since this country was declared independent of Britain. The wisdom and patriotism which dictated the declaration were well backed by the courage and fortitude that maintained it, and which after a glorious contest, finally effected a peace that had for its basis the independence of the United States.
>
> How far the lapse of a few years since that glorious period has brought us back towards the point whence we started in our career as a nation, let existing facts decide. Since the late treaty has become the law of the land it may be a doubt whether our independence be more than nominal; the British before the revolution insisted on taxing us; they now, under the slightest pretexts, capture and condemn our property on the high seas, and we cannot retaliate, our hands being tied by treaty.

Washington's administration had contributed much "towards re-colonizing us anew," he added. Yet he still believed that the "wishes of the People will . . . find their weight in time, even in the branches of our government most remote from their influence." And finally, in a conclusion that foreshadowed the remaining two years of his life and must have frightened rather than reassured most Americans, Bache declared that France, "to which we are bound by so many ties of gratitude, may again consolidate our liberties by her victories in Europe, and we may yet have substantial cause to do homage to the spirit which dictated" the Declaration of Independence.[84]

Notes

1. B. F. Bache to Wm. Bache, Feb. 26, 1795, Bache Papers, Castle Collection, American Philosophical Society, Philadelphia.

2. These issues are addressed in varying degrees in Bradford Perkins, *The First Rapprochement: England and the United States, 1795–1805* (Philadelphia, 1955); Alexander DeConde, *Entangling Alliance: Politics & Diplomacy under George Washington* (Durham, N. C., 1958); Joseph Charles, *The Origins of the American Party System* (New York, 1956), 91–122; Jerald A. Combs, *The Jay Treaty: Political Battleground of the Founding Fathers* (Berkeley, Calif., 1970); and Albert Hall Bowman, *The Struggle for Neutrality: Franco-American Diplomacy During the Federalist Era* (Knoxville, Tenn., 1974), esp. 198–261.

3. British-American conflict through early 1794 is discussed well in Charles R. Ritcheson, *Aftermath of Revolution: British Policy toward the United States, 1783–1795* (Dallas, Tex., 1969), 289–313. On Jefferson's Report see Dumas Malone, *Jefferson and the Ordeal of Liberty* (Boston, 1962), 154–60; and Bowman, *The Struggle for Neutrality*, 139–42. Tench Coxe's central role in preparing that Report and Jefferson's revealed liberalism are detailed in Jacob E. Cooke, *Tench Coxe and the Early Republic* (Chapel Hill, N. C., 1978), 224–31, 252–55. Even more emphatic about Jefferson's broad liberal support of commerce and manufacturing, as revealed in the Report on Commerce and consistently elsewhere, is John R. Nelson, Jr., *Liberty and Property: Political Economy and Policymaking in the New Nation, 1789–1812* (Baltimore, 1987), esp. 74 on the Report. Lord Dorchester's fears and blunders are discussed in J. Leitch Wright, Jr., *Britain and the American Frontier, 1783–1815* (Athens, Ga., 1975), 86–102. The nature, scope, and effect of the British Orders and depredations are examined in Anna C. Clauder, *American Commerce as Affected by the Wars of the French Revolution and Napoleon, 1793–1812* (Philadelphia, 1932), 30–37. See also Ritcheson, *Aftermath of Revolution*, 299–304. On January 8, 1794, a new Order-in-Council corrected the November distention of the Rule of 1756, allowing neutral vessels the right to trade with the French West Indies to the extent they had been allowed to before the war, while also allowing Americans to carry goods from the West Indies to France if first landed in an American port.

4. For a wide view of these arguments see *Gen'l. Adv.,* Jan. 6, 7 ("corres." from a Boston paper), 8 ("Cato" from the N. Y. *Diary*), Feb. 4, 6 ("Cato" from the N. Y. *Diary*), 7 ("A Few Plain Questions and Home Answers"), 8 ("corres."), 14 ("corres." and an extract), 15 ("corres." from a Boston paper), Mar. 1, 3 ("corres."), 8 ("corres."), 10 (Report of a Merchant Committee considering British depredations), 11 ("corres."), 13 ("A Nose of Wax"), 15, 17 ("corres."), 18 (Bache and "corres."), 22 ("corres."), 24 ("corres."), 25 (Bache and "corres."), 26 ("corres."), 27, 29, Apr. 2, 9, 11, May 3, 13 ("corres."), 31, 1794.

5. *Ibid.,* Mar. 28, 1794.

6. *Ibid.,* Apr. 18, 1794.

7. *Ibid.,* Apr. 11, 1794.

8. On Federalist maneuvers and the Jay appointment see Charles R. King, ed., *The Life and Correspondence of Rufus King* (New York, 1894–1900. Cited here N. Y., 1971), I, 517–23; and Frank Monaghan, *John Jay, Defender of Liberty* (Indianapolis, 1935), 364–68.

9. Details on the negotiation strategy devised by Rufus King can be found in King, ed., *Life and Correspondence*, I, 517–23; and Robert Ernst, *Rufus King, American Federalist* (Chapel Hill, N. C., 1968), 198–99. Jay's selection and nomination are discussed in Samuel Flagg Bemis, *Jay's Treaty: A Study in Commerce and Diplomacy* (New Haven, Conn., 1923), 265, 269–70; Alexander De Conde, *Entangling Alliance: Politics & Diplomacy under George Washington* (Durham, N. C., 1958), 103–104; Monaghan, *John Jay*, 364–68; Broadus Mitchell, *Alexander Hamilton. The National Adventure, 1788–1804* (New York, 1962), 331–34; John J. Reardon, *Edmund Randolph: A Biography* (New York, 1975), 261–63; and Harry Ammon, *James Monroe: The Quest for National Identity* (New York, 1971), 111–12.

10. For these denunciations of Jay's fitness see *Gen'l. Adv.*, Apr. 19 ("corres."), 28 (letter), May 9 ("corres."), 1794.

11. *Ibid.*, Apr. 19 ("corres."), 25 ("corres."), May 2, 6, 15, 17, Dec. 30 ("The Querist" from the *Ind. Gaz.*), 1794; Mar. 17, 1795. Fenno ridiculed Bache's March 17 editorial on the Chief Justice with a long doggerel poem by "Peter Short Metre," *Gazette of U. S.*, Mar. 18, 1795. Two of Bache's contributors in early 1794 mildly supported Jay's appointment. *Gen'l. Adv.*, Apr. 30 (letter), May 1 ("A Citizen"), 1794.

12. *Ibid.*, Apr. 29, May 1, 2, 17, 1794. For an omnibus attack incorporating most of these arguments see the editorial in *ibid.*, Apr. 29, 1794.

13. *Ibid.*, May 28, 1794; and *Gaz. of U. S.*, May 30, 1794.

14. *Gen'l. Adv.*, June 2, 6, 4 ("corres."), 7 ("corres."), 17 ("corres."), 1794. On Monroe's appointment see Ammon, *Monroe*, 112–14; and Edward Angel, "James Monroe's Mission to France, 1794–1796," (unpub. Ph.D. diss., George Washington Univ., 1979), 154–66.

15. *Gen'l. Adv.*, Aug. 28, and Sept. 5, 1794. The *Advertiser* chorus of writers also continued Bache's steady contention that whatever settlement was exacted from Great Britain would come as a consequence of French victories, not British fraternity. See *ibid.*, Aug. 29 ("corres."), Nov. 19 ("corres."), 1794. The British had not learned of growing resentment against the Orders-in-Council, Madison's resolutions, the embargo, or even Lord Dorchester's speech to the Indians, until early June 1794. On these early stages of negotiation see Bemis, *Jay's Treaty*, 282–86; Combs, *Jay Treaty*, 143–50; Ritcheson, *Aftermath of Revolution, 317–20; De Conde, Entangling Alliance*, 105; and Monaghan, *Jay*, 372–74.

16. *Gen'l. Adv.*, Oct. 9, 1794. On the progress of negotiations to September 30 see Bemis, *Jay's Treaty*, 287–97, 333–45; De Conde, *Entangling Alliance*, 105–107; John C. Miller, *Alexander Hamilton: Portrait in Paradox* (New York, 1959), 415–25; Mitchell, *Hamilton*, 336; Monaghan, *Jay*, 368–69; and Reardon, *Randolph*, 271, 287–93.

17. *Gen'l. Adv.*, Oct. 27 ("corres."), Nov. 1 ("A." from the *N. Y. Jour.*), 3, 18 ("Philo-Republicanus"), 1794; Jan. 23, 1795.

18. *Aurora*, Nov. 8 ("A." from the *N. Y. Jour.*), 11 (communication from N. Y.), 12, 18 ("Philo-Republicanus"), Dec. 5 ("A Hint"), 1794. Two writers mildly defended Jay's good intentions and conduct. See *ibid.*, Nov. 24 ("Moderation"),

Dec. 3 ("Reflections on the mission of Mr. Jay"), 1794. Compare all of the editorials cited in this paragraph with those written after revelation of the Jay Treaty on the same matter, when Jay was further portrayed as an enemy of France and a sycophant of the British court. The entire administration, furthermore, were held culpable for the negotiation, were accused of being the Treaty's real authors, and were blamed for not keeping Monroe and Pinckney informed in Europe. See *ibid.*, June 30 ("A SONG" from the *Del. Gaz.*), Aug. 15, Dec. 22 ("A Trip to St. James, 1794"), 1795; Jan. 12, Mar. 17 ("An Enemy to Oppression"), May 1 ("An American" from the Charleston *City Gaz.*), 1796. At different times Grenville, Washington, and Hamilton were charged with being the Treaty's real authors. See, for example, *ibid.*, July 15 ("corres."), 21, Aug. 12, 1795.

19. *Ibid.*, Feb. 2, 3 ("corres."), 6, Mar. 19 ("corres." from a Bennington paper), June 4 ("Political Observations"), 1795.

20. *Ibid.*, Feb. 2 ("corres."), 6, 7, 9 ("T. L." and a "corres."), 10 (letter), 11, Mar. 4, 19 ("Franklin" from the *Ind. Gazeteer*), Apr. 13 (letter and Bache), 15, 18 (Bache and "corres."), 30 (ed. from a Boston paper), May 4, 7, 16 ("corres."), 1795. For various editorial comment in the France-versus-England argument see *Aurora*, Feb. 26, ("Philanthropos"), Mar. 24, 30 (letter), 31 ("corres."), Apr. 1 ("corres."), May 15 ("A. B."), and 16 ("Yorick's" rebuttal to "A. B."), June 3 ("Political Observations"), 6, 18 (communication from a Boston paper), 22 ("Sidney"), 1795. On "Franklin" see *ibid.*, Mar. 19, 20, 25, 27, 31, Apr. 10, 13, 16, 20, 24, May 10, 26, June 8, 10, 12, 1795.

21. G. Washington to Sec. of Treas., June 24, 1796, John C. Fitzpatrick, ed., *The Writings of George Washington* (Washington, D. C., 1931–1944), XXXV, 95–96, hereafter cited as Fitzpatrick, ed., *Writings of Washington*. On the special envoy issue see G. Washington to Alex. Hamilton, June 26, 1796, *ibid.*, 101–104.

22. Ed. Randolph to J. Adams, Apr. 2, 1795, Microfilm of the Adams Papers, 1639–1889. Reel 379.

23. Receipt of the treaty is discussed in John Alexander Carroll and Mary Wells Ashworth, *George Washington: First in Peace* (New York, 1957), 236–39; Reardon, *Randolph*, 288–94; and Combs, *Jay Treaty*, 160. Hamilton's complaints are discussed in Miller, *Hamilton*, 422; and Mitchell, *Hamilton*, 338–41. Forrest McDonald, *Alexander Hamilton. A Biography* (New York, 1979), 315–16, argues that Hamilton was more supportive of the treaty. For the support of Wolcott and Pickering see O. Wolcott, Jr. to O. Wolcott, Sr., June 27, 1795; and O. Wolcott, Jr. to Jebediah Morse, July 16, 1795, George Gibbs, ed., *Memoirs of the Administrations of Washington and Adams* (New York, 1846. Cited here, N. Y., 1971), I, 200–201, 212, hereafter cited as Gibbs, ed., *Wolcott Papers;* and Gerald H. Clarfield, *Timothy Pickering and American Diplomacy, 1795–1800* (Columbia, Mo., 1969), 22–23. Bemis, *Jay's Treaty*, 371; A. L. Burt, *The United States, Great Britain and British North America . . .* (New Haven, Conn., 1940), 152–53, 156; Perkins, *First Rapprochement*, 1; and Ritcheson, *Aftermath of the Revolution*, 357–59, defend the treaty to varying degrees. Combs, *Jay Treaty*, 187, believes it led to political warfare at home. De Conde, *Entangling Alliance*, 108–10; and Bowman, *Struggle for Neutrality*, 261, define the treaty in terms of producing the schism with France.

24. "Corres.," *Aurora*, June 18, 1795. On secrecy, renunciation of a treaty with America's old enemy, and a new call for retaliation see *ibid.*, June 11 ("Caution" from the *Ind. Chron.*), 13 ("corres."), 16 ("corres."), 17 ("Sidney"), 18 ("corres."), 19 ("Sidney"), 20 ("corres." and communication from a Boston paper), 23 ("corres."), 26 ("Sidney"), 1795. Fenno defended Senate secrecy and charged the *Aurora* with interfering in the constitutional process of ratification merely to give Bache's Democratic club a chance to attack the treaty. *Gaz. of U. S.*, June 22 ("corres."), 23 ("corres."), 25 (letter), 1795. Senate dealings with the treaty are reviewed in Combs, *Jay Treaty*, 161; Perkins, *First Rapprochement*, 31–33; De Conde, *Entangling Alliance*, 112; Carroll and Ashworth, *Washington*, 250–53; and Miller, *Hamilton*, 422.

25. *Aurora*, June 24, 25, 1795. The treaty had been signed formally in London on October 28, 1795. The new British Order was not a revival of the November 6 Order but a secret attempt by the British to re-assert their right to condemn and buy foodstuffs headed for the enemy under their old June 8, 1793 and January 8, 1794, Orders. See Combs, *Jay Treaty*, 164–65; and Anna Cornelia Clauder, *American Commerce as Affected by the Wars of the French Revolution and Napoleon, 1793–1812* (Philadelphia, 1932), 37.

26. *Aurora*, June 26, 27, 1795.

27. *Ibid.*, June 26, 1795. King later defended himself in the *Aurora*, claiming that after Senate approval and adjournment the Senate had freed its members from confidence, allowing them to show the Treaty to others providing they did not reveal it for publication. *Ibid.*, Dec. 15, 1795. On the Butler-Madison connection see Gaillard Hunt, ed., *The Writings of James Madison* (New York, 1906), VI, 234n, hereafter cited as Hunt, ed., *Writings of Madison*. Perkins, *First Rapprochement*, 33, claims several persons had seen the treaty.

28. See Alex. Hamilton to O. Wolcott, Jr., June 26, 1795; and same to same, June 30, 1795, Harold C. Syrett, *et al.*, eds., *The Papers of Alexander Hamilton* (New York, 1961–79), XVIII, 388–89, 392–93, hereafter cited as Syrett, *et al.*, eds., *Hamilton Papers*. For another narrative of Bache's revelation of the Treaty and the government's plans for publication see *ibid.*, 389–92n. On Randolph and treaty publication see Reardon, *Randolph*, 296; Ed. Randolph to R. King, July 6, 1795, King, *Life and Correspondence*, II, 15. See also Randolph's "Memorandum," July 14, 1795, on giving Adet a copy of the treaty in Fitzpatrick, ed., *Writings of Washington*, XXXIV, 245n.

29. *Aurora*, June 29, 1795. Bache advertised authentic copies of the treaty for the first time in *ibid.*, July 1, 1795. Bache printed and sold two editions of the treaty, the first containing Senator Stevens Thomson Mason's reasons for revealing the treaty, the second containing Burr's motion in the Senate to renegotiate the treaty, and Senator Henry Tazewell's motion and reasons for demanding defeat of the treaty by the Senate. U. S., *(Authentic). Treaty of Amity, Commerce and Navigation, Between His Britannic Majesty, and the United States* (Philadelphia, 1795).

30. On Mason's statement see Stevens T. Mason to Benj. Franklin Bache, *ibid.*, 2. Adet's confession is in P. Adet to the Committee of Public Safety, July 3, 1795, in Frederick Jackson Turner, ed., "Correspondence of the French Ministers to the

United States, 1791–1797," in *Annual Report of the American Historical Association for the Year 1903* (Washington, D. C., 1904), II, 741–42. On this matter see also Bowman, *Struggle for Neutrality*, 204 and 204n.

31. M. H. Bache to B. F. Bache, July 2, 1795; B. F. Bache to M. H. Bache, July 3 (two letters), 6, 1795, Bache Papers, Castle Collection, American Philosophical Society, Philadelphia. On Fenno's charge see *Gaz. of U. S.*, July 14, 1795.

32. For Bache's descriptions of the countryside and cities see B. F. Bache to M. H. Bache, July 3, 6, 15, 1795, Bache Papers, Castle Coll., Am. Philos. Soc. On the political affairs described see *ibid.*, July 6, 10, 1795.

33. *Ibid.*, July 10, 15, 1795.

34. *Ibid.*, July 15, 1795. See also Stephen Higginson to T. Pickering, July 14, 1795, J. Franklin Jameson, "Letters of Stephen Higginson, 1783–1804," *Annual Report of the American Historical Association for the Year 1896* (Washington, D. C., 1897), I, 787–88.

35. B. F. Bache to M. H. Bache, July 18, 19, 21, 1795, Bache Papers, Castle Coll., Am. Philos. Soc. On Hamilton and the New York meeting see Combs, *Jay Treaty*, 162–63; Miller, *Hamilton*, 424; and Mitchell, *Hamilton*, 341–44.

36. Communication, *Aurora*, July 14, 1795. For editorials on the Fourth of July see *ibid.*, July 3 ("A Militia Man"), 9 (ed. from *Ind. Gaz.*), 14 (ed. from N. Y. *Argus*), 16, 23 ("Death of Independence," from *Vir. Gaz.*), 1795. Fenno used a poem to ridicule the *Aurora*'s audacity in denying celebrations of independence. See *Gaz. of U. S.*, July 3, 1795. Reports on protest meetings appeared in the *Aurora* on July 16, 25, 28, 29, 31, Aug. 1, 8, 10, 15, 17, 1795. The Boston meeting in particular was discussed in detail on July 13, 15, 17, 18, 22, 24, 25, 1795.

A colorful description of reactions against Jay and the treaty is offered in Monaghan, *Jay*, 390–97. On the Philadelphia meeting see O. Wolcott, Jr. to the President, July 26, 1795, in Gibbs, ed., *Wolcott Papers*, I, 217; Tinkcom, *Republicans and Federalists in Pennsylvania*, 89; and Miller, *Philadelphia, The Federalist City*, 71–72. Protests in the South are described in Lisle A. Rose, *Prologue to Democracy: The Federalists in the South, 1789–1800* (Lexington, Ky., 1968), 114–21; Delbert Harold Gilpatrick, *Jeffersonian Democracy in North Carolina, 1789–1816* (New York, 1931. Cited here, N. Y., 1967), 67–71; John Harold Wolfe, *Jeffersonian Democracy in South Carolina* (Chapel Hill, N. C., 1940), 84–85; Richard R. Beeman, *The Old Dominion and the New Nation, 1788–1801* (Lexington, Ky., 1972), 140–41; and Norman K. Risjord, *Chesapeake Politics, 1781–1800* (New York, 1978), 454–61. Individual Federalist reactions can be found throughout the correspondence of Oliver Wolcott, Jr. in Gibbs, ed., *Wolcott Papers*, 209–224; and King, *Life and Correspondence*, II, 22–25. On the New York Chamber of Commerce see R. King to Chris. Gore, July 24, 1795, *ibid.*, 16.

37. See *Gaz. of U. S.*, July 25 ("corres."), 27 (two "corres."), 29 ("corres."), 1795.

38. For *Gazette* editorials on this matter see *ibid.*, July 30 ("Y."), 31 ("P."), 1795. For the *Aurora* see July 27 ("corres."), 29 (ed. and "M."), 30, 1795. Both papers were probably wrong. A crowd that had the luxury of spreading out (as Fenno contended) also needed to hear the speaker. A reasonable compromise

would be four to six square feet per person, which would have placed attendance at between 1,800 and 2,700 persons.

39. On the N. Y. Chamber see *ibid.*, July 27 ("corres." from a N. Y. paper), 29 (ed. from N. Y. *Argus*), Aug. 5 ("Mercator" from N. Y. *Daily Adv.*), 1795. On the Flemington petition see "Vive la République," *ibid.*, Aug. 3, 1795. And on the right to protest see *ibid.*, July 31 ("A Detestable Faction" and Bache), Aug. 1, 3 (communication), 5 ("Detector"), 6, 17, 24 ("Passive Obedience and Non Resistance"), 1795. This latter charge was revived in later months *ibid.*, Sept. 4 ("Atticus" from *Ind. Gaz.*), Nov. 26, Dec. 11 ("A Federalist"), 1795.

40. On Virginia see *Aurora*, Aug. 14 (ed. from Richmond *Gaz.*), and 17 ("corres." and Bache), 1795. See also *ibid.*, July 31 ("Solon"), Aug. 3 ("corres."), 4 ("Minerva Reviewed"), 5 (Minerva Reviewed" and "corres."), 1795. For examples of the changed Federalist attitude see O. Wolcott, Jr., to Alex. Hamilton, July 30, 1795; O. Ellsworth to O. Wolcott, Jr., Aug. 20, 1795, Gibbs, ed., *Wolcott Papers*, I, 219–20, 226; S. Higginson to T. Pickering, Aug. 13, 16, 1795, *Annual Report of the Amer. Hist Assoc. for the Year 1896*, I, 788–93; and James M. Banner, Jr., *To the Hartford Convention: The Federalists and the Origins of Party Politics in Massachusetts, 1789–1815* (New York, 1970), 20.

41. *Ibid.*, Aug. 15, 22 ("C." and "Old Delaware Man"), 25 ("No Pendulum"), 26, 27 (ed. from *Ind. Chron.* and "Hancock"), 29 (two "corres."), 31 ("One of the Swinish Multitude"), 1795.

42. *Ibid.*, Aug. 3, 6, 10, 1795. Fenno and Webster protested that they were the true friends of the President, although "Chronus" argued that the President should not deny two-thirds of the Senate when under other circumstances the Congress could override a veto with a two-thirds vote. See *Gaz. of U. S.*, Aug. 5, 12 ("Chronus"), 1795; *American Minerva*, Aug. 6, 1795.

43. Combs, *Jay Treaty*, 160, 164–68, 193–96; De Conde, *Entangling Alliance*, 419–27; and Bowman, *Struggle for Neutrality*, 198–218. On Washington, the treaty, and Randolph see Carroll and Ashworth, *Washington*, 249–98. On the Randolph affair in particular see Reardon, *Randolph*, 307–315; William H. Masterson, *Tories and Democrats: British Diplomats in Pre-Jacksonian America* (College Station, Tex., 1985), 26; Clarfield, *Pickering and American Diplomacy* (Columbia, Mo., 1969), 23–30; and Gerard H. Clarfield, *Timothy Pickering and the American Republic* (Pittsburgh, 1980), 158–60.

On Randolph's clumsy attempt to vindicate himself see Edmund Randolph, *A Vindication of Mr. Randolph's Resignation* (Philadelphia, 1795); and Edmund Randolph, *Political Truth: or, Animadversions on the Present State of Public Affairs* (Philadelphia, 1796). William Cobbett ridiculed Randolph mercilessly in "A New Year's Gift for the Democrats," in John M. and James P. Cobbett, eds., *Selections from Cobbett's Political Works* (London, 1835), I, 85–113. In modern times Irving Brant, "Edmund Randolph, Not Guilty," *William and Mary Quarterly*, 3d Ser., VII (1950), 179–98, has defended Randolph's innocence while Forrest McDonald, *The Presidency of George Washington* (Lawrence, Kan., 1974), 165, believes Randolph never offered a "satisfactory explanation." John J. Reardon cautiously suggests that Randolph did not successfully exonerate himself. See Reardon, *Randolph,* esp. 329, 333. For more on the historiography of the affair see Bowman, *Struggle for Neutrality*, 217–18n.

44. *Aurora*, Aug. 15, 18 ("A Federalist"), 21, 1795. The partisan consequences of Washington's ratification have been frequently noted. See, for example, Joseph Charles, *The Origins of the American Party System* (New York, 1956), 107; and William O. Lynch, *Fifty Years of Party Warfare, 1789–1837* (Indianapolis, 1931), 53–54.

45. *Aurora*, Aug. 22 ("corres."), 27, 1795. The attack on Washington is taken up in greater detail in Chapter 10.

46. Alexander Hamilton and leading Federalists were eager to disclose the authorship of these letters. See especially Alex. Hamilton to O. Wolcott, Jr., Sept. 20, 1795, Syrett, *et al.*, eds., *Hamilton Papers*, XIX, 278. Fenno denied that the *Aurora* writers could be native Americans, and said these letters were the work of one man or a small clique of men. See "Civis," *Gaz. of U. S.*, Sept. 17, 18 ("corres."), Oct. 26, 27, 1795. A. J. Dallas, accused by William Willcocks of writing the "Valerius" letters, denied writing any essays for Bache's paper. See *Aurora*, Dec. 22 (letter from A. J. Dallas), 1795; and Jan. 6 (letter by Wm. Willcocks from N. Y. *Argus*), 1796. According to Edmund and Dorothy Smith Berkeley, *John Beckley: Zealous Partisan in a Nation Divided* (Philadelphia, 1973), 120, Beckley had begun to work closely with Bache by 1795 and was "suspected of being author of the 'Pittachus,' 'Belisarius,' and 'Valerius' letters." Next to Leib, Beckley would remain Bache's closest friend and ally until Bache's death in 1798. On Beckley's activities in this period see also Philip S. Marsh, "John Beckley: Mystery Man of the Early Jeffersonians," *Pennsylvania Magazine of History and Biography*, LXXII (1948), 59–60; and Gloria Jahoda, "John Beckley: Jefferson's Campaign Manager," *Bulletin of the New York Public Library*, LXIV (May, 1960), 247–53.

47. *Aurora*, Aug. 21 ("Hancock"), 22 ("Valerius"), 31 ("An Old Soldier of 1776"), Sept. 3 ("Hancock"), 7, 8 ("Hancock"), 11, 18 ("Pittachus"), 21 ("Atticus"), 28 ("Pittachus"), 1795.

48. *Ibid.*, Sept. 11, 1795. On general arguments see also *ibid.*, Aug. 20 ("corres."), 22, Sept. 1 (ed. and "Valerius"), 8, 12 ("Millions" from *Ind. Chron.*), 14 ("Pittachus" and Bache), 15 ("Belisarius"), 23 ("Pittachus"), Oct. 1 ("An Observer"), 12 (letter), 22 ("Atticus"), 26 ("Pittachus"), 1795. Webster denied Washington's infallibility but believed that the President had made few mistakes and would be backed by the people. *Am. Minerva*, Sept. 3, 15, 1795; Feb. 4, 1796. Both the *Minerva* and Fenno's *Gazette* staunchly defended the President's firm conduct throughout the fall of 1795.

49. *Aurora*, Aug. 26 ("A short string of modern logic . . ." from *Phila. Minerva*), Sept. 12 ("Millions" from *Ind. Chron.*), 14 ("Pittachus" and Bache), 16 ("corres." and "Diplomaticus" from *Ind. Chron.*), 26 ("Atticus" and "Diplomaticus"), Oct. 14 ("Belisarius"), 22 ("Atticus"), Nov. 17 ("A Citizen of Maine" from *Gaz. of Maine*), 1795; Jan. 26 ("A Freeman" and ed. from *Ken. Gaz.*), 1796.

50. *Ibid.*, Jan. 13, 1796. For other editorials on this theme see *ibid.*, Jan. 4, 7, 9 ("Candor" from *Ind. Chron.*), 13, 23, 1796.

51. *Ibid.*, Jan. 12, 16, 23, 1796.

52. On Madison's view of the *Aurora* see J. Madison to [?], Aug. 23, 1795, Hunt, ed., *Writings of Madison*, VI, 239–53. On Jefferson and Madison in general see Thos. Jefferson to J. Madison, Sept. 21, 1795, Paul Leicester Ford, ed., *The Writings of Thomas Jefferson* (New York, 1895), VII, 32–33, hereafter cited as Ford, ed., *Jefferson's Writings*. On this matter see also Dumas Malone, *Jefferson and the Ordeal of Liberty* (Boston, 1962), 246–49; and Brant, *Madison*, 425–26, 431–39.

53. On oppositionist writing in general see especially Donald H. Stewart, *The Opposition Press of the Federalist Period* (New York, 1969), 177–235. On Dallas see Raymond Walters, Jr., *Alexander James Dallas: Lawyer, Politician, Financier, 1759–1817* (Philadelphia, 1943. Cited here, N. Y., 1969), 66–68. The "Camillus" letters are most easily accessible in Henry Cabot Lodge, ed., *The Works of Alexander Hamilton* (New York, 1904. Cited here, N. Y., 1971), V, 188–491, and VI, 3–197. See also Miller, *Hamilton*, 427–30. The "Vindication of the treaty . . ." by "Curtius" is available in Noah Webster, *A Collection of Papers on Political, Literary, and Moral Subjects* (New York, 1843. Cited here, N. Y., 1968), 179–224. William Cobbett's *A Little Plain English*, in John W. and James P. Cobbett, eds., *Selections from Cobbett's Political Works . . .* (London, 1835), I, 53–85, defended British policies as much as the value of the treaty to Americans. The *Aurora* sometimes criticized "Curtius" or "Camillus," usually stressing the ponderous length and pretended expertise of these essays. See *Aurora*, Aug. 12 ("E."), 15 ("corres."), Oct. 1 ("corres."), 27 (letter from N. Y. *Argus*), Nov. 17 ("corres."), 1795; Jan. 6 (ed. from N. Y. *Argus*), 1796. The most available source is "The Jay Treaty. Treaty of Amity, Commerce, and Navigation, . . ." as quoted from Hunter Miller's *Treaties and Other International Acts of the United States of America*, II, 245–67, cited in Bemis, *Jay's Treaty*, 453–87.

54. *Aurora*, Dec. 19, 1795. See also *ibid.*, July 15 (ed. from N. Y. *Jour.*), 21 ("Caius"), Aug. 1 and 8 ("Atticus" from *Ind. Gaz.*), Dec. 19 ("Not one of your constituents"), 1795; Aug. 4, 1796.

55. *Ibid.*, July 20 ("Civis"), 21 ("Caius"), Dec. 2 ("corres."), 1795; Apr. 14, 1796. On slaves see *ibid.*, July 15 (ed. from N. Y. *Jour.*), 20 ("Civis"), 21 ("Caius"), 24 ("No Englishman"), Aug. 8 ("Atticus" from *Ind. Gaz.*), Dec. 19 ("Not one of your constituents"), 1795.

56. *Ibid.*, Sept. 5, 1795; Apr. 23, 1796.

57. On sequestration see *ibid.*, July 20 ("Civis"), 21 ("Caius"), Aug. 3 ("Americanus"), Nov. 14, ("Tully"), 1795. On land ownership see *ibid.*, July 17 (ed. from *Ind. Chron.*), Aug. 27 ("John Doe" from Charleston *Gaz.*), 1795. Two correspondents who obviously had not read Article XXVIII of the treaty carefully, erroneously assumed that if nothing were done to revise the unratified twelfth article, only the first ten articles would go into effect. See *ibid.*, July 6 ("Americanus"), 1795; Feb. 8 ("A Citizen" from *Ken. Gaz.*), 1796. On commercial provisions see *ibid.*, July 15 (ed. from N. Y. *Jour.*), 20 ("Civis"), 21 ("Caius"), Aug. 3 ("Americanus"), 8 ("Atticus"), Oct. 23, Dec. 10 ("Brutus"), 1795. On Article XII see *ibid.*, July 1, 10 (ed. from N. Y. *Argus*), 20 ("Civis"), Aug. 3 ("Americanus"), 1795. On impressment, boundaries, and piracy see *ibid.*, July 8 ("Impartial"), 21 ("Caius"), 29 ("A Citizen of Maine" from *Columbian Centinel*), 1795; Mar. 3 ("Scipio"),

1796. According to the *Aurora,* the English people and press believed the treaty's particular provisions were so bad for the United States that no one in England believed the Americans would ratify it. See *ibid.,* July 10 (ed. from London *Diary*), 31, 1795.

58. "Americanus," from *Ind. Gaz., ibid.,* July 25, 1795.

59. *Ibid.,* July 25, Aug. 6 (eds. from Boston and N. Y.), 7, 11, 17 (news from N. Y. and Newport, R. I.), 18 ("A Loyalist of '75' from N. Y. *Argus*), 26, 27, Sept. 12 and 26 (eds. from Boston paper), 29 ("corres."), Oct. 2, 3, 8, Nov. 7, 9, Dec. 29 ("A Plebian"), 1795; May 19 (communication), 27 ("Alarm" from *Vermont Gaz.*), 1796. For Washington's observations on the *Africa* incident see G. Washington to the Sec. of War, Sept. 28, 1795, Fitzpatrick, ed., *Writings of Washington,* XXXIV, 319. On Webster see *Amer. Minerva,* Dec. 8, 1795.

60. *Aurora,* Dec. 22, 1795. Other early editorials on impressment are in *ibid.,* Aug. 8, Oct. 20 ("Tully"), Dec. 11 ("An American Seaman Pressed on board the British fleet, and lately escaped), 22, 23, 1795; Mar. 1, 15, 29 (report on a bill to aid Amer. seamen), Apr. 7 ("An American"), 19 (communication from N. Y.), May 4 (ed. from Baltimore *Jour.*), 1796. Beginning May 4, 1796, Bache began a fairly regular column entitled "Evidences of British Amity," which ran to number CXLIII by the time it disappeared October 18, 1796.

61. *Col. Cent.,* May 25, 1796.

62. Noah Webster admitted Great Britain's continued hostility toward the United States and argued, therefore, that "war is an infinitely greater evil than the injuries we have endured." *Am. Minerva,* Sept. 5, 1795. In 1796, as the treaty was being discussed in the House of Representatives, Fenno argued that the *Aurora's* political hopes actually depended on rejection of the treaty and on war with Great Britain. See *Gaz. of U. S.,* Apr. 25, 1796. There is no evidence that war would have followed rejection of the treaty. Grenville informed Hammond that rejection of the treaty would simply mean a new negotiation in which the United States could not expect any better terms than it got the first time. Lord Grenville to G. Hammond, Aug. 31, 1795, in *Instructions to the British Minister to the United States, 1791–1812.* Vol. III of the *Annual Report of the American Historical Association for the Year 1936* (Washington, D. C., 1941), 92–94. *Aurora* editorials on the threat-of-war argument are in *Aurora,* July 4, Aug. 3 (communication), Sept. 9 ("Valerius"), 12 (ed. from *Ind. Chron.*), 15, 16 ("corres."), 17 ("Valerius"), Dec. 8, 1795; Jan. 11 ("A Prussian Patriot"), 14 ("Detector" from N. Y. *Argus*), Mar. 23 ("A Friend to the treaty"), 29, Apr. 20, 21 ("M." from *Diary*), 29 ("Pax"), 30 (letter from *Ind. Chron.*), Aug. 31, Sept. 8 (communication from *Ind. Chron.*), 1796.

63. *Ibid.,* Sept. 12, 1795.

64. On Monroe's initiative in authorizing news for the *Aurora,* see J. Monroe to G. Logan, June 24, 1795, in Berkeley, *Beckley,* 108. See also Angel, "James Monroe's Mission," 377–78. For editorials on the French issue see July 17 and 23 ("Atticus" from *Ind. Chron.*), Aug. 11, 12 ("corres."), 27, Sept. 16 ("Atticus" from *Ind. Chron.*), Oct. 10 (two "corres."), 12, 17, 19 ("A Political Watchman," from *Jersey Chron.*), 21 ("A Republican" from *Ind. Chron.*), Nov. 12, Dec. 22, 1795; Jan. 7, 1796. On Fenno see *Gaz. of U. S.,* Oct. 7 ("corres."), 1795.

65. On pre-election posturing see *Aurora*, Oct. 5 ("Justitia"), 8, 9 ("A Federal Democrat" and "A Friend to Good Government"), 12, 13 ("A Constitutionalist"), 13 ("Sleep" and Bache), 1795. For post-election editorials see *ibid.*, Oct. 15, 17, 24 ("Cleon"), 1795. For a full summary of the election see Miller, *Philadelphia, The Federalist City*, 75–78.

66. *Aurora*, Sept. 7 ("A Yeoman from Delaware," from *Del. Gaz.*), 19 (communication from Lexington), 28, Oct. 3 ("Belisarius"), 6, 16, 17 ("Pittachus"), 20 ("Mentor" from *Lancaster Jour.*), Nov. 13 (petition from *Petersburgh Intelligencer*), Dec. 8, 1795; Feb. 2, 1796.

67. For the general positions of Fenno and Webster see, for example, *Gaz. of U. S.*, Sept. 18 ("corres."), 1795; Jan. 28 ("Civis"), 1796. *Amer. Minerva*, Dec. 7, 1795. On the Sullivan issue see *Aurora*, Dec. 29, 1795; Jan. 5, 1796.

68. On South Carolina see *ibid.*, Jan. 2, 1796. On Virginia see *ibid.*, Feb. 2, 20, Mar. 12 ("A Spectator"), 1796. The *Gazette* claimed Virginia's legislators hated both the administration and the Constitution. "Corres." *Gaz. of U. S.*, Feb. 24, 1796. See also Risjord, *Chesapeake Politics*, 458. Reaction to Virginia's resolutions throughout the United States is described in Stephen G. Kurtz, *The Presidency of John Adams: The Collapse of Federalism, 1795–1800* (Philadelphia, 1957), 24–30. On Massachusetts and Sam Adams see *Aurora*, Feb. 2, 3 (communication from Boston), 5, 20, Mar. 12 ("A Spectator"), 1796. Fenno charged the *Aurora* with distortion in the affair; a quorum of the Massachusetts legislature had been present for the vote, Fenno argued, and many of that state's 300 legislators never, or rarely attended the sessions. "Corres.," *Gaz. of U. S.*, Feb. 8, 1796.

69. Miller, *Philadelphia, The Federalist City*, 78–79, cites the figures at 2,200 opposed to the treaty and 1,400 for it. For *Aurora* editorials on petitions see Apr. 15, 16 ("corres." "A Hint," and "E."), 19, 20 (three "corres."), 21, 23 (two "corres." and "A Friend to Order"), 25 (four "corres.") 27 ("Freeman" from N. Y. *Argus,* and "corres."), 28 ("Cato," "M." from N. Y. *Diary* and communication), 29 ("corres."), 30, 1796. The *Gazette* denied that all merchants were merely seeking their own self-interest in the petitions. "Civis," *Gaz. of U. S.*, Apr. 27, 1796.

Aurora editorials occasionally attacked merchant petitions in other cities. *Aurora*, Apr. 29 ("A Mechanic" from *Maryland Jour.*), May 4 ("A Maryland Yeoman," from *Baltimore Tele.*,), 7 ("An Observer"), 1796. The Massachusetts clergy were also attacked for exercising an unnatural influence over their congregations in opposing Sam Adams's election and supporting pro-treaty petitions. See *ibid.*, May 11 (two eds.), 13 (ed. from Boston), 1796.

70. *Ibid.*, Aug. 24 ("Hancock" from *Ind. Chron.*), Sept. 11 (ed. from Boston), 17, Oct. 29 ("Valerius"), Nov. 9 ("corres."), 16 ("corres."), 17, Dec. 7 ("Codrus"), 1795.

71. *Ibid.*, Jan. 19 and 21 ("Scipio"), Feb. 2 (letter), 11 ("Scipio"), 23 ("corres."), 27, Mar. 3 ("corres."), 1796. In rebuttal a *Gazette* correspondent argued that most state legislatures supported the treaty because they had been recently elected, while Congress had been elected in 1794 and been "congregated long enough to be organized into systematic opposition to the executive." Communication, *Gaz. of U. S.*, Mar. 28, 1796.

72. The best detailed account of House action on the treaty is in Combs, *Jay Treaty,* 171–88. See also De Conde, *Entangling Alliance,* 133–40. Republican organization against the treaty is described in Noble E. Cunningham, Jr., *The Jeffersonian Republicans: The Formation of Party Organization, 1789–1801* (Chapel Hill, N. C., 1957), 76–85; William Nisbet Chambers, *Political Parties in a New Nation: The American Experience, 1776–1809* (New York, 1963), 84–91; and Charles, *Origins of the American Party System,* 91–122. Federalist arguments in defense of the treaty and Washington's refusal to submit the Jay Treaty papers can be found in Carroll and Ashworth, *Washington,* VII, 345–78; Miller, *Hamilton,* 430–34; Mitchell, *Hamilton,* 346–49; Richard E. Welch, Jr., *Theodore Sedgwick, Federalist. A Political Portrait* (Middleton, Conn., 1965), 142–53.

73. On Bache's "Advertisement," see *Aurora,* Mar. 5, 1796. See also *ibid.,* Mar. 15 ("Codrus" and "corres."), 18 ("The Constitution") 19 ("corres."), 21 ("Codrus"), 23 ("corres." and Bache), 25, 29 (letter and "The Constitution"), 1796.

74. "Corres.," *ibid.,* Mar. 28, 1796. The *Gazette* was not surprised that the President's reply "should give offence to those who generally act without consideration." See Communication, *Gaz. of U. S.,* Mar. 30, 1796. The *Gazette* also believed the House was exceeding its prerogatives in calling for the papers even though it acknowledged that the House could withhold appropriations. Communication, *ibid.,* Mar. 21, 1796.

75. "The People," *Aurora,* Apr. 4, 1796.

76. *Aurora,* Apr. 2 ("Loyal Englishman," "corres.," and two eds.), 4 ("corres."), 11 ("corres."), 1796.

77. "Corres.," *ibid.,* Apr. 1, 1796. The *Gazette* shot back, asking why none of the ten senators who voted against the treaty had not revealed these "horrors." *Gaz. of U. S.,* Apr. 1, 1796. On Bache's cynicism see *Aurora,* Apr. 5, 1796.

78. *Ibid.,* Apr. 6 (ed.), 7 ("The People"), 11 ("The People" and Bache), 16 ("The People" and two "corres."), 21 (communication), 23 and 25 and 26 ("Harrington"), 28 ("corres."), 29, 1796.

79. *Ibid.,* Apr. 12, 1796.

80. *Ibid.,* Apr. 26, 1796. "Order & c.," *Gaz. of U. S.,* Apr. 26, 1796.

81. *Aurora,* Apr. 21, 16 (two "corres."), 28 ("corres."), 30 ("Sidney" and a "corres."), 1796.

82. *Ibid.,* May 3 ("corres."), 5 (Bache, ed. from *Baltimore Journal,* and letter from *Ind. Chron.*), 6 (reply to the *Minerva*), 7, 11 ("Locke"), 16 ("corres."), 19 (ed. from *Ind. Chron.*), 24 ("Paulding"), 26 (ed. and "Federal Republican"), July 18 ("An Agriculturist"), Aug. 1 ("Iconoclastes"), 1796. The *Gazette* labeled the *Aurora*'s attacks on petitioners for the Treaty as contradictory to *Aurora* principles, since the Democratic Societies, the "hot-bed of sedition," had opened the petitioning against the treaty. *Gaz. of U. S.,* May 6, 1796. Webster simply charged the *Aurora* with re-opening an unfair and systematic attack on the President. *Am. Minerva,* June 11, 1796.

83. See for examples of these charges, *Am. Minerva,* Oct. 1, 22, 1795; *Gaz. of U. S.,* Feb. 26, Mar. 12, 1796.

84. *Aurora,* July 4, 1796.

10. Partisan Rage: The Assault on Washington and the Election of 1796

> "Profession costs nothing, and it will be remembered that the present administration has been an administration of profession only . . . in a word the profession of honor, justice, candor, dignity and good faith, when dishonor, injustice, treachery, meanness and perfidy have given a hue to our public proceedings. What an eight year glorious administration!!"
> (*Aurora,* Dec. 17, 1796)

IT MAY HAVE SURPRISED NO ONE that the Jay Treaty blinded Bache with a hatred of George Washington that knew few bounds. But the seemingly unrestrained expression of that hatred in the columns of the *Aurora* in 1795 and 1796, and in a polemic written and published by Bache in 1797, entitled *Remarks Occasioned by the Late Conduct of Mr. Washington as President of the United States,* clearly shocked a nation not yet habituated to such extreme degrees of journalistic vituperation. More remarkable is the fact that the relentlessness of the attack would remain startling even in later eras more attuned to radical rhetorical violence. What drove such a sustained rage? Why did Bache and his closest allies persist in an impractical campaign that threatened to ruin what credibility the *Aurora* possessed?

Part of the answer lay in the destructive impact the Jay Treaty promised to have on Franco-American relations. But there were other reasons for Bache's conduct as well. Some were purely personal and developmental. When Washington ratified the Jay Treaty in August, 1795, Bache had just turned twenty-six years of age. An uneasy apprenticeship as the editor of an "advertiser" dependent on merchant support that never arrived, had given way to publication of the *Aurora,* an independent newspaper religiously dedicated to the dawn of a new day. While family resources probably helped to keep the presses running, Bache was no longer dependent on any family member for his personal identity and purpose. Even partisan allies like Jefferson and Madison, who had stayed at more than arm's length from the Jay Treaty conflict, had no claims on him. He was a young radical beholden to no one, driven by a romantic vision of a world cleansed and begun anew through republican revolution.[1]

Then there was George Washington. Well before 1795, Washington's aloofness, aristocratic bearing, and insistence on executive prerogatives had drawn fire from Bache. But only with Washington's ratification of the Jay Treaty could Bache manufacture a full and clear portrait of the President. Washington represented an elitist, gentry ethic opposed to Bache's democratic one. And while generational differences formed part of the ideological polarity between Washington's world and Bache's, more significant to Bache was Washington's unwavering commitment to an antique sociology of historical continuity and established orders, of a natural and permanent hierarchy in society, and of an executive autonomy that appeared free from the will of the people.[2]

Historically, the things Bache found objectionable in Washington, when viewed from a different perspective would sustain a myth of Washington. From John Marshall and Mason Weems to the present, Washington has been portrayed as standing on a stage of impartiality, stoically maintaining a posture of independence in the midst of political strife.[3] Washington's contemporaries recognized the value in trading on Washington's image, and modern interpreters of Country-Court, classical republican, and "patriot president" ideas have subtly sustained the myth. Washington was "a sacred possession" in his own generation, it has been claimed, not only a patriot king but a man who then and forevermore personified "public virtue, disinterestedness, moderation, resoluteness, private virtue, and piety."[4]

Bache and his contemporaries sensed the significance of the developing iconography and worried that Washington's symbolic significance might be successfully exploited by Federalists in a manner that would forever foreclose America's political options. Thus, those who attacked Washington were less infected with moral turpitude or splenetic derangement—as is implied in most casual analyses of the attacks Washington suffered—than filled with the frustrated rage of men who embraced an ideal of democracy and republicanism that a king-like Washington had threatened to undermine. Furthermore, Washington's pretended insensitivity to the attacks, his unwillingness to engage the attackers or admit his partisanship, and his *hauteur,* made him appear to Bache and others as a *poseur.* Even William Cobbett, admittedly much more a Tory than a Federalist, could not stomach the contrived image. "Never was the world so deceived, so shamefully duped, as to the character of any human being," Cobbett declared privately in 1800, as the myth of Washington was emerging more fully. "Mahomet was a more bold, but not a more consummate, imposter," Cobbett concluded, "which you will see most amply proved one day or other."[5]

Like Cobbett, Bache also sensed a vulnerability in the Washington façade. Still young enough to have the adolescent's keen instincts for vulnerability, he was not yet old enough or intelligent enough to attack those vulnerabilities to advantage and with credibility. As noted in earlier chapters, Bache was sometimes oblique and cautious, often self-contradictory and silly, in his early attacks on Washington. In April, 1795, for example, while merely nipping at the political heels of a President whom he had not yet thoroughly damned, Bache sent Washington an invitation to a civic festival in honor of French victories in Holland. Unamused, the President was at least troubled enough by the attack to remark, "Intended as an Insult it is presumed."[6] Some of the strangeness of these early attacks came into focus, however, after August, 1795, when it no longer seemed bizarre to charge the President with setting himself above the people. From late 1795 on, the assault on Washington took on a life of its own as Bache and his correspondents—"Valerius," "Portius," "Belisarius," "Pittachus," "Atticus," Thomas Paine, and others—unleashed unconditional warfare on Washington the man and the myth.[7]

The monarchical tendencies in Washington's character and behavior were the subject first revived after the issue of treaty ratification receded. "The President began his political career as if he had inherited a kingdom," said "Pittachus," "his port has been that of a Monarch, and the customs which he introduced are those of a Sovereign."[8] But *Aurora* writers also attempted to show that Washington had no right to appeal for public gratitude for past services in order to shield himself from criticism. "We know what he was in seventy-five," one writer claimed, "but we are likewise entitled to enquire what he is in ninety-five."[9] "Valerius," perhaps Washington's sharpest critic, accused the President of possessing neither talent nor intelligence, of being neither Tory nor Whig in the Revolution, and, while President, of taking the easy course of listening only to "ministerial communications" which were the "echoes of his own thoughts." By April, 1796, Bache acknowledged that Washington had been born in a land of freedom, "but it has become a problem whether he received his education in it."[10]

Aurora writers ignored few issues that might be used against the President, even those politically sensitive to Republicans. Attacks by the *Gazette* on Virginia slaveholders were turned against Washington; if he were infallible, why did he own slaves?[11] Washington's appointments were deemed partisan and unrepublican. Jefferson was the only Republican appointee, "Valerius" argued, yet he had been forced to withdraw when Washington never took his advice.[12] Washington was again accused of hating France and the French Revolution.[13] When the President received a new French flag from Minister Adet in a ceremony before Congress, and then deposited that flag in the archives of the United States rather than display it in Congress, the *Aurora* used the affair to prove Washington's disaffection for France.[14] A few writers tried to catalog all of Washington's crimes. Probably the most summary and notorious of these catalogs was "The Political Creed of 1795," which charged Washington with holding "his fellow citizens at an awful distance" and with desiring kingship, because he chose "advocates of kingly government as his first councillors and advisers." The author concluded with Paine-like rhetoric, declaring that "a blind confidence in any men who have done services to their country, has enslaved, and ever will enslave, all the nations of the earth," and harshly observing that "a good joiner may be a clumsy watchmaker; that an able carpenter may be a blundering taylor; and that a good General may be a most miserable politician."[15]

A few *Aurora* contributors believed that Washington should either resign or be impeached. "Scipio" was most direct in asking Washington to

> retire immediately; let no flatterer persuade you to rest one hour longer at the helm of state. You are utterly incapable to steer the political ship into the harbour of safety. If you have any love for your country, leave its affairs to the wisdom of your fellow citizens; do not flatter yourself with the idea that you know their interests better than other men; there are thousands amongst them who equal you in capacity, and who excel you in knowledge.[16]

These general *Aurora* attacks could be dismissed by Federalists as the work of men disappointed by the Jay Treaty's ratification. One extended attack did, however, produce apprehension and anxiety among the President's supporters. The issue was Washington's salary. When Washington assumed office in 1789, he had refused the $25,000 salary granted him by Congress. Instead, the President adopted the habit, with acquiescence from Congress and the Treasury, of having his private secretaries withdraw household and living expenses from funds appropriated for his salary. From the start, these withdrawals always consumed the entire annual appropriation made by Congress. In 1793, Congress further regularized the issuance of this money by directing the Treasury to dispense this appropriation in quarterly installments. Though the principle was never stated outright,

Congress apparently intended to facilitate Washington's expense withdrawals rather than force the President to wait until the end of each year to receive any funds.

Because few people had access to the Treasury records, the President's salary had seldom been a subject of criticism. John Beckley, clerk of the House, did see the records and attempted to use them to damage the President's public reputation. The method he used was a series of letters which he submitted to the *Aurora* in October and November over the pseudonym "A Calm Observer." "A Calm Observer" opened the attack on October 23, charging Secretaries of the Treasury Oliver Wolcott, Jr. and Alexander Hamilton with malfeasance. Specifically, the Treasury Department was accused of overpaying the President in the fiscal years of 1790–1791 and 1792–1793 and in the first quarter of the year beginning in March 1793. By the end of his first term, it was claimed, Washington had overdrawn his salary by $1,037; by early June 1793 this sum had increased to a total of $5,787. "Will not the world be led to conclude that the mask of political hypocrisy has been alike worn by a CAESAR, a CROMWELL and a WASHINGTON?" he concluded.[17] Federalists had long attacked the *Aurora* for "trivial" criticisms of the President, Bache now added, but the "Observer"'s attacks were different. "Coaches and six are not there the theme; but breaches of the laws, of the constitution and of a solemn oath are there talked of. The subject deserves the serious consideration of the Free Citizens of America, if their Constitution, the safeguard of their liberties is worth preserving."[18]

On October 26, Secretary Wolcott offered the angry public reply in the *Aurora* that "not one dollar has been advanced at any time for which there was not an existing appropriation by law," and demanded an explanation for the *Aurora*'s continual abuse of the government.[19] "A Calm Observer" quickly responded, noting that Wolcott had not refuted the charges. Was it not a violation, he insisted, for the President to receive more than $6,250 a quarter, or more than $25,000 a year, or more than $100,000 in four years? Wolcott followed with another letter on October 28, denying "evasion" and repeating that no advances had exceeded any existing appropriation. But "A Calm Observer," in two more letters, repeated his charges, stating that the Treasury had illegally anticipated the President's salary in several different years and quarters.[20]

The salary issue backed Federalist printers against the wall. The *Gazette* avoided the issue and, as Bache predicted, turned to invective against the *Aurora*. Webster defended the Treasury, not only by claiming that the

President could legally draw a quarter's salary in advance but by alleging that advances had been made in the same way to the Speaker of the House and other government officials. The *Aurora* categorically denied Webster's arguments: members of Congress received salaries only after they had earned them; the President was the only one to receive an advance, even though most people had been led to believe that he had refused any compensation whatsoever.[21]

In the meantime, Wolcott and Hamilton hurriedly compared notes. Although Washington avoided direct entanglement, Hamilton saw the need to offer a spirited and convincingly reply to the "vile insinuations." Hamilton and Wolcott privately agreed that the President had received advances of money not yet earned, although Wolcott denied that these ever extended beyond a yearly appropriation. They apparently agreed as well that congressmen had never received advances. And they concluded that Beckley, with former Secretary of State Randolph's aid, had written the "Calm Observer" letters. In order to offer a strong response to the *Aurora,* Hamilton also asked Wolcott for all pertinent Treasury materials on the subject.[22]

On November 18, after the furor had begun to subside, Hamilton published an exhaustive defense of the President and the Treasury. In general, Hamilton argued that the spirit of the Constitution and the laws had not been violated by advancing Washington money before it had been earned, and that all advances had come under some appropriation. In fact, Hamilton declared that by October, 1795 the government actually owed the President $846. But, relying on published Treasury records, Hamilton was unable to hide the fact that the President had frequently overdrawn his salary in previous years. The records showed, for example, that by March 31, 1795, Washington had been advanced $6,154 more than he had earned. For one of the few times in its six-year history, the *Aurora* at least felt that it held the upper hand in a political controversy while relying on concrete and accurate facts to make its case.[23]

Most of the attacks outlined above were designed to discredit the President and to encourage the House to defeat the Jay Treaty. Yet, even after the failure of the fight in the House, Bache continued and intensified his campaign.[24] For example, in late May, 1796 "Paulding" opened a potentially destructive attack on Washington's policies toward France. "Paulding" accused Washington of ignoring Genet's request in 1793 for a new Franco-American treaty, and of falsely telling Genet that no negotiation could proceed with the Senate out of session (as it was at the time of Genet's request). A few days later, after noting that Fauchet was also refused a treaty at the same time that Jay was negotiating one in England, "Paulding" published the entire text of thirteen questions submitted by Washington to his Cabinet in 1793. Because Washington, in these questions, appeared to doubt the validity of the 1778 treaty with France as well as the wisdom of receiving Genet as French Minister, the revelation of this state document threatened to do real damage to Washington's reputation.[25]

The Cabinet questions issue embittered and depressed the President. Soon after "Paulding"'s disclosure, Washington began to complain of press attacks on his character. He told Hamilton that every act by the President was "misrepresented" and "tortured." One reason he wanted to resign, he said, was to stop being "buffited [sic] in the public prints by a set of infamous scribblers." In a communication to James McHenry, he complained that the *Aurora* "arraigned" all executive acts, and he confided to Wolcott that, "Mr. Bache will continue his attacks on the Government, there can be no doubt, but that they will make no Impression on the public mind is not so certain, for drops of water will Impress (in time) the hardest Marble." A fortnight later he described the *Aurora*'s and "Paulding"'s attacks as "indecent as they are void of truth and fairness." According to Washington, Bache was trying to prove that the government was both "unfriendly" and "unjust" toward France. Denying any unfriendliness, Washington asked Pickering to consider some means of giving the lie to Bache's "misrepresentation and mutilated authorities."[26] When Jefferson assured Washington that he, Jefferson, had not been the source of the *Aurora*'s information on the Cabinet questions, Washington replied that he had never doubted his former Secretary's innocence, then plunged into a discourse of self-pity, charging his vilifiers with having no scruple for truth in their attacks and claiming that he had never been a party man himself.[27]

Washington's final address to Congress, given on December 7, 1796, revived *Aurora* charges that the President was partial to England and opposed to France. The address did not mention British relations but Washington did draw Congress's attention to difficulties with France. Washington's pledge "to maintain cordial harmony and a perfect friendly understanding" with France only convinced *Aurora* writers that Washington had the audacity to say what he did not truly feel.[28] Bache accused Washington of being calm and mild when the British seized American ships; but when the French assaulted American commerce, "he swaggers and struts the hero," posing in a warlike stance of firmness. The President's "professions" of warmth for France meant nothing.

Profession costs nothing, and it will be remembered that the present administration has been an administration of profession only; the profession of
republicanism, but the practice of monarchy and aristocracy; the profession
of sympathy and interest for a great nation and an ally struggling for liberty,
but a real devotion to the cause of the combined despots; the profession of a
neutral character, cold and indifferent to the warring power, but a warm and
sincere attachment to Great Britain . . . in a word the profession of honor,
justice, candor, dignity and good faith, when dishonor, injustice, treachery,
meanness and perfidy have given a hue to our public proceedings. What an
eight years glorious administration!![29]

In one of the best remembered diatribes directed against Washington, a
correspondent helped Bache close the year on another infamous and contemptuous note by declaring,

If ever a nation was debauched by a man, the American nation has been
debauched by WASHINGTON. If ever a nation was deceived by a man, the
American nation has been deceived by WASHINGTON. Let his conduct
then be an example to future ages. Let it serve to be a warning that no man
may be an idol, and that a people may confide in themselves rather than in an
individual. Let the history of the federal government instruct mankind, that
the masque of patriotism may be worn to conceal the foulest designs against
the liberties of a people.[30]

Editorials did not remain Bache's only means of attacking Washington.
In late 1796, after the presidential election had been decided, Bache published a pamphlet written by Thomas Paine containing several bitter, abusive letters to the President. The pamphlet was the end product of Paine's
trials and tribulations in France. With the fall of the Brissotins in late 1793,
Paine had been imprisoned. Until Monroe arrived as American minister to
France, Paine had languished in prison, weakened and ill, unable to convince Monroe's predecessor, Gouverneur Morris, or Washington that he
was an American citizen and eligible for release on those grounds. Monroe
reclaimed Paine as a citizen in late 1794, taking the disputatious revolutionary into his home in an act of remarkable (and undoubtedly painful)
charity. Throughout 1795, Paine worked on his *Dissertation on First Principles of Government* and completed the second part of *The Age of Reason*. He
then commissioned Bache to be the sole American distributor of both
works.[31] In the meantime, Paine's hatred of Washington festered. On
February 22, 1795, he wrote a bitter letter to the President which Monroe
persuaded him not to send. On September 20, he wrote another and sent it

to Washington indirectly through Bache. Receiving no reaction, he composed a new letter on July 20, 1796, attached his earlier letters and some additions, and sent the entire package off to Bache for publication. In a confidential aside to Bache, Paine declared that he was "sorry" the letters to Washington needed to be published "but it is necessary to speak out. The American character is so much sunk in Europe that it is necessary to distinguish between the Government and the Country."[32]

Published in late 1796, the pamphlet was a rambling tirade against the President.[33] Washington was accused of deliberate treachery for keeping Paine in a French prison and for refusing Paine's rightful claim to American citizenship. "I cannot understand your silence upon this subject upon any ground, than as a connivance at my imprisonment," Paine complained. According to him, Washington had ignored pleas for his release in order to "gratify the English government," to create the opportunity to "exclaim the louder against the French Revolution," or, through Paine's convenient absence from America, to have "less opposition in mounting up the American government." Moving far afield from his personal grief, Paine attacked the President's character, politics, and policies, condemning Washington's lack of accomplishment in the Revolution, his pro-British and pro-monarchical posturing, and his unfriendliness to France. Although Washington attempted to portray his own character as "a sort of non-describable, cameleon-coloured thing, called prudence," Paine claimed that the President's entire administration was marked by perfidy and deceit. Washington quietly avoided responding to Paine, except to complain that the letters were part of a general plan to "knock" him down. Bache believed, however, that Paine's letters told "galling truths" about the President which could not be countered by "vulgar abuse" from the Federalists.[34]

But if Washington was troubled by Paine's letters, he was outraged at another maneuver by Bache. It was an outrage that had built since 1795, when Bache republished the forged or "spurious" letters attributed to Washington during the Revolution. Allegedly written by Washington to his wife, Lund Washington, and a few others, the letters were first published in the winter of 1777–1778 in England and were reprinted shortly thereafter in New York. In general, the letters portrayed Washington as a lukewarm patriot at best, a loyal subject of George III at worst, and at least a skeptic concerning independence.[35]

When Washington finally felt free to deny the authenticity of the letters in 1797, *Aurora* writers dropped the issue. But the denial stimulated another antique charge. A writer claimed that Washington, while a young officer fighting the French in 1754, fired on a small group of French soldiers, killing a French officer named Jumonville, and was thereby guilty of murder. Webster ridiculed the weak and wretched charge. "To what a desperate ebb must a man be reduced," Webster exclaimed, "to ransack the musty French Journals of 1755, to find lies to wound the reputation of General Washington: One would think he might find an ample supply of lies of a more recent date."[36]

In a private letter written in January, 1797, Washington reviewed the history of the forged letters, completely denied their authenticity, and charged the *Aurora* with "malignant industry, and perservering [sic] false-hoods . . . in order to weaken, if not destroy, the confidence of the Public." In one of his last acts as President, Washington made his denial public and official by sending a deposition to the Secretary of State.[37] Bache published the denial on March 11, 1797. But in subsequent references to the forged letters, Washington revealed his anger at Bache's meanness. "This man [Bache] has celebrity in a certain way," he told a correspondent upon his retirement, "for His calumnies are to be exceeded only by his Impudence, and both stand unrivalled."[38]

Washington's Farewell Address brought on the final stage of Bache's defamation campaign. Although the Address drew little editorial attention in the *Aurora* itself, Bache did publish a pamphlet entitled *A Letter to George Washington* written over the pseudonym "Jasper Dwight." Unknown by angry Federalists at the time, "Jasper Dwight" was actually William Duane, an obscure, poor, friendless writer who had arrived in Philadelphia in October, 1796. Born in America in 1760, Duane had spent his youth in Ireland, rebelling against the Catholic Church. In the 1780s he educated himself as a printer, worked in London for a time, and then, at age twenty-six, left his Protestant wife behind and sailed for India out of "curiosity and ambition." A stolid defender of press freedom, and a warm-hearted but defensive man who was quick to sense injustice, Duane initially supported the British Government in India, despite the need for English reforms. But as publisher of a good, solid newspaper, the *World*, Duane eventually ran afoul of British authorities, attacking Great Britain while his personal support for the French Revolution grew. Deported from India to London in 1795 and discovering England closed to dissent, Duane joined the radical London Corresponding Society and was quickly labeled an Irish nationalist by the authorities. With the passage of a sedition act specifically designed for men of his opinions, Duane left England for good in 1796, part of that large contingent of English-Irish radicals who would, with Bache help shape the patterns of American democratic journalism.[39]

Duane's *A Letter to Washington,* published by Bache late in 1796, would be only the first of Duane's associations with Bache. In 1797 and 1798, while in the employ of various newspaper owners, Duane followed Bache's political line closely. Yet it was not until the summer of 1798—when he found himself unemployed and when his wife had recently died of cholera—that Duane was hired at the *Aurora*. When Bache died in September 1798, Duane, well schooled in Bache's ideology and journalism, helped Bache's widow run the *Aurora;* he eventually married her. "Like Bache," claims one student of journalism, "Duane preferred a tidied up version of the language of the people to 'classical' English in his daily columns, and he used it with sincerity and trenchant style."[40]

A Letter to Washington spoke of "incalcuable [sic] evils" in the Farewell Address, and asserted that some of Washington's measures had "an alarming and pernicious tendency" and were "repugnant to the purest maxims of liberality, wisdom and morals." Astonished at the silence that had followed the publication of the Address, Duane objected to what he considered the President's vagueness on the permanency and indivisibility of the union, to his attitude toward parties and civil liberties, and to his statements on foreign policy. More specifically, Duane attacked Washington for lacking "candor" in the British Treaty affair; ever since the President's promulgation of the Treaty, he added, "the enemies of Liberty in your Country called you their own, and the name of WASHINGTON sank from the elevated rank of SOLONS and LYCURGUSES to the insignificance of a Venetian Doge or a Dutch Stadtholder!" Duane noted at great length how Washington had adopted a narrow, unrepublican attitude toward parties, free speech, and dissent. Finally, he claimed that Washington had already abandoned his own advice on non-entangling alliances by ratifying the Jay Treaty and violating America's treaty with France.[41]

As 1797 opened and Washington's retirement approached, the *Aurora* echoed a few of Duane's charges.[42] But the worst and most infamous attack was written by a correspondent on March 4 and printed two days later. According to Robert Carr, one of Bache's journeyman printers, the editorial was written by Dr. James Reynolds with Michael Leib's help while Bache was out of town, and upon Bache's return to Philadelphia he was angry and annoyed that the editorial had been published. No matter what the circumstance, the writer blamed Washington for "all the misfortunes of our country." "If ever there was a period for rejoicing this is the moment— every heart, in unison with the freedom and happiness of the people ought to beat high with exaltation, that the name of WASHINGTON from this day ceases to give currency to political iniquity; and to legalize corruption."

Washington's administration, he concluded, had destroyed republicanism and enlightenment, and, therefore, "this day ought to be a jubilee in the United States."[43]

Federalists were disgusted. Bache had forgotten the virtues of his grandfather, Fenno declared, and allowed his paper to become the "pestilential retailer of sedition."

> It seems that Mr. Bache would wish to be thought the leader of that party which is unceasingly endeavoring to sap the foundation of our government, and sow discord among us. Dead to every normal sentiment that ought to animate the soul—he seems to take a kind of hellish pleasure in defaming the name of WASHINGTON.
>
> That a man who was born in America, and is part of the great family of the United States, could thus basely aim his poisoned dagger at the FATHER OF HIS COUNTRY is sorely to be lamented.

Webster believed that the attack "exceeds in virulence all the blackness and infamy, that have stained the annals of republican ingratitude. Even France, in the murderous history of Jacobinism, exhibits nothing more spiteful." The attack was, he concluded a "libel which amounts to a charge of high treason."[44]

But Bache was not finished. The attack was ultimately capped by a long, discursive pamphlet written by Bache himself. The only extensive political review directly attributable to Bache, *Remarks Occasioned by the Late Conduct of Mr. Washington,* was both a thorough condemnation of Washington and an analysis of those political subjects which Bache believed were most significant in shaping America's future, including the Jay Treaty, relations with France, and the proper nature of republican government. After discussing the Jay Treaty, Bache warned Americans against the tendency of young nations to imitate old, established governments. Aristocratic and monarchical usurpation of power was habitual in Europe, he said, and American aristocrats had already moved to imitate Europe by conspiring to make Washington an infallible monarch. Although Washington had not consciously participated in this design, the President had aided the antidemocratic cause by accepting flattery, behaving in a haughty manner, encouraging pomp, exciting ingratitude toward France, and forming a party. Americans were safe from such bad tendencies, he added, as long as property, numbers, and knowledge were arrayed on the side of democracy. But undue praise of the President and quiet acquiescence to his policies "renders it incumbent to recall the generous loan of public attachment from one, who had been averse to pay for it [with] even the slender interest of neutrality."

Bache then began a long, often tedious review of Washington's personal shortcomings, beginning with Washington's incompetence as a military leader. Compared to officers in the French Republic's war against Europe, Washington "would be like a puny shrub in the midst of a stupendous forest." Bache charged that after the American Revolution, Washington had encouraged the aristocratic Society of Cincinnati, promoted funding at a high interest rate, favored speculators, crushed a "petty insurrection" of excise protestors, timidly submitted to British depredations and policies, and ratified a treaty which "disgraced the American character in politics . . . and made national interests subservient to his little passions." Washington might have had some private virtues, Bache later admitted. He had been "firm" and sometimes "brave" in the Revolution. But, altogether, Washington was merely, "A Virginia planter by no means that most eminent, a militia-officer ignorant of war both in theory and useful practice, and a politician certainly not of the first magnitude." Claiming that Washington was dull, uninspiring, and wedded to authority, order, and pomp, Bache concluded, "He is but a man, and certainly not a great man."[45]

Bache's assault on Washington ended with this pamphlet. The *Remarks* confirmed the idea that the *Aurora* existed to peddle defamation against its foes, and established Bache's reputation as a scurrilous journalist to the exclusion of other facets of his ideological endeavors. Elizabeth Hewson, Polly's daughter and the woman Franklin once jokingly hoped would become Benny's wife, remarked in 1796, as the assault on Washington began, that, "At the time of Dr. F[ranklin]'s death Ben was universally beloved and esteemed and now he is as much despised even by some who are warm democrats." Eight months later she added that Bache "is now considered in the most despicable light by the most respectable part of his fellow citizens, and by almost every one whom he might formerly have considered as his particular friends."[46]

Most of Hewson's "respectable" citizenry and those *she* identified as Ben's "particular friends" were, in fact, Federalists by 1796. With his decision to attack Washington unrelentingly, Bache had taken on responsibility to challenge the entire phalanx of Federalism. Yet he may not have fully appreciated the fact that international forces and his journalistic pique had caused him to descend from the high, broad road of democratic evangelism to the low, narrow road of crisis politics, personal defamation, and event-driven accusation and response. While he was fighting the constant brush-fires of partisanship, Bache's efforts to fuel the constructive development of a democratic society became obscured.

Alexander Hamilton, whose popularity had fallen with both Congress and the public after his resignation from the Treasury, was one of many foes whose crimes—ranging from failings of personal character to funding to involvement in the Whiskey Rebellion suppression to support of the British Treaty—became the subject of lavish attacks.[47] Bache identified Hamilton as the head of the Federalist Party. "Artful, well informed, intriguing, and indefatigable amidst the ramblings of party spirit," Bache said, "he [Hamilton] has dexterously seized the reins, and it is believed guides the motions of the Executive branch of our government."[48] When "A. B." later attacked Franklin's reputation in Fenno's *Gazette,* Bache's rage nearly resulted in his disclosure of Hamilton's tawdry sexual affair with Mrs. James Reynolds (later made public by John Beckley and James T. Callender). In June, 1796, Bache merely commented, "He [Hamilton] might be proved, under his own hand, a seducer of a married woman tho' himself a married man,—and more might be proved."[49]

Lesser Federalists were not allowed to escape attack when they revealed themselves. Theodore Sedgwick, an outspoken critic of democracy and France, was charged with calling the people "the herd," promoting a consolidated government, and supporting the federal government's unlimited power to raise armies and taxes. Robert Goodloe Harper, considered a political trimmer and adventurer because he abandoned the Charleston Democratic Society in favor of the Federalists, was ridiculed for delivering long, senseless speeches in Congress. And, without naming them, Bache also attacked Pickering and Wolcott as talentless Hamiltonian sycophants who deserved no increase in their meager governmental salaries. "Neither of them could in private life, earn a fourth part of what they now receive from the public," Bache stated flatly.[50]

These attacks naturally drew Bache into a heightened battle with his old journalistic antagonists, Webster and Fenno. Noah Webster's open declaration that good and bad governments could be found in both republican and monarchical societies especially angered *Aurora* contributors. Webster obviously favored despotism and monarchy, hated popular opinion and representative government, and had no faith in America's republican future, proclaimed Bache's correspondents.[51]

John Fenno (referred to as the "Witch of Endor" and his newspaper attacked as the "Grub-Street Gazette" after mid-1795) was dismissed as a partisan who continually slandered the people. Yet Bache was continually drawn into hopeless jousts with Fenno's correspondents, one angering Bache so much that Bache challenged him to a duel. Throughout his attacks, Bache described Fenno as a "tool" of the British, while "A Citizen" charged Fenno with being paid by the British to distribute 900 copies of the *Gazette* through the country.[52]

By 1796, an earlier reluctance to contend with William Cobbett had begun to disappear. Until 1796, Cobbett had written editorials for Fenno's *Gazette* as well as published his own pamphlets, using the pseudonym "Peter Porcupine." But in that year Cobbett opened his own printing shop on Second Street and began to gain wider notoriety, eventually publishing *Porcupine's Gazette* in 1797.[53] *Aurora* writers denounced Porcupine as a foreigner and a Tory who candidly wanted to restore the British monarchy in America. Portrayed as an obscene, unprincipled opportunist, he was accused of being booted out of England, being whipped for insubordination while in the British Army and deported from France for stealing, and refusing to pay his taxes in Philadelphia.[54] He was, concluded others, a "hireling wretch," a "manufacturer of lies, and a retailer of filth," an "English burglar," and a "reptile."[55]

Bache's Federalist and journalistic opponents were predictably eager to retaliate. Webster lumped Bache in with other opposition writers and defined them all as anti-federalists, Jacobins, and Democrats who, through fanaticism, violence, and the repetition of false charges, hoped to tear down the government and attach the United States to France. According to Webster, these men represented "a collection of the discontended [sic], disappointed, restless and irritable passions, perpetually in action, and operating successfully on great numbers of weak, credulous minds and drawing them into the turbulent vortex of party."[56] Fenno's writers, generally referring to the *Aurora*'s contributors as the "Hollow Ware Company," also contended that *Aurora* editorials were the work of Jacobins, foreigners, and anarchists. Instead of upholding the government and supporting majority rule, they charged, Bache and his kind opposed the Constitution and used the mob for their own purposes. "Plain Dealing," noting the *Aurora*'s attacks on the President and Congress, mockingly urged Bache to reveal his "great plan of political redemption," anticipating that Bache would in all probability institute Robespierre's code and a new reign of terror.[57]

Fenno, Cobbett, and others were equally eager to establish Bache's villainy through what they thought was guilt by association. "An American Farmer," while bemused by Franklin's inventive genius and pretending to tolerate Franklin's deism, compared grandfather to grandson, discovering in that comparison that Bache was a grumbling malcontent who made his living by peddling six or seven hundred newspapers a day to the French ministry. At virtually the same time, "Porcupine" used the *Gazette*'s columns to condemn Bache's publication of Paine's *Age of Reason*, proof positive to Cobbett that Bache was following in the footsteps of Franklin and Paine in adopting deism and in peddling the poison of Paine's "blasphemous" works.[58]

By 1795 and 1796, more remote critics, especially those from or in New England, were unable to explain Bache's radicalism except by discovering a link between the *Aurora* and the French government. In the fall of 1795, for example, the *Columbian Centinel* stated flatly that French Minister Fauchet subscribed to four hundred copies of the *Aurora*. Later that year, Secretary of State Timothy Pickering was informed that Bache regularly sold 800 copies of the *Aurora* to Fauchet. Pickering relayed this information to Webster, asking the New York publisher not to reveal this information to anyone while at the same time telling Webster that the *Minerva* would replace the *Aurora* as one of the American newspapers designated for distribution to American ministers abroad. And in early 1797 the *Connecticut Courant* offered its own version of what would become a standard charge against Bache in 1797–1798. This time the *Courant* claimed that a French Agent of Marine named Penevert was the purchaser of copies of the *Aurora* for free distribution in New England. A month later the *Courant* retracted its charge completely.[59]

Attacks on Washington and rhetorical volleys between partisans and editors did not always appear to have a clear purpose. But, as the presidential election approached in the fall of 1796, Bache undoubtedly sought a more constructive goal that would make his rhetoric count for something. On September 13, four days before Washington's announced retirement, Bache scooped his journalistic opponents for the second time. Correctly guessing that the announcement of Washington's retirement was a carefully calculated Federalist move to influence the election, Bache regretted that "those who seem to think themselves exclusively interested in affairs of state" had known about the retirement for some time without informing the public. In calling upon voters to be careful in their selection of electors, he further observed that,

It requires no talent at divination to decide who will be candidates for the chair. THOMAS JEFFERSON & JOHN ADAMS will be the men, & whether we shall have at the head of our executive a steadfast friend to the

Rights of the People, or an advocate for hereditary power and distinction, the people of the United States are soon to decide.[60]

With these few words, the *Aurora* described much of its vision of the presidential contest. Although Jefferson had expressed hopes in 1794 for Madison's possible candidacy and could at least pose as a reluctant candidate, there had been little doubt that Republicans, especially in the South, would rally behind Jefferson. If anything, Jefferson's candidacy, coincidentally embraced by Republicans everywhere, was as close as politics would ever come to confirming Bache's belief in the spontaneity and unanimity of democratic action among a free and enlightened people. And, while Madison wrote a few letters of advice to Republicans in Virginia and other states, real campaigning fell to lesser men at the state and local level—men like Michael Leib, John Beckley, and Bache in Philadelphia.[61]

John Adams's candidacy was more problematic for the Federalists, as Bache well knew. Adams believed he had some right of succession to the presidency, and many New Englanders and rank and file Federalists had little difficulty supporting him. But in the South many Federalist candidates did not even dare to enlist Adams's name in the campaign. Pessimistic about the future of the republic and convinced that they were the only true friends of government, Federalists worked harder to deny Jefferson the election—as "Phocion"'s twenty-five letters to the *Gazette* attest—than to elect Adams. Gripped more than any other Federalist with the need to defeat Jefferson, Hamilton settled on the idea of promoting more pliable candidates, first turning to Patrick Henry, and then to Thomas Pinckney, for a place on the ticket. What followed was a strange quasi-*coup* attempt in which Hamilton tried to insure—through Adams-Pinckney ticket solidarity in the East, and perhaps a Federalist electoral preference for Pinckney in the South—that Jefferson would win neither the presidency nor the vice-presidency, with Pinckney likely to finish ahead of Adams.[62]

The *Aurora* took special care to defend and promote Jefferson. Early in 1796, before it was certain there would be any choice for the presidency, Bache had portrayed Jefferson as the probable savior of the United States from Federalist policies. In the general election campaign itself and after, Jefferson was recommended to voters as a man of integrity and simplicity, a friend to liberty, toleration, republicanism, and the rights of man, and an enemy of monarchy. Writers further claimed that Jefferson was knowledgeable about commerce and agriculture, had received a sound understanding of foreign affairs as Secretary of State, and had a good reputation in both

America and Europe. Jefferson alone, they hinted, was a friend of France and competent to mend the schism in Franco-American relations.[63]

Jefferson's supposed weaknesses were addressed as well. In response to persistent Federalist charges that Jefferson had deserted his post as governor of Virginia in the Revolution, *Aurora* writers noted Jefferson's pacific nature and his honest belief during the Revolution that others could administer the war effort better. Jefferson's resignation from the State Department was further defended on the basis of Jefferson's being, above all, a man of principle. Others argued that Jefferson's philosophical interests did not impede his ability to be a practical public servant. Denials were made of Jefferson's alleged apologies for excesses in the French Revolution. And Jefferson was portrayed as a moderate on the issue of slavery.[64]

A much larger group of *Aurora* writers relied on a distorted and exaggerated negative campaign against John Adams. Most of these concentrated on Adams's political philosophy. Repeating the same arguments again and again, correspondents quoted Adams's *Defense* and *Davila* essays out of context, consistently referring to passages which implied Adams's love of aristocracy, monarchy, and hereditary government. Adams was an opponent of pure republicanism, they claimed, and an admirer of British monarchy. Because Adams believed that three orders existed naturally in all societies—the one, the few, and many—these men charged Adams with seeking a permanent, hereditary executive and nobility to check the will of the majority. Apparently hoping not to antagonize Adams in case he was elected, and recognizing that Adams held a secure place among revolutionary patriots, the *Aurora* remained silent in evaluating Adams as either an anglophile or a francophile.[65]

Given the momentousness and complexity of the election, Bache tried to prepare the public mind fully for the contest. In late October, for example, Bache reminded voters of the 1796 Pennsylvania election law which provided that they were to choose fifteen electors, a law that invited politicos like Beckley and Leib to spring into action and circulate a Republican "ticket." Republicans in predominantly Republican areas could not afford to be apathetic, he warned. "The occasion is all important," Bache stated gravely, "it will determine the bias of our politics for years to come, it may be the casting dye [sic] which shall determine whether we shall remain independent, or be colonized anew; whether we shall continue to enjoy a republican government, or be brought under the yoke of a master."[66] At the same time, Bache issued a broadside that urged people to vote, that contained a list of fifteen Republican electors drawn up by Leib, Beckley, Rittenhouse, McKean, Gallatin, and others, and that quoted Thomas Paine on Adams's love of hereditary monarchy.[67]

Those who expected something more than the mere repetition of standard political postures from Bache and the *Aurora* were not disappointed. With less than a week remaining before the general election, Bache published the first of three letters from French Minister Pierre Adet to the Secretary of State. The letters dealt with the rupture in Franco-American relations, and dramatically laid full blame for that rupture at the feet of the Federalist Party and the Washington administration. Believing, as had his predecessors, that a majority of Americans were pro-French, Adet determined to expose the Jay Treaty as counter to that majority's interest and the American government as unrepresentative of the people. Adet's first letter announced that the French Republic, having decided that the United States had violated the Treaty of 1778, would henceforth "treat the flag of neutrals in the same manner as they [the United States] shall suffer it to be treated by the English." The second called on all true Frenchmen to wear, by "order" of the Directory, the badge of the Revolution—the tri-colored cockade. The third and longest letter detailed American violations of the 1778 treaty, labeled the Jay Treaty an abrogation of neutrality and "equivalent to a treaty of alliance" with England, and announced Adet's suspension as minister to the United States.[68]

As matters developed, the Adet letters did help to expose Secretary of State Pickering as a man who "showed not the slightest concern for either the diplomatic repercussions or the domestic political implications of his French diplomacy." Pickering, who clearly loathed Adet, curtly and incredibly responded that the United States did not claim any validity in international law for the freedom of the seas doctrine (which Adet legitimately claimed Americans had given up in the Jay Treaty), and even defended British impressment of American seamen.[69] But beyond that, Adet, who also believed that Washington's Farewell Address would expose the entire Federalist faction, had miscalculated; and so had Bache. Bache denied that the letters were intended to influence the election, lamely excusing himself by noting that he had merely published information handed down from the Directory and contending that the letters were published too late to influence the election in any case.[70] Never fully able to understand that Americans were developing an ethos of nationalism founded on nonentanglement, Bache still apparently believed that a majority of Americans wanted their nationalism strengthened through the sisterhood of republics, and that they would not tolerate this warning of the imminent collapse of Franco-American relations.

Despite Pickering's clumsy response, the Adet-Bache scheme failed everywhere. The *Gazette* found Adet's actions worse than the threat by Genet to appeal to the people, and charged the *Aurora* with telling the American people that Adams's election would mean war. Webster blamed Bache for deceiving and alarming the public as he had in disclosing the Jay Treaty. Cobbett responded with a work entitled the *Diplomatic Blunderbuss,* which accused Adet and France of chicanery in their relations with the United States.[71]

While Washington accused Adet of trying to "sway the government and control its measures," Samuel Chase, the Supreme Court Justice who would become notorious for his Sedition Act prosecutions at the end of the decade, argued that Bache "ought to be indicted for a false & base Libel on the Government."[72] Most importantly, moderate voters, who had seen at least the first letter before the election, and some electors who had seen them all, apparently identified the Adet letters with meddling in an American election.

Presidential politics were not Bache's only concern in the fall of 1796. Special attention was directed at the bell-wether race between Swanwick and Federalist Edward Tilghman. Tilghman was simply denounced as an aristocrat and a former Tory. Swanwick, under attack for first saying he would support the Jay Treaty and then voting against its implementation, was generally defended as a consistent Republican.[73] And, for the first and only time in his life, Bache also found himself a candidate for office. Nominated as the representative of mechanics and artisans at several small nominating meetings, Bache became a candidate for the city's Common Council. In Philadelphia's election of local, state, and congressional officers held in early October 1796, Bache finished well down the list, placing thirty-fifth out of forty candidates in the at-large election. Although the contest was a close one (according to *Aurora* statistics Bache's 1,113 votes were only six shy of election to the Council), the vote showed that Bache must have been supported by mechanics and artisans alone and unable to draw much or any vote from Elizabeth Hewson's "respectable" society.[74] Yet Bache was not unhappy, claiming that Swanwick had carried the city by 70 votes and that Republican candidates in general held a 520 vote majority in the county of Philadelphia.[75]

With the general elections completed in October and November, the *Aurora* turned again to the presidential election. Gloating over a 2,100 vote majority for Jefferson in the city and county of Philadelphia, Bache accused Fenno and the Federalists of an unsuccessful attempt to use wealth, governmental influence, and scurrilous attacks on the people to defeat Jefferson. And by the end of November Bache happily reported Republican ascendancy in early returns from the west.[76]

Bache's jubilation soon ended. According to Pennsylvania law, Governor Mifflin was to open all returns fourteen days after the election. But after the election no returns arrived from Fayette, Westmoreland, and Greene counties in the west. Without these the Republicans stood to lose all fifteen electors. After submitting the matter to the state supreme court, which delayed and then re-affirmed that the returns should be counted fourteen days after the election, the returns from Fayette and Westmoreland, which arrived a day late, were counted. Greene County did not report in time, thereby allowing the success of two Adams electors.[77] Bache and his writers were enraged. The *Aurora* charged that returns from Fayette and Westmoreland had been mailed two weeks before being received by Mifflin and had been waylaid in Pittsburgh by the Federalists for a week. Although Mifflin was praised for waiting for the late returns in the face of Federalist threats and pressures, one correspondent asked, "Is it a principle with 'federal republicans' to endeavour to trick the people out of their rights?"[78]

Through this confusing maze of election returns, Bache and his correspondents cautiously predicted a victory for Jefferson. Early analysis of the probable electoral vote revealed slight miscalculations in states divided between Federalists and Republicans, and a false anticipation that returns for Adams in Vermont would be invalidated—circumstances resulting in the prediction in late November that Jefferson would be elected 82 to 52. By mid-December, matters had changed. Bache was delighted that Eastern Federalists had shunned Pinckney, and that the Southern Federalists were prepared to support Pinckney and abandon Adams. But Jefferson was now given only a slight chance of victory, and Bache began to wonder if the election would go to the House. Adams's election did not seem probable to the *Aurora* until later that month, and the *Aurora* did not even print the final electoral count until February, 1797.[79]

The elevation of John Adams to the presidency did not produce paroxysms of political grief and rage at the *Aurora* or among the Republicans in general. Not only practical men like Madison and Jefferson but more radical observers like William Branch Giles and French Minister Pierre Adet were fairly optimistic about the new presidency. Immediate events played a considerable role in the quest for harmony. The juggernaut of executive administrative power that had developed behind the cloak of Washington's unassailable mythic stature and through the clever partisan connivance of Hamilton seemed to be at an end in late 1796 and early 1797. And the anticipation that Adams would turn out of office and influence such men as Pickering, Wolcott, and McHenry produced the prospect of a far different structure and moral complexion in executive government, despite Adams's political theories. Even if Adams did not turn out to be imbued with a strong democratic sensibility, or to appreciate Bache's faith in enlightened popular sovereignty, the crusty New England-er's hatred of a Hamilton who had conspired against him in the election seemed to guarantee a new open-mindedness in the presidency, the prospect for a return of congressional authority, and, above all, the *sine qua non*, Franco-American reconciliation.

Jefferson responded immediately. In a December 28 letter he described Adams as his senior in every way, waxing so conciliatory that Madison counseled against sending the letter at all since it compromised Republican views too thoroughly if reconciliation failed. But Madison did urge Jefferson to cultivate friendship with Adams. And Adams, whose emotions could run hot and cold, reciprocated warmly in his inaugural address, an address that resurrected the image of the American Revolution, proclaimed the sovereignty of the people, and—in a language and style not unfamiliar to the pages of Bache's *Aurora*—demanded that other nations respect American commerce. Furthermore, pledging himself to pursue peace and neutrality, Adams proclaimed his "personal esteem" for France. His desire to remain friendly with that country, he promised, would lead him to deal with France through "amicable negociation," and to deal openly with the American people.[80]

As early as December, 1796, the *Aurora* was comparing Adams to Washington. A preference for Adams was "plain and desirable," one correspondent observed. He was not a "puppet"; he had "integrity" and "would not sacrifice his country's interest at the shrine of party."

> In addition to these considerations, it is well known that ADAMS is an Aristocrat only in theory, but that WASHINGTON is one in practice—that ADAMS has the simplicity of a republican but that WASHINGTON has the ostentations of an eastern bashaw—that ADAMS holds none of his fellow men in slavery, but that WASHINGTON does.

After the inauguration, Adams was further praised for his republican virtue, his opposition to mock royalty, his simplicity, and his independence.[81] Although some writers were hard pressed to articulate how they had opposed Adams so vociferously in the campaign but supported him after it, they managed some rationalizations. Adams had never been a party to Washington's policies, they declared, yet Adams's true republicanism had never been revealed in the campaign. Republicans had mistakenly believed that Hamilton supported Adams, when Hamilton actually supported Pinckney. Adams's inaugural speech proved he was a friend to equality, republicanism, and France.[82] In an attempt to woo Adams away from the Federalists, one writer rhapsodized,

> It is universally admitted that Mr. ADAMS is a man of incorruptible integrity, and that the resources of his own mind are equal to the duties of his station; we may then flatter ourselves, that his measures will be taken in prudence, that he will not become the head of a party, and that he will not be the tool of any man or set of men. His speech on his inauguration augurs well to our country. Let it be compared with any of his predecessor's, & they must hide their diminished heads in the comparison. He declares himself the friend of France and of peace, the admirer of republicanism, the enemy of party, and he avows his determination to let no political creed interfere in his appointments. How honorable are these sentiments; how characteristic of a patriot![83]

Bache's willingness to court Adams was based on both a genuine belief that Adams could be a friend of France and republicanism, and a sly desire to manipulate, insofar as he could, an impressionable, friendless, pliable President. Federalists, overly cynical as usual, believed the underlying reasons for Bache's "conversion" were transparently obvious. Webster charged the *Aurora* with "shameless, unblushing effrontery," and predicted that "the bait is too thinly disguised to beguile that old and cautious statesman." Fenno mundanely added that "the only credit that any man can derive from that paper [*Aurora*], (which has been not inaptly styled the 'Infernal Gazette') is to receive its abuse."[84]

A casual observer would be justified in suggesting that from the attack on Washington through the attempted reconciliation with Adams, Bache had utterly abandoned his support of the "impartial press" for the machinations and manipulations of modern party politics. Between 1795 and early 1797, few if any editorials can be found that one might interpret as a defense of administration or Federalist policies, even when one includes the praise of Adams. Conversely, Republicans (with the exception of Swanwick in the election of 1796) were never criticized. Some historians have seen these developments as the natural evolution of loose partisan behavior into cohesive party discipline. Captured by a paradigm of consensus, these historians have implied that this evolution, as it related to the newspapers, was a reflection of an impartial press reduced to becoming the rhetorical tool of a larger party machine. On the basis of such evidence as party tickets and nominations, partisan polarities in general elections, and the emergence of party solidarity in congressional votes, they concluded that a first party system existed and that journalists like Bache were the servants of that system.[85]

Yet we have been appropriately reminded that, compared to later parties, "the Federalists and Republicans remained half-developed and not explicitly institutionalized," that "Federalist and Republican organizations did not take on a life of their own," and that prior to the 1820s "National organizations and campaigns did not exist."[86] It is also well known now that political journalists were generally not dumb followers of party policies and tactics, not sycophants of party lines or tools of party "superiors." The partisan press was not "devoted to parties *per se*. They were devoted to sets of ideas which generally were identified with and disputed by the parties."[87] Newspaper owners like Bache were jealous guardians of their political as well as their entrepreneurial independence.

But with cohesive party structure poorly developed and a modern sense of party loyalty absent in the 1790s, how do we explain the anomaly that Bache behaved as a thorough-going partisan, manipulating rhetoric and the public mood, promoting candidates, denouncing the opposition, and planning strategy with many of America's early national politicos? The definition of "party" is important in answering this, and Americans had at least three different definitions of party with which they might be familiar in the 1790s. The first was a Burkean definition, in which parties were a natural consequence of social hierarchies and ancient interests, embodiments of kinship and status which Burke found synonymous with patriotism and principled behavior. This kind of party was permanent and exclusive, not liberating or open. Bache did not find this idea of party appealing, but rather retrograde and static. It was this type of party that he referred to when he declared the Federalists to be an aristocratic faction who "would sooner bring us back to a state of British colonization, than lose their ascendancy in government."[88]

A second, more modern yet more skeptical view of party, a "qualified anti-party view," was that of Hume and Madison, in which the foundation of party could be found in the passions and the interests—the former being bad, the latter, "when men exercise their reason coolly and freely," being an inevitable basis of differing opinion and party formation. But such interests, and the parties that were their vehicles, had to be checked and kept from forming a majority that would in turn create a tyranny over the minority. Some of Bache's correspondents defined interest and party in this fashion, one asserting in early 1795, "That there never did and never will exist a real and pure republican government, without, and independent of parties."[89] But Bache, who could and did use varying definitions of interests and party, was never a regular or consistent subscriber to this idea of party. Insofar as he did embrace this view, he seemed to confine his concern for rationally divergent interests to the realm of minor disagreements over taste and opinion, subordinate to over-arching ideological positions of much greater moment and significance.

Burkean and Madisonian views of party have done much to obscure the idea of party that Bache and like-minded Republicans held. But the hegemonic structure that Country-Court and classical republican ideology has attempted to impose on the 1790s has further clouded the definition of party. Proponents of Country-Court Party ideology, unwilling to admit the newness of ideological vision in the 1790s, have identified Republican Party members from Jefferson down as seeking little more than an antique "virtue" that pre-dates any modern ideal of party, suggesting that Republicans nostalgically embraced a pre-modern ideal of patriot-kings, agrarian virtue, unanimity of sentiment, and singular moral purpose.[90]

This classical republican view of party has sometimes obscured other ideological bases for party in the early republic. Men like Bache and James Monroe, whose ideologies were closely aligned, have consequently been catalogued with a conservative tradition that was foreign to them. While they held in common with classical republicanism the ideal of no-party, the basis of their single-party ideology was a new view of individual and collective interest; faith in the shared, intuitive knowledge of liberated citizens; and confidence in the intelligence of a people more than in their virtue.[91] Bache's progress toward this view of party is clear. His early genuflections toward the supremacy of representative government alone, toward a constitutionally defined process that would leave no need for party, ended with what he identified as the usurpation of representation by the executive administration. With the rise of the Democratic Societies and the defeat of the Whiskey Rebellion, therefore, a more insistent language of popular sovereignty appeared in Bache's paper, replacing deference to constituted, representative authority. By the time Washington signed the Jay Treaty in August, 1795, the more potent word "democracy" began to appear as frequently as the word "republicanism" in *Aurora* rhetoric. And after 1795 democracy was exclusively associated with Republicans whose election—to Congress, to the state houses, and even to city councils—was imperative for the maintenance of both republicanism and democracy. Representative republicanism with its implication of deference had evolved into democracy with its implications of equality as the irreducible ethic, the inescapable test of legitimacy in Bache's eyes.[92] The idea of party and authentic citizenship reflected a definitional tautology that admitted no room for essential varieties of faith and belief or legitimacy of opposition. True citizens were democratic republicans, and true democratic republicans were Republicans.

Notes

1. Although convinced of Washington's partisanship, Jefferson advised Republicans not to risk an attack on Washington's seemingly invincible character until the President had retired. See Dumas Malone, *Thomas Jefferson as a Political Leader* (Berkeley and Los Angeles, 1963), 17.

2. On the gentry ethic see Robert H. Wiebe, *The Opening of American Society* (New York, 1984), 3–109. The elitism of the Federalists as well as their desire to maintain a deferential political order, secure the revolution, and avoid the chaos of the French Revolution is articulated best in Richard Buel, Jr., *Securing the Revolution: Ideology in American Politics, 1789–1815* (Ithaca, N. Y., 1972).

3. John Marshall, *The Life of George Washington* (Philadelphia, 1807); Mason L. Weems, *The Life of Washington,* ed. Marcus Cunliffe (Cambridge, Mass., 1962); and Washington Irving, *Life of George Washington* (Cited here, New York, 1900), either stated outright that Washington was above partisanship or implied that he was. Neither Marcus Cunliffe, *George Washington: Man and Monument* (Boston, 1958), nor Bernard Mayo, *Myths and Men: Patrick Henry, George Washington, Thomas Jefferson* (New York, 1963), two modern attempts to correct myths about Washington, succeeds in suggesting that Washington ever acted as a political partisan. One of the few strong claims of partisanship laid against Washington is in Joseph Charles, *The Origins of the American Party System* (Williamsburg, Va., 1956). On the creation of the mythical Washington see also William Alfred Bryan, *George Washington in American Literature, 1775–1865* (New York, 1952).

Jared Sparks, *The Life of George Washington* (New York, 1902), 420–21, claimed that Washington was assaulted "with a perseverance and sometimes with an acrimony, for which the best of causes could hardly afford an apology." John Bach

McMaster, *A History of the People of the United States from the Revolution to the Civil War* (New York, 1936), II, 53, covered the attacks on Washington in the greatest detail and rightly saw Washington as sensitive to these attacks. Nevertheless, McMaster wrongly contends that Philip Freneau's "abuse of Washington makes that afterward poured out by Benjamin Franklin Bache seem almost decent." John Alexander Carroll and Mary Wells Ashworth, *George Washington. First in Peace* (New York, 1957), seldom dwell on any attack on Washington for more than a few lines, generally avoiding editorial commentary, labeling most attacks as filled with "invective" and "slanders." However, John C. Miller, *The Federalist Era, 1789–1801* (New York, 1960), which is still regarded as the standard secondary source on the 1790s, takes a dim view of the attacks on the basis of decency and morality as well as politics.

4. L. Douglas Good, "Theodore Dwight: Federalist Propagandist," Connecticut Historical Society *Bulletin*, 39 (1974), 89–90. See also Barry Schwartz, "The Character of Washington: A Study in Republican Culture," *American Quarterly*, 38 (1986), 202, 205; and on the "patriot-king" ideal see Ralph Ketcham, *Presidents Above Party: The First American Presidency, 1789–1829* (Chapel Hill, N. C., 1984), 89–93.

5. W. Cobbett to Jonathan Boucher, Apr. 19, 1800, in Thomas Debevoise III, ed., "Another Cobbett Letter from America," *Yale University Library Gazette*, 53 (1978), 35.

6. John C. Fitzpatrick, ed., *Writings of George Washington* (Washington, D. C., 1931–44), XXXIV, 174n, hereafter cited as Fitzpatrick, ed., *Writings of Washington*.

7. Much of the material on the attack on Washington offered here previously appeared in James D. Tagg, "Benjamin Franklin Bache's Attack on George Washington," *Pennsylvania Magazine of History and Biography*, C (1976), 191–230.

8. "Pittachus," *Aurora*, Nov. 23, 1795. See also *ibid.*, Sept. 30 ("Portius"), Oct. 17 ("Timothy Turn-Penny" from *Jersey Chron.*), 21 ("Valerius"), Dec. 23 ("Pittachus" and "A Querist" from N. Y. *Argus*), 1795; and Jan. 27 ("Cosca" from *Petersburgh Gaz.*).

9. "Corres.," *ibid.*, Sept. 2, 1795. See also *ibid.*, Sept. 11 ("Belisarius"), 14 ("corres."), 1795.

10. *Ibid.*, Oct. 21 ("Valerius"), 1795; and Apr. 4, 1796. See also *ibid.*, Sept. 24 ("Portius"), 26 and Oct. 1 ("Pittachus"), 1795.

11. *Ibid.*, Oct. 21, Dec. 29 ("corres.," and communication from Bost.), 1795; Apr. 11 ("Consistency"), 1796.

12. "Valerius," *ibid.*, Nov. 11, 1795. Hamilton believed the Federalists could use this letter to reveal clear designs by the Republicans to contrast Jefferson with the President and thereby elevate Jefferson in public esteem for partisan reasons. Alex. Hamilton to O. Wolcott, Jr., Nov. 12, 1795, George Gibbs, ed., *Memoirs of the Administration of Washington and John Adams* (New York, 1846. Cited here N. Y., 1971), I, 262–63, hereafter cited as Gibbs, ed., *Wolcott Papers*. Other editorials attacking Washington's appointment policies include *Aurora*, Sept. 9 ("Plain Truth" from *Vermont Gaz.*), Nov. 19 and Dec. 1 ("Valerius"), 1795. Carl E. Prince, *The*

Federalists and the Origins of the U. S. Civil Service (New York, 1977), 270, points out that only six percent of Washington's appointees were Republicans.

13. *Aurora*, Sept. 18 ("Gracchus" from *Petersburgh Intelligencer*), Nov. 5 ("Pittachus"), 1795; Jan. 1 and 13 ("Pittachus"), 1796. "Pittachus" relied heavily on Edmund Randolph's *Vindication* for Washington's anti-French attitudes and statements.

14. *Ibid.*, Dec. 29 ("corres."), 1795; Jan. 13 ("Pittachus"), 1796. An American flag had been presented to the French National Convention earlier by Joshua Barney and had subsequently been hung in a place of prominence in that chamber. For details on the exchange of flags see Alexander De Conde, *Entangling Alliance: Politics and Diplomacy under George Washington* (Durham, N. C., 1958), 436, 496; and Harry Ammon, *James Monroe: The Quest for National Identity* (New York, 1971), 120–21. Washington was also attacked for not mentioning American affection for France in his address to Congress in December 1795. See *Aurora*, Dec. 15 ("An Old Soldier," "Pittachus," and "1776)" from the N. Y. *Argus*), 1795; Mar. 30, Apr. 12, 1796. Webster and Fenno both answered that the President ignored France in his message because no new developments in Franco-American relations had taken place in the past year. *American Minerva*, Dec. 15, 1795; and *Gazette of U. S.*, Jan. 2, 1796.

15. See "The Political Creed of 1795," *Aurora*, Nov. 23, 1795. Other catalogs were offered in *ibid.*, Oct. 16 ("Cosca," from *Petersburgh Intelligencer*), and Dec. 1 ("Valerius"), 1795.

16. "Scipio," *ibid.*, Nov. 20, 1795. See also "Pittachus," *ibid.*, Nov. 18, 26, 1795.

17. "A Calm Observer," *Aurora*, Oct. 23, 1795. A detailed account of the affair is in Edmund and Dorothy Smith Berkeley, *John Beckley: Zealous Partisan in a Nation Divided* (Philadelphia, 1973), 120–29. See also Carroll and Ashworth, *Washington*, 320–22; and John C. Miller, *Alexander Hamilton: Portrait in Paradox* (New York, 1959), 441–42.

18. *Aurora*, Oct. 24, 1795.

19. "Oliver Wolcott, *ibid.*, Oct. 26, 1795. Bache, in response to Wolcott's accusation about attacks on the government, simply said that the *Aurora* would "remain free, unbiased by the smile, and unawed by the frowns of any man or set of men." *Ibid.*

20. See respectively *ibid.*, Oct. 27 ("A Calm Observer"), 28 (Wolcott), 29 ("A Calm Observer"), and Nov. 5 ("A Calm Observer"), 1795. For other *Aurora* responses see *ibid.*, Oct. 28 ("One of the People"), 30 ("Philo-Oliver," "Honestus," and "corres."), 31 ("A Countryman"), Nov. 2 (letter), 3 ("Pittachus" and "A Citizen"), 16 ("Pittachus"), 1795.

21. On *Gazette-Aurora* exchanges see the *Gaz. of U. S.* for October and November, 1795; and *Aurora*, Oct. 30 ("corres." and ed.), 1795. On Webster and the *Aurora* see *Am. Minerva*, Oct. 29, 1795; and *Aurora*, Nov. 2, 1795.

22. Alex. Hamilton to O. Wolcott, Jr., Oct. 26, 1795, Harold C. Syrett, *et al.*, eds., *The Papers of Alexander Hamilton* (New York, 1961–1979), XIX, 350–53, hereafter cited as Syrett, *et al.*, eds., *Hamilton's Papers*. Alex. Hamilton to O. Wol-

cott, Jr., Oct. 27, Nov. 15, 1795; and O. Wolcott, Jr. to Alex. Hamilton, Oct. 29, Nov. 2, 9, 19, 1795, Gibbs, ed., *Wolcott Papers*, I, 261–65, 268.

23. "Alexander Hamilton," from *Gaz. of U. S.*, repr. in *Aurora*, Nov. 18, 19, 20, 21, 1795. The *Aurora* followed Hamilton's analysis with variations on the already well-developed theme. See, for example, *ibid.*, Nov. 21 ("Pittachus" and "corres."), 24 ("Camillus Simplex"), 28 ("Longinias," and a reply to the *Minerva*), 1795.

24. Many *Aurora* editorials repeated previous charges, although the language of ridicule and contempt increased as the campaign grew old. For examples of *Aurora* editorials assaulting the President after mid-1796 see *ibid.*, June 24 ("A Comet"), July 23, Dec. 17 (communication), 23 ("corres."), 27 ("Queries"), 31 ("Jasper Dwight"), 1796. Washington's birthday in 1797 provided opportunity for further *Aurora* ridicule of monarchical praise of the President. See *ibid.*, Feb. 23, Mar. 9, 1797.

25. See "Paulding," *Aurora*, May 30 and June 9, 1796. Bache claimed the document uncovered a "nefarious conspiracy" against republicanism. For the text of these questions see Fitzpatrick, ed., *Writings of Washington*, XXXII, 419–20. For further development of "Paulding"'s charge that Washington hated France and the French Revolution see "Paulding," *Aurora*, June 15, 18, 22, and July 22, 1796.

26. See respectively G. Washington to Alex. Hamilton, June 26, 1796; G. Washington to David Humphreys, June 12, 1796; G. Washington to Sec. of War, July 1, 1796; G. Washington to Sec. of the Treasury, July 6, 1796; and G. Washington to Sec. of State, July 18, 1796, Fitzpatrick, ed., *Writings of Washington*, XXXV, 102–103, 91–92, 110, 125–26, 144–45.

27. Thos. Jefferson to G. Washington, June 19, 1796, Paul Leicester Ford, ed., *Writings of Thomas Jefferson* (New York, 1895), VIII, 81–81, hereafter cited as Ford, ed., *Jefferson's Writings;* and G. Washington to Thos. Jefferson, July 6, 1796, Fitzpatrick, ed., *Writings of Washington*, XXXV, 118–20. Washington believed that Randolph had disclosed the thirteen questions addressed to the Cabinet. See Carroll and Ashworth, *Washington*, 391–92; and Dumas Malone, *Jefferson and the Rights of Man* (Boston, 1962), 269.

28. Eighth Annual Address, Dec. 7, 1796, in James D. Richardson, *A Compilation of Messages and Papers of the Presidents* (New York, 1897), I, 195, hereafter cited as Richardson, *Messages and Papers*. For *Aurora* disgust with the replies of the Senate and the House, see *Aurora*, Dec. 14, 15, 17, 1796; Jan. 6 ("Semper Idem"), 1797.

29. *Ibid.*, Dec. 17, 1796.

30. "Corres.," *ibid.*, Dec. 23, 1796.

31. On Bache's business interests with Paine in this period see Thos. Paine to B. F. Bache, July 13, Sept. 20, 1795, Bache Papers, Castle Collection, American Philosophical Society, Philadelphia; and Thos. Paine to Col. John Fellows, Jan. 20, 1797, Philip S. Foner, ed., *Complete Writings of Thomas Paine* (New York, 1945), 1384. Details of Paine's life in this period are provided best in David Freeman Hawke, *Paine* (New York, 1974), 295–316.

32. Thos. Paine to B. F. Bache, Aug. 7, 1796, Bache Papers, Castle Coll., Am. Philos. Soc. For secondary accounts of Paine's attacks see Hawke, *Paine*, 319–21;

Moncure David Conway, *The Life of Thomas Paine* . . . (New York, 1909), II, 111–80; and Alfred O. Aldridge, *Man of Reason: The Life of Thomas Paine* (Philadelphia, 1959), 205–246. John Adams believed Paine's letters were the weakest writings ever published by Paine, and claimed Bache had held back their publication until late 1796 because they would do nothing to aid the Republican cause in the election. J. Adams to Mrs. Adams, Dec. 8, 1796, Charles Francis Adams, ed., *Letters of John Adams Addressed to His Wife* (Boston, 1841), II, 233. Adams seemed amused that Bache had taken out a "patent" for the "exclusive privilege of publishing the pamphlet"—a reference perhaps to Paine's request of Bache for copyright protection. J. Adams to Mrs. Adams, Dec. 4, 1796, *ibid.*, 232.

33. Material in this paragraph is taken from Thomas Paine, *Letters to George Washington* (Philadelphia, 1796).

34. G. Washington to David Stuart, Jan. 8, 1797, Fitzpatrick, ed., *Writings of Washington*, XXXV, 354. On the other hand, Washington said that William Cobbett's attack on Paine in the *Political Censor* of December 1796 was "not a bad thing." *Ibid.*, 360, 360n. On Bache's comments see *Aurora*, Dec. 22, 1796; Feb. 2, 1797.

35. See *Letters from General Washington to Several of His Friends, in June and July, 1776* (Philadelphia, 1796). Bache was not the only one to revive the letters. The *New York Daily Gazette* also reprinted and declared the authenticity of the letters in November 1795. Details on the twenty-year history of the forged letters can be found in Douglas Southall Freeman, *George Washington. A Biography* IV (New York, 1954), 582 and 582n; and Carroll and Ashworth, *Washington*, 321, 435–36, 439. "Pittachus," *Aurora*, Nov. 13, 1795, used the letters to re-open charges about Washington's "frigidity" regarding independence.

36. Letter, *ibid.*, Mar. 13, 14, 1797. The author tried to prove Washington's guilt by quoting a vague and prejudicial surrender document which was written by the French and which Washington had been forced to sign. On Webster's reply see *Am. Minerva*, Mar. 17, 1797.

37. G. Washington to Benj. Walker, Jan. 12, 1797; and G. Washington to Sec. of State, Mar. 3, 1797, Fitzpatrick, ed., *Writings of Washington*, XXXV, 363–65, 414–16.

38. G. Washington to Jeremiah Wadsworth, Mar. 6, 1797, *ibid.*, 420. See also Washington to William Gordon, Oct. 15, 1797, *ibid.*, XXXVI, 50.

39. Biographic material on Duane largely comes from Kim Tousley Phillips, "William Duane, Revolutionary Editor," (unpub. Ph.D. diss., Univ. of California, 1968), 4–56. On the radical migration and its influence see Michael Durey, "Thomas Paine's Apostles: Radical Emigrés and the Triumph of Jeffersonian Republicanism," *William and Mary Quarterly*, 3d. Ser., XLIV (1987), 661–88.

40. Ray Boston, "The Impact of 'Foreign Liars' on the American Press (1790–1800)," *Journalism Quarterly*, 50 (1973), 727. Phillips is careful to note that "historians have inferred that Duane had been Bache's colleague over a long period and was his natural successor. In fact he had been regularly employed on the paper only two months before Bache's death, and his selection as editor was by no means inevitable." Phillips, "Duane," 56.

41. [William Duane], *A Letter to George Washington . . . Containing Strictures . . . by Jasper Dwight* (Philadelphia, 1796). Phillips, "Duane," 50–51, claims Bache agreed to print the *Letter* and sell it for twenty-five cents.

42. *Aurora*, Jan. 26 ("corres."), Mar. 4 ("E."), Apr. 19 ("corres."), 1797.

43. "Corres.," *ibid.*, Mar. 5, 1797. Robert Carr's claim first appeared in J. Thomas Scharf and Thompson Westcott, *History of Philadelphia, 1609–1884* (Philadelphia, 1884), I, 489.

44. *Gaz. of U. S.*, Mar. 7, 1797; and *Am. Minerva*, Mar. 9, 1797.

45. All material summarized here is from Benjamin Franklin Bache, *Remarks Occasioned by the Late Conduct of Mr. Washington as President of the United States* (Philadelphia, 1797).

46. Eliz. Hewson to Thos. T. Hewson, Oct. 24, 1796; June 5, 1797, Hewson Family Papers, Amer. Philos. Soc., Philadelphia.

47. See, for example, *Aurora*, Sept. 5 ("Gracchus" from *Petersburgh Gaz.*), 1795; Jan. 23 ("Onecrophilus"), 26 ("A Friend to Onecrophilus"), Apr. 4, May 13, Dec. 30 (communication), 1796. "Onecrophilus" discovered twenty-nine crimes attributable to Hamilton.

48. See Bache's parody on Webster's attack on Albert Gallatin in *ibid.*, Apr. 9, 1796.

49. *Ibid.*, June 11, 1796. How much Bache knew about the historically much-belabored Reynolds Affair is uncertain. In late 1792, Congressmen Monroe, Muhlenberg, and Venable had learned of the affair and interviewed Hamilton about it. Monroe informed Beckley about the affair, and Beckley undoubtedly peddled the gossip to Bache and possibly others, ultimately aiding James Thomson Callender in exposing the affair in Callender's *History of the United States for 1796*. Bache's warning may have reduced further attacks on Franklin in all but the renegade Cobbett's newspaper. On Beckley's role in the affair see Berkeley, *Beckley*, 75–85, 92–95. See also Forrest McDonald, *Alexander Hamilton. A Biography* (New York, 1979), 227–30; Miller, *Hamilton*, 333–42, 458–64; Ammon, *Monroe*, 158–60; and Edward Angel, "James Monroe's Mission to France, 1794–1796" (unpub. Ph.D. diss., George Washington Univ., 1979), 408–19.

50. On Sedgwick see *Aurora*, May 9 (Bache's reply to editorials in the *Farmer's Library*, a Vermont paper), 1796; Feb. 27 ("Sketches of the Political Character of Theodore Sedgwick" from the *American Annual Register*), Mar. 1 ("Castigation"), 1797. On Harper see *ibid.*, June 7, 1796; Feb. 27 ("corres."), 28 ("corres."), 1797. On Pickering and Wolcott see *ibid.*, Feb. 3, 1797.

51. For attacks on Webster and the *Minerva* see *ibid.*, Apr. 18, 30 ("corres."), Sept. 10 (letter from *Del. Gaz.*, and Bache), 12 ("L." from *Del. Gaz.*), 19, 1795; Jan 6 (communication from N. Y.), 1797.

52. See, for examples, *ibid.*, June 6 ("A Citizen"), 18 ("corres."), Sept. 16, 19, 22 ("Civis" from the *Gaz. of U. S.*), Dec. 24, 1795; June 9, and Dec. 31, 1796.

53. Daniel Green, *Great Cobbett: The Noblest Agitator* (London, 1983), 143–47; George Spater, *William Cobbett: The Poor Man's Friend* (Cambridge, 1982), I, 68–78; G. D. H. Cole, *Life of William Cobbett* (London, 1924), 51–64; Mary Elizabeth Clark, *Peter Porcupine in America: The Career of William Cobbett, 1792–*

1800 (Philadelphia, 1939), 46–93; and William Reitzel, "William Cobbett and Philadelphia Journalism: 1794–1800," *PMHB*, LIX (1935), 223–44. Cobbett's life was consumed with pamphleteering and attacking a variety of foes between 1795 and 1797, including his own publisher, Thomas Bradford. In *A Bone to Gnaw for the Democrats*, Pt. II (1795), he attacked Bache's defense of French revolutionary violence by portraying the brutality of the Lyons massacre. *A New Year's Gift . . .* (1796) attacked Randolph's *Vindication* and defended the Jay Treaty, as did *The Bloody Buoy . . .* (1796). The *Life and Adventures of Peter Porcupine* (1796) describes his emigration to America while taking periodic swipes at Benjamin Franklin.

54. *Aurora*, Feb. 25, Apr. 13 (ed. from Norfolk paper), June 25 (letter), July 8 ("Snub"), 1795; June 21 ("Q."), 13 ("A Virginian" from Fredericksburg *Republican Citizen*), 16 ("Truth"), 23 ("An American" from N. Y. *Argus*), Aug. 8 ("corres."), 11 ("A Native American"), 12 ("corres."), 17, Sept. 8 ("corres."), 13, 16, 17 ("Veritas"), 22, 1796.

55. *Ibid.*, May 25 (communication), June 9 ("Paul Hedgehog"), July 23 ("An American" from N. Y. *Argus*), 1796.

56. *Am. Minerva*, July 11, 1795. For the full catalog of charges see also *ibid.*, Sept. 16, Nov. 25, 1795; and Feb. 24, 1796.

57. See *Gaz. of U. S.*, Sept. 16 ("corres."), 18 ("Plain Truth" and "Plain Dealing"), Oct. 29 ("corres."), 1795; Mar. 16 ("corres."), May 12 (communication), 1796. On the "Hollow Ware Company" charge see, for example, *ibid.*, Nov. 20 (three "corres."), 1795.

58. *Ibid.*, June 3 ("An American Farmer"), 7 ("Paine's Age of Reason," A Critique by Peter Porcupine), 1796.

59. See respectively, Communication, *Col. Cent.*, Sept. 30, 1795; M. Rochefontaine to T. Pickering, Dec. 6, 1795, in Timothy Pickering Papers, Massachusetts Historical Society, Boston; and T. Pickering to N. Webster, Feb. 18, 1796, Emily E. F. Ford, comp. and ed., *Notes on the Life of Noah Webster* (New York, 1912. Cited here N. Y., 1971), I, 405; and *Connecticut Courant*, Jan. 23, Feb. 13, 1797.

60. *Aurora*, Sept. 13, 1796.

61. Jefferson's personal protests against his candidacy, both real and partially feigned, are clearly shown in Malone, *Jefferson and the Rights of Man*, 273–94; Adrienne Koch, *Jefferson and Madison: The Great Collaboration* (New York, 1950), 163–73; Thos. Jefferson to J. Madison, Dec. 17, 1796; Thos. Jefferson to E. Rutledge, Dec. 27, 1796; Thos. Jefferson to J. Adams, Dec. 28, 1796; Thos. Jefferson to J. Madison, Jan. 1, 1797, Ford, ed., *Jefferson's Writings*, VII, 91–92, 93–94, 95–97, 98–99. Madison's role is detailed in Irving Brant, *James Madison, Father of the Constitution, 1787–1800* (Indianapolis, Ind., 1950), 440–47; and Ralph Ketcham, *James Madison: A Biography* (New York, 1971), 365–67.

62. John Adams's candidacy is covered at length in Gilbert Chinard, *Honest John Adams* (Boston, 1933), 248–57; Manning J. Dauer, *The Adams-Federalists* (Baltimore, 1953), 78–110; Stephen G. Kurtz, *The Presidency of John Adams* (Philadelphia, 1961), 78–113; and Page Smith, *John Adams* (Garden City, N. Y., 1962), II, 887–922. On Adams's misfortunes in the South see Norman K. Risjord, *Chesapeake Politics, 1781–1800* (New York, 1978), 507–510. William L. Smith, with Hamilton's aid, composed the "Phocion" letters which appeared in the *Gaz. of U. S.*, Oct. 15–Nov. 24, 1796. See George C. Rogers, Jr., *Evolution of a Federalist:*

William Loughton Smith of Charleston (1758–1812) (Columbia, S. C., 1962), 292–93. Hamilton's scheming is discussed in Miller, *Hamilton*, 445–50; and McDonald, *Hamilton*, 327.

63. *Aurora*, Feb. 10, Sept. 27 ("Albert Russell" from *Alexandria Gaz.*), Oct. 12 ("An Observer" from *Ind. Chron.*), 18 ("A Whig"), Nov. 5 ("An Elector of Electors" from Pittsburgh), 12 ("Dialogue between an Aristocrat and a Republican"), 17 ("corres."), Dec. 14 (letter), 1796.

64. See, for example, *ibid.*, Oct. 28 ("Cassius" from *Petersburgh Intelligencer*), Nov. 8 ("corres."), 11, 12 ("Cassius" from *Petersburgh Intelligencer*), 14; and Dec. 5, 12, 13 and 14 ("A Federalist" from *Gaz. of U. S.*), 1796; Mar. 8 ("corres."), 1797. "A Federalist" was Tench Coxe.

65. *Ibid.*, Oct. 6 ("Sidney"); Oct. 6, 7, and 12 (communication from *New World*); 17 ("Extract of a letter from Thomas Paine," of July 30, 1796), 20 ("Publius" from *New World*, and "Sidney"), 21 ("Prudence"), 22 ("Sidney"), 24 ("A Western American" from *Baltimore Tele.* and "Honestus" from *Alexandria Gaz.*), 25 ("Franklin," "Cato" from *New World*, letter from *Lancaster Jour.*, and ed.), 27 ("Americanus" from *Baltimore Tele.*), 29 ("Stentor" from *Ind. Chron.* and "One of the People"), Nov. 1 ("A Friend to Equal Rights" and "Detector"), 2 (communication), 8 ("Polybius" from N. Y. *Argus*), 9 ("corres."), 22 ("corres."), 24 ("A Unitarian"), 30 ("corres." from *New World*); Dec. 1 and 2, 3, 6, and 10 ("A Federalist" from *Gaz. of U. S.*); 19 (ed. from *Ind. Chron.*), 1796; Jan. 10, 13 ("Henry Hoblin"), 1797.

66. *Ibid.*, Oct. 28, 1796. On Pennsylvania's "general" election law see Harry M. Tinkcom, *The Republicans and Federalists in Pennsylvania, 1790–1801* (Harrisburg, Pa., 1950), 162, 168. The extensive activities of Leib and Beckley in forming tickets and distributing them are covered in Noble E. Cunningham, Jr., "John Beckley: An Early American Party Manager in the United States; Pennsylvania in the Election of 1796," *PMHB*, LX (1936), 381–86; Richard G. Miller, *Philadelphia, The Federalist City: A Study of Urban Politics, 1789–1801* (New York, 1976), 87; and, Berkeley, *Beckley*, 136, 143–51.

67. Pennsylvania, *Public Notice. Friday the Fourth Day of November Next, is the Day Appointed by Law, for the People to . . . Choose . . . Electors . . . of a President . . .* (Philadelphia, 1796).

68. Adet's letters were dated Oct. 27, Nov. 1, and Nov. 16. The first and third were addressed to Secretary of State Pickering. Bache published these in the *Aurora* on Oct. 31, Nov. 5, and Nov. 16, 1796. The latter letter, which was printed in its entirety in *Claypoole's Gazette* on November, took up ninety-four columns in that paper and was only reprinted in part in the *Aurora* on November 16, with Bache offering a lengthy summary of the entire letter on November 18. Bache immediately published these letters for the French Minister as a pamphlet. See France, *Notes addressées par le citoyen Adet* (Philadelphia, 1796). On the significance and background of the Adet letters see especially De Conde, *Entangling Alliance*, 471–80; and Albert Hall Bowman, *The Struggle for Neutrality: Franco-American Diplomacy During the Federalist Era* (Knoxville, Tenn., 1974), 264–66.

69. The quotation is from Gerard H. Clarfield, *Timothy Pickering and the American Republic* (Pittsburgh, 1980), 172. On Pickering's anti-French actions and his response see *ibid.*, 172–76.

70. *Aurora*, Nov. 18, 1796.

71. *Gaz. of U. S.*, Nov. 3 ("Brutus"), 22, Dec. 26 (communication), 1796; *Am. Minerva*, Nov. 23, 1796; and William Cobbett, "Diplomatic Blunderbuss," cited from John M. and James P. Cobbett, eds., *Selections from Cobbett's Political Works* (London, 1835), I, 115–29. Bache replied to Webster that the danger of war was real, and carefully noted that Adet's attack was against the executive administration, not against the House of Representatives.

72. G. Washington to David Stuart, Jan. 8, 1797, Fitzpatrick, ed., *Writings of Washington*, XXXV, 358; and Samuel Chase to James McHenry, Dec. 4, 1796, Bernard C. Steiner, *The Life and Correspondence of James McHenry* (Cleveland, Ohio, 1907), 203.

73. *Aurora*, Sept. 17 ("A Citizen"), 20 ("corres."); 28 and 29 (election notices); Oct. 10, 11 ("corres." and Bache), Dec. 29, 1796. Bache also printed some editorials criticizing Swanwick. See *ibid.*, Sept. 12 ("Consistency" and "F. T."), 27 ("Romulus"), Oct. 11 ("A Native & a Freeman"), 1796.

74. *Ibid.*, Oct. 7 ("A Citizen"); 8 and 10 (election notices), 14, 1796.

75. *Ibid.*, Oct. 13, 18, 19 ("corres."), 1796. Miller, *Philadelphia, The Federalist City*, 82, reports that 45% of eligible voters voted in 1796, and that Swanwick won with a slim 51.2% of the votes cast. Swanwick's win was based on anti-British, anti-excise sentiment plus the support of artisans and unskilled labor. In the election of twenty common councillors Federalist candidates received 60.2% of the vote. *Ibid.*, 86.

76. *Aurora*, Nov. 8, 25, 1796.

77. Tinkcom, *Republicans and Federalists in Pennsylvania*, 168–74. Federalist elector Samuel Miles ultimately voted for Jefferson.

78. Ed., *Aurora*, Nov. 29, 1796. See also *ibid.*, Nov. 30 (two "corres."), Dec. 3 (communication), 6 (two "corres."), 7 ("corres."), 1796. For other election irregularities, see *ibid.*, Nov. 25 ("corres."), 30 ("corres."), Dec. 2 ("corres."), 1796; Mar. 10 and 14 ("A Brief History of the Election of Electors"), 1797. Berkeley, *Beckley*, 149, claims that Bache was not always accurate in his returns in 1796.

79. *Aurora*, Nov. 29, Dec. 12, 13, 14, 16, 28, 1796; Feb. 9, 1797.

80. Reconciliation and Adams's inauguration are discussed in Chinard, *Adams*, 258–62; Smith, *Adams*, 917–22; Kurtz, *Presidency of John Adams*, 209–38; Dauer, *Adams-Federalists*, 112–18; and Malone, *Jefferson and the Rights of Man*, 293–301. Jefferson's hopes for reconciliation are clear in Thos. Jefferson to J. Adams, Dec. 28, 1796; Thos. Jefferson to J. Madison, Jan. 1, 1797; Thos. Jefferson to Arch. Stuart, Jan. 4, 1797; Thos. Jefferson to J. Madison, Jan. 22, 1797; Thos. Jefferson to J. Langdon, Jan. 22, 1797; Thos. Jefferson to J. Madison, Jan. 30, 1797; Thos. Jefferson to E. Gerry, May 13, 1797, Ford, ed., *Jefferson's Writings*, VII, 95–97, 98–99, 101–103, 107–109, 111, 115–16, 119–21. On Madison's desire for reconciliation but reluctance to send Jefferson's letter to Adams see J. Madison to Thos. Jefferson, Jan. 15, 1797, Gaillard Hunt, ed., *Writings of James Madison* (New York, 1906), VI, 302–304, hereafter cited as Hunt, ed., *Writings of Madison*. Adams's anger at Hamilton and the High Federalists who opposed him can be seen in J. Adams to E. Gerry, Feb. 13, 1797; J. Adams to Henry Knox, Mar. 30, 1797, *ibid.*,

524, 535–36. Adams's inaugural address is in Richardson, ed., *Messages and Papers*, I, 218–22.

81. *Aurora*, Dec. 21 ("corres."), 1796; Mar. 10 ("Remarks on the President's Address" from N. Y. *Argus*), 14 ("corres."), 17 ("corres."), 18 ("corres."), 20 ("corres." and ed.), Apr. 28 ("corres."), 1797.

82. *Ibid.*, Mar. 16 (from N. Y.), 18 ("corres."), 20 ("corres."), 1797.

83. "Corres.," *ibid.*, Mar. 14, 1797.

84. *Am. Minerva*, Mar. 11, 1797; and, *Gaz. of U. S.*, Mar. 14, 1797.

85. Coming in the period of the most extensive publication of 1790s political literature, the lasting significance of this school has been considerable. For prominent examples of this type of literature see, for examples, Raymond Walters, Jr., "The Origins of the Jeffersonian Party in Pennsylvania," *PMHB*, LXVI (1942), 440–58; Koch, *Jefferson and Madison*; Joseph Charles, *The Origins of the American Party System* (New York, 1956); Noble E. Cunningham, Jr., *The Jeffersonian Republicans: The Formation of Party Organization, 1789–1801* (Chapel Hill, N. C., 1957); John C. Miller, *The Federalist Era, 1789–1801* (New York, 1960); and William Nisbet Chambers, *Political Parties in a New Nation. The American Experience, 1776–1809* (New York, 1963).

More recent quantitative studies have confirmed a growing tendency toward bloc voting and therefore apparent party conformity, in the 1790s. See Mary P. Ryan, "Party Formation in the United States Congress, 1789–1796: A Quantitative Analysis," *WMQ*, 3d. Ser., XXVIII (1971), 523–42; and Jerald A. Combs, *The Jay Treaty: Political Battleground of the Founding Fathers* (Berkeley, Calif., 1970). Rudolph M. Bell, *Party and Faction in American Politics: The House of Representatives, 1789–1801* (Westport, Conn., 1973), 185–91, discovers, as does Combs, the emergence of party machinery and polarization with the Jay Treaty battle in the House. It was not until 1797, however, that party voting consistently polarized. Bell contends that with increased partisan activity the Republicans concentrated more on winning offices than on establishing policy. *Ibid.*, 189–90.

86. Ronald P. Formisano, "Federalists and Republican: Parties, Yes—System, No," in Paul Kleppner, *et al.*, eds., *The Evolution of American Electoral Systems* (Westport, Conn., 1981), 66; and Ronald P. Formisano, *The Transformation of Political Culture* (New York, 1983), 10.

87. Besides my own work on Bache see William David Sloan, "The Party Press: The Newspaper Role in National Politics, 1789–1816" (unpub. Ph.D. diss., Univ. of Texas, 1981), 279. William Frank Steirer, Jr., "Philadelphia Newspapers: Years of Revolution and Transition, 1764–1794" (unpub. Ph.D. diss., Univ. of Penn., 1972), 380, reports that by 1794 the newspaper owner believed his newspaper "was solely his responsibility and creation, that the newspaper was indeed his."

88. *Aurora*, June 24, 1796. Other pertinent references to Federalists as an exclusive aristocratic faction attempting to hold authority at all costs can be seen in *ibid.*, Feb. 27, June 25, 1796. On this form of party see Richard Hofstadter, *The Idea of a Party System: The Rise of Legitimate Opposition in the United States, 1780–1840* (Berkeley, Calif., 1969), 29–33.

89. "Candidus," *Aurora*, Apr. 13, 1795. On the Humean-Madisonian view of

party see Hofstadter, *Idea of a Party System,* 24–29. Man reasoning "coolly and freely" is from Madison's "Federalist Paper No. 50," in Jacob Cooke, ed., *The Federalist* (Middletown, Conn., 1961), 346. On the early modern definitional division of the "passions" and "interests" and the subsequent tendency in the eighteenth century to recognize that these two qualities were the same, see Albert O. Hirschman, *The Passions and the Interests: Political Arguments for Capitalism Before Its Triumph* (New York, 1977).

90. For promotion of this thesis see especially Lance Banning, "Jeffersonian Ideology and the French Revolution: A Question of Liberticide at Home," *Studies in Burke and His Time,* XVII (1976), 5–26; Lance Banning, *The Jeffersonian Persuasion: Evolution of a Party Ideology* (Ithaca, N. Y., 1978); and Ketcham, *Presidents Above Party.* Professor Banning modifies his views somewhat in Lance Banning, "Jeffersonian Ideology Revisited: Liberal and Classical Ideas in the New American Republic," *WMQ,* 3d. Ser., XLIII (1986), 3–19.

91. Hofstadter, *Idea of a Party System,* 22–23, for example, places Monroe in the Patriot-King category. The best exposition of the liberal ideological scheme can be found in Joyce Appleby, *Capitalism and a New Social Order* (New York, 1984). On the role of Paine in this ideology see Durey, "Paine's Apostles," *WMQ,* XLIV (1987), 661–88. In analyzing the partisan ideology of Tench Coxe—a close compatriot of Bache in the partisan political activity in the late 1790s—Jacob Cooke, *Tench Coxe and the Early Republic* (Chapel Hill, N. C., 1978), 280, tellingly remarks that Coxe was as interested in the "intelligence" in the American people as much as "virtue." Sean Wilentz, *Chants Democratic: New York City and the Rise of the American Working Class, 1788–1850* (New York, 1984), 95, implies that this democratic ideology was not simple liberalism because artisanal republicans in general held "a vision of a democratic society that balanced individual rights with communal responsibilities—of independent, competent citizens and men who would soon win their competence, whose industry in the pursuit of happiness, as in politics, was undertaken not for personal gain alone but for the public good."

92. For the transformation of this ideology in general see Regina Ann Markel Morantz, " 'Democracy' and 'Republic' in American Ideology, 1787–1840 " (unpub. Ph.D. diss., Columbia Univ., 1971).

11. The French Crisis, 1797–1798

"War is inevitable between my country and France; our government has really lost their head."
(Benjamin Franklin Bache to Louis Gabriel Cramer,
June 27, 1798)

EVENTS CONSPIRED TO DESTROY the *Aurora*'s reconciliation with Adams long before the latter's inauguration, giving the strategy a cynical cast it did not entirely deserve. Those events involved the growing crisis with France. American enthusiasm for France, so resplendent in 1793, had become a dim memory by 1797, except among francophiles like Bache. After the Genet affair, Bache had attempted to carry the torch for France, despite suspension of the republican constitution in June, 1793, and despite arrival of news of the Terror in early 1794. But for most Americans, even French victories could no longer be celebrated with enthusiasm as the sharper image of the guillotine dulled all other visions. While men like Wolcott and Webster predictably abandoned France for its instability and despotism, moderates also fell away, leaving the public defense of France and republican sisterhood to radicals like Bache.[1]

Yet Bache had forged ahead in the mid-1790s. The *Advertiser* and *Aurora* almost daily reported the course of the European war, activities of the National Convention, and "reforms" initiated by the Committee of Public Safety, while Bache kept his print shop busy publishing reports and state papers released by the National Convention for propaganda purposes. Emphasizing the corruption of France's enemies, his editorials defended the imperialism of the Great Republic and predicted that England had to treat with France or be defeated.[2]

Bravado was less convincing in Bache's defense of France's internal politics. Initially, he claimed "rigorous measures" were needed to "baffle the intrigues" of counter-revolutionaries. But when Danton was guillotined in April, 1794, Bache appeared confused, first casting Danton as an innocent victim, then claiming the revolution was larger than one man, and finally condemning Danton, using the unproven Jacobin charges that he had taken a bribe.[3]

Robespierre's fall was also difficult to appraise. Bache first claimed that Robespierre was a victim of partisanship or blind ambition. But a week later, he catalogued a number of abuses, describing him as a passionate man who had carried his purge too far and had become a virtual dictator. Nevertheless, Bache re-assured his readers with his usual fallback argument, "that the French Republic or the liberties of any people do not rest on the existence of any man. Principles and not men have ever been the objects of their attachment."[4]

While he tried to interpret the Thermidorean Reaction as merely the restoration of stability, moderation, and peace, he soon found himself a victim of the wildfire changes of the Revolution once again. Party violence in France could not be ignored, and Bache even had to admit ultimately that his "moderates" sponsored much of that violence.[5] Slow to recognize the utter collapse of the Jacobins in this process, the *Aurora* continued to express pleasure with Jacobin reforms in education, the arts, and religion, and Bache also published and promoted the new French calendar.[6] Perhaps hoping to see a Girondist resurgence, Bache willingly deceived himself by claiming that the new French Constitution (not formally proclaimed as the Constitution of the Year III until September 23, 1795) established full democracy and universal suffrage when in fact it established a new engine for executive corruption, the Directory.[7] To the political right of the Jacobins himself, Bache defended them as real patriots well after their demise, blamed most excesses on the royalists and on Gracchus Babeuf's "Conspiracy of Equals," and denied that the democratic clubs of France had been abolished by law.[8] Aside from some light taunts about Bache and other defenders of the Revolution, Fenno summed up Federalist press reaction in succinct, Burkean tones: "Every species of crime has found apologists and applauders in the writings of some persons who call themselves friends of France, friends of mankind."[9]

In 1795 and 1796, as in 1794, the *Aurora* felt it could take comfort in, and discover the best means of promoting France through, French military progress. Victories in Holland and Italy, Prussian recognition of French independence, and Spain's withdrawal from the coalition were celebrated, while Webster and Fenno fretted over the likely consequences of French imperialism.[10] News from Europe was used to substantiate Bache's belief that England would either sue for peace or fall from a French attack. Attributing the failure of England's furtive peace feelers of late 1795 to

England's unjust demand that France relinquish conquered lands, rather than to the true reason, France's renewed arrogance, Bache predicted in September, 1796, that French invincibility would force England to seek peace. Without peace, Bache warned, France would consolidate and pacify all of Europe, and then have an easy time defeating England.[11] Remarkably insensitive to the fear that many Americans felt in contemplating an all-powerful, imperialist French state, Bache even welcomed the prospect of France's again possessing Louisiana, a circumstance he claimed would be of "utmost advantage" to Americans. Louisiana in French hands, he declared naively, would serve

> as an exemplary warning against the growing spirit of Aristocracy among us . . . as an aid against the wicked arts of Britain to entrap us into an offensive and defensive alliance . . . [and] as a safe and free asylum from tyranny in the event of the majority of our fellow citizens being betrayed into so diabolical an alliance, as the tame surrender of Republican freedom at the feet of Aristocracy & Kingly pageantry.[12]

To complement this specter of French omnipotence, Bache focused on English cruelty, ascribing full blame to England for the death and destruction of the European war, and for the vast sums of money consumed by that war. With the failure of Congress to defeat the British Treaty, Bache also began to print a series entitled "Evidences of British Amity." Altogether, one hundred and fifty instances of British depredations, impressments, and cruel and harsh treatment of Americans by the British were detailed.[13] But the new assault on England, replete with editorials condemning British seizures of American ships after the British Treaty had been ratified, and buttressed by British insistence that it could seize enemy goods on neutral ships and unilaterally apply the Rule of 1756, was undercut by the great lessening in British depredations after early 1796.[14] Bache had more success portraying the evils of impressment, which the British prosecuted with vigor in 1796, seizing Americans both in ports and on the high seas. Holding up the Jay Treaty as a document that licensed impressment, the *Aurora* offered dire predictions on the future of American commerce, and placed special emphasis on Britain's unjust contention that American seamen who had emigrated to the United States from England after the American Revolution were still British subjects, American naturalization laws notwithstanding.[15]

The unspoken reasons for these strident attacks on British behavior were self-contradictory—to justify a changed French policy toward the United

States, and to deflect attention from that policy. Defending French policy toward the United States had been a preoccupation of Bache's since the Genet fiasco. In 1794, the *Advertiser* had met increased French interference with neutral trade, and the seizure of American ships at Bordeaux, with hollow pleas to aid France and retaliate against Great Britain.[16]

Joseph Fauchet's arrival in February, 1794, at the head of a new French commission did little to bolster Bache's flagging cause. Fauchet assiduously avoided radicals like Bache, kept his views private, and through his demure style even made himself acceptable to Hamiltonian Federalists. When Bache's feigned hope that Fauchet's "principles and instructions may be such as to suffer us to pursue with tranquility our happiness under the shield of our neutrality" proved too accurate regarding the French Minister's accommodationism, Bache had no other recourse than to charge the administration with inconsistency and mean-spiritedness toward Genet. But Fauchet's conduct and an increase in French depredations against American shipping allowed the *Advertiser* little scope for furthering Franco-American brotherhood in 1794 or early 1795.[17]

Events in 1795 did nothing to reverse the growing rift. In the spring of 1795 the foreign debt owed to France was converted into a domestic debt and by the summer Federalists like Secretary of the Treasury Oliver Wolcott, Jr. happily saw all monetary obligations to France disappear. By the fall of 1795, with France angry but unclear about the fate of the Jay Treaty, and already harboring suspicions that American merchants were conspiring to avoid French condemnation of goods directed toward England, the Directory superseded the old Committee of Public Safety as the formulator of French foreign policy. This, along with Fauchet's return to Paris in December, 1795, his disavowal of the conciliatory instructions he had been forced to work under in America, and the return of Girondist influence in foreign policy, primed the French for a more vigorous assertion of their interests.

By early 1796, the new Foreign Affairs Minister, Charles Delacroix, had settled on a plan that set the tone for French policy toward the United States until the Convention of 1800. The Jay Treaty had placed France in a state of war with the American government, Delacroix advised in January, and France should, therefore, negotiate with the American people, whose sentiments were believed to be pro-French. That "negotiation" should take the form of encouraging separation of the United States from Great Britain, causing a rupture of relations and perhaps war. This would re-orient trade toward France, and the United States could retake Canada for France.

Although Adet had anticipated French strategy by protesting the Jay Treaty in the fall of 1795 and was subsequently instructed to work Delacroix's foreign policy revolution in America, Adet was to be recalled and replaced by a temporary representative of France at a designation below minister. In February, 1796, a beleaguered James Monroe was informed by the French that the alliance between France and the United States was considered to be at an end and that an Envoy Extraordinary would be sent to America to replace Adet.

A stunned Monroe soon faced new problems. French maritime decrees ranged between the dangerous and broad declaration that neutral vessels would be treated "in the same manner as they shall suffer the English to treat them" (July 2, 1796), and the later decree that announced a long list of contraband items as well as a requirement that neutrals keep a careful list of their crews (March 2, 1797). Unarmed by useful advice from his own government, Monroe offered the few feeble arguments he could in favor of the Jay Treaty. In November, 1796, a still pro-French Monroe learned that he would be replaced in France by Charles Cotesworth Pinckney, and the same month Adet turned over French affairs to Consul General Joseph Philippe Létombe.[18]

During 1796, the *Aurora,* while admitting some French culpability, generally argued that American merchants, having supported British interpretations of neutral rights in the Jay Treaty, had it coming. Even in May, 1796, before French retaliation was in full swing, Bache had warned,

> We have frequently hinted, that it could not be expected that France would long remain quiet sufferers under the effects of our partial neutrality. It is undeniable that every invasion of our rights by the British, which remained unredressed, encouraged further injury, and that so far as our trade with France was concerned, she must have suffered from our pusillanimity. Retaliation was consequently to be expected; it is deserved.[19]

When Bache applied this argument to the French capture of the American ship *Mount Vernon,* Treasury secretary Wolcott rightly predicted that Bache had laid out what would become the standard apology to be followed by France and the Republican press.[20]

Bache's publication of Adet's letters to Pickering in the fall of 1796 heightened the battle between the *Aurora* and the Federalists over France's right to retaliate. Adet's appeal to the people was defended. It was again suggested that the British plundered American commerce more than France did. And it was argued that the treaty of 1778 gave France reciprocal rights to treat the United States as England treated her. Bache's pamphlet attack on Washington, written in early 1797 with the French crisis in mind, also accused the administration of setting a double standard in negotiations with France.[21]

In late 1796, Bache offered the first of many angry *Aurora* charges that the British faction was conspiring to start a war between the United States and France.

> The object of the British party in this country is to irritate and machinate the French into direct hostility—an alliance offensive and defensive with Britain would be the necessary consequence; such an alliance would in the most effectual manner reduce us to our former condition of British Vassals: and undo all that France has done for us.[22]

Through early 1797, other editorials echoed this warning. The Jay Treaty and the French crisis, it was contended, flowed from the out-going administration's false belief that France would fall as well as from the British faction's anxious desire to establish a British dominated economy and a monarchy. But war would destroy republicanism, the *Aurora* added. America's favorable balance of trade with France would end, produce would rot on the wharves, the Mississippi River would be closed, the public debt would soar; fraud would replace frugality in wartime corruption, and the executive power would be strengthened.[23] If England and France successfully negotiated peace while the United States declared war on France, Bache reasoned, England would resume her harsh policies against the United States while Americans would suffer the full force of French might. Fenno again denied *Aurora*'s speculation: France would not declare war on the United States while she enjoyed the opportunity to plunder American commerce, and Bache was despicably trying to terrorize Americans into submission to France.[24]

But the crucial issue in the early months of 1797 was the fate of Pinckney's mission. Leaving for France in September, 1796, Pinckney promised to be a safe Federalist replacement for James Monroe, who, in Secretary of State Pickering's eyes, was no better than a disloyal apologist for France. Although given hollow orders to remove jealousies and restore friendship with France, Pinckney was really sent to demand redress of American grievances from a France that felt itself, not the United States, to be the aggrieved party.

Pickering's overt partisanship and open hatred of France promised to destroy the mission from the start. But even before Pickering vented his spleen, the Directory had determined not to recognize or receive another representative from the United States until that country had redressed French grievances. France allowed Monroe the courtesy of introducing Pinckney to Delacroix on December 9, but then announced its unwillingness to deal with him a couple of days later, and finally, on January 23, ordered Pinckney to leave the country at once. Although the American administration anticipated the mission's failure by early 1797, they probably did not receive verification of Pinckney's rebuff until mid-March.[25]

The *Aurora* was consistent in its analysis of the Pinckney mission from the start. Because Pinckney had been appointed before Adet's suspension and been given no extraordinary powers, he would not be received, the paper argued. America's only hope lay in sending an envoy extraordinary or in granting Pinckney new powers. But a letter of instruction of January 16 from Pickering to Pinckney, displaying the Secretary's overt hostility toward France, was published by the Federalists, thereby helping to destroy the possibility of a new negotiation. The *Aurora*'s writers described the letter as a party tract; it was a device to inflame France intentionally, to introduce monarchy, and to establish a British alliance with the United States. Others admitted Pickering's claim that self-interest drove French foreign policy, but France's right to American friendship, gratitude, and good faith was also maintained. By February, Bache was so depressed that he believed that the French, seeing Pickering's letter, would refuse even an envoy extraordinary. Bache even went out of his way to quash a rumor in mid-February that Pinckney had been accepted.[26]

On March 13, Bache simply stated that he had proof that the mission had failed. More somber than prophetic, he first tried to deny that Pinckney had been asked to leave France; later he predicted that the French would in due course ask Pinckney to leave when they saw Pickering's letter; and finally he justified the verified news of Pinckney's departure with the weak observation that French rudeness was probably a reaction against Pinckney's haughty insult of a Directory cool to American views. Clearly alarmed at the harshness of French actions, Bache tried to backtrack a little by April, no longer claiming that Pickering's letter meant the end to any further negotiations. In his final analysis, Bache declared:

> We have not a doubt but that an Envoy Extraordinary would remove every difficulty, and restore the wonted harmony between Sister Republics. In spite of all the efforts of the faction among us to involve this country in a war with France, for the advantage of Britain, and the ruin of America, we feel confident that pacific measures will be pursued.[27]

Bache's dismissal of the Pinckney mission, which was after all a vestige of the Washington administration, and his insistence that an opening still remained for negotiation were directed at influencing a new Adams administration whose policy on France was not yet formed by April. At the same time, most Federalists imagined themselves at the edge of war—some troubled by the prospect, others not entirely unpleased. Unaware of the March 2, 1797, decree, Adams's Cabinet—especially Wolcott and Pickering—believed war was inevitable, while a more deliberate Hamilton sought a staged response built on his earlier cautious calculations: a three man commission to France, including either Jefferson or Madison, bolstered by a broad program to protect American honor, commerce, and security, arouse American sentiment against France, establish an embargo, arm merchantmen, raise a navy, and create a 25,000-man army.[28]

The victim of the internal contradictions and forces of his own personality—one part drawn toward autonomy, leadership, and peace; the other driven by uncertainty, envy, and jealousy, a quest for affection, and the need to maintain national honor—President John Adams was caught in the middle. Indirectly aided by Hamilton's plan, Adams had determined on a new mission to France even before his inauguration. But early efforts to enlist Jefferson or Madison for the mission were blocked by Jefferson's refusal, and Wolcott threatened the resignation of the entire Cabinet if Madison were appointed. As one historian puts it, "Adams missed his best chance of maintaining peace abroad and harmony in his official household by not accepting Wolcott's offer."[29] Although undeterred in his demand for a mission, Adams turned to his Cabinet for advice on its make-up, called a special session of Congress for May 15, and wrote an address which, Adams told his wife, would soon acquit him of "*Aurora* praise."[30]

From the inauguration until Adams's speech to Congress in May, the *Aurora* generally supported the new President. Its writers continued to flatter Adams as an independent, peace-loving patriot, and predicted that Congress would support better relations with France.[31] Believing that Hamilton was behind the Federalist war-whoop, Bache exclaimed that "Adams has the welfare of his country too much at heart to give in to the measures of that political desperado." Adams's convocation of Congress, Bache stated further in late April, occurred because Adams "wished the more immediate representatives of the people to have an opportunity of deliberating, before he proceeded to act."[32]

Aurora writers also tried to convince the public of the necessity of sending an envoy extraordinary to France. France did not want war, they claimed as if party to the views of French representatives like Pierre Adet who were still in America, but an envoy armed with power to deal with France's just grievances was needed to avoid the calamities facing the United States if a war ensued. Fenno answered that a new negotiation would be absurd, resulting in further insults from the French, and attacked Bache for trying to bury the policies of the Washington administration.[33] Employing the *hauteur* of the French government itself, other correspondents in the *Aurora* spoke often of Napoleon's successes and French might, while suggesting Britain's imminent financial collapse and denouncing the degeneracy of British impressment. Americans were warned again about the machinations of the British faction for war.[34]

Adams was correct about the impact of his address of May 16; it ended the honeymoon with Republicans like Bache. Defending Pinckney's instructions and tracing French rebuffs of the American minister, Adams described French refusal to accept Pinckney as a "denial of right." Working to "separate the people of the United States from the Government," France also wished to subjugate American honor and independence, Adams suggested. And, while recommending peace through negotiation, Adams also called for measures of defense and a strict neutrality. In replies of May 24 and June 2 respectively, the Senate and the House published Federalist responses that flattered Adams's sense of firmness and national honor.[35]

For Bache the speech was a bellicose betrayal of true American desires for peace. *Aurora* restraint, no matter how calculated and cynical, disappeared for the last time in Bache's life. Adams was accused of sounding more like some foreign ministers than the American President. He had kow-towed to the British faction, the *Aurora* now charged, and had adopted the same reproaches against France that the coalition had spewed forth in 1792. Aiming at Adams's psychological vulnerabilities and the President's arch-Federalist Cabinet, one writer observed:

> From the temper which a great man shewed in his speech on Tuesday to a great assembly we are unavoidably led to believe that his man [sic] TIMO-THY and OLIVER have fed him upon pepperpot these three weeks in order to bring his nerves to a proper anti-gallic tone. The effects which aromatics or high seasoned food produce upon a cold northern constitution every quack can tell.[36]

More specifically, Adams was grossly wrong in saying France had no right to refuse Pinckney; it was argued that Pinckney had no extraordinary powers and a sovereign nation could refuse whomever it wished. Renewed negotiations were dismissed as a sham and deception to salve American consciences until war preparations were secured. Congress had been called into session, Bache now concluded, to whip up war fever.[37]

The Federalist press yelped with joy over the effect of the Address on the *Aurora*. Cobbett ridiculed "Bache's Bow-Wow," and said of Bache's turnabout, "Who would have imagined, that there was a wretch in existence capable of such barefaced baseness!" A more cautious and moderate Noah Webster, wary by this time of Cobbett's naked militancy, claimed the Address was moderate and would, therefore, eventually silence both Bache and Cobbett.[38]

Adams's Address to Congress opened a long and anxious period that stretched over the summer through the fall of 1797. On May 31, employing advice given by his Cabinet, the President named Pinckney, John Marshall, and Francis Dana to be envoys extraordinary to France. All were correct Federalists. Pinckney was already objectionable to France because he harbored personal resentment over his recent treatment there. Marshall had been the leading defender of the Jay Treaty in Virginia. Only Dana's refusal to serve allowed Adams to appoint a moderate, his old friend Elbridge Gerry, despite earlier objections to Gerry by the Cabinet. Meanwhile, the Federalists clamored for defense measures in Congress, where they were resisted by House Republicans under Albert Gallatin's leadership. Outside the House, Federalists privately complained of the public's lassitude in not responding to the crisis with outrage. As the summer passed, a Congress once enthusiastic for defense measures dragged its feet, recommending the construction of some fortifications, the completion of naval frigates, and the establishment of an 80,000-man militia—measures short of Hamilton's ambitious and more permanent plan of defense.[39]

The immediate response of the *Aurora* to the sending of envoys was cynical denunciation. Two days after the announcement of the envoys' names, a writer compared the appointment to that of Jay in 1794, bluntly stating that, "If he [Adams] was desirous of reconciliation, he would not have nominated characters who would have carried with them a temper in hostility to the French Republic." Another argued that Adams's speech "manifests the temper of a man divested of his reason, and wholly under the dominion of his passions."[40] Still others denounced Adams as a hypocrite, a deceiver, and a sycophant of Great Britain. John Marshall's inability to speak French and his reliance on histories of the *ancien régime*, rather than of the Republic, to prepare him for his mission were ridiculed.[41]

After republishing a letter from Rufus King, American minister to Great

Britain, in which King described the depressed state of England and the country's need for peace, Bache recommended the extravagant solution of recalling the envoys and forcing Adams to resign. The United States should pursue its own self-interest, he elaborated on June 19, yet Adams had "committed himself too far to retract"; he was too attached to war and England to change. Therefore, the American people were urged to "come forward in a manly tone of remonstrance to induce Mr. Adams to resign the helm to safer hands before it be too late to retrieve our deranged affairs."[42]

Although no new events re-kindled *Aurora* hatreds in the summer and early fall, the *Aurora* was unrelenting in portraying the Adams administration to be as virtueless as the preceding administration.[43] Accordingly, American hopes were entirely dependent on the course of France's external and internal affairs. Bache again reveled in French military victories as thoroughly as did the Directory, implying with vengeful delight that every French gain made matters more difficult for the envoys to be successful. Napoleon, though recognized as an enigmatic figure, was defended, even hailed as the symbol of France's terrible might, while predictions of the fall of France, especially those of Noah Webster, were ridiculed. Bache's favorite ploy was to compare French military might with English power, and to describe the American envoys as powerless pawns whose success—or more probable failure—depended on the outcome of Anglo-French negotiations.[44]

Because of these anticipated negotiations, Bache predicted in October that the envoys would be received with "cold civility" but would be put off until peace negotiations at Lisle were completed. Enraged by Bache's audacious prediction—one might say invitation to the French—the *Columbian Centinel* described this "Jacobin" editorial as "a sample of the foul water which continually issues through that sewer [the *Aurora*]." On the other hand, Oliver Wolcott, believing that Bache had been "prophetic of the course of French policy" in the past, tended to think Bache's prediction was accurate.[45]

Changes in France's internal affairs did not brighten the picture in Bache's view; he correctly claimed that Charles Pichegru's election to the presidency of the Directory, immediately following the coup of 18 Fructador (September 4, 1797), would do nothing for peace, and denied reports of the election of the pro-American aristocrat L. P. Segur to the Directory. As long as Adams was president, the *Aurora* reasoned, no French government would respect American neutrality.[46] The election of the old nobleman and career diplomat François Barthélemy to the Directory caused

Bache to reverse himself briefly in August; the *Aurora* grudgingly admitted that Adet, having left the United States before Adams's May 16 address, might have counseled the French toward moderation. Webster wryly noted that Bache was despondent to learn that conditions in France had stabilized and that France was willing to deal with the envoys.[47] But by September Bache had returned to his "I-told-you-so" pessimism, noting that Tall-eyrand, appointed the new French Foreign Minister in mid-July, and the Directory, by this time headed by reactionaries like Merlin, hated America.[48]

The pro-Jacobin Directory's *coup d'état* of September 4 (18 Fructidor) against a legislative assembly that had chastised the Directory for its provocations of American anger, and the ensuing purge that left Jacobins in firm control of the Directory, confirmed Bache's contention that the envoys' mission was in trouble. Perhaps belatedly aware that the pro-American Council of 500 had become conservative and even royalist through the spring elections of 1797, Bache feebly defended the coup, claiming that it resulted from real royalist threats and arguing that exiled royalists had been humanely treated. Webster, with some justification, charged Bache with having no principles in supporting any French government and any excesses. Fenno carefully noted that the Directory had purged its opponents, not royalists, and he accused Bache of actually supporting a French government that hated republicanism and liberty.[49]

French depredations gave Bache even more trouble. The *Aurora* had to admit that French seizures did violate American neutrality and were severe. But in order to deflect blame, England was accused of initiating the rapacious policy of seizures. American bad faith and the Jay Treaty stimulated French retaliation, claimed correspondents. A republican France, they added, was simply trying to stop goods from getting to Great Britain. All that the merchants could do, advised the *Aurora,* was give in to French decrees, including French demands that a neutral carry a *rôle d' équipage.*[50] The hostile decree of January 18, 1798, which defined neutral vessels as good prizes if they carried any article of English merchandise or touched on any English port, was justified as poorly as the March 2 decree. Bache weakly suggested that it at least applied equally to all neutrals as well as to France's allies, Holland and Spain.[51]

An editorial in June, 1797, expressed the general tone of despair in Bache's many editorials that year. After reporting the rumor that the Directory had advised war with the United States but that the Council of 500 had rejected it, Bache replied,

We are tempted to believe the information founded, from the nature of it. The injuries and insults France has endured from us during the war; the bad faith and perverseness of our executive could produce no other fruit. Almost a year ago the directory expressed their sense of our conduct towards them, by recalling the minister here, and from that time to this no sincere disposition for a preservation of peace has been manifested, no serious step has been taken to maintain it.

If Timothy Pickering's letter has not been sufficient to excite a spirit of resentment in France, from its being considered as the last desperate effort of an expiring administration, the speech of John Adams will bring about this consummation so devoutly wished for by the British faction, who have by artifice and treachery obtained the direction of our affairs.[52]

Prior to the cataclysm of the XYZ affair, Bache and his supporters were as active in attacking administrative policies and Federalists in general and defending domestic republicanism and Republicans as they were in defending France and attacking Britain. Although the *Aurora* cheered Republican attempts to quash Federalist defense measures in Congress, criticized the expense of building frigates and developing a navy, attacked the arming of merchantmen as a hostile act, and charged Federalists with holding Congress in session for no better reason than to encourage a drift toward war, surprisingly few editorials actually delved deeply into the defense-measure struggle.[53]

Instead of dwelling on Congress, *Aurora* writers repeated or embellished tired arguments to convince the public that Adams and the British faction, now filled with new scoundrels like Robert Goodloe Harper and William Loughton Smith, were conspiring for war. Bache summarized the sentiment of most of these editorials in one catalog in June, 1797. Some Federalists, with nothing to lose, hoped to gain by "fishing in troubled waters," Bache argued. Other Federalists hated France, loved England, sought an alliance with England, desired "lucrative jobs" or "patronage" as a consequence of war, hoped to form a standing army, wanted to destroy representative government, and conspired to create a new and large public debt that would have to be funded. Bache concluded with a tone of paranoia:

Various passions and interests will combine to drive or drag this country into a war. The ambitious and the avaricious of every shade and complexion are at this moment straining every nerve to accomplish the object; and they will accomplish it, if the people continue to sleep.[54]

One method of confirming *Aurora* suspicions about the covert desires of the Federalists was to discover their conspiracy in other current events. Republican Senator William Blount's conspiracy to separate Spain from her possessions in Louisiana and Florida drew the *Aurora*'s attention because it so clearly implicated the hated British Minister, Robert Liston, in the plan. When the plot unraveled in early 1797, *Aurora* correspondents eagerly asked pointed questions about British involvement.[55]

Fascinated by Pickering's extreme anglophilism, Bache tried to fix further the Secretary's bias in the public mind by focusing on another clash, this time between Pickering and Don Carlos Martínez d'Yrujo, the Spanish Minister to the United States. The Pickering-Yrujo clash had stemmed from Spanish refusals to comply with provisions of the Pinckney Treaty through which a new boundary line for Florida was to be struck and Spanish posts at Walnut Hills and Natchez were to be given up to the Americans. While Pickering accused Yrujo of stalling, Yrujo accused Pickering of being a British agent and the Federalist administration of conspiring with the British to seize Spanish lands. The *Aurora* added little to the debate, believing that by publishing Pickering's letters of July and August and Yrujo's replies provided enough evidence to convict Pickering of being a puppet of the British.[56] Most Americans did not know, however, that an *Aurora* contributor named "Verus," who caustically abused the administration's pro-British policies and Pickering, was in fact Yrujo. Pickering learned this when he noticed that a bitter letter he had received from Yrujo on November 22 was printed in Bache's *Aurora* the following day under the pseudonym "Verus." Pickering then advised David Humphreys, the American Minister in Spain, to use this information to obtain Yrujo's recall.[57]

Most of Bache's spiteful retaliation was less hidden. From May, 1797, until his death in 1798, Bache published a steady barrage of criticism against Adams in somewhat the same manner as he had attacked Washington. Old arguments about Adams's love of monarchy and aristocracy were revived, and the President's war-mongering was attacked.[58] Bache and his correspondents also tried personal attacks against the President's known vulnerabilities, as in reminding Adams of his slim victory in 1796.[59]

Bache was especially cruel in attacking Adams for appointing his son John Quincy for missions to Prussia, Berlin, and Sweden, implying the Adamses were lining their pockets in the process. Fenno and Cobbett thought the assault was a low attack. Abigail Adams privately condemned Bache's "billingsgate" (i.e., vulgarity) and audacity, suggested that Republicans check Treasury books on her son's expense account, and wished that the Grand Jurors of Philadelphia would indict Bache for his criminal statements. John Quincy pretended to be unbothered by Bache's attacks, and told his brother, "My old schoolfellow Bache has become too thoroughbred a democrat to suffer any regard for ancient friendship, or any sense of generosity for an absent enemy to suspend his patriotic scurrility." In 1798, as politics heated up, Abigail Adams could not resist using her son's "schoolfellow" letter to shame Bache, sending this quotation from the letter to Benjamin. She added the preface that she was "shocked" by *Aurora* "misrepresentations," and closed with the dagger that "this communication is only to his [Bache's] own Heart. . . ." Abigail misjudged. "Old boy" connections meant little to Bache by 1797 and 1798.[60]

Bache also tried to work on the President's vanity and jealousy. He ridiculed Adams's quick departure from Philadelphia when yellow fever struck in the fall of 1797, and claimed that the President had not received warm receptions in other cities on his journey to Braintree. He further attacked those who planned to welcome Adams back to the city in November, and then claimed that the Federalist press had exaggerated the size of the military parade that escorted the President. The President's wife was ready with her own pithy observations as usual, declaring, "Ben Bache is as usual abusing the President for forcing the respect of the people, degrading this city by representing the military parade as all forced."[61] Knowing the ambivalence and discomfort Adams felt toward Washington, Bache was mischievously delighted when Adams's birthday passed unnoticed in January, 1798. He felt doubly pleased when Adams refused to attend a Federalist-sponsored celebration for Washington's birthday in February. For once, Bache's connivances pleased the President's wife. Abigail claimed she was not "sorry" to see Bache publish her husband's curt rejection of their invitation to attend the Birth Night Ball for Washington. The rejection, she vengefully confided, "threw a Gloom & damp" over the celebration. Altogether, however, *Aurora* attacks on the President troubled Abigail, and she often interpreted Bache's most severe attacks as a consequence of his lying, satanic character.[62]

While Bache worked to expose the designs of the administration and the Federalist leadership, he was also compelled to defend a Republican leadership that was under attack. In May, 1797, for example, Noah Webster published the famous letter from Jefferson to Phillip Mazzei, in which Jefferson identified an "anglican, monarchical, & aristocratical party" in the United States which was tied to British ideals, capital, and interests. Although as vice-president Jefferson was unable to comment, Bache was, seconding virtually everything Jefferson had said. In reply to Webster's foolish charge of treason, Bache virtually taunted the Federalists. Daring and inviting them to address the issue further, Bache pontificated, "If the contents of that letter are treasonous, every page of the *Aurora,* for several years back, has been nothing but treason."[63]

A more difficult problem was the vindication of James Monroe. President Washington's initial desire to appoint someone friendly to France in 1794 had led to the radical Virginian's appointment. But as the Jay Treaty controversy grew, the quest for friendship for France was not strong enough to overwhelm partisanship. Monroe had become a Federalist liability by 1795. He had also worked toward digging his own grave. In late 1794, he nobly re-claimed Thomas Paine as a United States citizen, allowing Paine to live in the Monroe household for the next one and a half years.

Paine's influence and the deterioration of Franco-American relations also led Monroe into clandestine partisan activity. On June 23, 1795, Monroe wrote a partisan letter to George Logan and other Republicans in which he sketched the status of the Revolution in France, re-affirmed his faith in that Revolution's ultimate success, and condemned the Jay Treaty. Monroe then gave Logan and Beckley permission to insert this letter in the *Aurora.* Although the letter was published only as a letter "From a Gentleman in Paris to His Friend in this City" in the August 13, 1795, edition of the *Aurora,* Pickering obtained a copy, and used it to help convince Washington that Monroe was, indeed, an untrustworthy tool of a faction. In 1797, Pickering remarked further that Monroe, Beckley, and Bache were "those most notoriously hostile to the government of the United States," and that these men were all confidential friends. The Paine, Bache, Beckley, Logan connections were too much for the Secretary of State and simply added to Pickering's overall view that Monroe espoused American friendship for France too warmly and had been too slow to defend the Jay Treaty. By mid-1796, Pickering had convinced Washington of the need to recall Monroe, a recall that befuddled Republican critics with its lack of specificity.[64]

After Fenno announced the recall in late August, 1796, Bache defended Monroe against Fenno's charge that Monroe was more devoted to France than to America, and declared that the recall was ill-timed. And, when Monroe finally completed his journey home, arriving in Philadelphia in June, 1797, Bache made a point of showing how warmly Monroe had been received and celebrated for his conduct in France.[65] Meanwhile, Monroe pressed Pickering for documents regarding his mission to France. Having begun preliminary work on his self-defense as early as the summer of 1796, Monroe was all the more determined to vindicate himself by the time he left Philadelphia in August, 1797. By then he had chosen his fellow ideologue, Bache, to publish his vindication.[66]

As Monroe's correspondence in late 1797 and early 1798 attests, he was obsessed with writing and rapidly distributing a pamphlet that would unveil the treachery of Federalist policy completely. At first he was optimistic he would do so. In late September, Monroe reported to Madison that, although writing a thorough, accurate account of the mission was difficult, Bache had been able to print forty pages a week of the official correspondence. Two weeks later, Monroe made his official offer to Bache of exclusive copyright of the book. In addition Bache was given a phenomenally large six hundred dollar advance to defray printing costs. Monroe's only stipulations were that Bache would give up the copyright when he had been "amply compensated" through sales and that Bache would repay the loan in a year since, as Monroe confided, he (Monroe) needed the money badly.[67]

By mid-October, Monroe announced that he was almost prepared to send his entire narrative to Bache immediately, thereby completing Monroe's end of the work. Revealing his own anxieties and his sense of the political importance and timing of the work, he warned Bache that no copy should "escape you so as to get in the hand of the Adm. since be assured they will bribe our men to get one." By November 6, although Monroe had still failed to send the entire manuscript, he was harping about Bache's need to fill in dates on published correspondence, to insert errata, and to "let not a single error if possible creep in to the narrative." Adding that he would shortly send along an appendix, Monroe commented without levity of any kind, "All that you have to do is to have your hands in readiness to work day & Night when you get the residue." A week later he was chiding Bache because he had received nothing since page 368 of the documents, again reminding Bache to "take out a copy right immediately." By November 21, Monroe had instructed Bache on all sorts of detail, adding, "Regulate the price as you please for your advantage without preventing the sale."[68]

Monroe's *A View of the Conduct of the Executive* appeared in mid-December, 1797. It was an exhaustive book of four hundred seven pages, only sixty-three of which were Monroe's own narrative. It showed Monroe to be consistent in his dealings with the French government. It demonstrated his efforts to keep the Directory from issuing harsh decrees, and his success in preventing a vindictive new French mission with Michel Mangourit as the new chargé. It also demonstrated his firm belief that France and the United States were sister republics, and that France alone stood between European monarchies and American liberty. Jefferson was pleased, as were Madison, Robert R. Livingston, and John Taylor. Federalists thought it proved Monroe's intrigue. Cobbett alone hit the nail on the head; it was a tedious, expensive work (Bache decided to sell it for an enormous one dollar-fifty cents) which Cobbett believed would soon recede into oblivion.[69]

When the work failed to sell, Monroe grew disappointed and blamed Bache. Bache deserved some of the blame, as he did in almost every large printing venture he attempted. He was never meticulous and was always distracted or pressed for time. According to Jefferson, Bache had planned to send two or three hundred copies of the book to Richmond in December. The books never arrived, and Monroe complained that a grand opportunity to distribute them had passed, since the Virginia legislature had adjourned without getting a chance to see it. In fact, Monroe added, by late January only one copy had arrived in Virginia. A subsequent attempt by Bache to send five hundred copies to Virginia by ship failed when the Philadelphia port was closed by ice; for some reason, Bache was unable to send them by stage.[70]

By early 1798, Monroe apparently began to worry about his six hundred dollar advance to Bache, and asked Bache for payment. Finally, in March, he wrote a curt letter to Bache in which he demanded that Bache remit the money through a Mr. Dawson, who had been authorized by Monroe to collect the entire sum immediately. Bache was probably unable to repay Monroe by this time, and correspondence between Monroe and Bache ended as the entire venture collapsed in financial and political failure.[71]

Defending Jefferson and Monroe might be seen as a noble act, but Bache was drawn down to wallow in low politics as the Federalist hysteria increased. First, while inspecting the frigate *United States,* he was assaulted by the son of the ship's architect. Badly bruised from blows to his head and confined to his home for two days, Bache brought charges of assault and battery against his assailant, Clement Humphries. When the case finally reached court nine months later, Humphries tried to claim that Bache's verbal assault on Washington and the *Aurora*'s charge that shipyard workmen had been bribed by Federalists to vote for them in 1796 constituted provocation and libel. A. J. Dallas, representing Bache, easily countered these charges, and Humphries was fined fifty dollars.[72]

When Cobbett, thinly disguised as "Peter Porcupine," raged in reply to the Humphries decision, calling Bache an "impudent dog" for imagining "that his carcass is worth more than fifty dollars," it was as if all journalistic restraints had been lifted. Having begun *Porcupine's Gazette* in 1797 partly as an "antidote" to the *Aurora,* other editors felt either that they had to match Cobbett's visceral rhetoric, or else that they were somehow liberated from old rules by it.[73] For example, after Bache accused Fenno of receiving a five hundred dollar loan from James Greenleaf of New York to libel Jefferson, Fenno's son, John Ward Fenno, given the opportunity to edit his father's paper for a few days, attacked Bache as a "poor, silly, emaciated dupe of French villainy," "a base, unnatural, patricidal villain," and "a miserable tool of the most abandoned faction that ever disgraced a free country." As Cobbett goaded young Fenno on from his own newspaper, Bache weakly countered, claiming young Fenno was unrivaled in "ribaldry and billingsgate," proving himself "a living witness to the falsity of Buffon's assertion, that the powers of man degenerate in America; for he surpasses his father in the art of blackguardism."[74]

Cobbett bluntly labeled Bache a "liar" and a "scoundrel"; issued tirades against earlier *Aurora* editorials that had accused Cobbett of being whipped while in the British Army; and dismissed Bache as a low, mean newsmonger whose motto "I rise to be useful" meant useful to France and to himself.[75] Unable to rouse Bache with this assault, Cobbett moved on to portray the *Aurora*'s publisher as a carbon copy of his grandfather, who was a known atheist and a clever, conniving political dupe of France. Bache was described as an utter failure who was steadily losing subscribers and was unable to pay even a five-dollar Mayor's Court debt. In one grand libel, published well before the hysteria of the XYZ affair, Cobbett summarized Bache's career and character. Beginning by confusing Benjamin with his father Richard, who had sought office under Washington, he accused Bache of turning on the man who would not give him a sinecure, and added,

> He was born a hireling, and therefore when he found he could not obtain employ in one quarter, he sought it in another. The first effect of his paw being greased, appeared soon after Genet's arrival, and he has from that time to this been as faithful to the cut-throats of Paris, as ever a dog was to his master.
>
> He is an ill-looking devil. His eyes never get above your knees. He is of sallow complexion, hollow-cheeked, dead-eyed, and has a toute en semble, just like that of a fellow who has been about a week or ten days in a gibbet.[76]

Described by another Federalist newspaper as "Printer to the French Directory, Distributor General of the principles of Insurrection, Anarchy and confusion; the greatest fool, and most stubborn sans culotte in the United States," Bache came back with even broader attacks, accusing the Federalists of replacing liberty, democracy, republicanism, and the Constitution with aristocracy, monarchy, and a British alliance.[77] Revealing the range of his radicalism and the sweep of his passion, Bache added that,

> True liberty, according to their [Federalist] understanding, is the liberty in the few tyrannizing over the many, of living by extortion on the toil of the useful classes. They wish to see a gradation of classes: An aristocracy feeding on the miseries of the people, and a monarch, a golden CALF supported by that aristocracy, again at the expense of the People's substance and the People's rights.[78]

By early 1798, journalistic hyperbole and growing partisan rifts brought Bache into even closer conflict with the administration and with Congress. A poor judge of the temper of the times, Bache made Pickering his target. According to an *Aurora* writer later identified as Bache's friend, Dr. James Reynolds, the Secretary of State had violated law and proper conduct by exacting a five-dollar fee from a citizen requesting a passport. Pickering publicly denied the charge in the *Aurora*. On later review Pickering discovered the charge was true, that two clerks in the State Department had received payment for passports. Both were dismissed.[79]

Smarting from his loss, Pickering sought revenge. In a private letter he reviewed the incident, calling attention to the "general slanders" he had received from the *Aurora* for the past two years. Truth was no defense against the "Jacobins," he argued, and he complained that the public listened to the original charge but ignored his rebuttal. Pickering then made it clear that he would prosecute Reynolds and Bache for libel if, after consultation with two or three attorneys, it was decided that the matter was actionable. Either his friends in law discouraged him or his temper cooled; neither Reynolds nor Bache was brought to court on the charge.[80] Federalist spectators were as angry as Pickering. Abigail Adams blasted James Reynolds's reputation and, referring to both Bache and Reynolds, added, "I hope the Rascals will be persued [sic], to the extent of the Law." Washington congratulated Pickering on his firmness, but reflected that "the more the views of those who are opposed to the measures of our Government are developed, the less surprised I am at the attempt and the means, cowardly, illiberal and assasin like, which are used to subvert it; and to destroy all confidence in those who are entrusted with the Administration thereof."[81]

As Bache unwittingly flirted with prosecution in the Pickering passport business, the infamous Lyon-Griswold affair occurred. Matthew Lyon, a controversial Vermont congressman who had been accused by the *Columbian Centinel* of abusing the franking privilege by sending several hundred copies of the *Aurora* a week to his constituents, held to radical, democratic doctrines similar to Bache's. But Lyon was a man of many parts and a controversial past. He was a Vermonter first, eager to exploit his state's rise at the expense of emergent nationalism. This had made him consider siding with the British at the end of the Revolution. And although Lyon ended the Revolution as an officer in good standing, earlier in the Revolution he had been forced to carry a wooden sword in humiliation after his regiment mutinied. Crude and violent tempered, Lyon was an easy verbal target for House Federalists. Goaded to spit into Federalist Roger Griswold's face through Griswold's taunts about his "wooden sword," Lyon seemed to be equally vulnerable to physical abuse. Three days later he was attacked by Griswold; neither the Federalist Speaker, Jonathan Dayton, nor the Federalist dominated Committee on Breach of Privileges were moved to act against Griswold at the moment of attack or later.[82]

Sensitive to Lyon's less than polished image, the *Aurora* nevertheless reported the affair in detail, charging the Federalist press with a double standard in attacking Lyon's crassness while scurrilously abusing Lyon themselves. Lyon's foreign birth and poverty, the *Aurora* claimed, provided no cause to attack the Vermont congressman. Special attention was given to the growing nativist attitudes of the Federalists, and some *Aurora* writers lampooned the Federalist claim to be friends of order and good behavior. The attempt to expel Lyon, Bache argued on February 13, "was . . . a party attempt to get rid of his vote."[83]

Bache turned most of his attention to Speaker Dayton, administering heavy attacks on the Speaker for not calling the House to order when Griswold attacked Lyon.[84] Having acted as his own congressional reporter for some time, Bache had grown disturbed at Dayton's increasingly partisan remarks and rulings in the House. The issue came to a head in the midst of the Lyon affair when Dayton charged that some newspapers (obviously alluding to the *Aurora*) had distorted and misrepresented remarks made by Federalists in the debate on Lyon's expulsion. According to Dayton, Congress should have passed a rule demanding that reporters submit their notes to House members for "correction" before they were published. Because Congress had not acted, Dayton arbitrarily ruled that reporters who did not have their notes on the Lyon expulsion debate censored by House members would no longer receive the "indulgence" of the Speaker to record debates from the floor of the House.[85]

Bache admitted a week later that custom not right had allowed reporters to record debates from window recesses or other niches along the floor of the House rather than having to strain to hear from the gallery. But he was outraged. Dayton's ruling was "highly dangerous," he declared in lofty paragraphs defending free speech, and he promised to continue his reports on the Lyon affair in violation of the order. But, in effect Bache tried to work out a halfway solution. He retired to the public gallery in early February during the debate on Lyon's expulsion, only attempting to return on February 12. Dayton was waiting for him. He told Bache that the *Aurora* alone had violated the Speaker's ruling, and that he would not be allowed back on the floor of the House to record future debates.[86]

The *Aurora* chorus rose as one against Dayton. The Speaker was accused of indiscretion, of violence in speech and manner, and of standing by and allowing Griswold to cane Lyon. Testimony was given to prove that Dayton had arbitrarily ordered two Quakers out of the gallery for refusing to take their hats off inside the House. Months later, in his pamphlet *Truth Will Out,* Bache accused Dayton of attempting "To injure his press and to prevent a free and firm statement of the proceedings" from meeting the "public eye."[87]

There was a *dénouement.* On February 15, John Dawson of Virginia moved that a standing rule be adopted to allow all reporters on the floor of Congress, and to strip the Speaker of his former prerogative in making discretionary rulings on the subject. The motion was tabled. Four days later it was sent to a select committee which, in late February, recommended against the motion. The committee report was not discussed until March 21. When it was, John Nicholas charged Dayton with using the ruling as a means of attacking Bache, while Albert Gallatin took the high ground, claiming that the Speaker should not have the extraordinary power to exclude reporters inequitably. The Dawson motion failed by a party vote of 50 to 36, and Dayton retained his privilege.[88] Expelled from the floor, Bache was just beginning to feel the approaching hurricane of anti-French hysteria.

The crisis of 1798, founded psychologically on the Federalists' fascination with purging America of a democratic opposition and installing a permanent Anglo-American ethnocentrism in place of francophilism, was also a consequence of French errors. Two critical events of 1797 set the stage for the XYZ affair of the following spring. The first was the appointment of Charles Maurice de Talleyrand as foreign minister on July 18. Too aristocratic to have accepted or understood American society fully when he lived there in the mid-1790s, too single-minded in conniving his own rather than the public's success, and so cynical as to be naive, Talleyrand's failings were ones of character more than of policy. From a policy standpoint, he did not know something of America, and heavily relied on the professional diplomatic advice of those other Frenchmen who understood America best. Though he had concluded that American cultural and linguistic ties to England could never be severed, he also believed that the United States could be encouraged to remain neutral and free of alliances with Great Britain. To keep the United States neutral meant that the two republics had to remain at peace, a goal Talleyrand consistently sought.

The second event was the *coup d'état* of eighteen Fructidor (September 4, 1797), when the Directory consolidated its power, eliminating pro-American directors like François Barthélemy and Lazare Carnot from their midst, and Claude Pastoret and Jean Charles Pichegru from the Council of 500. Ready to exploit both the collapse of the First Coalition with the Treaty of Campo Formio and the collapse of peace negotiations with Great Britain at Lille (both occurring in October, just as the American envoys had arrived), offended at both the Jay Treaty and Adams's bellicose address of May, 1797, and confident that a large, powerful state could cow a small one, the Directory was recklessly prepared to push the United States, through commercial plunder, to the edge of war or beyond.

Talleyrand, therefore, was caught between his own basic desire for peace and his employers' impetuosity. His solution was to stall. Given his assumption that the American commissioners would never sacrifice their country's need for peace, "stall" meant demanding an "explanation" from the commissioners for the President's address, making the "request" for a loan through agents W,X,Y, and Z (as the American administration so artfully labeled them for moral effect), and suggesting a bribe be paid to Talleyrand himself. Although Talleyrand pled ignorance when his intricate web of delay, securing his own pecuniary advantage, and humbling the United States was revealed, he was not entirely disingenuous in portraying the scandal as of only slight importance in the delicate process of Franco-American negotiations.[89]

Attempting to read vague signals, Bache determined to follow a shopworn *Aurora* strategy—deliver the bad news before the President did, and blame the administration for the bad turn of affairs. Thus, on November 21, 1797, Bache predicted that Adams would not refer this time to "encreasing prosperity," and claimed further that the administration had counted on a successful royalist overthrow of the French Republic to save the negotiation when in fact the Great Republic had remained alive, healthy, and angry at the United States. "The crisis is fast approaching," Bache warned, "when the people will feel, that they [the administration] have led them to the brink of a precipice from which the same men cannot possibly save them, without a change in their sentiments and conduct which is not to be expected from their candour or their honesty."[90]

Although the *Aurora* undoubtedly scored few points for revelation, the Annual Address of November 22 did have an underlying tone of gloom based on the mixed messages Adams had received from his son John Quincy, in Prussia, and from William Vans Murray, recently appointed to replace young Adams at The Hague. Cautiously optimistic in the summer, they had grown worried in the fall, believing the French wanted peace but predicting the American mission would fail. Anticipating the continuation of the war in Europe, the President used his address to predict that American commerce left unprotected would continue to be plundered, then recommended that Congress place commerce and the country in a "suitable posture of defense," and asked that the cost of defense measures be defrayed by "immediate taxes, and as little as possible by loans." Attacking what it could, trying to keep its readers' eyes focused on politics at home, not abroad, the *Aurora* declared sarcastically,

> we shall be taxed up to the eyes and souzed in debt over head & ears to defend ourselves against the inroads of immorality and irreligion. The British Don Quixote fought windmills till he is tired; our Sancho now takes the field. He is chock full of fight Sirs.[91]

In the period of hiatus between the President's address and the first arrival of dispatches, Federalist defense measures languished in Congress, and the Blount impeachment and the Lyon-Griswold affairs became the temporary side-shows for a society wound tight with anticipation. Bache, meanwhile, continued his desperate policy of predicting events, preparing the public mind as he wished, and assigning ultimate blame for the crisis. In late November, for example, Bache reported a wild rumor that France planned to send three commissioners to America, commissioners who would demand a large indemnity for losses suffered when the United States abandoned the modern law of nations in the British Treaty. Using this rumor as his foil, Bache argued instead that France would recognize legitimate compensation claims by Americans; would demand indemnification from the United States in turn for not protecting the French West Indies islands and for abandoning the free ships, free goods doctrine; and would insist that the United States revive the modern law of nations two years after termination of the European war. Bache believed that if these demands were not met France would be justified in no longer viewing the United States as a friend.[92]

At the end of 1797, Bache again blamed the administration for placing false hopes in British might and for miscalculating the stability and resiliency of the French Republic. To bolster this view, he translated and published former French Minister Joseph Fauchet's sketch of Franco-American relations. Fauchet catalogued French grievances against the United States, including American violations of the treaties of 1778, and American abrogation of the modern law of nations in the Jay Treaty. While admitting French mistakes in such matters as the Genet affair, Fauchet blamed the Washington administration and the Federalist press for promoting pro-British policies.[93]

By early 1798, as President Adams began to receive early reports of the mission's failure, Bache increased his speculations. On January 1, he correctly predicted that France would not enter discussions until her negotiations with Austria were completed (as they had been at Campo Formio in October). A few days later, he firmly denied Federalist reports that the envoys had been arrested. The envoys would be successful, he claimed with audacity and probable accuracy, if they were not "bound down to the President's ideas of the honor and interest of this country."[94] Then, assuming Fauchet's arguments as their own, *Aurora* contributors detailed the terms of accommodation that France could legitimately claim. The French had a right to full compliance with the treaties of 1778, they argued, and the United States would be compelled to abrogate the section of the British Treaty dealing with neutral rights, or would unilaterally have to abandon the treaty altogether. Responsibility for this high price of peace was ascribed entirely to Federalist policy makers and the Federalist press, who had negotiated the Jay Treaty, given away neutral rights, divided the American people, supported royalism in France, and made intemperate remarks about France. According to Bache, the sponsors of the Jay Treaty had driven themselves into a corner and the country into an insoluble crisis.[95]

By mid-January, Bache had concluded that the envoys, operating under their original instructions, had failed. "What is to be done?" he moaned. Would the administration "sacrifice their private feelings and their private views" and change the envoys' instructions, or would they "brave the storms" and risk an open rupture with France? Radical action had to be taken, Bache believed.

> They have brought their country to a critical situation; from which, we fear they have neither the wisdom nor prudence to extricate it. The only step still in their power to heal the mischief they have done, is to retire & leave to more skillfull and fortunate pilots to save the vessel of state.

Bache must have known how politically absurd his remedies had become. But, for a few days in early March, Bache thought he saw a brief break in the clouds. Because the envoys had remained in France, Bache reasoned that the new instructions he had long called for had been sent to them. "If an amicable discussion is entered into in consequence of supplementary instructions," he promised, "we shall hear the pacific disposition of the Executive echoed through our land; but if, on the contrary reconciliation is not likely to take place, all the imps of darkness will be conjured up to blast the French Republicans."[96]

The "imps of darkness" were about to be "conjured up." By March, President Adams had learned of the Treaty of Campo Formio and had been told by Murray that the envoys had failed. Anticipating the worst, Adams had already asked his Cabinet in late January what policy should be pursued if the envoys were refused. None took Bache's advice to send new instructions. Pickering favored war but, like Secretary of War McHenry, turned to Hamilton for advice. Hamilton's views still coincided with the President's. Public sentiment would not support war, Hamilton believed, but firm defense measures should be adopted. Then, on March 4, Adams received the first dispatches from the envoys. Since everyone had waited so long for official news, the President went before Congress the next day, announced that it would take several days to decipher most of the dispatches, and gave Congress the dispatch that detailed France's severe January decree on neutral shipping.[97]

Announcement of the French decree was a bitter and unexpected blow for Bache and *Aurora* correspondents. Admitting that the decree spelled the defeat of the mission, Bache vented his anger on the Federalists again. "To this miserable plight have the United States been reduced by the masterly politics of the Tory party," he charged on March 6. Other editorials shifted the blame for the decree to the executive, to Pickering's earlier instructions to Pinckney, to Pinckney's contempt for France, and to Francophobic editorials in the Federalist press.[98] But there was a hollow ring to Bache's claim that the British Treaty had finally been unveiled for what it was, and to his conclusion that "people begin to see their madness in preferring John Adams and a French war to Thomas Jefferson with a French peace." Forced to grasp for straws, Bache fell into the High Federalists' trap early, arguing on March 14 that Adams and Pickering were "afraid" to disclose the dispatches.[99]

On March 19, the President surprised everyone again. Having examined the dispatches, Adams told Congress that the mission had failed and that the United States government had done everything in its power to reach accord with France. Exhorting Congress to pass defense and revenue measures to suit the crisis, Adams also announced that merchantmen would henceforth be allowed to arm and defend themselves. Republican leaders called the message a maniacal call to war. Bache was outraged, charging the President with "making" war even though Congress had the exclusive right to declare it, asking again why the envoys' dispatches were not released, and blasting Adams's decision on armed merchantmen as an unjust act of war.[100]

Always weak at incisive, detailed criticism, *Aurora* authors began to fight a futile holding action. Some aimed their appeal at enlightened self-interest, contending that arming merchantmen would lead to unnecessary clashes with the belligerent powers on the high seas and eventually to war. Commerce and agriculture would be ruined, it was argued, and Congress was called upon to reverse the President's ruling. War would not only destroy trade, they continued, but raise taxes, draw America into the vortex of European politics, create a high public debt, and place severe economic burdens on America's honest producing classes as well. "Columbia" offered the extravagant argument that the United States should protect her national honor by ignoring France rather than retaliate. Commercial violations on American trade were not sufficient cause for war, he noted, since England had also prosecuted attacks on American commerce. War would cost more, he concluded, than anticipated American losses in commerce. Without any real national gains to be made in a war with France, he suggested that the government compensate merchants for losses and reopen negotiations.[101]

Lavish generalizations and proposals began to appear as transparently desperate as they were. "Madness itself is the order of the day," wailed one correspondent who declared that the people's rational desire for peace was being drowned out by Federalist passions and the administration's false sense of injured pride. Bache returned to an earlier extreme solution: Adams could resign.

He must be sensible, himself, that at this time he is unfit to be trusted with the interests of a peaceful nation. His personal pride has been wounded by the information contained in the last dispatches of our commissioners to France, and this leads him to do what it never can be the interest of this country to suffer. Let him manage his own passions on the occasion; and, without him our councils will manage our differences with France.

Adams's narrow election in 1796, Bache hinted, had not taught him "moderation," nor had French victories in Holland, Belgium, Austria, and Prussia taught him "wisdom."[102] Like other Republicans, Bache apparently calculated that nothing could turn public anger around but the disclosure of dispatches that surely must contain some hint of French willingness to negotiate or some proof of perfidy on the part of the envoys. The *Aurora* claimed, therefore, that Adams's refusal to disclose the dispatches confirmed "the most violent suspicions against him," and that the dispatches would place the war faction in disrepute.[103]

Bache miscalculated. Fortunately for Adams, militant Federalist and Republican calls for the dispatches allowed the President to ignore the safety of the envoys and deliver the most stunning political blow since Bache's revelation of the Jay Treaty almost three years earlier. On April 2, the House voted 65 to 27 to see the entire dispatches. After substituting the letters W, X, Y, and Z for the names of Talleyrand's agents, Adams complied with the House request. Federalists who had waited for their chance to strike did not waste their sudden advantage. By April 9, both houses of Congress had agreed to print 1,200 copies of the dispatches for distribution throughout the country.[104]

The effect of the dispatches was stunning. The Federalists could not be restrained in seizing their advantage to qualify republicanism, re-affirm a hierarchical society of orders, and destroy their political enemies while snuffing out the last remnants of sympathy for France and the French Revolution. During the spring and summer of 1798 a broad-based program for retaliation against France and national defense was begun. Bache's beloved treaties of 1778 were abrogated; a navy and a provisional army were established; orders were issued allowing American ships to attack and capture all armed French vessels; harbor and fortification bills were passed; a direct property tax was instituted; and alien and sedition acts were imposed.[105]

Militant Federalists now set the tone, knowing full well that their fortunes were tied up with the maintenance of anti-French hysteria and a broad assault on American francophiles and Republicans. One Federalist pamphleteer vented his rage by calling the French "lawless barbarians," and describing pro-French Americans as "artful insidious foes," "abandoned vagabonds," and "fortune hunting foreigners," whose object of opposition to the administration was "the same as that of the midnight ruffian who fires a city that he may plunder in the midst of the conflagration, and rob the poor creatures of that little which the flames might spare." "Hail Columbia" and "Adams and Liberty" replaced the "Marseillaise" and "Ça Ira" at the theater, and the black cockade became the badge whereby "loyal" Federalists distinguished themselves from "disloyal" pro-French wearers of tricolor ribbons. According to the President's wife, Philadelphia was a tinderbox where "materials for a Mob might be brought together in 10 minuts [sic]." But she now believed that at least the violence and abuse of Bache's paper might be checked and "terminate in Good."[106]

Republicans were angry and broken. A despondent Albert Gallatin, watching his fellow Republican congressmen head for home in the early summer, could do little more than restrict his arguments against Federalist war measures to the high costs of such programs. At least Gallatin fought the battle in public. Jefferson and Madison moped behind the scenes, lamenting Talleyrand's "stupidity" and Adams's willingness to truckle to young militants in Philadelphia.[107]

Bache once again attempted to control the public mood, and this time limit potential damage, by an early disclosure. On the morning of April 4, before Congress had released the dispatches to the public, he printed a sketchy report of French agents attempting to secure a bribe from the envoys. Distraught by these revelations and having no ready answer to the charges, Bache instead mumbled his congratulations to the President for "having the courage to break thro' the trammels of his predecessor's example" by delivering the dispatches to the House. Braving it out and sticking to his democratic values, Bache further argued that it was Congress's duty "to give the whole to the people, that they may read & judge for themselves." Fenno claimed Bache had gotten his information from "confidential" friends in Congress, and sneeringly suggested that Bache need not have been surprised by events since Bache himself had experience with French bribes.[108]

During the months following disclosure of the XYZ dispatches, the *Aurora* recovered somewhat and tried to show that France had not closed the door on negotiation. Federalist desires for war were again identified as the root cause of the current crisis. Without qualification, Bache and others claimed that there was absolutely no connection between the informal agents and the Directory. Although circumstantial evidence implicated Talleyrand with these agents, there was no evidence, some argued, that even he was involved in the bribe demand. Even if Talleyrand was guilty in the affair, it was argued, the corruption of one official was insufficient cause to break negotiations and plunge head-long into war. A few tried to distance republicanism from Talleyrand, showing that the Foreign Minister, during his exile in America, had been a friend of Hamilton, King, and other High Federalists.

The *Aurora* also attempted to demonstrate that the envoys had acted precipitately and had not made a sincere effort to negotiate. Why had the envoys allowed themselves to become the dupes of swindlers in the first place, some asked. After all, they suggested, the envoys had received cards of hospitality and Talleyrand had complained that the envoys seemed reluctant to deal with the Foreign Ministry. Instead of negotiating in good faith, the *Aurora* argued, the envoys had foolishly gotten involved with those "foreigners" who posed as informal agents of the French government, and had then insulted Talleyrand by trying to go over his head to the Directory itself. It was also pointed out that when Gerry finally began informal talks with Talleyrand, no mention of a bribe was raised. All that Talleyrand demanded was a large loan and an apology for the President's bellicose speech of May 16, 1797. The French request for a loan, the *Aurora* contended weakly, was not an indecent proposal; the loan would be repaid; the United States would gain indemnification for seized cargoes and ships; and the loan would cost less than the expenses of continued depredations or war. As for the French demand for an apology for the President's address, *Aurora* writers noted that they had long argued for such an apology and had predicted that the failure to offer one would be a major roadblock to negotiation.[109]

Except for Gerry, the *Aurora* did not believe the envoys had made more than a token attempt at negotiation. In fact, by mid-summer Bache had begun to discover Gerry as America's last hope for peace. Gerry was independent, a true republican, and a courageous man, the *Aurora* proclaimed. But, although it was insisted on several occasions that Gerry might mend the rift between the two countries, Bache was certain "that his [Gerry's] efforts can be of no avail when the late conduct of our administration, and the unprecedented intemperance of our chief executive magistrate is known in Europe."[110]

Aurora analyses and arguments suffered from several problems. In trying to deny French hostility and blame, they were often inaccurate. Although there were good reasons to attack the anti-French views of Marshall and Pinckney, the *Aurora* was over-reaching in claiming these men were primarily at fault. And, in recommending apologies for Adams's May 16 speech and hinting at peace-at-all-cost measures, writers were recommending actions impossible for a public indignant over injustice and charged with nativist and nationalist rage. No matter how the *Aurora* strained to define and impose a not entirely inaccurate interpretation on the affair, concrete proof was beyond Bache's reach.

Rather than draw American attention toward France, Bache tried to accuse the Federalists of manufacturing a crisis. The Federalists, hiding behind the excuse that disclosure of the dispatches would endanger the envoys' personal safety, had let the Republicans do the necessary thing of demanding the dispatches, the *Aurora* maintained. Once they were disclosed, the argument ran, the Federalists had used them to attack the Republicans and whip up war hysteria. Linked to this argument was the charge that subsequent dispatches received after April were withheld when they did not suit the political tone set by the Federalists.

President Adams, too, was accused of political manipulation. Rather than humbly seeking some new method of solving the crisis, the *Aurora* contended, Adams had intentionally aroused public anger at France, had foolishly relied on the creation of a new European coalition against France, and then had dramatically pushed the crisis to the brink by insisting that France prove her sincere desire to negotiate before another American minister would be sent. Once again Bache argued that radical measures were needed to stop the President. "We are doomed to feel the horrors of war," he predicted, "unless the People step forward with one voice and induce the chief magistrate to retire, or their Representatives in Congress to impeach him, for having provoked a war, which he has not the constitutional power to declare." A day later, Bache wrote to Louis Gabriel Cramer in Geneva that, "War is inevitable between my country and France; our government has really lost their head." But, he added after describing his financial and political "difficulties," "I'm determined to do at whatever the price, what I believe to be my duty, as a printer and ardent friend of liberty."[111]

Federalists, depending on how secure they were in the belief that the envoys' dispatches had turned the tide irrevocably in their favor, were amused at Bache's resiliency, contemptuous of the *Aurora*'s audacity, or enraged at Bache's "disloyal" support of France. George Washington was certain the dispatches would "open the eyes of the blindest," and scorned the way in which Bache resolved the contents of the dispatches "into harmless chit-chat and trifles, less than was, or ought to have been expected from the misconduct of the Administration." Fenno's *Gazette* publicly emphasized the unbelievable manner in which Bache was trying to blame the administration for what was obviously the fruit of republican radicalism in France and America. On April 12, Fenno published a mock obituary: the "French faction has died, as it lived, a violent and disorderly end." And on May 29 Fenno concluded that Bache was undone:

> "Rise," cries Bache, "ere it be too late" "Rise and redress your wrongs." But ah! he cries in vain. . . . If Bache is ever exalted, it will be to the station of Prometheus, where the excruciating vultures of public scorn, . . . will amply punish the disgraces and injuries heaped on his country, by the venality, perfidy and malice of a base and unnatural miscreant.

No one with brains or decency, *Porcupine's Gazette* chimed in, could believe Bache's justification of France in the XYZ affair. The *Gazette*'s "No Doctor Leib" explained Bache's defense of Talleyrand in May: Bache would soon have to flee the United States and go to France, the author contended, and, once there he could use his editorials for proof of his devotion to France.[112]

But these attacks were mild compared to those that would soon follow. On June 16 Bache printed his last great newspaper "scoop," Talleyrand's March 18 reply to the envoys. In that reply, Talleyrand restated French grievances against the Jay Treaty, denounced American newspapers for attacking France, and suggested that the United States had not sent envoys conciliatory toward France after the manner in which they had sent Jay to Great Britain. In a statement designed for American public consumption, Talleyrand calculated on shifting blame from himself and the Directory to the American administration by employing a tone that made France appear more ready for negotiation than she was, and the United States only desirous of war. Already grasping for support, the *Aurora* took the letter at face value, arguing that it proved Talleyrand's willingness to negotiate and the administration's defiant refusal to meet the French half-way.[113]

Bache's source was never conclusively identified. Although he later claimed that he had been given the letter by someone in Philadelphia, he probably received it indirectly from Létombe, to whom the dispatch of March 18 had been sent with orders to give it all possible circulation in America. According to Pickering, the State Department had not received the letter and accompanying dispatches until June 14. When Bache published it two days later, Pickering stated, a government translator was still working on the document. Pickering's private belief was that Talleyrand feared the Federal Government would not disclose the letter and had, therefore, sent it to Bache for publication.[114]

The Talleyrand letter convinced Federalists that Bache was guilty of what they loosely and broadly defined as treason. Some Republicans in Congress and Bache's street allies in Philadelphia would come to his defense as he stood at the partisan political center of the whirlwind in the summer of 1798. But for most Americans Bache had become a political leper. Yet the *Aurora* plunged ahead, reviewing foreign relations historically. Washington's administration was charged with erring in not treating with Genet, signing a ruinous treaty with England, and foolishly recalling Monroe from France at a critical time. Adams was attacked for not reappointing Monroe, for making rash statements designed to antagonize France, and for unconstitutionally prosecuting a war that only Congress could declare.[115]

French military success in Europe was imminent, *Aurora* writers argued as they had so many times before. Frequent references were made to the impending French invasion of Ireland and England, an invasion that would end in French dominance on the high seas and that would leave the United States stranded against an omnipotent France. Economic ruin was again offered as the probable result of declared or undeclared war.[116] Trade to France would end and agricultural prices would fall, they argued again. But when it came to alternatives to war, *Aurora* writers had few ideas. Mention was made of reviving Madison's resolutions of 1794—this time against France—and writers sometimes alluded to pursuing perfect neutrality and isolation from Europe. Most *Aurora* supporters, however, seemed to believe that the United States had more cause to fight England than France.[117]

At least Federalist defense measures provided new subject matter for protest. Congressman Samuel Sitgreaves's resolution to arm merchantmen and allow them to resist seizure by French cruisers was considered by Bache a declaration of "war to all intents and purposes." Six days later, after passage of the motion, Bache wailed, "We are now, by the mad measures of our administration, on the eve of war, if not actually at war." When the Federalists followed the Sitgreaves motion with a recommendation to abrogate the treaties with France, Bache was thoroughly despondent. Only a few days before inheriting Federalist wrath through his disclosure of the Talleyrand letter, Bache remarked that the tide toward war could only be turned if all Republican representatives returned to Congress and the people petitioned their representatives for peace.[118] As the Federalist fury for full-scale military preparedness continued unchecked into the summer, the *Aurora* fought a holding action against the new provisional army and the new navy with the stance that the former threatened civil liberties while the latter would only drag the United States into European affairs.[119]

Bache's undisguised contempt for Federalist policies meant that the personal conflicts he faced in 1797 and early 1798 were turned up a notch in the spring and hot summer of 1798. This new stage began in March, before the XYZ affair had broken, with the President's proclamation of May 9, as a day of fasting and prayer. Ridiculing the whole idea, Bache interpreted the President's motives on March 29: "Mr. Adams wants to have the first hearing; and to make every pulpit resound with declamations against France." Exposing their own religious views, Bache and his writers condemned fasting days as imposing archaic, barbaric practices that infringed on an individual's religious and political liberty, practices that even impeded the flow of information from publishers to their readers. Such irreligion did not escape the ever observant Abigail Adams, who believed that Bache would not be able to make the day look ridiculous "with his Atheistical doctrines spreading French principles far and wide," because Americans would never "forget that it is Righteousness which exalteth a Nation, whilst Sin is their Reproach."[120]

The *Aurora* also fought a losing battle over petitions and addresses to the President, claiming there were few petitioners, and charging those who did support the President with self-deception or monarchism. Adams's replies to this flattery, the *Aurora* contended, showed that the President favored executive infallibility and party government, and that the President still did not believe that France had established a viable republican government.[121] In two replies by Adams to the citizens of Philadelphia, the President lamented the fall of the "old republics" of Europe and criticized the "ignorance," "cruel intolerance," "bloody superstitions," and "absurd dogmas" that were being forced on Europe by the sword. Adams also noted that the United States itself had "scarcely had time to . . . decide its own practicable form," and called upon Philadelphians to continue their "approbation" of the government. Adams's beloved "old republics," places such as Holland and the Swiss cantons, were not republics but aristocracies, Bache claimed. Adams did not understand or welcome the "new order of things," Bache asserted, and was consequently duping the American people on the nature of European politics. Bache also noted how Adams's replies exposed the Achilles heel of the Federalists—pessimism about the future of republicanism. "Where is the citizen," Bache asked, "who does not feel indignant when he hears the chief magistrate of his country doubt the practibility [sic] of the form of government, which the People have chosen to adopt and which he has sworn to support."[122]

The broad public issue of lost affection for France was a further personal grief to Bache. In late April, Federalists were charged with trying to cram Adams down everyone's throats by insisting that theater-goers sing the President's March, and then, through intimidation, preventing the orchestra and audience from playing and singing "Ça Ira." The Federalist press rebutted by claiming that only a few "feeble" voices—Bache's and Callender's, they claimed—called for "Ça Ira" rather than the "President's March" or "Hail Columbia." Bache was but a liar, they claimed, who was determined to cause "riot and tumult" at the theater.[123] Bache stepped up the battle over symbols shortly thereafter by accusing Cobbett of encouraging Americans to wear a pro-British black cockade. The black cockade, he charged, was an invitation to inflame political passions and violence. On the other hand, he defended Republicans who chose to wear red and white ribbons, failing to mention that these were emblematic of support for France. In August Bache summarized what he saw as the importance of political symbols.

> A man must sing "Hail Columbia" and wear a black cockade, or he is called by them a disorganizer, a Jacobin, a pensioned tool of the French; and many do not chuse to wear the cockade because they consider it simply as a badge of devotion to the executive, and see in their favorite song more of idolatry than of patriotism. It would seem really the view of some of the loudest vociferators for union to excite a civil war in our country; they cannot expect, that by their denunciations, their insults & their abuse they can bully the republicans into silence or an acquiescence in their sentiments or measures.[124]

What Bache failed to realize was that his opponents were not going to stop at "denunciations," "insults," and "abuse." Cobbett sounded the tocsin publicly for stronger retaliation against the *Aurora* editor, calling Bache a liar whose "baseness," "perfidy," "falshoods," and "insolence" had justly brought the *Aurora* to bankruptcy.

> No man is bound to pay the least respect to the feelings of Bache. He has outraged every principle of decency, of morality, of religion and of nature. I should have no objection to the boys spitting on him, as he goes along the street, if it were not, that I think they would confer on him too much honour.[125]

Congressman John Allen of Connecticut, who on several occasions had been accused by the *Aurora* of being an opponent of republicanism and a proponent of war, apparently came to the same conclusion at the same time. Unable to check his rage, Allen delivered a long speech to the House on the same day as Cobbett's editorial, in which he strenuously argued for arming vessels and fortifying American harbors. Frustrated by Republican obstruction of these measures, Allen then launched into a bitter attack on Gallatin and John Nicholas, an attack that fell just short of calling these men traitorous French agents. Losing control in the midst of his speech, Allen turned on Bache as well. He labeled the *Aurora* a "vile incendiary paper . . . which constantly teems with the most atrocious abuses of all the measures of the government and its administrators." Allen next claimed that the House franking privilege had been abused by congressmen in sending Bache's paper into all corners of the country. "No nation, no government was ever so insulted," Allen concluded. "In another country this printer and his supporters would long ago have found a Fourth of September, and this paper is well known always to speak the sentiments of, and to be supported by certain gentlemen in this house."[126]

Bache may not have found his Fourth of September, but he had found his twentieth of April. Trying to brush off Allen's allegations, he claimed that he had never received foreign aid, and that the *Aurora* had never spread "discord" and "dissention," as Allen had charged. Allen's attack, Bache said, was proof "that loose calumny and low abuse are the only props of a bad cause," adding the fillip that Allen, in a recent speech in Litchfield, had expressed doubts about the permanency of the federal government and had referred to the people as "rascals."[127]

A week later the violence that lay just under the surface of such rhetoric emerged. On May 7, a group of young, intoxicated Philadelphians who had that morning addressed the President and had, in turn, received Adams's approbation went to Bache's house, shouted "imprecations and threats" at the occupants, and battered the house and windows with stones. Bache, who had not been home during the incident, claimed he would not be intimidated. Hinting that the President was responsible for arousing these young men to violence and for asking them to take up arms, Bache noted "how early they dive into excesses."

They are now called upon to arm themselves; what are we to expect from them? The sincere friends to order and the laws should look to those things. It might, indeed, be a gratification to some, that I should have my throat cut, without the trouble of going through the tedious and uncertain forms of law. To be sure this, in itself, would be no very mighty matter; but the work of blood once begun who will say where it would stop.[128]

Bache had reached the end of his tether. Anger, disgust, frustration, and fear flooded over him the remainder of the summer. In June, he went out of his way to reply privately and at length to a subscriber who wanted his subscription ended. Bache noted that if the subscriber became known to the President, "it may probably recommend you to his good graces." "Any thing in the shape of persecution against the cause which I have espoused and which I shall never abandon but with my latest breath, be assured will meet with the countenance from our Federal Executive." Then he noted the "profligacy" of the President appointing Clement Humphreys, a man who had attacked him aboard the frigate *United States,* as a bearer of dispatches to France. He concluded darkly,

To take this marked a notice of a man who was yet under the penalty of the law (for he remained bound in a recognisance) for an action which nothing but party violence could attempt to extenuate would certainly be a disgrace to any government under the fuse; it is giving direct encouragement to assassination, and setting a price upon my head. You may suppose that in writing thus freely, I may expose myself to a further outrage.[129]

All partisan and rhetorical restraint had collapsed. Cobbett, who saw his sales of *Porcupine's Gazette* soar to 2,500 copies a day by August, 1797, cast a broader net of accusation when, in May, he published *Detection of a Conspiracy by the United Irishmen with the evident intention of aiding the tyrants of France.* Noah Webster, still deluding himself in believing he could discover a non-partisan middle in the midst of this violence, simply congratulated the "patriotic young men in Philadelphia" for their plan "to yoke Bache and Porcupine together, on the 4th of July and exhibit them as a show." New contributors to the partisan assault, made bold by the French crisis, began to come forward. The *Massachusetts Mercury* traced the history of the *Aurora,* condemned Bache's "slanders" on Washington, and accused Bache of being in "French pay." "It is from this paper," the *Mercury* concluded, "this fountain head and source of calumny that the various political streams have issued which have defiled our towns and cities."[130]

And then, there was still Bache's old nemesis, Fenno's *Gazette.* In the wake of the XYZ crisis Fenno and Bache seemed determined to destroy each other. As has been noted earlier, Bache accused Fenno of being in the pay of the British, or at least the British faction. But worse, in Bache's eyes, was Fenno's contempt for the common man. Fenno retaliated by claiming that the common man was the true patriot and supporter of the government, and that Bache's slipping subscriptions were proof of public sentiment. Bache's plan, Fenno implied, was to destroy the Constitution and the government by encouraging the people to "despise themselves," and by promoting violence. Fenno summarized his contempt for Bache most completely by printing a song, set to the tune of "Yankee Doodle," entitled A DEMOCRAT'S EDUCATION. Twenty-one verses of tedious doggerel were employed to accuse Bache of being schooled in French lies, corruption, immorality, atheism, and murder, and being bribed by Genet, Fauchet, and Adet to vilify the United States.[131]

Two weeks after disclosure of the XYZ dispatches, Fenno claimed that Bache was receiving his inside information on French affairs through "daily and secret conferences" with a man "infamous for his foreign correspondence"—meaning Thomas Jefferson. In June, Fenno further claimed that, because the *Aurora* was so near collapse, Jefferson was urging influential men in Virginia to subscribe to it. Bache replied that his paper had never been more prosperous, but added that it had never been a "lucrative establishment." At no time in the exchange did Bache deny that he had conferred with Jefferson.[132]

Jefferson did not react until August, when he privately complained that Congressman Allen had accused Jefferson of walking arm-in-arm with Bache, of holding "midnight conferences" with Bache, and of being "daily and nightly closeted" with the *Aurora*'s editor. Refusing to deny the charge publicly or to defend Bache, Jefferson tried to discover a middle-ground between loyalty to Bache and the damage that could be done if he were linked too closely to the notorious Republican editor.

> If the receipt of visits in my public room, the door continuing free to every one who should call at the same time, may be called closeting, then it is true that I was closeted with every person who visited me; in no other sense is it true as to any person. I sometimes received visits from Mr. Bache & Dr. Leib. I received them always with pleasure, because they are men of abilities, and of principles the most friendly to liberty & our present form of government. Mr. Bache has another claim on my respect, as being the grandson of Dr. Franklin the greatest man & ornament of the age and country in which he lived . . . I know that all my motions at Philadelphia, here, and everywhere, are watched & recorded. Some of these spies, therefore, may remember better than I do, the dates of these visits. . . . I know my own principles to be pure, & therefore am not ashamed of them.[133]

The dénouement of Bache's battles with the *Gazette* had nothing to do with Thomas Jefferson but again involved a clash, pitiful on both sides, with John Ward Fenno. In early August, Bache began to carry editorials concerning a Philadelphia Federalist named John Thomas, who, it was alleged, had been guilty of forgeries amounting to 20,000 dollars. Bache argued, that Thomas reflected the morality of the Federalists, and that Fenno the elder took up the cause of trying to cover up the scandal for his friend Thomas. John Ward Fenno, enraged by Bache's accusations, marched with a friend to Bache's office and demanded the name of the writer who had slandered his father. According to Bache, young Fenno's friend was ashamed of the confrontation and, at the end of the interview, Fenno, "the 'poor little foolish, fluttering thing'—literally ran away, with its mouth full of froth, and its knees trembling." The same day, August 8, John Ward Fenno testified in the *Gazette* that Bache stood "trembling and quaking" as he, Fenno, accused Bache of being a "lying, cowardly rascal." A fight did not break out, Fenno claimed, because Bache did not seem to have the "spirit" for it, and because Fenno's friend had intervened.[134]

The petty incident did not end there. On the same day that the *Aurora* and the *Gazette* published their varying accounts of what had happened, young Fenno met Bache walking with John Beckley on Fourth Street. Enraged by Bache's account of the first fracas, Fenno attacked Bache with his fists. Bache reported that Fenno did little damage in the attack, and that he, Bache, had countered with "a sound rap or two across the head and face." Bache also offered a more complete account of his first meeting with Fenno's "lad" on August 7. This time Bache said that Fenno had been so frightened that he was almost inarticulate, and that Fenno had accused Bache of slandering his father in the Thomas affair and in saying that the elder Fenno had received a gift from Greenleaf. John Ward Fenno had been so intemperate, Bache reported, that Fenno's friend had even felt compelled to apologize for the young man's behavior.[135]

John Ward Fenno naturally had his own account of the fight on Fourth Street. Although Bache had "brandished" a club, Fenno claimed that he himself had struck some good blows before Beckley and then others drew him off and held him back from further assaults. At the same time, the *Gazette* offered Bache a chance to recant all of the accumulated slanders against John Fenno and the *Gazette*. Bache did not recant. In a long editorial he instead reviewed his recent conflicts with the *Gazette*. Everything flowed from the fact that the elder Fenno had accused the editor of the *Aurora* of being in the pay of France, Bache reported. In retaliation for these false charges he had accused Fenno of being "sold to the British." He then reviewed young Fenno's attacks once again, clarifying that he had held Fenno off in the second encounter with a cane, not a club. In any case, Bache concluded, the *Gazette* and the Fennos had been the aggressors in verbal abuse and physical violence.[136]

The Bache-John Ward Fenno clash exemplified the degeneracy of politics in 1798. Whatever noble ideals, political credibility, democratic influence, and journalistic success Bache had acquired in earlier years were washed away in the flood of 1798. Commiserating with Louis Gabriel Cramer over lost fortunes, even Bache sensed the limits of his influence, lamenting that he had "worked nearly eight years for what I believed in, and still believe in, to be the good of my country; but no fortune." Instead, he admitted to being "exposed to political persecution of all types." All that was left, Bache concluded, were his children. "If I can't give them a fortune, I will always give them an education that will make them useful to themselves and their country," he remarked.[137] Much of his fall was of his own making. His youthful arrogance and indiscretions, his impertinence, his gratuitously insulting attacks, and his silly remedies to complex problems offended polite Americans well before the XYZ affair and provided them with a ready release of their pent-up rage. Defects in personality and character, in judgment and timing, constituted Bache's first failure in 1798.

Bache's second failure was his francophilism. Just as he had struggled to establish personal autonomy as a child and young man, he struggled to convince a broad public that he was his own man in relationship to France. But Bache's indomitable francophilism was generally defined as servility, perhaps conspiracy. His views were too coincidentally similar to French policies and propaganda. In the spring of 1797 he believed, as did Adet, that the Federalists wanted war and the French wanted peace. Like Jefferson (who had told Létombe that he would be waiting in the wings to correct American policy toward France in four years' time), Bache shared French outrage and understood their desire to stall until a more favorable administration emerged in the United States. Bache also supported a French invasion of England (which interested Jefferson as well), and did not oppose French designs on Louisiana. As if Bache's approval of French policies and his early receipt of official documents from France were not enough, his younger brother, William, had apparently signed up to serve on a French privateer in 1797.[138] Although Bache had never meddled in American foreign policy to the degree Hamilton had in his relations with

Hammond (partly because he never got the opportunity), although his francophilism was founded on the ideal of the sisterhood of republican nations, and although he never depended financially on any representative of France or felt obligated to do the bidding of France, he apparently failed to convince Federalists that he was not in the pay of France, or to convince moderates that he was not psychologically or philosophically beholden to France.

Bache's third failure was his journalism. By 1798 Bache had built the foundation of his publishing "success" on a clear set of journalistic first principles. These included extensive, accurate accounts of foreign affairs, and careful, full reports on the debates in Congress. Evidence suggests that Bache gave daily priority to examining and, when necessary, translating foreign news. When Congress was in session, he personally attended Congress and took down debates, as the Dayton affair attests. In 1798, neither of these resolute and forthright activities added up to any benefits or praise for Bache. Accurate reportage on such things as France's hostile Directory or the January 18 edict on commerce did the *Aurora*'s cause no good.

Beyond this foundation of accurate and extensive reportage, Bache embraced a secondary journalistic principle: report the news fast, before others had a chance to do so. Bache never succeeded at long term projects that required discipline, as his earlier failures at book publishing and his later failure in regard to Monroe's *View of the Conduct* illustrated. But when it came to the immediacy of modern journalism, Bache was a pioneer. His revelation of the Jay Treaty had even brought him the fleeting fame that we have come to associate with the journalism of modern democratic crises. The sense of being on top of things, of knowing the flow of events so well that one can anticipate momentous news, apparently exhilarated Bache and gave him journalistic credentials that his opponents were unable to take from him. But in 1798 that eagerness to reveal proved Bache's undoing. The *Aurora* had led the chorus in demanding that the sovereign public be able to see the envoys' dispatches. The President's revelation of the dispatches was more than a successful parry to Bache's thrust. Revelation of the XYZ dispatches proved that a Federalist administration could be open and public, and the dispatches gave an already aroused public the chance to empathize with Pinckney, Marshall, and Gerry as they struggled to maintain their country's interests in a distant and hostile land.

Desperate to recoup lost authority, Bache did not hesitate to publish Talleyrand's March 18 letter to the envoys—a letter that still reflected French arrogance and hostility and did not clearly demonstrate French desires to negotiate on terms of respect and equality. Thinking that most persons still desired some sign of good faith from France or at least some good reason to believe in the French Republic, Bache also made the fatal mistake of thinking that his view of American nationalism, a nationalism dependent on the success of French republicanism rather than separate from it, was shared by most Americans. The hurried translation and publication of Talleyrand's letter on June 16, therefore, presaged Bache's ultimate demise as a journalist. He was to score no points for journalistic diligence here. In the general public's eyes he now had too intimate an understanding of French affairs; he was too much the journalistic insider.

With the weapons of extensive news reporting, accurate accounts, and early revelations of events doing him no good, the force of the *Aurora's* editorials disintegrated as well. Bache was never a clever surgeon in analyzing pivotal events to partisan advantage, and always an ideologue who depended on the public's continued hatred of Great Britain and its love of liberty and republicanism as mirrored in America and France; now his general editorials sounded trite, out of fashion, and out of place. His strategies of feigned disbelief, of ridicule and sarcasm, of falsely predicting that things would either be better or worse than he knew they would be, seemed conniving and no longer prepared the way for political influence.

But for Bache the worst failure was yet to come. From June 1798 until his death in September, he would find himself preoccupied in his own defense. Unable to recover and orchestrate public opinion as he once had done, he was reduced to battling not only charges of sedition but also yellow fever.

Notes

1. On these aspects of the French Revolution see Georges Lefebvre, *The French Revolution*. Vol. I. *From Its Origins to 1793,* trans. Elizabeth Moss Evanson (London, 1962), 11–17, 39–136. For changes in American opinion in general see Charles Downer Hazen, *Contemporary American Opinion of the French Revolution* (Baltimore, 1897; cited here Gloucester, Mass., 1964), 253–78. On Wolcott and Webster see O. Wolcott, Jr. to Noah Webster, May 3, 1794, George Gibbs, ed., *Memoirs of the Administrations of Washington and John Adams* (New York, 1846), I, 135–36, hereafter cited as Gibbs, ed., *Wolcott Papers*. Webster's earlier support of the Revolution can be seen in *Amer. Minerva,* Dec., 1793–Sept., 1794. His transformation can be seen in a series of articles entitled "Revolution in France," *ibid.,* Oct. 1–Nov. 24, 1794. These were later republished in Noah Webster, *A Collection of Papers on Political, Literary, and Moral Subjects* (New York, 1843), 1–41.

2. Works printed and sold by Bache were [France. Republic.], *National Convention. Collection of the Heroic and Civic Actions of the French Republicans . . .* (Philadelphia, 1794); [France. Republic.], *National Convention. Report on the Means of Compleating and Distributing the National Library* (Philadelphia, 1794); [France. Republic.], *National Convention. Report on the Organization of the National Schools: To Complete a Republican Education* (Philadelphia, 1794); [France. Republic.], *National Convention. Report Upon the Principles of Political Morality Which Are to Form the Basis of the Administration of the Interior Concerns of the Republic* (Philadelphia, 1794). Bache also printed a description of the voyage of a grain convoy from the United States to relieve a starving France. See Jean Bon St. André, *A Summary Journal of the Cruise Undertaken for the Purpose of Protecting the Chesapeake Convoy . . .* (Philadelphia, 1794). For editorial comment see *General Advertiser,* May 30, June 5, 9, 21, Sept. 1, Oct. 7, 1794; and *Aurora,* Nov. 10, 1794; Jan. 10, Mar. 28, 1795.

3. *Gen'l. Adv.,* Jan. 25, 28 ("corres."), June 6, 7, 1794. Apparently unnerved by events and his own apologies, Bache snapped back at Fenno, denying charges of inconsistency and claiming impartiality in his summary of the Danton affair. See *ibid.,* July 12, 1794. He also took out his frustration on Webster, wondering "what . . . would be deemed a commendable revolution; and what punishment he would assign for traitors to their country, when that treachery tended to re-plunge the country into despotism." *Ibid.,* Aug. 26, 1794.

4. *Ibid.,* Oct. 20, 1794. See also *ibid.,* Oct. 10, 17 ("Fall of Robespierre"), 1794. Fenno again marveled at the *Advertiser's* capacity to reverse its stance. See *Gaz. of U. S.,* Oct. 14, 1794; Mar. 3, 1795.

5. See, for example, *Aurora,* Nov. 29, Dec. 6 ("Parties in France"), 1794; Mar. 25, 1795.

6. *Aurora,* Apr. 7, June 5, July 3, Aug. 1, Sept. 8, 23 ("An American" from *New World*), 1795. The revolutionary calendar was, in effect, an almanac describing French might and progress. See *Calendrier républicain pour l'an 5* (Philadelphia, 1796).

7. Bache clearly took a keener interest in these events than did most of his correspondents. See *Aurora,* Apr. 16, May 5, 13, 14, 15, 16, 25, 28, June 1, 9, 15, July 13 (communication), Aug. 26, 27, 29, 31 (Bache and two "corres."), 1795. For details on the French Revolution in 1795–1796 see Lefebvre, *French Revolution,* II, 137–63, 171–82.

8. *Aurora,* Sept. 2 (communication and Bache), Dec. 3, 22, 31 (reply to Webster), 1795; Jan. 12, 20, July 14, 15, 18 ("corres."), 20, Sept. 7 (ed. from *Ind. Chron.*), Nov. 9 ("The Patriot" from N. Y. *Diary*), 1796. When he learned the popular societies had been destroyed, Bache predicted the "worst consequences." *Ibid.,* Jan. 13, 1795.

9. *Gaz. of U. S.,* May 23, 1795. The best example of one of Fenno's taunts is in *ibid.,* May 18, 1795.

10. For a survey of French military successes in Europe in 1795 and 1796 see Lefebvre, *French Revolution,* II, 147–53, 167–69, 183–93. For Bache's interest in the French advance see *Aurora,* Apr. 3 ("corres."), 7, 10 ("corres."), 14, 17, 20,

May 2, 4, 12 ("Snub"), 22, June 12, Oct. 7, 8, 10, Nov. 12, 1795; July 7, 11, 26, 30, Aug. 4, 8 ("corres."), 27 ("Bion"), 29 (ed. from *New World*), Sept. 23, 28, Oct. 11, Nov. 29, 30 (communication), Dec. 2 ("corres."), 6 ("Franklin" from N. Y. *Argus*), 10, 28, 29, 1796; Jan. 23, 1797. On Fenno and Webster see *Gaz. of U. S.*, Aug. 2, 1796; and *American Minerva*, Sept. 3 ("The Cat O'Nine Tails"), 1796; Jan. 10, 1797.

11. *Aurora*, Apr. 7, 11, 18, May 7, June 4, Aug. 19 (Bache and "corres."), Sept. 8, 25, Oct. 6, 12, Dec. 12, 1795; Jan. 7, 18, 19, Feb. 10, June 1, 6, 7, 9, July 26, Oct. 11, 1796.

12. *Ibid.*, Dec. 29, 1796. France had begun negotiations with Spain for retrocession of West Florida and Louisiana in early 1796. See Albert Hall Bowman, *The Struggle for Neutrality: Franco-American Diplomacy during the Federalist Era* (Knoxville, Tenn., 1974), 245.

13. On British blame for the war see *ibid.*, Oct. 24, 1796. The "Evidences of British Amity" series was published in the *Aurora* from May through mid-September, 1796, with only a couple of subsequent essays in the series appearing in October and November.

14. For further editorials on British depredations beyond "Evidences of British Amity" see *Aurora*, June 21 ("Montgomery"), July 1, 26 ("Nichomedus"), 29 ("British Protection" and Bache's reply to Fenno), Sept. 23 ("A Jacobin"), Oct. 4, Dec. 13 (communication from N. Y. and Bache), 1796. The Jay Treaty and a decline in trade with France reduced the incidence of British seizures from early 1796 through 1799. See Bradford Perkins, *The First Rapprochement: England and the United States, 1795–1805* (Philadelphia, 1955. Cited here, Berkeley, Calif., 1967), 80–91; and Anna Cornelia Clauder, *American Commerce as Affected by the Wars of the French Revolution and Napoleon, 1793–1812* (Philadelphia, 1932), 47–49.

15. *Aurora*, June 4, 8 (reply to a Baltimore paper and "corres."), 17, 20, 21 ("All Hands a Hoy"), 25, 30, Sept. 2 ("Paulding"), Dec. 19, 1796; Jan. 4, 1797. Webster criticized Bache when the latter used the British interpretation of inalienability of citizenship as an excuse for French seizures. *Am. Minerva*, June 20, 1796. On impressment in general see Perkins, *First Rapprochement,* 61–69; and James Fulton Zimmerman, *Impressment of American Seamen* (New York, 1925. Cited here N. Y., 1966), 47–51.

16. Those items supporting aid to France include *Gen'l. Adv.,* Jan. 3 ("A Farmer of the Back Settlements"), Feb. 6 (Petition of the Constitutional Society of Boston to Congress), 28 ("Observations on the Present Commercial Systems of France with regard to the U. S."), 1794. Those charging ingratitude and attacking neutrality include *ibid.,* Jan. 3, 16 (letter), 22, 23 ("corres."), Feb. 1 ("Mr. T. Xang Xung"), 1794. Surprisingly, Bache still allowed some criticism of his stand on French relations to be printed. See "An American," *ibid.,* Feb. 5, 1794.

17. On the Fauchet mission see especially Alexander De Conde, *Entangling Alliance: Politics & Diplomacy under George Washington* (Durham, N. C., 1958), 392–422; Joseph Fauchet, "Mémoire sur les États Unis d'Amérique," ed. and intro. Carl Ludwig Lokke, in the *Annual Report of the American History Association for the Year 1936* (3 vols.; Washington, D. C., 1938), I, 83–123; and Bowman, *Struggle for*

Neutrality, 154–71. For editorials on the Fauchet mission see *Gen'l. Adv.,* Feb. 21, 25 (ed. and "corres."), 26 (Bache and "corres."), 28 ("corres."), 1794. Fenno and Webster defended the administration against inconsistency. See *Gaz. of U. S.,* Feb. 25, 1794; and *Am. Minerva,* Mar. 3, 1794. For Washington's favorable impression of Fauchet see G. Washington to Richard Henry Lee, Apr. 15, 1794, John C. Fitzpatrick, ed., *The Writings of George Washington* (Washington, D. C., 1931–44), XXXIII, 331, hereafter cited as Fitzpatrick, ed., *Writings of Washington.*

18. The best source on this topic is Bowman, *Struggle for Neutrality,* 228–78. See also Gardner W. Allen, *Our Naval War with France* (New York, 1909), 30–33; Clauder, *American Commerce,* 42–46; De Conde, *Entangling Alliance,* 378–80, 457; and Alexander De Conde, *The Quasi-War: The Politics and Diplomacy of the Undeclared War with France, 1797–1801* (New York, 1966), 8–10. The critical clauses of the March 2, 1797, decree are discussed in Allen, *Naval War,* 298–99; and Bowman, *Struggle for Neutrality,* 243–44. On Monroe's efforts in this period see especially Edward Angel, "James Monroe's Mission to Paris, 1794–1796," (unpub. Ph.D. diss., George Washington Univ., 1979), 239–381.

19. *Aurora,* May 20, 1796. For other comments on French seizures see *ibid.,* Mar. 29 (ed. from *Ind. Chron.*), Apr. 6, May 4, 21, June 20 (communication from N. Y. *Argus*), 30 ("Paulding" and Bache), July 8, 16 ("Anticipation" from *Ind. Chron.*), 23 ("Mercator" from *Ind. Chron.*), 28 ("Consistency" from *Ind. Chron.*), 30, Aug. 10, Sept. 5 (ed. from *Courier Français*), 16 ("An Independent Democrat" from *Conn. Gaz.*), Oct. 19 (ed. from *Ind. Chron.*), 1796. Fenno responded by calling Bache a transparent apologist for all that France did. See *Gaz. of U. S.,* May 19, 20 ("corres."), July 7 (communication), Dec. 29, 1796.

20. On the capture of the *Mount Vernon* by the French privateer *Flying Fish* see *ibid.,* June 14 (letter), 16, 18, 28 (ed. from *Md. Jour.*), 29 ("corres." from Alexandria and Bache), 1796. For Wolcott's claim see O. Wolcott, Jr. to Alex. Hamilton, June 14 and 17, 1796, George Gibbs, ed., *Memoirs of the Administrations of Washington and John Adams* (New York, 1846. Cited here N. Y., 1971), I, 359, 361, hereafter cited as Gibbs, ed., *Wolcott Papers.*

21. See *Notes addressées par le citoyen Adet* (Philadelphia, 1796); and B. F. Bache, *Remarks Occasioned by the Late Conduct of Mr. Washington as President of the United States* (Philadelphia, 1797). For *Aurora* editorials surrounding the Adet strategy see *Aurora,* Nov. 4 (communication), 14 ("Dialogue"), 15 ("corres."), 18 ("corres."), 21 ("corres."), Dec. 27, 28, 31 ("A Friend to Peace"), 1796; Feb. 25, 1797.

22. *Ibid.,* Dec. 19, 1796.

23. *Ibid.,* Dec. 24 ("A Watchman"), 27 ("An Old Soldier"), 30, 1796; Jan. 4 ("Hancock"), 7 (communication) 14 ("Hancock" from *Ind. Chron.*), 20, 21 (ed. from *Ind. Chron.* and Bache), 24, 27, 28 ("corres."), 31 ("corres." and "Numa"), Feb. 4, 22 (communication), Mar. 10 (communication from N. Y. *Argus*), 1797.

24. "Negociations for Peace," *Ibid.,* Feb. 15, 1797. From the *Gazette* see "True Blue," *Gaz. of U. S.,* Jan. 5, 1797. The *Aurora*'s forebodings did not seem outrageous to Bache's Republican contemporaries. Madison embraced similar views and argued privately that the Federalists were pushing Adams toward war and an alliance with Great Britain. See J. Madison to Thos. Jefferson, Jan. 29, 1797,

Gaillard Hunt, ed., *The Writings of James Madison* (New York, 1906), III, 307, hereafter cited as Hunt, ed., *Writings of Madison.*

25. Monroe's recall and the Pinckney mission are addressed in Harry Ammon, *James Monroe: The Quest for National Identity* (New York, 1971), 151–56; W. P. Cresson, *James Monroe* (Chapel Hill, N. C., 1946), 151–54; Angel, "Monroe's Mission," 372–81; Bowman, *Struggle for Neutrality,* 257–63; John Alexander Carroll and Mary Wells Ashworth, *George Washington. First in Peace* (New York, 1957), 383–93, 399–400; De Conde, *Entangling Alliance,* 378, 380–89, 482–83; and Marvin R. Zahniser, *Charles Cotesworth Pinckney, Founding Father* (Chapel Hill, N. C., 1967), 136–49. Pickering's unremitting hatred of France is described by his biographer; see Gerard H. Clarfield, *Timothy Pickering and the American Republic* (Pittsburgh, 1980), 175–78.

26. For editorials condemning the Pickering letter see *Aurora,* Jan. 24 (communication), Feb. 1 (communication), 6 (communication from N. Y.), Mar. 3 (communication), 1797. The most complete attack was by "A Citizen," reprinted in *ibid.,* Feb. 2, 9, 14, 16, 18, 23, and Mar. 24, 1797, from *American Daily Advertiser.* Bache's predictions of failure for the mission are in *ibid.,* Jan. 24, 26, Feb. 3, 14, 17, 1797. Cobbett called Bache a spy and Fenno called him a lackey of Adet in the letter episode. See *Porcupine's Political Censor for January, 1797* (Philadelphia, 1797); and *Gaz. of U. S.,* Jan. 26, 1797.

27. *Aurora,* Apr. 21, 1797. His other editorials on news of Pinckney's rejection are in *ibid.,* Mar. 13, 25, 28, 1797.

28. See S. Higginson to T. Pickering, Mar. 25 and May 11, 1797, J. Franklin Jameson, ed., "Letters of Stephen Higginson, 1783–1804," in the *Annual Report of the American Historical Association for the Year 1896* (Washington, D. C., 1897), 769–99; O. Wolcott, Jr. to O. Wolcott, Sr., Mar. 29, 1797; O. Wolcott, Jr. to Alex. Hamilton, Mar. 31, 1797; F. Ames to O. Wolcott, Jr., Apr. 24, 1797, Gibbs, ed., *Wolcott Papers,* I, 482, 485–86, 497–99; Alex. Hamilton to J. McHenry, Mar. [?], 1797; Alex. Hamilton to T. Pickering, Mar. 22, 29 and May 11, 1797; Alex. Hamilton to O. Wolcott, Jr., Mar. 30, 1797; Alex. Hamilton to Wm. L. Smith, Apr. 5, 1797, Harold C. Syrett, *et al.,* eds., *The Papers of Alexander Hamilton* (New York, 1961–1979), XX, 574–75, 545–47, 556–57, 567–68; XXI, 20–21, hereafter cited as Syrett, *et al.,* eds., *Hamilton Papers.*

29. Bowman, *Struggle for Neutrality,* 280.

30. J. Adams to His Wife, Apr. 24, 1797, Charles Francis Adams, ed., *Letters of John Adams Addressed to His Wife* (Boston, 1841), II, 254. Administration activities between early March and May 16, 1797, are covered in Bowman, *Struggle for Neutrality,* 279–82; De Conde, *Quasi-War,* 11–24; Page Smith, *John Adams.* Vol. II. *1784–1826* (Garden City, N. Y., 1962), 923–30; Manning J. Dauer, *The Adams Federalists* (Baltimore, 1953), 124–30; Gerard H. Clarfield, *Timothy Pickering and American Diplomacy, 1795–1800* (Columbia, S. C., 1969), 90–105; and Bernard C. Steiner, *The Life and Correspondence of James McHenry* (Cleveland, 1907), 209–18.

31. *Aurora,* Mar. 9, 11 (three eds. from N. Y.), 14 (ed. from Bost. and Bache), 23 ("corres."), Apr. 13 (communication), 17; 18 and 24 (communication from Boston), 26, 1797.

32. *Ibid.*, Mar. 9, Apr. 26, 1797.

33. *Ibid.*, Mar. 6 (reply to Dublin *Diary*), 17, 22 (ed. from N. Y. *Diary*), Apr. 24 (ed. from Bost.), May 6, 1797. On Fenno's rebuttals see *Gaz. of U. S.*, Feb. 7 (communication), Apr. 4 (two communications), May 8 ("A Friend to Truth"), 1797.

34. On French invincibility see *Aurora*, Feb. 11, 13, 14, Mar. 1, Apr. 1, 3 (Bache and "corres."), 5 ("corres."), 10, 11, 14, 15 ("Plain Truth" from *Ind. Chron.*), 21, 24; and Apr. 21, 22, 24, 26, and 28 (a series by "Fabius" from *New World*), 1797. On British degeneracy see *ibid.*, Feb. 10, Apr. 12 (communication), 20 (ed. from *Ind. Chron.*), 22 (communication from *New World*), 25, 27, 29 ("An American" from *Gaz. of U. S.*), Mar. 9, 13, 1797.

Warnings against war, in which Bache and Fenno accused each other of changing their respective views on the desirability of war between the crisis of 1794 with Britain and the 1797 crisis with France, can be seen in *ibid.*, Mar. 31, Apr. 7 ("corres."), 15 (ed. from Bost. and "corres."), 24 (communication from *Ind. Chron.*), 26, May 1 (reply to the *Gaz. of U. S.* and Bache), 2 ("corres."); May 3 and 5 (replies to the *Gaz. of U. S.*), 16 ("Benedict Arnold"), 1797. Fenno's charge is in *Gaz. of U. S.*, May 1, 1797. William Cobbett made no attempt to hide his support for war. See "Corres." *Porcupine's Gazette*, Mar. 13, 1797.

35. James D. Richardson, ed., *A Compilation of Messages and Papers of the Presidents* (New York, 1897), I, 223–34. For the partisan House battle over the reply to the President see De Conde, *Quasi-War*, 26–27; and Raymond Walters, Jr., *Albert Gallatin: Jeffersonian Financier and Diplomat* (New York, 1957), 104.

36. *Aurora*, May 18, 1797.

37. Attacks on Adams's address can be seen in *Aurora*, May 17 ("corres."), 18 (two "corres."), 19, 22, 24 ("corres."), 25 ("corres."), 1797.

38. *Porc. Gaz.*, May 18, 1797; and, *Am. Minerva*, May 19, 1797.

39. The period from May through November 1797 is traced from different angles in Bowman, *Struggle for Neutrality*, 282–305; De Conde, *Quasi-War*, 25–35; Gilbert Chinard, *Honest John Adams* (Boston, 1933), 265–68; Dauer, *Adams Federalists*, 130–35; Smith, *Adams*, II, 932–41; Stephen G. Kurtz, *The Presidency of John Adams: The Collapse of Federalism* (Philadelphia, 1957. Cited here, N. Y., 1961), 286–90; John C. Miller, *Alexander Hamilton: Portrait in Paradox* (New York, 1959), 453–54; Clarfield, *Pickering and American Diplomacy*, 106–139; Gibbs, ed., *Wolcott Papers*, I, 405–574; Steiner, *McHenry*, 212–18, 224–89; Dumas Malone, *Jefferson and the Ordeal of Liberty* (Boston, 1962), 315–38; Henry Adams, *The Life of Albert Gallatin* (New York, 1879. Cited here, N. Y., 1943), 183–84; and Walters, *Gallatin*, 104–105. The futile attempt by the Federalists to establish a permanent standing army before 1798 is considered at length by Richard H. Kohn, *Eagle and Sword: The Federalists and the Creation of the Military Establishment in America, 1783–1802* (New York, 1975), 191–303. High Federalist views of France and the crisis are expressed most clearly and completely in Robert Goodloe Harper, *Observations on the Dispute Between the United States and France* (Philadelphia, 1797).

40. *Aurora*, June 2 (communication), 6 ("corres."), 1797.

41. *Ibid.*, June 6 ("corres."), 30, July 5 ("Honesty the Best Policy"), 19, 1797. Bache grudgingly admitted that Hamilton recognized the danger of war and, out of this necessity alone, had been active in influencing the administration. *Ibid.*, July 17, 1797.

42. *Ibid.*, June 15, 19, 1797.

43. See, for example, *ibid.*, Oct. 19 and 20 ("Review of M. de Balow's Remarks on the U. S."); 21, 24 (ed. from N. Y. *Diary*), Nov. 21, 22 ("American Independence Prostrated"), 1797.

44. Many of the editorials promoting French imperialism were offered to taunt Noah Webster, who remained pessimistic about the future of the French Revolution. See *ibid.*, June 3, 5, 15, 27, Aug. 12, 14, 15, Sept. 12, 13, 16, 18, Oct. 4, 16, Dec. 22, 1797. Bache was so thoroughly committed to the military spread of republicanism that he was eventually dismayed when Napoleon's Treaty of Campo Formio left Venice in Austrian hands. *Ibid.*, Jan. 15, 1798.

45. *Ibid.*, Oct. 16, 1797; *Col. Cent.*, Oct. 25, 1797; and O. Wolcott, Jr. to the President, Oct. 24, 1797, Gibbs, ed., *Wolcott Papers*, I, 571.

46. *Aurora*, July 20, 21 (two eds.), 24, 1797.

47. *Ibid.*, July 25, Aug. 21, 1797; and *Am. Minerva*, Aug. 28, 1797. Even the astute observer John Quincy Adams believed that Barthélemy's election and the reconstruction of the Council of 500 to include more conservative moderates, even royalists, would lead to the envoys' success. J. Q. Adams to J. Adams, June 7, 1797, Worthington Chauncey Ford, ed., *The Writings of John Quincy Adams* (New York, 1913–1917), II, 177. On the shifts in French politics in the summer of 1797 and what they meant to American relations see Bowman, *Struggle for Neutrality*, 299–302.

48. *Aurora*, Sept. 16 (two eds.), 18 (two eds.), 1797.

49. *Ibid.*, Nov. 9, 11, 14, 15 (two eds.), 16, 22, 1797. *Commercial Advertiser*, Nov. 11, 23, 1797; and *Gaz. of U. S.*, Nov. 18, 20 (two eds.), 1797. On the September 4 coup itself see Bowman, *Struggle for Neutrality*, 297, 302–303; De Conde, *Quasi-War*, 39; and J. Q. Adams to J. Adams, Sept. 21, 1797, Ford, ed., *Writings of John Quincy Adams*, II, 210–16.

50. For comments on depredations from May, 1797, to revelation of the XYZ dispatches see *Aurora*, May 11, June 17, 29, July 13, 28 ("Cato"), Oct. 20 (ed. from N. Y. and Bache), Dec. 15 ("An American"), 1797; Feb. 10 ("An American"), 20, Mar. 17, 1798.

51. *Ibid.*, Mar. 13, 1798. Details on the decree of January 18 are in Bowman, *Struggle for Neutrality*, 320–21; Allen, *Naval War*, 33–35, 299. John Quincy Adams predicted the January decree would create a "passive," "unproclaimed" war. J. Q. Adams to Sec. of State, Jan. 15, 1798, Ford, ed., *Writings of John Quincy Adams*, II, 239.

52. *Aurora*, June 17, 1797.

53. *Ibid.*, June, 2, 3, 8 ("corres."), 10 (two eds.,) 12, 13 ("corres."), 24, 28, Sept. 28 (communication), 29, 30 (ed. from *Ind. Chron.*), 1797; Jan. 18, Feb. 13 ("Caution" from *Ind. Chron.*), Mar. 2, 6 ("Contradictions and Inconsistencies by Mr. Harper"), 14, 1798. Bache was apparently active behind the scenes in convinc-

ing Congressman William Smith of Pennsylvania to vote with the Republicans on a crucial issue. See W. L. Smith to Ralph Izard, May 29, 1797, Ulrich B. Phillips, ed., "South Carolina Federalist Correspondence, 1789–1797," *American Historical Review*, XIV (1909), 789.

54. *Aurora*, June 20, 1797. For other editorials see *ibid.*, May 18 ("corres."), 20 ("corres."), 23 ("Peace"), 27 ("Democritus"), 29, 31 ("corres."), June 1, 2 ("Investigator"), 7 ("Castigator"), 8 ("1776" and "corres."), 9, 13 (communication and Bache), 16, 22 (communication), 24 ("Obadiah Cornplanter"), 28 (communication), July 1 (communication), 8, 11, 14 ("Cato"), 15 ("corres."), 17 ("Citizen"), 20 (communication), Aug. 8, Sept. 8 ("A Republican"), 13 (communication from N. Y. *Argus*), 26 ("A Friend to Peace"), 30 ("Tully" from *Ind. Chron.*), Oct. 3, Nov. 17, Dec. 5 (ed. from *Ind. Chron.*), 1797; Jan. 29 (communication from *Ind. Chron.*), Feb. 20, 21 ("British Captures"), 27 (letter), 28, Mar. 3 ("corres."), 14 (communication), 1798.

55. See William H. Masterson, *William Blount* (Baton Rouge, La., 1954; cited here, N. Y., 1969), 302–23; Thomas P. Abernethy, *The South in the New Nation, 1789–1819* (Baton Rouge, La., 1976), 169–91; William H. Masterson, *Tories and Democrats: British Diplomats in Pre-Jacksonian America* (College Station, Tex., 1985), 37–41; Perkins, *First Rapprochement*, 99–101; Smith, *Adams*, 939–40. *Aurora* editorials on the affair are in *Aurora*, July 6 (five eds.), 10 (two communications), 11 (two eds. and "Cato"), 12 (Bache and "Cato"), 13, 14 ("Leonidas"), 15, 17, 26 ("Cato"), 28 ("corres."), 31 ("Cato"), Aug. 8 ("Cato"), 18 ("Aristides" and Bache), 22, 24, 26, 31, Sept. 1 ("One of Us"), Dec. 9 1797; Feb. 5, 6, Mar. 12 ("corres."), 1798. Weak Federalist attempts to affiliate Blount with France and the mainstream of the Republican Party can be seen in *Porc. Gaz.*, July 7 ("A Member of the House of Representatives"), 10, 13 (two eds.), 26 (two eds.), Aug. 31 (two "corres."), Sept. 1, 1797; and *Gaz. of U. S.*, July 7, Aug. 14 ("Aristides"), 22 ("corres."), 27, 1797.

56. The Pickering-Yrujo clash is covered extensively in Clarfield, *Pickering and American Diplomacy*, 120–39. For *Aurora* involvement see *Aurora*, July 13 (Pickering to Yrujo); 14 and 15 (Yrujo to Pickering); Oct. 23–25 (Pickering to Yrujo, Aug. 18, 1797), 1797. For editorials on the affair see *ibid.*, May 15 ("D. A."), July 19 ("Cato"), 25 ("Heraclitus"), 26 (communication from N. Y.), Aug. 28 ("An American"), Nov. 27 (communication), 1797.

57. See "Verus," in *ibid.*, July 18, 25, 27, 29, Aug. 3, 15, and Nov. 23, 1797; and Sec. of State to Col. Humphreys, Dec. 7, 1797, in the Timothy Pickering Papers, Massachusetts Historical Society, Boston.

58. *Aurora*, Mar. 5, 1798. See also *ibid.*, May 27, June 9, Oct. 12 ("Mentor"), Sept. 9 (ed.), 29 ("Tully" from *Ind. Chron.*), Oct. 28, Nov. 29 (communication), 30 (ed. from N. Y. *Time Piece*), Dec. 15 ("corres." from Boston paper), 1797; Feb. 27 ("corres." and Bache); May 17 and 22 ("Nestor"); June 8 and 25 ("Democritus" from Carey's *U. S. Recorder*); July 18 and 30 ("Senex"); July 28, Aug. 17 (two eds.), 1798. On war-mongering see *ibid.*, May 27 ("corres."), and June 8, 1797.

59. *Ibid.*, May 22 (communication), 23 ("corres."), July 18, 20, Aug. 14 ("Cato"), 1797.

60. *Aurora,* May 26 ("Presidential Conundrums"), July 8, 17 (communication), 1797; Mar. 16, 17, May 22, 1798. Fenno's and Cobbett's rebuttals are in *Gaz. of U. S.,* Mar. 16 ("A Member of the Senate" and "Junius"), May 27 ("Monitor"), 1797; and *Porc. Gaz.,* Mar. 17, 1798. Adams family reactions are in A. Adams to Her Sister, Mar. 20 and Apr. 21, 1798, Stewart Mitchell, ed., *New Letters of Abigail Adams, 1788–1801* (Boston, 1947), 146–47, 159–60; J. Q. Adams to A. Adams, July 29, 1797; and J. Q. Adams to Charles Adams, Aug. 1, 1797, Ford, ed., *Writings of John Quincy Adams,* II, 193–94, 196. On Abigail Adams's letter to Bache see [Abigail Adams] to [B.] F. Bache, Mar. 17 [1798], Bache Papers, Castle Collection, American Philosophical Society, Philadelphia.

61. *Aurora,* Aug. 24 ("corres."), Sept. 12, Nov. 1, 4 ("An Old Soldier"), 7, 10 ("No Idolator," "An Old Whig," and two eds.), 11, 13 ("An Old Soldier"), 14 ("Veritas" and communication), 1797. Abigail's response is in A. Adams to Her Sister, Nov. 15, 1797, Mitchell, ed., *New Letters,* 110–13. Fenno, Cobbett, and Webster dismissed the attack as that of a party hack jealous of Adams's firmness and defense of the Constitution. See *Gaz. of U. S.,* July 28, 1797; *Porc. Gaz.,* Nov. 6, 1797; and *Commercial Adv.,* Nov. 16, 1797.

62. *Aurora,* Jan. 16, Feb. 23, Mar. 1 ("Hem! Hem!"), 1798; and A. Adams to Her Sister, Feb. 28, 1798, Mitchell, ed., *New Letters,* 137. For examples of Abigail's views of Bache's character see A. Adams to Her Sister, May 24, June 3, 8, Dec. 12, 1797; *Ibid.,* 91–92, 94–95, 96–97, 115–17, 118–20.

63. See Thos. Jefferson to Phillip Mazzei, Apr. 24, 1796, Paul Leicester Ford, ed., *Writings of Thomas Jefferson* (New York, 1895), VII, 75–76, hereafter cited as Ford, ed., *Jefferson's Writings.* The letter was translated into Italian, then into French for the Paris *Moniteur,* and finally back into English. The version Webster published was accurate in spirit, if not in detail and language. See *ibid.,* 74–77n. The reaction of Federalist journalists can be found in *Am. Minerva,* May 2, 4, 1797; "A Friend to Truth," *Gaz. of U. S.,* May 6, 1797; *Porc. Gaz.,* May 5, 1797, June ?, 1797. For Bache's taunt see, *Aurora,* May 5, 8, 1797. For other *Aurora* comments on the Mazzei letter and Federalist attacks see *ibid.,* May 12 (two eds.), June 7 ("An Enemy to Traitors"), 1797. For a sketch of the Mazzei letter controversy in relation to Jefferson see Malone, *Jefferson and the Ordeal of Liberty,* 302–307.

64. On the extensive involvement of Paine with Monroe in France see Angel, "Monroe's Mission," 180–82, 362–64; David Freeman Hawke, *Paine* (New York, 1974), 304–21. Monroe's June 23, 1795 letter is in J. Monroe to [Thos. Jefferson, G. Logan, A. Burr, J. Beckley], June 23, 1795, Stanislaus M. Hamilton, ed., *The Writings of James Monroe* (New York, 1898–1903], II, 292–304, hereafter cited as Hamilton, ed., *Writings of Monroe.* On Pickering's reaction quoted above see T. Pickering to Ed. Carrington, Dec. 9, 1797, Timothy Pickering Papers, Mass. Hist. Soc. On the influence of the letter in general see G. Washington to Sec. of State, July 8, 1796, Fitzpatrick, ed., *Writings of Washington,* XXXV, 127–28 and 128n; Carroll and Ashworth, *Washington,* 343; De Conde, *Entangling Alliance,* 384; Tolles, *Logan,* 142–44; and Berkeley, *Beckley,* 108.

Details on the slow progress toward Monroe's recall are in Beverly W. Bond, Jr., *The Monroe Mission to France, 1794–1796* (Baltimore, 1907), 10–79; Angel, "Monroe's Mission," 315–81; Ammon, *Monroe*, 112–56; Cresson, *Monroe*, 127–54; Carroll and Ashworth, *Washington*, 393–400; and De Conde, *Entangling Alliance*, 347–89.

65. *Aurora*, Sept. 13, 1796; July 3, 1797. Details on Monroe's reception in Philadelphia are in Ammon, *Monroe*, 157–58; and Angel, "Monroe's Mission," 398–99.

66. Pickering refused to offer a full official explanation for the recall. Ammon, *Monroe*, 157–62; Angel, "Monroe's Mission," 401–404.

67. J. Monroe to J. Madison, Sept. 24, 1797, Hamilton, ed., *Writings of Monroe*, III, 86; J. Monroe to B. F. Bache, Oct. 9, 1797, Bache Papers, Castle Coll., Am. Philos. Soc.

68. J. Monroe to B. F. Bache, Oct. 8, 15, Nov. 6, 21, 1797, *ibid.;* and J. Monroe to B. F. Bache, Nov. 13, 1797 [with postscripts for Nov. 20 and 23], Manuscripts Division, University of Virginia Library, Charlottesville, Va.

69. On the work's contents and initial reception see J. Monroe, *A View of the Conduct of the Executive* (Philadelphia, 1797); and Angel, "Monroe's Mission," 430–47.

70. Thos. Jefferson to J. Monroe, Dec. 21, 1797, Ford, ed., *Jefferson's Writings*, VII, 180; J. Monroe to [B. F.] Bache, Jan. 28, 1798, in the Etting Papers, Hist. Soc. of Penn.; Thos. Jefferson to J. Madison, Feb. 8, 1798, Ford, ed., *Jefferson's Writings*, VII, 195.

71. J. Monroe to B. F. Bache, Mar. 26, 1798, Bache Papers, Castle Coll., Am. Philos. Soc. Dawson reported in 1800 that Monroe would take books in exchange for the remaining claim, adding that Bache had made one payment of four hundred dollars on the loan. See J[ohn] Dawson to [Wm. Duane], Nov. 25, 1800, *ibid.*

72. For Bache's preliminary description of the attack and the subsequent court record of the attack see *Aurora*, Apr. 6, Dec. 9 ("The Commonwealth of Pennsylvania versus Clement Humphries, for an assault and battery on Benjamin Franklin Bache"), 1797. In rebuttal see *Porc. Gaz.*, Apr. 6 ("Measure for Measure"), 12 ("Clement Humphries"), 1797.

73. On the "carcass" quotation see *Porc. Gaz.*, Dec. 13, 1797. *Porcupine's Gazette* was begun in March, 1797. Karen K. List, "The Role of William Cobbett in Philadelphia's Party Press, 1794–1799" (unpub. Ph.D. diss., Univ. of Wisconsin-Madison, 1980), 180, claims that *Porcupine's Gazette* was begun as an "antidote" to Bache, and she argues convincingly through her work that Cobbett was more a Tory than a Federalist.

74. The *Aurora*'s original charges against John Fenno can be seen in *Aurora*, Apr. 29, May 29 ("corres."), Sept. 21, 1797; Mar. 9, 10, 17, 21, 30, Apr. 4, 19 ("corres."), 1798. John Ward Fenno's assault and Cobbett's support of him are in *Gaz. of U. S.*, Sept. 20, 22, 1797; and *Porc. Gaz.*, Sept. 30, 1797. Bache's "Buffon" allusion is in *Aurora*, Oct. 18, 1797.

75. *Porc. Gaz.*, Mar. 4, 7 ("corres."), 17 ("Rusticus"), Apr. 10, 1797.

76. *Ibid.*, Nov. 16, 1797. For other attacks on Bache by Cobbett see *ibid.*, June 29 (communication), Sept. 1, Nov. 16, 20, Dec. 4, 1797; Jan. 12, Feb. 26, Mar. 22, 23, 1798.

77. The Federalist quotation cited here is an "Extract" from the *Federal Gazette* republished in *ibid.*, Mar. 12, 1798. The *Aurora's* general charges against Federalists are in *Aurora*, May 29, Sept. 5 (reply to "Darius Moffat"), 8 (two eds.), 28 ("Tully" from *Ind. Chron.*), 23 (ed. from New York *Time Piece*), Nov. 14 ("corres."), 21, 1797; Jan. 11, 24 ("corres."), 29 (ed. from New York), Feb. 2 (criticism of *Federal Gazette*), 15 ("One of the People"), Mar. 21 ("A Citizen of Pennsylvania to His Friend in Baltimore"), Apr. 25 (communication), 1798.

78. *Ibid.*, Nov. 21, 1797.

79. *Ibid.*, Jan. 24 ("South Front Street"), 26 ("Timothy Pickering"), 29 ("James Reynolds"), Feb. 5, 27, 1798.

80. Pickering also referred to both clerks as steady and industrious. See T. Pickering to Rev. John Clark, Jan. 26, 1798, Timothy Pickering Papers, Mass. Hist. Soc. Pickering also repeated details of the affair to Washington. See T. Pickering to G. Washington, Jan. 27, 1798. *Ibid.*

81. A. Adams to Her Sister, Feb [1–5], 1798, Mitchell, ed., *New Letters,* 128; and G. Washington to the Sec. of State, Feb. 6, 1798, Fitzpatrick, ed., *Writings of Washington,* XXXVI, 157.

82. Lyon apparently even compared his newspaper, *The Farmer's Library,* to the *Aurora.* On Lyon's character and the Lyon-Griswold affair see Aleine Austin, *Matthew Lyon: 'New Man' of the Democratic Revolution, 1749–1822* (University Park, Pa., 1981), 17–19, 27–29, 73–102. See also J. Fairfax McLaughlin, *Matthew Lyon: The Hampden of Congress, A Biography* (New York, 1900), 212–37. The *Centinel's* accusations against Lyon are in "An Island Farmer," *Col. Cent.,* Jan. 28, 1798. As an illustration of the full circle of Republican intimacy, it is interesting that Lyon boarded in Philadelphia with Steven T. Mason and John Nicholas, the two radical congressmen from Virginia, and that Gallatin, the Republicans' loyal chief debater, stood by Lyon completely.

83. *Aurora,* Jan. 31, Feb. 2 (two eds.), 8 (reply to *Gaz. of U. S.*), 10 ("corres."), 11 (ed. from N. Y.), 13, 14, 1798.

84. *Ibid.*, Feb. 16 (five eds.), 22, Mar. 1, 8, 9, 1798.

85. *Debates and Proceedings in the Congress of the United States* (Washington, D. C., 1824–56), 5th Cong., 2d Sess., VIII (Feb. 6, 1798), 963, hereafter cited as *Annals.* For a profile on Jonathan Dayton see Rudolph and Margaret C. Pasler, Jr., *The New Jersey Federalists* (Rutherford, N. J., 1975), 207–208.

86. *Aurora,* Feb. 7, 14; Feb. 24 and Mar. 28 (eds. from a Newark paper); Mar. 24 ("A Reporter"), 1798. The *Annals* of Congress are silent on Bache's confrontation with Dayton, but subsequent House actions substantiate the narrative of the affair as told in the two Newark editorials.

87. *Ibid.*, Feb. 13 ("A Lover of Order"), 15 ("Junius"), 17 ("Nohum"), Feb. 24 and Mar. 8 (eds. from Newark); Mar. 5, 13 ("A Member of the Pennsylvania Legislature"), 24, 1798; and B. F. Bache, *Truth Will Out* (Philadelphia, 1798), ii.

88. The House debate and action on the Dawson motion is in *Annals,* 5th Cong., 2d Sess., VIII (Feb. 15, 19, 28, Mar. 21, 1798), 1036, 1044–45, 1068, 1286–96.

89. Bowman, *Struggle for Neutrality,* esp. 306–25, 334–47; and William

Stinchcombe, *The XYZ Affair* (Westport, Conn., 1980), esp. 13–76, 106–24, supersede all previous work on the complexities of Franco-American negotiation except De Conde, *Quasi-War,* 36–58. The most recent biographers of the American envoys all defend their subjects, leaving us still with partisan views of the principal actors. Zahniser, *Pinckney,* 165–85; and Leonard Baker, *John Marshall: A Life in Law* (New York, 1974), 213–90, either contend outright or hint that no resolution with France was possible and their subjects were realists. George Athan Billias, *Elbridge Gerry: Founding Father and Republican Statesman* (New York, 1976), 245–93, presents Gerry as a latter-day classical republicanist who acted honorably in staying in France and who, although sometimes predicating his actions on false assumptions and decisions, nevertheless contributed to the ultimate resolution of conflict.

90. *Aurora,* Nov. 21, 1797. On the difficulty in reading Adams's desires and views see Stinchcombe, *XYZ,* 13–31.

91. *Ibid.,* Nov. 24, 1797. The President's First Annual Address to Congress, November 22, 1797, is in Richardson, ed., *Messages and Papers of the Presidents,* I, 240–44. Compare J. Q. Adams's optimistic letter to his father on June 7, 1797, to a later letter to his father on Sept. 21, 1797, in Ford, ed., *Writings of John Quincy Adams,* II, 177, 210–216. On Murray see Worthington C. Ford, ed., "Letters of William Vans Murray to John Quincy Adams, 1797–1803," *Annual Report of the American Historical Association for the Year 1912* (Washington, D. C., 1914), *passim.*

92. *Aurora,* Nov. 29, 1797. On the mood of this period in general see De Conde, *Quasi-War,* 60–61; and Dauer, *Adams Federalists,* 137–40.

93. *Aurora,* Dec. 5, 26, 1797; and Jean Antoine Joseph Fauchet, *A Sketch of the Present State of Our Political Relations with the United States . . .* (Philadelphia, 1797).

94. *Aurora,* Jan. 1, 4, 1798.

95. *Ibid.,* Jan. 12, 1798. See also Jan. 9, 11, 15, 16, 17, 27 ("Fiat Justitia"); Feb. 6 and 7 ("An American Merchant"—Tench Coxe), 16 (communication from *Ind. Chron.*), 17 ("corres."), 1798.

96. See respectively, *ibid.,* Jan. 17, 22, Mar. 2, 1798.

97. De Conde, *Quasi-War,* 63–66; Smith, *Adams,* II, 947–48; Clarfield, *Pickering and American Diplomacy,* 140–46; and Steiner, *McHenry,* 291–95. The President's request for Cabinet advice is in J. Adams to Heads of Depts., Jan. 24, 1798, Charles Francis Adams, ed., *The Works of John Adams* (Boston, 1854), VIII, 561, hereafter cited as Adams, ed., *Works of Adams.* Hamilton's attitude and response can best be seen in Alex. Hamilton to T. Pickering, Mar. 17, 1798, Syrett, *et al.,* eds., *Hamilton Papers,* XXI, 364–66. The President's message to Congress is in Richardson, ed., *Messages and Papers,* I, 253–54.

98. *Aurora,* Mar. 6, 7, 20, 1798.

99. *Ibid.,* Mar. 12, 14, 1798.

100. The President's March 19 message is in Richardson, ed., *Messages and Papers,* I, 254–55. For Republican reaction see Thos. Jefferson to J. Monroe, Mar. 21, 1798, Ford, ed., *Jefferson's Writings,* VII, 221; J. Madison to Thos. Jefferson, Apr. 2, 1798, Hunt, ed., *Writings of Madison,* VI, 312–13; J. Monroe to

Thos. Jefferson, Apr. 8, 1798, Hamilton, ed., *Writings of Monroe*, III, 116–17. Bache's response is in *Aurora*, Mar. 20, 1798.

101. *Ibid.*, Mar. 24 ("A Centinel"), 25 ("A Fellow Citizen Who Does Not Believe in Executive Infallibility" from *Middlesex Gaz.*), 29, 30 ("corres."), Apr. 2 ("corres."), 3, 4 ("Columbia"), 1798.

102. *Ibid.*, Mar. 21, 23 ("Cetera Desunt"), 1798.

103. *Ibid.*, Mar. 27, 30, Apr. 3, 1798.

104. Adams's submission of the dispatches to Congress on April 3 is recorded in Richardson, ed., *Messages and Papers*, I, 255; De Conde, *Quasi-War*, 71–73.

105. De Conde, *Quasi-War*, 74–108; and 219–230, 277–303. See also Smith, *Adams*, II, 960–80; Chinard, *Honest John Adams*, 273–77; Clarfield, *Pickering and American Diplomacy*, 150–64; Miller, *Hamilton*, 467–72; Steiner, *McHenry*, 304–307; Richard E. Welch, Jr., *Theodore Sedgwick, Federalist. A Political Portrait* (Middletown, Conn., 1965), 170–74. Federalist defense measures nevertheless fell short of Hamilton's comprehensive program. For this program see Alex. Hamilton to T. Pickering, Mar. 17, 1798, Syrett, *et al.*, eds., *Hamilton Papers*, XXI, 364–66.

106. See respectively [Joseph Hopkinson], *What Is Our Situation? And What Our Prospects?* (Philadelphia, 1798); De Conde, *Quasi-War*, 82; and A. Adams to Her Sister, Apr. 7, 1798, Mitchell, ed. *New Letters*, 154.

107. Walters, *Gallatin*, 107–110; Malone, *Jefferson and the Ordeal of Liberty*, 373–75; and J. Madison to Thos. Jefferson, Apr. 15, 1798, and May 20, 1798, Hunt, ed., *Writings of Madison*, VI, 315, 321.

108. *Aurora*, Apr. 14, 1798; and *Gaz. of U. S.*, Apr. 4, 1798. Cobbett began publication of the dispatches on April 9, and Bache followed a day later.

109. Arguments summarized in the last two paragraphs are from *Aurora*, Apr. 6, 7, 9, 16 ("Sidney" and two "corres."); 20 and 23 ("Sidney"); 27 ("C."), May 1, 4 ("Anti-Machiavel"), 10, 12, 15 ("Brutus"), 18 ("Sidney"), 19; 21 and June 1 ("Sidney"); 6, Sept. 1, 3, 10 (two eds.), 1798.

110. *Ibid.*, June 21, 1798. See also *ibid.*, June 4, 6, 20, July 6, 20, Aug. 9 (ed. from *Ind. Chron.*), 15, 17, Sept. 3, 1798.

111. The Bache editorial is in *ibid.*, June 26, 1798. The letter to Cramer is in Lucien Cramer, *Les Cramer, une famille génévoise. Leurs relations avec Voltaire, Rousseau et Benjamin Franklin Bache* (Génève, 1932), 70–71. Examples of arguments used in the previous two paragraphs are in *Aurora*, Apr. 5, 13, 14 ("Sidney"), 23 ("Nestor"), 26, May 23, June 22, July 7, 17, 18, 24, 28 ("No Boaster" from *Herald of Liberty*), Aug. 1, 3, 1798.

112. G. Washington to the Sec. of State, Apr. 16, 1798; and G. Washington to the Sec. of War, May 6, 1798, Fitzpatrick, ed., *Writings of Washington*, XXXVI, 249, 254; *Gaz. of U. S.*, Apr. 6, 12, May 11 (four eds.), 29, 1798; *Porc. Gaz.*, Apr. 10, May 1 ("No Doctor Leib"), 1798.

113. *Aurora*, June 16, 18, 19 ("Tim Pick"), 1798. A summary of the letter and its place in the negotiation is in Bowman, *Struggle for Neutrality*, 323–24; and Stinchcombe, *XYZ*, 111.

114. *Aurora*, June 21; and T. Pickering to John Pickering, June 16, 1798, in the Timothy Pickering Papers, Mass. Hist. Soc., Boston.

115. These kinds of editorial can be seen in *Aurora,* Apr. 16, 17; 20 and 30 ("Nestor"); Apr. 24 ("corres."), 25 (letter), 26, 27 ("corres."), May 10 ("Candidus"), 11, 18 ("Lysander"), 23 (two eds. and "corres."), 26 ("Alfred"), 31, June 15, 19, 20 ("corres."), July 21 ("Circumspection" from *Ind. Chron.*), Aug. 22, 1798. In July, Bache reported that Federalist congressmen had caucused to determine if a declaration of war would pass; finding they were 10 votes short, they allowed the question to "sleep." *Ibid.,* July 14, 1798.

116. *Ibid.,* Feb. 9 (communication from Vermont paper), Mar. 14, 24 ("Prudence"), Apr. 7 ("Nicodemus"), 9, 13 ("Some Free Thoughts on the Present Situation of America"), 17 (communication), 26, 27 (quotation from Monroe's *View of the Conduct . . .),* May 7, June 2, 11 ("An American Lady"), 18, 20 ("An American" and Bache), 29, July 27, Aug. 13, 17, 22, 24, 27, Sept. 6, 1798.

117. For examples of anti-war sentiments see *ibid.,* Apr. 13 ("corres."), 18 (petition from Caroline County, Va.), May 10 ("Valerius"), 19 ("A Republican" from *Ind. Chron.*), 28 ("Lysander"), June 12 ("Apprehensions" from N. Y. *Gaz.*), Aug. 4, 6 ("Aristides" from Washington, Ky., *Mirror*), 20, 1798.

118. *Ibid.,* June 7, 1798.

119. On army issues see *ibid.,* May 11 ("A young, a very young Citizen"), July 3, 13, 21, 23, 30 ("One of the People"), 31 ("Queries" from *Vermont Gaz.*), Aug. 20, 1798. On the navy see *ibid.,* Aug. 2, 17, 20, 24, 29, 1798.

120. The President's call for a day of fasting was made in a March 23 proclamation. See Richardson, *Messages and Papers,* I, 258–60. *Aurora* attacks are in Mar. 29, 30 ("A Good Christian and an Enemy to Hypocrisy"), Apr. 27 ("Populus" from *Baltimore Intelligencer*), May 2 ("corres."), 9, 26, 1798. On Abigail Adams see A. Adams to Her Sister, Mar. 31, 1798, Mitchell, ed., *New Letters,* 150.

121. *Aurora,* Apr. 17, 19 (communication and "corres."), 27, May 12, 26 (ed. from Newark *Centinel*), 30 ("A Democrat" from Mass.), June 11 ("Pacificus"), July 3, 9 (two eds.), 10, Aug. 28 (letter), 1798.

122. For Bache see *Aurora,* Apr. 27, 1798. The President's replies are to The Mayor, Aldermen, and Citizens of the City of Philadelphia, Apr. ?, 1798; and to the Citizens of Philadelphia, the District of Southwark, and the Northern Liberties, Apr. 26, 1798, Adams, ed., *Works of Adams,* IX, 182–83.

123. *Ibid.,* Apr. 21 (two communications), 27, 1798; *Porc. Gaz.,* Apr. 27, 1798; and *Gaz. of U. S.,* Apr. 27 ("An American"), 28, 1798. Bache denied that Callender influenced *Aurora* editorials or had ever written more than a few editorials for the *Aurora. Aurora,* Apr. 30, 1798. One of James Thomson Callender's letters suggests that Bache had refused to publish some of Callender's work, and that the two men were far from being close friends. See J. T. Callender to Thos. Jefferson, Oct. 26, 1798, Worthington C. Ford, ed., "Thomas Jefferson and James Thomson Callender," *New Eng. Hist. and Genealogical Reg.,* L (1896), 330.

124. *Aurora,* Aug. 1, 1798. On the cockade and ribbon issue in general see also May 10, 11, 12, 1798.

125. *Porc. Gaz.,* Apr. 20, 1798.

126. *Annals,* 5th Cong., 2d. Sess., VIII (Apr. 20, 1798), 1476–88.

127. *Aurora,* May 4, 1798.

128. Bache reported the incident on May 9 in the *Aurora.*

129. [B. F. Bache] to a Subscriber in Washington, Pa., Bache Papers, Castle Coll., Am. Philos. Soc.

130. On Cobbett's activities see George Spater, *William Cobbett: The Poor Man's Friend* (Cambridge, Mass., 1982), 82–85; and Richard Buel, Jr., *Securing the Revolution: Ideology in American Politics, 1789–1815* (Ithaca, N. Y., 1972), 180. Webster's and the *Mercury's* comments are in *Comm. Adv.,* June 27, 1798; and *Massachusetts Mercury,* May 8 (letter), 1798.

131. *Aurora* attacks on the *Gazette* can be seen in *Aurora,* May 12, June 19 ("corres."), July 3 (Bache and "Fillip"), 12, 17, Aug. 29, 1798. Fenno's attacks on Bache are in *Gaz. of U. S.,* Apr. 24 ("An American"), May 3, 7 ("A DEMOCRAT'S EDUCATION"), July 31, Aug. 30, 1798.

132. Fenno's charges regarding Jefferson are in *ibid.,* Apr. 18, 19, June 4 ("HELP! OH! HELP!"), 1798. Seven months earlier, Webster had accused Jefferson of encouraging certain persons in Maryland to subscribe to the *Aurora. Comm. Adv.,* Oct. 4, 1797. Bache's replies to Fenno are in *Aurora,* Apr. 21, June 5, 1798.

133. For Allen's charges see *Annals,* 5th Cong., 2d Sess., VIII (July 5, 1798), 2100. On Jefferson's confession see Thos. Jefferson to Samuel Smith, Aug. 22, 1798, Ford, ed., *Jefferson's Writings,* VII, 276–77.

134. Bache's accounts are in the *Aurora,* Aug. 6, 7, 8, 10 and 13, 1798. Fenno's are in *Gaz. of U. S.,* Aug. 8, 1798.

135. *Aurora,* Aug. 9 (two eds.), 1798.

136. *Gaz. of U. S.,* Aug. 9, 1798; *Aurora,* Aug. 10, 1798. Cobbett was delighted that Bache had received a "very decent drubbing." *Porc. Gaz.,* Aug. 9, 1798.

137. B. F. Bache to Louis Gabriel Cramer, June 27, 1798, in Cramer, *Une Famille Genevoise,* 71.

138. On Létombe, Jefferson and Hauterive see Bowman, *Struggle for Neutrality,* 289–292. On William Bache see W[illiam] Bache to B. F. Bache, Jan. 6, 1796, Bache Papers, Castle Coll., Am. Philos. Soc.

12. Sedition

"The people as well as the government have certain rights pre-scribed by the constitution, and it is as much the sworn duty of the administration to protect the one as the other. If the government is instituted for the benefit of the people, no law ought to be made to their injury. One of the first rights of a freeman is to speak or to publish sentiments; if any government founded upon the will of the people passes any ordinance to abridge this right, it is as much a crime as if the people were, in an unconstitutional way, to curtail the government of one of the powers delegated to it."
(*Aurora*, July 16, 1798)

ONE WEEK BEFORE BACHE'S PUBLICATION of the Talleyrand letter, Massachusetts Federalist Stephen Higginson sent an anxious message to Timothy Pickering:

Seditions, conspiracies, seductions, and all the Arts which the french use to fraternize and overturn nations, must be guarded against by strong and specific Acts of Congress. You have already passed far the Rubicon, there can be no safety but in going forward, perhaps it may not be found even in that way; but a long pause, that shall damp the ardour, and give an opening for french intrigues to operate, will be dangerous indeed.[1]

As Bache would learn all too well, there would be no "long pause."

The initial "specific Acts of Congress" against aliens—in the Naturalization Act and the two alien acts—did not appear to touch Bache. When Harrison Gray Otis and Robert Goodloe Harper first attempted to curtail the merger of "the Democracy" and immigrants by placing a restrictive tax on certificates of naturalization in 1797, the *Aurora*, seeing the threat to republicanism and the Republican Party, defended the prime targets of naturalization—Otis's "wild Irishmen"—as supporters of the American Revolution, and more generally argued that the Federalists hated immigrants because they were opposed to tyranny and loved republicanism.[2] Having failed in 1797, Harper re-opened the naturalization controversy in

1798, calling for nativity as the sole credential for citizenship, and Otis argued in favor of forever barring aliens from public office and the right to vote. The Naturalization Act that was finally signed by the President on June 18 lengthened the residence requirement for citizenship from five to fourteen years without including Harper's and Otis's extremely ethnocentric provisions. Rightly portraying Harper and Otis as bigots who wanted to prevent aliens from gaining attachment to the nation and the Constitution, Bache believed that such attitudes would make the United States "a much less advisable asylum than Portugal, or Turkey."[3]

But naturalization was just part of a larger fabric of anti-alien legislation. More interested in alien "friends" and domestic enemies than in alien "enemies" (i.e., those who were nationals of countries at war with the United States), the Federalists did not spend their rage on the Alien Enemies Bill; they allowed the Republicans to take up that bill as their own, softening it where they could and passing it through the House on June 26 despite continued provisions for presidential discretion in identifying enemy aliens.[4] Alien "friends" were another matter. By early May, a long bill had been proposed in the Senate to address Federalist desires to banish, control, and keep surveillance over alien friends. The Senate bill was passed on June 8 and sent on to the House, where milder alien friends proposals had already been slipped into an omnibus bill dealing with alien friends and seditious practices. Therefore, when debate began in the House on June 16 it appeared the House would prefer its own somewhat milder alien bill over the Senate proposal.

But Saturday, June 16, was the beginning of a momentous long weekend. Three days earlier, Bache's radical compatriot, George Logan, had quietly left the country to begin his own unauthorized peace mission to France, and on Monday, June 18, Cobbett called everyone's attention to Logan's "seditious" plans. At the same time, June 16, Bache had further fueled Federalist wrath by publishing the Talleyrand letter. As if the weekend were the overture for a tragic opera, John Marshall entered Philadelphia on Monday, June 18, to receive a hero's welcome from the Federalists, while the President climaxed the affair by presenting Talleyrand's letter and the final envoy dispatches before Congress.[5]

The House was a different body when it reconvened on June 18. George Thacher and Harper immediately charged Bache with being a French agent; Harper claimed that he would soon be able to sort out the threads of a "plot"—presumably referring to Logan's mission—and alluded to a "treasonable correspondence" of a "criminal nature" that had taken place.[6]

Allen followed with a motion to postpone the House alien bill, recommending that the Committee of the Whole consider the more severe Senate bill on aliens as well as the sedition bill. On June 18, 19, and 21, the House debated the Senate alien bill. Because that debate degenerated into discussions of seditious citizens as much as dangerous aliens, allusions to Bache sometimes crept into statements made on the floor. Edward Livingston of New York, while giving an impassioned speech in which he claimed that no conspiracies had been uncovered, was interrupted by Otis, who argued that French agents had long been active in the United States. "Do not our bad citizens correspond with the agents of the Directory," Otis demanded, clearly referring to Bache, "and does not that Directory boast of its diplomatic means and, of course, calculate on individuals here to give efficiency to their means?" Joseph McDowell of North Carolina, one of the handful of Republicans to challenge Federalist allegations, replied to the "French press" charge that it was "trumped up for the purpose of assisting the passage of this bill." The Alien Friends Act, softened somewhat from the severe Senate version, passed by a vote of 46 to 40 the same day, June 21.[7]

Meanwhile, the *Aurora* simply tried to slow the course of events, first claiming with foolish confidence that the severe alien friends bill would not pass the Senate, and that if it did reach the House, "not twenty of the Representatives would vote for it." Dismayed especially by the clause punishing those who harbored or concealed aliens, Bache attempted one of his specious, distended arguments.

> A correspondent who resides upon one of the most frequented roads in Virginia, entertains, upon the average about an hundred aliens, in the course of a summer. He lives about an hundred thirty miles from the seat of government and it would by this notable bill, be necessary for him to dispatch a courier an hundred and thirty miles, before he durst give a dinner to a visitor from Europe.

Senators who spoke for the bill were ridiculed for their terror tactics and attacked for suggesting that even some American citizens and public officers should be deported by the President.[8] When it became obvious the alien bills would pass, the *Aurora* lamented the abuse of natural justice as well as the loss of talent, money, and property to society as a whole and to immigrants in particular. The *Aurora* also implied that the acts were purposefully directed against French aliens, for obvious reasons, and against Irishmen, for their liberal political views and their attachment to Catholicism.[9]

But the Naturalization Act and the two alien acts were minor issues for the country generally and Bache personally compared to the over-arching issue of sedition. For the Federalists no one more clearly revealed the need for action against sedition than did Benjamin Bache. As early as 1796, after Bache had published Adet's famous letters to the Secretary of State, some Federalists had begun to consider silencing the *Aurora*. Samuel Chase, who would become notorious for his conviction of Republican printers under the Sedition Act, said after publication of Adet's letters that Bache "ought to be indicted for a false and base Libel on our Government." "A free press is the support of Liberty and a Republican Govt.," he admitted, "but a licentious press is the bane of freedom, and the peril of Society, and will do more to destroy real liberty than any other Instrument in the Hands of knaves and fools."[10]

After disclosure of the XYZ dispatches, Abigail Adams had gone further, frequently clamoring in her correspondence for Bache's head. On April 21, 1798, the First Lady declared that

> Bache has the malice & falshood of Satan, and his vile partner the Chronical [sic] [Boston *Independent Chronicle*] is equally bad. But the wretched will provoke measures which will silence them e'er long. An abused and insulted publick cannot tollerate [sic] them much longer. In short they are so criminal that they ought to be Presented by grand jurors.

Claiming that Bache could not have been prosecuted for previous libels on the President and Congress, she had, by April 28, taken comfort in the belief that "the wrath of an insulted people will by & by break upon him," adding in early May that, "If that fellow [Bache] & his Agents Chronical [sic], and all is not surpressed [sic], we shall come to a civil war." At about the same time, Vice-President Jefferson noted that the Federalists were aiming at "the suppression of the Whig presses." And, he added, "Bache's [paper] had been particularly named."[11]

Most Federalists appeared to believe that the best means to get Bache and others like him was through a statutory act. On June 4 a House Committee recommended the omnibus alien and sedition bill mentioned above. The sedition provisions were stern. Persons could be convicted for forming combinations and conspiracies against the government; for speaking, writing, or printing material that threatened government officeholders; or for encouraging riots, insurrections, combinations, or unlawful assemblies. The bill even recommended conviction for those who combined to oppose measures of the government which had been duly ratified and executed. Altogether, the bill was a testament to the very limited understanding of civil liberties, natural justice, and the nature of free societies on the part of many Federalists. Under the sweeping application of this standardless bill, Bache could have been found guilty on several counts. In response, Bache demurred: he merely published the Defense Committee's proposal and, at the same time, quoted the First Amendment to the Constitution. Bache must have believed that two things were clear: the public had a more advanced notion of legitimate free speech than the Federalist sponsors of the bill, and the First Amendment was a primary and positive ascription of civil rights.[12]

Then came the long weekend of June 16 through 18. Only hours after the issue of the *Aurora* containing Talleyrand's letter had hit the streets, the omnibus bill initially laid before the House on June 4 was taken up for discussion. On Monday, June 18, the House having received the administration's translation of the Talleyrand letter and the envoys' dispatches, Harper and Thacher charged Bache and others with seditious practices. From June 19 through 21 House Federalists stoked the fires of partisan rage, allowing their arguments on aliens to spread frequently into the subject of sedition. On June 21, President Adams threw another log on the fire by declaring he would never send another minister to France without assurances that such a minister would be received.[13]

The House was not the only scene of Federalist infatuation. Logan's mission and Bache's publication of Talleyrand's letters had also provided catalysts for James Lloyd of Maryland, a Senator with only one year's service, to encourage his colleagues in the Senate to introduce a sedition bill. After its first reading on June 21, the bill was submitted for revision to a committee headed by Lloyd on June 27, and was finally ratified by a vote of 18 to 6 on July 4. Lloyd's original bill, describing France as an enemy of the United States and prescribing the death penalty for anyone who gave aid and comfort to France, was eventually amended to make no mention of France and to abandon a death penalty clause. But the major provisions dealing with sedition remained intact and were neatly tailored to fit Bache and a few other inveterate opponents of the Federalists.[14]

In response to the Senate's actions, Bache wondered, "Whether there is more safety and liberty to be enjoyed at Constantinople or Philadelphia?" At the same time, he attacked Lloyd and insisted on the primacy of the First Amendment.

> The constitution declares that 'Congress shall make no law abridging the freedom of speech nor the press'—the same constitution declares that every member of the Senate shall take an oath or affirmation to support the constitution. Quere, was Mr. Lloyd exempted from his oath?

A few days later, contemplating the passage of the Sedition Act, he asked if there was "any alternative between an abandonment of the constitution and resistance?" Unwilling to find merit in the modern theory of opposition politics, especially in regard to Federalist behavior, Bache defined a faction as a group of men who combined to violate the laws and the Constitution or injure the interests of the nation; nothing better illustrated the existence of an American faction, to his mind, than the sedition bills. When the Senate bill passed on July 4, Bache silently noted the irony by printing the entire Declaration of Independence.[15]

Senate passage of the sedition bill was applauded by most Federalists, and it encouraged House Federalists to drop their milder omnibus bill in favor of the Senate's more stringent one. Although Republican Edward Livingston moved that the bill be rejected when it was brought before the House on July 5, the House took up consideration of the bill in a heated, vicious debate. From the outset, Bache was a principal subject of Federalist hate and contempt. Speaking first, Allen of Connecticut vented his usual anger against the *Aurora*.

> If ever there was a nation which required a law of this kind, it is this. Let gentlemen look at certain papers printed in this city and elsewhere, and ask themselves whether an unwarrantable and dangerous combination does not exist to overturn and ruin the Government by publishing the most shameless falsehoods against the Representatives of the people of all denominations.

Allen then turned to specific editorials carried in Bache's *Aurora* and quoted liberally from them. Singled out for special attention were: Bache's charge of June 28 that the United States had not done everything in its power to negotiate with France, and Bache's suggestion that Gerry should be granted power to negotiate alone; Bache's statement two days later, in regard to Lloyd's sedition bill, that it was questionable whether more liberty existed in America than in Turkey; and Bache's query of July 3, whether there was "any alternative between an abandonment of the constitution and resistance." Allen then flew into a rage.

He [Bache] declares what is unconstitutional, and then invites the people to 'resistance.' This is an awful, horrible example of the 'liberty of opinion and freedom of the press.' Can gentlemen hear these things and lie quietly on their pillows? Are we bound hand and foot that we must he witnesses of these deadly thrusts at our liberty? Are we to be the unresisting spectators of these exertions to destroy all that we hold dear? Are these approaches to revolution and Jacobinic domination, to be observed with the eye of meek submission? No, sir, they are indeed terrible; they are calculated to freeze the very blood in our veins. Such liberty of the press and of opinion is calculated to destroy all confidence between man and man; it leads to a dissolution of every bond of union; it cuts asunder every ligament that unites man to his family, man to his neighbour, man to society, and to Government.[16]

Between reading *Aurora* editorials and delivering tirades, Allen accused the *Aurora* and four or five other newspapers (all remained nameless except the *Aurora* and the New York *Time Piece*) of being leagued in a combination against the United States and its government. Allen also seemed interested in tying congressmen into the combination. He noted, for example, that four days after Bache suggested that Gerry be given sole negotiating powers, Livingston had risen in the House and recommended the same thing. Then, a day after Livingston's "treasonous" resolution to reject the Senate's sedition bill, Bache had recommended resistance to the laws. In Allen's mind these things suggested a close connection between Livingston and Bache.

After a short digression on the evils of the press in France, Allen again returned to the *Aurora*, charging Bache with counseling Irishmen "not only not to defend this country, but to join our enemy." When Allen had gone so far as to charge that the *Aurora* was "the great engine of all these treasonable combinations, and must be strongly supported or it would have fallen long ago," William Claiborne of Tennessee rose to ask Allen if he did not subscribe to the *Aurora* himself.[17] Slightly embarrassed, Allen admitted he did, but only to see what "abominable things" could issue from "a genuine Jacobinic press." Quickly regaining his previous aggressive style, Allen then hinted that he did not support the *Aurora* in the same manner as Jefferson or some other Republican office-holders did. He did not, Allen noted, alluding to Jefferson, walk arm-in-arm with Bache or hold "midnight conferences" with the *Aurora*'s publisher. Concluding his attack on the *Aurora*, Allen charged that,

This paper is devoted to party; it is assiduously disseminated through the country by a party; to that party it owes its existence; if they loved the peace of our Zion, if they sought the repose of our country, it would cease to emit its filth; it has flourished by their smiles; it would perish by their frowns.[18]

Allen's views of what constituted seditious speech were lavish even by Federalist standards, and his inability to see the ideological independence of men like Bache suggests the insular political world that Allen occupied. No other House Federalist bothered to attack the *Aurora* specifically because there was little left to say, by way of rational or irrational accusation.

In the relatively short debate on the sedition bill, House Republicans occasionally risked a defense of the *Aurora*'s editor. Nathaniel Macon of North Carolina, apparently believing truth or falsehood could be established in political discourse, weakly argued that if the *Aurora* printed unfounded statements, these statements would be "contradicted" by other newspapers. McDowell was bolder. Avoiding mention of Bache's name, he referred to the *Aurora*'s editor as "a citizen of respectable character and connexions," accused Cobbett of being in the pay of the British, and attacked Fenno by name. John Nicholas of Virginia, one of the few members of the House who had developed a clear libertarian and modern sense of the primacy of free speech, explained that he subscribed to the *Aurora* because it was one of only four or five papers in the country that was willing to criticize the government and the executive.[19]

Albert Gallatin, the Republicans' most thorough and intelligent spokesman, offered the best defense. Avoiding the pitfalls of debating the *Aurora*'s merits or portraying Bache as a pure innocent victim, Gallatin simply noted that the *Aurora* editorials cited by Allen contained no seditious statements and were at worst "perhaps erroneous." The *Aurora* had a perfect right to claim that Gerry might be given the power to treat with Talleyrand, Gallatin continued. And Bache's speculation about more freedom existing in Constantinople than in Philadelphia would be proved true if the sedition bill were passed. Interrupting Gallatin's speech at this point, Allen made the incredible claim that he did not mean to suggest that these particular editorials left Bache vulnerable for indictment. With this admission, Gallatin exploded. Why had Allen brought the editorials before the House in the first place? Gallatin asked. Taking a broader view, Gallatin then blasted the Federalists for pouring a torrent of abuse on the Republicans and for using innuendo and baseless charges to prepare the way for the sedition bill.[20]

On July 14 the President signed the Sedition Act, which, among other things, established a penalty not to exceed two years in prison and a two-thousand-dollar fine for anyone writing, printing, or uttering "false, scandalous and malicious" writing against the United States, Congress, and the President, or for "intent to defame" or bring into disrepute the same institutions or persons. In this regard, both the nature of the offenses listed and the punishments ascribed were well tailored to Bache; his editorials could be interpreted to violate the act, and two years (or less) in prison and a two-thousand-dollar fine would close up his printing shop.[21]

Although the Act guaranteed truth as a defense and stipulated that the jury could retain the privilege of interpreting the law as well as the fact of the alleged libel, the Sedition Act was an ill wrought piece of legislation that ignored the idea of a legitimate opposition and naively assumed that truth was an absolute that could be teased out of even political disagreements of opinion. It destroyed any illusions of the primacy of the First Amendment, instituted what is generally defined as a bad tendency principle in regard to free speech, and created an ugly atmosphere of political persecution.[22]

The *Aurora* did not launch an extensive attack on the Sedition Act during the House debates. Perhaps writers feared that any comments they made would make them vulnerable to attack. Bache operated under his own ideological constraints. Although some men like Madison and Gallatin might appreciate the concept of political opposition and relative truth in political discourse, Bache believed there was an ultimate political truth as much as did some Federalists. In an early editorial, after citing Machiavelli on the dangers of a citizen's criticizing a prince, Bache alleged that the government, in "sapping and betraying the liberties of the people," had committed "treason."[23]

With the Sedition Act passed through Congress, Bache immediately warned "the good citizens of these States" to "hold their tongues and make tooth picks of their pens." Bache, of course, ignored his own advice, promoting a two pronged attack on the Act. Unlike some other Republicans who invoked state sovereignty in the area of seditious libel, Bache was a nationalist. As such, he necessarily condemned the Act as a gross violation of the First Amendment. But Bache was as much an ultra-democrat as he was a nationalist, and the major thrust of his argument addressed the need of a sovereign people to have the free and natural right to make their influence known to a government that was merely an agent for the people. On July 16 he summarized his views:

> The people as well as the government have certain rights prescribed by the
> constitution, and it is as much the sworn duty of the administration to protect

the one as the other. If the government is instituted for the benefit of the people, no law ought to be made to their injury. One of the first rights of a freeman is to speak or to publish his sentiments; if any government founded upon the will of the people passes any ordinance to abridge this right, it is as much a crime as if the people were, in an unconstitutional way, to curtail the government of one of the powers delegated to it. Were the people to do this, would it not be called anarchy? What name shall then be given to an unconstitutional exercise of power over the people? In Turkey the voice of the government is the law, and there it is called despotism. Here the voice of the government is likewise the law and here it is called liberty.

Only a few *Aurora* editorials ventured beyond Bache's comprehensive charges of unconstitutionality into the legal intricacies of the act.[24]

Most *Aurora* editorials addressed the broader concern that the Sedition Act was a tool designed to prosecute Republicans. Frequent references were made to government suppression, and Federalist papers were accused of spearheading this drive to silence the opposition. Threats against newspapers like the New York *Time Piece* and Thomas Adams's *Independent Chronicle* were duly recorded, as were meetings and toasts given in opposition to the alien and sedition acts.[25] The French threat was not a legitimate reason for the act, Bache argued. "Will a sedition bill redress French aggressions," he asked, "or an alien bill make the Directory listen to our terms? Will either prevent the French Republic from the pursuit of her own plans?"[26] A few days later, after noting that the President had said that opposition to the government was slight and political divisions were only a "difference of sentiment," Bache wondered why the alien and sedition acts had been passed.

> Is this not blowing hot and cold out of the same mouth? If it is only a difference of sentiment on public measures, why has he sanctioned measures to restrain the liberty of the press and in open violation of the constitution?[27]

Passage of the Sedition Act also stimulated a real sense of paranoia in Bache. On August 3, he printed an editorial by a New York writer who recommended that Republicans arm themselves "to defend their persons and property." Bache foolishly supported such actions, opening the door to further political hysteria and fear. After noting how the alien and sedition acts as well as Federalist speeches and parades had alarmed Republicans in New York, Bache applauded the formation of an "armed association" in New York City. "This prudent and proper step of the republicans has struck the tories with dismay," he naively declared, "They know, that if the arm of republicanism is once nerved to resistance, all their plans for the overthrow of the constitution, for assimilating our government to that of Britain and for dragging us into a connection with that country must vanish." Two weeks before his death, he seemed to have become more paranoid, advising "every republican . . . to provide himself with arms and to habituate himself to the constant use of them."[28]

Insofar as Bache was a primary target of the Act, the Sedition Act remained merely a weapon to be held in reserve and used if necessary. Impatient Federalists had already acted in Bache's case long before the Sedition Act was passed, instituting a common-law seditious libel suit against the *Aurora*'s editor in the federal district court of Philadelphia. Bache's publication of Talleyrand's March 18 letter to the envoys had provided the occasion for the seditious libel charge. Appearing in the *Aurora* on June 16 only two days before the State Department received the envoys' copy of it, the letter seemed belittling and arrogant in its assertion that the envoys had not done everything in their power to reach an accommodation with France. And it appeared meddlesome in recommending that the American government grant Elbridge Gerry full power to negotiate with the French foreign ministry. Bache's subsequent contention that the Talleyrand letter proved the President's true desire for war and demonstrated how the harsh words of Adams, Congress, and the Federalist press had undermined the entire negotiation from the start, only confirmed administration and Federalist beliefs that Bache was acting on behalf of a foreign and hostile state.[29]

Federalists were primarily interested in one thing: how had Bache received this letter? Pickering stated privately that the State Department did not receive its copy until June 14. The Secretary rightly speculated that Talleyrand had sent the letter to America for publication because of the French belief that the United States government might keep it concealed from the American people.[30] Federalist printers were thinking along the same line. Bache had finally made a fatal error, they proclaimed in unison, and had revealed himself as a French agent in direct communication with the French Foreign Minister. Unquestioning in their belief that even indirect communication with an officer of a foreign state constituted sedition, Fenno and Cobbett initiated the attack immediately.[31]

Cobbett, as usual, went to greater lengths than Fenno. He opened his article by describing Talleyrand as a violent atheist and accusing the French of robbing the United States of 25 million dollars, of reducing American trade, and of attempting to divide the American people. Having set the perfidious scene, Cobbett sneered that, "You ought to know that the diplomatic skill of France and the means she possesses in your country are sufficient to enable her, with the French Party in America to turn all the blame on the Federalists!!!" And then Cobbett concluded by training his sights on Bache:

> It is certain that BACHE has received this letter from France, or from a French agent here, for the express purpose of drawing off the people from the Government, of exciting discontents, of strengthening opposition, and to produce a fatal delay of preparations for war. The prostitute printer has announced, that he has struck an extraordinary number of the gazette which contains it, and the evident purpose of this is, to spread it all over the country. In consequence of this, I now express my determination to publish these remarks in several succeeding papers, and to strike some thousands besides upon white paper which I will sell for a cent each. These will be ready on Monday [June 18]. Ought not Bache to be regarded as an organ of the diplomatic skill of France? And ought such a wretch to be tolerated at this time?[32]

By Monday, June 18, Federalists everywhere were in a fury. In the House, Thacher charged that the French Directory had ordered Bache to print Talleyrand's letter, and that Bache was an agent of the French government. When Claiborne demanded proof, Thacher suggested that he would soon be able to produce proof. The following day, June 19, the House ratified Sitgreaves's extravagant proposal to print 10,000 copies of the Talleyrand letter and the envoys' dispatches presented to the House the day before, believing that these complete documents were needed to counter the harm Bache had done.[33]

Bache's initial comment was that the administration or the envoys, recognizing the damage Talleyrand's letter would do to the Federalist war effort, had withheld the letter.[34] With Thacher's accusation in the House, Bache vigorously replied that, "Few members could have been found in the house so devoid of honor and spirit as to have done the job which it fell to the lot of Mr. Thacher to perform." In addition to denying Thacher's charges completely and labeling Thacher with "cowardice," Bache called the attack against him a link in "the chain of persecution by which it is attempted to injure the *Aurora* and muzzle the press." Later editorials charged Thacher with being a "base calumniator," and when Thacher fell silent about proving the charge, Bache demanded that Thacher deny the charges or stand guilty of "concealing treason."[35]

Until the afternoon of June 18, Federalist accusations were based largely on conjecture. But then the Federalist press produced evidence which they believed could be used to indict Bache for conspiring with France. Details of the new Federalist charges appeared simultaneously (June 18) in the *Philadelphia Gazette* and Fenno's *Gazette of the United States*. According to the *Philadelphia Gazette,* a gentleman traveling on a ship from France to Philadelphia had privately testified that he had seen a packet bearing the seal of the French Foreign Office addressed to Benjamin Franklin Bache, and a similar packet addressed to someone in New York. Both packets, the witness testified, had been placed under the care of a Mr. Lee by a clerk in Talleyrand's office on March 18. Lee left the vessel, the witness reported, when it first arrived at New York. Fenno reported the same story, except that he identified a Mr. Keeder [John Kidder] as the witness only alluded to in the *Philadelphia Gazette*. Kidder had apparently arrived in Philadelphia on June 11 "with dispatches from the French Directory to Benjamin Franklin Bache . . . under the seal of Mr. Talleyrand." Fenno stated Kidder "punctually delivered" these dispatches to Bache, Fenno concluded, and also delivered a packet of material to a person in New York.[36]

Kidder's testimony, though reported differently in these two newspapers, suddenly gave credence to the Federalist assault on the *Aurora*. Bache vainly argued that the testimony was a "lie." The Talleyrand letter, Bache claimed for the first time, had not been received from Talleyrand. Furthermore, Bache defensively declared that the accounts carried in Fenno's paper and the *Philadelphia Gazette* did not "agree."[37]

When Kidder subsequently came forth with a full statement, it appeared Bache's charges about contradictions had been swept away. According to Kidder, whose June 18 clarification appeared in Cobbett's *Gazette* on June 19, he had had two packets addressed respectively to Bache and Genet, and bearing the seal of the French Foreign Office, placed under his care by a Mr. Lee [William Lee] on March 19 or 20, just as the vessel carrying Kidder and Lee was about to leave France for America. As Kidder recalled it, he had asked Lee what the packets contained. Lee had answered that they contained a pamphlet written by a young man in Talleyrand's office. Kidder then testified that, not knowing the political importance of the packets, he had unwittingly sent Genet's packet to the New York post office, and sent Bache's packet to the Philadelphia post office. After declaring his own innocence in the affair, Kidder concluded by saying that the public "may judge whether or not the French have their secret agents in this country."[38]

Fenno and Cobbett wasted little time in reconstructing Kidder's testimony and producing what they believed was a true narrative of events. "Junius" said in the *Gazette* that the envoys had sent Talleyrand's letter and their comments on Talleyrand's behavior to the Secretary of State in April. But, this writer went on, the vessel carrying the dispatches arrived at Cape Ann, Massachusetts, on June 8, and they were not delivered to Pickering until June 14. Talleyrand, hoping to "surprise" the American people and the American government, had sent his letter to America for publication at the same time, but Kidder's vessel had actually taken a long passage while the official dispatches had come by a shorter route. Bache, therefore, did not receive Talleyrand's letter until June 11, when Kidder deposited it in the post-office. According to "Junius," Bache then used the letter "to divide the people and weaken their opposition to French aggression and plunder." When the President sent the Talleyrand letter and the envoys' dispatches to Congress a short time later, "Junius" concluded, Bache had simply been forced to argue that the President had been withholding them.[39]

Cobbett believed that Kidder's letter conclusively proved that Bache was a French hireling. Adding guilt by association to circumstantial evidence, Cobbett declared,

> This is the traitor caught at last! This discovery accounts for all the villains conduct and for the continued connection that has been kept up with him by many persons in this country. JEFFRIES [Captain Jeffries, a Republican] was seen going into his house on the very day that the dispatches appeared; BACHE was the other day seen in company with YRUJO, the Spaniard, COLLOT, the French General, and T. S. MASON, a Senator from Virginia; and his connection with Dr. LOGAN and REYNOLDS the chief of the UNITED IRISHMEN, is notorious.

Delay could no longer be afforded, Cobbett declared. The French infiltrated countries and divided them internally, he argued. Having earlier painted a terrifying picture of the French Revolution, he now encouraged his readers to let their imaginations roam on the prospect of how a French force of 10,000 men could land in the South, free the slaves, and begin a war that would be both civil and foreign. Returning to Bache, Cobbett hysterically demanded action:

> in such a state of things, shall this atrocious villain, BACHE, be tolerated? Shall he be suffered to proceed in his career of defaming the government, misleading the people, exciting them to insurrection, when it is known, when it is proved, that he acts in concert with the foreign as well as domestic

enemies of the country? . . . The French faction must be crushed, or the government here MUST FALL.[40]

Hoping to sustain the assault, Cobbett printed a broadside the following day which contained the Talleyrand letter and Kidder's testimony. Cobbett again begged Americans to act.

> This AMERICANS, is the most awful warning you ever had. It is here proved, that the man, who, for six long years has been incessantly employed in accusing and villifying [sic] your government, and in justifying the French in all their abominable injuries and insults, is absolutely in close correspondence with the insolent and savage despots by whom those injuries and insults have been committed.[41]

Bache began his own campaign to clear himself of Federalist press charges on June 21. First, he presented his own sworn affidavit, issued on June 20 in the presence of the Mayor of Philadelphia, in which he declared, "That the letter signed Ch. Mau. Talleyrand . . . was not received by him from France; that it was delivered to him for publication by a gentleman in this city; and that he never received the letter said to have been put into the post office for him in a piece signed John Kidder." Realizing that most people would not accept the truth of his deposition, Bache reviewed the entire case. The Federalists, he declared at the outset, had made much of the "manner" in which the letter was received in order to "divert the public attention from its contents." As a result, he continued, the Federalists had "libelled him on the floor of Congress, as an agent of the French, and their venal presses attempted to fix the charge, by bringing forward something that looked like evidence, of his having received the letter in question from the French Department of Foreign Affairs." The only evidence the Federalists had produced, Bache pointed out, was Kidder's testimony. Yet, he noted, Fenno's allegation that Kidder had "punctually delivered" the packet did not conform to Kidder's own testimony a day later when Kidder admitted that he had only deposited the letter in the post-office.

Bache then reported that he had begun his own investigation into Kidder's testimony. After twice failing to find Kidder at home on June 18, Bache finally obtained an interview with Kidder on the 19th. Bache brought a witness, and Kidder was given the opportunity to correct Bache's written record of the meeting before publication. Kidder again stated that he had been given a packet addressed to Bache bearing the French Foreign Office seal, that Lee had given him the packet, and that Lee had stated that he believed the packet contained a pamphlet written by a young man employed in Talleyrand's office. Kidder denied that any air of "mystery" or "secrecy" was involved in Lee's request that Kidder deliver the packet. Although Kidder was unable to remember the name of the author of the alleged pamphlet, he agreed with Bache that it might have been Pichon. But then Kidder's memory got worse. When asked what he had done with the packet, Kidder said he "believed" it was dropped in the ship's letter bag and sent to the Philadelphia post office. Unsatisfied, Bache then said he thought it was "strange" that the packet had never reached the *Aurora*'s office. This prompted Kidder to speculate. Perhaps, he ventured, the packet had been taken when a British vessel intercepted Kidder's ship and seized some of Kidder's other papers. Or, Kidder reflected, it was even "probable" that Lee took the packets when Lee left the ship to take another vessel to Boston.

Pleased by Kidder's inability to verify anything, Bache analyzed the Kidder testimony himself. First, the *Aurora*'s editor admitted that he had met Louis Pichon, whom he described as an "intimate" friend, when Pichon was attached to the French mission to Philadelphia. Though no letter had turned up, either from Pichon or anyone else, Bache thought it was perfectly natural that Pichon would write a political pamphlet and send it to his friends in America. Because Pichon was an employee of the French foreign office, Bache argued, it was reasonable to assume that that department's seal would be on the packet.[42] Bache added that if Pichon or anyone else had been involved in sending material that constituted a "treasonable correspondence" he would not have been so foolish as to put the Foreign Office seal on it, and Lee would have been instructed to keep the delivery of the packet secret.

Bache then ridiculed Kidder's bad memory concerning delivery of the letter in Philadelphia. Kidder's testimony might contain some substance, Bache admitted, but he believed that the myriad of contradictions in that testimony were enough to make observers doubt if the packet had ever been delivered. To prove further that the packet had not been delivered, Bache, accompanied by two witnesses, confronted the letter carrier who delivered the *Aurora*'s mail. The letter carrier admitted that on June 11, the date Kidder had earlier claimed to have deposited the packet in the post office, Bache had not received a ship letter and that the only letter delivered to Bache on June 11 was a local letter.

In concluding his arguments of June 21, Bache stated his belief that the administration had already discovered from whom he had received the

Talleyrand letter. And, he said, the government was "welcome" to make their information known. He also believed that the government knew where the missing packet from France was, and he asked that it be returned to the *Aurora*. "Even if the seal should be broken or the letter defaced, I shall attribute it to accident, & never suspect them of having done either," Bache righteously proclaimed.[43]

Bache was close to the mark on everything, as the administration well knew. Although the President remained aloof from the case, secretaries Pickering and Wolcott were eager to discover more about the packets William Lee had brought from France to Republicans throughout the country. Pickering and Wolcott may have interviewed Kidder before public reports emerged but, after learning that Kidder no longer had any of the packets, and after Kidder referred to other packets still in Lee's possession, they hurriedly turned their attention to Lee.

William Lee, who sought a consulship in France and who was later refused appointment to the federal revenue service because Adams considered him too thorough a "jacobin," had left Paris for Bordeaux on March 18, and was accompanied by Kidder and Samuel M. Hopkins of New York. According to Lee's diary, all three men boarded the ship *William* bound for Philadelphia. In late May, Lee and Hopkins transferred to a vessel bound for Marblehead, hoping their transfer would speed the return home. Their ship arrived in Marblehead on June 2, and Lee immediately set out on a business trip to Boston.[44] Lee did not mention the famous packets in his diary, but evidence and testimony later showed that Lee, in his hurry to transfer ships, had left some of the packets with Kidder and taken the rest himself. Kidder, however, was not given the packet addressed to Bache. Kidder apparently believed that it was wise to confess his role as a courier and avoid Federalist wrath, although he did not even remember whether he had been given the Bache packet or not.

Pickering and Wolcott were on the right track, therefore, when they decided Wolcott should go to New York to encounter Lee and investigate the matter. Wolcott arrived on June 19 and, the following day, interrogated Lee at the home of fellow traveler Samuel Hopkins. According to a reliable observer, Lee, worried at the prospect of being considered a French agent, gave Wolcott the packets in his possession, including the one addressed to Bache. Wolcott then repeatedly asked if there were any letters for Jefferson, an important object of the secretaries' investigations. After being convinced that there were no further letters, Wolcott gave Lee a receipt for the packets received.[45]

Bache was saved from the charge that he was in direct communication with Talleyrand simply because Lee had not given the packet to Kidder, and because Lee had not posted the packet himself in New York. But Pickering and Wolcott were now in an embarrassing situation; they had intercepted mail addressed to private persons, and had failed to come up with any evidence concerning Bache's receipt of the Talleyrand letter.

Meanwhile, Samuel Hopkins and William Lee, having seen Kidder's letter reprinted in a New York newspaper, came to the conclusion that they should publicly defend their roles in the affair. On June 20, both men submitted letters to he *New York Gazette*. Hopkins stated that he had accompanied Lee and Kidder from Europe; all three men knew of letters addressed to Monroe, Bache, Genet, and others, he said. Hoping to get Lee off the hook, Hopkins said that Lee wanted to send these suspicious packets to the Secretary of State but, in changing ships, accidentally left some with Kidder. Lee, Hopkins hastened to add, "was one of the very few Americans of respectable character who have lately resided in France." Lee wasted few words in defending himself. He insisted that he had known nothing of the contents of the letters, nor did he know the source of the letters. He had taken little note of the letters while at sea, he said, and had given some of the letters to Kidder by mistake. The ones he had kept, Lee added, were "delivered up to the government."[46]

Cobbett used the Hopkins and Lee letters to make one last, bad attempt at proving that Bache was in "close correspondence with the old hopping apostate Bishop." Not knowing, as Wolcott did, that Bache had not yet received the packet from France, Cobbett claimed that the Hopkins-Lee letters corroborated Kidder's account of putting Bache's letter in the post office.[47]

Bache also commented on the Hopkins and Lee letters. He first drew attention to Kidder's foolish and contradictory testimony. Kidder, Bache argued, had been "prevailed upon to be the stalking horse in this pitiful contrivance to injure us, and has not had the brains to tell a straight story." As for the missing packet, Bache was convinced that it was in the administration's hands. Harper and Thacher had grown silent about their bold charges, Bache predicted, because the administration did not care to violate an individual's private letters by breaking the seal. "We have not a doubt but that finally, the letter directed to us will reach us safe and whole," he concluded.[48]

Bache did not have to wait long to learn what had happened. Sometime on Saturday, June 23, he received the missing packet. On the following

Monday, he drew all of the threads together in an editorial entitled, "The Plot Unravelled." Bitter and angry, he recalled again how Harper and Thacher had accused him of being a French agent, and how the Federalist presses "spread the poison far and wide." But truth had finally emerged victorious, he declared. The "mysterious packet," he reported, had been delivered by one of Pickering's messengers. Because the seal was intact, Bache said that he had kept the messenger at hand until two witnesses could be summoned. The packet was then opened, and was found to contain two pamphlets, one entitled "Lettre d'un Français à M. Pitt" and the other a "Seconde Lettre d'un Français à M. Pitt." Both had been sent by Pichon and there was no covering letter enclosed. Bache's witnesses also testified that two receipts had been written on the back of the packet: one read, "Received, June 20, from William Lee" and was signed by Wolcott; the other read, "Received in the mail from New York, June 22, 1798," and was signed by Pickering. Bache noted that it was ironic that the "calumnies" directed at him had all arisen from two pamphlets on English affairs, pamphlets that did not even mention the United States. He conveniently failed to mention from whom he had received the Talleyrand letter.

In the remainder of this June 25 editorial, Bache re-constructed the whole complex affair as he understood it. The administration, having learned that Lee had certain interesting packets, had been torn between finding out the contents of the packets and the hazards of opening another man's mail, Bache guessed. Wolcott had been dispatched to New York, he further speculated, to decide what to do. In the meantime, the government thought it wise to throw out rumors about Bache's activities and thereby injure the *Aurora*. Charging the government with a sinister conspiracy against the *Aurora*, Bache claimed that Wolcott would have destroyed the packet except for the fact that Kidder had implicated Lee, and that Lee had been forced to say that he had given the packets to the government. "While this base business of espionage" was going on, Bache continued, "Reports were industriously spread, that he was arrested,—that he was in jail, that he had fled." In fact, Bache said that he had learned that an order for his arrest had even been signed. Intimidation had been used to encourage him to flee, Bache argued, but he had resisted. "He will ever prefer death, as a victim," Bache said of himself, "to a flight that would render his innocence suspected."

Bache then contrasted his innocent conduct with the conduct of Wolcott and the administration, and the behavior of Harper and Thacher. Although Wolcott, realizing that the packets to Monroe, Genet, and Bache contained the same material, had apparently not opened any of them, Bache had no doubt about Wolcott's initial intent to open them. The implications were grave.

> So far as the Secretary Wolcott went in this business, he went not only without law, but against the law; and he has had the folly, by his receipt to give proof of it. The letter directed to the Editor was his property; What right had Oliver Wolcott to receive it? and then to send it to a third person? Who told him that we were willing to trust him with a letter? Suppose we should undertake to receive a letter directed to him, or any other property, detain it a time, and then transmit it to a third person, would he not consider himself injured, and could he not obtain redress?

Bache also wondered if other executive officers—obviously referring to Pickering—should be able to place themselves above the law. "If they are not brought before the courts of justice for their arrogance," Bache proclaimed triumphantly, "it is because the tribunal of the press is more formidable to them." Turning to Harper and Thacher, Bache contended that, although both men could plead immunity for their attacks in the House, both were honor bound to admit they were wrong.[49]

Bache's analysis of June 25 marked the end of the Talleyrand letter episode. Some Federalist newspapers took a few feeble passing shots at the *Aurora*'s editor, and tried with apparently limited success to revive the issue of where and from whom Bache had received the Talleyrand letter.[50] Bache never revealed who had given him the Talleyrand letter. He could do little else but play the unconvincing role of the injured innocent for as long as possible. Shortly after the Talleyrand letter incident, Bache compiled a pamphlet of the editorials and documents of the affair under the title, *Truth Will Out!* In the preface, Bache reviewed the "persecutions" he had suffered at the hands of his opponents, noting how his encounters with Humphries, Dayton, the young men of Philadelphia, and other Federalist combinations and persecutions had failed to drive away the *Aurora*'s subscribers and supporters. There were shades of pathos, self-pity, defeat, and fatigue in his words. No matter what he said, his paper was not prospering. And, as he admitted himself, other newspapers had been "dilatory" in printing his "vindication," thereby leaving the public with the lingering impression of his personal guilt.[51]

Federalists were neither impressed nor slowed by Bache's defense. Eager to prosecute Bache for sedition without waiting for final passage of the Senate sedition bill, Federalists conspired to have the radical editor arrested on June 26 under a warrant issued by Federalist Judge Richard Peters of the

Federal District Court of Philadelphia "on the charge of libelling the President, & the Executive Government in a manner tending to excite sedition, and opposition to the laws, by sundry publications and re-publications." Because Bache died before this charge of common law seditious libel could be tried in court, neither he nor anyone else mentioned what specific "publications" Peters had in mind. Bache only reported that he was called before Peters on Wednesday, June 27. Because Bache's counsel, Alexander James Dallas and Moses Levy, had not been given time to prepare for Peters's unexpected warrant, Peters agreed to suspend proceedings until the following Friday. In the meantime, Bache was placed on parole.[52]

On Friday, June 29, Bache appeared again before Peters. Delighted by Bache's predicament, Fenno ridiculed the entourage Bache brought with him to court. In addition to Dallas and Levy, Fenno noted that Thomas Leiper, a tobacconist, and Israel Israel, a tavernkeeper, had appeared and paid one thousand dollars each to cover Bache's bail. Robert Smith, a hatter, and Colonel Barker, a tailor, were Bache's "attending friends," Fenno added. Fenno clearly remained oblivious to the "new men" of American society and antagonistic to the emergence of a democracy of ordinary men.[53]

Bache and his attorneys were too busy to notice Fenno's social commentary as they tried to counter the government's charges. Levy and Dallas, in their appearance before Peters and United States District Attorney William Rawle, argued "that the Federal Courts had no common law jurisdiction in criminal cases." To uphold this opinion, they cited Judge Samuel Chase's initial view in *United States v. Worrall* that no federal common law existed or had been incorporated in the federal system of laws. In fact, the Bache case promised to be a reprise of the Worrall case, which had been heard only a few months earlier in April. Rawle had been the prosecutor and Dallas the defense attorney in that case as well. More importantly, Peters had sat on the federal circuit court with Chase during the Worrall case, firmly resisting Chase's opposition to a federal criminal common law and persuading Chase to acquiesce to Worrall's conviction. Although Chase's initial instincts against a federal common law would ultimately be confirmed in American constitutional law, Peters had a firmer grasp of the conventional wisdom of the day in 1798. A federal common law in criminal cases had been employed since 1793, and in 1797 Chief Justice Oliver Ellsworth had explicitly declared in *United States v. Smith* that a federal common law existed. In *United States v. Sylvester* (1799), Chase himself came around, openly agreeing to a federal common law.[54]

Aware of these constitutional nuances better than most, Peters was prepared for the argument posed by Levy and Dallas. He disagreed, Peters said, with the argument that there was no federal common law. He then advised Bache "to enter into recognizance for his appearance, . . . in order that his counsel might digest a mode of proceeding" and do "compleat justice" for their client. By such action, Peters continued, Bache's lawyers could "avoid if possible an injurious collision between the State and Federal Tribunals." Fixated on the issue of jurisdiction, not on the existence of federal common law or the legitimacy of a charge of seditious libel, Peters and Rawle suggested that Bache's attorneys could proceed in one of two ways: they could object to the federal district court's jurisdiction, or they could try "the legality of the imprisonment under a Writ of Habeaus Corpus, returnable before a State Judge, or Court." Peters further offered that by submitting to bail Bache did not give up his right to use these procedures. Peters did say, however, that he was "confirmed" in the opinion he had taken in the Worrall case. Bache was then requested to post a two-thousand-dollar "security," which was immediately paid, and two further "sureties" to "appear and answer," of one thousand dollars each.[55]

The day after his arrest, before the interview with Peters cited above, Bache confidently asserted that the prosecution could not succeed because of Chase's opinion in the Worrall case. But this was really Dallas speaking. Bache significantly added that he hoped the case would not be determined on the basis of jurisdiction but on "THE LIBERTY OF THE PRESS." Bache modified this argument somewhat in the preface to his pamphlet, *Truth Will Out!* He was, he claimed, still confident of victory "even if he [Bache] is obliged to submit to the assumed jurisdiction of the Federal Court, and be tried by a Jury summoned by an officer, appointed by the party that received the alleged injury."[56] Jurisdiction and partisan Federalist domination of the federal judicial system did bother him, but as usual Bache was unwilling or unable to offer a carefully reasoned argument against Federalist constitutional views.

In defending himself for publishing the Talleyrand letter, Bache had achieved a pyrrhic victory only. In terms of lasting effects, the defense was more interesting for what it revealed about the merits and idiosyncrasies of his decade-long journalism than for how it advanced political truth. His saga of the Pichon packet masterfully deflected attention from more central issues. His shrewd detective work and convincing analysis were credits to his ability to trace events. And the mystery of the lost packet allowed him to parade a convincing image of forthrightness and open, democratic journalism.

But when it came to defending himself and the democratic cause at a more profound level in 1798, Bache was a failure. While he implied a primary position for first amendment freedom of speech, he failed to destroy the philosophical underpinnings of seditious libel root and branch. He did not venture toward the libertarian idea just emerging in America that in a democratic society political opinion had to be left free regardless of truth or falsehood. He could not, because he subscribed to the political theory of his opponents, that there are ultimate political truths. For Bache, however, the path to that truth was enlightened and democratic. Stymied by his own political philosophy in rejecting the notion of seditious libel, he also failed to make the case that there was no sedition in publishing the Talleyrand letter, no matter where he had obtained it. As long as he was not an agent of a foreign state—which he was not—he might have simply portrayed his publication of the letter as nothing more nor less than the competent work of an aggressive journalist.

The hysteria of 1798 made such "could-have-beens" moot. Bache was not unlike any other Republican activist; the agenda of political discourse was out of his hands. The pathetic thing to Bache was into whose hands that agenda had fallen. All of the principals in the attack on Bache in 1798 represented a political ideology that he found abhorrent. Noah Webster and John Fenno had become pessimists regarding the future of unalloyed republicanism. William Cobbett was, for the time being, an intolerant Tory. Robert Goodloe Harper, a "pompous" and "pretentious" politico, was "the McCarthy of his generation." Harrison Gray Otis relied on "rhetoric rather than reason," and was a hopeless elitist who hated democracy and wished "jacobinism" were an indictable offense. John Allen, "remarkable for the width of his body and the narrowness of his mind," as David Hackett Fischer has written, consistently attacked the idea of democracy with "violence and vituperation." The "old Federalists" were as bad as the "new Federalists." Samuel Sewall believed liberty depended on security. George Thacher held a deep distrust of the democratic "mob." Stephen Higginson believed the people should be educated to revere their leaders. And, by 1806, Richard Peters would come to advocate legislative sessions behind closed doors.[57]

Bache must have been in despair to see persons with these beliefs rise to eminence in 1798. With death on his doorstep, there would be no comfort for Bache in the fact that the political ideas and the social conservatism of these men were about to fade in a new age of democracy.

Notes

1. S. Higginson to T. Pickering, June 9, 1798, J. Franklin Jameson, "Letters of Stephen Higginson, 1783–1804," in *Annual Report of the American Historical Association for the Year 1896* (Washington, D. C., 1897), I, 808.

2. *Aurora,* July 11 ("Republican"), Sept. 23, 25, 29, 1797. The best discussion of the problem of citizenship from the Revolution through the 1790s is James H. Kettner, *The Development of American Citizenship, 1608–1870* (Chapel Hill, N. C., 1978), 213–47. On the nativist campaign of 1797 see James M. Smith, *Freedom's Fetters: The Alien and Sedition Laws and American Civil Liberties* (Ithaca, N. Y., 1956), 23–25, which remains as a whole the best work on the naturalization, alien, and sedition acts of 1798.

3. On the Naturalization Act see *ibid.,* 26–33. A copy of the act is available in *ibid.,* 435–38. For Bache's response see *Aurora,* May 5, 1798. Bache also compared the United States unfavorably with despotic Russia, where immigrants were welcomed. See *ibid.,* May 11, 25, 1798. "A Naturalized Citizen," *ibid.,* May 15, 1798, portrayed immigrants as potentially more loyal citizens than many native born.

4. Smith, *Freedom's Fetters,* 35–49. Provisions of the Alien Enemies Act can be seen *ibid.,* 440–41. The Act passed the Senate on July 3 and was signed by the President on July 6.

5. As James Morton Smith has said, "From the fateful weekend on June 16–18, the Federalist extremists held control of the House until the end of the session," *ibid.,* 58. The Logan mission is discussed in *ibid.,* 101–103; and in Frederick B. Tolles, *George Logan of Philadelphia* (New York, 1953), 153–73. For Cobbett's accusations see *Porcupine's Gazett,* June 18, 1798.

6. *Debates and Proceedings in the Congress of the United States,* 5th Cong., 2d Sess., VIII (June 18, 1798), 1971, hereafter cited as *Annals.*

7. For Livingston, Otis, and McDowell see *ibid.,* 5th Cong., 2d Sess., VIII (June 21, 1798), 2017, 2021–22. For the entire House debate on the Alien Friends Bill see *ibid.,* 5th Cong., 2d Sess., VIII (June 18, 19, and 21), 1972–2029. See also Smith, *Freedom's Fetters,* 50–93. Provisions of the act can be found in *ibid.,* 438–40.

8. The "Virginia" quote is in *ibid.,* May 9, 1798. See also *ibid.,* May 30 (communication), June 14, 1798.

9. *Ibid.,* June 16 (communication), 19 ("corres."), July 4 ("Republican"), 16 (ed. from *Vermont Gazette*), 21 ("A Colonist"), Aug. 14, 1798.

10. S. Chase to McHenry, Dec. 4, 1796, in Bernard C. Steiner, *The Life and Correspondence of James McHenry* (Cleveland, 1907), 203.

11. A. Adams to Her Sister, Apr. 21, 26, 28, May 10, 1798, Stewart Mitchell, ed., *New Letters of Abigail Adams, 1788–1801* (Boston, 1947), 159, 165, 167, 172. And Thos. Jefferson to J. Madison, Apr. 26, 1798, Paul Leicester Ford, ed., *The*

Writings of Thomas Jefferson (New York, 1895), VII, 245, hereafter cited as Ford, ed., *Jefferson's Writings*.

12. For details of House action on sedition in May, and the Defense Committee's submission of an omnibus bill see *Annals*, 5th Cong., 2d Sess., VIII, 1771, 1868. See also Smith, *Freedom's Fetters*, 99–101. Bache's reaction is in *Aurora*, June 6, 1798.

13. House debates on alien friends and seditious citizens can be found in *Annals*, 5th Cong., 2d Sess., VIII (June 16, 18–19, 21, 1798), 1954–2029. See also Smith, *Freedom's Fetters*, 102–106. The President announced his refusal to send another minister to France in an address to Congress. See James D. Richardson, ed., *A Compilation of the Messages and Papers of the Presidents* (New York, 1897), I, 256.

14. Lloyd cited both Logan's mission and Bache's publications and activities in two letters to George Washington which are quoted and summarized in Smith, *Freedom's Fetters*, 107, 110. On Lloyd's inexperience and status see Norman K. Risjord, *Chesapeake Politics, 1781–1800* (New York, 1978), 531–32. On the Senate deliberations and passage of Lloyd's bill see *Annals*, 5th Cong., 2d Sess., VIII, 590–91, 596–99; and Smith, *Freedom's Fetters*, 106–11.

15. *Aurora*, June 29, July 3, 4, 1798.

16. *Annals*, 5th Cong., 2d Sess., VIII (July 5, 1798). For the *Aurora* editorials cited by Allen see *Aurora*, June 28, 29, July 3, 1798. Allen's bitter attack and its Burkean *dénouement* were quoted in the *Aurora* one and a half months later. In parallel columns, an *Aurora* writer gave Allen's "aristocratic" statement, altering only a few words in the column adjoining it to show how the speech might have been delivered by a Republican. Allen's mention of "revolution and Jacobinic domination" was replaced by "tyranny and executive domination." In place of Allen's words, "Such liberty of the press and of opinion is calculated to destroy all confidence between man and man," the *Aurora* writer wrote, "Such an alarming specimen of Star-Chamber policy is calculated to destroy all confidence between man and man." See *ibid.*, Aug. 20, 1798.

17. *Annals*, 5th Cong., 2d Sess., VIII (July 5, 1798), 2099–2100.

18. *Ibid.*, 2100. For the entire text of Allen's speech see *ibid.*, 2093–2101. Jefferson's reaction to Allen's attack was noted in Chapter 9. Bache merely reported that some *Aurora* editorials had been mentioned in a "stormy" session of the House. *Aurora*, July 6, 1798.

19. On the Macon, McDowell, and Nicholas defenses see respectively *Annals*, 5th Cong., 2d Sess., VIII (July 5, July 10), 2106, 2107, 2143.

20. *Ibid.*, 5th Cong., 2d Sess., VIII (July 5, 1798), 2107–2109.

21. The best account of the Sedition Act is in Smith, *Freedom's Fetters*, 94–155. Provisions of the Act are *ibid.*, 441–42.

22. On the matter of truth as a defense, Leonard Levy, *Emergence of a Free Press* (New York, 1985), 303, astutely observes, "Gallatin and Nicholas were among the first Americans on record to have rejected 'truth' as a defense because it inadequately protected the freedom of political opinion in cases of seditious libel." Levy further notes, however, that until at least 1799, even Gallatin and Nicholas retained with

other Americans the idea that seditious libel did exist. On the slow evolution of American thought on seditious libel see *ibid.*, esp. 220–349.

The use of the Act as a political weapon is documented in John C. Miller, *Crisis in Freedom: The Alien and Sedition Acts* (Boston, 1951), 74–85, and *passim;* Smith, *Freedom's Fetters,* 221–443; and Frank M. Anderson, "The Enforcement of the Alien and Sedition Acts," *Annual Report of the American Historical Association for the Year 1912* (Washington, D. C., 1913), 115–26. President Adams's complicity and role are described in Manning J. Dauer, *The Adams Federalists* (Baltimore, 1953), 159–61; Gilbert Chinard, *Honest John Adams* (Boston, 1933), 275–76; Page Smith, *John Adams.* Vol. II, *1784–1826* (Garden City, N. Y., 1962), 976.

23. *Aurora,* July 10, 1798.

24. *Ibid.,* July 16, 1798. For examples of legal arguments see *ibid.,* July 16 ("Senex"), Aug. 3, 1798.

25. *Ibid.,* July 14, 18 (four ed.), 20 (three eds.), 21 (ed from *Ind. Chron.*), 24 ("Americanus"), 27 ("Putnam" and communication), Aug. 4, 13 ("Obadiah"), 27, 1798.

26. *Ibid.,* July 17, 1798.

27. *Ibid.,* July 21, 1798.

28. *Ibid.,* Aug. 3 ("Brutus" from N. Y. *Argus*), 6, 30, 1798. The fact that Noah Webster endorsed the Act as necessary to combat factions, and that a writer in Cobbett's paper hoped the Act's "first operation will be upon the infamous Bache and his associates," did not lessen Bache's paranoia. See respectively *Commercial Advertiser,* July 30, 1798; and "A Jerseyman," *Porc. Gaz.,* Aug. 1, 1798.

29. See "IMPORTANT STATE PAPER, from the French Minister of Foreign Affairs to the American Commissioners, March 18, 1798," *Aurora,* June 16, 1798. *Aurora* editorials closely linked to the Talleyrand letter are in *ibid.,* June 18, 19 ("Tim Pick"), 20, 1798.

30. T. Pickering to John Pickering, June 16, 1798, in the Timothy Pickering Papers, Mass. Hist. Soc., Boston. In the same letter, Pickering remarked that war was "inevitable." Albert Hall Bowman, *The Struggle for Neutrality: Franco-American Diplomacy During the Federalist Era* (Knoxville, Tenn., 1974), 323–24, says that the "note was dispatched to Létombe . . . with instructions to give it all possible publicity in America. It was intended as much for the American people as for their representatives in the first place."

31. *Gaz. of U. S.,* June 16, 1798. Webster described Bache as a "traitor." See *Comm. Adv.,* June 19, 1798. See also *Columbian Centinel,* June 23, 1798.

32. "The Antidote," *Porc. Gaz.,* June 16, 1798. Cobbett's pamphlet appeared on June 18 as promised. See William Cobbett, *Remarks on the Insidious Letter of the Gallic Despots by Peter Porcupine* (Philadelphia, 1798).

33. *Annals,* 5th Cong., 2d Sess., VIII (June 18–19), 1971–73.

34. *Aurora,* June 18, 19 ("Z."), 1798. A later letter to the editor accused the administration of receiving Talleyrand's letter in April and withholding it until Congress had abrogated the French treaties. Letter, *ibid.,* June 22, 1798.

35. *Ibid.,* June 19, 20, 22, 1798.

36. *Philadelphia Gazette,* June 18, 1798; and *Gaz. of U. S.,* June 18, 1798. Both reports were printed in the *Aurora* the next day.

37. *Aurora,* June 19, 1798.

38. Kidder's letter was presented in "The Traitor Trap," in *Porc. Gaz.*, June 19, 1798; and in William Cobbett, *The Detection of Bache . . . June 18, 1798* (Philadelphia, 1798). This latter work was a one-penny broadside published and sold by Cobbett on June 20. *The Detection of Bache* was also printed in Cobbett's newspaper on June 20.

39. "Junius," *Gaz. of U. S.*, June 19, 1798. Cobbett concurred with "Junius" in "The Detection of Bache," *Porc. Gaz.*, June 20, 1798.

40. "The Traitor Trap," *ibid.*, June 19, 1798.

41. Cobbett, *The Detection of Bache.*

42. Twenty-eight-year-old Louis Pichon had been secretary to Genet and to Fauchet. In 1798 he was an employee in the American section of the French Foreign Office. Ironically, Pichon was to be a principal character in establishing a *rapprochement* between the United States and France after being charged by Talleyrand to open discussions with William Vans Murray at the Hague. See especially Bowman, *Struggle for Neutrality,* 350–59.

43. *Aurora*, June 21, 1798. After the scandal was over, Bache published these, and other editorials, in a chronological summary of the affair. See Benjamin Franklin Bache, *Truth Will Out!* (Philadelphia, 1798). Fenno and Cobbett seemed satisfied to ridicule Bache's sworn deposition and to insist that Kidder's testimony still linked Bache in a treasonable correspondence with the French. See *Porc. Gaz.*, June 21, 1798; and *Gaz. of U. S.*, June 21, 22 (communication), 1798.

44. See Mary Lee Mann, *A Yankee Jeffersonian: Selections from the Diary and Letters of William Lee of Massachusetts, Written from 1796 to 1840* (Cambridge, Mass., 1958), 50–52.

45. See *Diary of William Dunlap (1766–1839), The Memoirs of a Dramatist, Theatrical Manager, Painter, Critic, Novelist and Historian* (New York, 1929–31), I, 294.

46. The Hopkins and Lee letters of June 20 were published in *Porc. Gaz.*, June 22, 1798; and *Aurora*, June 23, 1798. Hopkins, who was never suspected of being a liaison for the French or pro-French Americans, had apparently written his letter as an act of friendship toward Lee. Lee's letter, however, was written in an off-hand manner that belied Lee's fear, and perhaps even his feelings of guilt at turning the letters over to Wolcott. Lee, as an office-seeking Republican, needed to clear himself of suspicion in the eyes of some Federalists. See, for example, S. Higginson to O. Wolcott, Jr., June 29, July 11, 13, 1798, George Gibbs, ed., *Memoirs of the Administration of Washington and John Adams* (New York, 1846. Cited here, N. Y., 1971), II, 68, 70, 72, hereafter cited as Gibbs, ed., *Wolcott's Papers.*

47. *Porc. Gaz.*, June 22, 1798.

48. *Aurora*, June 23, 1798.

49. "The Plot Unravelled," *ibid.*, June 25, 1798.

50. See, for example, *Gaz. of U. S.*, June 25, 1798, and Bache's reply in the *Aurora*, June 26, 1798. See also *Col. Cent.*, June 27, 1798.

51. B. F. Bache, *Truth Will Out!*, ii–iii. Bache surprisingly praised Webster for printing in the *Commercial Advertiser* some of the materials used in his vindication. See *Aurora*, June 29, 1798.

52. *Ibid.*, June 27, 1798.

53. *Gaz. of U. S.*, June 29, 1798.

54. *Aurora,* June 30, 1798. On the Worrall case see especially James Haw, Francis F. Beirne, Rosamond R. Beirne, and R. Samuel Jett, *Stormy Patriot: The Life of Samuel Chase* (Baltimore, 1980), 184–85. On Worrall and the constitutional background to federal criminal common law see Levy, *Emergence of a Free Press,* 276–78. Ironically, the Worrall case involved an attempt by an Englishman, Robert Worrall, to bribe Tench Coxe. Coxe, in the meantime, was writing editorials for the *Aurora* and would, by late summer 1798, be involved in financially bailing-out the *Aurora.* See Jacob Cooke, *Tench Coxe and the Early Republic* (Chapel Hill, N. C., 1978), 294–95, 338–47.

A year after the Bache case, President Adams, apparently responding to a newfound reluctance by District Attorney William Rawle to prosecute William Duane's *Aurora* for seditious libel, proclaimed Rawle unfit for the job if Rawle did not think the *Aurora's* criticisms had been and continued to be libelous. See J. Adams to T. Pickering, Aug. 1, 1799, Charles Francis Adams, ed., *Works of John Adams* (Boston, 1854), IX, 9.

55. *Aurora,* June 30, 1798.

56. *Ibid.,* June 27, 1798. Bache, *Truth Will Out!,* iii.

57. On "old" versus "new" Federalists see David Hackett Fischer, *The Revolution in American Conservatism: The Federalist Party in the Era of Jeffersonian Democracy* (New York, 1965). The lively political sketches of Allen, Harper, Otis, Higginson, Sewall, Thacher, and Peters abbreviated above are *ibid.,* 22–23, 36–38, 38–41, 5, 249–50, 256, 258, and 342–43, respectively.

13. Epilogue

> "So it is to have had a philosopher for a grandfather, for that idea
> was the food of much of his extravagance of mind, and placed him
> in a state of pretence where he was obliged to act a part for which he
> had not talents."
> (Wm. Vans Murray to J. Q. Adams, Nov. 27, 1798)

THE DAY AFTER HIS ARREST for seditious libel, Bache "pledged himself that
prosecution no more than persecution, shall cause him to abandon what he
considers the cause of truth and republicanism; which he will support, to
the best of his abilities, while life remains." The frenzy of the French crisis
and the Federalist drive to prosecute what they defined as sedition had
taken their toll. Elizabeth Hewson reported as early as June 20 that Bache
was "going fast to destruction," and was "very much embarrassed in his
circumstances." Only "violent democrats" associated with him any longer,
she gossiped, and "violent measures" were certain to follow if he remained
on the same course.[1]

In August, while denying that New York taverns were dropping their
subscriptions to the *Aurora,* Bache announced that he would try to publish
a three-day-a-week newspaper for distant subscribers. The evidence seems
clear, however, that he was headed toward bankruptcy. Years later, William
Duane, Bache's successor and an assistant to Bache by 1798, claimed that
Bache had spent between $14,700 and $20,000 to keep the *Aurora* alive. In
the spring of 1798, Jefferson had asked Madison to help round up subscriptions for the *Aurora* and Carey's *United States Recorder,* which "totter for
want of subscriptions. We should really exert ourselves to procure it for
them, for if these papers fall, Republicanism will be entirely browbeaten."
Alarmed at the financial condition of the *Aurora,* Tench Coxe, who later
claimed he had been writing a large share of the essays for that paper from
1797 on, was probably the motive force behind a campaign to raise funds
for Bache.[2]

Publishing difficulties were just part of the picture. In reply to an earlier letter from Margaret Bache, Francis Markoe expressed deep concern for what Margaret apparently described as a "distressed situation." The circumstances were already "serious enough," he wrote in early August, but he feared "the worst is yet to come." "You are certainly unhappy," he observed from far-away St. Croix, "& I would advise you to come to us immediately." Markoe then recommended that Bache sign his property over to Margaret and the children, with whom the property would remain safe from creditors.[3]

In August, yellow fever completed the tragedy. Always assuming a political view of the plague, Bache once again blamed the British for the importation of yellow fever, calling it "a present from the British." Unlike the situation in 1793, there were no partisan advantages to be reaped by such attacks in 1798. The fifth yellow fever plague of the decade, one which would kill over 3,500 persons in Philadelphia, was dreadful by its repetition alone. Victims, jaundiced and weakened from vomiting, were often abandoned and sometimes even found lying delirious in the streets. Businesses closed, people fled, and crime increased.[4]

For Bache the scene was poignant and pathetic. He was under arrest, his business was bankrupt, and his political views were seemingly under attack from all quarters. To make matters worse, his wife was pregnant with their fourth child. Perhaps economic necessity, more likely political ideology and commitment, compelled him to declare on September 7 that he would continue to publish until the "cruel malady" struck the *Aurora* office. It was a fatal decision. Late in the evening of September 10, Bache died of yellow fever. Elizabeth Hewson recalled the scene eight months later:

> A french doctor attended him who ordered frequent bathings. The tub leaked and there was that poor woman Margaret Bache just out of her bed continually in a room covered with water. It is a wonder she escaped with her life. She behaved with the greatest fortitude during his illness and after his death.

Hewson described the circumstances in a letter written nearer to Bache's death. Mrs. Bache had been in confinement only five days, Hewson explained, when her husband died. Bache's illness was "short and not severe," she reported. "He settled all his affairs . . . and died with the greatest composure."[5]

Only hours after her husband's death, Margaret had printed a black bordered notice of the death. It proclaimed:

The friends of civil liberty and patrons of the Aurora are informed that the Editor, BENJAMIN FRANKLIN BACHE, has fallen a victim to the plague that ravages this devoted city. In ordinary times the loss of such a man would be a source of public sorrow—in these times men who see, and think, and feel for their country and posterity can alone appreciate the loss—the loss of a man inflexible in virtue, unappalled by power or persecution—and who in dying knew no anxieties but what were excited by his apprehensions for his country—and for his young family.

Margaret then promised that the *Aurora* would reappear in a few days under her own direction, as soon as arrangements were made to "ensure its wonted character of intelligence and energy."[6]

The immediate reaction of friends and foes revealed the tensions of the times. Thomas Adams's Boston *Independent Chronicle* praised Bache for standing "firm at his post" and discharging "like an honest man the duties of his profession." Adams could "sincerely lament the loss of so valuable a citizen . . . but the indecent joy displayed at the receipt of the news around the door of the Insurance office [in Boston], in a broad grin on the countenance of some of our mushroom gentlemen, betrayed a disposition disgraceful even to swine." A later *Chronicle* correspondent eulogized Bache's virtues, praising his opposition to "aristocracy & Despotism" and his defense of "freedom and humanity" while noting the "brilliancy of his talents, the amiable qualities of his mind," and the "manly independence of his soul." These virtues, he concluded, should be admired and imitated by everyone.[7]

Philadelphia's Federalist printers seemed uncertain about what course to take. The *Gazette* and *Porcupine's Gazette* merely mentioned Bache's death in lists of other victims.[8] Cobbett, having received a vicious letter attacking Bache a week after the latter's death, refused to print it, claiming that the attack did no more than "mangle the carcass" of the victim. Cobbett added, however, that "this forbearance ought not . . . to shelter the character or conduct of the deceased from just censure, if that character or conduct should be hereafter held up as an example to, or if they should be imitated by, the survivors."[9] Cobbett kept his word on the caveat.

Massachusetts newspapers failed to employ even Cobbett's oblique politeness. The *Massachusetts Mercury,* a paper that had joined the extreme Federalist ranks after the XYZ affair, claimed that Bache had not been patriotic or courageous in staying at his post, but had continued to print out of "imperious necessity," adding that Bache would not "be suffered to sleep in peace" as long as "unjust and designing praise" was bestowed on

Bache by Republican printers. The *Columbian Centinel* reported that its correspondents were angered by the manner in which *Aurora* supporters had "made" Bache's widow announce the death. These contributors, Russell stated, believed that Bache's "memory ought to be held up to the execration of the whole earth, as a monster, who clutched a dagger prepared to stab the vitals of his country." Parading his own false display of decency, Russell then stated,

> We do not, ourselves, thus estimate his malignity. We never thought the country had much to fear from his exertions in the cause of anarchy, sedition, and French robbery; because they were open, and their origin palpable; and we are as indifferent as in recording his death, as we should be in noticing his escape from the pestilence.[10]

While the *Columbian Centinel* clearly believed Margaret Bache had been manipulated by political handlers, other Federalists truly hoped that she might be easier to deal with than her husband. The *Philadelphia Gazette,* trying to encourage Mrs. Bache toward moderation at least, attempted to flatter her by claiming she possessed a "mild and amiable temper, and an understanding highly cultivated." The *Gazette* then added that it was "impossible to believe, that a pure heart, and a clear head, can be the advocate of her country['s] degradation, or apologist of French usurpation, venality, and murder."[11]

The *Centinel* and the *Philadelphia Gazette* were wrong. The new *Aurora,* published for Margaret Bache until November 14, 1798, and thereafter for Bache's heirs, did not change course. Under the direction of both Margaret Bache and William Duane, the *Aurora* continued as the leader among Republican newspapers. Finances continued to be a problem, however. Mrs. Hewson said the paper had "ruined" Bache's character, that its profits were "triffling," and that Mrs. Bache stood to "make still less." In her mind, Mrs. Bache should sell the copyright. Instead, the *Aurora* was set with new type when it appeared on November 1, 1798, and the number of columns in the paper was increased. While retaining Bache's general format for editorials, Duane also increased the number of news items, making the *Aurora* into a more thorough repository of European and American information.[12]

Secret sources of funding must have promoted the *Aurora*'s maintenance and revival. In mid-1799, Cobbett even claimed that Duane was being paid a salary of eight hundred dollars to manage the paper, and that the paper was being kept afloat by Dr. Adam Kuhn, Margaret's stepfather, as well as by Richard Bache and Joseph Clay, a public office clerk. Since Cobbett was never especially brilliant at investigation, his analysis probably depended on gossip, but he may have been partially correct. According to Jacob Cooke, Tench Coxe had received a "confidential memorandum" from Bache upon the latter's contracting the fever. In it Bache pleaded with Coxe to keep the *Aurora* alive for the sake of his "'family, his country and mankind.'" Coxe apparently conveyed these wishes to Margaret on September 13, promising to prop up the paper himself or in concert with others. Somehow, possibly through Kuhn and Clay, who were executors of Bache's estate, and perhaps through Bache's political friends like Thomas Leiper, who had the means to support the paper, the *Aurora* was kept alive. It is unlikely that any support came from Richard and Sally Bache, both of whom had become estranged from their son before his death.[13]

In 1799, Margaret considered and rejected a proposal by Alexander James Dallas and other Republicans to buy the *Aurora*.[14] Other proposals apparently came from the Federalists as a means of silencing the paper. John Ward Fenno, whose own father was a victim of yellow fever, allegedly refused an offer by some Federalists to buy the *Aurora* out. And in 1799, writing behind a thin veil of anonymity, William Duane accused Alexander Hamilton of offering Margaret Bache $6,000 down toward the purchase of the paper. Claiming that the *Aurora* was worth between $15,000 and $20,000, and insinuating that Hamilton's source of revenue was "British secret service money" provided by British minister Robert Liston, Duane labeled Hamilton's plan to "suppress" the paper a "bungling piece of work." Outraged at the accusation and angry at the "malignant calumnies of the faction opposed to our government," Hamilton eagerly sought the "prosecution of the persons" who published this accusation.

David Frothingham, publisher of the New York *Argus,* served four months in jail for printing Duane's charges, which Frothingham had printed as an "Extract of a letter from Philadelphia, dated September 20." Charged with libel, Frothingham was refused by the court the opportunity to bring forward evidence to prove Duane's accusations, although the prosecution was willing to permit truth as a defense and although the Sedition Act had supposedly set a new "modern" standard of truth as a defense. Frothingham had been caught in the same net as Bache—hostility to ordered government was the important issue to the Federalists.[15]

Finances were only part of Margaret's hardships during her year-and-a-half tenure as editor of the *Aurora.* William Cobbett, displaying a kind of perverse and negative recognition of equality between the sexes, began to direct his attacks against the *Aurora*'s new editor shortly after Bache's death. Having promised to keep up his attack if the *Aurora* retained its former character, Cobbett made wide-ranging accusations. He accused Margaret and her deceased husband of hiring two apprentices who, in the exercise of "true Democratic principles," had been caught looting and stealing. He labeled the new *Aurora* a "disgrace" and called Duane a "wretch" who kept up Bache's "vile slanders." Mrs. Bache, or "Peg" as Cobbett derisively referred to her, was attacked as an indecent liar who "discovers a great degree of that sort of low, instinctive cunning, for which her down-looking husband was so famous."[16] Duane tried to shame Cobbett for attacking a dead man and a poor widow, but the ploy did not work. As late as May 1, 1799, Cobbett was still seething, still trying to destroy Margaret Bache and the *Aurora* utterly. Unwilling to let readers forget the Baches, Cobbett remarked on Margaret's announcement of Benjamin's death,

> HIS WIDOW had this notice . . . struck off before his corpse was cold! It was actually hawked about the city, before day-light had scarcely made it appearance, and long before the husband's dead body was put under the ground! There's 'delicacy,' there's 'sensibility' for you![17]

Cobbett's attacks did not go unanswered. Several Republican papers and writers eulogized Bache in both 1798 and 1799. Duane in particular was careful to protect his predecessor's image. In late 1799, Duane would declare that the *Aurora* under Bache's editorship,

> was the most formidable check upon ambition and false policy, which this nation has possessed for five years past. It cannot be questioned that the talents which this paper displayed under his direction; his timely and able developments and expositions of public measures, foreign and domestic— tended more to disseminate authentic information, and frustrate deception, than the most active efforts even of the spirit and various talents displayed in the Congress of the United States.[18]

Bache would have liked Duane's summary, and especially Duane's comparisons of his "talent" to those who sat in Bache's beloved democratic branch of government.

Porcupine's Gazette would disappear in 1799. A year later Thomas Jefferson's election to the presidency would make William Duane, who was married to Margaret by this time, the editor of an administration news-paper. Although Duane shared Benjamin Bache's general worldview, he was a different character. He was more narrowly self-interested than Bache. He sought material gain and political fame, eagerly pursuing the spoils of partisan politics. Admittedly, he had more opportunities to do so than Bache had. Quicker to anger than Bache, Duane would often become disappointed in allies as well as outraged at enemies. His newspaper columns reflected his more personal and visceral brand of journalism even though his writing style was probably more fluid and less idiosyncratic than Bache's had been.

Bache was a transitional figure in a transitional age. Though he was a product of elements we associate with the eighteenth-century past—Franklin's moral engineering, and Enlightenment thought and psychology—Bache's life and career foreshadowed the era that was to follow, an era that celebrated a new kind of autonomous action, a consistent democratic ethic, and a vision of progress. Yet there was a romantic hue in the passion of his vision not to be found among the many who embraced mere party politics after 1800. Part of this romanticism was an inheritance from his years in France and his later image of the "Great Republic." Part was a consequence of the ideal of Franklin, his education, and the influence of Paine. Still another part was a product of his personality.

Although only intending to be critical of Bache's arrogance, the Federalist William Vans Murray offered an astute analysis of Bache's character upon the death of the *Aurora*'s editor. "So it is to have had a philosopher for a grandfather," Murray told John Quincy Adams, "for that idea was the food of much of his extravagance of mind, and placed him in a state of pretence where he was obliged to act a part for which he had not talents."[19] Murray presumably meant that Bache was not intellectually competent to be a philosopher. Bache was not a philosopher; he was an ideologue who shared a democratic *mentalité,* an intuitive vision of a new order and a new way of thinking. He was an advocate of a new kind of self-interest, a self-interest built on a natural collective morality and individual, enlightened self-interest. He saw that his primary role in this process of social improvement, besides providing for his own children's education, was to inform the public on civic concerns through accurate reportage as well as editorial cautions and interpretations. If Thomas Paine provided a new voice for democratic ideology, Bache amplified that voice in a new popular journalism.

Many historians have dismissed Bache's journalism for its scurrility and for his outlandish attacks on George Washington, unable to look beyond their own ill-defined notions of acceptable partisanship and editorial rhetoric. But Bache's aims were not to offend polite sensibilities. His chief purpose was to protect republicanism and democracy from what he perceived as their enemies. As a consequence, he struggled to determine how the public could become informed, and how they could articulate their informed interests to their representatives in government. In the main, he was frustrated in this task. He was premature in supporting the ideal of a broadly cast democracy shouldered by an honest working class of farmers, artisans, and mechanics. He also fought a battle that he inevitably had to lose in trying to prevent the doors of Anglo-American ethnocentrism from closing out the rest of the world. As he discovered in 1797 and 1798, he embraced a view of the sisterhood of republics and a definition of American nationalism that Americans were unwilling and unable to accept. And he stepped outside society's legitimate bounds of political discourse in attacking the rise of federal executive and administrative authority.

This did not mean that Bache was not a partisan in a practical political sense. His newspaper scoops and his too clever attempts to manipulate the tone of political opinion were calculated to disadvantage Federalists and promote Republicans. Duane testified to Bache's cunning in 1802, while denouncing the political opportunism of James Thomson Callender. Apparently both Bache and Duane were angry that Callender had turned political trimmer and turned his attacks on Jefferson and the Republicans. Duane reported that in May or June 1798 Bache had become aware of a plan by British Minister Robert Liston to hire Callender to write on behalf of the Federalist and British cause. Troubled by Cobbett's abuse of society, Bache reportedly worried "that Callender added to him could not fail of ruining the morals and the decency of the press." To prevent that, Bache asked Duane to give up his ten-dollar-a-week salary so that Callender could be hired by the *Aurora*. The idea, as Bache outlined it to Duane, was to force Callender to write editorials that Bache could screen. Thus, "a check would be kept on his [Callender's] vulgarity."[20] Although Bache did not accept the modern idea of a loyal opposition as it applied to the Federalist-Republican division, he was perfectly willing and competent to embrace practical politics.

Would Bache have become a one-dimensional "politico" and party man if he had lived longer? His attachment to Jefferson and his firm commitment to Republican candidates and policies suggest he might have. But there had also been a radical element in his nature. He genuinely identified with mechanics and artisans, and considered himself to be one as well. Although he was bonded to an emerging idea of class through his own occupation, he was also influenced by radicals like Dr. Michael Leib, Thomas Leiper, and Dr. James Reynolds. Having risen to positions of privilege and means through their own industry, these men would be the early theorists of a new democratic and working-class radicalism that had not yet taken shape. It is not hard to believe that Bache would have been enthusiastic when Dr. James Reynolds, Bache's close associate in 1798, published the first socialist utopian tract in American history in 1802. It does not seem likely that he would have abandoned the radical vision of the mechanics, Irish radicals, and working class spokesmen who had long been his friends.[21] As it was, Benjamin Bache died a democrat attached both to partisanship and to radicalism.

Notes

1. *Aurora,* June 27, 1798; and Eliz. Hewson to Thos. T. Hewson, June 20, 1798, in the Hewson Family Papers, American Philosophical Society, Philadelphia.

2. On Bache's announcement see *Aurora,* Aug. 23, 24, 1798. On Duane's claims see *ibid.,* Apr. 22, 1800; and Aug. 11, 1802. On Jefferson see Thos. Jefferson to J. Madison, Apr. 26, 1798, Andrew A. Lipscomb, ed., *The Writings of Thomas Jefferson* (Washington, D. C., 1903–1904), X, 32. On Coxe see Jacob E. Cooke, *Tench Coxe and the Early Republic* (Chapel Hill, N. C., 1978), 345.

3. F. Markoe to M. H. Bache, Aug. 4, 1798, Bache Papers, Castle Collection, American Philosophical Society, Philadelphia.

4. On the importation of yellow fever from British Jamaica see *Aurora,* Aug. 21, 1798. On the 1798 yellow fever epidemic as a whole see J. Thomas Scharf and Thompson Westcott, *History of Philadelphia, 1609–1884* (Philadelphia, 1884), I, 459n.

5. *Aurora,* Sept. 7, 1798. Eliz. Hewson to Thos. T. Hewson, Oct. ? and 30, 1798, and May 10, 1799, in Hewson Family Papers, Am. Philos. Soc.

6. A typescript copy of the notice is in Bache Papers, Castle Coll., Am. Philos. Soc.

7. *Independent Chronicle,* Sept. 17, 20 ("Democritus"), 1798. Adams appended Mrs. Bache's September 11th eulogy to her husband in his obituary of September 17.

8. *Gaz. of U. S.,* Sept. 11, 1798. Apparently distracted by the yellow fever epidemic, Cobbett reported Bache's death six days later than the *Gazette,* and made the erroneous claim that Bache had died on September 12, *Porcupine Gazette,* Sept. 17, 1798.

9. *Ibid.,* Sept. 17, 1798.

10. *Massachusetts Mercury*, Sept. 18, 1798; and *Columbian Centinel*, Sept. 29, 1798.

11. *Phila. Gaz.*, Sept. 15, 1798.

12. Eliz. Hewson to Thos. T. Hewson, May 10, 1799, Hewson Family Papers, Am. Philos. Soc. Observations about improvements in the *Aurora* are based on a cursory survey of the *Aurora* for two years after Bache's death. On Duane's editorship the authoritative work is Kim Tousley Phillips, "William Duane, Revolutionary Editor," (unpub. Ph.D. diss., Univ. of California, 1968). Duane, whose wife had died of cholera in July 1798, married Margaret Bache in June, 1800. *Ibid.*, 54, 83.

13. For Cobbett's claim see *Porc. Gaz.*, July 8, 1799. On Coxe see Cooke, *Coxe*, 346 and 346n. Claude-Anne Lopez and Eugenia W. Herbert, *The Private Franklin: The Man and His Family* (New York, 1975), 312, raise the issue of estrangement.

14. A. J. Dallas to Margaret H. Bache, Nov. 2, 1799, Bache Papers, Castle Coll., Am. Philos. Soc.

15. On the Duane letter episode and the Frothingham case see especially Harold C. Syrett, *et al.*, eds., *The Papers of Alexander Hamilton* (New York, 1961–79), XXXIV, 5–6, 6n–7n; Leonard Levy, *Emergence of a Free Press* (New York, 1985), 254; Phillips, "William Duane," 60; and John C. Miller, *Alexander Hamilton: Portrait in Paradox* (New York, 1959), 486–87.

16. *Porc. Gaz.*, Oct. 17, Nov. 3 ("An American" and Cobbett), 6 ("MOTHER BACHE"), 30, 1798. Karen K. List, "Two Party Papers' Political Coverage of Women in the New Republic," *Critical Studies in Mass Communications*, II (1985), 152–65, finds Bache's attitudes toward women somewhat more liberated than Cobbett's. Cobbett, she points out, advised women to encourage their husbands to resist France and even to divorce them if they were democrats.

17. *Porc. Gaz.*, May 1, 1799.

18. *Aurora*, Sept. 21, 1799. For other praise and eulogies see *ibid.*, Nov. 1, 8 ("Monody on the Death of Benjamin Franklin Bache" by John D. Burk from N. Y. *Argus*), 13 ("Idylium"), 1798; Mar. 21 (toast), July 6 (two toasts), Dec. 21 (toast), 1799; July 7 (toast), 1800.

19. Wm. Vans Murray to J. Q. Adams, Nov. 27, 1798, Worthington Chauncey Ford, ed., "Letters of William Vans Murray to John Quincy Adams," *Annual Report of the American Historical Association for the Year 1912* (Washington, D. C., 1913), 489–90.

20. *Aurora*, Aug. 11, 1802. Duane did not claim that Callender failed to get anything published in the *Aurora* under this scheme, but he did claim that he, Duane, was the anonymous author of most of the correspondence and communications attributed to Callender. After Callender became an American citizen to avoid the alien acts and then fled to Virginia to avoid the Sedition Act on July 13, 1798, Duane was re-hired by Bache. Callender later expressed his bitterness that Bache had censured and rejected his material, and that Jefferson and the Philadelphia Republicans had abandoned him. See Phillips, "William Duane," 58.

21. On Reynolds see Richard J. Twomey, "Jacobins and Jeffersonians: Anglo-American Radical Ideology, 1790–1810," in Margaret and James Jacob, eds., *The*

Origins of Anglo-American Radicalism (London, 1984), 292–95. Radical emigrés are discussed expertly in Richard Jerome Twomey, "Jacobins and Jeffersonians: Anglo-American Radicals in the United States, 1790–1820" (unpub. Ph.D. diss., Northern Illinois Univ., 1974); and Michael Durey, "Thomas Paine's Apostles: Radical Emigrés and the Triumph of Jeffersonian Republicanism," *William and Mary Quarterly*, XLIV (1987), 661–88.

Index

99999999

Pennsylvania, 124, 128, 207–10, 218, 220–21; on the whiskey excise, 210, 213–14; on the Whiskey Rebellion, 210–13

• *economic views:* and artisans and mechanics, 294, 402–3; and Coxe's economic views, 161; on the economic potential of America, 90; on farming, 90; and free trade, 137; on Hamiltonian fiscal policies, 136, 161, 166, 214; and political economy, 136–37, 231–32n.2; on the poor, 89–90

• *elections and partisan politics:* and Adams's candidacy for the presidency, 290–95; and the Adet letters in the election of 1796, 293–94, 307n.68, 308n.71; adopts Freneau's partisanship, 161; attempts to influence Adams administration, 318; blames Federalists for French crisis, 341; as a candidate for the Philadelphia Common Council, 294; defines faction, 372; on disputed election returns in 1796, 295; and the election list for 1796, 292–93; and the election of 1792, 160; and the election of 1796, 290–95; and elections, 224, 231, 257, 259; and the Federalists, 225, 323, 330, 343, 365n.115, 381; and the Germantown Society for promoting Domestic Manufactures, 210–11; and an impartial press, 107–8, 192, 297, 302n.19; and Jeffersonian-Republicans, 300; and Jefferson's candidacy for the presidency, 290–95; lobbies Rep. William Smith, 358–59n.53; as non-partisan, 159–60; partisan parody of Allen's speech in congress, 391n.16; and partisanship, 166, 221–30, 287–88, 292–95, 297–300, 401–3; and Pennsylvania election law of 1796, 292; on petitions for and against the Jay Treaty, 258; political cunning of, 402; political enemies of, in 1798, 389; and political opponents, 222–30; and political parties, 226–27, 292–95, 297–300; and political satire, 226; and the Reynolds affair, 288, 305n.49

• *France, French Relations, and the French Revolution:* accused of being an agent of France, or in their "pay," 106, 290, 347, 349–50, 368–69, 377, 385; on Adams's French policy, 333–34; and Adams's speech on French foreign pol-

icy, 319–20, 323; Adet letters and, 294, 315–16; and America's losts affection for France, 345; asks administration to resign during French crisis, 336, 337–38; attacks Pickering's instructions to Pinckney, 323; and Danton's execution, 311–12, 353n.3; defends *coup d'état* of 18 Fructidor, 322; defends French foreign policy, 314–23; and Fauchet's sketch of Franco-American relations, 335; on France and Louisiana, 313; on France and the Jay Treaty, 263; Francophilism of, 197, 350; defends French seizure of the Mount Vernon, 315; and defense measures against, 337; and the Directory, 321–22; and the envoys' mission to France, 321–23, 335–37; and execution of Louis XVI and Marie Antoinette, 176, 180–81; and the Faucher mission, 314; and the French crisis, 334–35, 341, 344, 346–47, 376; and French depredations, 315–16, 334, 354n.15; and the French Revolution, 141–42, 171–97, 199n.9, 311–13, 353n.2, 353n.3; and the Genet mission, 185–97; and the Jacobins, 179, 312; and Monroe's appointment as minister to France, 242; and military victories of France, 312–13, 321; on neutrality, 187; and the Pinckney mission, 317–18; and parties in France, 175, 178; and political clubs in France, 220; and the president's replies to petitions against France, 344–45; and Talleyrand's letter to the envoys, 342–43, 368, 371; and Thermidorean Reaction, 312; and the threat of war in French crisis and, 323, 341, 343–44, 358n.41, 365n.115; and the Treaty of Campo Formio, 358n.44; on the War of the First Coalition, 177–78; and Washington's attitude toward France, 281–82; and XYZ affair, 337, 339, 341–42

• *Franklin:* and "A.B."'s attack on BF's reputation, 288; asks BF for books and a gold watch, 37; attempts cult of BF, 159; and *Autobiography* of BF, 67–69; as BF's "amanuensis," 66, 83–84n.38; and BF's political ideas and activities, 127–30; and BF's will, 75, 85n.52; impact of BF's death on, 74–75; influence of BF on, 56–57, 59; as inheritor of

This book has been set in Linotron Galliard. Galliard
was designed for Mergenthaler in 1978 by Matthew
Carter. Galliard retains many of the features of a sixteenth
century typeface cut by Robert Granjon but has some
modifications which gives it a more contemporary look.

Printed on acid-free paper.